Communications in Computer and Information Science

2772

Series Editors

Gang Li, *School of Information Technology, Deakin University, Burwood, VIC, Australia*
Joaquim Filipe, *Polytechnic Institute of Setúbal, Setúbal, Portugal*
Zhiwei Xu, *Chinese Academy of Sciences, Beijing, China*

Rationale

The CCIS series is devoted to the publication of proceedings of computer science conferences. Its aim is to efficiently disseminate original research results in informatics in printed and electronic form. While the focus is on publication of peer-reviewed full papers presenting mature work, inclusion of reviewed short papers reporting on work in progress is welcome, too. Besides globally relevant meetings with internationally representative program committees guaranteeing a strict peer-reviewing and paper selection process, conferences run by societies or of high regional or national relevance are also considered for publication.

Topics

The topical scope of CCIS spans the entire spectrum of informatics ranging from foundational topics in the theory of computing to information and communications science and technology and a broad variety of interdisciplinary application fields.

Information for Volume Editors and Authors

Publication in CCIS is free of charge. No royalties are paid, however, we offer registered conference participants temporary free access to the online version of the conference proceedings on SpringerLink (http://link.springer.com) by means of an http referrer from the conference website and/or a number of complimentary printed copies, as specified in the official acceptance email of the event.

CCIS proceedings can be published in time for distribution at conferences or as post-proceedings, and delivered in the form of printed books and/or electronically as USBs and/or e-content licenses for accessing proceedings at SpringerLink. Furthermore, CCIS proceedings are included in the CCIS electronic book series hosted in the SpringerLink digital library at http://link.springer.com/bookseries/7899. Conferences publishing in CCIS are allowed to use our online conference service (Meteor) for managing the whole proceedings lifecycle (from submission and reviewing to preparing for publication) free of charge.

Publication process

The language of publication is exclusively English. Authors publishing in CCIS have to sign the Springer CCIS copyright transfer form, however, they are free to use their material published in CCIS for substantially changed, more elaborate subsequent publications elsewhere. For the preparation of the camera-ready papers/files, authors have to strictly adhere to the Springer CCIS Authors' Instructions and are strongly encouraged to use the CCIS LaTeX style files or templates.

Abstracting/Indexing

CCIS is abstracted/indexed in DBLP, Google Scholar, EI-Compendex, Mathematical Reviews, SCImago, Scopus. CCIS volumes are also submitted for the inclusion in ISI Proceedings.

How to start

To start the evaluation of your proposal for inclusion in the CCIS series, please send an e-mail to ccis@springer.com

Constantine Stephanidis · Margherita Antona ·
Stavroula Ntoa · George Margetis ·
Gavriel Salvendy

Editors

HCI International 2025 – Late Breaking Posters

27th International Conference on
Human-Computer Interaction, HCII 2025
Gothenburg, Sweden, June 22–27, 2025
Proceedings, Part II

 Springer

Editors
Constantine Stephanidis
University of Crete and Foundation for
Research and Technology - Hellas (FORTH)
Heraklion, Crete, Greece

Margherita Antona
Foundation for Research and Technology -
Hellas (FORTH)
Heraklion, Crete, Greece

Stavroula Ntoa
Foundation for Research and Technology -
Hellas (FORTH)
Heraklion, Crete, Greece

George Margetis
Foundation for Research and Technology -
Hellas (FORTH)
Heraklion, Crete, Greece

Gavriel Salvendy
University of Central Florida
Orlando, FL, USA

ISSN 1865-0929   ISSN 1865-0937 (electronic)
Communications in Computer and Information Science
ISBN 978-3-032-12766-2   ISBN 978-3-032-12767-9 (eBook)
https://doi.org/10.1007/978-3-032-12767-9

© The Editor(s) (if applicable) and The Author(s), under exclusive license
to Springer Nature Switzerland AG 2026, corrected publication 2026

This work is subject to copyright. All rights are solely and exclusively licensed by the Publisher, whether the whole or part of the material is concerned, specifically the rights of translation, reprinting, reuse of illustrations, recitation, broadcasting, reproduction on microfilms or in any other physical way, and transmission or information storage and retrieval, electronic adaptation, computer software, or by similar or dissimilar methodology now known or hereafter developed.
The use of general descriptive names, registered names, trademarks, service marks, etc. in this publication does not imply, even in the absence of a specific statement, that such names are exempt from the relevant protective laws and regulations and therefore free for general use.
The publisher, the authors and the editors are safe to assume that the advice and information in this book are believed to be true and accurate at the date of publication. Neither the publisher nor the authors or the editors give a warranty, expressed or implied, with respect to the material contained herein or for any errors or omissions that may have been made. The publisher remains neutral with regard to jurisdictional claims in published maps and institutional affiliations.

This Springer imprint is published by the registered company Springer Nature Switzerland AG
The registered company address is: Gewerbestrasse 11, 6330 Cham, Switzerland

If disposing of this product, please recycle the paper.

Foreword

The HCI International (HCII) conference was founded in 1984 by Gavriel Salvendy (Purdue University, USA, Tsinghua University, P.R. China, and University of Central Florida, USA) and the first event of the series, "1st USA-Japan Conference on Human-Computer Interaction", was held in Honolulu, Hawaii, USA, on 18–20 August. Since then, HCI International has been held jointly with several Thematic Areas and Affiliated Conferences, with each one under the auspices of a distinguished international Program Board and under one management and one registration. Twenty-seven HCI International Conferences have been organized so far (every two years until 2013, and annually thereafter).

Last year, we celebrated 40 years since the establishment of the HCII conference, which has been a hub for presenting groundbreaking research and novel ideas and collaboration for people from all over the world. Over the years, this conference has served as a platform for scholars, researchers, industry experts, and students to exchange ideas, connect, and address challenges in the ever-evolving HCI field. The conference has evolved itself, adapting to new technologies and emerging trends, while staying committed to its core mission of advancing knowledge and driving change.

The 27th International Conference on Human-Computer Interaction, HCI International 2025 (HCII 2025), was held as an 'on-site' conference at the Gothia Towers Hotel and Swedish Exhibition & Congress Centre, in Gothenburg, Sweden, on June 22–27, 2025, with the additional option for 'on-line' participation. It incorporated the 21 thematic areas and affiliated conferences listed below.

A total of 7972 individuals from academia, research institutes, industry, and government agencies from 92 countries submitted contributions. 1430 papers and 355 posters (as short research papers) were included in the volumes of the proceedings published just before the start of the conference. Additionally, 439 papers and 104 posters were included in the volumes of the proceedings published after the conference, as "Late Breaking Work". The contributions thoroughly cover the entire field of human-computer interaction, highlight the evolving role of computers in diverse contexts, and demonstrate how HCI research is shaping and improving user experiences across a wide range of domains, influencing technological progress and its effective integration into various sectors. The volumes constituting the full set of the HCII 2025 conference proceedings are listed on the following pages.

I would like to thank the Program Board Chairs and the members of the Program Boards of all thematic areas and affiliated conferences for their contribution towards the high scientific quality and overall success of the HCI International 2025 conference. Their manifold support including paper reviews (via a single-blind review process, with a minimum of two reviews per submission), session organization, and their willingness to act as goodwill ambassadors for the conference is most highly appreciated.

This conference would not have been possible without the continuous and unwavering support and advice of Gavriel Salvendy, founder, General Chair Emeritus, and Scientific Advisor. For his outstanding efforts, I would like to express my sincere appreciation to Abbas Moallem, Communications Chair and Editor of HCI International News.

September 2025   Constantine Stephanidis

The original version of the book has been revised. The title of this book has been corrected. A correction to this book can be found at https://doi.org/10.1007/978-3-032-12767-9_44

HCI International 2025 Thematic Areas and Affiliated Conferences

- HCI: Human-Computer Interaction Thematic Area
- HIMI: Human Interface and the Management of Information Thematic Area
- EPCE: 22nd International Conference on Engineering Psychology and Cognitive Ergonomics
- AC: 19th International Conference on Augmented Cognition
- UAHCI: 19th International Conference on Universal Access in Human-Computer Interaction
- CCD: 17th International Conference on Cross-Cultural Design
- SCSM: 17th International Conference on Social Computing and Social Media
- VAMR: 17th International Conference on Virtual, Augmented and Mixed Reality
- DHM: 16th International Conference on Digital Human Modeling & Applications in Health, Safety, Ergonomics & Risk Management
- DUXU: 14th International Conference on Design, User Experience and Usability
- C&C: 13th International Conference on Culture and Computing
- DAPI: 13th International Conference on Distributed, Ambient and Pervasive Interactions
- HCIBGO: 12th International Conference on HCI in Business, Government and Organizations
- LCT: 12th International Conference on Learning and Collaboration Technologies
- ITAP: 11th International Conference on Human Aspects of IT for the Aged Population
- AIS: 7th International Conference on Adaptive Instructional Systems
- HCI-CPT: 7th International Conference on HCI for Cybersecurity, Privacy and Trust
- HCI-Games: 7th International Conference on HCI in Games
- MobiTAS: 7th International Conference on HCI in Mobility, Transport and Automotive Systems
- AI-HCI: 6th International Conference on Artificial Intelligence in HCI
- MOBILE: 6th International Conference on Human-Centered Design, Operation and Evaluation of Mobile Communications

Conference Proceedings – Full List of Volumes

1. LNCS 15766, Human-Computer Interaction — Part I, edited by Masaaki Kurosu and Ayako Hashizume
2. LNCS 15767, Human-Computer Interaction — Part II, edited by Masaaki Kurosu and Ayako Hashizume
3. LNCS 15768, Human-Computer Interaction — Part III, edited by Masaaki Kurosu and Ayako Hashizume
4. LNCS 15769, Human-Computer Interaction — Part IV, edited by Masaaki Kurosu and Ayako Hashizume
5. LNCS 15770, Human-Computer Interaction — Part V, edited by Masaaki Kurosu and Ayako Hashizume
6. LNCS 15771, Human-Computer Interaction — Part VI, edited by Masaaki Kurosu and Ayako Hashizume
7. LNCS 15772, Human-Computer Interaction — Part VII, edited by Masaaki Kurosu and Ayako Hashizume
8. LNCS 15773, Human Interface and the Management of Information: Part I, edited by Hirohiko Mori and Yumi Asahi
9. LNCS 15774, Human Interface and the Management of Information: Part II, edited by Hirohiko Mori and Yumi Asahi
10. LNCS 15773, Human Interface and the Management of Information: Part III, edited by Hirohiko Mori and Yumi Asahi
11. LNAI 15776, Engineering Psychology and Cognitive Ergonomics: Part I, edited by Don Harris and Wen-Chin Li
12. LNAI 15777, Engineering Psychology and Cognitive Ergonomics: Part II, edited by Don Harris and Wen-Chin Li
13. LNAI 15778, Augmented Cognition, Part I, edited by Dylan D. Schmorrow and Cali M. Fidopiastis
14. LNAI 15779, Augmented Cognition, Part II, edited by Dylan D. Schmorrow and Cali M. Fidopiastis
15. LNCS 15780, Universal Access in Human-Computer Interaction: Part I, edited by Margherita Antona and Constantine Stephanidis
16. LNCS 15781, Universal Access in Human-Computer Interaction: Part II, edited by Margherita Antona and Constantine Stephanidis
17. LNCS 15782, Cross-Cultural Design: Part I, edited by Pei-Luen Patrick Rau
18. LNCS 15783, Cross-Cultural Design: Part II, edited by Pei-Luen Patrick Rau
19. LNCS 15784, Cross-Cultural Design: Part III, edited by Pei-Luen Patrick Rau
20. LNCS 15785, Cross-Cultural Design: Part IV, edited by Pei-Luen Patrick Rau
21. LNCS 15786, Social Computing and Social Media: Part I, edited by Adela Coman and Simona Vasilache

45. LNCS 15810, Human Aspects of IT for the Aged Population: Part II, edited by Qin Gao and Jia Zhou
46. LNCS 15811, Human Aspects of IT for the Aged Population: Part III, edited by Qin Gao and Jia Zhou
47. LNCS 15812, Adaptive Instructional System: Part I, edited by Robert A. Sottilare and Jessica Schwarz
48. LNCS 15813, Adaptive Instructional System: Part II, edited by Robert A. Sottilare and Jessica Schwarz
49. LNCS 15814, HCI for Cybersecurity, Privacy and Trust: Part I, edited by Abbas Moallem
50. LNCS 15815, HCI for Cybersecurity, Privacy and Trust: Part II, edited by Abbas Moallem
51. LNCS 15816, HCI in Games, edited by Xiaowen Fang
52. LNCS 15817, HCI in Mobility, Transport and Automotive Systems: Part I, edited by Heidi Krömker
53. LNCS 15818, HCI in Mobility, Transport and Automotive Systems: Part II, edited by Heidi Krömker
54. LNAI 15819, Artificial Intelligence in HCI: Part I, edited by Helmut Degen and Stavroula Ntoa
55. LNAI 15820, Artificial Intelligence in HCI: Part II, edited by Helmut Degen and Stavroula Ntoa
56. LNAI 15821, Artificial Intelligence in HCI: Part III, edited by Helmut Degen and Stavroula Ntoa
57. LNAI 15822, Artificial Intelligence in HCI: Part IV, edited by Helmut Degen and Stavroula Ntoa
58. LNCS 15823, Human-Centered Design, Operation and Evaluation of Mobile Communications: Part I, edited by June Wei and George Margetis
59. LNCS 15824, Human-Centered Design, Operation and Evaluation of Mobile Communications: Part II, edited by June Wei and George Margetis
60. CCIS 2522, HCI International 2025 Posters — Part I, edited by Constantine Stephanidis, Margherita Antona, Stavroula Ntoa and Gavriel Salvendy
61. CCIS 2523, HCI International 2025 Posters — Part II, edited by Constantine Stephanidis, Margherita Antona, Stavroula Ntoa and Gavriel Salvendy
62. CCIS 2524, HCI International 2025 Posters — Part III, edited by Constantine Stephanidis, Margherita Antona, Stavroula Ntoa and Gavriel Salvendy
63. CCIS 2525, HCI International 2025 Posters — Part IV, edited by Constantine Stephanidis, Margherita Antona, Stavroula Ntoa and Gavriel Salvendy
64. CCIS 2526, HCI International 2025 Posters — Part V, edited by Constantine Stephanidis, Margherita Antona, Stavroula Ntoa and Gavriel Salvendy
65. CCIS 2527, HCI International 2025 Posters — Part VI, edited by Constantine Stephanidis, Margherita Antona, Stavroula Ntoa and Gavriel Salvendy
66. CCIS 2528, HCI International 2025 Posters — Part VII, edited by Constantine Stephanidis, Margherita Antona, Stavroula Ntoa and Gavriel Salvendy

85. CCIS 2772, HCI International 2025 — Late Breaking Posters: Part II, edited by Constantine Stephanidis, Margherita Antona, Stavroula Ntoa, George Margetis and Gavriel Salvendy
86. CCIS 2773, HCI International 2025 — Late Breaking Posters: Part III, edited by Constantine Stephanidis, Margherita Antona, Stavroula Ntoa, George Margetis and Gavriel Salvendy

https://2025.hci.international/proceedings

27th International Conference on Human-Computer Interaction (HCII 2025)

The full list with the Program Board Chairs and the members of the Program Boards of all thematic areas and affiliated conferences of HCII 2025 is available online at:

http://www.hci.international/board-members-2025.php

25th International Conference on
... (ICCT 2024)

HCI International 2026 Conference

The 28th International Conference on Human-Computer Interaction, HCI International 2026, will be held jointly with the affiliated conferences at the Montréal Convention Centre (Palais des congrès de Montréal), in Montreal, Canada, 26–31 July 2026. It will cover a broad spectrum of themes related to Human-Computer Interaction, including theoretical issues, methods, tools, processes, and case studies in HCI design, as well as novel interaction techniques, interfaces, and applications. The proceedings will be published by Springer (part of Springer Nature) in a multi-volume set. More information will become available on the conference website: https://2026.hci.international/.

General Chair
Constantine Stephanidis
University of Crete and ICS-FORTH
Heraklion, Crete, Greece
Email: general_chair@2026.hci.international

https://2026.hci.international/

Contents

AI-Powered and Decision Support Systems

Human-Centered Interaction Design and Experience

Smart Mobility and Transportation

Acceptance of Advanced Vehicle Technologies in Conditionally Automated Vehicles

Iris Jestin[1,2(✉)], Catherine Harvey[1], Michael Craven[1,2,3], Neil Chadborn[4], and Sarah Sharples[1,2,5]

[1] Human Factors Research Group, School of Engineering, University of Nottingham, Nottingham, UK
iris.jestin@nottingham.ac.uk
[2] Horizon Centre for Doctoral Training, University of Nottingham, Nottingham, UK
[3] NIHR MindTech Research Centre, Institute of Mental Health, University of Nottingham, Nottingham, UK
[4] NIHR Applied Research Collaboration, University of Nottingham, Nottingham, UK
[5] Department for Transport, London, UK

Abstract. Driver Monitoring Systems (DMS) in Conditionally Automated Vehicles (CAVs) can identify if the driver has an appropriate state of awareness to be taking control of the driving, if the vehicle requires them to do so, and then indicate this to the driver through Human Machine Interface (HMI). This has the potential to improve road safety by eliminating accidents caused by human error during transition of driving control between the vehicle and driver due to distraction, fatigue, and other undesirable driver states. However, the potential benefits and utility that these technologies can provide may be overlooked due to a lack of trust, which affects their acceptability. To explore current perceptions that affect the acceptability of DMS and HMIs in CAVs, a scenario-based survey that combines the Car Technology Acceptance Model (CTAM) with qualitative questions exploring the changes to technology that may increase its social desirability, was conducted with 63 respondents (32 females, 33 males). The data was compared against demographic characteristics of age, gender, frequency of driving and duration of holding a license. The quantitative results indicated that gender has a significant effect ($p = 0.043$) on anxiety experienced towards technology. The qualitative findings showed that the respondents would like to have more information about the working of the technology, including system states, provided through training, videos or other support suggesting a current lack of understanding of how such technologies work. The study offers some takeaways to vehicle manufacturers, related other equipment manufacturers and policymakers on the design and implementation of such technologies to increase acceptability.

Keywords: Driver Monitoring System · Human Machine Interfaces · Conditionally Automated Vehicles · Public Perceptions · Acceptance

© The Author(s), under exclusive license to Springer Nature Switzerland AG 2026
S. Sundarakannan and O. Knorpp (Eds.): HCII 2025, CCIS 2772, pp. 3–14, 2026.
https://doi.org/10.1007/978-3-032-12767-9_1

1   Introduction

With the current status of fully automated vehicles being developmental, there remain many barriers to its implementation on public roads. Hence, it is likely that it will be many more years before fully automated vehicles are widespread on our roads (Fisher et al. 2020; Endsley 2020). Until then, it is important that the driver has a good state of situational awareness and is capable of taking over control in conditionally automated vehicles (CAV) (Merat et al. 2019). With CAVs, the role of the driver changes to that of a supervisor of driving functions, which creates a need for additional aides in the vehicle, to help the human controller with their altered role. Drivers may need assistance in managing the driving control being transferred back from the automated system, since skill degradation and reduced situation awareness are known to accompany long periods of the automated system being in control (Endsley 2016; Trösterer et al. 2016). Hence, driver monitoring systems (DMS) will be a useful addition to the vehicle, where enhancing vehicle safety by detecting the driver's state is a necessity to reduce traffic accidents. At the current time, DMS that can be found in production vehicles are capable of monitoring 'states' such as fatigue/drowsiness and distraction/inattention. Technological developments will mean that future DMS will also be capable of monitoring stress, workload, mood/emotions, wellbeing, and many more characteristics of a driver's real-time condition (Guettas et al. 2019). But a lack of acceptance of the technology may lead to the consumer's disuse or indeed misuse of it, which in the context of DMS in CAVs, could mean switching off the DMS or automation technology where possible, using them in ways not intended by designers or simply not buying such vehicle technologies. This leads to negating all the predicted potential benefits of such technologies (Regan & Strayer 2014; Smyth et al. 2021). Hence, understanding public opinions in the lead up to the implementation of such technologies even if the public have had little to no exposure to them, is crucial to informing future planning by governments, in helping manufacturers to create products to the perceived needs of users and experts to conduct academic research in the area (Regan & Strayer 2014).

2   Related Work

Models of User Acceptance. The Unified Theory of Acceptance and Use of Technology (UTAUT) (Venkatesh et al., 2003) provides an integrated view of user acceptance of technology from other acceptance models. The UTAUT has four key determinants performance expectancy, effort expectancy, social influence and facilitating conditions. The use of UTAUT in most of literature extends itself according to context, to add some other determinants, the most common ones used to be Self-Efficacy, Attitude Towards Using Technology, Anxiety, and Behavioural Intention to Use the Technology. While the UTAUT was developed to explore acceptance in different contexts, it can be applied directly to examine acceptance in the context of AVs (Hewitt et al. 2019). The Car Technology Acceptance Model (CTAM) (Osswald et al. 2012, see Fig. 1), based on the UTAUT, was designed specifically for examining technology acceptance of information systems in the context of a car. The results of the work by Osswald et al. showed that safety is among the most mentioned topics when it came to the use of the system while driving, leading to the addition of Perceived Safety to the above-mentioned UTAUT determinants, to create the CTAM. Further, the CTAM reworded some of the questions adopted from the UTAUT to ensure consistency and to focus on in-car technology. With the focus of the current study being perceptions around advanced vehicle technologies, the CTAM was selected as an appropriate assessment tool.

Public Acceptance of AV Technology. Although there exist several studies in literature that explore the public opinions and acceptance of AV technology across different levels of automation and of in-vehicle HMIs in such vehicles, there seem to be fewer studies of public acceptance of DMS technology particularly in the context of these vehicles (Coyne et al., 2024; Smyth et al. 2021). Many of the studies exploring AV and related HMI acceptance have used an extension or combination of different acceptance models such as the TAM, UTAUT and CTAM, with modifications made to suit the context of the respective studies. Research suggests that despite the increasing prevalence of AV technology on roads, public opinion regarding it is still poor, with greater anxiety felt towards increasing levels of automation (Hewitt et al. 2019). Previous experiences with basic Advanced Driver Assist Systems (ADAS) such as lane departure warning and blind spot monitoring, that are a common standard in lower levels of automation, was seen to have positive effects on user acceptance and experience of AVs, leading to assumptions that more vehicles being equipped with ADAS might lead to an increased acceptance of automation in vehicles (Rödel et al. 2014). Previous research that investigated acceptance towards DMS has highlighted that users need to be aware and educated on the expected performance of a DMS to ensure use (Ghazizadeh & Lee 2014; Smyth et al. 2021). Research has previously shown that the acceptance towards technologies such as ADAS and AVs depends not just on the technology but also on characteristics of the driver such as age, gender and pre-experiences. This highlights the importance of considering the effects of these characteristics on the acceptance of the technology (Rödel et al. 2014), which has been considered in this research study. To ensure there is a suitable degree of monitoring of in-vehicle HMIs by the driver, and that important warnings are not missed, an informative and accurate DMS, which manages the human-HMI-vehicle link is required (Merat et al. 2019). This points to the importance of the joint working of both DMS and HMIs in AVs, which is addressed in this research. There have been numerous attempts previously in literature to explore the acceptance of ADAS features, of in-vehicle HMIs in AV and manual vehicles. But they have almost always been explored separately, with not much research having explored the joint working of DMS and HMIs in AVs. The current study tried to address this gap, by taking a step towards the early exploration of perceptions towards DMS and HMIs working together as a system with the driver, in potential CAV driving scenarios.

3   Exploratory Study Design

A questionnaire was used to explore the perceptions towards DMS and related HMIs in CAVs. Participants were asked to provide demographic information (age group, gender, nationality, country of residence), driving frequency and duration of holding a valid driving license. Definitions of the technologies – human machine interfaces, driver monitoring systems and conditionally-automated vehicles, that would be used through the course of the questionnaire were explained to ensure familiarity with the novel technologies. Inspired by the use of detailed scenarios to set context on the use of novel technologies for respondents before answering a questionnaire (Hewitt et al. 2019; Rödel et al. 2014), the definitions were followed by two driving scenario examples that used the above-mentioned technologies. The scenarios used simple words aiding the respondents to see themselves in the situation, employing typical scenarios of handover-takeover of driving control in CAVs. The scenarios specifically emphasised the relationship between HMI and DMS in potential CAV driving contexts as a system, to best convey to the participants how interaction with the novel technologies might be experienced. Participants were asked to read both scenarios and then complete questions based on their understanding of those scenarios and drawing from experiences with similar technologies. The first set of questions were taken from the CTAM (Osswald et al. 2012). The second set of questions, designed to complement the CTAM, explored the respondent's thoughts on the acceptance of technology. The online questionnaire was created on Microsoft Forms and distributed using opportunistic sampling, via social media, university email chains, word of mouth, direct or indirect friends, family and acquaintances. All participants were given information regarding the purpose of the questionnaire, data collection, storage and asked to give informed consent before completing the questionnaire.

4   Results

63 respondents filled in the online questionnaire out of which one participant entry was deleted due a response bias identified post-study. The demographic breakup of the responses can be seen in the following Table 1.

4.1   Quantitative Results

The following section which elaborates on the results from the quantitative questions which was based on the Car Technology Acceptance Model (CTAM), was analysed using inferential tests. All the question items of the CTAM scales were five-point Likert scale responses, from 1 (strongly disagree) to 5 (strongly agree). To ensure the reliability of the items measuring each scale, the Cronbach's Alpha value for each of the scales were computed. Due to how the CTAM items are worded, some of them needed to be reverse scored so that all the items of a specific scale were in the same direction measuring the scale. Following (Hewitt et al. 2019; Sarah Schwindt-Drews et al. 2023) approach to creating a composite score of different items in a specific scale, for all 9 scales of the CTAM, the mean values of the respective items in the specific scale were calculated for each of the participants. The assumption for homogeneity of variance and normality were tested using the Levene's test and the Shapiro-Wilk test respectively. As the assumptions for normality required for parametric tests were met by the dependent variables Social Influence, Anxiety and Perceived Safety for the independent variable Gender, the parametric test independent samples T-test was used. For the remaining dependent variable CTAM scales against Gender, the non-parametric, Mann Whitney U was conducted. For the independent variable, Age Group, four dependent variables, Facilitating Conditions, Attitude Towards Using Technology, Anxiety and Perceived

Table 1. Demographic Distribution.

Demographic	Levels	Frequency	Percent
Gender	Female	30	48.4
	Male	32	51.6
Age Group	20–30	32	51.6
	31–40	9	14.5
	41–50	8	12.9
	51–60	8	12.9
	61–70	5	8.1
Duration of Holding a License	Less than 5 years	5	8.1
	5–15 years	32	51.6
	16–25 years	10	16.1
	More than 25 years	15	24.2
Frequency of Driving	Less frequently	10	16.1
	At least once every couple months	5	8.1
	At least once a month	3	4.8
	At least once a week	14	22.6
	Almost everyday	30	48.4

Safety abided by the assumptions for parametric tests. Similarly, no violation of the assumptions was found for the dependent variable Perceived Safety when tested against both independent variables Duration of Holding a License, and Frequency of Driving. The parametric test One-way ANOVA was hence conducted on the above-mentioned variables. Owing to the violation of normality, the non-parametric Kruskal Wallis H was conducted on the remaining scales of the CTAM against the independent variable Age Group, Duration of Holding a License, and Frequency of Driving. The results of the study show that Gender ($p < 0.05$) has a significant effect on one of the nine scales of the CTAM; Anxiety towards the technology, which is defined as the degree to which an individual responds to a situation with feelings of uneasiness or apprehension. The independent samples T-test reported a significant effect of Gender on Anxiety, $t(60) = 2.066$, $p = 0.043$. Those identifying as female (n = 30, Mean = 3.01, Median = 3) experienced significantly more anxiety towards the use of the technology as opposed to those identifying as male (n = 32, Mean = 2.64, Median = 2.58). The qualitative results in the next section provided some more context to support this argument (Table 2).

Table 2. Effect of gender.

CTAM Scale	T-test	p-value	Female	Male
			Median	Median
Anxiety	2.066	0.043	3.0	2.58

4.2 Qualitative Results

The qualitative data was analysed using inductive thematic analysis to generate 7 themes. The themes were then categorised by age group to explore trends (see Table 3). Due to the small sample sizes in some of the age groups the results should be considered suggestive rather than definitive of said themes.

Table 3. Qualitative Results.

Themes	Age Groups	Quotes From Respondents
T1: Override Automation	61–70	"I need an option to turn it off."
	51–60	"A fully automated driving system should have an option to override."
T2: Discomfort in automation takeover without driver confirmation	51–60	"The suggestion that the system can do this apparently without confirmation from the driver made me wary".
	20–30	"There are certain worst-case scenarios where I could let it take over. But simply letting it take over because I'm distracted?" "I would be worried that it is taking over for me and not feel in control."
T3: Difficulty in making a decision to use the technology without trying it	51–60	"I would want to test a system under 'safe' driving conditions before using it more broadly."
	41–50	"I would like to try it first and then decide." "I would need to see it work in other settings/drivers first to be confident."
	31–40	"I believe a system like this could help with my driving, but I'd have to try it out and get used to it."
	20–30	"I would like to try the system first."
T4: Increase knowledge of the system.	61–70	"Some form of coaching to increase confidence levels."

(*continued*)

Table 3. (*continued*)

Themes	Age Groups	Quotes From Respondents
	31–40	"Greater explanation from the system on when it's important to focus attention, when the automated system is working and how it perceives the current environment." "I would like to know limitations of the system and their potential impact on my safety." "At least an icon should be visible showing that something is happening because of DMS."
	20–30	"Information on how the system works theoretically would make me feel more confident about the product itself." "Some test videos in place when the system is available to the public to familiarise oneself with how it works." "There is little real-world knowledge of how these technologies work. I think increasing knowledge in the general population around how they work (i.e. information, demonstrations) would make them seem less like a technology of the future and increase trust and awareness." "There should be clear reminder instructions each time the system is activated."
T5: Concerns around partial over full automation	41–50	"Either give me control or let me switch off altogether, don't expect me to stay alert if I'm not doing anything."
	20–30	"I do not believe that the majority of drivers will still pay attention when not in full control." "I feel people would pay less attention to the road, overly depending on the technology and zone out while in the car."
T6: Difficulty in answering questionnaire questions	61–70	"Impossible to answer as I don't know details about the system or how it will work or how I will respond and interact with it."
	51–60	"It's difficult to answer some questions - without a familiarity with the robustness of the system that I don't have."

(continued)

Table 3. (*continued*)

Themes	Age Groups	Quotes From Respondents
T7: Concerns around the safety of the technology	41–50	"I will use it if it makes my driving safer."
	20–30	"I will wait for more real-world tests and a safety focused standards organization to provide assurance I will use it."

There was a perceived need by the older age groups (51–70) to be able to override the vehicle's automation system (T1), with respondents stating a requirement of needing to be able to turn off the automation in the vehicle where they would presumably take back the driving control. The older age groups (51–70) also found it difficult to answer the questionnaire with just scenario-based questions (T6), indicating the need for a more ecologically valid experimental set-up to help them visualise the use-cases better.

A related theme to T1 was the expressed discomfort over the vehicle automation taking the driving control without driver confirmation (T2), due to a DMS-identified undesirable driver state, when the respondent was driving. A respondent stated that it would make them "wary" if this were to happen. Another mentioned "There are certain worst-case scenarios where I could let it take over. But simply letting it take over because I'm distracted?", confirming the discomfort experienced. Respondents across the different age groups expressed their inability to decide whether they intend to use automated vehicles that employ such technologies without being able to try such a vehicle or seeing it work successfully with other people (T3). There were quite a few comments in the qualitative responses to suggest the need for increased knowledge and understanding about the system (T4). While some responses suggested the need for training videos, others spoke about the requirement for understanding the system's state through notifications or explanations delivered in the vehicle. Some respondents suggested the need to increase public knowledge through awareness sessions. Others stated the need for more information around privacy and their data sharing from using the technology. There were three comments indicating concerns around partial automation in a vehicle (T5) stating that it would be impossible for drivers to not be in control of the vehicle's driving but be expected to maintain awareness enough to take over driving control when needed. Some other respondents based their decision to use the technology on the expectation that it would make their driving safer but had concerns over whether real-world tests have been conducted on such systems (T7). Out of the 62 responses, 13 answered 'No' to the question "If available to use, I intend to use a driver monitoring system which will allow for human-machine interfaces in conditionally automated vehicles to support me with my driving". It was interesting to note that out of the 13 responses on intention to use the technology, only 4 responses were Male (n = 32), and the remaining 9 responses were Female (n = 30). This further confirms the quantitative findings that align with existing literature that show females experience significantly more anxiety towards the use of the technology than males.

5 Discussion

The inferential tests on the CTAM results reported that females experienced significantly more anxiety about using the technology than males. The same was also seen in the qualitative data with more females reporting a 'No' to intention to use the technology. This finding is consistent with previous publications that found that males are more receptive to AV and related technologies than females and generally felt the expected benefits associated with AVs were more likely to materialize (Schoettle & Sivak 2014; Cunningham et al. 2019). The technology usage of old people is more affected by perceived behavioural control (Morris and Venkatesh, 2000). This can be seen in the qualitative results which interestingly point out that older respondents aged 51–70 displayed a lack of trust in the technology and a requirement for control over the vehicle's automation by needing to turn off the automation as they desired. This finding is consistent with existing research that states that it is important for older drivers to perceive that they can intervene to take over control of an AV at any time even when they are not controlling the vehicle, as driving is a habit that creates a sense of control over their lives (Li et al., 2019). Smyth et al. (2021) talks about how it must be considered that vehicle users are unlikely to be familiar with the technology within their vehicles, as the engineers who designed it will be. This is reinforced by the findings that highlight the ambiguity and lack of understanding around the working of the technology, including system states. The results highlighting the need to increase public awareness around the technologies through demonstration sessions and increasing understanding through the use of in-vehicle HMI support is in line with existing research. Classen et al. (2024) suggest demonstration rides, workshops and roundtable discussions to increase awareness for those who have not been exposed to the technology. Further there exists research that talks about the need for extensive, and regular, training of the human driver, to ensure they have a good understanding and mental model of system capabilities and limitations, which helps to better understand the behaviours and limitations of these new automated features (Endsley 2020; Merat & Louw, 2020). Endsley talks about human operators increasingly being unable to take over manual control when needed, the more robust and reliable automation is added to a vehicle (Endsley 2016). This is seen in the findings with respondents expressing their concerns over partial automation requiring them to stay alert even when not in control of the driving. This is a recognised problem with intermediate levels of automation, for example so-called level 2++ systems which support hands-off, feet-off, but eyes-on driving. With CAVs, the role of the driver changes to that of a supervisor, leading to a need for aides in the vehicle to help them with their altered role. The challenge faces by designers and human factors experts will be to ensure that users have the correct mental model of the system functionality so that their responsibility and expectations are clear (Fisher et al. 2020; Flemisch et al. 2011; Sarter & Woods 1995). The current study findings show that older adults needed a more real-life like experimental set-up to elicit responses. This can be related to research that states that exposure to AVs or simulators, along with surveys more accurately reveal perceptions of drivers (Classen et al. 2024) and further talks about the acceptance of AV technologies by older adults improves when exposed to the technology. Based on this study, the following key recommendations may support governments and manufacturers in effectively realising CAV and advanced vehicle technologies: 1. Alongside introducing these technologies, significant effort must go into building public awareness to foster understanding and trust. This could include public simulator demonstrations, accessible training for potential buyers, or intuitive in-vehicle support to aid comprehension. The study found that experiencing the technology or observing others use it positively influenced respondents' willingness to adopt it. Media coverage of successful implementations and publicising regulations like the Automated Vehicles Bill (2023–2024), which addresses liability, can also build trust. 2. Understanding users' current mental models is essential, so engineers can design according to perceived needs and expectations. This helps identify gaps between user understanding and actual technological capabilities. 3. As noted in this and other studies on AV acceptance, manufacturers should address anxiety-related concerns, especially to ensure gender-inclusive acceptance. 4. To elicit authentic responses during development, studies should use simulations with high ecological validity. This was particularly important for older drivers in the current study, who found scenario-based methods insufficient for providing reliable feedback.

6   Conclusion

The study found general enthusiasm for the technology, but highlighted that ambiguity, low awareness and anxiety, especially experienced by women may affect its acceptance. The use of a scenario-based approach by the exploratory questionnaire required imagination, which limited immersion especially by older participants and is acknowledged as a limitation of the study. The lack of further significance in the CTAM analyses might be explained by the lack of exposure to the technology. The study recommends improving public understanding and trust, suggesting future research on how mental models of DMS and HMIs in CAVs affect acceptability.

Disclosure of Interests.   The authors have no competing interests to declare that are relevant to the content of this article.

References

Automated Vehicles Bill: 167, House of Lords, UK Parliament (2024). https://commonslibrary.parliament.uk/research-briefings/cbp-9973/#:~:text=The%20Automated%20Vehicles%20Bill%20%5BHL,driving%20vehicles%20in%20Great%20Britain

Bonnefon, J.-F., Shariff, A., Rahwan, I.: The social dilemma of autonomous vehicles. Science. **352** (2016). https://doi.org/10.1126/science.aaf2654

Classen, S., Sisiopiku, V.P., Mason, J.R., Yang, W., Hwangbo, S.-W., McKinney, B., Li, Y.: Experience of drivers of all age groups in accepting autonomous vehicle technology. J. Intell. Transp. Syst. **28**(5), 651–667 (2024). https://doi.org/10.1080/15472450.2023.2197115

Cunningham, M.L., Regan, M.A., Horberry, T., Weeratunga, K., Dixit, V.: Public opinion about automated vehicles in Australia: results from a large-scale national survey. Transp. Res. A Policy Pract. **129**, 1–18 (2019). https://doi.org/10.1016/j.tra.2019.08.002

Coyne, R., Hanlon, M., Smeaton, A.F., Corcoran, P., Walsh, J.C.: Understanding drivers' perspectives on the use of driver monitoring systems during automated driving: Findings from a qualitative focus group study. Trans. Res. Traffic Psychol. Behav. **105**, 321–335 (2024). https://doi.org/10.1016/j.trf.2024.07.015

Davis, F.D.: Perceived usefulness, perceived ease of use, and user acceptance of information technology. MIS Q. **13**(3), 319–340 (1989). https://doi.org/10.2307/249008

Fisher, D.L., Horrey, W.J., Lee, J.D., Regan, M.A.: Handbook of Human Factors for Automated, Connected, and Intelligent Vehicles (2020). https://doi.org/10.1201/b21974

Endsley, M.: Situation awareness in driving. In: Horrey, W.J., Fisher, D.L., Lee, J.D., Regan, M.A. (eds.) Handbook of Human Factors for Automated, Connected, and Intelligent Vehicles, 1st edn, (2020). https://doi.org/10.1201/b21974

Endsley, M.R.: From here to autonomy: lessons learned from human–automation research. Hum. Factors. **59**(1), 5–27 (2016). https://doi.org/10.1177/0018720816681350

Flemisch, F., Heesen, M., Hesse, T., Kelsch, J., Schieben, A., Beller, J.: Towards a dynamic balance between humans and automation: authority, ability, responsibility and control in shared and cooperative control situations. Cogn. Tech. Work. **14**, 3–18 (2011). https://doi.org/10.1007/s10111-011-0191-6

Ghazizadeh, M., Lee, J.: Modelling driver acceptance: from feedback to monitoring and mentoring systems. In: Driver Acceptance of New Technology: Theory, Measurement and Optimisation, pp. 51–70 (2014). https://doi.org/10.1201/9781315578132-5

Guettas, A., Ayad, S., Kazar, O.: Driver state monitoring system: a review (2019). https://doi.org/10.1145/3372938.3372966

Sanaei, N.H., Ghofranipour, F., Kazemnejad, A., Khavanin, A., Tavakoli, R.: Evaluation of knowledge, attitude and behavior of workers towards occupational health and safety. Iran. J. Public Health. **38**, 125–129 (2009) http://eprints.bmsu.ac.ir/id/eprint/6942

Hewitt, C., Amanatidis, T., Sarkar, A., Politis, I.: Assessing public perception of self-driving cars: the autonomous vehicle acceptance model. In: IUI '19: Proceedings of the 24th International Conference on Intelligent User Interfaces (2019). https://doi.org/10.1145/3301275.3302268

Li, S., Blythe, P., Guo, W., Namdeo, A.: Investigation of older drivers' requirements of the human-machine interaction in highly automated vehicles. Trans. Res. Traffic Psychol. Behav. **62**, 546–563 (2019). https://doi.org/10.1016/j.trf.2019.02.009

Merat, N., Seppelt, B., Louw, T., Engström, J., Lee, J.D., Johansson, E., Green, C.A., Katazaki, S., Monk, C., Itoh, M., McGehee, D., Sunda, T., Unoura, K., Victor, T., Schieben, A., Keinath, A.: The "out-of-the-loop" concept in automated driving: proposed definition, measures and implications. Cogn. Tech. Work. **21**(1), 87–98 (2019). https://doi.org/10.1007/s10111-018-0525-8

Regan, M.A., Strayer, D.L.: Towards an understanding of driver inattention: taxonomy and theory. Assoc. Adv. Automot. Med. **58**, 5–14 (2014) https://pmc.ncbi.nlm.nih.gov/articles/PMC4001671/

Merat, N., Louw, T.: Allocation of function to humans and automation and the transfer of control. In: Fisher, W.J.H.D.L., Lee, J.D., Regan, M.a. (eds.) Handbook of human factors for automated, connected, and intelligent vehicles, 1st edn, p. 19 (2020). https://doi.org/10.1201/b21974

Osswald, S., Wurhofer, D., Trösterer, S., Beck, E., Tscheligi, M.: Predicting information technology usage in the car: towards a car technology acceptance model. In: AutomotiveUI '12: 4th International Conference on Automotive User Interfaces and Interactive Vehicular Applications (2012). https://doi.org/10.1145/2390256.2390264

Rödel, C., Stadler, S., Meschtscherjakov, A., Tscheligi, M.: Towards autonomous cars: the effect of autonomy levels on acceptance and user experience. In: AutomotiveUI '14: Proceedings of the 6th International Conference on Automotive User Interfaces and Interactive Vehicular Applications (2014). https://doi.org/10.1145/2667317.26673

Sarah Schwindt-Drews, K.S., Peters, S., Abendroth, B.: Acceptance and trust: drivers' first contact with released automated vehicles in naturalistic traffic. IEEE Trans. Intell. Transp. Syst., 1–10 (2023). https://doi.org/10.48550/arxiv.2312.08957

Sarter, N., Woods, D.: How in the world did we ever get into that mode? Mode error and awareness in supervisory control. Hum. Factors. **37**, 5–19 (1995). https://doi.org/10.1518/001872095779 049516

Schoettle, B., Sivak, M.: A survey of public opinion about connected vehicles in the U.S. In: The U.K., and Australia 2014 International Conference on Connected Vehicles and Expo (ICCVE), Vienna, Austria (2014). https://doi.org/10.1109/ICCVE.2014.7297637

Smyth, J., Chen, H., Donzella, V., Woodman, R.: Public acceptance of driver state monitoring for automated vehicles: applying the UTAUT framework. Transport. Res. F: Traffic Psychol. Behav. **83**, 179–191 (2021). https://doi.org/10.1016/j.trf.2021.10.003

Trösterer, S., Gaertner, M., Mirnig, A., Meschtscherjakov, A., McCall, R., Louveton, N., Tscheligi, M., Engel, T.: You never forget how to drive: driver skilling and deskilling in the advent of autonomous vehicles. In: Automotive 'UI 16: Proceedings of the 8th International Conference on Automotive User Interfaces and Interactive Vehicular Applications (2016). https://doi.org/ 10.1145/3003715.3005462

Venkatesh, V., Davis, F.D.: A theoretical extension of the technology acceptance model: four longitudinal field studies. Manag. Sci. **46**(2), 186–204 (2000). http://www.jstor.org/stable/263 4758

Venkatesh, V., Morris, M.G., Davis, G.B., Davis, F.D.: User acceptance of information technology: toward a unified view. MIS Q. **27**(3), 425–478 (2003). https://doi.org/10.2307/30036540

Thermal Comfort in Autonomous Vehicles: A Survey Study on Activity-Based Preferences and Climate Control Strategies

Manuel Kipp, Yijie Sheng[(✉)], Aysu Sözbir, and Klaus Bengler

Chair of Ergonomics, Technical University of Munich, 85748 Garching, Germany
`{manuel.kipp,yijie.sheng,bengler}@tum.de`

Abstract. The introduction of autonomous vehicles (AVs) presents significant challenges in achieving optimal thermal comfort for passengers. Conventional air conditioning (AC) systems, which are designed around a fixed, driver-centric layout, are not equipped to handle the diverse in-cabin activities that are characteristic of AVs. This paper presents a comprehensive, survey-based analysis of thermal comfort preferences across three primary activity modes: productivity, entertainment, and relaxation. A review of the fundamental principles of thermal comfort is conducted, and current ventilation strategies are examined with an emphasis on adaptive, personalized climate control and the concept of Non-Driving Related Activities (NDRAs). An extensive online survey is described, and the resulting data indicate a gender difference in thermal sensitivity and local ventilation preferences for NDRAs. The findings underscore the significance of adaptive climate control for future AVs, emphasizing the need for user-centered, energy-efficient solutions.

Keywords: Thermal Comfort · Autonomous Vehicles (AVs) · Adaptive Climate Control · Ventilation Strategies · Survey Study · Non-Driving Related Activities (NDRAs)

1 Introduction

AVs are increasingly recognized as a promising technology capable of reshaping personal mobility and transportation services [5]. Unlike conventional cars designed around a driver-centric layout, AVs allow flexible seating arrangements that enable occupants to engage in various NDRAs, such as working, socializing, or relaxing. This shift toward passenger-focused interiors creates new demands for in-cabin systems, particularly climate control [8].

Thermal comfort is a central aspect of the in-cabin experience, influencing alertness, productivity, and overall well-being [6]. However, satisfying the comfort

---

M. Kipp and Y. Sheng—These authors contributed equally to this work.

© The Author(s), under exclusive license to Springer Nature Switzerland AG 2026

S. Sundarakannan and O. Knorpp (Eds.): HCII 2025, CCIS 2772, pp. 15–26, 2026.
https://doi.org/10.1007/978-3-032-12767-9_2

requirements of multiple occupants simultaneously poses inherent challenges. One passenger might need targeted cooling to remain attentive during work, while another may prefer a warmer, more diffuse environment suited for relaxation. Existing mixing ventilation approaches, which distribute air uniformly, often fall short of accommodating these varying preferences, potentially causing discomfort from uneven airflow or localized temperature gradients [12].

Recent advances in sensor-based technologies and machine learning have enabled adaptive climate control that continuously adjusts airflow, temperature, and humidity for each occupant based on real-time data. Examples include infrared-based posture and heat mapping [18], and federated learning approaches for temperature prediction based on individual preferences [9]. However, many of these systems are still developed in lab-based or building-related contexts that do not fully reflect the diversity of activities and environmental dynamics in AV interiors [25].

2   State of the Art

This section provides an overview of the key factors that influence thermal comfort for occupants in AV interiors. It also examines the role of NDRAs in shaping occupant needs. Additionally, it reviews the limitations of conventional AC systems.

2.1   Fundamentals of Thermal Comfort

Thermal comfort is typically defined as an individual's subjective sense of satisfaction with the ambient thermal environment [6]. Core parameters include air temperature, humidity, radiant heat, and airflow velocity. These parameters can affect the human body's heat balance and perception of comfort [2]. In the context of vehicles, factors such as seat material, occupant anatomy, and posture are also known to influence localized thermal sensations [29]. Although the Predicted Mean Vote (PMV) was originally developed for the design of interior spaces, vehicle cabins present distinctive challenges. These include rapid changes in interior temperature and occupant position, which can compromise the direct application of building-centric standards [4].

Research into automotive climate control focused primarily on conventional driver-oriented setups, offering limited accommodation for multiple passengers or flexible seating [29]. As AVs evolve, seating may rotate or recline, and interior layouts are becoming more passenger-centered. These shifts present a unique challenge to maintaining thermal comfort because occupant activities can vary significantly. These activities range from productivity tasks that require high alertness to relaxation activities that favor warmer, calmer conditions [26]. Further research indicates that factors such as age, gender, and other individual attributes influence how occupants experience and adapt to cabin temperatures [7]. These complexities underscore the limitations of conventional climate systems in AV environments.

2.2 Non-driving Related and Occupant Activities

Recent studies emphasize that autonomous functionalities enable occupants to carry out activities beyond driving, often referred to as NDRAs [10,14,16]. Surveys and observational data have identified a variety of such tasks, ranging from simple media consumption to collaborative work sessions [10,16]. These tasks impose distinct demands on cabin comfort and tend to share broad comfort requirements.

Productivity tasks may require a cooler environment to sustain alertness. However, certain entertainment or relaxation activities may be compatible with warmer conditions and lower airflow velocity [21,26]. Demographic factors, such as age and cultural background, introduce additional complexities to these preferences. Research indicates that younger adults may be more comfortable with cooler cabin temperatures for activities such as gaming or media viewing. In contrast, older adults often prefer slightly warmer environments for social interactions or reading activities, as cited in the study by Foncesa [7].

2.3 Conventional Air Conditioning Systems and Their Limitations

The majority of current vehicles use mixing ventilation, which distributes conditioned air evenly throughout the cabin via a limited number of vents. While these designs are adequate for standard, driver-centered layouts, they are less effective in autonomous settings that feature a broader range of occupant activities and seating possibilities [19]. Passengers near windows often receive elevated solar heat, while those located farther from the main air outlets may experience insufficient airflow [20]. Rapid transitions between external environments, such as moving from direct sunlight into tunnels, present challenges for static air distribution strategies. These concerns highlight the importance of advanced systems capable of adjusting airflow and temperature according to individual occupant needs and in-room conditions.

3 Motivation and Research Questions

Despite the progress made in emphasizing the significance of occupant-centric climate control, several challenges remain. The existing literature frequently addresses occupant demographics, task diversity, and climate control methods as discrete topics. However, there is a lack of an integrated perspective on how these factors intersect in real-world AV scenarios. Furthermore, the majority of adaptive concepts remain in the preliminary stages of development, placing greater emphasis on technical feasibility rather than energy trade-offs, long-term comfort, and passenger acceptance.

The present work builds upon these identified gaps by examining how demographic factors and varied NDRA modes jointly shape occupant comfort in AV interiors. The survey-based approach is a comprehensive and empirical way to validate emerging hypotheses on adaptive ventilation's potential for enhancing comfort while maintaining efficiency. The objective is to inform the development of next-generation climate control systems capable of meeting the evolving requirements of autonomous mobility. To examine these issues systematically, three research questions guide the present investigation:

RQ1: How do gender difference influence thermal comfort in AV interiors?

RQ2: How do various in-cabin modes (productivity, entertainment, relaxation) affect perceived thermal comfort and preferences for ventilation concepts in AV interiors?

RQ3: Which ventilation strategies are most effective in providing personalized and adaptive climate control in AV interiors?

These questions structure the subsequent survey design and data analysis, offering a framework for understanding how user-centered comfort requirements can be integrated into next-generation autonomous vehicle interiors.

4   Methodology

This section outlines the questionnaire structure, sample details and data analysis. The survey was administered via LimeSurvey, a platform provided by the Chair of Ergonomics at TUM, and remained open for a period of four weeks. All participation was voluntary and without compensation. Ethical approval for this study was granted by the Ethics Commission of the Technical University of Munich under reference 701/21 S-NP.

4.1   Survey Design and Structure

The questionnaire is organized into four main parts to ensure a systematic collection of relevant data:

1. **Demographics.** Participants reported age, gender, geographical region, and typical vehicle usage patterns, following guidelines for comprehensive occupant profiling [22].
2. **Activity Modes.** Scenarios representing productivity, entertainment, and relaxation were presented, with each scenario containing items on temperature preferences, airflow needs, and perceived comfort for winter and summer conditions. These scenarios were informed by prior research on NDRAs in AV contexts [14, 16].
3. **Environmental Preferences.** Participants indicated the temperature ranges they found comfortable, and overall satisfaction ratings. This section was based on thermal comfort measurement methodologies adapted to vehicular applications [4].
4. **Ventilation Configurations.** Questions on global and local ventilation concepts for specific body parts were included to evaluate spatial factors that affect thermal perception.

4.2   Sample

A total of 213 individuals aged 18 years and above fully participated in the online survey, including 140 males, 71 females, and two individuals who preferred not to disclose their gender. The average age of the participants was 27.39 years ($SD =$ 9.45). The participants in the study ranged in age from 18 to 58 years, with the majority (72.30%) falling between the ages of 21 and 30. Most participants ($N = 120$) were from Germany, followed by 27 from the United States.

Regarding vehicle usage, the most common daily commute duration is 30–60 min (50 males, 22 females), followed by commuting for 10–30 min (32 males, 22 females). After excluding participants who did not own an automobile equipped with AC or who were uncertain about it, over 75% of both males and females reported using AC either 'always' or 'often'.

Given the focus of the study on NDRAs in AVs, participants were also asked about their knowledge of autonomous driving. According to the findings, over 80% of the respondents have dealt with this subject at least once. This approach ensured the reliability of the questionnaire responses, despite the fact that all AV-related scenarios were clarified in the survey.

4.3   Data Analysis

The survey data is analyzed using descriptive statistics and inferential statistical methods. The Mann-Whitney U test and the Friedman test are used for non-parametric and ordinal samples, while the chi-square test is employed for categorical data analysis. The following effect thresholds are used to present the magnitude of significant results: 0.1 for a small effect, 0.3 for a medium effect, and 0.5 for a large effect [3].

Due to the predominance of German residency and the under-30 age group, it was not feasible to conduct demographic comparisons based on the regional or age factors. Therefore, gender was the only demographic factor under discussion in this paper. The chi-square test and the Mann-Whitney U test were used to analyze gender differences in thermal sensitivity and comfort ($RQ1$). The Friedman test was then conducted to assess temperature preferences across various in-cabin activities in AVs, and the chi-square test was applied to analyze the preferences for local and global ventilation concepts across three activity modes ($RQ2$). Due to the limitations in sample size, data on local ventilation concepts for personalized and adaptive climate control were analyzed descriptively ($RQ3$). Unless otherwise stated, a significance value of $p < .05$ was applied to all inferential tests.

5   Results

5.1   Gender Differences in Thermal Perception and Preferences

Looking into the two gender groups, 67.1% of females reported freezing quickly compared to 30.7% of males. While 62.0% of males reported getting warm quickly

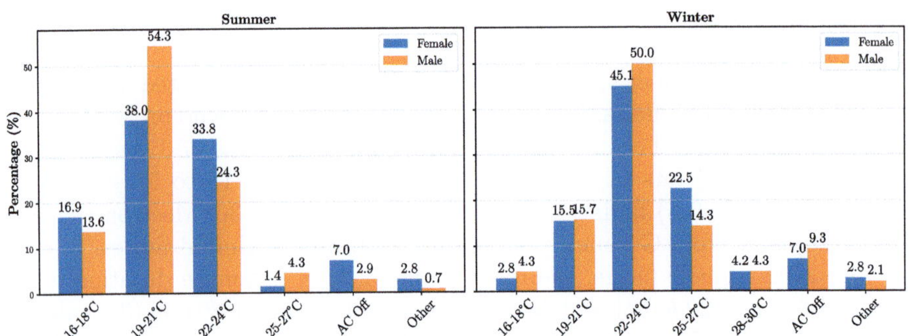

Fig. 1. Preferred AC temperature ranges under summer and winter conditions.

compared to 45.7% of females. Significant differences were observed in their sensitivity to cold ($\chi^2 = 4.76$, $p < .001$, $V = .353$) and warmth ($\chi^2 = 6.31$, $p = .043$, $V = .174$).

Regarding participants' preferred most comfortable AC temperature setting in traditional vehicles, as shown in Fig. 1, preferences were assessed separately for summer and winter conditions with a 5-point temperature scale ($0 = 16 - 18°C, 1 = 19 - 21°C, 2 = 22 - 24°C, 3 = 25 - 27°C, 4 = 28 - 30°C$). In summer, more than half of the male participants tended to set the AC temperature at $19 - 21°C$. Among female participants, 38.0% chose the same temperature range, while another 33.8% preferred a setting of $22 - 24°C$. In winter, most participants reported setting the AC temperature to $22 - 24°C$. No significant differences between gender groups were found in preferred AC temperature settings in both conditions ($summer : U = 4167, p = .660; winter : U = 3636, p = .303$)

5.2   Temperature and Ventilation Preferences Across In-Cabin Activities in AV Interiors

The same 5-point temperature scale was used to assess participants' temperature setting preference across three different activity modes. Figure 2 illustrates the seasonal distribution of preferred AC temperature across three activities. A clear temperature difference can be observed between summer and winter conditions.

In all three activities, approximately 50% of the participants preferred the temperature to be set at 19–21°C in summer, while in winter, the majority preferred it to be set at 22–24°C. However, no significant difference was found for the temperature preference among the three modes ($summer : \chi^2 = 5.80, p = .055; winter : \chi^2 = .403, p = .818$).

When further asked to indicate their preference between global and local ventilation for specific body parts across three modes, the majority preferred global ventilation (see Fig. 3). However, a chi-square test revealed a significant difference between activity type and ventilation preference ($\chi^2 = 10.04, p = .007, V = .125,$). A standardized residuals analysis provided further details of the distribution of preferences. A significant positive residual ($+2.33$) was observed

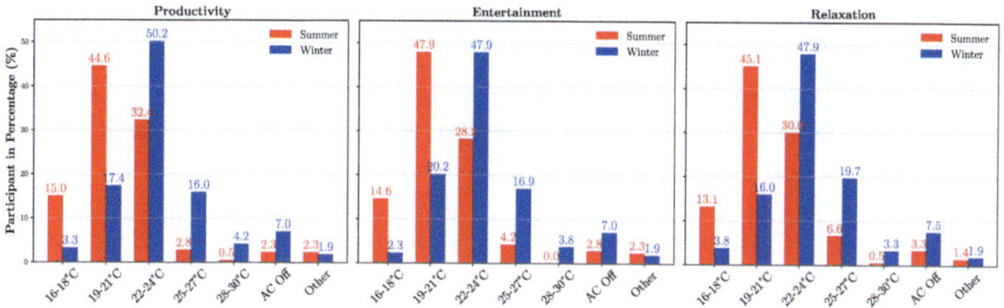

Fig. 2. Preferred AC temperature ranges across three activity modes

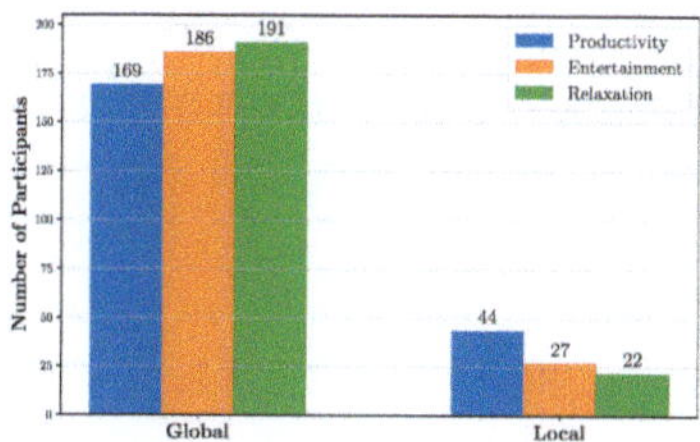

Fig. 3. Global and local ventilation preferences across three activity modes

for the productivity mode, while in the other two modes, no significant residuals were found (*Entertainment* : -1.62; *Relaxation* : -0.72).

5.3   Local Ventilation for Personalized and Adaptive Climate Control

Participants who chose local ventilation were further asked to indicate which body parts they wished to be ventilated. Figure 4 presents the distribution of these preferences across three activity modes.

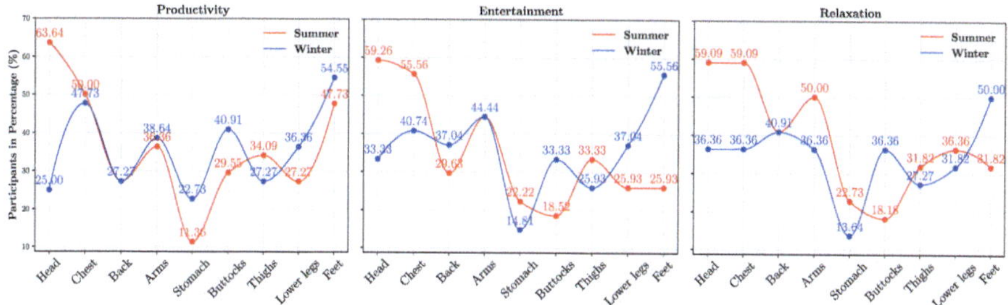

Fig. 4. Preferred ventilated body parts across three activity modes

Seasonal shifts were found in the head and feet areas. The majority preferred direct cooling airflow to the head during summer (63.64% in productivity,

59.26% in entertainment, 59.09% in relaxation). At the same time, it was less preferred to warm the head area in winter (25.00% in productivity, 33.33% in entertainment, 33.36% in relaxation). Feet ventilation became relatively more important in winter (54.55% in productivity, 55.56% in entertainment, 50.00% in relaxation). And notably, it was still favored during the productivity mode in summer.

Regarding activity-related differences, preferences for chest and arm ventilation remained relatively stable across all three modes. However, there was a strong seasonal contrast for the stomach ventilation during the productivity mode, with only 11.36% of respondents preferring it in summer compared to 22.73% in winter. In contrast, the other two modes demonstrated a distinct pattern, with the stomach being more frequently preferred in summer. A similar seasonal divergence was also found between productivity and the other two modes for the lower legs.

6   Discussion

The survey results analyzed gender differences in thermal comfort and demonstrated that ventilation preferences vary across seasons and activity types. This underscores the necessity for a customized ventilation strategy to address the diverse thermal demands observed in AV cabins.

While prior studies have indicated that females may be more sensitive to cold and males to warmth, the present survey did not reveal statistically significant differences in preferred comfortable in-cabin temperatures between genders. This finding aligns with the research by Kwak et al. [13], who reported gender-based physiological differences (e.g. skin temperature) without corresponding differences in overall thermal comfort ratings in vehicle environments. However, it is important to note that the analysis in this study was limited to gender due to sample composition, which was predominantly young and from the same geographical region. Consequently, other demographic factors, such as age or regional background, which may also influence thermal comfort preferences, could not be statistically evaluated in this survey [24, 30].

In the three modes of AVs, the preferred comfortable temperature range is consistent with the most common choice of 19–21°C in summer and 21–24°C in winter conditions. According to the comfort zones defined by ISO 14505-2 [4] and Nilsson [15], the summer range corresponds to the 'cold but comfortable' category, and the winter range falls within the 'neutral' category. This suggests that during summer months, cabin temperature may need to be set slightly cooler than the neutral range to meet passenger comfort expectations, as also found by Rolle [17] and Yun et al. [28]. It is important to note that preferences for ventilation concepts differed depending on the in-cabin activities. This preference is particularly evident in the productivity mode, where participants exhibited a stronger inclination for local ventilation. It can be assumed that targeted airflow on specific body parts may be valued when occupants are engaged in focused or task-oriented activities.

A subsequent investigation into the preferences for local ventilation revealed that preferences for specific body parts, such as the chest and arms, remained consistent across all three modes. During the summer months, participants placed greater emphasis on upper-body ventilation, while in the winter, their preferences shifted toward the lower body. This finding aligns with the results reported by Kipp et al. [11], which indicate that upper-body airflow under summer conditions contributes positively to overall thermal comfort.

The stomach received low priority for ventilation, especially during summer productivity mode. This may be attributed to concerns that exposure to cold airflow in this area could potentially trigger digestive issues. Furthermore, there is a trend towards more body parts being ventilated during productive tasks, indicating a need for more distributed airflow to maintain comfort and concentration under cognitively demanding conditions. In contrast, fewer ventilated regions were perceived as sufficient during entertainment and relaxation.

These findings also offer valuable insights for the future development of adaptive airflow management and climate control in AV interiors. Research on adaptive ventilation systems in building contexts has suggested efficiency gains and higher occupant satisfaction [27,31], suggesting similar outcomes may be attainable in fully autonomous vehicles. Furthermore, studies by Wang et al. [23] and Aryal at al. [1] have confirmed the energy-saving potential of personalized thermal comfort. Based on these insights, it is necessary to design activity-based adaptive airflow strategies for AV cabins, aiming to achieve both energy efficiency and optimal thermal comfort of occupants.

It is essential to confirm that DIN ISO 14505-2's comfort zones [4], with summer defined as 'cool but comfortable' and winter defined as 'neutral' reflect the activity and demographic variations observed. To ensure the validity of the findings, it is essential to validate the bands in a real AV setting. This involves recording in-cabin temperature and airflow alongside skin temperature or other physiological metrics from participants of diverse ages and backgrounds. This data will inform a new comfort model tailored to activity and gender, refine adaptive airflow algorithms, and guide the adaptation of DIN ISO 14505-2 [4] for vehicle use.

7   Limitations

While the survey and its supporting analyses provide valuable insights into potential avenues for adaptive climate control in AVs, it is important to note several limitations that require careful consideration. First, the use of self-reported data introduces an element of subjectivity and potential recall bias, as respondents may overestimate or underestimate their comfort preferences. Second, the lack of objective physiological or environmental measurements, such as in-cabin temperature logs or real-time airflow tracking, limits the precision of the findings. In the absence of these data streams, it remains challenging to verify whether the reports provided by occupants are in alignment with the actual thermal conditions.

The study's conclusions are derived from conceptual models and an online survey rather than from controlled or on-road experiments. Although simulations and user feedback can guide the early stages of system design, real-world testing in autonomous vehicle prototypes is essential to assess how factors like seat orientation, group dynamics, and changing external conditions impact overall comfort and energy usage.

8 Conclusions and Future Work

This paper has examined the multifaceted nature of thermal comfort in AV interiors. The survey findings indicate the existence of gender-based differences in thermal sensitivity, underscoring the necessity for adapting ventilation strategies according to NDRAs in AVs. It also highlights the importance of customized and adaptive ventilation solutions for enhancing thermal comfort and energy efficiency in future AV interiors.

Building on this foundation, future research should explore the influence of additional demographic factors and advance the development of modular heating, ventilation and air conditioning (HVAC) architectures to enable user-centered, personalized, and adaptive thermal comfort systems. To ensure the validation of performance, reliability, and user acceptance of these adaptive approaches, controlled on-road testing and long-term user studies are essential. As autonomous vehicles continue to transform the landscape of personal mobility, robust, human-centric climate solutions will play a pivotal role in promoting occupant well-being, user satisfaction, and environmental sustainability.

Acknowledgments. Support for this research was provided by the Chair of Ergonomics at the Technical University of Munich. The contributions of all survey participants and the extensive body of literature on automotive thermal comfort are gratefully acknowledged.

References

1. Aryal, A., Becerik-Gerber, B., Lucas, G.M., Roll, S.C.: Intelligent agents to improve thermal satisfaction by controlling personal comfort systems under different levels of automation. IEEE Internet Things J. **8**(8), 7089–7100 (2021)
2. ASHRAE. ASHRAE®Handbook - Fundamentals - Thermal Comfort (2017)
3. Cohen, J.: Statistical power analysis for the behavioral sciences. L. Erlbaum Associates, Hillsdale, N.J, 2nd ed edition (1988)
4. DIN EN ISO. DIN EN ISO 14505-2 Ergonomie der thermischen Umgebung Beurteilung der thermischen Umgebung in Fahrzeugen Teil 2: Bestimmung der Äquivalenttemperatur (ISO 14505-2:2006); Deutsche Fassung EN ISO 14505-2:2006 (2007). Number: 145050-2
5. Eluru, N., Choudhury, C.F.: Impact of shared and autonomous vehicles on travel behavior. Transportation **46**(6), 1971–1974 (2019)
6. Fanger, P.O.: Thermal Comfort: Analysis and Applications in Environmental Engineering. McGraw-Hill Book Company (1970)

7. Fonseca, E.: The Impacts of Temperature on Health and Comfort. PhD thesis, Ariozona State University (2013)
8. Gehringer, D., Kuthada, T., Wagner, A.: Thermal management system of the UNICARagil vehicles–a comprehensive overview. World Electric Veh. J. **14**(1), 6 (2022)
9. Gül, B.C., Devarakonda, N., Jazdi, N., Weyrich, M.: Personalized comfort features in software-defined vehicles using federated learning. In: 2024 IEEE 29th International Conference on Emerging Technologies and Factory Automation (ETFA), pp. 1–7, Padova, Italy, September (2024). IEEE
10. Hecht, T., Darlagiannis, E., Bengler, K.: Non-driving related activities in automated driving – an online survey investigating user needs. In: Ahram, T., Karwowski, W., Pickl, S., Taiar, R. (eds.) Human Systems Engineering and Design II, volume 1026, pp. 182–188. Springer International Publishing, Cham (2020). Series Title: Advances in Intelligent Systems and Computing
11. Kipp, M., Rolle, A., Bengler, K.: An innovative seat ventilation concept: does the seat provide overall thermal comfort in autonomous vehicles? In: Black, N.L., Neumann, W.P., Noy, I. (eds.) IEA 2021. LNNS, vol. 221, pp. 701–709. Springer, Cham (2021). https://doi.org/10.1007/978-3-030-74608-7_85
12. Kramer, T., Garcia-Hansen, V., Omrani, S., Zhou, J., Chen, D.: Personal differences in thermal comfort perception: observations from a field study in Brisbane. Aust. Build. Environ. **245**, 110873 (2023)
13. Kwak, J., Chun, C., Park, J.-S., Kim, S., Seo, S.: The gender and age differences in the passengers' thermal comfort during cooling and heating conditions in vehicles. PLoS ONE **18**(11), e0294027 (2023)
14. Naujoks, F., Befelein, D., Wiedemann, K., Neukum, A.: A review of non-driving-related tasks used in studies on automated driving. In: Stanton, N.A. (ed.) AHFE 2017. AISC, vol. 597, pp. 525–537. Springer, Cham (2018). https://doi.org/10.1007/978-3-319-60441-1_52
15. Nilsson, H.O.: Thermal comfort evaluation with virtual manikin methods. Build. Environ. **42**(12), 4000–4005 (2007)
16. Pfleging, B., Rang, M., Broy, N.: Investigating user needs for non-driving-related activities during automated driving. In: Proceedings of the 15th International Conference on Mobile and Ubiquitous Multimedia, pp. 91–99, Rovaniemi Finland. ACM (2016)
17. Rolle, A.D.: Objektive Bewertung des thermischen Komforts im Pkw Entwicklung von Methodiken für aktuelle und zukünftige Klimakonzepte. PhD thesis, Technische Universiteit München, Garching (2022)
18. Román, P., Knoch, E.M.: Wide-Angle Thermal Sensing for Personalized Climate Control: An Infrared Fisheye Camera Approach in Commuter Vehicles (2025)
19. Schmeling, D., Shishkin, A., Dehne, T., Lange, P., Gores, I.: Evaluation of thermal comfort for novel aircraft cabin ventilation concepts. Aerospace Europe Conference 2020, (2020)
20. Stuke, P.E.B.: Vertical interior cooling system for passenger cars: Trials and evaluation of feasibility, thermal comfort and energy efficiency. PhD thesis, Technische Universiteit München, Garching (2016)
21. Tamura, K., et al.: Physiological and subjective comfort evaluation under different airflow directions in a cooling environment. PLOS ONE **16**(4), e0249235 (2021)
22. Wadhwa, A., Kalsia, M.: A critical review on occupant's thermal comfort inside electric vehicle car cabin. In: 2023 2nd Edition of IEEE Delhi Section Flagship Conference (DELCON), pp. 1–7, Rajpura, India (2023). IEEE

23. Wang, J., Xie, X., Xingjun, H., Wang, B., Guo, P., Tianming, Yu.: Research on thermal comfort of human body under localized automotive air conditioning. J. Thermal Sci. Eng. Appl. **17**(1), 011002 (2025)
24. Yuxin, W., et al.: Age differences in thermal comfort and physiological responses in thermal environments with temperature ramp. Build. Environ. **228**, 109887 (2023)
25. Xin, X., Zhao, L., Yang, Z.: Prediction models of overall thermal sensation and comfort in vehicle cabin based on field experiments. Int. J. Automot. Technol. **26**(1), 269–282 (2025)
26. Ye, X.J., Lian, Z.W., Zhou, Z.P., Feng, J.M., Li, C.Z., Liu, Y.M.: INDOOR ENVIRONMENT, THERMAL COMFORT AND PRODUCTIVITY. Indoor Air (2005)
27. Yun, G.Y., Lee, J.H., Steemers, K.: Extending the applicability of the adaptive comfort model to the control of air-conditioning systems. Build. Environ. **105**, 13–23 (2016)
28. Yun, S., et al.: Prediction of thermal comfort of female passengers in a vehicle based on an outdoor experiment. Energy Build. **248**, 111161 (2021)
29. Zhang, H., Arens, E., Huizenga, C., Han, T.: Thermal sensation and comfort models for non-uniform and transient environments, part II: local comfort of individual body parts. Build. Environ. **45**(2), 389–398 (2010)
30. Zhang, N., Cao, B., Wang, Z., Zhu, Y., Lin, B.: A comparison of winter indoor thermal environment and thermal comfort between regions in Europe, North America, and Asia. Build. Environ. **117**, 208–217 (2017)
31. Zhang, W., Zhang, W., Zhang, H., Xuan, Y., Liu, X.: Effective improvement of a local thermal environment using multi-vent module-based adaptive ventilation. Build. Simul. **16**(7), 1115–1134 (2023)

Design of Automated Transport Equipment for Plant Factory Based on UJM-AHP-FAST

Bingxin Li and Li Xu[✉]

School of Art Design and Media, East China University of Science and Technology, Shang-hai, China
2298684060@qq.com

Abstract. The plant factory employing vertical agriculture exhibits short production cycles and high yields, necessitating an automated conveying system as the core element for ensuring capacity. This study segments the stages of automated transportation from a human-computer interaction perspective, utilizing the UJM-AHP-FAST analysis model to analyze and design automated transportation equipment. The aim is to systematically organize design requirements, rationally and scientifically evaluate the importance of sub-functions, and guide research and development investments. Initially, during the User Journey Map (UJM) construction, 16 design requirements across four modules are identified through in-depth research, forming a hierarchical model. The Analytic Hierarchy Process (AHP) is then used to weight these requirements. Subsequently, Functional Analysis System Technique (FAST) transforms the nine highest-weighted requirements into functional components, constructing the equipment's functional system model. Finally, guided by UJM-AHP-FAST, the design of automated transport equipment is completed, demonstrating the model's efficacy in logical analysis and emphasizing a user-centered, structured development approach.

Keywords: Plant factory · Automated transportation equipment · UJM · AHP · FAST

1 Introduction

The fully automated production mode has emerged as the developmental trajectory for vertical agricultural plant factories. Ensuring minimal damage rates, machines can transport each planting unit in just 2 min [1], operating over 10 times faster than manual labor, thus mitigating issues such as fatigue, high-altitude operational risks, and inefficiency associated with manual handling.

Stereoscopic automated transfer operations encompass ground transportation, lifting transfers, and in-rack transfers, involving equipment like conveyor belts, mobile robots, lifting racks, shuttle cars, and mechanical arm, typically orchestrated by a central dispatching system. The choice of transfer mode and equipment varies with the factory's production scale and investment capacity. Various studies and implementations have explored transfer modes. For instance, Tokimasa et al. [2] proposed a shuttle-mode

© The Author(s), under exclusive license to Springer Nature Switzerland AG 2026
S. Sundarakannan and O. Knorpp (Eds.): HCII 2025, CCIS 2772, pp. 27–37, 2026.
https://doi.org/10.1007/978-3-032-12767-9_3

seedling tray transportation system for localized progressive or reciprocating transportation in vertical plant factories. Sananbio's [3] unmanned vertical agricultural production system integrates shuttle cars with lifting platforms, wireless guided vehicle or conveyor belt, achieving high automation and flexibility, with commercialization success. Codema [4] utilizes the seedbed as the planting unit, designing an automatic seedbed conveying system to facilitate indoor transportation of large seedbeds, adopted by Shanghai Dadi Horticultural Seedlings Co., Ltd. for progressive transportation. Osaka Prefectural University [5] developed a gantry-type transfer device with tracks between seedling frames, ensuring high stability but limited mobility. Jones Food in the UK employs super-high forklifts for seedbed transportation between the planting frame and the sowing and harvesting area, simplifying logistics but increasing operational complexity and risk.

Leveraging IoT technology [6], intelligent dispatching systems can control and execute automatic transfers in plant factories. Wan Peng et al. [7] developed an automated potted plant transportation management system integrating equipment (AGV, conveyor) control and potted plant information management for greenhouse rice cultivation and transport. Huang Longxian's [8] intelligent dispatching system for vertical agriculture comprises six layers, enabling remote access and intelligent management via cloud platforms.

Improved automation in plant factories centers human - machine interaction on the control panel, requiring systematic organization of the user journey and interaction to analyze and extract design requirements. Due to high operational and maintenance costs, automated production demands robust system integration. As a complex functional entity, automated transportation equipment should scientifically assess the significance of its sub - functions to guide R&D investments effectively.

2   Materials and Methods

2.1   Establishment of the UJM-AHP-FAST Model Analysis Method

The User Journey Map (UJM) is capable of conducting an in-depth analysis of users' needs and pain points within specific usage scenarios. By integrating the AHP-FAST method [9, 10] on this basis, a complete closed-loop path from problem identification, analysis to solution can be established. In light of this, this paper aims to develop a design research methodology for automated transport equipment in plant factories based on the User Journey Map (UJM), Analytic Hierarchy Process (AHP), and Function Analysis System Technique (FAST), providing a clear and systematic path for product design and development. The entire process is illustrated in Fig. 1.

First, guided by user behavior, this study constructs a User Journey Map using research, observation, interviews, and human - machine interaction analysis. It precisely divides user behavior stages from an HCI perspective and identifies demand pain points at each stage. Then, the Analytic Hierarchy Process organizes design requirements, builds a hierarchical model and judgment matrix, determines and ranks demand indicator weights after a consistency test. Next, the Function Analysis System Technique transforms and integrates functions, creating a function tree model to define product structural modules and key technologies. Finally, conceptual design forms a complete, scientific design loop.

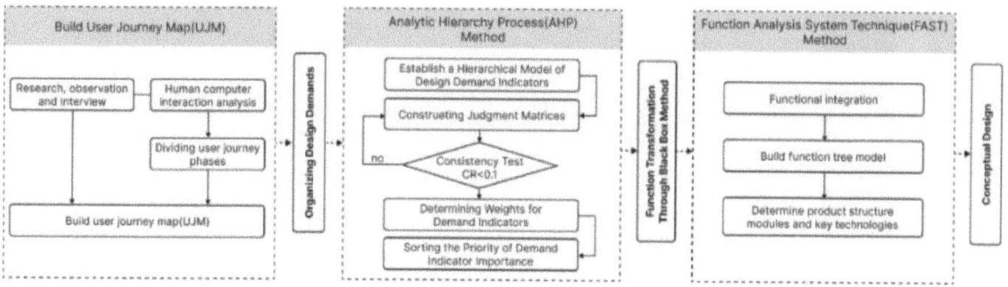

Fig. 1. Design process based on the UJM-AHP-FAST method.

2.2   Establishment of User Journey Map and Derivation of Design Requirements

HCI-Based User Journey Stage Division. In plant factory operation systems, good HCI design is vital for efficient, convenient operator - automated transfer equipment interactions. During HCI, when a user starts an operation and engages with the system interface or functions, the system should offer a user - friendly interface guide and clear prompts to accommodate the action and smoothly lead the user to subsequent interaction stages. This process helps divide user experience stages. The User Journey Map (UJM) then aids in understanding and optimizing interactions by analyzing information exchange, behavioral interactions, and emotional experiences between users and the system (software and hardware). Peter Wright et al. [11] note that user experience is a holistic, dynamic process needing in - depth study from a user - product interaction perspective, providing a theoretical basis for dividing user journey stages from an HCI viewpoint.

As shown in Fig. 2, this paper divides users' interactive behaviors during the entire lifecycle management of seedling trays (from transfer at the transplanting area to harvesting area) into seven stages: Transplant to cultivation area, Moving into cultivation rack, Inventory management, Cultivation and monitoring, Removal from cultivation area, Cultivation to harvesting area, and Inventory management. In each stage, users interact with the corresponding transfer operational systems for tasks like ground transport, vertical transfer, inter - rack movement, monitoring, and inventory recording. Notably, moving planting units into and out of cultivation racks are essentially opposite processes with reversed equipment routes and sequences. This HCI - related info will be integrated into the UJM to build a comprehensive map.

Establishment of User Journey Map. Based on preliminary research and the seven journey stages outlined earlier, user personas and a User Journey Map (UJM) were created, as depicted in Fig. 3. An analysis of the pain points underlying these emotions shows that tension in ground transportation and vertical transfer stems from unreliable equipment causing transport disruptions. The inventory recording stage's emotional dip is due to manual data entry errors and delayed updates. Cultivation's stable emotions result from mature environmental control technology, yet frequent adjustments to growth parameters remain a challenge.

In response, technicians have specified needs: reliable transportation equipment for ensuring production continuity, a simplified and user-friendly operation mode to reduce labor intensity, an automated inventory system for accurate data, and an intelligent

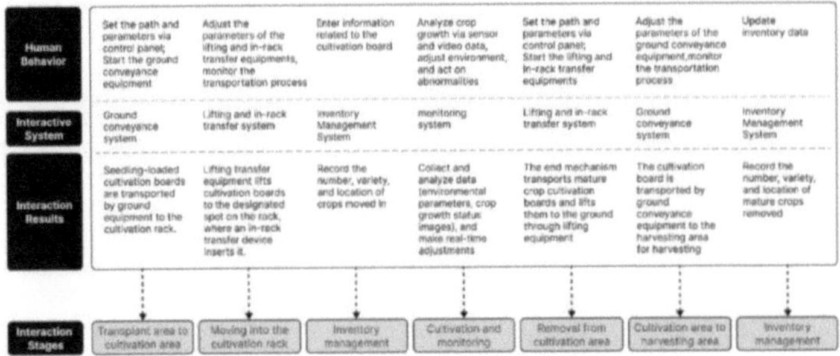

Fig. 2. HCI-based user journey stage division diagram.

environmental control system to optimize crop growth. This analysis of emotions, pain points, and needs provides a thorough foundation for subsequent design requirement analysis.

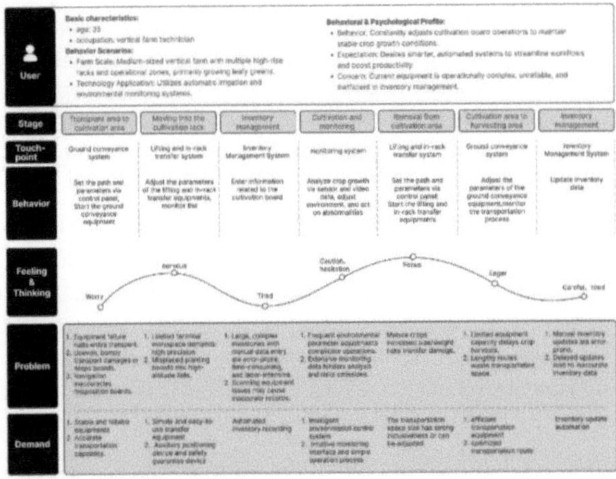

Fig. 3. User Journey Map: automated transfer in plant factories

Derivation of Design Requirements. Through integration, a total of 16 design requirements were ultimately deduced and a hierarchical model of design requirement indicators was constructed. In this model, the automated transport equipment in plant factories serves as the objective layer. The criterion layer is divided into four modules (A, B, C, D) according to different operational stages: ground transportation, vertical transfer, inter-rack movement, and intelligent functions. The sub-criterion layer consists of specific design requirements, namely 16 indicators (A1—D4), as illustrated in Fig. 4.

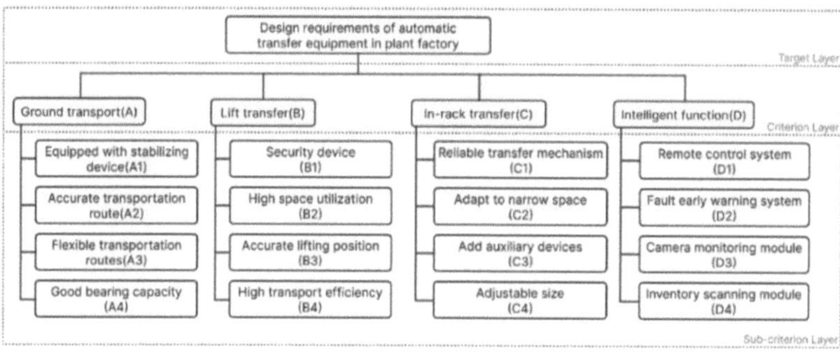

Fig. 4. Hierarchical model of design requirement indicators

2.3 AHP-Based Weight Determination of Design Requirements

Establishment and Computation of the Judgment Matrix. Nine experts in relevant fields were recruited to rate the importance of design requirement indicators. The 9-point scale method was employed for scoring. The indicators in both the criterion layer and the sub-criterion layer shown in Fig. 4 were compared pairwise by each expert.

During data processing, if an expert's score for a particular item failed the consistency test, that score was excluded. For the remaining scores, the geometric mean was calculated to obtain the weights. The weight calculation and consistency test were conducted using the online data analysis website SPSSAU (https://www.spssau.com/).

The weight values of the scores given by the nine experts were computed. The final results of the judgment matrix for the criterion layer are presented in Table 1, and those for the sub-criterion layer are shown in Table 2.

Table 1. Criterion layer judgment matrix and weight

Criterion layer	Ground transport	Lift transfer	In-rack transfer	Intelligent function	Wheight
Ground transport	1	0.891	0.918	0.742	0.21762
Lift transfer	1.122	1	0.891	0.794	0.23328
In-rack transfer	1.089	1.122	1	0.618	0.23080
Intelligent function	1.348	1.26	1.619	1	0.31830

Conformance Test. A consistency test was performed on experts' weighted scoring results. If the consistency ratio (CR) < 0.1, the test is passed; if CR ≥ 0.1, it fails. In case of failure, the scoring questionnaires of non - compliant experts need re - evaluation and analysis until the weight relationships pass.

Table 2. Subcriterion layer judgment matrix and weight

Ground transport	A1	A2	A3	A4	Wheight
A1	1	1.351	4.829	2.537	0.43298
A2	0.74	1	2.809	2.021	0.30751
A3	0.207	0.356	1	0.644	0.10042
A4	0.394	0.495	1.552	1	0.15910
Lift transfer	B1	B2	B3	B4	Wheight
B1	1	2.432	2.943	1.75	0.43091
B2	0.411	1	0.537	0.76	0.14871
B3	0.34	1.861	1	1	0.20803
B4	0.572	1.316	1	1	0.21235
In-rack transfer	C1	C2	C3	C4	Wheight
C1	1	0.953	2.605	2.608	0.36615
C2	1.049	1	2.172	1.809	0.32788
C3	0.384	0.46	1	1.201	0.15607
C4	0.383	0.553	0.833	1	0.14990
Intelligent function	D1	D2	D3	D4	Wheight
D1	1	2.268	1	1	0.30233
D2	0.441	1	1	0.693	0.18421
D3	1	1	1	0.794	0.23203
D4	1	1.442	1.26	1	0.28143

Table 3 shows the consistency test results for the criterion and sub - criterion layers. The CR values are all <0.1, passing the test. Thus, the relevant weight data can be used for further analysis.

Table 3. Conformance test results

	Criterion layer	Ground transport	Lift transfer	In-rack transfer	Intelligent function
Maximum characteristic root	4.014	4.007	4.066	4.025	4.06
CI value	0.005	0.002	0.022	0.008	0.02
RI value	0.882	0.882	0.882	0.882	0.882
CR value	0.005 < 0.1	0.003 < 0.1	0.025 < 0.1	0.009 < 0.1	0.023 < 0.1

Demand Weight Ranking and Analysis. The comprehensive weights were obtained by multiplying the weights of different design modules in the criterion layer with the weights of sub-requirements, and then a ranking was conducted, as shown in Table 4. The data results indicate that the priority order is Intelligent function > Lift transfer > In-rack transfer > Ground transport. The specific ranking is as follows: A × A3 < C × C4 < A× A4 < B × B2 < C × C3 < B × B3 < B × B4 < D × D2 < A × A2 < D × D3 < C × C2 < C × C1 < D × D4 < A × A1 < D × D1 < B × B1.

Table 4. Comprehensive weight ranking

Criterion layer and weight	Criterion layer indicators	Weight	Comprehensive weight	Sort
Ground transport (A)0.21762	A1	0.43298	0.09423	3
	A2	0.30751	0.06692	8
	A3	0.10042	0.02185	16
	A4	0.15910	0.03462	14
Lift transfer (B)0.23328	B1	0.43091	0.10052	1
	B2	0.14871	0.03469	13
	B3	0.20803	0.04853	11
	B4	0.21235	0.04954	10
In-rack transfer (C)0.23080	C1	0.36615	0.08451	5
	C2	0.32788	0.07567	6
	C3	0.15607	0.03602	12
	C4	0.14990	0.03460	15
Intelligent function (D)0.31830	D1	0.30233	0.09623	2
	D2	0.18421	0.05863	9
	D3	0.23203	0.07386	7
	D4	0.28143	0.08958	4

Therefore, the functions of the automated transport equipment in plant factories tend to lean towards the intelligent function module. Attention should be paid to functions such as remote intelligent control, inventory recording, and camera monitoring (C × C1, C × C3, C × C4). Meanwhile, demands related to the stability and precise routing of ground transportation (A × A1, A × A2), the safety and efficiency of lift transfer (B × B1, B × B4), as well as the mechanism reliability and spatial adaptability of in-rack transfer (C × C1, C × C2) should also be focused on.

2.4 Function Transformation and Solution Based on FAST

Basic Requirement Transformation Based on the Black Box Method. The four criterion - layer modules perform distinct tasks in the automated transfer process. When screening core requirements, we comprehensively considered both the comprehensive weight ranking and their even distribution across the four modules. Finally, nine core requirements were identified and converted into designable functional elements via the black - box method, as shown in Fig. 5.

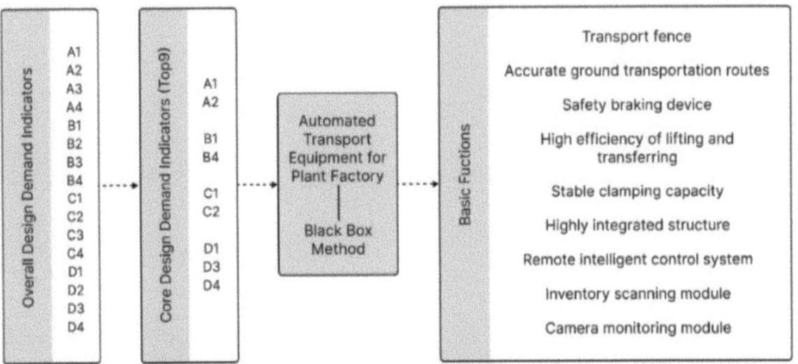

Fig. 5. Basic function transformation based on black box method

Construction of Fast Functional Model. The FAST functional modeling of automated transfer equipment in plant factories is depicted in Fig. 6. First, basic functions obtained via the black - box method were integrated into the FAST functional tree model for classification and decomposition. Functional elements from requirements A2, B4, C2, D1, and D2 (e.g., precise ground route planning, efficient lifting/transfer, integrated structure, remote intelligent control, intelligent storage) were identified as core functions and placed on the left. Secondary functions were then categorized into safety, cost and energy consumption, adaptability, and intelligence on the right. Safety - related elements from A1 and B1 (e.g., braking devices, guardrails) were expanded to include high load strength. The stable gripping ability from C1 was categorized under adaptability and extended to size adaptability. Intelligence - related elements from D1, D3, and D4 (e.g., inventory scanning, camera monitoring, intelligent scheduling) were expanded to provide crop data feedback. For cost and energy, the focus was on optimal paths and waterproof and anti - corrosion treatments.

These functions ultimately aim at the equipment's functionality in plant factories, forming a logical chain among functional systems at different levels and resulting in a comprehensive functional framework.

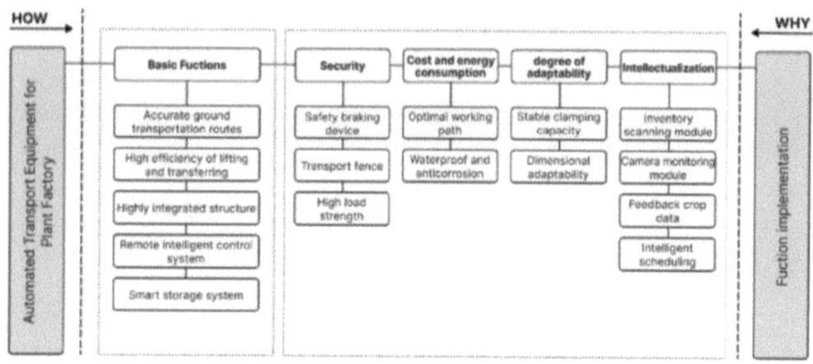

Fig. 6. Fast functional system analysis

3   Conceptual Design

Based on the preceding analysis and guided by the FAST functional link, a design scheme for the automated transfer equipment in plant factories was developed, resulting in a set of transfer operation equipment as shown in Fig. 7 and a user interface for the transfer process as illustrated in Fig. 8.

Functional Design of the Equipment. AGV robots are employed for ground transportation. Equipped with SLAM laser navigation systems [12], these robots can navigate precisely in factories without any pre - laid transportation infrastructure and optimize delivery routes [13]. Shuttle vehicles are utilized for vertical transfer and inter - rack movement. Capable of vertical and horizontal motion on the growth rack tracks [14], they can handle transfer tasks at any height. An annular rail and pallets are mounted on the top of the AGV robot. While meeting a certain delivery volume, the progressive transfer coordination with the shuttle vehicle is achieved through cyclic alternation, enhancing the cooperation efficiency and enabling efficient transfer, as depicted in Fig. 7. To accommodate visual recognition and technologies like RFID and barcode scanning [15], camera modules are designed on the tops of both the AGV robot and the shuttle vehicle for inventory recording and crop monitoring.

Structural Design of the Equipment. The AGV robot's annular rail is magnetic - driven, allowing pallet quantity adjustment based on crop height. The shuttle vehicle has retractable supporting structures for adapting to different crop heights, and its clamp - type forks extend/retract rapidly for cargo handling. Both the AGV robot and shuttle vehicle pallets have non - slip grooves to prevent tray slippage.

Appearance design of the equipment. It features a highly integrated, modular design. A black, white, and gray CMF scheme is chosen, using aluminum alloy and ABS plastic with a painting process for corrosion and water resistance.

Management mode design. The management module for the transfer process is divided into the transfer module, planting module, inventory module, and market module, as shown in Fig. 9. The transfer module handles equipment and route management. The planting module monitors crop growth. The inventory module tracks crop inflow and outflow. The market module boosts competitiveness by sharing crop data for consumer traceability. Based on the early user journey, management content is clearly defined to match user habits, enhancing human - machine interaction efficiency.

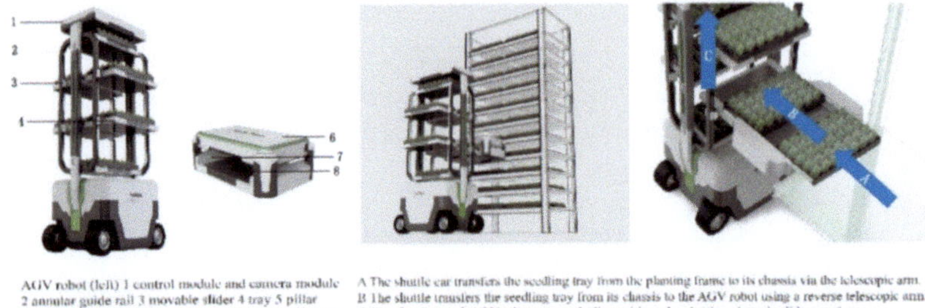

Fig. 7. Schematic diagram of product design and working process

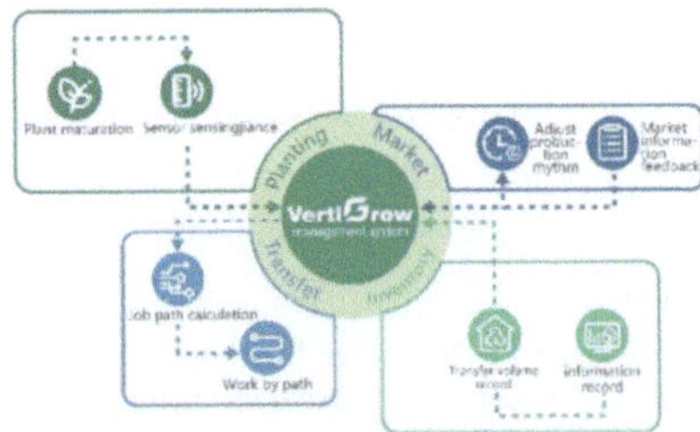

Fig. 8. Human computer interface

Fig. 9. Plant factory intelligent management system architecture

4   Discussion

This study utilized the UJM - AHP - FAST analytical model for a clear, reliable logical analysis of automated transfer equipment in plant factories, aiding the integration of practical - scenario - meeting requirements into R&D. It highlighted a user - centered, well - structured equipment development approach, offering a reference for future designs.

However, limitations persist: the small and less - diverse expert sample used in weight determination may have undermined the comprehensiveness and representativeness of the weight results, so future research should expand the sample to include more relevant fields like agricultural engineering and automation control for broader, balanced insights and accurate weighting; the model's applicability and effectiveness outside automated transfer equipment in plant factories, such as in other agricultural or industrial automation devices, are yet to be verified, hence subsequent studies should probe its transferability and adaptability across different scenarios; and as the research is currently at the theoretical and design - proposal stage without real - world plant - factory validation, it's difficult to gauge the design's performance, cost - effectiveness, and reliability, so the next steps should involve practical feedback - based design refinements to enhance its market value.

Acknowledgments. I am deeply grateful to my supervisor and friends for their invaluable assistance and expertise.

Disclosure of Interests.   The authors have no competing interests to declare that are relevant to the content of this article.

References

1. Ji, H., Gu, S.: Research Progress on stereoscopic conveying equipment in plant factories. Agric. Eng. Technol. **42**(04), 16–21 (2022)
2. Tokimasa, M., Nishiura, Y.: Automation in plant factory with labor-saving conveyance system. Environ. Control Biol. **53**(2), 101–105 (2015)
3. SANANBIO: Unmanned vertical agricultural production system. https://www.sananbio.com.cn/solutions/uplift.html, last accessed 2025/6/15
4. Yin, Y., Chen, Y., Cheng, R., et al.: Investigation and implications of intelligent production technology and equipment for facility horticulture in the Netherlands. Agric. Eng. Technol. **38**(34), 75–81 (2018)
5. Ohara, H., Hirai, T., Kouno, K., et al.: Automatic plant cultivation system (automated plant factory). Environ. Control Biol. **53**(2), 93–99 (2015)
6. Miao, X., Zhang, Y., Cheng, E., et al.: Design of Smart Warehousing and Logistics System Based on internet of things. Internet Things Technol. **14**(11), 92–96 (2024)
7. Peng, W., Yun, G., Hong, C., et al.: Design of an automated management system for potted plant transportation in greenhouses. In: Chinese Society of Agricultural Engineering(CSAE), Proceedings of the 2011 Academic Annual Conference of the Chinese Society of Agricultural Engineering, pp. 1013–1016., China (2011)
8. Huang, L.: Design and implementation of an intelligent dispatching system for vertical agriculture. Dig. Agric. Intell. Agric. Mach. **10**, 124–126 (2023)
9. Song, D., Xu, Y., Cui, T., et al.: Research on product concept innovation design mode based on AHP-FAST. Packag. Eng. **40**(24), 228–234 (2019)
10. Zhou, C., He, C., Ma, B.: Research on the design of bathroom fixtures for one-armed disabled people based on "B-AHP-FAST". Packaging Engineering. **41**(24), 143–149+161 (2020)
11. Wright, P., Blythe, M., McCarthy, J.: User experience and the idea of design in HCI. In: Gilroy, S.W., Harrison, M.D. (eds.) Interactive Systems. Design, Specification, and Verification. DSV-IS 2005. Lecture Notes in Computer Science, vol. 3941. Springer, Berlin, Heidelberg (2006)
12. Cai, D., Li, C., Ling, L., et al.: Architecture and application practice of laser SLAM navigation AGV system. Modern Inform. Technol. **9**(02), 163–170 (2025)
13. Yu, J.: Research on AGV path optimization for intelligent warehouse material handling system. Manufac. Upgrad. Today. **9**, 33–35 (2014)
14. BionicHive Company of Israel. https://www.chinaagv.com/shop/2273/index/. last accessed 2025/6/15
15. Chi, X.: Analysis of the application of intelligent shuttle cart system in plant factories. Logistics & Material Handling. **23**(01), 100–101 (2018)

Towards Optimized Remote Operation of Driverless Buses Using Virtual Reality to Evaluate Operator Performance with Different Viewpoints

Koki Masuda[1,2]([✉]), Yanbin Wu[1] [iD], and Naohisa Hashimoto[1] [iD]

[1] National Institute of Advanced Industrial Science and Technology (AIST), Tsukuba, Japan
{masuda.2713,wu.yanbin,naohisa-hashimoto}@aist.go.jp
[2] Tokyo University of Science, Tokyo, Japan

Abstract. Remote operation is considered a feasible solution to realize automated driving by covering those edge-cases. Virtual reality (VR) can simulate complex and rare driving environments, providing a controlled yet immersive experience for remote operators. In this preliminary study, cases difficult to reproduce in the real world were created using VR, and remote operator's performance was evaluated while different viewpoints were provided for supporting automated vehicles remotely. The results revealed that participants performed better when with a traditional driver's view than with a bird's view. VR based training and evaluation is considered a promising approach to optimize remote operation systems.

Keywords: Automated vehicles · Human factors · Human-machine interface · Virtual reality

1 Introduction

Automated vehicle (AV) technology stands at the forefront of revolutionizing public transportation systems, offering significant benefits such as enhanced accessibility and increased sustainability. Among the challenges that hinder the wide adoption of AVs, handling edge cases is one of the most significant [1]. Edge cases refer to rare, unusual, or complex driving scenarios that lie outside the "normal" operational conditions. By allowing a human operator to provide guidance in edge-case scenarios, remote operation systems have been explored to enhance the safety and functionality of AVs [2]. Herein, virtual reality (VR) can simulate complex and edge-case driving environments, providing a controlled yet immersive experience to train and evaluate remote operator's performance. While many of previous studies used VR to evaluate the effect of different interfaces on remote driving performance (e.g., [3]), in this paper, we aimed to use VR to evaluate operator performance with different viewpoints in the context of remote operation of driverless buses. Cases that occur infrequently and are difficult to reproduce in the real world were created using VR, and remote operator's performance was evaluated while different viewpoints were provided for them to provide guidance for AVs.

© The Author(s), under exclusive license to Springer Nature Switzerland AG 2026
S. Sundarakannan and O. Knorpp (Eds.): HCII 2025, CCIS 2772, pp. 38–43, 2026.
https://doi.org/10.1007/978-3-032-12767-9_4

2 Methods

2.1 Recreating Remote Operation Scenarios

The experiment focused on three operation tasks crucial for driverless buses but challenging or costly for automated systems to undertake. Table 1 shows the descriptions of the tasks. Each task has two kinds of scenarios, need stop' or 'good-to-go.' All scenarios were presented with two types of camera angles: the driver's view and the bird's view. Extensive research has been conducted on generating bird's views of vehicles, including methods that combine omnidirectional cameras and approaches using deep learning architectures to generate bird's-eye views from monocular images [3–5]. Based on insights from previous studies, we adjusted the height of the bird's view in our implementation.

Table 1 shows all scenarios, which were created in Unity. For each scenario, two types of videos – from the driver's view and the bird's view - were prepared, resulting in a total of 12 videos. In each scenario and from each viewpoint, the video captures the autonomous bus identifying the tasks described in Table 1 and stopping along the route. Examples of the actual videos used in the experiment are shown in Figs. 1 and 2.

Table 1. Descriptions of the remote operation tasks.

Task	Scenario	Description
Task 1: Lane clearance confirmation	Stop	A car parked on the lane
	Go	A car parked within road shoulder
Task 2: Obstacle object confirmation	Stop	Tree trunks on the lane
	Go	Falling leaves on the lane
Task 3: Bus stop confirmation	Stop	Passengers are waiting at a bus stop
	Go	No passenger is waiting at the stop

Fig. 1. Left: Driver's view when stopping is required for Task 1, as shown in Table 1. Right: Bird's view when stopping is required for Task 1, as shown in Table 1.

Fig. 2. Left: Driver's view when stopping is not required for Task 1, as shown in Table 1. Right: Bird's view when stopping is not required for Task 1, as shown in Table 1.

2.2 Description of PsychoPy

Response judgement time for evaluation using 12 different video types was measured for the evaluation. An interface for participants to make their judgment was necessary. We adopted PsychoPy, a tool commonly used in psychological experiments. PsychoPy is software that allows designing and conducting psychological experiments on a computer, presenting image and audio stimuli at specific timings, and precisely measuring participants' reaction times. We set up random video presentations and timing for keyboard input. We created a timing chart to build a system that records judgment times efficiently and accurately. The videos were designed to be presented in a randomized order among the 12 patterns. Keyboard input was enabled during video playback. After a participant responded, the next video automatically played, and keyboard input was reactivated for the following trial.

2.3 Procedure of the Experiment

14 participants participated in the experiment. The layout of the experimental setup is shown in Fig. 3. Before starting the experiment, participants were given an overview of the experiment, an explanation of the tasks and correct judgements, and the risks of making any failures. Specifically, it was emphasized that incorrect judgments could lead to accidents. Participants were instructed to react as quickly as possible only when they were confident in making correct judgments.

The formal experiment consisted of 4 blocks, each with 12 random trials of the remote operation tasks. For task 1, participants were instructed to confirm whether the lane was clear for the automated bus to pass through. For task 2, participants were instructed to confirm whether the obstacle hindered the automated bus's route. For task 3, participants were instructed to confirm whether the bus needed to stop for picking up the waiting passengers at the stop. Participants were instructed to press the corresponding key at the moment they were able to make the "Stop" or "Go" judgement. Before the formal experiment, participants completed a practice block consisting of 12 trials. This was followed by four blocks of the main experiment. After the experiment, participants answered a subjective scale on judgement easiness.

Fig. 3. Experimental setup.

3 Results and Discussions

Participants' response time and accuracy are used to quantify their performance with different viewpoints. As shown in Fig. 4, comparing to the bird's view, participants reacted significantly faster when with the driver's viewpoints for all the three tasks. This may be due to obstacles that are difficult to judge and their size. Murakami [6] showed that responses to local features increased with increasing visual stimuli, suggesting that the size of the obstacle affected judgment. In addition, Jonas [7] showed that the puddle scenario caused low perceived inability to work, while the loaded dock scenario caused high inability to work due to a lack of vision. It is possible that the lack of field of view made it difficult to grasp the details of the obstacle, resulting in an increase in judgement time. Furthermore, as shown in Fig. 5, the response accuracy tended to be lower when with the bird's view than with the driver's view. The presence or absence of a sense of depth may have influenced this result. Ito et al. [8] concluded that the driver's viewpoint is more likely to provide a certain sense of depth in the remote driving video environment.

Regarding the subjective report on the easiness of judgement, results were shown in Fig. 6. Similar to the performance metrics, the average rate of ease seems to be higher when with the driver's view than with the bird's view for task 1 and 2, while no differences could be found for task 3.

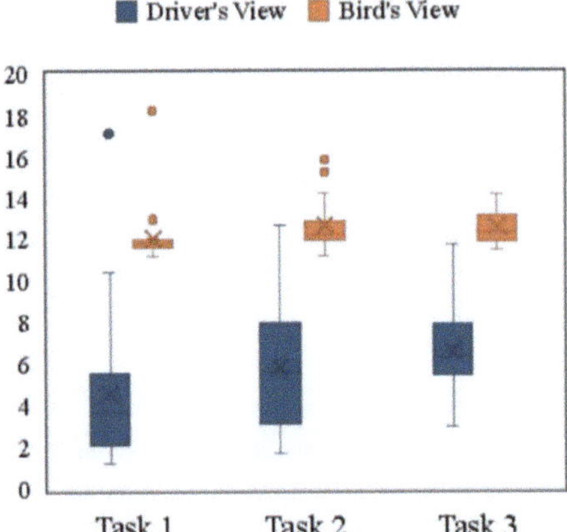

Fig. 4. Response time for each task.

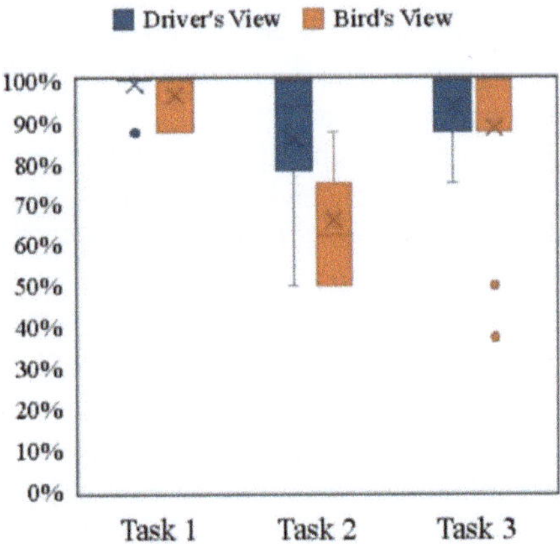

Fig. 5. Response accuracy for each task.

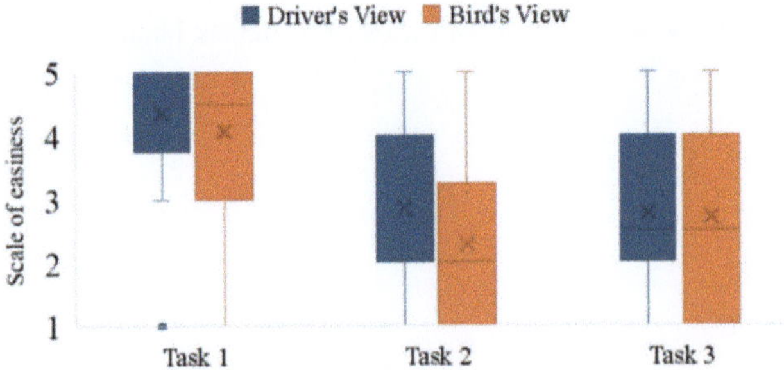

Fig. 6. Participants' subjective report of easiness (1 = very difficult 2 = difficult, 3 = either, 4 = easy, 5 = very easy) of different tasks.

4 Conclusions

By replicating three operation tasks using VR, this study preliminarily investigated the impact of viewpoints on remote operation performance. The results supported the adoption of a driver's view when asking the remote operator to make STOP-or-Go decisions. It should be noticed although a pure bird's view seemed to be less efficient, an adaptive switch between viewpoints, as suggested in the teleoperation of other objects, may enhance remote operator's performance. We expect to investigate this in future VR based studies.

Acknowledgments. This work has been supported by Ministry Economy Trade and Industry in Japan.

Disclosure of Interests. The authors declare that they have no competing interests relevant to the content of this article.

References

1. Wu, Y., Sugimoto, F., Kihara, K., Kimura, M., Yokoyama, T., Takeda, Y., Hashimoto, N.: The role of task-switching cost in remote operation of driverless vehicle fleet. In: IEEE Intelligent Vehicles Symposium (IV), pp. 37–42. IEEE (2024)
2. Kettwich, C., Schrank, A., Avsar, H., Oehl, M.: A helping human hand: relevant scenarios for the remote operation of highly automated vehicles in public transport. Appl. Sci. **12** (2022)
3. Boker, A., Lanir, J.: Bird's eye view effect on situational awareness in remote driving. Adjunct Proceedings of the 15th International Conference on Automotive User Interfaces and Interactive Vehicular Applications, pp. 36–41 (2023)
4. Roddick, T., Cipolla, R.: Predicting semantic map representations from images using pyramid occupancy networks. arXiv preprint arXiv:2003.13402. (2020)
5. Ehlgen, T., Pajdla, T.: Monitoring surrounding areas of truck-trailer combinations. In: Proceedings of the 5th International Conference on Computer Vision Systems (ICVS 2007), vol. 2007. Applied Computer Science Group, Bielefeld University, Bielefeld, Germany. ISBN 978-3-00-020933-8
6. Murakami, T.: Effects of mood on visual cognition of Navon stimuli of different sizes: the usefulness of threshold as an index. Jpn. J. Cogn. Psychol. **7**(2), 79–88 (2010)
7. Andersson, J., Rizgary, D., Söderman, M., Vännström, J.: Exploring remote operation of heavy vehicles—findings from a simulator study. In: Human–Intelligent Systems Integration. Springer (2022)
8. Ito, S., Sakano, Y., Fujino, K., Ando, H.: Remote controlled construction equipment by using high-resolution stereoscopic 3D images. J. Jpn. Soc. Civ. Eng. Ser. F3 (Civ. Eng. Inform.). **73**(1), 15–24 (2017)

Navibus-Enhancing the Accessibility of Bus Rapid Transit System for Visually Impaired Through Multimodal Interactions

Rishika Sood[✉], Vishwa Desai, and Amitha Mohandas

New Media Design, National Institute of Design, Gandhinagar, India
rishika_s@nid.edu

Abstract. This research addresses the challenges faced by visually impaired individuals while navigating through India's Bus Rapid Transit System (BRTS). Despite having infrastructure provisions and assistive technologies, visually impaired individuals continued to experience barriers in independently accessing and using public transport systems. They had to heavily rely on others for doing the basic tasks like identifying the right platform, boarding on the right bus. These small but critical moments of friction showcased the deeper issue of public transport system under looking the needs and necessities of the visually impaired

Rooted in a human-centered design approach, this study presents NaviBus, a thoughtful, inclusive mobility solution designed to restore a sense of autonomy and ease in public travel.

Key findings reveal systemic gaps in physical accessibility, digital usability, and sensory overload-highlighting a need for more responsive and context-aware interventions. Through immersive field work and stakeholder engagement, this research introduces a solution framework which is divided into three parts, encompassing a platform identification system with the help of vibro-sonic feedback, one handed gesture-based interaction and a simplified, high contrast user interface for users with low vision.

By leveraging inclusive design methods rooted in lived experiences, the study aims to empower visually impaired commuters and foster more equitable access to urban transportation in the Indian context.

Keywords: Passenger Information Systems · Accessible Design · Social Inclusion · Universal Design · Inclusive Design · Multi Modal Interaction · Vibration Design · Systems Design · User Centric Design · Problem Solving · Human Computer Interaction · User Experience (UX) · Interaction Design

1 Introduction

India accounts for approximately 25% of the global population of individuals with visual impairments [2], highlighting the critical need for inclusive public infrastructure that caters to this demographic. Current accessibility guidelines in India primarily emphasize

© The Author(s), under exclusive license to Springer Nature Switzerland AG 2026
S. Sundarakannan and O. Knorpp (Eds.): HCII 2025, CCIS 2772, pp. 44–51, 2026.
https://doi.org/10.1007/978-3-032-12767-9_5

tactile flooring and audio announcements [6, 9]. However, the practical implementation and contextual relevance of these measures for individuals with visual impairments remain a concern.

To address this gap, NaviBus is proposed as a Bus Rapid Transit System (BRTS) navigation solution tailored to enhance accessibility and independence for visually impaired users. In alignment with SDG Goal 10, which emphasizes the importance of inclusion and accessibility for individuals with disabilities to remove barriers preventing their full participation in society [8], NaviBus seeks to promote dignity, autonomy, and social inclusion. By enabling independent navigation within public transportation systems, it strives to foster equal opportunities in education, employment, and mobility for visually impaired individuals.

2   Research Methodology

2.1   Understanding the Users in BRTS Context

The research underpinning the design proposal was structured into two key phases: Empathize and Explore. The Empathize phase aimed to build a nuanced understanding of the lived experiences of visually impaired individuals. It began with secondary research that provided a foundational medical and psychological understanding of visual impairment. This was followed by immersive field visits to two significant institutions: The Blind People's Association [1] in Ahmedabad and the School for the Blind in Gandhinagar [3]. These visits enabled the research team to engage with users in context and employ a range of qualitative research methods including observation studies, directed storytelling, and role-playing exercises.

In the observation studies, participants were observed in their natural environments, with attention to how they navigated spaces, interacted with everyday objects, and managed daily tasks. Directed storytelling allowed the researchers to collect detailed personal narratives through guided prompts and follow-up questions, which offered insight into individual routines, emotional responses, and adaptive strategies. To build empathy and gain experiential insight, the team participated in the "Vision in the Dark" walkthrough at BPA, a carefully designed multisensory space simulating total blindness. This was supplemented by independent role-play in familiar environments, encouraging the team to explore how non-visual senses support navigation and sensemaking. These combined methods not only deepened the understanding of the sensory world of visually impaired individuals but also helped challenge the researchers' preconceptions and assumptions.

The Explore phase shifted the focus toward visually impaired individuals' interaction with urban public transport, specifically the Bus Rapid Transit System (BRTS) in India. A comparative analysis of BRTS systems across various Indian cities was conducted using secondary sources to identify infrastructural disparities and derive a comprehensive understanding of inclusive mobility [5]. This analysis helped highlight areas requiring improvement to make transit systems more accessible.

To contextualize the findings, a detailed space audit was conducted at an Ahmedabad BRTS station located near the Blind People's Association. This location was selected because it is regularly used by visually impaired commuters. The audit helped assess the physical infrastructure, tactile navigation cues, signage systems, and user flow, while also capturing interactions between different stakeholders. Complementing this, fly-on-the-wall observations were conducted to study real-time behaviour of visually impaired individuals at the bus stop-how they approached the station, navigated the space, and boarded the bus. These observations revealed systemic pain points and gaps in accessibility.

Semi-structured interviews were then carried out with seven individuals-five at the BRTS station and two from the school for the blind-to further explore user motivations, perceptions, and challenges. These conversations validated previous observations and uncovered deeper emotional and functional needs. Finally, usability testing of mobile navigation tools such as Google Maps and the GSRTC app was conducted. By observing real-time app usage, the team identified critical issues related to information clarity, audio feedback, and interaction complexity.

Together, the Empathize and Explore phases established a robust foundation of contextual and user-centric insights, essential for framing inclusive design interventions for visually impaired commuters.

2.2 Analysis of the Data Collected

To generate relevant and actionable insights, multiple mapping methods were employed to analyse the data collected during the field research. These tools helped structure observations, uncover latent needs, and reveal interconnections within the system.

System mapping enabled the team to visualize the broader ecosystem, helping identify relationships between processes, stakeholders, and user experiences across the BRTS infrastructure. This holistic perspective informed a more integrated design approach.

Journey mapping allowed the researchers to trace specific user journeys, highlighting pain points that occur at each stage of interaction with the BRTS system, from arrival at the station to boarding and traveling. These context-specific touchpoints revealed critical usability gaps.

Stakeholder mapping helped identify and engage relevant actors involved in the user experience, such as bus drivers, station staff, and app developers. Understanding their roles and perspectives informed the feasibility and impact of proposed solutions.

Behaviour mapping captured how visually impaired individuals interacted with the built environment. Particular focus was given to movement patterns, reliance on tactile cues, and adaptive strategies used in public spaces.

Cognitive mapping visually represented the mental models of visually impaired individuals, illustrating how they perceive, interpret, and navigate information in the absence of sight.

2.3 Key Insights Uncovered

Key insights from these methods revealed several recurring challenges:

- Visually impaired users often relied on companions or bystanders to guide them to the correct platform or bus.
- Tactile flooring was helpful, but not always consistently implemented.
- Individuals positioned themselves near platform gates to maintain orientation.

- Many needed assistance to identify platform or bus numbers, which were inaccessible due to screen-based schedules.
- Mobile phone usage required both hands, creating difficulty when also carrying bags or canes.
- The boarding process was frequently rushed and stressful, with minimal support available.
- Group travel was common, indicating a need for solutions that accommodate both individual and collective navigation.

These insights emphasized the importance of inclusive infrastructure, accessible digital tools, and support systems that empower visually impaired individuals to navigate public transport independently and with dignity.

Usability testing of existing applications like Google Maps and GSRTC revealed several issues:

- Overlapping audio outputs from TalkBack and navigation apps caused confusion.
- Multiple swipes and taps were needed to access key information.
- Overwhelming audio feedback and frequent tapping disrupted the navigation experience.
- Difficulty in quickly accessing estimated time and distance data.

2.4 Design Considerations

These findings informed key design considerations for NaviBus:

- Integration with existing assistive technologies.
- Minimal, non-intrusive audio feedback.
- Support for one-handed operation.
- Use of multimodal feedback (audio and haptic).
- A clean, uncluttered visual interface.
- Minimal learning curve to support ease of adoption.

Together, these research insights directly influenced the development of a solution tailored to the lived realities of visually impaired individuals navigating urban public transport systems.

3 Designing Bus Rapid Transit System for Visually Impaired

3.1 Designing Platform Identification System

The platform identification system utilizes proximity sensors integrated into platform gates to deliver vibro-sonic notifications directly through the NaviBus mobile application. This environment-initiated communication means the system informs the user automatically when they approach the correct platform, eliminating the need for users to seek assistance from peers or others. By reversing the traditional user-initiated interaction, this approach empowers users to independently locate their boarding platform with confidence (Fig. 1).

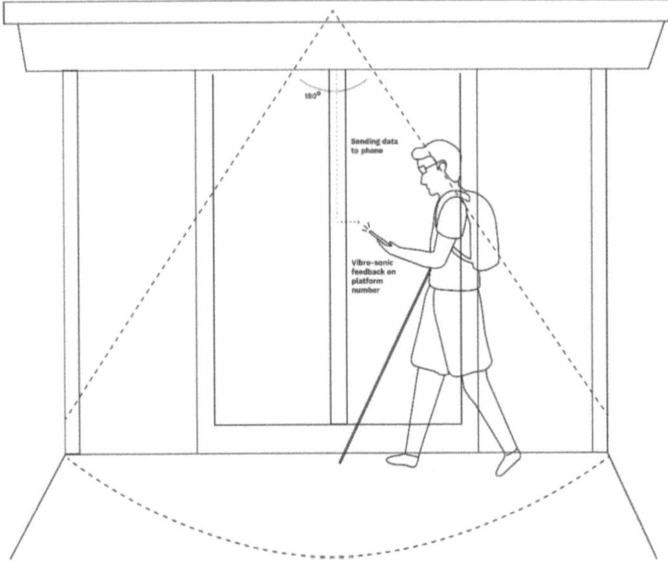

Fig. 1. Proximity based platform identification system.

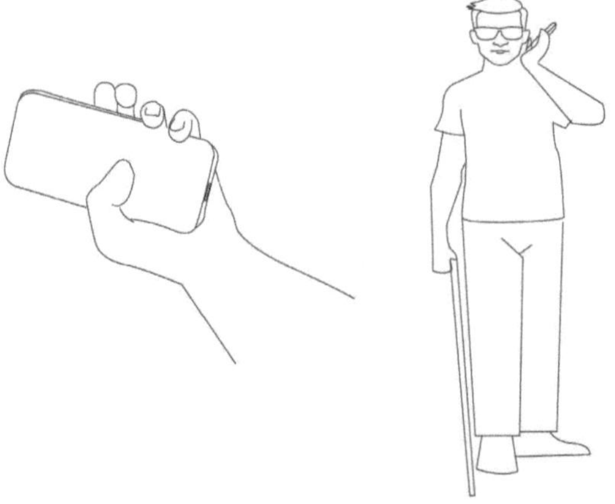

Fig. 2. Horizontal orientation for one-hand gestural input and accessible audio output.

3.2 Vibro-Sonic and Gestural Intuitive Feedback System

To facilitate seamless interaction with the application, the gesture and feedback design incorporates six intuitive one-handed gestures. Users hold their phones horizontally near their ear, enabling simultaneous reception of app audio feedback and attention to surrounding auditory cues critical for navigation. The feedback system employs a two-layer confirmation: a distinctive vibration unique from standard phone notifications, followed by a replayable audio message. This dual modality minimizes cognitive overload, addressing challenges posed by information saturation and ensuring clarity in communication (Figs. 2 and 3).

Fig. 3. Vibration feedback followed by replayable audio notification.

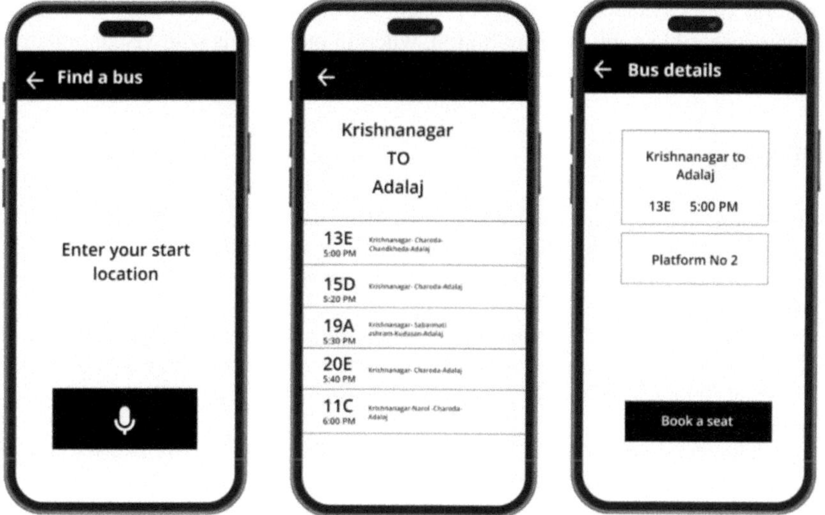

Fig. 4. High contrast visual design catering to people with low vision along with limited information per screen preventing information fatigue.

3.3   Visual Design of the Mobile Application

Recognizing the needs of users with low vision, the visual design prioritizes high contrast between backgrounds and foreground elements like text and buttons to aid visual differentiation. Large, bold fonts reduce eye strain, while clear spatial separation between interface components prevents clutter and enhances legibility. The interface limits information displayed per screen to avoid fatigue and incorporates voice-based input to eliminate the need for typing during critical situations. Together, these features make the system intuitive, efficient, and accessible, even under time-sensitive or stressful condition (Fig. 4).

Overall, the NaviBus framework harmonizes environmental sensing, user-friendly interaction, and thoughtful visual design to create an inclusive transit experience tailored to the diverse needs of visually impaired passengers.

4 Conclusion

The NaviBus system reflects a user-centered and context-sensitive design approach that aligns with the sensory preferences and cognitive models of visually impaired individuals. By facilitating independent navigation and enhancing overall user experience, the system has the potential to significantly improve quality of life, promote social inclusion, and reshape public perceptions of disability. Moreover, NaviBus can serve as a scalable model for enhancing accessibility in public transportation systems both within India and globally. The research demonstrates how design, grounded in extensive field research, can enable inclusive innovation in urban infrastructure. Through multimodal interaction and a systems-thinking approach, it presents a compelling vision for equitable and accessible public transportation, wherein individuals with visual impairments are empowered to navigate the world with autonomy and confidence.

References

1. BPA: Blind Peoples Association Ahmedabad India (n.d.). https://bpaindia.org/
2. Ehrlich, J.R., Arvind, A.: The prevalence of vision impairment and blindness among older adults in India: findings from the longitudinal ageing study in India. Nat. Aging. **2**(11), 1000–1007 (2022)
3. Freese, T.: This School's Unique Features Lets Blind Students Navigate Through Smell, Touch & Sound. The Better India (2024). https://thebetterindia.com/340084/gujarat-school-for-the-blind-and-visually-impaired-inclusive-design-architecture-by-anand-sonecha-sealabs/
4. Indian Roads Congress (IRC): Bus Rapid Transit (BRT) Guidelines for Indian Cities. Indian Roads Congress, New Delhi (2017)
5. Kathuria, A.P.: A review of bus rapid transit implementation in India. Cogent Eng. **3**(1) (2016)
6. Ministry of Housing and Urban Affairs (MoHUA): Harmonised Guidelines and Standards for Universal Accessibility in India. Government of India (2021)
7. Rao, P., Srinivas, S.: Designing BRT Systems for Universal Access, EMBARQ India, WRI (n.d.)
8. United Nations (UN): Reduce inequality within and among countries. United Nations, Department of Economic and Social Affairs (n.d.). https://sdgs.un.org/goals/goal10
9. United Nations (UNCRPD): United Nations Convention on the Rights of Persons. United Nations (2006)

10. Wai, W.: Web accessibility initiative WAI. Designing for Web Accessibility. (July 2024). https://www.w3.org/WAI/tips/designing/#:~:text=Provide%20sufficient%20contrast%20b etween%20foreground,and%20how%20to%20check%20contrast
11. World Health Organization (WHO): Blindness and vision impairment (Aug 2023). https:// www.who.int/news-room/fact-sheets/detail/blindness-and-visual-impairment#:~:text=Glo bally%2C%20at%20least%202.2%20billion,are%20refractive%20errors%20and%20cata racts

Workflow to Simulate In-Vehicle Display Interactions Using Mixed Reality

Thirumanikandan Subramanian and Wolfram Remlinger[✉]

Institute of Engineering Design and Industrial Design, University of Stuttgart,
Pfaffenwaldring 9, 70569 Stuttgart, Germany
`thiru.subramanian@iktd.uni.stuttgart.de`,
`wolfram.remlinger@iktd.uni-stuttgart.de`

1 Introduction

With the rapid advancement of automated vehicles, there has also been a parallel rise in the need for in-vehicle displays. Earlier, instrumentations were used to display the status of the vehicle systems, which were later on digitalized. This further extended with navigation function, infotainment and presently, displays also provide situational awareness by displaying current information of the vehicle and the environment together [1]. In automated vehicles, users tend to spend more time on activities that are not related to driving [2]. Therefore, the interactions with these in-vehicle displays are also significant. Development and testing of in-vehicle displays with physical prototypes are challenging in terms of cost and time [1].

Though methods of Virtual Reality(VR) or Mixed Reality (MR) have been implemented by Defence Industries and Automotive OEMs for driving simulations and design visualisations, simulating in-vehicle displays with enhanced realism and user interactions is still not explored [2, 3].

2 Methodology

This paper presents workflows to simulate the in-vehicle displays in MR environments, to analyse user interaction, usability aspects, type of information to be displayed, position of displays within the vehicle interior and visibility in various lighting conditions.

Unreal Engine (UE) is used to build the various scenarios involving vehicle interior consisting of 3D models of the cockpit, instrumentation and seating. The display elements were created using Unreal Motion Graphics (UMG) as interactable widgets within the game environment [4]. These widgets were designed based on the requirements and the information to be displayed.

As seen in Fig. 1, the type of content to be displayed decides the nature of the display projection within the game environment. For example, general instructions, safety messages and warnings were generated as images in PNG format, which were embedded on to the widgets as materials with emissive properties. When displays need information with animations, like the information cluster showing speed, battery level or other vehicle varying parameters, the sequencing function in UE can be implemented to create the

© The Author(s), under exclusive license to Springer Nature Switzerland AG 2026
S. Sundarakannan and O. Knorpp (Eds.): HCII 2025, CCIS 2772, pp. 52–55, 2026.
https://doi.org/10.1007/978-3-032-12767-9_6

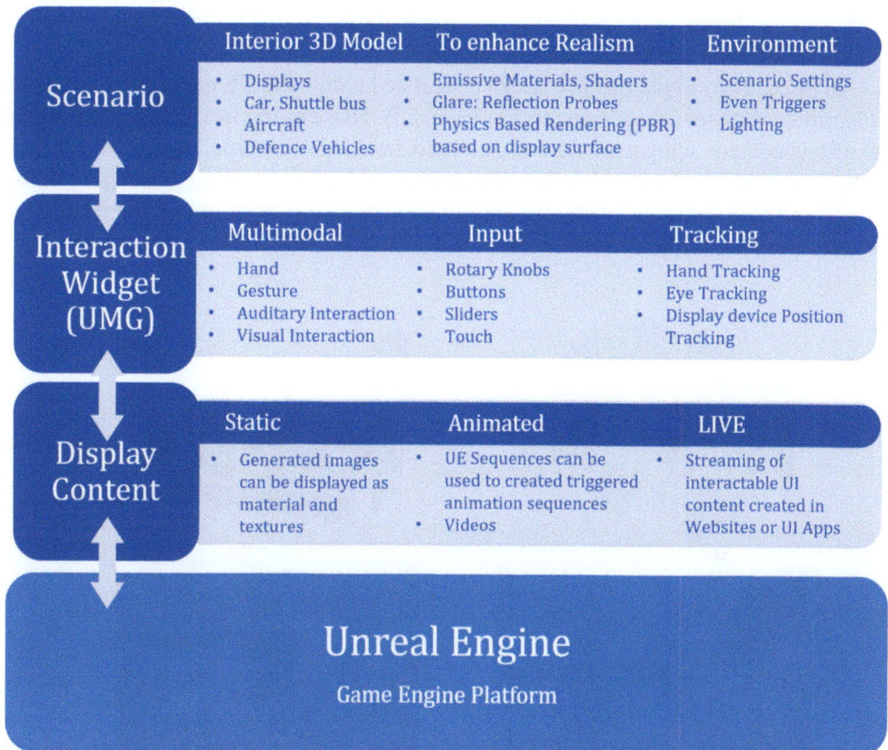

Fig. 1. Workflow to simulate In-Vehicle displays in MR environment.

necessary animations. To display real-time simulations such as weather forecasts, external sensor data from CAN signals, and live Google navigation, the streaming widget was used to stream content from external sources.

Using UMG, the types of displays generated using the above techniques can also be extended to be interactive and exchange data. Integrating interaction elements like sliders, knobs, buttons and touch can enable even static display elements to be interactive by swapping images on the same display element based on input replicating real interaction with a touch screen. By activating hand tracking, eye tracking and voice recognition modules within the UE in combination with the system of the Head Mounted Display (HMD), the user can also interact with the in-vehicle displays using hand gestures, touch, visual and auditory interactions.

For every simulation, a particular scenario has to be developed to yield better subjective evaluations [5]. To enhance the realism of the simulated environments, high-polygon 3d meshes of the corresponding vehicle interior created in Blender were imported into the UE game environment. Though the widget replicating the in-vehicle displays was developed by the above-mentioned methods, they need to be scaled and positioned into the right location in the vehicle interior. To enhance the realism of the displays, ray tracing techniques were used for better reflection, refractions, and glare and specific shaders were used to replicate different types of screen surfaces and textures and the corresponding behavior of the display for a particular lighting. This ray tracing technique is particularly important when simulating Head Up Display (HUD) [6].

All three layers explained above can be realized within the UE game environment by Blueprints, or the visual scripting technique in UE. These blueprints are used to program the widget content, widget interaction, scenario, tracking of external bodies with the help of the type of HMD deployed during simulation, reading and writing data from external files. These blueprints also make the environment dynamic, by enabling interaction and its corresponding impact on the environment visible.

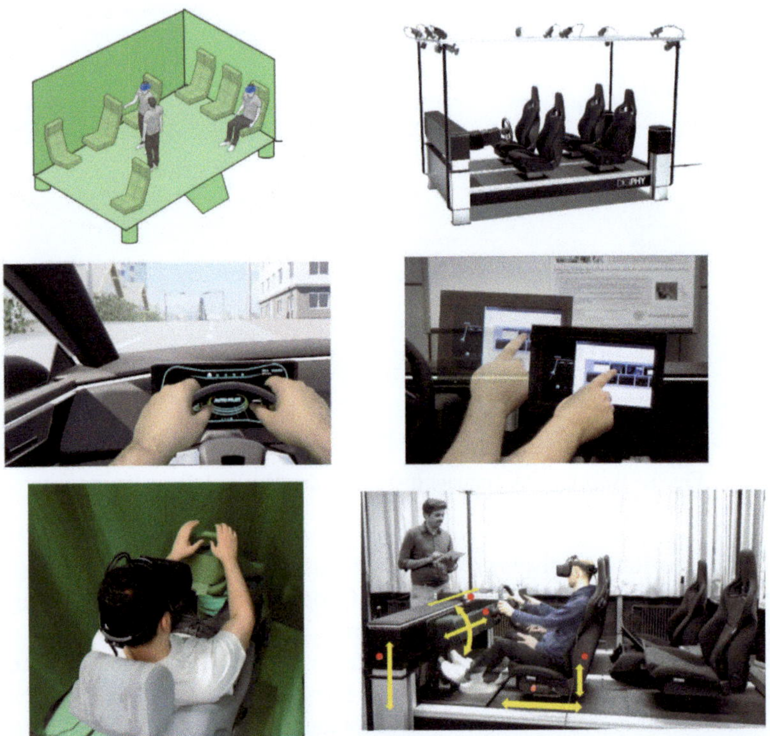

Fig. 2. Left: Simulation of vehicle interior using Green Cave, to integrate real hands into virtual environment. Right: Simulation of vehicle interior using DigiPHY, to precisely position both the user participant and the display to conduct ergonomic and accessibility analysis [2, 8].

As shown in Fig. 2, the workflow is integrated with physical mockups, such as the adjustable seating buck (DigiPHY, 4 seat system) [8], which sets into a particular vehicle seating configuration based on input and also in the green cave for MR simulations. These mockups are integrated with glass surfaces in place of the displays to enhance the realism of the interaction of the user. By using the greencave technology, real display-based devices could be integrated into the workflow simulating real display screens in a virtual environment [3].

3   Conclusion

This paper shows the methods to simulate in-vehicle displays in an MR environment based on type of display and user interaction. With this method, researchers and engineers working on human factor studies and the UX domain can simulate, refine and prototype automotive UI elements in an MR environment effectively. The workflow also provides the capability to evaluate aspects according to [7] such as usability, acceptance, workload determination, level of distraction for users, accessibility and intuitiveness of the in-vehicle displays in the early phase of development, reducing cost and time. Further studies are planned to compare the user interaction techniques to establish a correlation between types of displays, types of interaction and aspects to be analysed.

References

1. Chen, F., Kuo, J.: In-vehicle display technology. In: Li, Y., Shi, H. (eds.) Advanced Driver Assistance Systems and Autonomous Vehicles. Springer, Singapore (2022). https://doi.org/10.1007/978-981-19-5053-7_11
2. Subramanian, T., Schlichtherle, F., Remlinger, W.: Mixed reality tool to simulate and evaluate user interactions in the interior of automated vehicles. In: Adjunct Proceedings of the 15th International Conference on Automotive User Interfaces and Interactive Vehicular Applications, pp. 304–306 (2023, September)
3. Subramanian, T., Schlichtherle, F., Remlinger, W.: Workflow for evaluating vehicle interiors using serious gaming. In: 2024 IEEE Gaming, Entertainment, and Media Conference (GEM), pp. 1–4. IEEE (2024, June)
4. Unreal Motion Graphics. https://dev.epicgames.com/documentation/en-us/unreal-engine/umg-ui-designer-for-unreal-engine?application_version=5.2
5. Jeong, C., Kim, B., Yu, S., Suh, D., Kim, M., Suh, M.: In-vehicle display HMI safety evaluation using a driving simulator. Int. J. Automot. Technol. **14**, 987–992 (2013)
6. Li, L., Carlos, C.Q.J., Yang, Z., Ono, K.: Assessment of user preferences for in-car display combinations during non-driving tasks: an experimental study using a virtual reality head-mounted display prototype. World Electr. Veh. J. **15**(6), 264 (2024)
7. Alam, M.S., Subramanian, T., Martens, M., Remlinger, W., Bazilinskyy, P.: From A to B with ease: user-centric interfaces for shuttle buses. In: Adjunct Proceedings of the 16th International Conference on Automotive User Interfaces and Interactive Vehicular Applications, pp. 111–116 (2024, September)
8. DigiPHY: Adjustable seating buck. https://www.granstudio.com/digiphy

Enabling Sustainable Everyday Mobility: The Role of E-Cargo Bikes in Urban and Rural Contexts

Jan-Niklas Voigt-Antons[✉][iD], Miladin Ceranic[iD], and Francesco Vona[iD]

Hamm-Lippstadt University of Applied Sciences, Hamm, Germany
{Jan-Niklas.Voigt-Antons,Miladin.Ceranic,Francesco.Vona}@hshl.de

Abstract. E-cargo bikes are becoming more popular than motorized vehicles as cities grow and people look for greener modes of transportation. This is especially true for anyone who has to move goods or kids. The potential of e-cargo bikes to encourage the use of ecologically friendly modes of transportation in urban and rural areas is examined in this study. Using a qualitative, interview-based methodology, we investigate adoption-related perceptions, barriers, and facilitators among urban users. Participants include caregivers, small business owners, and people who need frequent mobility. The results show that city dwellers enjoy better infrastructure but still have trouble finding places to store their bicycles and negotiating traffic. People who live in rural areas face difficulties because of their isolation and the lack of bike-friendly roads. To provide insights into policy and customized design approaches, this study looks at infrastructure, psychological factors, and local norms.

Keywords: E-cargo bikes · Sustainable mobility · Urban transport · Rural transport · Adoption barriers

1 Introduction

More people are using micromobility options like electric cargo bikes (e-cargo bikes) because cities worldwide are moving toward more sustainable ways to get around. These vehicles are a space-saving and low-emission alternative to private cars, especially for short to medium-distance excursions like taking kids or goods. Even if e-cargo bikes are helpful, many places still think of them as a unique method of travel. People in cities and rural areas have extremely diverse views on infrastructure, which affects how many people adopt it. We need to develop better and more eco-friendly ways to travel around since traffic and air pollution are worsening, and we need to minimize greenhouse gas emissions. In multimodal mobility networks, e-cargo bikes are becoming more and more crucial. This is especially true for families, small business owners, and service providers who need to go around without cars. You may use them for many activities, like driving the kids to school, getting groceries, deliveries, and providing mobile services. The story of the environment is terrific, but many issues

© The Author(s), under exclusive license to Springer Nature Switzerland AG 2026
S. Sundarakannan and O. Knorpp (Eds.): HCII 2025, CCIS 2772, pp. 56–61, 2026.
https://doi.org/10.1007/978-3-032-12767-9_7

make it impossible for people to use it in real life. To improve the conversation on sustainable transportation, this study looks at the everyday experiences, perceived benefits, and significant obstacles faced by e-cargo bike users in urban and rural settings. We seek to discern the complex constraints and incentives that shape transportation behaviors by examining environmental and physical surroundings and the cultural and governmental frameworks that impact utilization. Our research includes a comparative analysis of migration patterns in rural areas and a qualitative interview study focused on urban consumers.

2   Related Work

Preceding studies have pinpointed numerous findings regarding the motivators, barriers, and suggestions for local governments to promote the adoption of cargo cycles. These findings emphasize regulatory frameworks, strategic city planning, infrastructure adaptations, pilot programs, cooperation with private entities, and knowledge-sharing platforms [7]. According to [2], measuring how businesses will respond to freight transport-related policies is possible. Additional research has highlighted that cycling can support public health [6]. Regarding user perception and behavior, [4] highlights that the availability of cycling infrastructure and safety perceptions are key determinants in whether people choose bicycles over cars. [5] contends that reallocating space is essential for enhancing urban ecosystems. This can be analyzed from multiple perspectives: social, health, environmental, and economic. However, there are shortcomings in the studies about the everyday use of e-cargo bikes for personal or family travel compared to commercial logistics. While some studies focus on parent cyclists [1] or the factors influencing the urban environment [3], there is a scarcity of research examining the lived experiences of individuals managing household transportation in diverse geographic and infrastructural settings.

3   Methods

A qualitative field study was performed in an urban environment with several potential users to ascertain the factors that facilitate or hinder the utilization of e-cargo bikes. The primary data collection method involved conducting intercept interviews with individuals approached in public locations where e-cargo bikes were likely utilized. Several of these locations were near playgrounds, local markets, elementary schools, and mixed-use communities recognized for their family-friendliness and abundant public transportation options. Individuals potentially interested were requested to participate in a brief, informal interview. The selection criteria targeted those who expressed a need for transportation that facilitated using an e-cargo bike (such as for transporting children, products, or equipment) or those who were already utilizing an e-cargo motorcycle at the time of contact. The semi-structured interviews included open-ended questions to ascertain individuals' perceptions, emotions, and experiences about e-cargo bikes. We sought to identify the factors that deter individuals from utilizing e-cargo bikes and the motivations that encourage their adoption. Respondents remained anonymous, and their answers were recorded promptly. Thematic analysis of the data facilitated the identification of prevalent themes and novel perspectives. The detected themes were categorized into two primary groups: (1) factors that complicate the usage of e-cargo bikes and (2) factors that facilitate their use (drivers). The principal data gathering took place in an urban environment. Contextual field notes and the related work enabled a comprehensive collection of the requirements and limitations of rural mobility.

4   Barriers to E-Cargo Bike Use

Many technological, infrastructural, social, financial, and cultural barriers make it hard to use e-cargo bikes. Many people interested in e-cargo bikes worry about the batteries' distance and range. People who make several journeys a day or have long commutes may not like the limited battery life. Another essential thing to consider is payload capacity, especially for people needing to transport large or heavy things. People often say that bad weather, like wind, rain, or snow, makes them start driving again. Some people also think that driving is faster and easier, especially in places where there aren't any bike lanes. Others might not be fit or strong enough to ride an e-cargo bike. People who aren't sure of themselves when riding motorcycles are less inclined to do so, especially if they don't know how to ride or have physical restrictions.

Many people are quite worried and see threats beyond just technological ones. People often worry that their bike or cargo will be stolen, especially in cities where parking is hard to find. People who don't know how to use e-cargo bikes may find daily use too expensive and time-consuming. Employers are worried that workers won't want to use e-cargo bikes because they think they are uncomfortable or hard to use.

However, the biggest problem we heard about during our interviews was inadequate infrastructure. Bike lanes aren't as beneficial when they're narrow or not well-kept, when there aren't any links between bike pathways, and when there aren't enough places to park cargo bikes. People say sharing the road with heavy or fast-moving motorized traffic makes them nervous. Users who aren't very good at fixing bikes feel even less safe because there isn't a professional service network for maintenance and repairs. Another problem with inadequate infrastructure is that it can damage the payload, especially when bicycles go on bumpy or pothole-filled roads.

You can't ignore hurdles that have to do with money. E-cargo bikes usually cost a lot more up front than regular bicycles. Also, cities and towns have high debts, making it harder to build sustainable transportation infrastructure or give incentives.

There are also a lot of real and imagined worries about safety. Riding next to big cars, having difficulties getting youngsters to sit down, or being fearful of getting attacked or harassed can all make people feel unsafe. People who are older or belong to a minority group, and who may already have trouble getting around, are especially affected. These feelings make it less likely that people will switch from driving to more environmentally friendly ways to get around.

Cultural and societal attitudes provide more deeply rooted challenges. People grow doubtful of other choices and back policies that are good for cars. People think e-cargo bikes are strange or useless, which makes it hard for them to become popular. These biases lead to investment patterns that favor autos.

It can be hard to use e-cargo bikes because of how cities are set up. Many individuals can't use them because of steep hills, severe traffic, and insufficient room for infrastructural changes. Some cities, especially those with old layouts, have difficulty upgrading their infrastructure since there isn't enough public space.

5 Positive Influencing Factors (Drivers) for E-Cargo Bike Use

Notwithstanding these challenges, various advantages may render using e-cargo bikes more attractive and beneficial. The economic viability is frequently cited as a primary argument. E-cargo bicycles are significantly more economical to operate and maintain than private automobiles. They are exempt from paying for parking, road tolls, or congestion charges in many locations. The Total Cost of Ownership (TCO) per kilometer is significantly less than that of motorized vehicles. E-cargo bikes are suitable for cost-conscious individuals, small businesses, and urban areas.

Users assert that numerous "soft" benefits extend beyond economic considerations. These encompass improved health for you and your staff, as cycling promotes more physical activity. Individuals frequently discuss how diminished dependence on automobiles provides them a sense of liberation and contentment, along with consistent journey durations unaffected by traffic conditions. Utilizing e-cargo bikes can enhance a business's public image and demonstrate its commitment to environmental sustainability, aligning with its corporate social responsibility objectives.

E-cargo bicycles are most effective in urban environments, offering several notable advantages. They are ideal for navigating areas where automobiles are prohibited, such as pedestrian zones, low-traffic neighborhoods, and vehicle-free campuses. E-cargo bikes surpass cars in speed for brief journeys in numerous congested urban places, and they can park in proximity to their destinations, hence reducing travel time. This is particularly advantageous for families or businesses with hectic schedules and delivery services.

The e-cargo bike sector has shown substantial growth in recent years. Many enterprises are interested in bicycles, and bike-sharing programs are emerging in urban areas. These programs mitigate entrance barriers by allowing individuals to utilize bicycles temporarily without the necessity of purchase. An increasing number of individuals are using these bicycles, enhancing public awareness and willingness to adopt them. Government rebate initiatives and legal backing, such as including e-cargo bikes in Mobility as a Service (MaaS) platforms, are facilitating the integration of e-cargo bikes into standard transportation systems.

Social and health-related factors further enhance the positive news. E-cargo bikes promote physical activity and improve cardiovascular fitness, mental health, and overall well-being. Cargo bikes are renowned for their social inclusivity, accommodating individuals of all ages, being gender-neutral, and being accessible to those with diverse physical abilities. For example, front-loading designs can accommodate multiple children or groceries while remaining accessible.

A compelling rationale is its environmental benefits. E-cargo bikes generate negligible greenhouse gas emissions compared to conventional automobiles and trucks. They also contribute to reducing noise and air pollution in urban areas. They assist cities in reducing traffic jams and optimizing the utilization of road space and land.

6   Discussion

The results of this study highlight the intricate interaction of environmental, infrastructural, cultural, and psychological factors that influence the viability and appeal of e-cargo bike utilization. In cities with bike lanes and other traffic-calming measures, users find it easier to get around and fit biking into their daily lives. However, they have trouble with crowded public transportation, not enough storage space at home, and safety issues when interacting with motorized vehicles.

The study's main contribution is finding universal traits true no matter where you are, like cost-benefit analyses, dependence on the weather, and perceived safety. When making sound policy, these obstacles and facilitators must be considered. Policymakers should work on tailored solutions, such as better infrastructure in crowded cities.

The results underscore the importance of integrating e-cargo bikes into transportation frameworks. This could include shared mobility platforms, extra services like training and maintenance, and urban design projects that focus on making it easier for people to use more than one mode of transportation. Interventions must tackle social norms and perceptions to normalize the utilization of e-cargo bikes and diminish the cultural preeminence of car-centric ideologies.

7   Conclusion

E-cargo bikes are an effective and environmentally friendly way to get around cities and rural areas, primarily for carrying goods and kids. According to a wealth of data, they can lower emissions, improve urban livability, and advance public health. However, realizing this potential requires a thorough understanding of the challenges that impede their widespread adoption and the factors that facilitate uptake.

This study demonstrates that physical and economic constraints and broader socio-cultural and policy-related influences shape these obstacles and facilitators. People's willingness and ability to use e-cargo bikes depend on the financial support, local infrastructure, weather, terrain, and cultural openness.

To make mobility systems more fair and sustainable, policy efforts should focus on making it easier for people to use e-cargo bikes. This includes building special bike lanes, giving people financial help to buy bikes, raising public awareness, and getting transportation planners, healthcare professionals, and community leaders to work together. Future research should continue to investigate user demands and preferences progression over time, and assess the enduring impacts of initiatives incorporating e-cargo bike mobility into the mainstream.

Acknowledgment. The authors used ChatGPT4.0, QuillBot, and Grammarly for grammar and spell-checking. After using these tool(s)/service(s), the authors reviewed and edited the content as needed and take full responsibility for the publication's content.

References

1. Aldred, R., Jungnickel, K.: Why culture matters for transport policy: the case of cycling in the UK. J. Transp. Geogr. **34**, 78–87 (2014)
2. Anderson, S., Allen, J., Browne, M.: Urban logistics–how can it meet policy makers' sustainability objectives? J. Transp. Geogr. **13**(1), 71–81 (2005)
3. Chatziioannou, I., Bakogiannis, E., Karolemeas, C., Kourmpa, E., Papadaki, K., Vlastos, T.: Urban environment's contributory factors for the adoption of cargo bike usage: a systematic literature review. Future Transp. **4**(1), 92–106 (2024)
4. Fishman, E.: Bikeshare: a review of recent literature. Transp. Rev. **36**(1), 92–113 (2016)
5. Gössling, S.: Why cities need to take road space from cars-and how this could be done. J. Urban Des. **25**(4), 443–448 (2020)
6. Oja, P., et al.: Health benefits of cycling: a systematic review. Scand. J. Med. Sci. Sports **21**(4), 496–509 (2011)
7. Rudolph, C., Gruber, J.: Cargo cycles in commercial transport: potentials, constraints, and recommendations. Res. Transp. Bus. Manag. **24**, 26–36 (2017)

Aesthetic and Emotional Preferences in Wheel Hub Design for New Energy Vehicles

Yi Wang[1], Meiyu Zhou[1], Weilin Cai[1], and Zhengyu Wang[2](✉)

[1] East China University of Science and Technology, Meilong Road NO.130, Xuhui District, Shanghai 200237, China
{Y12232175,Y10220200}@mail.ecust.edu.cn, myzhou@ecust.edu.cn
[2] Industrial Design Institute, COMAC Shanghai Aircraft Customer Service Co., Ltd., Shanghai 200241, China
wangzhengyu1@comac.cc

Abstract. Wheel hub form for new energy vehicles (NEVs) is undergoing significant changes that may affect consumers' aesthetic and emotional preferences. However, there is still a lack of research in this area. This paper aims to investigate consumers' aesthetic and emotional preferences for NEVs wheel hub shape design and provide valuable insights for automotive designers and manufacturers. The study first collected and processed a series of wheel hub images, from which design experts selected 34 representative samples and identified key features. Through literature analysis and expert interviews, Kansei words related to consumer sentiment were identified as perceptual factors. Subsequently, a semantic difference questionnaire was constructed to investigate users' Kansei evaluation and preference for NEVS wheel hubs. Finally, multiple linear regression and Pearson correlation analysis were used to process the collected data to elucidate consumers' emotional preferences and styling expectations of NEVS wheel hubs. The study results show that the wheel hub design with decoration significantly enhances consumers' emotional experience and liking. At the same time, the hollow area does not have a significant effect on emotional preference. Consumers preferred wheel hubs with a sense of fashion, luxury, and technology, and no significant differences were found in the preferences for fragility and solidity. The sense of eco-friendly shows a particular trend in consumer preference, but the related design elements are not prominent. This study provides an important consumer orientation for the design of NEVS wheel hubs, emphasizing the importance of incorporating emotional experience and aesthetic value in the design process to meet the diverse needs of modern consumers.

Keywords: Wheel Hub Morphology Design · Kansei Engineering · Aesthetic Preferences · Regression Analysis · Quantification-I Theory

1 Introduction

With the global emphasis on environmental protection and sustainable development, NEVS is becoming an important direction for the future development of the automotive industry [1]. At the same time, modern consumers not only pay attention to the performance and economy of the vehicles but also pay more attention to the aesthetics and

© The Author(s), under exclusive license to Springer Nature Switzerland AG 2026
S. Sundarakannan and O. Knorpp (Eds.): HCII 2025, CCIS 2772, pp. 62–69, 2026.
https://doi.org/10.1007/978-3-032-12767-9_8

emotions conveyed by the appearance of the vehicles [2]. In this context, the appearance design of NEVs is crucial, and they must be differentiated from traditional fuel vehicles to meet changing consumer needs [3].

As one of the key features of NEVs, the wheel hub has an important impact on consumer satisfaction [4]. There have been many studies related to wheel hubs in the past. Luo et al. evaluated the correlation by analyzing the semantic differences between the body and the wheel hub to provide design references for the wheel hub-matching selection of different vehicles [5]. Li and Lu researched the morphology of the wheel hub based on shape semantics, branding, and structural optimization. They developed an automated, bi-directional, and morphological parameter transformation mechanism [6]. Chen et al. used linear regression to explore the matching relationship between the Kansei words and the morphological elements of the wheel hub of the sedan [7]. However, all of these studies are based on the wheel hubs of traditional energy vehicles.

With technological development and aesthetic trends, we observe that the wheel hub design of NEVs is undergoing significant changes. More and more wheel hubs are now adopting closed shapes to minimize wind resistance, improve aerodynamic performance, and extend driving range. At the same time, the decoration of wheel hubs is also increasing. However, the specific impact of these morphological changes on consumers' aesthetic and emotional preferences has not been thoroughly studied.

Therefore, this study aims to investigate consumers' aesthetic and emotional preferences for wheel hub shape design in NEVs. Based on the theories of Kansei Engineering (KE) [8] and Quantification-I Theory [9], the study employs multiple linear regression and Pearson correlation analysis through qualitative and quantitative analytical methods to reveal how different design elements affect consumers' emotional responses and preference levels. This study helps to provide valuable insights for automotive designers and manufacturers and points out the direction for the future wheel hub design of NEVs.

2 Methods

2.1 Subjects

Eighty subjects aged between 18 and 30 (mean 26.63 years old) were recruited for this study, with a male-to-female ratio close to 1:1 (38 males and 42 females). All subjects had some knowledge of NEVs, had normal or corrected-to-normal vision, and were in good health. Subjects were randomly recruited through online and offline channels, signed an informed consent form, and were paid for participation at the experiment's end. The study strictly followed ethical norms, and all personal information was handled confidentially.

2.2 Materials

The materials for this experiment included two core categories: NEV wheel hub samples and Kansei words, which were used in the visual and linguistic perception evaluation sessions of the semantic difference experiment, respectively.

NEV Wheel Hub Samples. The picture sample consists of 34 pictures of different types of NEV wheel hub appearance, which guide the subjects to perceive and evaluate the target stimuli, as shown in Fig. 1. These pictures were selected from the wheel hub samples of actual vehicles and were strictly screened to ensure picture quality and content consistency. The screening criteria included a resolution of no less than 1024*1024 pixels and a uniform shooting angle (all of which were the wheel hubs on the front side of the vehicle). In addition, to eliminate the interference of additional variables such as color, lighting, and redundant interfering elements, all pictures were post-processed (e.g., uniform resolution, adjusting the hue to grey, removing the background and brand logos) to ensure that the subjects could focus on the exterior features of the wheel hubs of the NEVs. The image samples were intentionally selected to encompass a wide range of categories of wheel hubs from various mainstream NEVs (e.g., sedan, SUV, sports car), aiming to maximize the representativeness of the experimental data and improve the generalizability of the findings.

Fig. 1. Samples of NEV wheel hub.

In order to qualitatively and quantitatively analyze the samples, the target product is usually divided into several design elements using morphological methods [10]. During the sample selection and evaluation process, 15 focus group members specializing in industrial design conducted a comprehensive feature deconstruction of the selected wheel hub samples. The team members referred to the previous literature on the splitting methods of traditional ones [11]. Combined with NEV wheel hubs' unique design trends and styling changes, they constructed a comprehensive set of feature parameter systems, as shown in Table 1.

Kansei Words. In this study, Kansei words were selected to capture subjects' perceptual perceptions and emotional responses to the design features of NEV wheel hubs. After extensive literature research and interviews with experts, the researchers finally selected five pairs of representative Kansei words to describe the attributes of NEV wheel hubs. These words were presented as positive and negative extreme antonyms to help subjects

Table 1. Feature parameter system of NEV wheel hub.

Feature parameters	Parameter attributes		
Spoke Numbers	3、4、5、6、7、8、10、12、20、25、28、30		
Curvature Level	Straight	mixed	Curved
Rotation Mode	non-rotational	rotational	
Shape Form	geometric	V-type	Y-type
Spoke Width	Thin	Medium	Wide
Hollow Area	Small	Medium	Large
Decorations	Few	Medium	Many

accurately express their emotional attitudes during the assessment process. Table **2** lists the Kansei words obtained from the screening.

The sentiments embodied in K1-K4 are derived from consumers' perceptions of the wheel hubs of conventional energy vehicles and have been widely used in previous studies. Given the eco-friendly nature of NEVs, the pair of terms K5 was added to reflect consumers' perceptions of wheel hubs in terms of eco-friendliness. Subjects could assess whether the design of the wheel hubs was in line with the concept of eco-friendliness, which helped to understand their affective attitudes towards the environmental characteristics and sustainability of the wheel hubs of NEVs. The above five pairs of Kansei words will be used as key evaluation indicators in the experiment.

Table 2. Representative Kansei words.

Code	Kansei words
K1	Conservative - Fashion
K2	Affordable - Luxury
K3	Fragile - Solid
K4	Traditional - technological
K5	Polluting - Eco-friendly

2.3 Semantic Differences Experiment

We combined the 34 wheel hub samples with five pairs of Kansei words into a semantic difference scale to assess subjects' perceptions of NEV wheel hubs. The scale was designed in a 7-point Richter format to facilitate subjects to rate each pair of Kansei words, thus reflecting their affective attitudes towards each wheel hub sample.

Each pair of words in the scale represents two opposing affective dimensions. When completing the questionnaire, subjects were asked to select a value on a scale of 1 to 7 to indicate the extent to which they agreed with the particular wheel hub sample on the affective dimension. A value of 1 indicated a 'complete preference for the left-hand side of the vocabulary,' and a value of 7 indicated a 'complete preference for the right-hand side of the vocabulary.'

In addition, we added a "favorite value rating" dimension to the scale. Subjects were asked to rate each sample wheel hub according to their preference on a scale ranging from 1 to 7, where 1 means' dislike very much' and 7 means' like very much.' This rating helped explore the potential relationship between Kansei words and user preferences.

The questionnaire was distributed to 80 subjects. After collection and screening, we finally recovered 50 valid questionnaires.

3   Results and Discussion

3.1   Multiple Linear Regression Analysis

We used the method of multiple linear regression to analyze the data. The design features of the NEV wheel hubs were considered the dependent variable, while the Kansei words associated with them were used as the independent variable. Table 3 summarises the results of the multiple linear regression analysis.

K1 (Conservative-Fashionable): the model has significance (P = 0.035) and reasonable explanatory power (R^2 = 0.558) for regression analysis. In the regression coefficients, the positive effect of Decorations is significant (B = 0.117***), indicating that increasing decorative designs will improve users' fashion perceptions. In addition, increasing Curvature Level and Hollow Area also show a small but positive trend.

K2 (Affordable-Luxury): The model is statistically highly significant (P = 0.002) and has good explanatory power (R^2 = 0.611) for regression analysis. Among them, Decorations (B = 0.105***) and Spoke Numbers (B = 0.006*) significantly affect the perception of luxury. In addition, the Y-type Spoke also somewhat enhances the perception of luxury. This result implies that adding sophisticated design elements can attract luxury-seeking consumers.

K3 (Fragile-Solid): The model exhibits a high level of significance (P = 0.000) and explanatory power (R^2 of 0.734), suggesting that the model can keenly capture changes in the data and make predictions. On the one hand, Rotation Mode (0.094***), Y-type Spoke (0.068**), increasing Spoke Width (0.046**), and Decorations (0.059***) can significantly enhance the sense of solidity. On the other hand, a higher Curvature Level (−0.027*) reduces the feeling of solidity and gives the user a sense of fragility.

K4 (Traditional – technological): The model is insignificant (P = 0.219) and has limited explanatory power (R^2 = 0.354), which is unsuitable for regression analysis. However, Decorations (0.106**) still showed a strong significance level, suggesting that an increase in the decorations can positively affect the feeling of technology.

K5 (Polluted-Environmental): The model is insignificant (P = 0.402) and has limited explanatory power (R^2 = 0.291), unsuitable for regression analysis, indicating that the design features were ineffective in communicating environmental awareness. Designers should consider how to reflect the eco-friendly features practically in future design solutions to enhance consumers' awareness and attention to this feature.

Table 3. Results of multiple linear regression analysis.

Features	K1	K2	K3	K4	K5
	Non-standardized Coefficient B				
Spoke Numbers	0.006	**0.006***	0.002	0.005	−0.003
Curvature Level	0.037	0.016	**−0.027***	0.028	−0.002
Rotation Mode	−0.042	0.008	**0.094*****	−0.033	0.007
geometric	−0.11	−0.107	−0.047	−0.069	−0.053
V-type	−0.106	−0.092	0.023	−0.089	−0.044
Y-type	0.027	0.043	**0.068****	0.028	0.006
Spoke Width	−0.04	−0.058	**0.046****	−0.046	0.008
Hollow Area	0.031	−0.026	−0.025	0.008	0.008
Decorations	**0.117*****	**0.105*****	**0.059*****	**0.106****	0.009
Constant	**0.454****	**0.534*****	**0.52*****	**0.477***	**0.597*****
R^2	0.558	0.611	0.734	0.354	0.291
Adjusted R^2	0.337	0.466	0.634	0.111	0.025
p	**0.035****	**0.002*****	**0.000*****	0.219	0.402

Note: ***, **, and * represent 1%, 5%, and 10% significance levels, respectively.

In summary, we found a significant difference in the impact of different design features on user preferences. The regression coefficients for Decorations are significantly positive across multiple Kansei words, especially in K1 and K2, suggesting that an increase in Decorations positively correlates with a sense of fashion and luxury. Increasing the Spokes Number enhances the sense of luxury. Increasing the Curvature Level has a slight positive effect on enhancing fashion and luxury but increases fragility. The significance of the effects shown by the design features for the K4 and K5 is yet to be improved, suggesting that future design efforts should respond to consumer expectations and demands for technology and environmental awareness.

3.2 Correlation Analysis

We used Pearson correlation analysis to explore the relationship between individual emotion (K1 to K5) and user preference values (A). Pearson correlation analysis is a commonly used statistical method for assessing the strength and direction of a linear relationship between two variables. By calculating the correlation coefficient (r), we can quantify the influence of different perceptual dimensions on user preferences, thus revealing their interrelationships.

In order to demonstrate more visually the correlation between each perceptual term and the user preference value, we used a heat map (Fig. 2). The heat map displays the magnitude of the correlation coefficient r through the shade of the color, and we can understand more intuitively how different affective preferences affect the user's preference level.

Our analysis found that the correlations between K1, K2, K4, and A were 0.827, 0.819, and 0.793, respectively, showing strong correlations. This result suggests that enhancing the sense of fashion, luxury, and technology can significantly enhance users' liking of NEV wheel hubs.

In addition, the correlation between K5 and A is 0.574, suggesting that, to a certain extent, the conveyance of a sense of eco-friendliness can enhance user favoritism. With the increase in environmental awareness, consumers are increasingly concerned about the environmental characteristics of products when purchasing.

Comparatively, the correlation between K3 and A is only 0.325, showing that fragility and solidity do not significantly affect user preference.

Overall, our analyses reveal multiple considerations for users when choosing wheel hubs for NEVs, highlighting the importance of emotional communication in design elements. In order to gain users' favor, future designs should focus more on fashion, luxury, and technology while incorporating a combination of environmental values to meet modern consumers' pursuit of aesthetics and functionality.

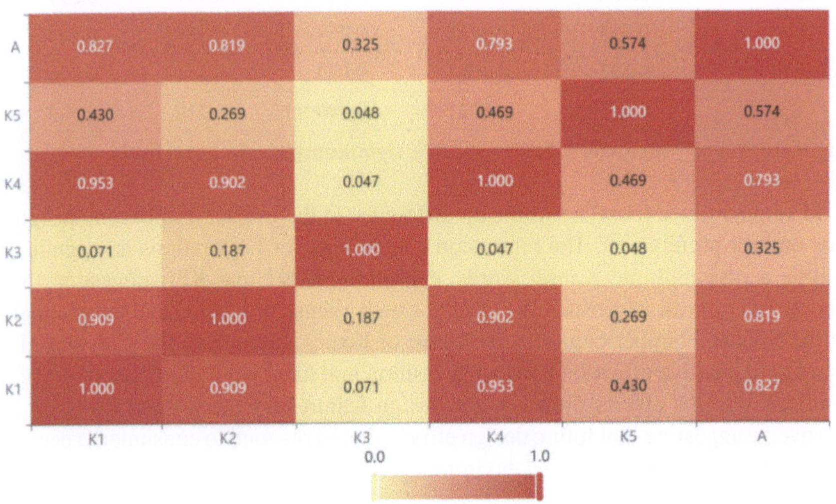

Fig. 2. Heat map of correlation analysis.

4 Conclusion

This study explored consumers' aesthetic and emotional preferences for the design of NEVs wheel hubs, combining KE and quantification-I theory. The study results show that the decorations of the NEVs wheel hubs have a significant positive correlation with consumers' perceptions of fashion, luxury, and solidity, especially in enhancing user satisfaction. The hollow area of the wheel hub did not affect users' emotions and preferences. Enhancing the wheel hub shape's fashion, luxury, and technology can gain consumers' favoritism. In addition, the influence of eco-friendliness as an important aspect of modern consumers' concerns is gradually increasing. However, the current design features fail to evoke this emotion and awareness effectively. Overall, the study not only provides valuable insights for automotive designers and manufacturers but also points out the direction for the future design of NEVs wheel hubs, contributing theoretical support to promoting the sustainable development of the automotive industry.

References

1. Wang, Z., Niu, S., Fu, C., Hu, S., Huang, L.: Advancing data-driven sustainable design: a novel NEV form design approach in China's market. J. Clean. Prod. **461**, 142626 (2024)
2. Hou, X., Gou, B., Chen, D., Chu, J., Ding, N., Ma, L.: A method to assist designers in optimizing the exterior styling of vehicles based on key features. Expert Syst. Appl. **254**, 124485 (2024)
3. Lai, X., Zhang, S., Mao, N., Liu, J., Chen, Q.: Kansei engineering for NEV exterior design: an internet big data mining approach. Comput. Ind. Eng. **165**, 107913 (2021)
4. Kang, X.: Combining rough set theory and support vector regression to the sustainable form design of hybrid electric vehicle. J. Clean. Prod. **304**, 127137 (2021)
5. Luo, S., Lin, H., Hu, Y., Fang, C.: Preliminary study on the aesthetic preference for taillight shape design. Int. J. Ind. Ergon. **87**, 103240 (2022)
6. Li, W., Lu, Z.: Feature transformation method for wheel hub shape based on target detection and geometric analysis. Electronics. **12** (2023)
7. Chen, Y., Peng, Q., Huang, R., Shao, J.: Evaluation of parametric sedan wheel hub based on Kansei Engineering and regression analysis. Metaverse. **5** (2024)
8. Nagamachi, M.: Kansei Engineering: A new ergonomic consumer-oriented technology for product development. Int. J. Ind. Ergon. **15**, 3–11 (1995)
9. Dunia, R., Joe Qin, S.: Joint diagnosis of process and sensor faults using principal component analysis. Control. Eng. Pract. **6**, 457–469 (1998)
10. Chang, Y.-M., Chen, C.-W.: Kansei assessment of the constituent elements and the overall interrelations in car steering wheel hub design. Int. J. Ind. Ergon. **56**, 97–105 (2016)
11. Liu, J., Zhi, Q., Ji, H., Li, B., Lei, S.: Wheel hub customization with an interactive artificial immune algorithm. J. Intell. Manuf. **32**, 1305–1322 (2021)

Enhancing User Trust and Comprehension in Autonomous Driving: The Role of Strategic HMI Design

Ornella Ziino[(✉)], Giulia Losi, and Buse Tezçi

RE:LAB s.r.l., Reggio nell'Emilia RE, Italy
ornella.ziino@re-lab.it

Abstract. Trust and comprehension are critical for the successful adoption of Automated Driving Systems (ADS). This study empirically investigated how Human-Machine Interface (HMI) design influences user trust across different automation levels. Nine participants experienced three automation levels (3–5) in a driving simulator, with each level implementing different degrees of system proactivity and adaptivity. Quantitative analysis revealed consistently high trust scores ($M = 5.31$–5.89) with no significant differences between levels ($F(2.16) = 1.57, p > 0.05$). However, qualitative analysis uncovered critical insights: information overload at intermediate automation, appreciation for transparency, and polarized responses to full automation. Results suggest trust depends less on automation level than on specific interface design choices. Key implications include balancing information provision with cognitive load and ensuring clear control communication. Despite sample size limitations, findings provide empirical indications for user-centered HMI design in automated vehicles .

Keywords: Automation · Trust · HMI · User Interface · Automotive

1 Introduction

The rapid advancement of automated vehicle technology promises transformative benefits for transportation safety, efficiency, and accessibility. As vehicles transition from manual control to increasing levels of autonomy, the fundamental relationship between human users and their vehicles undergoes profound changes (Paden et al., 2016). Central to the successful adoption and safe operation of these systems is the level of trust that users place in Automated Driving Systems (ADS). Trust, defined as the attitude that a system will help achieve an individual's goals in situations characterized by uncertainty and vulnerability, serves as a crucial prerequisite for effective human-automation collaboration (Lee & See, 2004). The challenge lies in calibrating this trust appropriately, as both under-trust (leading to disuse) and over-trust (resulting in misuse or complacency) pose significant risks to safety and system effectiveness (Lee & See, 2004).

Extensive research has investigated trust in automation from multiple perspectives, examining its antecedents, development, and consequences for human-automation interaction (Hoff & Bashir, 2015). Studies have explored various factors influencing trust,

© The Author(s), under exclusive license to Springer Nature Switzerland AG 2026

S. Sundarakannan and O. Knorpp (Eds.): HCII 2025, CCIS 2772, pp. 70–80, 2026.
https://doi.org/10.1007/978-3-032-12767-9_9

including system reliability, transparency, predictability, and even anthropomorphic design features (Kim et al., 2024). However, while this body of work provides valuable theoretical insights, a notable gap remains in translating these concepts into specific, actionable HMI design strategies tailored to the unique challenges of automated driving (Wei et al., 2024). Current literature often addresses trust at conceptual levels or investigates broad interface characteristics without providing detailed design guidelines that practitioners can implement.

This study addresses this gap by empirically investigating how strategic HMI design principles influence user trust and comprehension across different automation levels. We move beyond theoretical frameworks to examine how specific interface implementations affect user experience in realistic driving scenarios. By testing carefully designed interfaces that embody key trust-building principles, we provide empirical evidence for effective HMI design in automated vehicles.

1.1   Defining Trust and Comprehension in Automated Driving

Trust in automated vehicles represents a multifaceted construct that extends beyond simple confidence in system reliability. It encompasses users' beliefs about the system's competence, predictability, and alignment with their goals, particularly in uncertain and potentially hazardous situations (Lee & See, 2004). This trust is not static but rather dynamic, evolving continuously based on user experiences, system performance, and the quality of information provided through the HMI (Ekman et al., 2018).

Comprehension, equally critical yet often overlooked, refers to users' understanding of the ADS's current state, its perception of the environment, its planned actions, and the rationale behind its decisions (Endsley et al., 2003). Effective comprehension enables users to maintain appropriate situational awareness, anticipate system behavior, and intervene effectively when necessary. The absence of adequate comprehension can lead to anxiety, inappropriate trust calibration, and delayed or incorrect responses in critical situations (Endsley et al., 2003).

Hoff and Bashir's influential three-layered model provides a framework for understanding trust complexity in automated systems (Hoff & Bashir, 2015). Dispositional trust reflects individual tendencies to trust technology generally. Situational trust emerges from specific context and system characteristics. Learned trust develops through accumulated experience with the system. This framework helps explain why users might respond differently to identical automation levels and why trust calibration remains challenging across diverse user populations.

1.2   The Critical Role of HMI Design

The Human-Machine Interface serves as the primary conduit for information exchange between the ADS and the user, making it instrumental in shaping trust and comprehension (Kim et al., 2024). A well-designed HMI can transform abstract system operations into understandable, actionable information that builds user confidence and maintains appropriate engagement. Conversely, poor HMI design can create confusion, erode trust, and potentially lead to dangerous situations (Raats et al., 2020).

Research has demonstrated that effective HMIs must balance multiple considerations. Transparency in system operations helps users understand automation decisions but must be implemented carefully to avoid information overload (Ekman et al., 2018). Multimodal feedback leveraging visual, auditory, and haptic channels can enhance information processing and maintain user attention (Hoff & Bashir, 2015). The timing and presentation of information prove as critical as its content, particularly during control transitions where ambiguity can have serious safety implications (Endsley et al., 2003).

1.3 Research Approach and Automation Framework

To investigate these design challenges empirically, we developed and tested HMI prototypes based on six key principles derived from literature: (1) contextually relevant information delivery, (2) multimodal feedback systems, (3) continuous system status feedback, (4) judicious use of anthropomorphism, (5) adaptive interface capabilities, and (6) clear control transition communication.

We adapted Sheridan and Verplank's seminal automation taxonomy (Sheridan & Verplank, 1978) to create five distinct levels focusing specifically on system proactivity:

- Level 1 - Manual: No system assistance; full user control
- Level 2 - Guided Support: System suggests options, user confirms before execution
- Level 3 - Automatic Execution with Intervention: System executes after timeout unless user intervenes
- Level 4 - Transparent Automation: Autonomous operation with explanations provided
- Level 5 - Full Automation: Complete autonomy without explanations

This framework enabled systematic investigation of how varying degrees of system initiative and information provision influence user trust and comprehension.

2 Methodology

2.1 Participants

Nine participants (N = 9) were recruited from an Italian technology company with approximately 150 employees. The sample intentionally included both HMI specialists and employees from non-technical departments to capture diverse perspectives. This recruitment strategy provided insights from both expert users familiar with interface design principles and typical end-users who represent the broader driving population. Participant diversity in technical background proved valuable for understanding how different user groups respond to automation interfaces.

2.2 Experimental Design and Scenario

The study employed a within-subjects design where each participant experienced three automation levels (3–5, and). Levels 1 and 2 were excluded from formal testing as they involve minimal system proactivity, making trust measurement less relevant. The core scenario involved a critical driving situation: while traveling on an urban road, an unexpected obstacle (a broken-down vehicle) suddenly appears, requiring an evasive maneuver. This scenario was selected because it represents a realistic situation where trust in automation becomes critical for safety.

The automated system's response varied by level. At Level 3, the system suggested an overtaking maneuver and initiated it after a countdown, allowing user intervention. Level 4 executed the maneuver while providing real-time explanations of its decision-making process. Level 5 performed the maneuver automatically without explanations. This design enabled direct comparison of how different information strategies influence trust and comprehension during safety-critical events (Figs. 1, 2, and 3).

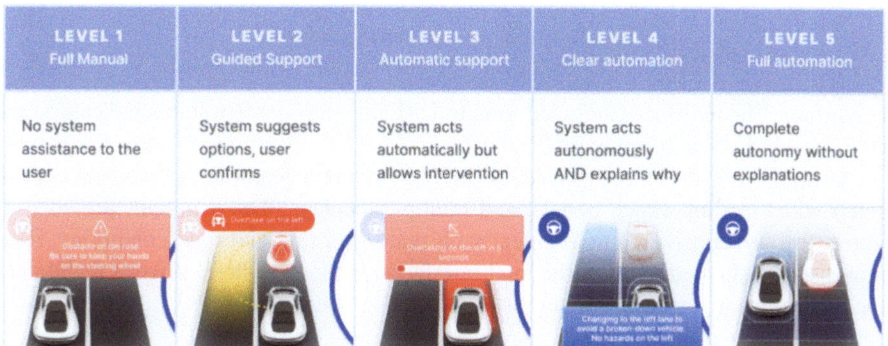

Fig. 1. Strategic variations in user interface design across different levels of automation.

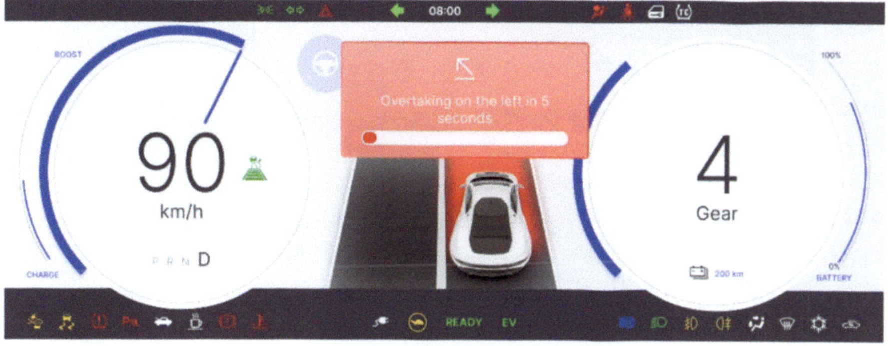

Fig. 2. Cluster image scenario of level 3.

2.3 Materials

Interface prototypes were developed using Figma (https://www.figma.com/), incorporating the six design principles identified in our literature review. Each prototype was carefully crafted to represent its automation level while maintaining visual consistency across

Fig. 3. Cluster image scenario of level 5.

conditions. The interfaces included a central driving view, system status indicators, and context-appropriate information displays.

Testing occurred in a high-fidelity driving simulator featuring a complete cockpit setup with steering wheel, pedals, and multiple displays. The simulator provided an immersive urban driving environment with realistic traffic and road conditions. Head unit displays showed the experimental interfaces, while peripheral screens maintained the driving scene, creating a naturalistic interaction context (Fig. 4).

Fig. 4. Driving simulator setup cluster scenario prototype displayed.

2.4 Procedure

Participants first completed the Affinity for Technology Interaction (ATI) (Franke et al., 2017) scale to assess baseline technology comfort. After simulator familiarization, they experienced each automation level in sequence. Each level scenario lasted approximately 2 min, with the critical event occurring at a predetermined point.

Following each scenario, participants completed the Trust of Automated Systems Test (TOAST) (Wojton et al., 2020), a validated 9-item scale measuring trust through understanding and performance dimensions. Additionally, they answered three open-ended questions addressing: (1) their understanding of system actions, (2) their experience using the system, and (3) their satisfaction with the interaction. This mixed-methods approach enabled triangulation of findings and revealed nuances that quantitative measures alone might miss.

3   Results

A repeated measures Analysis of Variance (ANOVA) was used to examine trust differences across automation levels. Effect sizes were calculated to assess practical significance. Qualitative responses were analyzed thematically, with two researchers independently coding responses into emergent categories. Discrepancies were resolved through discussion. Response frequencies were calculated to identify predominant themes within each automation level.

3.1   Affinity to Technology

ATI scores revealed considerable diversity in technology affinity among participants ($M = 4.31$, $SD = 1.10$, range: 2.67–5.67). Two participants demonstrated very high affinity (scores >5.0), four showed moderately high affinity (4.0–5.0), two exhibited low affinity (<3.0), and one scored in the neutral range. This distribution reflects expected variability in the general population and provides confidence that findings are not limited to technology enthusiasts.

3.2   Trust in Automation

Repeated measures ANOVA revealed no significant main effect of automation level on overall trust scores ($F(2,16) = 1.57, p > 0.05, \eta^2 = 0.06$). The small effect size indicates minimal practical impact of automation level on quantitative trust ratings. Mean trust scores remained consistently high across all conditions: Level 3 ($M = 5.83, SD = 0.80$), Level 4 ($M = 5.49, SD = 1.68$), and Level 5 ($M = 5.57, SD = 0.73$).

Examining subscales revealed interesting patterns. Level 3 showed the highest scores for both understanding ($M = 5.75$) and performance ($M = 5.89$). Level 4 demonstrated greater variability ($SD = 1.68$), suggesting mixed responses to transparency. Level 5 presented a notable divergence: the lowest understanding score ($M = 5.31$) paired with high performance trust ($M = 5.78$), indicating users trusted the system's capability despite not understanding its operations (Fig. 5).

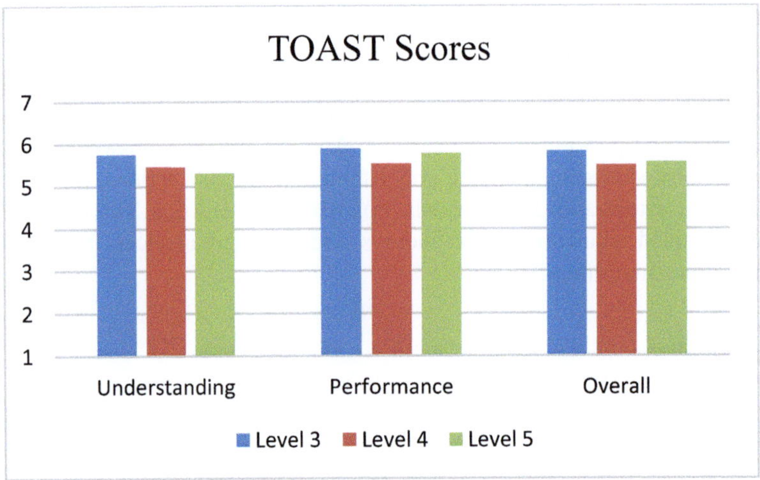

Fig. 5. TOAST Scores over three levels of automation that shows, understanding, performance and overall scores.

3.3 Qualitative Findings

Thematic analysis revealed distinct response patterns for each automation level, providing rich insights into user experience beyond trust ratings.

Level 3 - Automatic Execution with Intervention. Information overload emerged as the dominant theme, with 44% of participants (4/9) reporting distraction from multiple notifications and visual elements. One participant articulated: *"There's too much happening at once - time bars, pop-ups, warnings. I'm more focused on the interface than the road."* Control confusion affected 22% of participants (2/9), who expressed uncertainty about when the system versus the user maintained control. Another noted: *"This interaction would be fine if I'm already in autonomous mode, but if there's potential danger and I'm driving, why take control at this precise moment?"*

Despite these challenges, 33% (3/9) appreciated specific features, particularly the safety distance monitoring. This suggests that relevant safety information is valued when presented appropriately, but the overall implementation at Level 3 created cognitive overload that undermined its benefits.

Level 4 - Transparent Automation. Responses to transparent automation were notably more positive, though still mixed. Users consistently recognized and valued the system's explanatory approach. Comments indicated that understanding the system's reasoning helped build confidence even as it assumed greater control. One participant stated: *"I appreciate knowing why it's making decisions. Even if I'm not controlling, I feel more comfortable."* However, some users found the explanations added to their cognitive load during critical moments, suggesting that transparency implementation requires careful consideration of timing and presentation.

Level 5 - Full Automation. Full automation elicited the most polarized responses. Some participants expressed complete comfort with system control: *"This time I don't* *do anything, it does everything. That's actually relaxing once you accept it.*" Others felt uncomfortable with the lack of information: "*I trust it's working, but I want to know what it's thinking. The silence makes me nervous.*" This division appeared unrelated to general technology affinity, suggesting that preferences for automation transparency represent a distinct individual difference that HMI design must accommodate.

4 Discussion

The contrast between high quantitative trust scores and diverse qualitative experiences reveals important insights about trust measurement and user experience in automated driving systems. While TOAST scores suggested uniform high trust across automation levels, participant comments exposed significant concerns and preferences that standardized measures failed to capture. This discrepancy highlights the complexity of trust in automation and the need for nuanced evaluation approaches.

Our findings reveal a fundamental problem in HMI design that is the need to provide sufficient information for situational awareness while avoiding cognitive overload. Level 3's attempt at comprehensive information delivery, intended to support user understanding and control, paradoxically created confusion and distraction. This aligns with Endsley's framework on situational awareness (Endsley et al., 2003), which emphasizes that information must be not just available but cognitively manageable.

The negative response to information density at Level 3 suggests that designers must prioritize information hierarchy and timing over completeness. Critical information for immediate decisions should take precedence, with secondary details available on demand rather than simultaneously presented. These finding challenges assumptions that more information necessarily builds more trust.

Level 4's relative success in user acceptance validates theoretical arguments for transparency in automation (Lee & See, 2004). Users appreciated understanding system reasoning, which helped maintain their sense of involvement even when not actively controlling the vehicle. However, the implementation of transparency requires sophistication beyond simply exposing system logic. Effective transparent automation must consider when explanations add value versus when they may distract from critical tasks.

Our findings suggest that transparency should be adaptive, providing detailed explanations during routine operations but simplifying during critical events. This aligns with principles of adaptive automation (Parasuraman et al., 2000) but extends them to information presentation strategies.

The polarized responses to Level 5's full automation reveal that users vary fundamentally in their comfort with system autonomy, independent of their general technology affinity. Some users readily embraced complete automation, finding relief in relinquishing control. Others maintained a strong need for system insight even when their intervention was neither required nor possible.

These differences suggest that future HMI designs must accommodate varying user preferences through customizable information levels. Rather than imposing a single information strategy, systems should allow users to select their preferred level of system visibility, ranging from minimal interfaces for those comfortable with full automation to detailed displays for those requiring ongoing system awareness.

4.1 Design Implications

Our findings point to several crucial design considerations for automated vehicle HMIs. First, information architecture must prioritize cognitive efficiency over comprehensiveness. Designers should employ progressive disclosure, presenting essential information prominently while making details available through user request. Second, multimodal feedback strategies should reinforce rather than duplicate information, using each modality's strengths to create coherent communication.

Control transition communication emerged as particularly critical. The confusion expressed at Level 3 highlights that users need unambiguous, persistent indicators of who maintains control authority. These indicators should be visually distinct and positioned to remain visible without demanding constant attention. Haptic feedback through the steering wheel could provide an additional channel for control status, creating redundancy without visual clutter.

5 Conclusions

This empirical investigation of HMI design's role in automated driving trust provides evidence that interface design choices profoundly influence user experience, often more than automation level itself. While users demonstrated generally high trust in automated systems, their comprehension, comfort, and preferences varied significantly based on how information was presented and control was communicated.

Key findings challenge several assumptions in current HMI design. The information overload at Level 3 demonstrates that comprehensive information provision can undermine rather than support user trust. The appreciation for transparency at Level 4 validates theoretical predictions while revealing implementation challenges. The polarized responses to full automation at Level 5 highlight individual differences that transcend general technology affinity.

These results yield specific design recommendations. Interfaces must balance information richness with cognitive manageability through careful hierarchy and progressive disclosure. Transparency should be implemented adaptively, adjusting to situational demands. Control status requires persistent, multimodal communication that remains clear without demanding constant attention. Most importantly, systems should accommodate individual preferences through customizable information levels.

Several limitations constrain our findings' generalizability. The small sample size (N = 9) severely limits statistical power, likely contributing to non-significant quantitative results. This prevents definitive conclusions about population-level trust differences across automation levels. The within-subjects design, while enabling direct comparisons, may have introduced order effects influencing later responses.

The simulator environment, though high-fidelity, cannot replicate the full complexity and consequences of real-world driving. Participants' trust ratings might differ substantially when actual safety is at stake. Brief exposure to each automation level may not reflect trust evolution over extended use, as trust calibration is known to develop through accumulated experience (Muir & Moray, 1996).

Another important factor is the duration of the interaction with the system. All participants interacted with the system for a short period of time, however, the study did not investigate the changes in the trust level over a duration of time, that might impact the trust level.

These limitations point to several research priorities. Large-scale studies with sufficient power to detect meaningful trust differences should be conducted across diverse populations. Longitudinal research examining trust evolution over weeks or months would provide insights into how initial responses translate to sustained acceptance. Field studies using actual automated vehicles would enhance ecological validity and reveal trust dynamics in genuine risk contexts.

Development of advanced trust measurement instruments represents another crucial direction. These should capture trust's multidimensional nature, potentially combining physiological measures, behavioral indicators, and sophisticated self-report instruments. Real-time trust assessment during driving could reveal moment-to-moment fluctuations missed by post-hoc evaluations.

Research into adaptive HMI systems that dynamically adjust to user preferences and states offers promising possibilities. Machine learning could optimize information presentation for individual users, learning from their interactions to provide personalized interfaces that maintain appropriate trust while minimizing cognitive load.

Despite its limitations, this study contributes insights that effective HMI design in automated vehicles requires sophisticated understanding of human information processing, trust dynamics, and individual differences. As automated vehicles progress toward deployment, such human-centered design research becomes increasingly critical for ensuring safe, trusted, and effective human-automation collaboration on our roads.

Disclosure of Interests.   The authors have no competing interests to declare that are relevant to the content of this article.

References

Ekman, F., Johansson, M., Sochor, J.: Creating appropriate trust in automated vehicle systems: a framework for HMI design. IEEE Transactions on Human-Machine Systems. **48**(1), 95–101 (2018). https://doi.org/10.1109/THMS.2017.2776209

Endsley, M.R., Bolte, B., Jones, D.G.: Designing for Situation Awareness: an Approach to User-Centered Design, 1st edn. CRC Press (2003). https://doi.org/10.1201/9780203485088

Franke, T., Attig, C., Wessel, D.: Assessing affinity for technology interaction – the affinity for technology interaction (ATI) scale. Scale Description – English and German Scale Version. (2017). https://doi.org/10.13140/RG.2.2.28679.50081

Hoff, K.A., Bashir, M.: Trust in automation: integrating empirical evidence on factors that influence trust. Hum. Factors. **57**(3), 407–434 (2015). https://doi.org/10.1177/0018720814547570

Raats, K., Fors, V., Pink, S.: Trusting autonomous vehicles: an interdisciplinary approach. Transp. Res. Interdiscip. Perspect. **7**, 100201 (2020). https://doi.org/10.1016/j.trip.2020.100201

Kim, S., He, X., van Egmond, R., Happee, R.: Designing user interfaces for partially automated vehicles: effects of information and modality on trust and acceptance. Transp. Res. F Traffic Psychol. Behav. **103**, 404–419 (2024). https://doi.org/10.1016/j.trf.2024.02.009

Lee, J.D., See, K.A.: Trust in automation: designing for appropriate reliance. Hum. Factors. **46**(1), 50–80 (2004). https://doi.org/10.1518/hfes.46.1.50_30392

Muir, B., Moray, N.: Trust in automation. Part II. Experimental studies of trust and human intervention in a process control simulation. Ergonomics. **39**(3), 429–460 (1996). https://doi.org/10.1080/00140139608964474

Paden, B., Čáp, M., Yong, S.Z., Yershov, D., Frazzoli, E.: A survey of motion planning and control techniques for self-driving urban vehicles. IEEE Transactions on Intelligent Vehicles. **1**(1), 33–55 (2016). https://doi.org/10.1109/TIV.2016.2578706

Parasuraman, R., Sheridan, T.B., Wickens, C.D.: A model for types and levels of human interaction with automation. IEEE Trans. Syst. Man Cybern. Syst. Hum. **30**(3), 286–297 (2000). https://doi.org/10.1109/3468.844354

Sheridan, T.B., Verplank, W.L.: Human and computer control of undersea teleoperators. DTIC Document, Tech. Rep. (1978)

Wei, D., Zhang, C., Fan, M., Ge, S., Mi, Z.: Research on multimodal adaptive in-vehicle interface interaction design strategies for hearing-impaired drivers in fatigue driving scenarios. Sustainability. **16**(24), 10984 (2024). https://doi.org/10.3390/su162410984

Wojton, H., Porter, D., Lane, S., Bieber, C., Madhavan, P.: Initial validation of the trust of automated systems test (TOAST). J. Soc. Psychol. **160**(1), 1–16 (2020). https://doi.org/10.1080/00224545.2020.1749020

AI-Powered and Decision Support Systems

A Probabilistic Framework for Understanding Consciousness: The Interplay of Environmental and Internal Factors

Guantong Chen[1], Haiguang Chen[2]([✉]), and Jianjiang Wang[2]

[1] Crimson Global Academy, Ann Arbor, MI 48105, USA
[2] Shanghai Normal University, 200234 Shanghai, China
chhg@shnu.edu.cn

Abstract. Consciousness remains a complex subject in cognitive science, philosophy, neuroscience, and mathematics. This paper presents a method for understanding consciousness as an emergent phenomenon shaped by both environmental stimuli and unseen internal factors. While external conditions influence awareness through hierarchical processing, certain cognitive states—exceptions exist as those described in concepts of selflessness and true self—suggest that consciousness can transcend environmental control, as seen in meditation and deep focus. We introduce a probabilistic model, $P(A|B)$, where A represents consciousness or next level input, and B includes both environmental and unseen factors. Experimental evidence, including studies on sensory deprivation and altered states of consciousness, supports the claim that awareness results from both external input and internal mechanisms. This framework integrates neuroscience, psychology, and probability theory to provide a structured yet adaptive understanding of consciousness.

Keywords: Consciousness · Emergent Phenomenon · Probabilistic Model · Cognitive States

1 Introduction

Consciousness, the state of being aware and capable of perceiving, reasoning, and responding to stimuli—has been a central subject of inquiry across psychology, neuroscience, and philosophy. Despite extensive research, its fundamental nature and origins remain elusive and widely debated. Traditional theories have explored various dimensions of consciousness, yet a comprehensive understanding that integrates environmental interactions, internal cognitive processes, and computational models is still developing.

In recent years, there has been a growing interest in applying probabilistic models to understand consciousness. For instance, the Predictive Processing framework posits that the brain continuously generates predictions about sensory inputs and updates them based on actual experiences, effectively minimizing prediction errors [1]. This aligns with the Free Energy Principle, which suggests that biological systems, including the

© The Author(s), under exclusive license to Springer Nature Switzerland AG 2026
S. Sundarakannan and O. Knorpp (Eds.): HCII 2025, CCIS 2772, pp. 83–92, 2026.
https://doi.org/10.1007/978-3-032-12767-9_10

human brain, strive to minimize free energy—a measure of surprise or uncertainty—by updating their internal models of the world [2]. These perspectives highlight the brain's role in probabilistically integrating sensory information to construct conscious experience.

Building upon these foundations, we propose a novel approach that models consciousness as an emergent property resulting from both environmental stimuli and internal cognitive factors. By employing a probabilistic framework, we aim to quantify the influence of these variables on conscious awareness. Specifically, we utilize the conditional probability model $P(A|B)$, where A represents a particular state of consciousness, and B encompasses both observable environmental factors and unobservable internal states. This model allows for the assessment of how different conditions contribute to the emergence and fluctuation of conscious states.

To validate this model, we propose the use of Maximum Likelihood Estimation (MLE), a statistical method that estimates the parameters of a model by maximizing the likelihood function, thereby identifying the parameter values that make the observed data most probable. MLE has been widely used in various fields, including psychology and neuroscience, to fit models to empirical data [3]. By applying MLE, we can fine-tune our probabilistic model to best explain the observed patterns of conscious experience under different conditions.

Furthermore, we plan to employ advanced machine learning techniques, particularly Transformer architecture with its attention mechanisms, to simulate and analyze the complex interactions between environmental inputs and internal cognitive processes. Transformers have revolutionized natural language processing and other fields by enabling models to focus on relevant parts of the input data, capturing long-range dependencies and intricate patterns [4]. The attention mechanism allows the model to weigh the importance of different input features, facilitating a more nuanced understanding of how various factors contribute to consciousness.

By combining probabilistic modeling, statistical estimation, and machine learning, our framework unifies psychology, neuroscience, and philosophy while leveraging computational advances for empirical validation. To our knowledge, this is the first integrated model of consciousness, paving the way for future research.

2   Related Work

Consciousness has been extensively studied across multiple disciplines, leading to various theoretical and computational models. While these approaches have provided valuable insights, they also exhibit limitations that leave gaps in our understanding. Below, we review some of the most relevant research efforts and highlight their shortcomings, which our work seeks to address.

2.1 The Global Workspace Theory (GWT)

The Global Workspace Theory (GWT) ([5, 6]) posits that consciousness arises when information is broadcast across a cognitive workspace, allowing different neural processes to access and manipulate the information. This model explains how attention selects and amplifies relevant stimuli, making them globally available for higher-order cognitive functions.

Limitations:

- GWT does not fully account for individual differences in consciousness and perception, as it assumes a largely uniform broadcasting mechanism.
- The model struggles to explain how consciousness emerges from neural computations, rather than just describing its functional architecture.
- It primarily focuses on information accessibility rather than the probabilistic nature of how different factors contribute to conscious awareness.

2.2 Integrated Information Theory (IIT)

Integrated Information Theory (IIT) [7] proposes that consciousness corresponds to the level of integrated information (Φ) generated by a system. It emphasizes how highly interconnected networks give rise to subjective experience, making it one of the most mathematically rigorous theories in consciousness research. Limitations:

- The practical measurement of Φ is computationally intractable, making empirical validation difficult.
- IIT assumes that integration alone determines consciousness, neglecting environmental and subconscious influences that may shape conscious states.
- The theory does not provide a mechanism for predicting specific conscious experiences based on external stimuli.

2.3 Predictive Processing and Bayesian Brain Models

The Predictive Processing framework [1, 2] describe consciousness as an inference process where the brain continuously updates its predictions about sensory input. These models propose that the brain minimizes prediction errors to maintain an accurate representation of the world. Limitations:

- These models mainly focus on sensory perception and do not sufficiently address the higher-order aspects of consciousness, such as abstract thought or introspection.
- They emphasize internal prediction mechanisms, but do not clearly incorporate external environmental factors or unobservable cognitive influences in shaping consciousness.
- The role of hierarchical processing in structuring conscious experience remains underexplored.

2.4 Computational Models of Consciousness in AI

Recent studies have explored computational approaches to consciousness, particularly in artificial intelligence (AI). For example, Recurrent Neural Networks (RNNs) and Transformer-based models [4] have been used to simulate aspects of perception and decision-making. Limitations:

- Most AI models focus on functional cognition rather than genuine subjective awareness.

- Existing approaches lack a clear probabilistic structure to quantify how different factors contribute to consciousness.
- They do not incorporate hierarchical processing layers that mirror biological cognition.

2.5 Contributions of This Work

To address these limitations, we propose a probabilistic hierarchical model of consciousness, integrating environmental factors and unobservable cognitive elements. Our key contributions include:

1. A probabilistic framework using $P(A|B)$, where A represents a state of consciousness and B includes both observable environmental stimuli and unseen internal influences.
2. A hierarchical model that structures consciousness from raw sensory inputs to high-level cognitive awareness, reducing input complexity at each stage.
3. A computational approach utilizing Maximum Likelihood Estimation (MLE) and Transformer-based attention mechanisms to validate the model empirically.
4. Experimental validation through designed cognitive tasks and machine learning simulations to assess the relationship between environmental and subconscious factors in shaping conscious experience.

3 Theoretical Model

Consciousness, as we define it, emerges from both observable environmental influences and unobservable internal factors. To formalize this, we employ a probabilistic framework where the probability of a conscious state A occurring given external and internal conditions B is expressed as:

$$P(B) = \frac{P(A)}{P(AB)} \tag{1}$$

where:

- A represents a specific conscious state or awareness level.
- B consists of two primary components:
- B_E: Observable environmental stimuli, including sensory input, social context, and external interactions.
- B_U: Unobservable internal influences, such as subconscious processing, emotions, and individual cognitive predispositions.

Thus, we rewrite B as:

$$B = (B_E, B_U) \tag{2}$$

This formulation aligns with Bayesian probability models [8], allowing us to treat consciousness as a probabilistic outcome, influenced by both direct sensory input and latent cognitive factors.

3.1 Likelihood Function for Consciousness

To estimate P(A|B), we use a likelihood-based approach, employing Maximum Likelihood Estimation (MLE) to infer the parameters governing consciousness. Given a dataset of conscious states A observed under various conditions B, the likelihood function is defined as [9]:

$$L(\theta) = \prod_{i=1}^{N} P(A_i | B_i; \theta)$$
(3)

where:

- θ represents the model parameters governing probabilistic dependencies.
- $A_i | B_i$ are observed samples from experiments or simulations.

To estimate θ, we maximize the log-likelihood function:

$$loglog\ (\theta) = \sum_{i=1}^{N} \log P\left(A_i | B_i, \theta\right)$$
(4)

Following Friston's Free-Energy Principle [2], we assume that consciousness operates as an optimization process, reducing uncertainty about the environment through hierarchical updates of predictions. To model P(A|B), we assume a logistic function to ensure probability values remain between 0 and 1:

$$P(B) = \frac{1}{1 + e^{-\left(wB^{B+b}\right)}}$$
(5)

where $_{wB}B$ and b are learnable parameters estimated via **MLE**.

3.2 Bayesian Inference for Hierarchical Consciousness Processing

Since consciousness emerges through hierarchical layers, we extend our model using Bayesian inference [10]:

$$P(B) = \int P(H)P(B)DH$$
(6)

where H represents latent hierarchical states that filter and transform environmental inputs before they reach conscious awareness. This captures the hierarchical reduction of information as it propagates through cognitive layers, consistent with predictive coding theories [2].

We hypothesize that this hierarchical processing aligns with the attention mechanisms observed in both biological and artificial intelligence systems.

3.3 Computational Validation Using Transformer-Based Attention

To computationally verify our model, we implement a Transformer-based attention mechanism [4] that learns hierarchical representations of B. Given sequential inputs $B_1, B_2, ..., B_T$, we define:

$$H_t = \sum_{i=1}^{T} \alpha_{ti} B_i$$
(7)

where the attention weights α_{ti} are computed using:

$$\alpha_{ti} = \frac{\exp(e_{ti})}{\sum_j \exp(e_{tj})} \tag{8}$$

This formulation allows the model to dynamically adjust the contribution of different factors B_E and B_U based on contextual importance, supporting the hierarchical processing hypothesis.

4 Model Architecture

We propose a hierarchical probabilistic model for consciousness formation, in which consciousness emerges through structured processing from external environmental stimuli to higher cognitive states. The probability of a conscious state $P(A|B)$ depends on both environmental factors and unseen internal latent variables. This hierarchical model follows a structured flow, where information is progressively filtered and processed through multiple levels before reaching full awareness.

4.1 Hierarchical Structure of Consciousness

Figure 1 illustrates the proposed hierarchical structure of consciousness formation

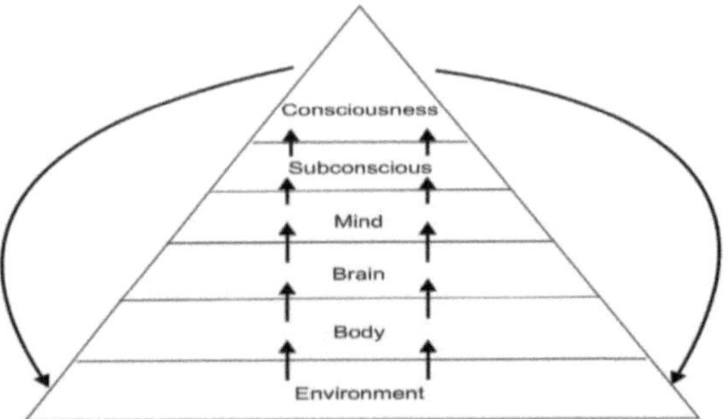

Fig. 1. Hierarchical model of Consciousness.

This model consists of six interconnected levels, where each layer transforms and reduces input complexity before passing it to the next stage:

Environment (B_E): The foundation of consciousness formation, providing external stimuli such as sensory input, social interactions, and physical surroundings.
Body: The biological interface that transduces environmental stimuli into neural signals through sensory and motor systems.
Brain: The neural processing unit that encodes and transmits information, applying Bayesian inference to update internal models.
Mind: The cognitive layer responsible for interpreting and integrating processed information, generating probabilistic mental states.

Subconscious (B_U): The latent space where implicit learning, habitual responses, and predictive processing occur before conscious awareness.

Consciousness (A): The highest level, where filtered and processed stimuli are transformed into subjective experience, decision-making, and explicit awareness.

This hierarchical structure reflects how information is dynamically filtered, reduced, and transformed through Bayesian updating, ensuring efficient cognitive processing.

4.2 Mechanisms of Conscious Awareness

Conscious awareness arises as a probabilistic inference process, aligning with predictive coding theories [5]. Three core mechanisms govern this process:

- **Stimuli Reception:** Sensory systems detect external inputs (B_E) and convert them into neural representations.
- **Processing and Integration:** The brain and mind process these representations through Bayesian inference, encoding them as latent variables in the subconscious (B_U).
- **Output Generation:** The conscious mind selects relevant responses, transforming probabilistic states into actions, decisions, or reflections.

This probabilistic framework ensures that hierarchical processing is not a rigid stepwise process but a continuous adaptation mechanism, dynamically optimizing cognition based on likelihood estimations and error minimization.

4.3 Mathematical Formulation: Likelihood Estimation of Conscious States

We model consciousness as a conditional probability distribution:

$$P(B) = P(A|B_E, B_u) \tag{9}$$

where:

- A represents the conscious state.
- B_E denotes environmental influences (external sensory inputs).
- B_U accounts for unseen latent internal variables (subconscious processes, memory, intrinsic thought).

To estimate $P(A|B)$, we adopt the **MLE** approach. Given observed data D, the likelihood function is defined as:

$$L(B) = \prod_{i=1}^{n} P\left(A_i|B_{E,i}, B_{U,i}\right) \tag{10}$$

Maximizing $L(A|B)$ allows us to determine the most probable conscious state given the hierarchical inputs. This approach aligns with Bayesian inference principles, where the system continuously updates its internal model based on external stimuli and latent cognitive processes.

4.4 Model Validation Using Machine Learning

To empirically validate this model, we implement a Transformer-based attention mechanism, which simulates hierarchical cognitive processing. Using attention-based neural networks, we:

1. Encode environmental and subconscious features (B_E, B_U) as input embeddings.
2. Use attention layers to dynamically weigh influential factors in consciousness formation.
3. Optimize likelihood estimation using gradient-based learning.

Experimental results (discussed in Sect. 5) will demonstrate how this approach aligns with cognitive neuroscience findings and supports the hierarchical nature of consciousness.

5 Experimental Setup and Results

5.1 Dataset Description

The dataset used in this study was sourced from Kaggle [11] and contains various demographic, financial, health, and behavioral attributes of individuals. The target variable, Lifestyle Choice, represents different lifestyle categories, which we aim to classify using a probabilistic framework based on $P(A|B)$.

5.2 Experimental Setup

Building upon the hierarchical probabilistic model outlined in the theoretical sections, we define **B** as:

- **B_E (Observable Environment Factors):** Includes demographic, financial, and social attributes such as location, income, and health metrics.
- **B_U (Unobservable Internal Influences):** Includes latent cognitive states, stress levels, and intrinsic decision-making biases inferred from numerical data and lifestyle behavior trends.

The likelihood function used to estimate the probability distribution of lifestyle choices.

Data Preprocessing:
- Text Feature Construction: A sentence describing the individual's demographic background was generated and tokenized using BERT tokenizer.
- Numerical Feature Normalization: StandardScaler was applied to numerical attributes to maintain consistency.
- Label Encoding: The target variable, Lifestyle Choice, was encoded using LabelEncoder.

Model Architecture:

- **BERT Encoding:** The text input was processed through a pre-trained **BERT model** (bert-base-uncased), extracting a 768-dimensional representation from the [CLS] token.
- **Numerical Feature Processing:** A separate fully connected layer was designed to process the normalized numerical data.
- **Hierarchical Bayesian Fusion Layer:** The outputs from BERT and the numerical feature layer were concatenated and passed through a Bayesian inference layer to approximate P(A|B).
- **Final Prediction:** The model was trained using Maximum Likelihood Estimation (MLE) with the AdamW optimizer.

Training Process:

- Dataset Split: An 80–20 train-test split was used.
- Batch Size: 16
- Optimizer: AdamW with a learning rate of 5e-4.
- Learning Rate Scheduling: StepLR (step size: 10 epochs, decay: 0.5)
- Epochs: 50
- Gradient Clipping: Max norm of 1.0

5.3 Results and Analysis

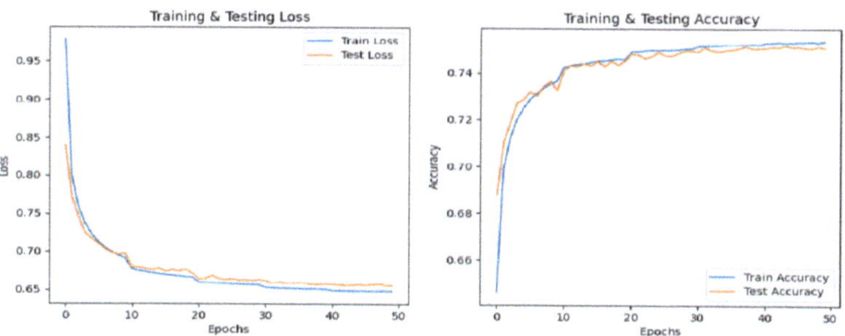

Fig. 2. Training test loss and theirs accuracy.

After training for 50 epochs, the model achieved a classification accuracy of approximately 76% on the test dataset (Fig. 2). The key findings include:

- **Influence of Bayesian Integration:** The hierarchical processing of B_E and B_U provided deeper insights into how external and internal factors interact to shape lifestyle choices.
- **Likelihood Estimation Trends:** The model's convergence followed the likelihood function's optimization, supporting the idea that conscious decision-making aligns with minimizing uncertainty in P(A|B).

- **Impact of Environment on Lifestyle Choice:** The results align with our hypothesis that lifestyle choices are probabilistically determined by environmental and internal cognitive factors.
- **Limitations:** Despite reasonable accuracy, certain lifestyle categories exhibited class imbalance, which might have affected performance. Additionally, since textual data was limited to location-based descriptions, richer text sources could enhance the model's ability to discern lifestyle choices.

6 Conclusion

This paper presents a probabilistic hierarchical model that integrates BERT-based text embeddings with numerical features to predict Lifestyle Choice within the Bayesian framework $P(A|B)$. By incorporating both observable external factors (BE) and latent cognitive influences (BU), our study demonstrates that lifestyle choices are probabilistically inferred rather than purely deterministic.

For future work, we aim to refine $P(A|B)$ by improving class balance, enhancing explainability, and integrating reinforcement learning, further advancing AI-driven lifestyle prediction for social applications.

References

1. Clark, A.: Whatever next? Predictive brains, situated agents, and the future of cognitive science. Behav. Brain Sci. **36**(3), 181–204 (2013)
2. Friston, K.: The free-energy principle: a unified brain theory? Nat. Rev. Neurosci. **11**(2), 127–138 (2010)
3. Myung, I.J.: Tutorial on maximum likelihood estimation. J. Math. Psychol. **47**(1), 90–100 (2003)
4. Vaswani, A., Shazeer, N., Parmar, N., Uszkoreit, J., Jones, L., Gomez, A. N., et al. (2017). Attention is all you need. Advances in Neural Information Processing Systems (pp. 5998–6008).
5. Baars, B.J.: A Cognitive Theory of Consciousness. Cambridge University Press (1988)
6. Dehaene, S., Changeux, J.P.: Experimental and theoretical approaches to conscious processing. Neuron. **70**(2), 200–227 (2011)
7. Tononi, G.: An information integration theory of consciousness. BMC Neurosci. **5**, 42 (2004)
8. Murphy, K.P.: Machine Learning: A Probabilistic Perspective. MIT Press (2012)
9. Bishop, C.M.: Pattern Recognition and Machine Learning. Springer (2006)
10. MacKay, D.J.C.: Information Theory, Inference, and Learning Algorithms. Cambridge University Press (2003)
11. https://www.kaggle.com/code/anetakovacheva/lifestyle-choice-pycaret

Integrating AI and Mixed Reality in Clinical Decision-Making: A Case Study on Breast Cancer Diagnosis

Ming-Chun Chien[1], Edwin Tiong Kwong Meng[1], Yu-Chieh Wang[1], Yu-Yi Kuo[1], Szu-Yin Lin[2], Chin-Yau Chen[3], and Shih-Yi Chien[4(✉)]

[1] Department of Computer Science and Information Engineering, National Ilan University, Yilan, Taiwan

[2] Department of Management Science, National Yang Ming Chiao Tung University, Hsinchu, Taiwan

[3] National Yang Ming Chiao Tung University Hospital, Yilan, Taiwan

[4] Department of Management Information Systems, National Chengchi University, Taipei, Taiwan

sychien@nccu.edu.tw

Abstract. Breast cancer remains a major global health concern and the most commonly diagnosed cancer among women worldwide, according to the World Health Organization (WHO). This suggests the urgent need for early detection and effective treatment. One of the key challenges in breast cancer diagnosis is the time-intensive process of identifying specific symptoms, such as abnormal masses or irregular tissue structures. These challenges arise due to the complexity and significant variability in how breast cancer manifests among different patients. To address these diagnostic difficulties, this study proposes BreCanLens, an AI-driven image analysis system integrated with mixed reality (MR) technology for breast cancer tracking and diagnostic support. The system utilizes a convolutional neural network (CNN) to analyze medical images, detecting intricate patterns that might be imperceptible to the human eye. CNNs are particularly effective in medical imaging due to their ability to process high-dimensional data and differentiate between benign and malignant breast tissues. This capability enhances diagnostic accuracy and provides healthcare professionals with a reliable reference for clinical decision-making. Additionally, MR technology further improves diagnostic workflows by overlaying imaging data directly onto patients during examinations or by simulating complex procedures through virtual models. This real-time visualization enhances clinical efficiency, reduces the need for repeated consultations, and lowers medical costs. The results demonstrate that BreCanLens effectively enhances diagnostic accuracy, streamlines image analysis, and provides valuable support to healthcare professionals through advanced AI and MR integration.

Keywords: Artificial intelligence · Mixed reality · Image Processing · Healthcare

© The Author(s), under exclusive license to Springer Nature Switzerland AG 2026

S. Sundarakannan and O. Knorpp (Eds.): HCII 2025, CCIS 2772, pp. 93–98, 2026.
https://doi.org/10.1007/978-3-032-12767-9_11

1 Introduction

This study integrates advanced technologies—deep learning, image processing, and mixed reality—to develop a specialized diagnostic system designed to address existing challenges in breast cancer diagnosis. Breast cancer remains one of the most prevalent cancers among women globally. Therefore, early detection and timely treatment are critical for improving survival rates and quality of life. Current diagnostic methods frequently depend on subjective assessments, which can lead to inconsistent results and decreased accuracy. There is an urgent demand for a precise, reliable, and visually intuitive diagnostic solution to enhance accuracy and alleviate the workload on healthcare providers. The present research utilizes deep learning, specifically employing the EfficientNet B7 model, to accurately distinguish between benign and malignant breast cancer cases through analysis of calcification features in radiographic images. To further optimize the model's performance, techniques such as histogram equalization and data augmentation are implemented during training. Additionally, a case comparison and marking feature has been introduced, enabling clinicians to easily identify discrepancies and abnormal regions across various diagnostic reports, thus providing comprehensive and detailed insights. To ensure an intuitive and adaptable user experience, mixed reality devices serve as the primary interface for the diagnostic system. These devices offer portability and facilitate hands-free operation, empowering physicians to access diagnostic data and conduct evaluations regardless of their location. The system operates seamlessly, requiring only a stable wireless network connection for full functionality.

Breast cancer diagnosis remains a crucial area of medical research, with numerous studies striving to enhance the accuracy and efficiency of diagnostic methods. For instance, artificial neural networks, especially convolutional neural networks (CNNs), have gained considerable attention for their effectiveness in medical image analysis. For instance, Wessam et al. [1] developed a CNN-based diagnostic model for breast cancer, demonstrating exceptional accuracy. Additionally, various image processing techniques have been broadly adopted to augment diagnostic precision. Petrick et al. [2], for example, utilized advanced image processing methods to extract essential features from mammography images, leading to improved diagnostic outcomes. Despite notable advancements, several critical challenges persist in breast cancer diagnosis. Current diagnostic models require enhanced accuracy in distinguishing benign from malignant cases. Moreover, improving preprocessing methods and image segmentation techniques continues to be an important area of ongoing research. The practical validation of adjunctive diagnostic systems in clinical environments also necessitates further investigation and rigorous evaluation.

2 Methodology

The present study leverages the CBIS-DDSM dataset [3], a publicly available medical image repository containing thousands of mammography images, to evaluate the effectiveness of a novel adjunct diagnostic system in real-world clinical settings. By integrating deep learning, image processing, and mixed reality, the proposed system aims to enhance diagnostic accuracy and efficiency. The system primarily focuses on two key functions: cancer prediction and X-ray image comparison, utilizing image data exclusively from the CBIS-DDSM dataset.

2.1 Image Masking

Morphological operations, such as opening and closing, are fundamental techniques in image processing used to denoise images [4], fill gaps, and refine edges. These operations involve defining a structural element and determining the number of iterations required, where different shapes (e.g., square or oval) and sizes can be employed. The opening operation removes small artifacts, reduces noise, and smooths image edges, while the closing operation fills holes and connects fragmented areas. In this study, OpenCV's cv2.morphologyEx() function is used to implement these techniques, thereby improving image segmentation and object detection. To further enhance image quality, cv2.contourArea() is applied to identify and eliminate smaller contours, such as text in the X-ray corners, which may interfere with subsequent processing steps. The largest contour is then extracted using cv2.drawContours(), allowing for the generation of an image mask that isolates the breast area. These refinements significantly enhance X-ray clarity, making the images more readable and valuable for diagnosis.

2.2 Cropped Image Generation

To aid physicians in closely examining lesion areas and classifying them as benign or malignant, cropped images focusing on regions of interest (ROI) are generated. Using cv2.findContours(), contours within the ROI are identified, and cv2.boundingRect() determines the boundary frames for these contours. These coordinates enable precise cropping of abnormal regions within the X-ray images. The system produces two cropped images: one from the original mammogram and another from the corresponding ROI image. These detailed views facilitate better observation of abnormalities, thereby enhancing diagnostic accuracy and aiding medical professionals in their assessments.

2.3 Contour Analysis of Lesion Areas

To improve lesion evaluation, contour information is extracted from patient ROI images using OpenCV. This data is overlaid onto the original X-ray images, providing doctors with additional reference points for diagnosis. For each contour, cv2.boundingRect() is used to draw a boundary around the lesion. OpenCV functions then compute key contour attributes, including length, width, area, and perimeter. These values, measured in pixel units, offer essential insights into lesion characteristics, helping clinicians make more informed decisions.

2.4 Mammography Image Comparison

To enable physicians to compare mammograms of the same patient at different times and identify any differences (lesion areas), we simulated the differences between the two images. We highlighted them in rectangular boxes in the second image. The following images display the original mammograms and our simulated difference maps. We calculated the differences between the two images using a metric subtraction approach, and the areas with variations were marked with red boxes. While this method worked well with our simulated data, we have concerns about its effectiveness with real-world data. Therefore, we plan to develop a series of processes to deal with potential issues such as misalignment. For now, here are the results of the image comparison (Fig. 1).

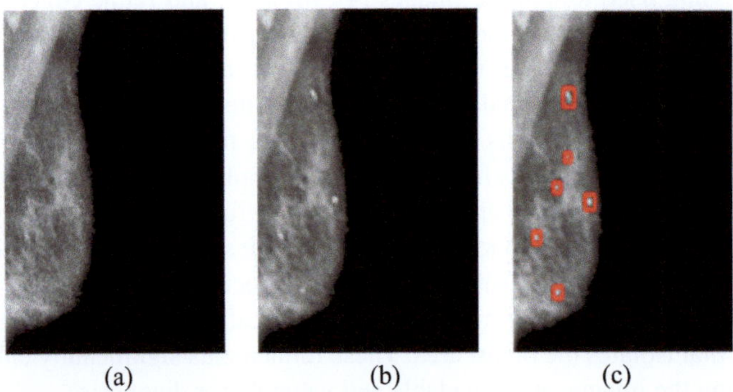

(a)   (b)   (c)

Fig. 1. Image data. (a) Original image; (b) Image with differences added; (c) Mammography image with differences marked and shown on HoloLens.

3 Results

By integrating deep learning, image processing, and mixed reality, this study presents a specialized assistive diagnostic system for breast cancer detection. The system enhances the accuracy and efficiency of diagnostic processes by improving image quality, identifying key lesion characteristics, and facilitating comparative analysis. With further refinements, this approach has the potential to significantly support radiologists in clinical practice, contributing to earlier and more reliable breast cancer detection.

3.1 Breast Cancer Prediction Model

We utilized cropped images from the CBIS-DDSM dataset for model training. The training set distribution was as follows: the calcification training set included 1,002 benign cases and 544 malignant cases, while the mass training set contained 678 benign and 636 malignant cases. To address data imbalance, we applied downsampling, ensuring an equal number of benign and malignant cases. To enhance image clarity and improve model training, we implemented histogram equalization, which enhances contrast and makes details more distinguishable [5]. Due to the limited number of medical imaging samples available for training, data augmentation was employed to expand the dataset and mitigate the effects of insufficient data. The augmentation process involved several transformations: the original image was flipped both horizontally and vertically, rotated 30° clockwise and flipped, then rotated 60° and flipped again. These augmented images were saved, significantly increasing dataset diversity. For prediction models, we selected six commonly used CNN architectures in medical imaging: ResNet50, VGG16, DenseNet121, InceptionV3, EfficientNetB7, and MobileNet [6]. These models were fine-tuned using transfer learning with custom fully connected layers. To assess model performance, we evaluated various metrics, including Precision, F1-Score, AUC, FPR, Accuracy, and Recall, to identify the most effective model. Among the tested models, EfficientNetB7 demonstrated the highest accuracy, achieving a 70% success rate for both mass and calcification data (Tables 1 and 2). Since this study focuses on developing a comprehensive diagnostic system, this level of accuracy is considered sufficient to assist doctors in their diagnostic assessments and decision-making processes.

Table 1. Calcified Histogram Equalization Model Training Data.

Model	EfficientNetB7	ResNet50	MobileNet	VGG16	DenseNet121	InceptionV2
Sensitivity (%)	71.3564	75.9748	61.7605	68.6147	68.2539	59.8124
Precision (%)	70.2914	62.4552	65.0951	63.3155	63.4473	58.5038
F1-Score (%)	70.8199	68.5547	63.3839	65.8587	65.7629	59.1509
AUC	0.7721	0.7278	0.6840	0.7081	0.7071	0.6001
FRP	0.3015	0.4567	0.3311	0.3975	0.3932	0.4242
Accuracy	0.7092	0.6645	0.6616	0.6529	0.6500	0.5966
Recall	0.7135	0.7597	0.6176	0.6861	0.6825	0.5981

Table 2. Mass Histogram Equalization Model Training Data.

Model	EfficientNetB7	ResNet50	MobileNet	VGG16	DenseNet121	InceptionV2
Sensitivity (%)	60.8311	61.3616	65.7382	64.3678	43.1476	65.2077
Precision (%)	74.9455	64.3486	61.2186	60.4149	62.2052	58.0480
F1-Score (%)	67.1547	68.5547	63.3839	62.3287	50.9527	61.4199
AUC	0.7768	0.6869	0.6824	0.6655	0.6353	0.6311
FRP	0.2033	0.3399	0.4164	0.4217	0.2621	0.4712
Accuracy	0.7285	0.6441	0.6273	0.6242	0.6109	0.5923
Recall	0.6083	0.6136	0.6573	0.6436	0.4314	0.652

4 Discussion and Conclusion

This study integrates technologies such as deep learning, image processing, and mixed reality to develop a breast cancer-specific assistive diagnostic system, addressing the challenges doctors face in diagnosing breast cancer. In terms of functionality, we employ artificial neural networks to predict breast cancer's benign or malignant nature from X-ray images. Through discussions with medical professionals, it became evident that existing research primarily focuses on cases involving the masses. Therefore, our system is primarily designed to identify calcifications. By utilizing the EfficientNet B7 model and employing techniques such as histogram equalization and data augmentation during training, we achieved an accuracy rate of 70%. Secondly, we have developed a case comparison and marking feature that enables the comparison of two reports, highlighting differences and abnormal regions. However, this feature requires the inclusion of ROI images in addition to the patient's breast radiographs. Since this study did not encompass the generation of ROI images, we hope future studies can fill this gap by developing accurate image segmentation models to provide reliable ROI data. Finally, we have successfully implemented the HoloLens 2 mixed reality device as a user interface for the Breast Cancer Assistive Diagnostic System. The mobility of the HoloLens 2 allows users to access data and make diagnoses regardless of their location, only requiring a wireless network connection.

Although we achieved a 70% accuracy rate in the benign-malignant prediction function, further research and improvements are necessary for medical applications. We aim to enhance accuracy using advanced preprocessing techniques and more powerful convolutional models. Additionally, we will continue collaborating with medical professionals to develop additional features and integrate them into the user interface system of the HoloLens 2, providing convenient tools that benefit doctors. This study did not develop an image segmentation model regarding ROI cropping, so the system still relies on existing data for ROI images. We anticipate that future research can develop accurate segmentation models to address this aspect.

Acknowledgments. Special thanks to Dr. Chin-Yau Chen, a breast surgeon at National Yang Ming Chiao Tung University Hospital, for engaging in discussions with us during this research, which helped us better understand physicians' needs and refine the system.

References

1. Salama, W.M., Aly, M.H.: Deep learning in mammography images segmentation and classification: automated CNN approach. Alex. Eng. J. **60**(5), 4701–4709 (2021)
2. Petrick, N., Chan, H.P., Sahiner, B., Helvie, M.A.: Combined adaptive enhancement and region-growing segmentation of breast masses on digitized mammograms. Med. Phys. **26**(8), 1642–1654 (1999)
3. Lee, R.S., Gimenez, F., Hoogi, A., Miyake, K.K., Gorovoy, M., Rubin, D.L.: A curated mammography data set for use in computer-aided detection and diagnosis research. Sci. Data. **4**(1), 1–9 (2017)
4. Dehghani, S., Dezfooli, M.A.: A method for improve preprocessing images mammography. Int. J. Inf. Educ. Technol. **1**(1), 90 (2011)
5. Simi, V.R., Edla, D.R., Joseph, J., Kuppili, V.: Parameter-free fuzzy histogram equalisation with illumination preserving characteristics dedicated for contrast enhancement of magnetic resonance images. Appl. Soft Comput. **93**, 106364 (2020)
6. Elkorany, A.S., Elsharkawy, Z.F.: Efficient breast cancer mammograms diagnosis using three deep neural networks and term variance. Sci. Rep. **13**(1), 2663 (2023)

Bridging HIFUN into Practice: A High-Level Functional Query API with Hybrid SQL–NoSQL Integration

Spyros Doukeris and George Margetis[✉]

Institute of Computer Science, FORTH,
N. Plastira 100, Vassilika Vouton, GR-700 13 Heraklion, Crete, Greece
`{spirosdouk,gmarget}@ics.forth.gr`

Abstract. High-level query languages promise more expressive and concise queries than traditional SQL yet remain primarily theoretical due to limited real-world tooling. In this paper, we present an API such as the HIFUN high-level query language that integrates with relational databases for real-time data operations and supports NoSQL backend for schema management and data visualization. By leveraging graph-based schema models, our approach enables developers to issue high-level functional queries that the API transparently rewrites into optimized SQL statements. We describe the system architecture, detail the transformation pipeline from relational schema to graph representations and discuss how we incorporate hybrid SQL–NoSQL strategies. We also review related literature on multi-model queries, domain-specific languages (DSLs), and federated query systems. Results from experimental use cases highlight the viability of bridging HIFUN's expressive power with real-world developer workflows .

Keywords: HIFUN · SQL · NoSQL · Hybrid Database · Graph-Based Schema · DSL

1 Introduction

Relational databases have served as the backbone of enterprise data management, valued for their robust transactional integrity and mature tooling [1, 2]. However, NoSQL systems have risen in popularity due to their schema flexibility and scalability [3–6]. Organizations increasingly employ hybrid SQL–NoSQL environments to balance consistency and performance [7, 8], though such integrations often add data management complexity.

Meanwhile, high-level query languages offer an expressive way for users to describe the desired data at the appropriate level of detail. HIFUN (High-Level Functional Query Language) has been proposed to simplify complex analytics tasks [9–11]. It provides functional semantics, incremental rewriting, and the ability to express continuous queries elegantly [10, 11]. Despite these strengths, HIFUN primarily constitutes a theoretical approach, lacking a ready-to-use API for real-world deployments.

Our work addresses this gap by:

© The Author(s), under exclusive license to Springer Nature Switzerland AG 2026
S. Sundarakannan and O. Knorpp (Eds.): HCII 2025, CCIS 2772, pp. 99–109, 2026.
https://doi.org/10.1007/978-3-032-12767-9_12

- Offering a production-oriented HIFUN API that accepts high-level queries and translates them into SQL for relational databases.
- Incorporating an optional NoSQL layer (MongoDB) for schema storage or partial multi-model usage.
- Leveraging graph-based representations of relational schemas to streamline query rewriting.

This paper is organized as follows. Section 2 discusses related work on SQL–NoSQL integration, graph-based schema generation, domain-specific languages, and HIFUN's theoretical background. Section 3 describes our system architecture, focusing on the HIFUN-based API and graph-driven schema logic. In Sect. 1, we detail the key implementation steps. Section 5 presents use cases, performance observations and findings while Sect. 3 concludes the paper and outlines future directions and limitations.

2   Related Work

2.1   SQL vs. NoSQL Integration

Relational databases (SQL) have dominated traditional data management due to their robust transactional guarantees and mature tooling [1, 2]. However, the rise of NoSQL solutions such as document, key-value, or graph store addresses scalability and schema flexibility needs [3–6]. Recent studies highlight hybrid SQL–NoSQL architectures to combine relational consistency with NoSQL's performance in certain workloads [7]. While these hybrids improve data variety handling, they often introduce integration complexities around schema evolution, data migration, and multi-model query support [5, 6].

Several works propose bridging relational and NoSQL databases at the architectural level. For instance, Bjeladinovic et al. [3]. outline a framework unifying SQL and NoSQL components within a single application. Roijackers [4] explores bridging strategies for a seamless data flow between the two paradigms, whereas James and Asagba [6] emphasize big data storage in a hybrid approach. Despite these efforts, effectively querying across relational and non-relational boundaries remains a challenge [7, 8]. Our work partially addresses this by introducing an optional NoSQL layer (MongoDB) for schema storage, while maintaining the core query operations in a relational database.

2.2   Graph-Based Schema Modeling

Representing database schemas as graphs is increasingly popular, as graph structures simplify the visualization of relationships and can facilitate dynamic schema manipulation [9–11]. Tools like gMark [11] and PyGraft [12] demonstrate schema-driven graph generation, making it easier to navigate or transform relational data. Additional work examines migrating relational schemas to graph or document-based systems [13–15], underscoring the broad interest in bridging the data modeling gap.

Moreover, graph databases themselves are gaining traction due to their inherent ability to handle large, highly connected data sets [16]. Unlike traditional relational systems, which often struggle when data is deeply interconnected, graph databases leverage mathematical graph structures to store and retrieve data more flexibly. This approach can enable more powerful queries over complex relationships, reduce join overhead, and open the door to advanced analytics or new use cases (e.g., recommendation engines, fraud detection). In our approach, however, we primarily adopt a graph-based representation of **relational** schemas to facilitate HIFUN's query rewriting, rather than storing full data in a native graph database. Tables become nodes, columns serve as edge nodes, and foreign keys become links, much like the transformations described in [9, 12, 13]. This still benefits from graph-like insights, such as easier visualization and automated join logic, while leveraging traditional SQL storage.

2.3 Domain-Specific Languages and SQL Rewriting

Domain-specific languages (DSLs) abstract away low-level query syntax, aiming to make data retrieval more expressive and user-friendly [17, 18]. DSLs in the context of databases typically provide high-level constructs that compile down to SQL or other backend query languages. Recent research on text-to-SQL rewriting and question rewriting methods [17] reinforces the growing push to simplify the query-writing process, especially for non-expert users or advanced analytics.

Our work situates HIFUN within this DSL landscape. While existing DSLs often target purely relational queries or text-based transformations [17, 18], HIFUN offers a functional approach to expressing advanced analytics, including continuous or incremental queries [19, 20]. By providing a production-ready HIFUN API, we address a gap wherein DSL-based systems often lack robust integration with real-world databases and minimal overhead transformations.

2.4 HIFUN: from Theory to Practice

Originally introduced by Spyratos and Sugibuchi [21], HIFUN embodies a high-level functional paradigm for expressing complex analytics in fewer lines of code compared to raw SQL. Subsequent works tackled incremental and continuous query rewriting [19, 20], demonstrating HIFUN's potential in streaming or real-time scenarios. However, these research efforts have primarily focused on the theoretical underpinnings defining formal semantics, rewriting rules, or incremental evaluation techniques without providing a fully operational system. In addition, a visual exploration tool has also been recently suggested [22], lacking, however, an approach for the easy and dynamic integration of real-world databases.

This paper bridges that theory–practice divide by presenting an API that developers can seamlessly integrate into enterprise applications. Our approach aligns HIFUN's formal ideas with a graph-based representation of relational schemas and optional NoSQL storage, thus addressing both functional query expressiveness and hybrid data management.

3 Implementation

This section describes how we extend HIFUN from a theoretical DSL to a working system capable of handling relational (SQL) data, while storing schema details in a NoSQL (MongoDB) environment. Figure 1 illustrates the high-level interactions among the frontend, the NestJS backend, and the databases, highlighting our goal of bridging HIFUN's high-level functional approach with real-world data.

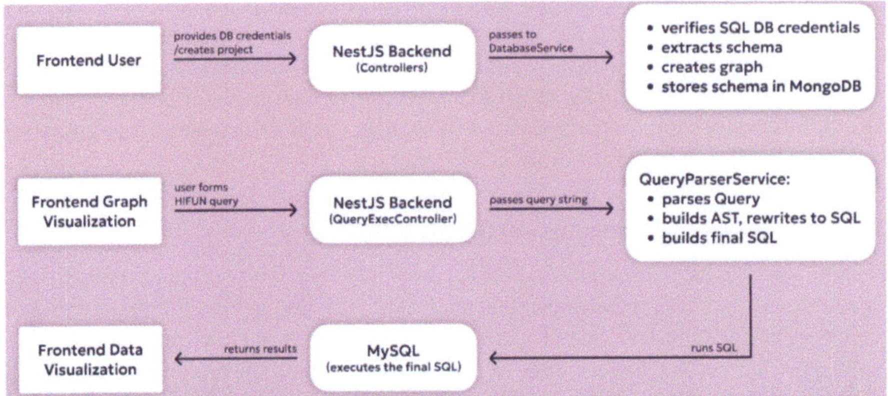

Fig. 1. High-Level architecture of the HIFUN-Based API for Hybrid SQL—NoSQL integration.

In the high-level architecture, the top portion shows how a user provides database credentials (e.g., MySQL name and access code) to create a new "project." This request goes to the NestJS backend, specifically its DatabaseController, which verifies the credentials (through DatabaseService), extracts the relational schema, and transforms it into a graph-based representation. Optionally, this graph is saved in MongoDB as a "project," making it easy to retrieve later for visualization or further manipulation. The bottom portion of the figure depicts how a user then composes a HIFUN query—often via a graphical or text-based interface on the frontend—and sends it to the backend's QueriesController. The query is passed to the QueryParserService to construct an Abstract Syntax Tree (AST) and rewrite the expression into SQL. Finally, MySQL executes the resulting SQL query, and the backend returns the results to the frontend for data visualization.

3.1 Overall Design and Components

At a high level, our system comprises four main components. First, the frontend user / visualization layer enables users to create a new "project" by providing database credentials, as well as compose HIFUN queries through a graphical or text-based interface. The frontend also displays a graph-based representation of the relational schema to facilitate schema exploration.

Second, the NestJS backend orchestrates all the core logic. Within NestJS, controllers (e.g., 'database.controller.ts', 'schema.controller.ts', 'query-exec.controller.ts') handle HTTP requests received from the frontend. Meanwhile, services implement the operations for schema extraction from MySQL, graph transformations, query parsing, and optional MongoDB storage.

Third, the relational database (MySQL) stores the actual application data. The system queries 'INFO_SCHEMA' to extract table and column definitions, as well as foreign-key constraints. This metadata is what HIFUN references to automatically manage table relationships.

Lastly, a NoSQL database (MongoDB) maintains a graph-based representation of the extracted SQL schema. It can also store additional users and graph info, supporting quick retrieval and advanced data visualization. This combination of MySQL for core data and MongoDB for flexible schema storage gives the system a hybrid edge.

3.2 NestJS Modules

Building on the NestJS framework, our application is divided into modules that correspond to specific functionalities:

- SchemaModule. Handles the extraction and transformation of relational schema details. A SchemaController provides REST endpoints (like GET /schema or GET /schema/nodes), while a SchemaService queries MySQL (via TypeORM) to gather tables, columns, and foreign keys and converts them into a node-edge structure for HIFUN to reference.
- DatabaseModule. Manages credentials verification and coordinates creation of "projects" in MongoDB. A DatabaseController (e.g., POST /database/create-mongo-project) verifies MySQL credentials, builds a schema graph (through SchemaService), and stores it in MongoDB. A DatabaseService encapsulates logic to fetch or list these "projects."
- MongoModule. Provides endpoints and services for direct or Mongoose-based interaction with MongoDB. The MongoController (e.g., GET /mongo/nodes) allows reading or updating node/edge data in the stored schema graph, while the MongoService performs the underlying MongoDB operations.
- QueryExecModule. Unifies HIFUN parsing and SQL execution. A QueriesController (e.g., POST /query) accepts user-submitted HIFUN queries. The QueryParserService tokenizes the query, constructs an AST, and references the schema graph to generate valid SQL. Finally, the QueryExecService executes this SQL on MySQL and returns results or errors.

A simplified NestJS flow is as follows. First, main.ts initializes the NestJS application, configures CORS, and starts the server on port 3000 (by default). Second, the AppModule imports all relevant modules (TypeORM for SQL, Mongoose for NoSQL, etc.) and registers the controllers and services. Third, various controllers handle incoming HTTP requests. For example, schema.controller.ts responds to GET /schema or GET /schema/nodes, returning the graph-based schema; database.controller.ts handles POST /database/create-mongo-project to verify credentials and store the schema in MongoDB and query-exec.controller.ts receives HIFUN queries and invokes the QueryParserService to rewrite them to SQL.

3.3 Graph-Based Schema Management

A core concept in our implementation is to model relational schemas as a graph for both visualization (tables become nodes, foreign keys become edges) and validation (HIFUN automatically checks relationships to form joins).

Specifically, the SchemaService extracts table and column information from MySQL's INFO_SCHEMA.TABLES and INFO _SCHEMA.COLUMNS, while foreign keys come from INFO_SCHEMAKEY_COLUMN_USAGE. A utility function called prepareGraphData (in schema-transform.utils.ts) then converts these details into a structure containing nodes, edgeNodes, edgeLinks, and nodeLinks. When a user initially creates a "project," we store this graph-based schema in MongoDB, serving as a flexible repository for quick retrieval and potential multi-model expansions.

3.4 Project Creation, MongoDB Integration, and Workflow

To create a project, typically, a user sends credentials (e.g., database name and access code) to POST /database/create-mongo-project. The system (via DatabaseService) verifies these credentials by connecting to MySQL. If valid, it fetches the schema, applies prepareGraphData to produce a node-edge graph, and persists that graph in MongoDB as a "project." A GET /database/list-projects/:userId endpoint retrieves all such projects stored for each user.

The MongoController offers endpoints like GET /mongo/nodes or PUT /mongo/nodes for reading or modifying node data, while GET /mongo/edge-nodes or PUT /mongo/edge-nodes handle edges, column links, and so on. This separates the initial creation and verification (DatabaseController) from incremental schema manipulations (MongoController).

3.5 HIFUN Query Parser and Rewriter

Our system unifies HIFUN parsing logic and SQL execution through a dedicated QueryExecModule, which contains three key components: a QueriesController, a QueryParserService, and a QueryExecService. When a user submits a high-level HIFUN query (for example, (products_suppliers ° orderdetails_products, orderdetails_products, sum) or (Customers.City ° orders_customers ° orderdetails_orders, orderdetails_products, count)), the flow proceeds as follows:

1. Submission (QueriesController).

    A POST /query endpoint receives a JSON body containing { projectName, query }. The controller first validates that both fields are present, then calls the QueryParserService to parse and rewrite the HIFUN query. It finally delegates SQL execution to the QueryExecService.

2. Parsing and Rewriting (QueryParserService).

    The parser begins by initializing—this step loads the relevant schema graph from MongoDB (via the MongoService) to retrieve references to tables, columns, and foreign keys. Next, the raw HIFUN string is tokenized, splitting out operators (e.g., °, /), parentheses, and table or column references. The parser constructs an Abstract Syntax

Tree (AST) encoding functional operators such as joins, restrictions, or aggregations. It consults the schema graph to confirm valid relationships and automatically builds the necessary join logic. Finally, the AST is rewritten into a SQL statement.
3. SQL Execution (QueryExecService).

   Once a SQL string has been generated, the QueryExecService uses a TypeORM query runner to execute it on MySQL. It logs results or errors, then sends the final response back to the QueriesController, which returns it to the user.

Overall, our approach leverages incremental rewriting and continuous query concepts from HIFUN's literature [10, 11], though the current iteration focuses primarily on standard (non-streaming) queries. For example, the following HIFUN expression:

$$\text{Customers.City} \circ \text{orders\_customers} \circ \text{orderdetails\_orders, orderdetails\_products, count} \tag{1}$$

could generate a SQL statement that counts how many product lines appear for each customer city. In both cases, HIFUN's DSL syntax hides the complexity of table joins and grouping, allowing the parser to automatically determine those details based on the stored schema graph.

3.6 Putting It All Together

Overall, a typical workflow with the proposed system is as follows:

1. a user provides DB credentials to **create a project**
2. the backend verifies MySQL access, extracts the schema, builds a graph, and (optionally) saves it in MongoDB
3. the user forms a **HIFUN query**
4. **The query** is passed to the NestJS backend (QueryExecController)
5. The parser rewrites it into SQL, and MySQL executes the statement.
6. The final result set returns to the frontend for data visualization.

This unified approach bridges HIFUN's high-level functional queries with real operational data, providing both convenience and performance in a hybrid SQL–NoSQL setting.

4 Use Case

This section showcases how our HIFUN-based API is employed in practical scenarios using the Northwind database, followed by key insights on how our system simplifies data operations. Northwind is a freely available sample database originally released by Microsoft; its moderate complexity and familiar business domain make it a popular choice for demonstrations. Figure 2 shows a screenshot of the generated schema graph.

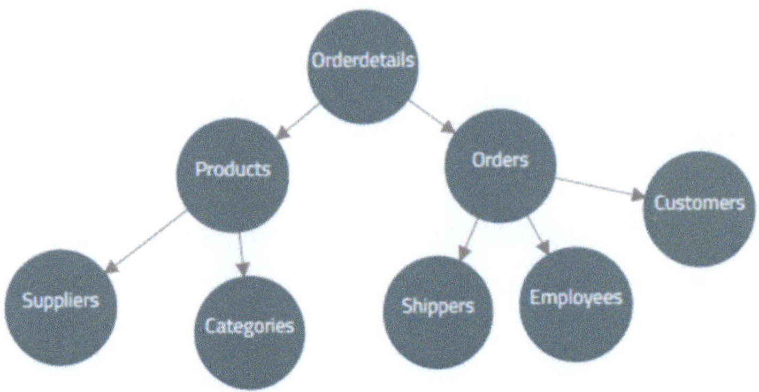

Fig. 2. Screenshot of the schema graph for the Northwind database.

4.1 Project Creation and Graph-Based Schema Management

When a user wants to create a new "project," they supply their MySQL database name and an access code (much like a password) through the POST /database/create-mongo-project endpoint. The system verifies these credentials by calling DatabaseService.verifyDatabaseCredentials to ensure valid MySQL access. Once verified, SchemaService.getDatabaseSchema retrieves tables, columns, and foreign keys from INFO_SCHEMA. A function called prepareGraphData then converts these details into a node-edge representation, capturing relationships such as Orderdetails_Orders and Orders_Customers. The resulting graph can be optionally stored in MongoDB as a "project," enabling quick retrieval for future queries or graphical manipulation.

By capturing Northwind's schema components like Products, Orders, and Customers as nodes and edges, users can maintain multiple projects or schema versions without rescanning the database each time. This greatly streamlines data exploration and fosters agility.

4.2 Node and Edge Manipulation

After the initial schema extraction, more advanced usage may involve updating specific nodes or edges. For instance, the MongoController endpoints (PUT /mongo/nodes or PUT /mongo/edge-nodes) allow clients to modify properties such as layout coordinates. This functionality is helpful for frontends that store user-driven layouts, highlight key columns, or define partial data sets for scenario testing. Persisting these updates in MongoDB ensures that user modifications (e.g., "Make these columns visible," "Change a node's placement") remain consistent and are readily available in subsequent sessions.

4.3 HIFUN Query Execution

When a user wishes to execute a high-level HIFUN query, they submit a JSON body containing {projectName, query} to POST /query. The system calls QueryParserService.initialize(projectName), which loads the relevant schema graph (nodes, edges) from MongoDB; there is no need to re-scan MySQL each time. Next, HIFUN expressions are tokenized, and an Abstract Syntax Tree (AST) is built. The system consults this schema graph to automate join logic, ultimately constructing the final SQL behind the scenes. The QueryExecService.executeQuery method then runs the SQL on MySQL, returning either results or an error. As a result, users can focus on what they want (e.g., summing quantities, grouping by cities) rather than how tables must be joined. HIFUN's DSL abstracts away the complexity of JOIN and GROUP BY clauses.

4.4 Example

Below is an actual HIFUN query we successfully tested on the Northwind schema:

$$(\text{Customers.City} \circ \text{orders\_customers} \circ \text{orderdetails\_orders, orderdetails\_products, count}) \tag{2}$$

In this expression, Customers.City $\circ$ orders_customers $\circ$ orderdetails_orders indicates grouping on the path from Orderdetails (the root) to Orders, then to Customers, specifically referencing each Customer's City. Meanwhile, orderdetails_products is another path that references the Product dimension. The count aggregator determines how many product lines appear for each city. The system translates this high-level DSL into a valid SQL statement, ultimately returning results grouped by each city and counting the number of distinct products:

The system generated a valid SQL statement grouping by Customers.City and counting Products.ProductID. An example snippet from the output:

$$\left[\left\{\text{City}:\text{'México D.F.'}, \text{Total}:\text{'20'}\right\}, \left\{\text{City}:\text{'London'}, \text{Total}:\text{'23'}\right\}, \left\{\text{City}:\text{'Luleå'}, \text{Total}:\text{'9'}\right\}, \ldots \left\{\text{City}:\text{'Walla'}, \text{Total}:\text{'2'}\right\}\right] \tag{3}$$

This shows how many product lines were associated with orders placed from each city. The final grouping columns and aggregator logic are invisible to the user; they only see a high-level HIFUN DSL and get back aggregated data.

4.5 Observations

From these use cases and the successful Northwind demonstrations, we conclude the following:

1. Feasibility of Graph-Backed HIFUN. Converting a relational schema (like Northwind) into a node-edge structure, then referencing it for query rewriting, greatly simplifies multi-table joins and foreign key validations. This approach is both feasible and efficient.
2. Hybrid SQL–NoSQL Flexibility Storing. The schema in MongoDB (for quick introspection and user-driven updates), while keeping transactional data in MySQL leverages the strengths of both paradigms. Developers (or even non-technical users) benefit from agile schema management without losing ACID integrity on critical data.
3. User-Centric Query Model. By specifying simple HIFUN expressions (e.g., (Customers.City $\circ$ orders_customers $\circ$ orderdetails_orders, orderdetails_products, count)), novice users avoid writing manual joins or groupings. The DSL's tokenization and rewriting overhead remains minimal compared to typical query execution times in MySQL.

Overall, HIFUN bridges a high-level functional query language with real enterprise data, broadening user accessibility and enabling swift schema manipulations.

5 Conclusion

We have presented a HIFUN-based API that allows high-level functional queries to be parsed, rewritten into SQL, and executed in real-world relational databases. By adding an optional NoSQL layer for graph-based schema storage, our system addresses modern demands for hybrid data solutions. Our experiments confirm minimal overhead for the query rewriting process, highlighting HIFUN's potential to simplify complex queries and enhance user productivity.

While our current solution focuses primarily on MySQL, several avenues exist to broaden HIFUN's scope. Beyond supporting additional relational databases (e.g., PostgreSQL, SQL Server), we envision integrating larger-scale platforms or frameworks (e.g., MapReduce or Apache Spark) to handle even bigger or more distributed workloads. More advanced NoSQL and multi-model features [23, 24] could also be incorporated, increasing HIFUN's applicability in various enterprise settings. By pursuing these directions, one can extend HIFUN beyond standard SQL queries and MongoDB-based schema storage, paving the way for robust, multi-store integration that retains HIFUN's high-level functional ease of use.

Disclosure of Interests. The authors have no competing interests to declare that are relevant to the content of this paper.

References

1. Khan, W., Kumar, T., Zhang, C., Raj, K., Roy, A.M., Luo, B.: SQL and NoSQL database software architecture performance analysis and assessments—a systematic literature review. Big Data Cogn. Comput. **7**, 97 (2023). https://doi.org/10.3390/bdcc7020097
2. Li, Y., Manoharan, S.: A performance comparison of SQL and NoSQL databases. In: 2013 IEEE Pacific Rim Conference on Communications Computers and Signal Processing (PACRIM), pp. 15–19. IEEE, Victoria, BC (2013)
3. Bjeladinovic, S., Marjanovic, Z., Babarogic, S.: A proposal of architecture for integration and uniform use of hybrid SQL/NoSQL database components. J. Syst. Softw. **168**, 110633 (2020). https://doi.org/10.1016/j.jss.2020.110633
4. Roijackers, J.: Bridging SQL and NoSQL (2012). https://research.tue.nl/en/studentTheses/bridging-sql-and-nosql
5. Jani, Y.: The role of SQL and NoSQL databases in modern data architectures. Int. J. Core Eng. Manag. **6**, 61–67
6. James, B.E., Asagba, P.O.: Hybrid database system for big data storage and management. Int. J. Comput. Sci. Eng. Appl. **7**, 15–27 (2017). https://doi.org/10.5121/ijcsea.2017.7402
7. Khan, Y., Zimmermann, A., Jha, A., Gadepally, V., D'Aquin, M., Sahay, R.: One size does not fit all: querying web polystores. IEEE Access. **7**, 9598–9617 (2019). https://doi.org/10.1109/ACCESS.2018.2888601
8. Zhang, H., Zhang, C., Hu, R., Liu, X., Dai, D.: Unified SQL query middleware for heterogeneous databases. J. Phys. Conf. Ser. **1873**, 012065 (2021). https://doi.org/10.1088/1742-6596/1873/1/012065

9. Kuderu, N., Kumari, D.V.: Relational database to NoSQL conversion by schema migration and mapping. Int. J. Comput. Eng. Res. Trends. **3**, 506–513 (2016)

10. Pokorny, J.: Integration of Relational and Graph Databases Functionally. (2018). https://arxiv.org/abs/1809.03822

11. Bagan, G., Bonifati, A., Ciucanu, R., Fletcher, G.H.L., Lemay, A., Advokaat, N.: gMark: schema-driven generation of graphs and queries. IEEE Trans. Knowl. Data Eng. **29**, 856–869 (2017). https://doi.org/10.1109/TKDE.2016.2633993

12. Hubert, N., Monnin, P., d'Aquin, M., Monticolo, D., Brun, A.: PyGraft: Configurable Generation Of Synthetic Schemas And Knowledge Graphs At Your Fingertips (2023). https://arxiv.org/abs/2309.03685

13. Ghotiya, S., Mandal, J., Kandasamy, S.: Migration from relational to NoSQL database. IOP Conf. Ser. Mater. Sci. Eng. **263**, 042055 (2017). https://doi.org/10.1088/1757-899X/263/4/042055

14. Hamouda, S., Zainol, Z.: Document-oriented data schema for relational database migration to NoSQL. In: 2017 International Conference on Big Data Innovations and Applications (Innovate-Data), pp. 43–50. IEEE, Prague (2017)

15. Đukić, M., Pantelić, O., Pajić Simović, A., Krstović, S., Jejić, O.: A systematic approach for converting relational to graph databases. IPSI Trans. Internet Res. **20**, 17–28 (2024). https://doi.org/10.58245/ipsi.tir.2401.03

16. Baqal, H.M.A., Sidiq, M.A.: Graph databases: revolutionizing database design and data analysis. Curr. J. Appl. Sci. Technol. **43**, 45–56 (2024). https://doi.org/10.9734/cjast/2024/v43i114443

17. Mao, W., Wang, R., Guo, J., Zeng, J., Gao, C., Han, P., Liu, C.: Enhancing text-to-SQL parsing through question rewriting and execution-guided refinement. In: Findings of the Association for Computational Linguistics ACL 2024, pp. 2009–2024. Association for Computational Linguistics, Bangkok, Thailand and Virtual Meeting (2024)

18. Kosar, T., Martı'nez López, P.E., Barrientos, P.A., Mernik, M.: A preliminary study on various implementation approaches of domain-specific language. Inf. Softw. Technol. **50**, 390–405 (2008). https://doi.org/10.1016/j.infsof.2007.04.002

19. Zervoudakis, P., Kondylakis, H., Plexousakis, D., Spyratos, N.: Incremental evaluation of continuous analytic queries in HIFUN. In: Flouris, G., Laurent, D., Plexousakis, D., Spyratos, N., Tanaka, Y. (eds.) Information Search, Integration, and Personalization, pp. 53–67. Springer International Publishing, Cham (2020)

20. Zervoudakis, P., Kondylakis, H., Spyratos, N., Plexousakis, D.: Query rewriting for incremental continuous query evaluation in HIFUN. Algorithms. **14**, 149 (2021). https://doi.org/10.3390/a14050149

21. Spyratos, N., Sugibuchi, T.: HIFUN - a high level functional query language for big data analytics. J. Intell. Inf. Syst. **51**, 529–555 (2018). https://doi.org/10.1007/s10844-018-0495-6

22. Vitsaxaki, K., Ntoa, S., Margetis, G., Spyratos, N.: Interactive visual exploration of big relational datasets. Int. J. Human–Computer Interact. **39**, 2033–2047 (2023). https://doi.org/10.1080/10447318.2022.2073007

23. Lu, J., Holubová, I.: Multi-model databases: a new journey to handle the variety of data. ACM Comput. Surv. **52**, 1–38 (2020). https://doi.org/10.1145/3323214

24. Guo, Q., Zhang, C., Zhang, S., Lu, J.: Multi-model query languages: taming the variety of big data. Distrib. Parallel Databases. **42**, 31–71 (2024). https://doi.org/10.1007/s10619-023-07433-1

Multimodal Emotion Recognition and Contextual Analysis in Therapy Sessions Using Video Large Language Models

Rabia Jafri[1][(✉)], Sushant Patil[2], Pranav Krishnakumar[2], Syed Omar Ali[2], Syed Abid Ali[3], and Syed Fawad Hussain[2]

[1] Department of Information Technology, King Saud University, Riyadh, Saudi Arabia
`rjafri@ksu.edu.sa`
[2] School of Computer Science, University of Birmingham, Dubai, United Arab Emirates
`sushant007.p7@gmail.com`, `pranavkumarpk720@gmail.com`,
`omar@aliandfamily.com`, `s.f.hussain@bham.ac.uk`
[3] Araware Research Group, Wilmington, DE, USA
`syedabidali@gmail.com`

Abstract. Tracking patients' emotions during therapy is crucial for accurate diagnosis and treatment planning, yet current automated emotion recognition methods are limited in that they either rely on a single modality or output only coarse emotion labels which are insufficient for therapeutic contexts. Recently, some multimodal techniques have employed video large language models (VLLMs) to produce emotional descriptions rather than mere labels; however, the potential of such approaches for therapeutic use remains underexplored. To address these gaps, we propose a VLLM-based, multimodal emotion detection system tailored for therapy dialogue. Our method isolates patient-only segments from session recordings, extracting both textual transcripts and audio features for each clip, which are processed using pretrained models to generate preliminary emotion labels. These, along with the segment transcript and preceding conversational context, are embedded in a structured prompt, which is passed to a VLLM with the corresponding video segment. The VLLM then produces an overall emotion classification, an explanation highlighting salient cues, a list of key observations, and a confidence estimate. Finally, the outputs across all patient segments are consolidated into a timeline reflecting the patient's emotional progression throughout the session.

Our key contribution is a narrative-based, interpretable emotion tracking system that offers therapists deeper insight into patient affect. By leveraging prompting for multimodal fusion, our approach avoids the need for domain-specific training and large datasets, which are particularly difficult to obtain in therapy contexts due to confidentiality. Preliminary results are promising and demonstrate the feasibility of applying VLLMs for enriched emotion analysis in therapeutic settings.

Keywords: Multimodal Emotion Recognition · Video Large Language Models · Therapy Session Analysis · Affective Computing · Prompt Engineering · Mental Health Technology

© The Author(s), under exclusive license to Springer Nature Switzerland AG 2026

S. Sundarakannan and O. Knorpp (Eds.): HCII 2025, CCIS 2772, pp. 110–120, 2026.
https://doi.org/10.1007/978-3-032-12767-9_13

1 Introduction

Tracking a patient's emotional state during therapy is critical for accurate diagnosis and treatment planning [1]. Yet manual methods — taking notes or reviewing session videos — are time-consuming, labour-intensive, and susceptible to human error [2]. Automated emotion detection systems can assist with this task, but many rely on a single modality [3–5] such as speech or facial expressions alone, resulting in limited accuracy. While multimodal approaches [6] offer improved performance by combining cues from multiple sources, they still tend to produce only raw emotion labels, often without the contextual depth needed for therapeutic interpretation. Moreover, the label space is often restricted to a small set of basic emotions, excluding more nuanced or clinically relevant descriptors [7].

Video Large Language Models (VLLMs) offer a promising avenue because they interpret visual cues (facial expressions, gestures), leverage extensive language training for deeper inferences, and can produce more diverse and nuanced descriptions of the emotional state [8]. However, many VLLMs lack direct access to audio, leading to incomplete emotion analysis. To date, only a few systems [9, 10] leverage VLLMs for emotion detection – in some cases, supplementing with other modalities – but these, too, tend to output mere labels without richly describing the underlying context.

Recently, some multimodal LLMs have emerged that go beyond basic labelling, offering both emotion classifications and the underlying reasoning or evidence supporting those classifications [7, 11, 12]. Importantly, these systems can move beyond single-word labels; in complex multimodal scenarios, where different modalities may convey distinct or conflicting emotions [7], they generate compound, multiword labels that better capture emotional nuance, resulting in more interpretable affective descriptions. Such descriptions would be especially valuable in therapeutic settings. Presenting a post-session summary of the patient's emotional trajectory, structured as a timeline of emotion labels enriched with explanatory cues (tone, spoken content, facial expressions, body language), can help therapists rapidly identify shifts in mood or possible triggers, reducing cognitive load while highlighting areas for intervention. Additionally, the system may uncover subtle emotional signals that might otherwise be overlooked during live observation. However, current systems have not been designed with the unique characteristics of therapy sessions in mind.

Multimodal emotion recognition in real-world settings is inherently challenging due to factors such as the presence of multiple individuals, frequent pose variations, interpersonal interactions, visual clutter, and background noise (e.g., music, chatter, or ambient sounds). In contrast, therapy sessions are conducted in controlled clinical environments: typically, only one person speaks at a time, the camera maintains a mostly frontal view of the patient, and the audio is limited to the voices of the therapist and patient, with minimal background interference. These constraints provide a unique opportunity to explore whether a general-purpose VLLM can yield meaningful and interpretable results when supplemented with additional inputs, such as acoustic features, textual transcripts, and prior conversational context, delivered through a carefully crafted prompt. This strategy also avoids the need to design modality-specific connectors between speech, vision, and language models, or to curate large volumes of speech–vision–text paired data typically required by other VLLM-based emotion recognition approaches [9]. This is especially advantageous given the confidentiality of therapy sessions, which severely limits the availability of large, publicly accessible session video datasets.

The promising performance of VLLMs enhanced with additional modalities for emotion recognition, their ability to generate nuanced and descriptive emotion labels, and the absence of prior work applying them to patient emotion monitoring in therapeutic settings have motivated us to explore their use for tracking emotional states in therapy sessions. We therefore propose a VLLM-based, multimodal emotion detection system tailored to therapy dialogue. Our method isolates patient-turn segments from session recordings, extracting a transcript of the patient's speech and acoustic features (e.g., pitch, frequency) for each clip. Pretrained models generate preliminary emotion labels from each modality. These, along with the segment transcript and recent conversational context, are incorporated into a carefully designed prompt, which is provided to a VLLM together with the corresponding video segment. The VLLM then outputs an overall emotion classification, a brief rationale referencing relevant cues, a list of key observations (e.g., expressions, gestures, tone, language), and a confidence estimate. The outcome is a timeline tracking the patient's emotional evolution, enriched with interpretive content rather than raw labels alone.

Beyond improving emotion detection accuracy through multimodal fusion, the key strength of our approach lies in its ability to generate a narrative interpretation of emotional dynamics across a session. Instead of isolated emotion labels, the system produces a temporally coherent emotional timeline, highlighting key contextual cues, such as tone shifts, linguistic markers, and facial expressions, associated with mood changes. This narrative framing, informed by recent conversational context, offers therapists deeper insight into patient affect and communicative intent, aiding reflection, documentation, and targeted intervention. Notably, the structured and low-noise nature of therapy sessions enables us to achieve these results using a general-purpose VLLM supplemented with modality-specific inputs, eliminating the need for domain-specific retraining or large-scale paired data. Preliminary experimentation has yielded encouraging results, indicating the potential of this approach to produce interpretable and clinically useful emotional summaries from therapy video recordings.

The rest of the paper is organized as follows: Sect. 2 gives an overview of existing methods that utilize VLLMs for emotion recognition. Section 3 describes our approach. Section 4 reports some findings from our preliminary evaluation. Section 5 concludes the paper and identifies some directions for future work.

2   Related Work

Though several unimodal [3–5] and multimodal [6] solutions for emotion recognition have been presented, the use of VLLMs for this purpose has only recently begun to be explored. Xu et al. [9] utilize pre-trained models to extract the speech transcript and a speech emotion caption based on acoustic features and employ Video-ChatGPT [13] to extract a visual description of the video; these features are integrated into a prompt fed to a pre-trained LLaMA3–8 B model that outputs emotion words describing the video. Vaiani et al. [10] employ three methods to obtain emotion reaction intensities for seven emotion categories in a video: direct querying of the Video-LLaVA VLLM [14], probing with fine-tuning on the embeddings produced by Video-LLaVA [14], and integration of textual features extracted from generated video descriptions into the multimodal VIPER framework [15].

However, the above approaches output only emotion labels or intensity scores for emotion categories and do not provide any contextual explanations. Recently, some systems have aimed to generate not only labels or scores but also provide evidence and reasoning behind the predicted emotion. For example, Yang et al. [11] integrate additional face and audio encoders with an existing VLLM, LLaVA-OneVision-7B [16], and then use task-specific prompts to guide the model in generating either emotion labels alone or label-explanation pairs. Cheng et al. [12] introduce the Emotion-LLaMA model that employs specialized encoders – HuBERT [17] for audio processing and multiview visual encoders (MAE [18], VideoMAE [19], EVA [20] for facial details, dynamics, and context) – which are aligned with a LLaMA-based language model [21] to produce an emotion label with a corresponding explanatory sentence that rationalizes the emotional cues.

However, none of these VLLM-based systems have been adapted for domain-specific contexts such as therapy sessions. Some earlier studies have explored the use of automated emotion recognition tools for therapy support [2, 22, 23], but to the best of our knowledge, the use of VLLMs for emotion recognition in this domain has yet to be fully examined.

3   Method

Our approach integrates pretrained text and audio emotion classifiers with a general-purpose VLLM via structured prompting to generate a timeline of interpretable, multimodal summaries that trace the progression of the patient's emotional states during a therapy session.

Our method consists of the following steps: First, the therapy session video is segmented by speaker, and patient turns are extracted. For each patient segment, acoustic features and textual transcripts are processed using pretrained models to generate preliminary emotion labels. These, along with the segment transcript and preceding conversational context, are embedded in a structured prompt, which is passed to the VLLM alongside the corresponding video segment as a separate input. The VLLM then produces an overall emotion classification, an explanation highlighting salient cues, a list of key observations, and a confidence estimate. Finally, the outputs across all patient segments are consolidated into an emotion timeline that reflects the emotional evolution of the patient throughout the session.

The individual steps of this process are described below.

3.1   Segmenting the Video to Extract Patient Turns

The audio stream of the therapy session video is first transcribed using Whisper [24], a pretrained automatic speech recognition model. This transcript is then processed by Pyannote [25], a pretrained speaker diarization model, which identifies individual speaker turns, labels each turn as either patient or therapist, and assigns start and end timestamps. These timestamps are then used to extract matching video clips from the full recording, thereby isolating the segments where the patient is speaking. The outcome is a sequence of patient-turn video segments, each aligned with its corresponding transcript and audio.

3.2 Generating Emotion Labels and Contextual Descriptions

Each patient video segment is analyzed to generate preliminary emotion labels from two distinct modalities: text and audio. The transcript of the segment is processed using a pretrained text emotion classifier to obtain a text-based label, while the segment's audio is analyzed using an audio-based classifier to derive a label from vocal cues.

After some initial prompt tuning, we finalized a structured prompt that includes the current patient transcript, inferred audio and text emotion labels, and the two most recent preceding utterances (one from the therapist and one from the patient) to provide conversational context. The prompt also specifies the response format.

This prompt and the corresponding video segment are input into the LLaVA NeXT Video 7B model [26], a general-purpose VLLM. The model processes these multimodal inputs and produces a structured response consisting of an overall emotion label (using nuanced or compound terms where appropriate), a rationale explaining the inference based on verbal, visual, and vocal cues, a list of key observations (such as tone, gestures, and linguistic features), and a qualitative confidence score (high, medium, or low). Figure 1 shows the system prompt and Fig. 2 provides an overview of this pipeline.

Model selection: We selected LLaVA NeXT Video 7B [26] due to its strong performance on recent multimodal benchmarks and open-source accessibility. For text and audio emotion classification, we used pretrained models from Hugging Face [27], michellejieli/emotion_text_classifier [28] and ehcalabres/wav2vec2-lg-xlsr-en-speech-emotion-recognition [29], both of which are specifically trained for emotion recognition tasks. These choices enabled rapid development and evaluation without the need for domain-specific fine-tuning, making them well suited for our exploratory study.

Data preprocessing and computational setup: All experiments were conducted using Google Colab [30] (free tier), equipped with a T4 GPU, 12.7 GB of RAM, and 15 GB of VRAM. The VLLM was run using default generation parameters, except for setting max_new_tokens to 512, which was chosen to allow sufficient space for the structured output format while preventing excessively long or unfocused responses. Frame extraction from each video segment was limited to a maximum of 8 frames using linear sampling across the clip duration. Audio was converted to WAV format and segmented based on speaker diarization timestamps. All inputs were converted to PyTorch tensors and passed to the model using the standard HuggingFace processor interface.

3.3 Constructing the Session Timeline

The VLLM outputs for each patient segment are arranged chronologically to create an emotion timeline for the session. Each entry includes the detected emotion, a supporting rationale, key cues (e.g., tone, language, expressions), and a confidence rating. This timeline provides a coherent narrative of the patient's emotional progression, helping

```
    You are an advanced vision-language model specialized in analyzing
human emotions in counseling sessions.

    You will be given:
    1. A short video clip showing a patient speaking during a therapy
session.
    2. The transcript of what the patient says in that clip.
    3. The last two utterances before the clip (to provide conversa-
tional context).
    4. Emotion labels detected by external models from the patient's
transcript and audio (these may be fallible and are only provided for
reference).

    Your task is to analyze the patient's emotional state based on fa-
cial expressions, body language, voice tone, and spoken content.
    Give a holistic interpretation and do not simply merge the
text/audio results. Use your own multimodal understanding of the vid-
eo.

    Your output should contain the following:
    overall_emotion: Primary emotion being expressed, using nuanced or
compound terms if appropriate,
    rationale: Brief explanation of how you inferred this emotion (men-
tioning visual, vocal, and textual cues),
    key_cues: ["List of specific observed cues - facial expressions,
gestures, tone, language used"],
    confidence: high / medium / low

    Note: No preamble or any words other than what you've been asked to
output.
```

Fig. 1. System prompt used.

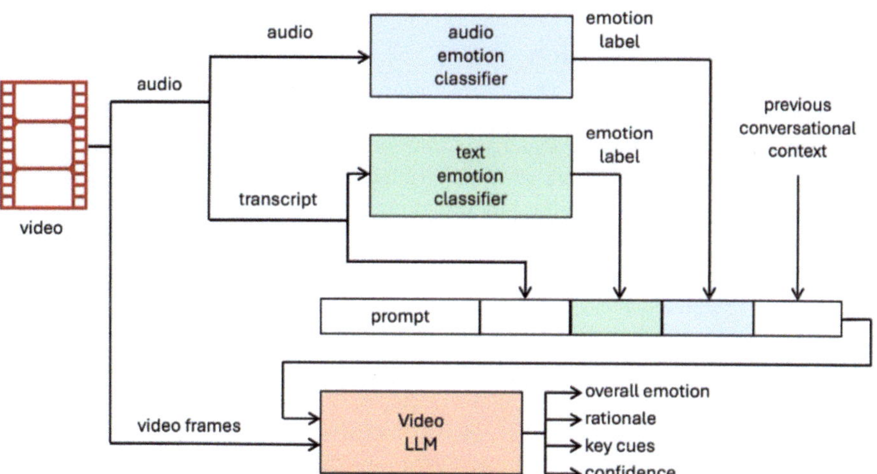

Fig. 2. Overview of the emotion recognition pipeline for a video segment.

therapists identify mood shifts, potential triggers, and areas for intervention. By combining multimodal signals with contextual prompting, the system offers an interpretable and clinically useful summary of affective dynamics.

The sample timeline in Fig. 3 is included solely to illustrate the type of output our system aspires to generate. While our system cannot yet consistently produce outputs like the one shown below, our preliminary evaluation (detailed in the next section) suggest that its behavior is aligned with this goal and can be improved through further refinement.

Timestamp	Overall Emotion	Rationale	Key Cues	Confidence
00:00–00:15	Hesitant and withdrawn	The patient's minimal eye contact, soft voice, and fragmented speech suggest uncertainty and social discomfort at the start of the session.	Avoidant gaze, low volume, fragmented speech: "I don't know... maybe it's nothing"	Medium
00:26–00:41	Defensive frustration	The sharper tone and crossed arms, along with accusatory language, indicate frustration directed at others.	Crossed arms, eye rolling, raised tone: "They always act like I'm the problem"	High
01:03–01:18	Defeated and ashamed	The patient lowers their head and speaks in a whisper, expressing regret over academic failure, suggesting self-directed shame.	Head lowered, whispering, lip biting: "I didn't even turn in the assignment"	High
01:45–01:55	Momentary optimism	Upright posture and a slight smile accompany a rare positive comment, indicating a brief moment of confidence and hope.	Upright posture, soft smile, relaxed tone: "But I did really well in math last week"	Medium

Fig. 3. Sample emotion timeline (fictional session). (*Note: This example illustrates the type of output the proposed system aims to produce. Actual results will vary based on model performance.*)

4   Preliminary Evaluation

We conducted initial experimentation with our approach using publicly available mock therapy videos licensed under Creative Commons on YouTube [31]. A small number of representative segments were reviewed by human evaluators to assess whether the system's outputs aligned with the emotional content of each clip. Fig. 4(a) shows an example where the model performed well. Although the audio classifier incorrectly predicted "disgust," the transcript and visual cues clearly conveyed sadness. The VLLM successfully integrated these signals to produce the correct overall label ("sadness") along with an appropriate rationale, demonstrating the robustness of our multimodal approach when one modality is noisy or misleading. In contrast, Fig. 4(b) presents a failure case. Here, although the patient's facial expressions and posture suggested sadness, the VLLM output "disgust", likely influenced by the incorrect label from the audio classifier. This highlights a limitation in how the model weighs conflicting input signals.

We observed that the audio classifier was a frequent source of error, often mislabeling segments and negatively impacting final predictions. A notable pattern across examples was its tendency to overpredict "disgust," possibly due to flat or subdued speech patterns common in therapeutic contexts. This overuse led to emotion labels that were not contextually appropriate and, in some cases, appeared to unduly influence the VLLM's final

<table>
<tr><td>

Transcript: "Yeah, I guess I have to figure out things for myself and for my parents who need my help a lot."

Context_Therapist: N/A (because beginning of video)

Context_Patient: N/A (because beginning of video)

Audio Emotion: Disgust

Text Emotion: Sadness

</td><td>

Transcript: "Yeah, and my parents, they don't understand that I can't do schoolwork, not because I'm not trying, but because my problems, understanding English."

Context_Therapist: "As well, you're worried about how your parents might respond when they find out you've failed two courses and that they might actually make you study more."

Context_Patient: "Yeah, and with everything happening right now I just don't know where to start."

Audio Emotion: Disgust

Text Emotion: Neutral

</td></tr>
<tr><td>

VLLM output:
overall_emotion: Sadness
rationale: The patient's body language, specifically the slumped posture and downward gaze, along with the tone of voice, suggests a sense of sadness. The mention of needing to help their parents and the implication of responsibility for their well-being further emphasizes this emotion.
key_cues: Slumped posture, downward gaze, subdued tone of voice
confidence: High

</td><td>

VLLM output:
overall_emotion: Disgust
rationale: The patient's facial expression shows a slight twist of the mouth and a furrowed brow, which are common indicators of disgust. The tone of voice is also slightly raised and tense, suggesting a negative emotional state.
key_cues: Facial expression includes a slight twist of the mouth and a furrowed brow, tone is slightly raised and tense.
confidence: Medium

</td></tr>
<tr><td align="center">*c+</td><td align="center">*d+</td></tr>
</table>

Fig. 4. Example outputs from the proposed system. (a) A correct prediction of sadness despite an incorrect audio-based label. (b) A misclassification as disgust, likely influenced by the audio model. Video segment sourced from: https://www.youtube.com/watch?v=JGMGXtfAX7U.

prediction, particularly when textual and visual cues were ambiguous. While the VLLM generally behaved robustly when modalities provided overlapping signals, it sometimes over-relied on the audio input when modalities conflicted. This highlights the need for more balanced modality integration or prompt-level guardrails to avoid over-weighting any single input. Encouragingly, in some "neutral" segments, the VLLM explicitly noted the absence of visible emotional cues and correctly withheld interpretation demonstrating restraint and interpretability that rule-based systems often lack. Replacing the audio classifier with a more accurate model or using one that jointly analyzes textual and acoustic cues may further improve performance. Additionally, despite our instruction to use "nuanced or compound terms if appropriate," the VLLM consistently returned a single dominant emotion. This not only constrained the granularity of emotional interpretation but also appeared to cause the model to retroactively tailor the rationale and cues to justify the selected label. This indicates that further prompt engineering is needed to encourage more descriptive, multiword emotional terms; for instance, in-context learning [32] can be employed where a few examples could show the model how to use compound emotion descriptors.

Overall, the results are promising and suggest that the proposed approach merits further exploration. As the capabilities of VLLMs and audio- and text-based emotion recognition models continue to evolve rapidly, we anticipate this framework will deliver increasingly accurate and nuanced outputs. In the meantime, we plan to address current limitations by experimenting with alternative audio emotion classifiers and refining the prompt design.

5 Conclusion and Future Work

We presented a novel multimodal approach for assisting therapists in tracking patient emotional trajectories during therapy sessions by leveraging an existing advanced general-purpose VLLM alongside pretrained audio- and text-based emotion recognition models. Preliminary results are encouraging, demonstrating the feasibility of this framework for therapeutic intervention and justifying further exploration.

Future work will focus on replacing the current audio emotion classifier with a more reliable alternative or with a model that jointly integrates acoustic and textual signals and refining the prompt design to encourage the generation of more nuanced, multiword emotion labels. As VLLMs and audio- and text-based emotion recognition models continue to advance rapidly, we expect this system to yield increasingly accurate and insightful results. We also plan to conduct a formal evaluation using a small dataset of therapy session videos manually annotated with emotion labels and descriptions. In parallel, we aim to run a user study with therapists to assess the system's perceived usefulness and gather feedback to better align its outputs with clinical needs. By delivering context-aware emotional interpretations, our approach has the potential to support therapists in monitoring patient mood shifts, enhance clinical decision-making, foster more effective human-AI collaboration in mental health care, and extend to broader applications such as digital therapy support and emotion-aware well-being tools.

References

1. Khanna, R., Robinson, N., O'Donnell, M., Eyre, H., Smith, E.: Affective computing in psychotherapy. Adv. Psychiatry Behav. Health. **2**(1), 95–105 (2022)
2. Liu, Y., Zhang, Y., Wang, Y.: Application of deep learning-based image processing in emotion recognition and psychological therapy. Traitement Signal. **41**(6), 2923 (2024)
3. Chowanda, A., Iswanto, I.A., Andangsari, E.W.: Exploring deep learning algorithm to model emotions recognition from speech. Procedia Comput. Sci. **216**, 706–713 (2023)
4. George, S.M., Ilyas, P.M.: A review on speech emotion recognition: a survey, recent advances, challenges, and the influence of noise. Neurocomputing. **568**, 127015 (2024)
5. Ballesteros, J.A., Ramírez, V.G.M., Moreira, F., Solano, A., Pelaez, C.A.: Facial emotion recognition through artificial intelligence. Front. Comput. Sci. **6**, 1359471 (2024)
6. Kalateh, S., Estrada-Jimenez, L.A., Nikghadam-Hojjati, S., Barata, J.: A systematic review on multimodal emotion recognition: building blocks, current state, applications, and challenges. IEEE Access. **12**, 103976–104019 (2024). https://doi.org/10.1109/ACCESS.2024.3430850

7. Lian, Z., Sun, H., Sun, L., Gu, H., Wen, Z., Zhang, S., Chen, S., Xu, M., Xu, K., Chen, K.: Explainable multimodal emotion recognition. arXiv preprint arXiv:230615401. (2023)

8. Li, F., Zhang, R., Zhang, H., Zhang, Y., Li, B., Li, W., Ma, Z., Li, C.: Llava-next-interleave: tackling multi-image, video, and 3d in large multimodal models. arXiv preprint arXiv:240707895. (2024)

9. Xu, Y., Zhou, Y., Cai, Y., Xie, J., Ye, R., Wu, Z.: Multimodal emotion captioning using large language model with prompt engineering. In: Proceedings of the 2nd International Workshop on Multimodal and Responsible Affective Computing, pp. 104–109 (2024)

10. Vaiani, L., Cagliero, L., Garza, P.: Emotion recognition from videos using multimodal large language models. Future Internet. **16**(7), 247 (2024)

11. Yang, Q., Bai, D., Peng, Y.-X., Wei, X.: Omni-emotion: extending video MLLM with detailed face and audio modeling for multimodal emotion analysis. arXiv preprint arXiv:250109502. (2025)

12. Cheng, Z., Cheng, Z.-Q., He, J.-Y., Wang, K., Lin, Y., Lian, Z., Peng, X., Hauptmann, A.: Emotion-llama: multimodal emotion recognition and reasoning with instruction tuning. Adv. Neural Inf. Proces. Syst. **37**, 110805–110853 (2024)

13. Maaz, M., Rasheed, H., Khan, S., Khan, F.S.: Video-chatgpt: towards detailed video understanding via large vision and language models. arXiv preprint arXiv:230605424. (2023)

14. Lin, B., Ye, Y., Zhu, B., Cui, J., Ning, M., Jin, P., Yuan, L.: Video-llava: learning united visual representation by alignment before projection. arXiv preprint arXiv:231110122. (2023)

15. Vaiani, L., Quatra, M.L., Cagliero, L., Garza, P.: ViPER: video-based perceiver for emotion recognition. In: Proceedings of the 3rd International on Multimodal Sentiment Analysis Workshop and Challenge, Lisboa, Portugal, pp. 67–73. Association for Computing Machinery (2022). https://doi.org/10.1145/3551876.3554806

16. Li, B., Zhang, Y., Guo, D., Zhang, R., Li, F., Zhang, H., Zhang, K., Zhang, P., Li, Y., Liu, Z.: Llava-onevision: easy visual task transfer. arXiv preprint arXiv:240803326. (2024)

17. Hsu, W.N., Bolte, B., Tsai, Y.H.H., Lakhotia, K., Salakhutdinov, R., Mohamed, A.: HuBERT: self-supervised speech representation learning by masked prediction of hidden units. IEEE/ACM Trans. Audio Speech Lang. Process. **29**, 3451–3460 (2021). https://doi.org/10.1109/TASLP.2021.3122291

18. Sun, L., Lian, Z., Liu, B., Tao, J.: MAE-DFER: efficient masked autoencoder for self-supervised dynamic facial expression recognition. In: Proceedings of the 31st ACM International Conference on Multimedia, Ottawa ON, Canada, pp. 6110–6121. Association for Computing Machinery (2023). https://doi.org/10.1145/3581783.3612365

19. Tong, Z., Song, Y., Wang, J., Wang, L.: Videomae: masked autoencoders are data-efficient learners for self-supervised video pre-training. Adv. Neural Inf. Proces. Syst. **35**, 10078–10093 (2022)

20. Fang, Y., Wang, W., Xie, B., Sun, Q., Wu, L., Wang, X., Huang, T., Wang, X., Eva, C.Y.: Exploring the limits of masked visual representation learning at scale. In: Proceedings of the IEEE/CVF Conference on Computer Vision and Pattern Recognition, pp. 19358–19369 (2023)

21. Touvron, H., Martin, L., Stone, K., Albert, P., Almahairi, A., Babaei, Y., Bashlykov, N., Batra, S., Bhargava, P., Bhosale, S.: Llama 2: open foundation and fine-tuned chat models. arXiv preprint arXiv:230709288. (2023)

22. Rasool, A., Aslam, S., Hussain, N., Imtiaz, S., Riaz, W.: nBERT: harnessing NLP for emotion recognition in psychotherapy to transform mental health care. Information. **16**(4), 301 (2025)

23. Nixon, D., Mallappa, V.V., Petli, V., HosgurMath, S., Kiran, K.S.: A novel AI therapy for depression counseling using face emotion techniques. Global Trans. Proc. **3**(1), 190–194 (2022). https://doi.org/10.1016/j.gltp.2022.03.008

24. Radford, A., Kim, J.W., Xu, T., Brockman, G., Mcleavey, C., Sutskever, I.: Robust speech recognition via large-scale weak supervision. In: Andreas, K., Emma, B., Kyunghyun, C., Barbara, E., Sivan, S., Jonathan, S. (eds.) Proceedings of the 40th International Conference on Machine Learning, Proceedings of Machine Learning Research, pp. 28492–28518. PMLR (2023)
25. Plaquet, A., Bredin, H.: Powerset multi-class cross entropy loss for neural speaker diarization. In: Proceedings of Interspeech 2023, pp. 3222–3226 (2023). https://doi.org/10.21437/Interspeech.2023-205
26. Zhang, Y., Li, B., Liu, H., Lee, Y.J., Gui, L., Fu, D., Feng, J., Liu, Z., Li, C.: LLaVA-NeXT: A Strong Zero-Shot Video Understanding Model (2024). https://llava-vl.github.io/blog/2024-04-30-llava-next-video/. Accessed June 11, 2025
27. Hugging Face – The AI community building the future. https://huggingface.co/. Accessed June 16 2025
28. Li, M.: Michellejieli/emotion_text_classifier (Hugging Face Model). Hugging Face (2023). https://huggingface.co/michellejieli/emotion_text_classifier. Accessed June 11 2025
29. Calabres, E.H.: wav2vec2-lg-xlsr-en-speech-emotion-recognition (Hugging Face Model). Hugging Face (2023). https://huggingface.co/ehcalabres/wav2vec2-lg-xlsr-en-speech-emotion-recognition. Accessed June 11 2025
30. Google Colaboratory. https://colab.research.google.com/. Accessed June 16 2025
31. YouTube: YouTube (2025). https://www.youtube.com. Accessed June 14 2025
32. Min, S., Lyu, X., Holtzman, A., Artetxe, M., Lewis, M., Hajishirzi, H., Zettlemoyer, L.: Rethinking the role of demonstrations: What makes in-context learning work? arXiv preprint arXiv:220212837. (2022)

Exploring Factors Influencing Perceived Usefulness and Adoption Intention for Financial AI Services Across User Experience Levels

Eunbi Kang[1] [iD], Soyeong Choi[1] [iD], Xu Li[2] [iD], and Hyesun Hwang[1 (✉)] [iD]

[1] Department of Consumer Science, Convergence Program for Social Innovation, Sungkyunkwan University, Seoul, South Korea
h.hwang@skku.edu
[2] Department of Consumer Science, Sungkyunkwan University, Seoul, South Korea

Abstract. This study examines user acceptance of AI technologies in financial services to promote inclusive and user-centered AI design. By analyzing perceived usefulness and adoption intention, it compares users with and without prior experience in using financial AI services. Using survey data from 6352 Korean adults from the 2023 Digital Divide Survey (conducted by the National Information Society Agency of Korea), the study addresses two research questions: (1) What factors influence the perceived usefulness of financial AI services among users with and without prior experience? (2) What factors influence the adoption intentions of financial AI services among users with and without prior experience? Findings reveal that for perceived usefulness, users with prior experience benefit from positive AI perceptions and both bonding and bridging social capital. Among users without prior experience, positive AI perceptions, digital self-efficacy, and bonding social capital are significant predictors, while bridging social capital is not. Logistic regression results reveal contrasting adoption determinants. For users with prior experience, positive AI perceptions and bridging social capital significantly influence adoption, with the latter having a negative effect. In contrast, for users without prior experience, positive AI perceptions and both bonding and bridging social capital are critical. These findings highlight the role of user experience in shaping attitudes and intentions, emphasizing the need for tailored strategies in human-computer interaction. Experienced users benefit from social networks and targeted information, while users without experience require self-efficacy support and reduced perceived barriers. This study contributes to the design of inclusive AI-driven financial systems by addressing diverse user needs and fostering broader AI adoption.

Keywords: Artificial intelligence · Financial service · Adoption intention

1 Introduction

Artificial intelligence (AI) services in finance, where individual knowledge and expertise are highly valued, enhance inclusiveness by improving consumer accessibility [1]. Consumers previously excluded due to limited financial literacy can now access diverse,

© The Author(s), under exclusive license to Springer Nature Switzerland AG 2026
S. Sundarakannan and O. Knorpp (Eds.): HCII 2025, CCIS 2772, pp. 121–132, 2026.
https://doi.org/10.1007/978-3-032-12767-9_14

tailored information through AI-based financial services, along with personalized recommendations [2]. Consequently, despite financial services being a specialized domain, AI significantly lowers entry barriers, enabling more user-friendly and inclusive services [3, 4].

However, even such highly accessible services may pose entry barriers as new technologies [5]. As per the technology acceptance model (TAM), adoption timing varies with individual disposition, resource availability, and external environments [6]. Despite living in the AI era, financial AI services have yet to achieve widespread adoption [7], making it relevant to analyze these services based on user experience. As the discussions shift from the traditional digital divide to emerging AI technologies, it is important to investigate whether a new digital gap is emerging, examine its underlying causes, and explore ways to develop a more inclusive society in the AI era before these disparities become entrenched. While financial AI services aim to enhance inclusivity by lowering entry barriers, it is essential to assess whether they truly achieve inclusivity for all.

Prior research has examined user responses to AI services across domains; however, research on financial AI services and the differences between experienced and non-experienced users remain limited. This study investigates how consumer perceptions and behavioral responses toward financial AI services are formed, emphasizing the impact of self-efficacy and social capital.

It examines differences in factors influencing perceived usefulness and adoption intentions of financial AI services between users with and without prior experience. Specifically, it analyzes the disparity between early adopters (who readily embraced AI-based financial services, which require significant cognitive effort and specialized knowledge) and non-adopters. By focusing on advanced and emerging technologies, the study sheds light on the evolving digital divide in the AI era, exploring new dimensions of technology acceptance. Ultimately, it offers insights for developing more inclusive and accessible financial AI service systems.

2　Literature Review

2.1　AI Perception

As AI grows increasingly prevalent, focus is shifting from the technology itself to user perspectives on incorporating AI into their daily lives [8, 9]. Unlike traditional technologies, AI demonstrates human-like thinking capabilities, enabling more flexible and personalized user interactions [10]. This personalized engagement necessitates examining both internal and external user reactions, including emotional responses, cognitive processes, perceptions, attitudes, and behaviors before, during, and after AI usage [11]. While AI's human-like intelligence enables highly accessible and quality service delivery, it also raises concerns about job displacement or potential social disruption [12, 13]. The recognition of AI's benefits and drawbacks, including its potential risks, are not mutually exclusive [14]. These perceptions manifest as attitudes, significantly influencing subsequent user behaviors [15].

2.2 Digital Self-Efficacy

Self-efficacy refers to an individual's belief in their ability to effectively perform a specific task, closely linked to self-confidence [16, 17]. Rooted in Bandura's Social Cognitive Theory, self-efficacy significantly influences an individual's capability to successfully accomplish various tasks [17]. In the digital age, this concept is adapted as 'digital self-efficacy,' particularly relevant for tasks involving digital devices or learning new digital technologies [17, 18].

In other words, digital self-efficacy is crucial for individuals to follow, accept, and adapt to the rapidly emerging technologies and the swiftly changing modern society [19]. Individuals with high digital self-efficacy exhibit greater confidence in learning new skills and are likelier to adopt new technologies [20]. Conversely, those with low digital self-efficacy tend to be passive toward new digital technologies [21]. This difference in behavior and attitude can lead to disparities in digital usage, potentially exacerbating structural digital divides [22]. Digital self-efficacy is particularly relevant in specialized domains like financial services, which demand greater knowledge and engagement from consumers [23]. This necessitates examining digital self-efficacy within the context of financial AI services, an emerging domain requiring both acceptance of advanced technologies, like AI, and substantial financial knowledge.

2.3 Social Capital

Social capital refers to the resources individuals or groups can access through their social networks [24, 25] and is broadly divided into bonding and bridging social capital [26]. Bonding social capital is built on strong ties within homogeneous groups such as family, friends, or those with similar backgrounds and interests [26, 27]. It is characterized by high levels of trust and emotional support stemming from deep, intimate connections [26, 28]. In contrast, bridging social capital refers to connections across heterogeneous groups or individuals from diverse backgrounds [29]. Although these ties tend to be weaker, bridging social capital broadens social networks, providing access to diverse perspectives and information [30, 31].

Social capital significantly influences decision-making in daily life [24, 25], particularly in shaping attitudes and behaviors toward accepting new technologies [32–35]. Bonding social capital, characterized by deep bonds and trust, drives technology adoption through recommendations and learning within close connections [32]. For example, elderly individuals—often digitally vulnerable—learn to use digital devices from their children [33].

Conversely, high bridging social capital, characterized by broad connections among diverse individuals, enables rapid access to information about emerging technologies. Adoption of these innovations by a substantial portion of society can lead to their acceptance evolving into a social norm, further promoting widespread adoption [34, 35].

Moreover, the expansion of AI services offers a context to examine user responses to new technologies, which are similarly influenced by social capital [36]. In specialized fields like finance, where independent skill development demands significant resources, support from social capital becomes critical [3, 37].

Building on this theoretical foundation, this study hypothesizes that perceptions of AI, digital self-efficacy, and social capital (bonding and bridging) influence the perceived usefulness and adoption intention of financial AI services. These factors are expected to manifest differently between users with and without prior experience, leading to the following research questions:

RQ 1. What factors influence the perceived usefulness of financial AI services among users with and without prior experience?
RQ 2. What factors influence the adoption intentions of financial AI services among users with and without prior experience?

3   Methods

This study used data from the 2023 Digital Divide Survey conducted by the National Information Society Agency of Korea (NIA). This annual survey assesses the digital competency of Korea's digitally vulnerable populations and lays the groundwork for more effective strategies to close the digital divide. The survey served as the primary data source for this study on digital inclusion, focusing on a sample of 6,352 Korean adults.

The dependent variables were perceived usefulness and adoption intention for financial AI services, with AI perception, digital self-efficacy, bonding social capital, and bridging social capital serving as the primary explanatory variables.

Perceived usefulness was measured by asking respondents to indicate the extent to which they felt the service was beneficial. For users, this reflected their actual experience, and for non-users, it reflected expected benefits. *Adoption intention* was measured as a binary variable indicating whether respondents planned to use financial AI services in the future.

AI perception was evaluated through five items assessing positive perceptions (AI's beneficial impact on daily life) and three items measuring negative perceptions (concerns about AI causing social problems). *Digital self-efficacy* was measured by respondents' confidence in using digital devices and learning new technologies. *Bonding social capital* was captured by questions about the presence of close and deep relationships, while *bridging social capital* focused on the connectivity and breadth of respondents' wider social networks.

All items were measured using a 4-point Likert scale (1 = Strongly disagree, 4 = Strongly agree). To examine differences between individuals with and without prior experience using financial AI services, respondents were classified into two groups based on a binary item assessing their prior use of these services.

The study first employed descriptive statistics to examine the general characteristics of the sample. To address RQ 1, the perceived usefulness of financial AI services (treated as a continuous variable) was analyzed separately for individuals with and without experience using multiple regression analysis. For RQ 2, logistic regression analysis was conducted for each group, with adoption as the binary dependent variable.

4   Results

4.1   Descriptive Statistics

Table 1 summarizes the descriptive statistics for the study sample of 6,352 respondents, with 51.7% male and 48.3% female. In terms of age, 19.3% were in their 20 s, 20.3% in their 30 s, 25.0% in their 40 s, 24.7% in their 50 s, and 10.8% in their 60 s (the smallest group). Over half (54.6%) had completed high school education. Regarding occupation, professional workers comprised the smallest group (5.5%), whereas service/sales workers were the largest (35.5%). In terms of monthly income, 13.2% earned less than three million KRW, while the majority (59.4%) fell within the three–six million KRW range. Finally, 46.6% of the respondents resided in metropolitan areas.

Table 1. General Characteristics of Participants (N = 6,352).

Variables	Freq	%	Variables	Freq	%
Gender			Occupation		
Male	3,285	51.7	Professionals	349	5.5
Female	3,067	48.3	Office worker	1,647	25.9
Age			Service/sales	2,258	35.5
20s	1,224	19.3	Skilled/manual worker	918	14.5
30s	1,288	20.3	Others	1,180	18.6
40s	1,586	25.0	Monthly income		
50s	1,570	24.7	Less than 3M KRW	837	13.2
60s	684	10.8	Between 3 – 6M KRW	3,771	59.4
Education			Higher than 6M KRW	1,774	27.5
Less than HS Grad	193	3.1	Metropolis	2,963	46.6
HS Grad	2,690	42.2			
Higher than HS Grad	3,469	54.6			

Notes. Freq = Frequency, HS Grad = high school graduation, M = million, 1 USD = 1,447.50 KRW (March 17, 2025)

4.2   Perceived Usefulness of Financial AI Services

Table 2 presents the multiple regression results for RQ 1, which examined whether the factors influencing the perceived usefulness of financial AI services differ between users with and without prior experience. In both groups, positive perceptions of AI and bonding social capital demonstrated a statistically significant positive effect on perceived usefulness ($p < 0.01$). However, differences emerged regarding digital self-efficacy and bridging social capital. For digital self-efficacy, the effect was non-significant for users with prior experience ($\beta = -0.010$, $p = 0.777$) but showed a significant positive effect for users without prior experience ($\beta = 0.114$, $p < 0.001$). While bonding social capital was positively correlated with perceived usefulness in both groups (with prior experience: $\beta = 0.100$, $p < 0.01$; without prior experience: $\beta = 0.102$, $p < 0.001$), bridging social capital had a significant positive effect only for users with prior experience ($\beta = 0.114$, $p < 0.01$). No significant relationship was observed for users without prior experience ($\beta = 0.009$, $p = 0.699$). These results indicate that factors affecting perceived usefulness differ between individuals with and without experience in using financial AI services.

Table 2. Analysis of Perceived Usefulness of Financial AI Services.

	Financial AI Service Perceived Usefulness					
	Group 1: With Prior Experience			Group 2: Without Prior Experience		
	B	S.E	β	B	S.E	β
Socioeconomic Variables						
Gender (Male = 1)	0.005	0.041	0.004	0.002	0.031	0.001
Age	0.000	0.002	−0.003	0.001	0.001	0.024
Education	−0.099	0.043	−0.076[*]	−0.002	0.033	−0.001
Occupation (ref: skilled worker)						
Professionals	0.086	0.092	0.034	0.092	0.072	0.032
Office worker	0.097	0.068	0.07	−0.021	0.055	−0.013
Service/sales	0.069	0.064	0.048	−0.056	0.051	−0.036
Others	−0.031	0.075	−0.017	0.009	0.058	0.005
Monthly Income	0.027	0.032	0.025	−0.022	0.024	−0.018
Metropolis	−0.145	0.038	−0.110[***]	−0.023	0.030	−0.016
Digital Self-Efficacy	−0.011	0.040	−0.010	0.136	0.030	0.114[***]
AI Perception						
Pros	0.344	0.054	0.215[***]	0.341	0.042	0.185[***]
Cons	−0.007	0.040	−0.005	−0.038	0.031	−0.025
Social Capital						
Bonding	0.162	0.058	0.100[**]	0.186	0.043	0.102[***]
Bridging	0.163	0.051	0.114[***]	0.015	0.038	0.009
F	11.771 [***]			16.341 [***]		
R^2 (Adj. R^2)	0.132 (0.121)			0.092 (0.086)		

[*] $p < 0.05$, [**] $p < 0.01$, [***] $p < 0.001$

4.3 Adoption Intention for Financial AI Services

To examine whether the factors influencing adoption intention differ between users with and without prior experience (RQ 2), a logistic regression analysis was conducted for each group using adoption intention as the binary dependent variable. The results (Table 3) indicate that similar to the findings for perceived usefulness, positive AI perceptions significantly increased adoption likelihood in both groups (prior experience users: $\exp(B) = 1.611$, $p < 0.01$; without prior experience: $\exp(B) = 1.587$, $p < 0.001$). In contrast, negative AI perceptions had no significant impact on adoption intention for either group (prior experience: $\exp(B) = 0.823$, $p = 0.149$; without prior experience: $\exp(B) = 0.964$, $p = 0.688$). While digital self-efficacy previously showed a significant positive effect on perceived usefulness among users without prior experience, its influence on adoption intention was not statistically significant in either group (prior experience: $\exp(B) = 0.934$, $p = 0.612$; without prior experience: $\exp(B) = 0.851$, $p = 0.064$). Moreover, the role of social capital differed between the groups. Among the users with prior experience, only bridging social capital significantly affected adoption intention, exhibiting a negative relationship ($\exp(B) = 0.614$, $p < 0.01$). Conversely, among users without prior experience, both bonding and bridging social capital were significant predictors: bonding social capital was positively associated with adoption intention ($\exp(B) = 1.607$, $p < 0.001$), while bridging social capital showed a significant negative effect ($\exp(B) = 0.707$, $p < 0.01$). These results demonstrate that the factors influencing adoption intention operate differently between users with and without experience.

Table 3. Determinants of Adoption Intention for Financial AI Services.

	Financial AI Service Adoption Intention					
	Group 1: With Prior Experience			Group 2: Without Prior Experience		
	B	S.E	Exp (B)	B	S.E	Exp (B)
Socioeconomic Variables						
Gender (Male = 1)	0.054	0.136	1.056	0.025	0.091	1.025
Age	−0.009	0.006	0.991	0.009[*]	0.004	1.009
Education	0.094	0.145	1.098	0.194[*]	0.098	1.214
Occupation (ref: skilled worker)						
Professionals	−0.753[*]	0.313	0.471	0.059	0.212	1.061
Office worker	−0.628[**]	0.232	0.534	0.374[*]	0.160	1.453
Service/sales	−0.290	0.221	0.748	0.186	0.149	1.204
Others	−0.499	0.256	0.607	−0.083	0.169	0.920
Monthly Income	−0.025	0.108	0.976	−0.017	0.071	0.983
Metropolis	0.457[***]	0.129	1.579	0.141	0.087	1.152
Perceived usefulness of financial AI services	0.449[***]	0.104	1.566	0.325[***]	0.062	1.384
Digital Self-Efficacy	−0.069	0.135	0.934	−0.162[†]	0.087	0.851
AI Perception						
Pros	0.477[*]	0.185	1.611	0.462[***]	0.125	1.587

(continued)

Table 3. (*continued*)

| | Financial AI Service Adoption Intention | | | | | |
	Group 1: With Prior Experience			Group 2: Without Prior Experience		
Cons	−0.195	0.135	0.823	...−0.037	0.091	0.964
Social Capital						
Bonding	0.013	0.197	1.014	0.474***	0.129	1.607
Bridging	−0.488**	0.176	0.614	−0.347**	0.115	0.707

† $p < .10$, * $p < .05$, ** $p < .01$, *** $p < .001$

5 Discussion and Implications

This study aimed to identify factors shaping users' intentions to adopt financial AI services. The findings revealed that key determinants differ between the two user groups, emphasizing the need for tailored strategies in specialized fields like finance.

5.1 Discussion

For users without prior experience, digital self-efficacy emerged as a significant factor—those more confident in their ability to use digital technologies tended to perceive AI financial services as more useful. This implies that fostering self-efficacy is particularly important for individuals new to these advanced technologies. Moreover, only bonding social capital positively influenced perceived usefulness, suggesting that information or recommendations from family and close friends can enhance the perceived benefits of financial AI services.

In contrast, digital self-efficacy did not significantly influence perceived usefulness among users with prior experience. They benefited from both bonding and bridging social capital, with broader social networks also contributing positively. This indicates that exposure to diverse information and positive social norms reinforces the perceived benefits among those already familiar with the service.

These findings suggest that financial AI service promotion strategies should be tailored accordingly. For users without prior experience, efforts should focus on enhancing self-efficacy and leveraging close personal ties, whereas for users with prior experience, broader social networks reinforcing positive norms may be more effective.

The analysis of adoption intention (RQ2) revealed differences between the two groups, though the results diverged from those for perceived usefulness. While digital self-efficacy significantly influenced perceived usefulness among users without prior experience, it had no significant effect on adoption intention. This suggests that the underlying mechanisms shaping the evaluation of a service's benefits and the behavioral intention to adopt it differ. Although self-efficacy is theoretically expected to drive behavioral change and influence the future adoption intentions of users without prior experience, this was not observed. This may be attributed to the use of secondary data, where the available digital self-efficacy measure may not specifically assess AI-related competence. Consequently, confidence in general digital competencies may not directly translate to the perceived usefulness of novel AI-integrated financial services.

In terms of social capital, the results differed from those observed for perceived usefulness. Among users with prior experience, only bridging social capital had a significant negative effect on adoption intention. A wider social network correlated with higher perceived usefulness, yet it corresponded to a lower adoption intention. This may be because a broader network exposes individuals to diverse information and perspectives, potentially reducing the perceived necessity of adopting AI in financial services [3, 32, 37]. Bridging social capital expands networks with new and diverse contacts, broadening an individual's outlook and providing access to various informational resources [29, 30]. In finance, advice and information from multiple experts beyond AI may lead individuals to decide against adopting financial AI services [3, 37]. This negative influence of bridging social capital was also significant among users without prior experience. Meanwhile, for users without prior experience, bonding social capital had a significant positive effect on adoption intention, mirroring its effect on perceived usefulness. Their judgments about a service's usefulness and adoption intention were strongly influenced by close personal relationships. Those who have not yet directly used financial AI services, representing an earlier stage in the technology adoption cycle, appear particularly affected by close and intimate social ties when considering the adoption of new technologies [32, 33].

Regardless of the user group or dependent variable, only positive perceptions of AI had a significant positive impact, while negative perceptions showed no significant effect. This indicates that individuals' positive expectations regarding AI's benefits more directly influence both perceived usefulness and adoption intention than their concerns about its risks [38]. In the current era of AI, people are more likely to base their attitudes and behaviors on AI's anticipated benefits than on risk avoidance [9].

5.2 Implications

This study lays the groundwork for inclusive strategies in the AI era by examining the differences between users with and without prior experience in financial AI services. In domains requiring specialized knowledge like financial AI, it is particularly important for users with prior experience—or early adopters—to have access to robust social networks and appropriate information [4, 5]. Even within expansive networks offering diverse perspectives, tailored and relevant information appears more beneficial for this group. Conversely, for non-experience users, enhancing digital self-efficacy and delivering information through close, supportive contacts may prove more effective. To advance toward a more inclusive AI era, lowering entry barriers is crucial when these individuals express interest in adopting new technologies [1, 2]. Notably, while digital self-efficacy contributes to perceived usefulness for his group, it does not directly translate into adoption intention, highlighting the need for strategies to boost self-efficacy in the AI context [5, 14, 18]. These findings are expected to inform the design of more inclusive, AI-based financial systems.

5.3 Limitations

Several resolved issues warrant further attention. Digital self-efficacy did not have a significant impact on adoption intention for either user group. In the group without prior experience, it even showed a marginally negative effect on the adoption intention (exp(B) = 0.851, p = 0.064), which raises further questions. Although prior research suggests that digital self-efficacy positively influences new technology adoption, the possibility of a negative effect is intriguing [20, 21]. Future studies should examine the conditions under which digital self-efficacy exerts either a positive or negative effect on new technology adoption, especially among users without prior experience. Moreover, the use of secondary data somewhat limited the scope of the questionnaire. Future research should develop and refine surveys to capture more detailed perspectives.

References

1. Yasir, A., Ahmad, A., Abbas, S., Inairat, M., Al-Kassem, A.H., Rasool, A.: How artificial intelligence is promoting financial inclusion? A study on barriers of financial inclusion. In: 2022 International Conference on Business Analytics for Technology and Security (ICBATS), pp. 1–6. IEEE (2022)
2. Aishwaryalaxmi, N. S., Rathod, P.: Artificial intelligence (AI) as a moderating variable in the relationship between financial inclusion, digital adoption, and financial literacy in developing economies. In: ITM Web Conf., vol. 68, p. 01034. EDP Sciences (2024)
3. Dudley, E.: Social capital and entrepreneurial financing choice. J. Corp. Finan. **70**, 102068 (2021)
4. Kumari, R., Sharma, K., Kumar, R.: Social and ethical implications of AI in finance for sustainability: convergence of culture in the banking sector after adaptation of artificial intelligence. In: Social and Ethical Implications of AI in Finance for Sustainability, pp. 141–155. IGI Global (2024)
5. Jisham, M., Selvaraj, V., John, A.: Navigating Behavioural barriers to Fintech Chatbot adoption: an extended innovation resistance theory approach. Colombo Bus. J. **15**(1), 80–104 (2024)
6. Davis, F.D.: Technology acceptance model: TAM. Al-Suqri MN Al-Aufi AS: Inform. Seek. Behav. Technol. Adopt. **205**(219), 5 (1989)
7. Schwaerzler, C., Carrasco, M., Daniel, C., Bollyky, B., Niwa, Y., Bharadwaj, A., Awad, A., Sargeant, R., Nawandhar, S., Kostikova, S.: The AI Maturity Matrix: Which Economies Are Ready for AI? Boston Consulting Group (2024)
8. Noy, S., Zhang, W.: Experimental evidence on the productivity effects of generative artificial intelligence. Science. **381**(6654), 187–192 (2023)
9. Virvou, M.: Artificial intelligence and user experience in reciprocity: contributions and state of the art. Intell. Dec. Technol. **17**(1), 73–125 (2023)
10. Yang, J., Yoon, S.: Beyond ChatGPT: entering the era of generative AI—cases of media and content creation AI services and strategies to secure competitiveness. Media Issue Trend. **55**, 62–70 (2023)
11. Ma, Y.M., Dai, X., Deng, Z.: Using machine learning to investigate consumers' emotions: the spillover effect of AI defeating people on consumers' attitudes toward AI companies. Internet Res. **34**(5), 1679–1713 (2023)
12. Ahmad, Z., Kaiser, W., Rahim, S.: Hallucinations in ChatGPT: an unreliable tool for learning. Rupkatha J. Interdisc. Stud. Hum. **15**(4), 12 (2023)

13. Eng, P.H., Liu, R.L.: Will intelligent technologies replace humans in the future? An exploratory study for likelihood of intelligent technologies to replace humans in the future. In: Current and Future Trends on Intelligent Technology Adoption: Volume 2, pp. 171–202. Springer, Cham (2024)

14. Schwesig, R., Brich, I., Buder, J., Huff, M., Said, N.: Using artificial intelligence (AI)? Risk and opportunity perception of AI predict people's willingness to use AI. J. Risk Res. **26**(10), 1053–1084 (2023)

15. Shin, D.: User perceptions of algorithmic decisions in the personalized AI system: perceptual evaluation of fairness, accountability, transparency, and explainability. J. Broadcast. Electron. Media. **64**(4), 541–565 (2020)

16. Bandura, A.: Social foundations of thought and action. Englewood Cliffs. **2**(2), 23–28 (1986)

17. Bandura, A.: Self-Efficacy: the Exercise of Control. Macmillan (1997)

18. Compeau, D.R., Higgins, C.A.: Computer self-efficacy: development of a measure and initial test. MIS Q. **19**(2), 189–211 (1995)

19. Ulfert-Blank, A.S., Schmidt, I.: Assessing digital self-efficacy: review and scale development. Comput. Educ. **191**, 104626 (2022)

20. Venkatesh, V., Bala, H.: Technology acceptance model 3 and a research agenda on interventions. Decis. Sci. **39**(2), 273–315 (2008)

21. Hsia, J.W., Chang, C.C., Tseng, A.H.: Effects of individuals' locus of control and computer self-efficacy on their e-learning acceptance in high-tech companies. Behav. Inform. Technol. **33**(1), 51–64 (2014)

22. Eastin, M. S., LaRose, R.: Internet self-efficacy and the psychology of the digital divide. J. Comput.-Mediat. Commun. 6(1), JCMC611 (2000)

23. Mindra, R., Moya, M., Zuze, L.T., Kodongo, O.: Financial self-efficacy: A determinant of financial inclusion. Int. J. Bank Mark. **35**(3), 338–353 (2017)

24. Putnam, R.: Bowling alone: America's declining social capital. J. Democr. **6**(1), 65–78 (1995)

25. Ikeda, S.: The meaning of "social capital" as it relates to the market process. Rev. Austrian Econ. **21**, 167–182 (2008)

26. Putnam, R.: Bowling Alone: The Collapse and Revival of American Community. Touchstone, New York, NY (2000)

27. Onyx, J., Leonard, R.: The conversion of social capital into community development: an intervention in Australia's outback. Int. J. Urban Reg. Res. **34**, 381–397 (2010)

28. Castro Torres, M.E., Vargas-Piérola, P.M., Pinto, C.F., Alvarado, R.: Serial mediation model of social capital effects over academic stress in university students. Eur. J. Investig. Health Psychol. Educ. **12**(11), 1644–1656 (2022)

29. Woolcock, M., Narayan, D.: Social capital: implications for development theory, research, and policy. World Bank Res. Obs. **15**(2), 225–249 (2000)

30. Burt, R.: The contingent value of social capital. Adm. Sci. Q. **42**(2), 339–365 (1997)

31. Evans, M., Syrett, S.: Generating social capital? The social economy and local economic development. Eur. Urban Reg. Stud. **14**(1), 55–74 (2007)

32. Rey-Moreno, M., Medina-Molina, C.: Social capital in e-services adoption. Psychol. Mark. **33**(12), 1151–1158 (2016)

33. Warburton, J., Cowan, S., Bathgate, T.: Building social capital among rural, older Australians through information and communication technologies: a review article. Australas. J. Ageing. **32**(1), 8–14 (2013)

34. Huijboom, N.: Social capital and ICT adoption in the public sector. In: ACM International Conference Proceeding Series, vol. 228, pp. 140–147 (2007)

35. Lee, B.C., Cho, J., Hwang, D.: An integration of social capital and tourism technology adoption—A case of convention and visitors bureaus. Tour. Hosp. Res. **13**(3), 149–165 (2013)

36. Inaba, Y., Togawa, K.: Social capital in the creation of AI perception. Behaviormetrika. **48**(1), 79–102 (2021)

37. Noonpakdee, W.: The adoption of artificial intelligence for financial investment service. In: 2020 22nd International Conference on Advanced Communication Technology (ICACT), pp. 396–400. IEEE (2020)
38. Alanzi, T., Almahdi, R., Alghanim, D., Almusmili, L., Saleh, A., Alanazi, S., et al.: Factors affecting the adoption of artificial intelligence-enabled virtual assistants for leukemia self-management. Cureus. **15**(11) (2023)

Applying Jobs-To-Be-Done Framework to Design AI Applications for Women in Menopause Transition

Jennie Lai[✉] and Ritcha Ranjan

PeriHealth, New York, NY 10024, USA
`jennie@reculturehealth.com`

Abstract. While modest advancements have been made in designing applications for women's healthcare, a structured approach to designing AI applications for women in menopause transition represents a notable gap. This critical life stage impacts over 75 million women in the U.S., yet these women remain underserved by evidence-based research, clinician knowledge, and personalized products. Health disparities across race and ethnicity are also contributing to these challenges. This study uses the Jobs-To-Be-Done (JTBD) framework to better understand the diverse and unique experiences of women in menopause transition with a focus on their functional, emotional, and social contexts. We conducted in-depth interviews with eight participants through purposive sampling from a beta test group. The qualitative research identified a "purpose-driven" segment that is motivated by the functional outcomes of feeling healthy with preference to focus on their health goals rather than perimenopause. These participants demonstrate stronger motivation when their health goals align with emotional and social benefits. The JTBD framework provides an actionable blueprint for designing women-centered AI applications with key considerations on the challenges (trust in AI technology) and benefits (potential to reduce bias) of the use of AI. This approach offers a pathway to design AI applications that help women in menopause transition accomplish their health goals while providing emotional and social support throughout their journey.

Keywords: Jobs-To-Be-Done · Women's Health · Healthcare Technology · Artificial Intelligence · User-Centered Design · Perimenopause

1 Introduction

Approximately 75 million women are experiencing perimenopause, menopause, or post-menopause in the U.S. [1]. Globally, an estimated 1.2 billion women will be experiencing these different menopausal stages by 2030 [2]. This is the most pivotal transition for women given the increased health risks for Alzheimer/dementia, depression/anxiety, heart diseases, and osteoporosis—all known health conditions associated with hormonal changes [3]. The transition to menopause can start as early as women's 30s to their early 50s, and it can last 5–10 years. Yet there are critical gaps in evidence-based research, clinician knowledge, and personalized products to support women on this journey.

© The Author(s), under exclusive license to Springer Nature Switzerland AG 2026
S. Sundarakannan and O. Knorpp (Eds.): HCII 2025, CCIS 2772, pp. 133–142, 2026.
https://doi.org/10.1007/978-3-032-12767-9_15

As critical as these gaps may be, they only reflect the general state of health research on perimenopause and menopause. When examined closely, there are notable differences in these experiences—including perimenopause symptoms that can start as early as age 30, premature menopause before age 40, or early menopause between ages 40–45 [4, 5]. The health disparities are also evident across racial and ethnic groups—Black and Hispanic women tend to experience more severe symptoms and more frequent rates of premature or early menopause than White women in the U.S. [6].

These gaps and disparities are driven by the systematic exclusion of women of color from health research, lack of trained clinicians on menopause, and one-size-fits-all products in the market [7, 8]. This results in inadequate access to perimenopause education that could empower women to take actions on preventive care early. Given the recent National Institute of Health funding cuts to women's health research, it is clear that technology innovation in perimenopause care represents a critical opportunity to bridge these gaps and address the health disparities [9].

Our goal for this paper is to present a structured approach to designing AI applications for women ages 30–49 in menopause transition. It leverages the Jobs-To-Be-Done (JTBD) framework with a focus on the functional, emotional, and social needs of these underserved women. The user insights from this research informed the design of a women-centered AI application that addresses their health goals (related to perimenopause) and desired health outcomes, while providing early validation of product-market fit for distinct user segments.

2 Background

2.1 Current State of Menopause Transition

According to the Menopause Society, perimenopause (also known as menopause transition) is defined as the transition period before natural menopause. Natural menopause marks the permanent end of menstruation and fertility for women [5]. While the average age of natural menopause is 51, a recent study from UVA Health and Flo health app shows 55% of U.S. women ages 30–35 are already experiencing "moderate" or "severe" perimenopause symptoms [4]. The proportion increased to 64% for women ages 36–40. The Menopause Rating Scale (MRS) was used in their study to measure the severity of perimenopause symptoms. Notably, the MRS has also been validated internationally for use in different regions and over time [10].

In addition to the trend of younger women experiencing perimenopause symptoms starting in their 30 s, the experience is also different for women of color. The investigators of the Study of Women's Health Across the Nation (SWAN)—a U.S. longitudinal study on women's health and menopause transition since 1994—found Hispanic and Black women reach menopause earlier and experience perimenopause symptoms longer (i.e., 10 or more years) compared to White women [6]. They also found Asian women (specifically Chinese and Japanese) experience less symptoms compared to Black, Hispanic, and White women [3].

2.2   Perception of AI in Healthcare

When considering the use of artificial intelligence in health and medicine, adults in the U.S. have a mix of positive and negative sentiments. According to the Pew Research Center, 60% of Americans would feel "uncomfortable" if their own health provider used AI to diagnose disease and recommend treatments [11]. However, there are demographic differences for those who would be "comfortable" if their healthcare provider used AI. Men (46%) would feel more comfortable than women (33%). Similarly, Hispanics (43%) would feel more comfortable than Black (38%) and White (37%) adults. Younger adults ages 30–49 (42%) are more open to AI compared to ages 50 or older (35%). Additionally, adults with higher levels of education, income, and knowledge of AI are also more open to the use of AI in healthcare.

On the other hand, over half of Americans (51%) believe the problem with racial and ethnic bias in healthcare would get "better" if AI was used to diagnose disease and recommend treatments for patients. When specifically asked about bias and unfair treatment based on patients' race or ethnicity, about a third of Americans (35%) reported it's a "major" problem. Black adults (64%) were far more likely to report it is a "major" problem compared to Hispanics (42%), Asians (39%), and Whites (27%). Among adults who believe there is a problem, 51% overall think AI would make the issue "better" compared to 40% of Black adults.

While there are promising sentiments that AI could potentially address bias and unfair treatment, there is still a fair amount of skepticism stemming from lack of knowledge of AI or bias in data used by AI. These insights from Pew Research helped inform our research approach and contextualize the similar mix of promise and skepticism shared by the participants in this study. Being transparent about AI's role in healthcare, such as diagnosing diseases and recommending treatments vs. personalizing health information or app experience based on their health data, is critical to help users gain trust in a new product or service.

2.3   Jobs-To-Be-Done (JTBD) Framework

To better understand the diverse and unique experiences of women in menopause transition, we leverage the JTBD framework for product design and research. Clayton Christensen developed the JTBD framework to anchor product innovation on the underlying reasons of why customers want to "hire" a product or service to get a "job" done. It is a "theory that helps innovators understand *how* and *why* people make decisions" [12]. It goes beyond the surface such as demographic characteristics or company attributes, by exploring the functional, emotional, and social context behind customers' hiring decisions for their unmet needs.

To provide more context for each of the three dimensions, we offer an illustrative example to demonstrate the theory to a use case. Christensen's *functional job* focuses on the utilitarian aspect of what the customer wants to accomplish with the product or service. For many women in menopause transition, their top concern or the problem they want to solve is often related to sleep issues. The *emotional job* focuses on the feelings and emotions customers want to experience or avoid while accomplishing the functional job. Women with sleep issues want to improve their sleep quality. Some use wearable devices to track their sleep quality, but a poor sleep score can cause more anxiety than being helpful to them. Lastly, the *social job* focuses on how customers want to be perceived by others such as their family, friends, or co-workers. The lack of sleep may make them feel they are not the optimal version of themselves at home or at work.

The JTBD methodology was used to uncover the full picture of different challenges women are experiencing during their menopause transition. We also identified the common job patterns across specific segments of women to personalize the solution based on their unmet needs and desired outcomes. It is a journey but not the end for these women. Understanding these different contexts—functional, emotional, and social—in addition to openness to AI is critical to develop a solution that will solve their problems and keep them motivated on their health goals throughout the journey.

3 Healthcare Jobs-To-Be-Done (JTBD)

3.1 JTBD Methodology

Following Christensen's JTBD methodology, we set out to uncover the full story of women in menopause transition and common job patterns with specific groups of women. In-depth interviews were conducted with eight participants recruited from a beta test group with PeriHealth for early feedback on product concepts. Participants were recruited through purposive sampling using three criteria: (1) "moderate" or "severe" symptoms using the Menopause Rating Scale, (2) ages 30–54, and (3) different racial and ethnic backgrounds including Asian, Black, Hispanic, and White women. Purposive sampling, a method commonly used in qualitative research, allowed for targeted selection of participants within the constraints of available resources [13].

The one-on-one sessions between the researcher and participant were one hour, semi-structured interviews conducted online using open-ended questions. All interviews were recorded strictly for data analysis purposes with informed consent from participants. The interviews were transcribed using Looppanel and the researcher analyzed the data by assigning tags for "functional", "emotional", "social", etc. to identify the underlying contexts to what participants want to accomplish and the outcomes they expect for measure of success.

The discussion guide was grounded in the principles of JTBD to convey a concise story by framing it in a JTBD statement ("When [situation], I want to [motivation] so I can [expected outcome]"). Each interview was also summarized into these statements to clearly identify the underlying contexts of what they want to accomplish and how/why they want to hire a product or service to accomplish it. While the eight interviews are sufficient to identify common job patterns, the findings by race and ethnicity are not generalizable to the general population. Hence their qualitative feedback is used to contextualize their perception of AI in healthcare in addition to the research from Pew. There is a follow-up plan for larger-scale quantitative segmentation research to validate these findings at scale.

3.2 JTBD Implementation

During the planning phase of this study, we intentionally included women with both menopause and perimenopause status to evaluate their unmet needs and products or services they may use to manage their symptoms. It became clear early on that those in menopause (age 50 or older in our sample) are more *overserved* compared to those in perimenopause when considering the research available about their symptoms, their accessibility to clinicians, and products or services personalized to them. Women with perimenopause status (ages 30–49 in our sample) are far more *underserved* given disproportionately less research published on their symptoms, knowledge gaps of clinicians on perimenopause, and products or services tailored to their experience. In fact, when reviewing the menopause-related published papers on PubMed, ~84% is focused on natural menopause or post-menopause, followed by ~10% on perimenopause, and the rest on early or premature menopause.

Based on the unmet needs and product gaps for those with perimenopause status, the paper will therefore focus on this segment of women ages 30–49. The three outcomes expected from the JTBD research include (1) understanding their specific health concerns and the goals they want to achieve; (2) speaking to the functional outcomes of what achieving their goals mean to them; and (3) speaking to the social and emotional outcomes of how they want to feel or be perceived when they have accomplished their goals.

The JTBD statements help to better understand the specific circumstances of what each participant wants to accomplish while analyzing the common themes. These statements can also help product designers think about these participants as personas—personified representations of real information about the target audience so they can design with real customers in mind [14]. The underlying contexts of the functional, emotional, and social jobs can be translated to product features that will not only help the target segment accomplish their goals in a functional context but also keep them motivated for the long journey.

4 Discussion

4.1 The JTBD Segments

The interviews and analysis helped to uncover common sets of health-related jobs for four distinct segments of women along with other social determinants of health (e.g., economic stability, healthcare access). The "solution-focused" segment is made up of women ages 50 or older and have already taken action on treatment for their more severe menopause symptoms. They are part of the overserved segment with access to healthcare and personalized products or services in the market. Next, the "mindfully-informed" segment is younger than age 50 and they are not yet in perimenopause or in the early stage of perimenopause. Their symptoms are less severe and prefer to avoid information that raises their anxiety or fear. They are also less trustful of AI and rely heavily on healthcare providers for their care plans. The "casually-attentive" segment is a mix of the two aforementioned segments. They are mostly ages 50 or older but not experiencing severe perimenopause symptoms. While they want to know what to expect when fully transitioning to menopause, they tend to be less motivated to learn more on their own.

The fourth segment is known as the "purpose-driven" segment which will be our target segment to focus on for several reasons. They are between the ages 30–49 and motivated by a specific purpose related to their health. They are open to AI in healthcare to learn more about their "moderate" or "severe" perimenopause symptoms and find a care plan that is personalized to them. Yet they are the most underserved compared to the solution-focused segment. For the rest of this paper, we will focus on the key research findings for the "purpose-driven" segment and examples of their jobs (as shown in Table 1).

- **Driven by purpose as their source of motivation.** These participants are motivated by specific health concerns such as Alzheimer's disease in the family that fuels the desire to take action or fertility challenges that can make them feel isolated. The functional outcomes on different aspects of feeling healthy are only one driver of behavioral change. There's also a deeper sense of purpose (i.e., emotional jobs) when their health goals are also aligned with benefits to those who are important to them such as their friends, family, or co-workers (i.e., social jobs).

- **Focus on purpose, not perimenopause.** The topic of perimenopause remains a social stigma for some of the participants in the sample even with their family or friends. The avoidance of the topic is often related to the negative perception of aging and/or a taboo topic that is not discussed in the family or with friends for certain cultures. It is also worth noting that some participants were more engaged with the research topic after reframing the interview on their health goals (during their menopause transition) rather than making their perimenopause experience as the primary topic. The emotional context is important in order to help keep them engaged on their health goals for the long term.

- **Open to AI and technology for healthcare.** We also evaluated these participants' openness to AI and technology for healthcare. Based on both market research from Pew and user research from this study, this segment is more digitally engaged, so they are more likely to use mobile health apps and participate in health discussions. Some participants of Black race and Hispanic ethnicity also noted AI may be more objective or less biased towards their physical characteristics. The concerns on data privacy, security, and potential bias in AI systems are still top of mind for them. Hence trust in AI is a critical area to focus on for product design.

Table 1. Examples of JTBD Statements and Contexts.

Participant	JTBD statement	Underlying contexts
P1 Age 45–49, Perimenopause status	When a close family member was diagnosed with Alzheimer's, I want to stay up-to-date with the latest research on menopause's impact on brain health, so I can consider the right preventive treatments early on.	Functional job: Accessing the most relevant health information related to menopause and Alzheimer's. Emotional job: Feeling empowered to take action on preventing a hereditary disease in the family. Social job: Maintaining an active lifestyle to stay healthy for the family and keeping up a demanding career.
P2 Age 35–39, Perimenopause status	When facing fertility challenges during perimenopause, I want to learn from mothers with similar challenges so I can connect with a community and feel less isolated.	Functional job: Evaluating different fertility options with unexpected challenges of perimenopause. Emotional job: Feeling less lonely during the fertility journey while juggling work and family life. Social job: Connecting with a community of mothers with similar experiences of secondary infertility.

5 Applications for Product Design

The JTBD framework drove three critical decisions for product design. First, the interviews helped us understand *who* is the most underserved so we can prioritize the features based on what's not currently available in the market and fill the unmet needs of women ages 30–49 during their menopause transition. Next, the JTBD statements detailed *what* their functional, emotional, and social jobs these participants wanted to accomplish so we can keep the right personas in mind for product design. Lastly, the different job contexts were adapted to product features on *how* we can meet their needs in a functional way and keep them motivated for the long term through emotional and social support in the app (as shown in Table 2).

We will address the table stakes (i.e., areas we must address) by anchoring on their health goals and expected outcomes in addition to a personalized action plan to help accomplish their goals. As noted by the Christensen Institute on JTBD for healthcare, "only with a clear understanding of where people are coming from and what outcomes they seek can we effectively communicate to change their behavior" [15]. Generative AI can be a tool for behavioral change by leveraging health data (with user consent) and lifestyle patterns to personalize an action plan with real-time recommendations.

Behavioral science will also play a key role in giving users agency (feeling empowered) and nudging them towards their goals along the way.

For areas that are currently underserved, we will add value by making science-backed research accessible and connect users with a community where they can choose to share or learn from. For the first added-value, make research content accessible and actionable with AI in two ways: curate the most relevant information based on their user profile (e.g., age, race/ethnicity, health preferences, etc.) and simplify the content in an easy-to-consume format via text and illustrations. For the second added-value, offer access to a community where they can participate in health discussions by specific topics (e.g., fertility during perimenopause) or self-formed identity groups (e.g., by race or ethnicity). Generative AI can also increase social proof effectiveness by sharing how other users with similar profiles and purposes are achieving their goals (or matching them in a community to learn and share with each other).

Table 2. JTBD Applications for Product Design.

Product features	Functional job [help users…]	Emotional job [help users…]	Social job [help users…]
Health goals & tracking related metrics	Anchor on their health goals rather than their symptoms	Elicit positive emotions on the desired health outcomes	Present a healthy version of themselves to their friends & family
Personalized care plans to achieve health goals	Collect health data to personalize plans and ensure AI transparency	Trust AI recommendations with transparent process	Be informed when communicating with their doctors about their health
Research content both accessible and actionable	Understand how hormonal changes can impact mental & physical health	Access science-backed research most relevant & relatable to them	Learn how women similar to them achieve their health goals
Topic or identity based community for connection	Normalize conversations on perimenopause and aging	Feel less alone for women without an outlet to share their experiences	Participate in a safe & private space for them to share and learn

6 Conclusion

6.1 Limitations

This study recognizes several key limitations when interpreting these findings and implications for AI application design. The small sample size is not generalizable to the broader population of women experiencing perimenopause. There's a potential selection bias of participants recruited from a beta test group already engaged with digital health tools and being open to AI for healthcare. The study also focuses primarily on women experiencing perimenopause in the U.S. which will vary across different countries and healthcare systems. This initial research is the first phase of gathering qualitative data to inform the second phase of quantitative segmentation research and validate the findings at scale. The product expansion plan will include local research using the JTBD framework to compare differences of perimenopause experiences, cultural attitudes toward menopause/aging, and openness to AI/technology for healthcare. Future research will include larger, diverse samples and longitudinal data to validate these preliminary findings.

6.2 Future Implications

For many women ages 30–49, they believe they are too young to be experiencing perimenopause symptoms. Consequently, most of them do not seek treatment for these symptoms until they are well into their 50 s. This delay in getting early screening and/or appropriate treatment increases the risks for bone, brain, cardiovascular, and mental health decline. By understanding the functional, emotional, and social contexts through the JTBD framework in addition to their openness to AI for healthcare, it provides a blueprint on designing an AI application to help women achieve their goals while providing emotional and social support along the way. Beyond the initial design phase, the JTBD framework can continue to inform product design and growth in three ways: (1) broaden product-market fit through local segmentation, (2) develop personas for local markets using the JTBD statements, and (3) prioritize product features based on the different job contexts with cultural considerations and openness to AI.

References

1. Lapp, L., Ruprecht, K., Hsu, A., Jabeen, S., Kazyak, S.: Advancing Menopause Research and Care. American Medical Association Women Physicians Section Resolution (I-24) (2024). https://www.ama-assn.org/system/files/i24-wps-menopause.pdf
2. Hill, K.: The demography of menopause. Maturitas. **23**(2), 113–127 (1996). https://doi.org/10.1016/0378-5122(95)00968-X
3. El Khoudary, S.R., Greendale, G., Crawford, S.L., Avis, N.E., Brooks, M.M., Thurston, R.C., Karvonen-Gutierrez, C., Waetjen, L.E., Matthews, K.: The menopause transition and women's health at midlife: a progress report from the study of women's health across the nation (SWAN). Menopause. **26**(10), 1213–1227 (2019). https://doi.org/10.1097/GME.0000000000001424
4. Cunningham, A.C., Hewings-Martin, Y., Wickham, A.P., Prentice, C., Payne, J.L., Zhaunova, L.: Perimenopause symptoms, severity, and healthcare seeking in women in the US. NPJ Womens Health. **3**, art. 12 (2025). https://doi.org/10.1038/s44294-025-00061-3
5. Perimenopause. The Menopause Society. https://menopause.org/patient-education/menopause-topics/perimenopause. Accessed May 31, 2025
6. Harlow, S.D., Burnett-Bowie, S.A.M., Greendale, G.A., et al.: Disparities in reproductive aging and midlife health between black and white women: the study of women's health across the nation (SWAN). Womens Midlife Health. **8**, art. 3 (2022). https://doi.org/10.1186/s40695-022-00073-y

7. Reeves, A., Elliott, M.R., Karvonen-Gutierrez, C.A., Harlow, S.D.: Systematic exclusion at study commencement masks earlier menopause for black women in the study of women's health across the nation (SWAN). Int. J. Epidemiol. **52**(5), 1612–1623 (2023). https://doi.org/10.1093/ije/dyad085

8. Carter, B.: Women in Menopause Often Go Untreated. AARP Public Policy Institute Spotlight (2025). https://doi.org/10.26419/ppi.00362.001

9. Menopause Research is Globally Underfunded: It's time to change that. Nat. Editor. **627** (2025). https://doi.org/10.1038/d41586-025-00150-y

10. Heinemann, K., Ruebig, A., Potthoff, P., Schneider, H.P., Strelow, F., Heinemann, L.A., Do, M.T.: The menopause rating scale (MRS) scale: a methodological review. Health Qual. Life Outcomes. **2**, art. 45 (2004). https://doi.org/10.1186/1477-7525-2-45

11. Pew Research Center: 60% of Americans Would Be Uncomfortable With Provider Relying on AI in Their Own Health Care. (Feb. 22, 2023). https://www.pewresearch.org/science/2023/02/22/60-of-americans-would-be-uncomfortable-with-provider-relying-on-ai-in-their-own-health-care/. Accessed May 31, 2025

12. Christensen Institute: Jobs to Be Done Theory. https://www.christenseninstitute.org/theory/jobs-to-be-done/. Accessed May 31, 2025

13. Palinkas, L.A., Horwitz, S.M., Green, C.A., Wisdom, J.P., Duan, N., Hoagwood, K.: Purposeful sampling for qualitative data collection and analysis in mixed method implementation research. Adm. Policy Ment. Health Ment. Health Serv. Res. **42**(5), 533–544 (2015). https://doi.org/10.1007/s10488-013-0528-y

14. Nielsen Norman Group: Personas: Study Guide. https://www.nngroup.com/articles/personas-study-guide/. Accessed May 31, 2025

15. Behavior change is impossible if you don't understand the Job to Be Done. Christensen Institute Blog. https://www.christenseninstitute.org/blog/behavior-change-is-impossible-if-you-dont-understand-the-job-to-be-done/. Accessed May 31, 2025

Harnessing Image to Text Models for Clinical Case Report Generation

Sabah Mohammed$^{(\boxtimes)}$ (iD) and Jinan Fiaidhi (iD)

Lakehead University, Thunder Bay, ON P7B 5E1, Canada
{mohammed,jfiaidhi}@lakeheadu.ca

Abstract. The advancement in generative artificial intelligence (GenAI) in medicine, involving the use of multimodal AI models (narratives to text and image to text) and workflow tools play a crucial role in assisting clinicians towards understanding health trends, answering clinical questions, personalizing treatment, and compiling medical case reports. These advancements are only possible due to the development in several technical areas like meta-transformers, large-scale medical datasets, image captioning, optical character recognition and new loss functions. The rapid demand for these GenAI is due to clinician burnout, growing interlinked medical knowledge, staff shortages and an aging population. However, the current content management for clinical case report generation often lacks built-in tools for generating detailed image descriptions and relevant hash tags, leading to time-consuming manual work and potential inconsistencies. This short paper investigates the effectiveness of learning from two fine-tuned clinical vision-language models (BLIP-2 and Florence-2) for grounding textual descriptions to image regions that can contribute to compiling a clinical case report. Our investigation to learn from these two models is based on a popular Roco-2 Image and Text medical dataset. Our comparison shows the superiority of Florence-2 over BLIP-2

Keywords: Image-to-Text Models · Multimodal Transformers · BLIP2 · Florence-2

1 Introduction

Clinical practitioners often need to compile a case report to provide quality care planning based on the best available evidence from sound medical literature or clinical trials. Usually such report describes a novel clinical occurrence and it contains an extensive review of the relevant literature on the topic. The case report is a rapid short communication between busy clinicians who may not have time or resources to conduct large scale research [1]. However, the growing number of medical publications, clinical training datasets and clinical trials are sharply increasing which makes it extremely difficult to stay updated [2]. The best available practice of collecting clinical evidences is to present clinical questions around the clinical case that requires answers and imaging interpretations. Usually clinicians tend to use the PICO format for synthesizing their clinical

© The Author(s), under exclusive license to Springer Nature Switzerland AG 2026
S. Sundarakannan and O. Knorpp (Eds.): HCII 2025, CCIS 2772, pp. 143–147, 2026.
https://doi.org/10.1007/978-3-032-12767-9_16

questions [3] and later to conduct web literature search from medical sound repositories like PubMed or WebMD and go through the medical materials including images and try summarizing their finding before compiling the final case report [4]. However, this manual process of compiling a clinical case report is time consuming requires specific filtering skills and resources to manage the retrieved information [5]. Skilled physicians may use assistive question answering applications like AskHERMES [6], MiPACQ [7], MEANS [8], MedQA[9] or HONqa [10] to shorten the searching and filtering time, however, these applications hide the details of finding the clinical answers as well as their tested reliability is not acceptable in many cases according to notable scholars [11, 12]. A promising knowledge acquisition solution, however, emerged from research areas like Question Answering (Q&A), Image-to-Text models, Text Summarization and Generative AI (GenAI) based on transformers which can automatically identify relevant clinical articles or trials based on clinical description and their associated PICO questions [13]. The reported success of Q&A techniques in answering some focused clinical questions based on training information scrapped from the web from sites like WebMD, HealthTap, eHealthForums, patientslikeme, PubMed, Medical Encyclopedia and iCliniq encouraged researchers to investigate using this new artificial intelligence Q&A technique for providing more evidence-based clinical answers [14].

In this short paper, we are reporting an investigation into using two different deep learning technologies to answer PICO question related to medical images from sound medical repositories like PubMed containing variety of medical images as well their captions and sound medical imaging and their description using the Roco-2 dataset [15]. The first investigated technology utilizes the BLIP-2 to provide answers to given PICO questions [16] and the second technology utilizes the Florence-2 technology [17] for Q&A automatic image interpretation. Figure 1 illustrates the framework used in our investigation.

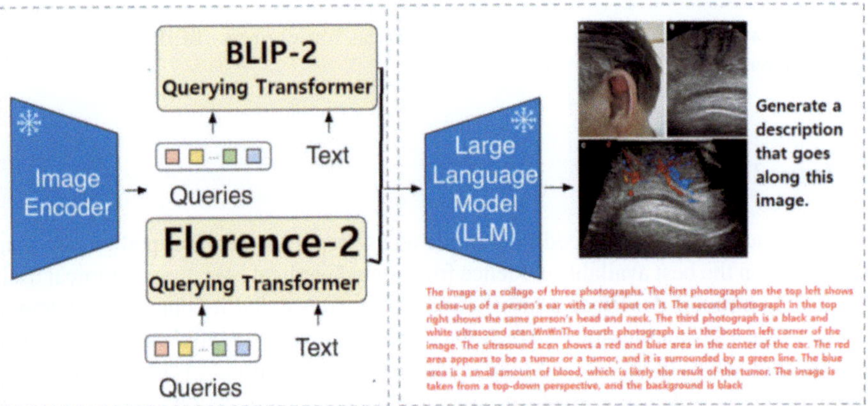

Fig. 1. The Framework of Using Two Grounding Image-to-Text Models in Medical Report Generation.

2   Blip-2 Versus Florance-2 Clinical Image Interpretation

These two models are characterized by their massive parameter scales and advanced architectures, exhibit remarkable performance vision to text interpretation. BLIP-2 can flexibly switch between visual-language understanding tasks and generation tasks, and effectively utilize noisy data through bootstrapping. However, Florence-2 follows in the footsteps of LLMs, leveraging a unified architecture and simple training paradigm paired with a vast amount of data to become competent at many different tasks. Florence-2 can be considered a sort of GPT-V4 - being able to perform tasks like:

- Captioning
- Optical Character Recognition
- Object Detection
- Region Detection
- Region Segmentation
- Vocabulary Segmentation

and more with one set of weights and no architectural modifications by providing special task tokens to the model at inference. With the image-text pairs of the ROCO-2 dataset at hands, for each model, we calculated the list of image, text and multimodal vector embeddings. In this direction we focused on a subset from Rocov2 called MURA [18] that contains only 100 images (see Table 1) distributed on the following modalities:

Table 1. The Mura Subset from ROCOv2.

CT		40
	Abdomen and pelvis	15
	Chest	14
	Brain	10
	Spine	1
MRI		31
	Brain	15
	Spine	16
X-ray		29
	Chest	10
	Abdomen	3
	Skeletal	16

Our comparison between the BLIP-2 and Folrence-2 is based on the traditional metrics (BLEU, ROUGE, and METEOR [19]) used to compare the ground truth images captions and the generated captions form each of the models using the Mura dataset.

Table 2 illustrates our comparison between the two models based on their performance in different image contexts (Abdomen, Chest, Brain and Spine). The Florence 2 model exhibited better performance across all NLG metrics. For example the Florence 2 model achieved the highest METEOR scores in all the context images.

Table 2. Comparing BLIP2 and Florence2 using Caption Performance Metrics.

Model		BLEU_1	BLEU_2	BLEU_3	BLEU_4	ROUGE	METEOR
BLIP2	Abdomen	0.164	0.048	0.015	**0.003**	0.171
	Chest	0.099	0.016	0.004	0.000	0.103
	Brain	0.057	0.007	0.002	0.000	0.057
	Spine	0.022	0.002	0.000	0.000	0.029
Florence2	Abdomen	0.169	0.037	0.007	0.000	**0.180**
	Chest	0.116	0.025	0.006	0.000	**0.137**
	Brain	0.061	0.014	0.004	0.001	**0.085**
	Spine	0.025	0.005	0.001	0.000	**0.045**

3   Conclusions

In this short paper, we compared the performance of generating meaningful description to provided medical images using two models (BLIP2 and Florence2). The heat map of the correlation among the various caption scoring for the two models is shown in Fig. 2. The color intensity indicates the strength of correlation, with darker shades representing higher correlation which means Florence2 have better performance in providing descriptions to given medical images.

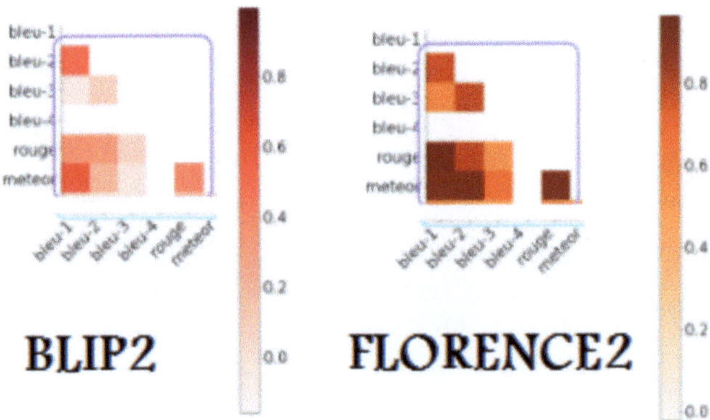

Fig. 2. Heat map for Comparing the Performance of BLIP2 with Florence 2 Models.

We are continuing our research into testing these models and others for clinical case report generations. Our first steps in implementing our comparison method can be found in our Github Week 12 and 13 (https://github.com/TennoSerra/QL4POMR/tree/main).

References

1. Riley, D.S., Barber, M.S., Kienle, G.S., Aronson, J.K., von Schoen-Angerer, T., Tugwell, P., Kiene, H., et al.: CARE guidelines for case reports: explanation and elaboration document. J. Clin. Epidemiol. **89**, 218–235 (2017)
2. Bastian, H., Glasziou, P., Chalmers, I.: Seventy-five trials and eleven systematic reviews a day: how will we ever keep up? PLoS Med. **7**(9), e1000326 (2010)
3. Leonardo, R.: PICO: model for clinical questions. Evid. Based Med. Pract. **3**(115), 2 (2018)
4. Lacasse, M., Lafortune, V., Bartlett, L., Guimond, J.: Answering clinical questions: what is the best way to search the web? Can. Fam. Phys. **53**(9), 1535–1536 (2007)
5. EbEll, M.H.: How to find answers to clinical questions. Am. Fam. Physician. **79**(4), 293–296 (2009)
6. Cao, Y., Liu, F., Simpson, P., et al.: AskHERMES: an online question answering system for complex clinical questions. J. Biomed. Inform. **44**(2), 277–288 (2011)
7. Cairns, B.L., Nielsen, R.D., Masanz, J.J., et al.: The MiPACQ clinical question answering system. AMIA Annu. Symp. Proc. **2011**, 171–180 (2011)
8. Abacha, A.B., Zweigenbaum, P.: MEANS: a medical question-answering system combining NLP techniques and semantic web technologies. Inform. Process. Manag. **51**(5), 570–594 (2015)
9. Zhang, X., Wu, J., He, Z., Liu, X., Su, Y.: Medical exam question answering with large-scale reading comprehension. Proc. AAAI Conf. Artif. Intell. **32**(1) (2018)
10. Wong, W., Thangarajah, J., Lin, P.: Health conversational system based on contextual matching of community-driven question-answer pairs. In: Proceedings of the 20th ACM International Conference on Information and Knowledge Management, pp. 2577–2580 (2011)
11. Schwartz, D.G., Abbas, J., Krause, R., Moscati, R., Halpern, S.: Are internet searches a reliable source of information for answering residents' clinical questions in the emergency room. In: Proceedings of the 1st ACM International Health Informatics Symposium, pp. 391–394 (2010)
12. Ni, Y., Zhu, H., Cai, P., Zhang, L., Qui, Z., Cao, F.: CliniQA: highly reliable clinical question answering system. In: Quality of Life through Quality of Information, pp. 215–219. IOS Press (2012)
13. Stylianou, N., Vlahavas, I.: Transformed: end-to-end transformers for evidence-based medicine and argument mining in medical literature. J. Biomed. Inform. **117**, 103767 (2021)
14. Faris, H., Habib, M., Faris, M., Alomari, A., Castillo, P.A., Alomari, M.: Classification of Arabic healthcare questions based on word embeddings learned from massive consultations: a deep learning approach. J. Ambient Intell. Humaniz. Comput., 1–17 (2022)
15. Rückert, J., Bloch, L., Brüngel, R., Idrissi-Yaghir, A., Schäfer, H., Schmidt, C.S., Koitka, S., et al.: Rocov2: radiology objects in context version 2, an updated multimodal image dataset. Sci. Data. **11**(1), 688 (2024)
16. Li, J., Li, D., Savarese, S., Hoi, S.: Blip-2: bootstrapping language-image pre-training with frozen image encoders and large language models. In: International Conference on Machine Learning, pp. 19730–19742. PMLR (2023)
17. Xiao, B., Wu, H., Xu, W., Dai, X., Hu, H., Lu, Y., Zeng, M., Liu, C., Lu, Y.: Florence-2: Advancing a unified representation for a variety of vision tasks. In: Proceedings of the IEEE/CVF Conference on Computer Vision and Pattern Recognition, pp. 4818–4829 (2024)
18. Rajpurkar, P., Irvin, J., Bagul, A., Ding, D., Duan, T., Mehta, H., Yang, B., et al.: Mura: large dataset for abnormality detection in musculoskeletal radiographs. arXiv preprint arXiv:1712.06957. (2017)
19. Chatoui, H., Ata, O.: Automated evaluation of the virtual assistant in Bleu and Rouge scores. In: 2021 3rd International Congress on Human-Computer Interaction, Optimization and Robotic Applications (HORA), pp. 1–6. IEEE (2021)

LLM-Powered Interpretable 3D Gait Visualization and Analysis Platform for Interdisciplinary AI Applications

Haocong Rao[1], Jiachen Zhao[2], and Chunyan Miao[1,2]($\boxtimes$)

[1] College of Computing and Data Science, Nanyang Technological University, 50 Nanyang Ave, Singapore 639798, Singapore
`{haocong001,ascymiao}@ntu.edu.sg`
[2] Joint NTU-WeBank Research Centre on Fintech, Nanyang Technological University, 50 Nanyang Ave, Singapore 639798, Singapore

Abstract. 3D skeleton based gait representations have been widely applied to various areas with many advantages, while most existing models lack the ability to provide intuitive or human-understandable explanations for the effectiveness of learned representations. In this work, we propose a general 3D skeleton based Gait Visualization and Analysis (3DGVA) platform, which can not only *interactively* present unified skeleton-based gait patterns but also provide the visualization of feature-based gait ranking for qualitative evaluation. Moreover, 3DGVA synergizes large language models (LLMs) to perform automatic gait analysis to facilitate users' model assessment with explainable reasoning. Our 3DGVA platform is able to visualize and analyze different state-of-the-art skeleton-based models for person re-identification, gait score prediction, disease prediction tasks, and can be potentially extended to more related interdisciplinary applications.

Keywords: Gait Visualization · 3D Skeletons · LLM · Person Re-Identification · Gait Score Prediction · Disease Prediction · Interdisciplinary AI

1 Introduction

Human gait is one of the most significant motor symptoms in sports science, pathology, and biometrics, which has been extensively studied and utilized in interdisciplinary AI applications, ranging from gait-based identity prediction to disease diagnosis [1–3]. The recent advancement of economical, non-obtrusive, and accurate skeleton-tracking devices such as Kinect [4] has established 3D skeleton data a common and adaptable data modality for various gait-related applications [5,6]. Compared with traditional methods that rely on appearances or foot force signals (*e.g.*, ground reaction force) to capture gait, 3D skeletons

---

H. Rao and J. Zhao—The two authors contribute equally

© The Author(s), under exclusive license to Springer Nature Switzerland AG 2026
S. Sundarakannan and O. Knorpp (Eds.): HCII 2025, CCIS 2772, pp. 148–158, 2026.
https://doi.org/10.1007/978-3-032-12767-9_17

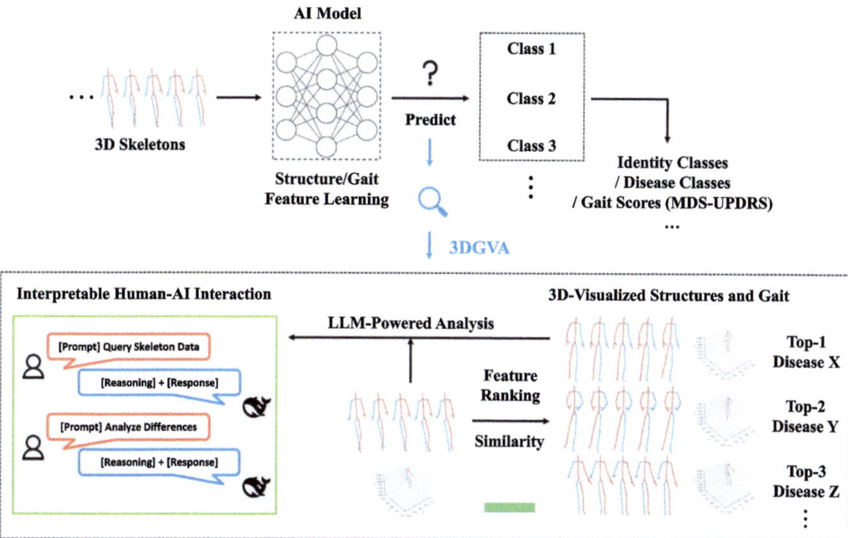

Fig. 1. Schematic diagram of skeleton-based AI models (top) and 3DGVA platform (bottom): First, the AI model exploits 3D skeletons to learn body structure and gait features for different prediction tasks. Then, the 3DGVA platform visualizes 3D skeletal structures and gait patterns of both query (probe) and gallery skeleton samples, with a similarity ranking of feature representations learned by the AI model. It provides an interactive and user-friendly interface, supporting varying class types, trained models, sequence lengths, and probe selection (illustrated in Fig 2 and 3). The state-of-the-art LLMs, including DeepSeek-R1 with transparent reasoning, are integrated into 3DGVA to support both data query and interpretable analysis of key differences between skeleton sequences.

can model human body structure, poses, and gait patterns simultaneously using *only* 3D positions of numerous key body joints, which enjoy many unique merits such as small data size, enhanced privacy safeguard (*e.g.*, without using appearances), and good robustness against view variations [7]. They can not only offer detailed spatial 3D coordinates and their temporal dynamics for statistical gait analysis, but also enable intuitive body representations (*e.g.*, pose visualization) that reveal variations in gait [3].

Despite the success of existing skeleton-based models in interdisciplinary AI applications such as identity, gait score or disease prediction (see Table 2, 3, 4 and 5), they typically cannot provide either intuitive (*e.g.*, interactive) visualization for gait analysis, or human-friendly explanations that allow users to evaluate the effectiveness of the models. This opacity in the models may increase the risk of incorrect predictions and hinder their large-scale adoption. To address these challenges, we propose a general **3D** skeleton based **G**ait **V**isualization and **A**nalysis (3DGVA) platform[1] (illustrated in Fig. 1) that supports different models to **(1)**

---

[1] A video demo of 3DVGA platform is available here.

Interactively visualize static body structure (referred to as *"sequential structure"*) and dynamic walking poses (referred to as *"gait patterns"*) for comprehensive gait assessment (see Fig. 3); **(2)** Rank skeletons in the database (denoted as "gallery") based on *model-specific* feature distance between them and query (denoted as "probe") skeletons to show the top predictions for qualitative correctness evaluation (see Fig. 4); **(3)** Leverage a large language model (LLM) to automatically analyze key similarities and differences between different skeleton sequences to facilitate users' examination in an explainable manner (see Fig. 5). Furthermore, we provide the 3DGVA workflow (shown in Fig. 2) with visualization examples (see Fig. 3, 4, and 5) and a video demo to assist users in operating the platform, and supplement quantitative evaluation results of interdisciplinary skeleton-based applications, including person re-identification (re-ID), gait score prediction, and gait-based disease prediction, to facilitate comprehensive model comparison.

The 3DGVA platform provides key benefits in efficiency, scalability, security (privacy), and interpretability: It employs 3D skeletons to efficiently model human gait while avoiding the use of appearance or facial data that disclose identities, and it supports flexible integration of new trained models for diverse interdisciplinary gait-related tasks. The integration of DeepSeek-R1 and other LLMs into 3DGVA enables automatic and interpretable 3D skeletal gait analysis with a transparent reasoning process, *i.e.*, revealing how AI thinks and why it gives such solution step by step. We also envision the potential application of interpretable 3DGVA in broader interdisciplinary fields, such as explainable medical gait analysis, and hope this platform can bring new insights to researchers across disciplines as well as expedite future skeleton-based research.

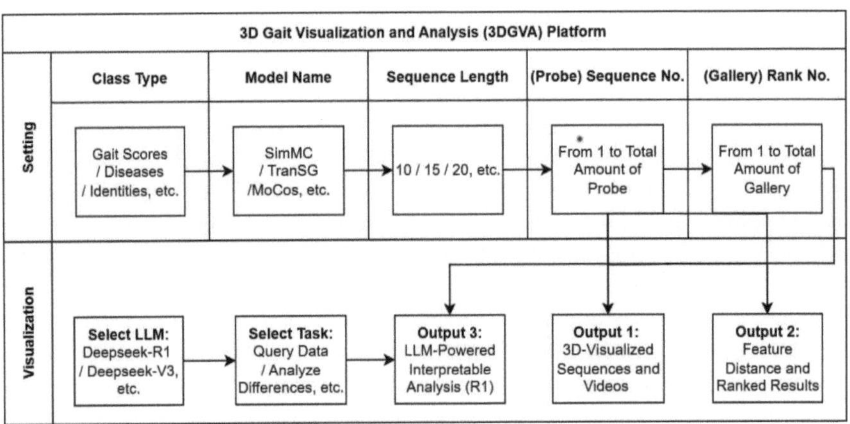

Fig. 2. Workflow of 3DGVA platform with different settings of class types, model names, sequence lengths, probe sequence numbers, gallery rank numbers, and LLMs used for data query and difference analysis.

2   Related Works

3D skeleton data have been extensively applied to learning spatial-temporal human gait features for person re-ID [8]. Early methods manually extract 3D skeleton features from anthropometric and gait aspects to depict human body and motion patterns [9,10]. Most recent mainstream methods leverage deep neural networks to perform automatic skeleton representation learning [5,6,11–16]. For example, [11] utilize an encoder-decoder model with attention mechanisms (AGE) to encode skeleton-based gait patterns, while its extension SGELA [6] further enhances skeleton semantic learning with diverse skeletal pretext tasks and inter-sequence contrastive mechanisms for the person re-ID task. In [15], a skeleton graph transformer is devised to learn both skeleton and sequential graph features for person re-ID. Despite their success, they rely on massive weight parameters to learn numerical features, and typically cannot provide intuitive visualization for gait analysis, or human-friendly explanations that allow users to evaluate the effectiveness of the models.

In the interdisciplinary areas such as disease diagnosis and emotion recognition, skeleton-based deep learning models have also been explored to assess disease risk (*e.g.*, probability) while protecting privacy without using appearance features [3,17,18]. However, although a few advanced models like LLMs are utilized for multi-modal analysis and interaction [19], most existing skeleton-based models lack the ability to intuitively interpret 3D skeleton sequences, their gait patterns and effectiveness, which might increase the risk of incorrect predictions and hinder their large-scale adoption in high-stake fields. Hence, we devise a general 3D skeleton based gait visualization and analysis (3DGVA) platform to help users verify the effectiveness of different models by intuitively and interactively presenting, ranking, and analyzing the gait patterns based on skeleton sequences.

3   Method

3.1   Unified Gait Representation and Visualization

To accommodate models across different application scenarios, we adopt *3D skeleton sequences* that can demonstrate body structure and motion patterns as the unified gait representation. Formally, we denote a 3D skeleton sequence as $\boldsymbol{S} = (\boldsymbol{s}_1, \cdots, \boldsymbol{s}_f) \in \mathbb{R}^{f \times J \times 3}$, where f is the number of skeletons in the sequence and $\boldsymbol{s}_i \in \mathbb{R}^{J \times 3}$ represents the ith skeleton with 3D coordinates of J body joints. Each sequence $\boldsymbol{S}$ belongs to a class label $y \in \{1, \cdots, L\}$ and L is the number of different class labels corresponding to a downstream task. For example, the labels are different identity classes for person re-ID tasks, while the labels are different disease categories for disease diagnosis tasks. In skeleton-based tasks, the training set, probe set, and gallery set are defined as $\Phi_{\mathrm{T}} = \left\{ \boldsymbol{S}_i^{\mathrm{T}} \right\}_{i=1}^{n_1}$, $\Phi_{\mathrm{P}} = \left\{ \boldsymbol{S}_i^{\mathrm{P}} \right\}_{i=1}^{n_2}$, and $\Phi_{\mathrm{G}} = \left\{ \boldsymbol{S}_i^{\mathrm{G}} \right\}_{i=1}^{n_3}$, which respectively contain n_1, n_2, and n_3 skeleton sequences of different classes collected from different scenes or views. The model (denoted

Table 1. Prompt templates to instruct LLMs for skeleton data query as well as automatic gait analysis in terms of similarities and differences. $< \cdot >$ denotes placeholders for pre-defined variables or related mathematical operations.

Query Skeleton Data

Q: Give data of two normalized sequences of 3D skeletons with <J > joints' 3D positions, please answer user's questions based on them.

I will first introduce the indices are:

<joint-0 name > 0, <joint-1 name > 1, ... <joint-J name > <J > .

The First Sequence: $< \boldsymbol{S}_i^{\mathrm{P}} >$

The Second Sequence: $< \boldsymbol{S}_k^{\mathrm{G}} >$

The first sequence is the $< i >$ -th sequence of the probe set and the second sequence is its rank-$< k >$ -th most similar sequence in the gallery set.

Please answer questions based on them and user's query.

A: ......

Analyze Differences

Q: Give statistical data (mean, min, max, median, standard deviation, variance) of two normalized sequences of 3D skeletons with 25 joints' 3D positions, please compare them and analyze. I will first introduce the indices are:

$< \text{joint-0 name} > 0, < \text{joint-1 name} > 1, ... < \text{joint-J name} > < J >$

The First Sequence:

Mean: $< \mathrm{Mean}(\boldsymbol{S}_i^{\mathrm{P}}) >$

Max: $< \mathrm{Max}(\boldsymbol{S}_i^{\mathrm{P}}) >$

Min: $< \mathrm{Min}(\boldsymbol{S}_i^{\mathrm{P}}) >$

Median: $< \mathrm{Median}(\boldsymbol{S}_i^{\mathrm{P}}) >$

Standard Deviation: $< \mathrm{Std}(\boldsymbol{S}_i^{\mathrm{P}}) >$

Variance: $< \mathrm{Var}(\boldsymbol{S}_i^{\mathrm{P}}) >$

The Second Sequence:

Mean: $< \mathrm{Mean}(\boldsymbol{S}_k^{\mathrm{G}}) >$

Max: $< \mathrm{Max}(\boldsymbol{S}_k^{\mathrm{G}}) >$

Min: $< \mathrm{Min}(\boldsymbol{S}_k^{\mathrm{G}}) >$

Median: $< \mathrm{Median}(\boldsymbol{S}_k^{\mathrm{G}}) >$

Standard Deviation: $< \mathrm{Std}(\boldsymbol{S}_k^{\mathrm{G}}) >$

Variance: $< \mathrm{Var}(\boldsymbol{S}_k^{\mathrm{G}}) >$

Please shortly summarize the key similarity and difference between these two sequences in terms of $< J >$ joints.

A: ......

---

as function $f(\cdot)$) target is to encode skeleton sequences into effective latent representations: $f(\boldsymbol{S}_i) = \boldsymbol{V}_i$, where $\boldsymbol{V}_i \in \mathbb{R}^H$ and H is the dimension of features, so that we can query the correct class of each skeleton sequence representation (denoted as $\{\boldsymbol{V}_i^{\mathrm{P}}\}_{i=1}^{n_2}$) in the probe set via matching it with the sequence representations (denoted as $\{\boldsymbol{V}_i^{\mathrm{G}}\}_{i=1}^{n_3}$) in the gallery set.

The developed 3DGVA platform provides a unified, interactive, and user-friendly interface for different learned models (Note that 3DGVA is designed for visualizing results of trained models without need for training or fine-tuning). As shown in Fig. 3, it can present corresponding 3D skeleton sequences $\boldsymbol{S}$ to assess their 3D sequential structure and gait patterns, and can function with varying class types (*i.e.*, different L), trained models (*i.e.*, different $f(\cdot)$) or sequence lengths f, allowing users to select arbitrary probe sequences in $\varPhi_{\mathrm{T}}$ and their ranked matching results within gallery $\varPhi_{\mathrm{G}}$ (detailed in Fig 2).

3.2   Visualization of Ranking

As the effectiveness of a skeleton-based model can be evaluated through its quality to rank the query (*i.e.*, probe) sequence for correctly matching the gallery sequence label, we propose to visualize the top ranking results of a model based on learned features, so as to conduct similarity comparison and analyze the effects of true and false positive samples on model performance. We integrate different state-of-the-art skeleton-based AI models (*e.g.*, MoCos [20]) trained

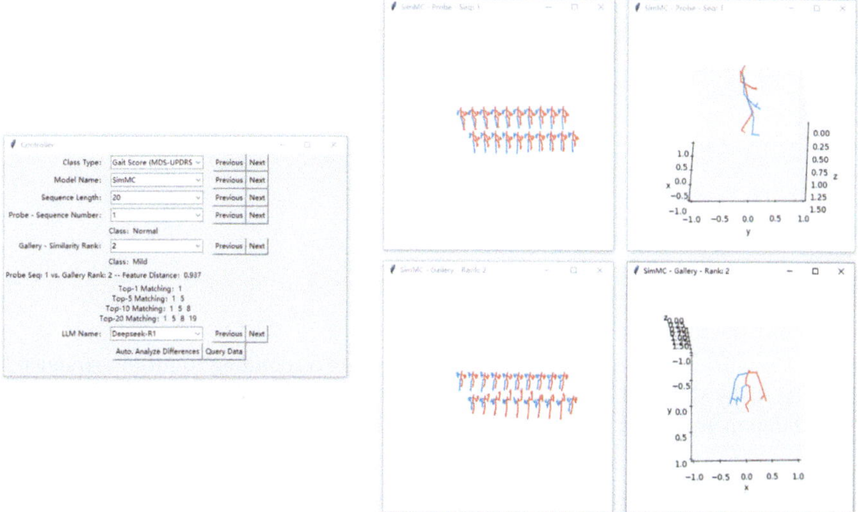

Fig. 3. An example (rotated view) of 3DGVA platform that visualizes 3D skeletal structures and gait patterns of the 1st sequence in the probe and its rank-2 similar sequence in the gallery.

for varying tasks, including gait score prediction, disease prediction, and identity prediction, into the proposed 3DGVA platform. Specifically, we rank the gait representations of 3D skeleton sequences in the gallery Φ_G using the same evaluation protocol of dowsnstream tasks (*i.e.*, based on the similarity between their features $\{V_i^G\}_{i=1}^{n_3}$ and the feature V_i^P of the query skeleton sequence in Φ_P), and provide the corresponding visualization of most likely prediction and its close results. In this way, 3DGVA help users explore the most distinct gait patterns related to true positive prediction via interactive visualization, while assisting in discovering the easily-confused skeleton sequences and gait patterns from the false positive samples.

3.3   LLMs for Automatic Gait Analysis

To enable automatic and explainable analysis of 3D skeletal gait, we incorporate state-of-the-art LLMs (*e.g.*, DeepSeek-R1 [21]) into the 3DGVA platform to achieve interpretable human-AI interaction. As shown in Table 1, we devise prompts based on statistical properties (*e.g.*, raw data, variance) of skeleton sequences, where we perform the operations Mean(S), Max(S), Min(S), Median(S), Std(S), Var(S) $\in \mathbb{R}^{J \times 3}$ to compute the mean value, maximum value, minimum value, median value, standard variation, and variance of the input skeleton sequence S over the temporal dimension. Then, we instruct the LLMs to summarize the key similarity and difference between the query sequence (*i.e.*, i^{th} probe sequence S_i^P) and the rank-k most similar sequence in the gallery

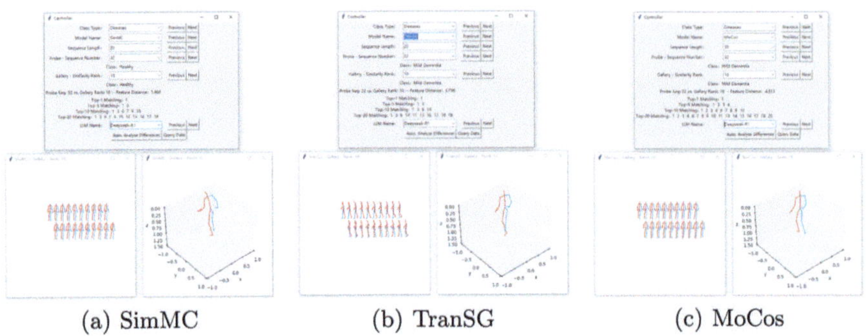

(a) SimMC   (b) TranSG   (c) MoCos

Fig. 4. Visualization of rank-10 gallery sequence (corresponding to probe sequence No. 32) inferred by different state-of-the-art models (SimMC [14]), TranSG [15], MoCos [20]). Different matching results are shown in the platform interface.

set (denoted as S_k^G for convenience), so as to help users automatically analyze the most common and distinct gait patterns in these sequences.

The proposed 3DGVA offers not only real-time responses to users' query about skeleton data but also detailed *reasoning* about the key differences between probe and gallery skeleton sequences (see Fig. 5), so as to facilitate in-depth assessment of model effectiveness and reliability. 3DGVA can be flexibly extended with different instruction and prompt templates to support more diverse tasks.

Table 2. Quantitative evaluation results of different skeleton-based AI models for the application of person re-ID on two benchmarks (KS20 [22] and KGBD [9]). R1, R5, R10, mAP denote Rank-1 accuracy, Rank-5, Rank-10, and mean average precision respectively.

Task	Method	R1	R5	R10	mAP
20-Class	SimMC [14]	66.4	80.7	87.0	22.3
Identity	TranSG [15]	73.6	86.3	90.2	46.2
Prediction (KS20)	MoCos [20]	76.0	87.1	90.2	50.8
164-Class	SimMC [14]	54.9	66.2	70.6	11.7
Identity	TranSG [15]	59.0	73.1	78.2	20.2
Prediction (KGBD)	MoCos [20]	62.0	75.2	79.6	26.1

4   Results

As shown in Table 2, 3, 4, and 5, we evaluate different state-of-the-art skeleton-based models, including SimMC [14], TranSG [15], MoCos [20], on person re-ID,

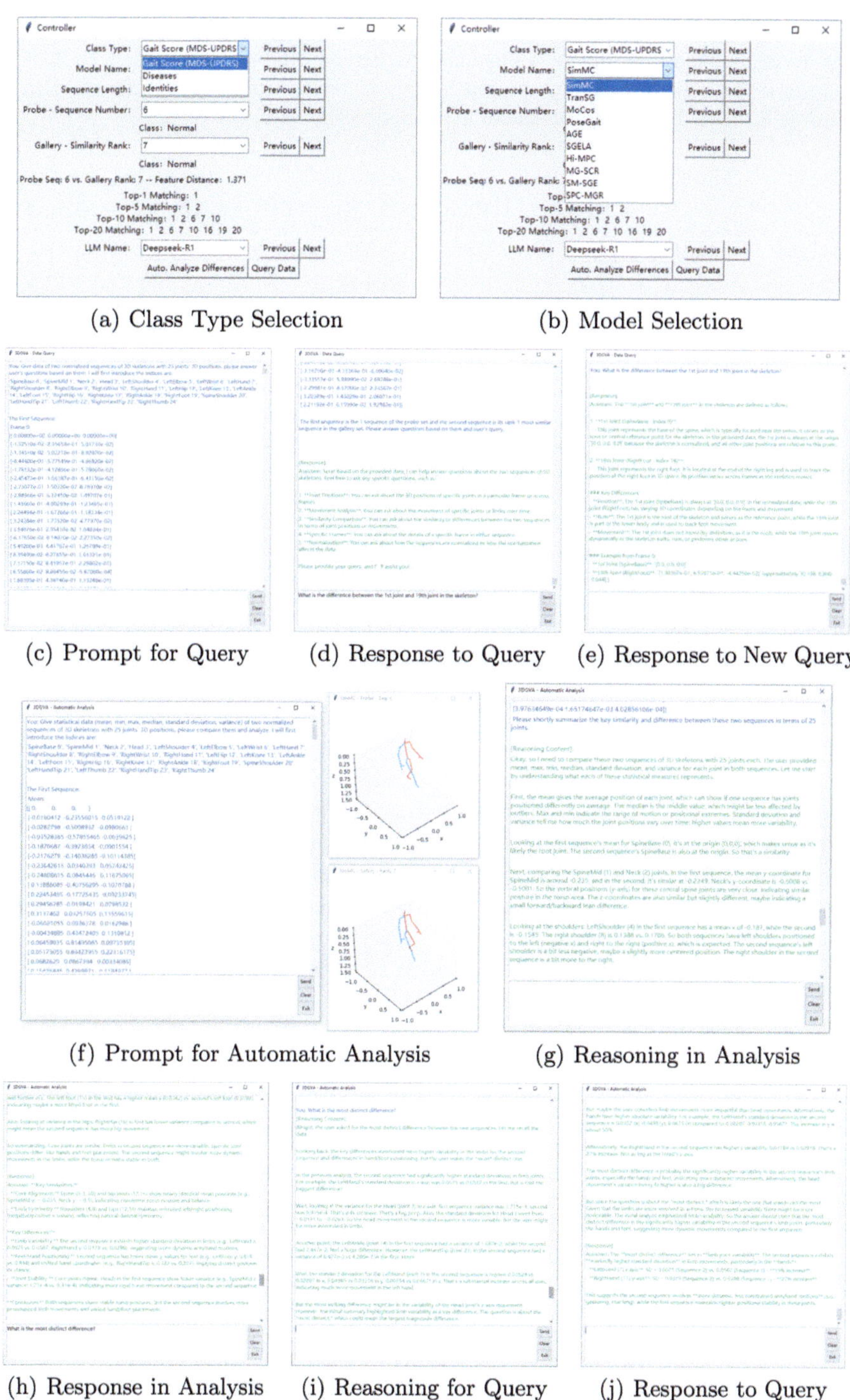

(a) Class Type Selection

(b) Model Selection

(c) Prompt for Query

(d) Response to Query

(e) Response to New Query

(f) Prompt for Automatic Analysis

(g) Reasoning in Analysis

(h) Response in Analysis

(i) Reasoning for Query

(j) Response to Query

Fig. 5. Examples for class and model settings ((a)-(b)), "Query Data" ((c)-(e)), "Automatically Analyze Differences" ((f)-(j)) in the 3DGVA platform.

Table 3. Quantitative evaluation results of different skeleton-based AI models for the application of 3-class (Healthy, Dementia, Alzheimer) disease prediction on 3DGait benchmark [17] with different sequence length f. R1, R5, R10, mAP denote Rank-1 accuracy, Rank-5, Rank-10, and mean average precision respectively.

Task	Method	$f = 20$				$f = 15$				$f = 10$			
		R1	R5	R10	mAP	R1	R5	R10	mAP	R1	R5	R10	mAP
3-Class	SimMC [14]	60.2	73.4	78.9	55.3	39.0	69.9	84.8	44.2	45.3	68.4	77.3	41.9
Disease	TranSG [15]	62.5	71.9	72.7	54.5	46.1	72.7	87.9	45.3	49.7	69.9	82.4	42.4
Prediction	MoCos [20]	62.5	75.0	75.8	56.7	57.8	76.6	85.2	46.7	53.1	78.5	86.7	42.6

Table 4. Quantitative evaluation results of different skeleton-based AI models for the application of 5-class (Normal, Slight, Mild, Moderate) gait score (MDS-UPDRS Gait III) prediction on 3DGait benchmark [17] with different sequence length f. R1, R5, R10, mAP denote Rank-1 accuracy, Rank-5, Rank-10, and mean average precision respectively.

Task	Method	$f = 10$				$f = 15$				$f = 20$			
		R1	R5	R10	mAP	R1	R5	R10	mAP	R1	R5	R10	mAP
4-Class	SimMC [14]	44.5	74.6	92.2	36.7	55.5	81.3	91.4	36.3	30.5	50.0	51.6	29.4
Gait Score	TranSG [15]	48.8	68.8	75.8	38.5	48.4	68.0	84.4	42.3	18.8	26.6	38.3	30.7
Prediction	MoCos [20]	46.1	67.6	78.5	39.8	51.6	71.1	85.2	46.6	36.7	51.6	70.3	36.2

disease prediction, and gait score prediction tasks. In Fig. 4, the skeleton representations learned from these models and corresponding skeleton sequences are integrated into the 3DGVA platform, which enables users to visualize skeleton-based gait patterns corresponding to different features ranked by the trained models. Here we take three state-of-the-art models as examples, while the 3DGVA platform can be flexibly extended to other skeleton-based models such as PoseGait [5], AGE [6], Hi-MPC [16], etc.

As presented in Fig. 5, the 3DGVA platform can leverage different LLMs such as DeepSeek-R1 to query skeleton data and perform automatic gait analysis with a transparent reasoning. This enhances the interpretability of model evaluation and can be potentially applied to more interdisciplinary gait-related tasks.

Table 5. Quantitative evaluation results of different skeleton-based AI models for the application of 5-class (Healthy, Mild Dementia with Lewy Bodies, Mild Alzheimer's Disease, Severe Dementia with Lewy Bodies, Severe Alzheimer's Disease) disease prediction on 3DGait benchmark [17] with different sequence length f. R1, R5, R10, mAP denote Rank-1 accuracy, Rank-5, Rank-10, and mean average precision respectively.

Task	Method	$f = 20$				$f = 15$				$f = 10$			
		R1	R5	R10	mAP	R1	R5	R10	mAP	R1	R5	R10	mAP
5-Class	SimMC [14]	33.6	49.2	61.0	34.1	30.5	34.4	45.3	39.5	23.8	44.1	50.8	25.8
Disease	TranSG [15]	39.8	50.8	57.0	34.1	32.0	42.2	54.7	42.2	28.5	43.8	53.1	33.4
Prediction	MoCos [20]	43.0	52.3	53.1	37.2	38.3	55.5	76.6	44.3	32.0	46.5	56.6	35.2

5   Conclusion

This paper proposes a scalable and interpretable 3DGVA platform to interactively visualize 3D gait representations to help evaluate the effectiveness of models across different fields. A unified gait representation based on 3D skeleton sequences is visualized, while their feature-based ranking results in prediction are presented to help analyze the distinct and easily-confused gait patterns. It further integrates LLMs for query and automatic gait analysis with explainable reasoning. 3DGVA can be applied to different state-of-the-art skeleton-based models, and can be potentially extended to diverse gait-related applications.

Acknowledgements. This research is supported by the National Research Foundation, Singapore under its AI Singapore Programme (AISG Award No: AISG2-PhD/2022-01-034[T]).

References

1. Murray, M.P., Drought, A.B., Kory, R.C.: Walking patterns of normal men. J. Bone Joint Surg. **46**(2), 335–360 (1964)
2. Sethi, D., Bharti, S., Prakash, C.: A comprehensive survey on gait analysis: history, parameters, approaches, pose estimation, and future work. Artif. Intell. Med. **129**, 102314 (2022)
3. Rao, H., Zeng, M., Zhao, X., Miao, C.: A survey of artificial intelligence in gait-based neurodegenerative disease diagnosis. Neurocomputing (2025)
4. Shotton, J., et al.: Real-time human pose recognition in parts from single depth images. In: Proceedings of the IEEE/CVF Conference on Computer Vision and Pattern Recognition (CVPR), pp. 1297–1304 (2011)
5. Liao, R., Yu, S., An, W., Huang, Y.: A model-based gait recognition method with body pose and human prior knowledge. Pattern Recogn. **98**, 107069 (2020)
6. Rao, H., et al.: A self-supervised gait encoding approach with locality-awareness for 3D skeleton based person re-identification. IEEE Trans. Pattern Anal. Mach. Intell. **44**(10), 6649–6666 (2021)

7. Han, F., Reily, B., Hoff, W., Zhang, H.: Space-time representation of people based on 3D skeletal data: a review. Comput. Vis. Image Underst. **158**, 85–105 (2017)
8. Rao, H., Miao, C.: Recognizing identities from human skeletons: A survey on 3D skeleton based person re-identification (2025). https://arxiv.org/abs/2401.15296
9. Andersson, V.O., Araujo, R.M.: Person identification using anthropometric and gait data from Kinect sensor. In: Proceedings of the AAAI Conference on Artificial Intelligence (AAAI), pp. 425–431 (2015)
10. Munaro, M., Fossati, A., Basso, A., Menegatti, E., Van Gool, L.: One-shot person re-identification with a consumer depth camera. In: Person Re-Identification. Springer, pp. 161–181 (2014)
11. Rao, H., et al.: Self-supervised gait encoding with locality-aware attention for person re-identification. In: International Joint Conference on Artificial Intelligence (IJCAI), vol. 1, pp. 898–905 (2020)
12. Rao, H., Xu, S., Hu, X., Cheng, J., Hu, B.: Multi-level graph encoding with structural-collaborative relation learning for skeleton-based person re-identification. In: International Joint Conference on Artificial Intelligence (IJCAI), pp. 973–980 (2021)
13. Rao, H., Hu, X., Cheng, J., Hu, B.: SM-SGE: a self-supervised multi-scale skeleton graph encoding framework for person re-identification. In: Proceedings of the 29th ACM International Conference on Multimedia, pp. 1812–1820 (2021)
14. Rao, H., Miao, C.: SimMC: simple masked contrastive learning of skeleton representations for unsupervised person re-identification. In: International Joint Conference on Artificial Intelligence (IJCAI), pp. 1290–1297 (2022)
15. Rao, H., Miao, C.: TranSG: transformer-based skeleton graph prototype contrastive learning with structure-trajectory prompted reconstruction for person re-identification. In: Proceedings of the IEEE/CVF Conference on Computer Vision and Pattern Recognition (CVPR) (2023)
16. Rao, H., Leung, C., Miao, C.: Hierarchical skeleton meta-prototype contrastive learning with hard skeleton mining for unsupervised person re-identification. Int. J. Comput. Vision **132**(1), 238–260 (2024)
17. Wang, D., Zouaoui, C., Jang, J., Drira, H., Seo, H.: Video-based gait analysis for assessing Alzheimer's disease and dementia with Lewy bodies. In: MICCAI Workshop on Applications of Medical AI. Springer, pp. 72–82 (2023)
18. Zhang, Z., Liang, F., Wang, W., Zeng, R., Leung, V.C., Hu, X.: Skeleton-based pre-training with discrete labels for emotion recognition in IoT environments. IEEE Internet of Things Journal (2025)
19. Lu, H., Chen, J., Liang, F., Tan, M., Zeng, R., Hu, X.: Understanding emotional body expressions via large language models. Proc. AAAI Conf. Artif. Intell. **39**(2), 1447–1455 (2025)
20. Rao, H., Miao, C.: Motif guided graph transformer with combinatorial skeleton prototype learning for skeleton-based person re-identification. In: Proceedings of the AAAI Conference on Artificial Intelligence (AAAI) (2025)
21. Guo, D., et al.: DeepSeek-R1: Incentivizing reasoning capability in LLMs via reinforcement learning. arXiv preprint arXiv:2501.12948 (2025)
22. Nambiar, A., Bernardino, A., Nascimento, J.C., Fred, A.: Context-aware person re-identification in the wild via fusion of gait and anthropometric features. In: International Conference on Automatic Face & Gesture Recognition, pp. 973–980. IEEE (2017)

Artificial Empathy in Divinatory Interaction: The Case of "SelfJourneon"

Po-Yao Wu[1(✉)] and Ya-Lun Tao[2]

[1] International Intercollegiate Ph.D. Program, Division of TechArt,
National Tsing Hua University, Hsinchu City, Taiwan
`r3a2t10@gapp.nthu.edu.tw`
[2] Graduate Institute of Technology and Art, College of Arts,
National Tsing Hua University, Hsinchu City, Taiwan

Abstract. This paper reexamines AI-powered divination not as a predictive tool, but as a symbolic and emotional interface. While existing systems reduce divination to deterministic output, traditional practices like Tarot operate as rituals of self-reflection, rich in metaphor and ambiguity. We introduce *"SelfJourneon,"* a prototype that integrates artificial empathy with the archetypal grammar of the Tarot. By positioning AI as a divinatory companion rather than an oracle, *"SelfJourneon"* fosters emotionally resonant dialogues through visual-symbolic interaction. Drawing from Jungian psychology, Campbell's Hero's Journey, and recent research in affective computing, we argue for a reconfiguration of AIhuman interaction centered on narrative co-construction and emotional attunement. This study proposes that large language models, when designed for symbolic participation, may serve as vessels for collective unconscious material–transforming AI into a mythopoetic guide for introspection. We present the system's design and interaction flow to demonstrate how AI can embody ambiguity and support participatory meaning-making through ritualized interface.

Keywords: AI Divination · Artificial Empathy · AI-Human Interaction · Tarot Archetypes · Hero's Journey

1 Introduction: AI as Divinatory Companion

The rise of generative artificial intelligence (AI) has redefined how humans engage with symbolic systems of meaning, extending its influence into domains once considered spiritual or mystical–such as divination [2,5,8–10]. Increasingly, AI is being used to generate Tarot readings, astrological forecasts, and other divinatory outputs.

Historically, divination has never been solely about forecasting. Rather, it serves as a narrative and symbolic interface through which individuals externalize inner questions, gain psychological insight, and navigate uncertainty. Tarot in particular, with its archetypal imagery and mythic sequence, provides a

© The Author(s), under exclusive license to Springer Nature Switzerland AG 2026
S. Sundarakannan and O. Knorpp (Eds.): HCII 2025, CCIS 2772, pp. 159–164, 2026.
https://doi.org/10.1007/978-3-032-12767-9_18

metaphorical mirror for the user's emotional and existential state. When AI is tasked with simulating such rituals, it risks becoming a black-box oracle–projecting a false aura of objectivity and mystical authority.

Contemporary critiques have noted how AI's opacity encourages spiritual projection. Davies describes this convergence as a "ludomantic" turn, where algorithmic output is reimagined as divine intervention [5]. McFadden calls this "enchanted determinism" [9], while Lee's theory of "rational superstition" explains how users respond more to symbolic resonance than to technical credibility [7]. Rather than rejecting these responses as misguided, this paper suggests rechanneling them: reimagining AI not as a passive oracle, but as an active participant in symbolic meaning-making.

2   Reframing Divination: From Prediction to Symbolic Dialogue

To transform AI divination into a reflective and participatory process, we must move beyond the dominant predictive paradigm. AI has traditionally been understood as reinforcing deterministic logics. When applied to divination, this tendency leads to outputs being interpreted as final and unambiguous. This framing diminishes the symbolic and psychological functions of divination, which thrive on interpretive multiplicity and emotional ambiguity. Divination, at its core, is not answer-giving–it is world-making.

Emerging research in affective computing proposes an alternative vision. Pataranutaporn's "3W" framework–Wellbeing, Wisdom, and Wonder–frames AI as a co-evolving ally in human development, emphasizing reflection over resolution [12]. Systems like "Future You" exemplify this shift, enabling users to engage with future-facing narratives that deepen temporal self-continuity [13]. Within this reconfiguration, artificial empathy plays a central role: not as emotional mimicry, but as an interactive capacity to resonate with tone, metaphor, and inner narrative [4].

Tarot offers a structured yet open-ended symbolic system ideal for such AI interactions. Each Major Arcana card corresponds to archetypal stages of transformation, aligned with Jungian theory and Campbell's Hero's Journey [3,6,14]. Computationally embodied, these cards become narrative nodes that AI can use to co-construct emotionally meaningful interactions. Rather than answering questions, the AI invokes symbols–The Fool, Death, The Star–as invitations for reflection.

This convergence of AI and Tarot suggests a novel interactional paradigm. AI becomes not a predictor, but a symbolic co-narrator–one capable of hosting affective dialogue, prompting identity reconfiguration, and surfacing unconscious material. Ackerman and Shihadeh frame language models as vessels of the collective unconscious [1], while O'Lemmon's notion of the "soft singularity" captures AI's transformation into an emotionally saturated symbolic medium [11].

To explore this reframing in practice, the next section presents *"SelfJourneon"*: an AI divination system that operationalizes symbolic dialogue, artificial

empathy, and archetypal language to support self-reflection through ritual interaction.

3   System Overview: *"SelfJourneon"*

"SelfJourneon" is a dialogic divination system that fuses Tarot's symbolic grammar with the design principles of artificial empathy (Fig. 1). Its name–blending
Self, Journey, and Neon–suggests a digitally mediated path of inner exploration.
Departing from the model of AI as a deterministic oracle, *"SelfJourneon"* positions AI as an emotional mirror and narrative catalyst, where mythic imagery
and psychological projection converge in interactive dialogue.

Here, divination is not prediction but co-creation–a symbolic conversation
that evokes emotional resonance and introspective insight. By shifting AI interaction from passive reception to reflective engagement, *"SelfJourneon"* becomes
a ritual interface for meaning-making, guiding users through archetypal language
toward deeper self-understanding.

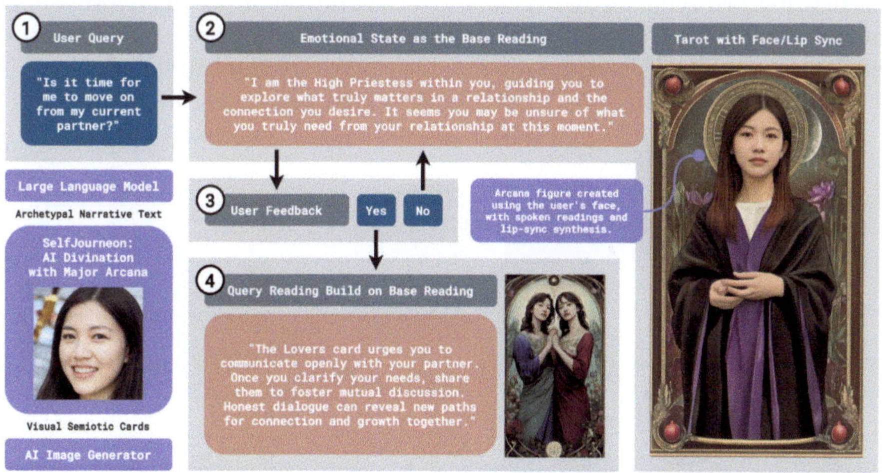

Fig. 1. *"SelfJourneon"* System Interaction Sample.

3.1   System Architecture and Interaction Flow

"SelfJourneon" is an immersive AI-based divination system that weaves together
symbolic archetypes, empathic dialogue, generative visuals, and voice synthesis
into a ritualized interactive experience. The process (Fig. 2) begins when the user
submits a personal question alongside a facial image. The system then initiates
a simulated shuffle and randomly draws a Major Arcana card, which functions

as the core archetype–mirroring the user's current psychological or emotional state.

The selected Tarot card becomes a narrative canvas. Through algorithmic processing, the user's face is embedded into the visual structure of the card's archetypal figure–be it The Fool, The High Priestess, or The Magician–symbolizing the user's entry into a personalized hero's journey. In doing so, the system not only retains the symbolic resonance of the original card but also forges a psychological link between the user and the mythic role they now inhabit.

In the subsequent stage, the composite portrait is animated via voice synthesis and facial reenactment technologies. The Tarot figure speaks directly to the user in the first person. The interaction unfolds in two parts: the first focuses on attuning to the user's emotional state; the second guides the user through the symbolic meanings encoded in the drawn card, prompting further reflection and dialogic engagement.

Rather than offering definitive answers, the system mobilizes the symbolic vocabulary of Tarot and the generative capacities of AI to elicit metaphorical thinking and affective resonance. In this way, *"SelfJourneon"* reconfigures AI from a tool of prediction into a companion of emotional presence. Through participatory storytelling and symbolic co-construction, it fosters a form of divinatory interaction grounded in artificial empathy–inviting users into a transformative process of self-interpretation and psychological integration.

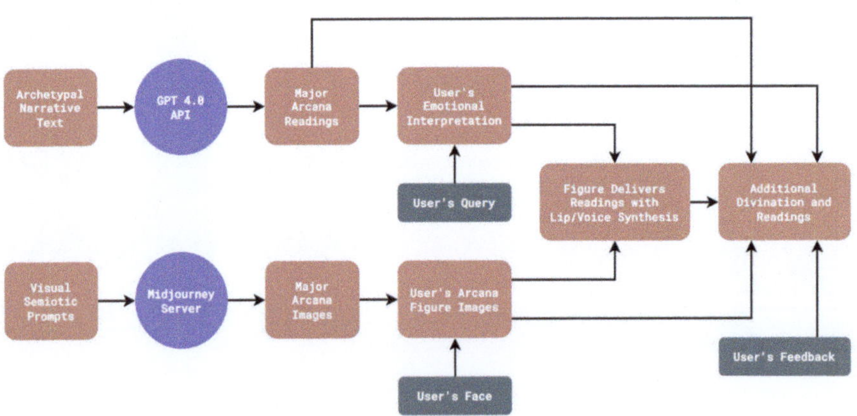

Fig. 2. The System Design Framework of *"SelfJourneon."*

3.2 Artificial Empathy in Practice

In its system architecture, *"SelfJourneon"* adopts a three-tiered strategy for implementing artificial empathy–redefining the role of AI within divinatory interaction, shifting its function from predictive authority to that of an emotional companion and narrative co-facilitator:

1. **Symbolic Guidance:** Tarot's visual grammar, the system activates archetypes that mirror users' emotions, using metaphor-driven prompts to guide self-reflection.
2. **Affective Feedback:** The AI's tone modulation and linguistic feedback aim to simulate empathic presence, creating a space of co-regulated emotional clarity.
3. **Non-Directive Design:** Instead of fixed answers, the system poses open-ended prompts to foster introspection, symbolic ambiguity, and narrative flexibility.

Together, these three strategies establish a linguistic and symbolic field that extends artificial empathy beyond mere emotional recognition–toward a dynamic practice that supports psychological processes and narrative generation. Through this approach, *"SelfJourneon"* enables AI not only to evoke emotional resonance and promote self-awareness but also to serve as a mediating agent for narrative activation and symbolic participation.

4   Conclusion

In this paper, we challenged the dominant paradigm of AI divination as a predictive engine, proposing instead that AI can function as a symbolic and emotional companion. Through *"SelfJourneon"*, we explored how AI systems might facilitate introspection by invoking archetypal structures and multimodal empathy, engaging users in reflective, co-constructed narratives rather than delivering deterministic answers. Grounded in the visual grammar of the Tarot and the psychological arc of the Hero's Journey, our system leverages artificial empathy not for imitation, but for ritual participation–inviting users to project meaning, process uncertainty, and navigate inner transformation.

This reframing situates AI as a mediating presence in symbolic dialogue, capable of surfacing unconscious material and mirroring the complexity of human emotion. As generative models increasingly shape intimate and identity-forming experiences, their design must support interpretive openness, psychological depth, and narrative agency. We offer *"SelfJourneon"* as an early but concrete step toward a more emotionally literate and symbolically grounded future of AI interaction.

References

1. Ackerman, M., Shihadeh, J.: The collective mind: exploring our shared unconscious via AI. Religion **1**(8), 19 (2024)
2. Banerjee, P., Sindhu, B., Sindhu, S., et al.: Exploring the intersections of AI (artificial intelligence) in psychology and astrology: a conceptual inquiry for human well-being. J. Psychol. Clin. Psychiatry **15**(1), 75–77 (2024)
3. Campbell, J.: The hero with a thousand faces, vol. 17. New World Library (2008)
4. Chao, C., Fu, Z., Chen, Y.: Multidisciplinary review of artificial empathy: from theory to technical implementation and design. In: International Conference on Human-Computer Interaction, pp. 195–209. Springer (2024)

5. Davies, H.: From I-Ching to AI: interrogating digital divination. In: Proceedings of International Symposium on Electronic Art (ISEA) (2024)
6. Jung, C.G.: The concept of the collective unconscious. Collect. Works **9**(1), 42 (1936)
7. Lee, E.: The power of perception in human-AI interaction: Investigating psychological factors and cognitive biases that shape user belief and behavior. arXiv preprint arXiv:2409.15328 (2024)
8. Lustig, C., Rosner, D.: From explainability to ineffability? ML tarot and the possibility of inspiriting design. In: Proceedings of the 2022 ACM Designing Interactive Systems Conference, pp. 123–136 (2022)
9. McFadden, C.: Practices of prediction: tarot as a lens for disrupting ml eventfulness. In: Proceedings of International Symposium on Electronic Art (ISEA) (2024)
10. Michelson, R., Lustig, C., Rosner, D., Hoy, J., Santos, D.R.: Worlding with tarot: Design, divination, and the technological imagination. In: Proceedings of the 2024 ACM Designing Interactive Systems Conference, pp. 638–652 (2024)
11. O'Lemmon, M.: The technological singularity as the emergence of a collective consciousness: an anthropological perspective. Bull. Sci. Technol. Soc. **40**(1–2), 15–27 (2020)
12. Pataranutaporn, P.: Cyborg Psychology: The Art & Science of Designing Human-AI Systems that Support Human Flourishing. Ph.D. thesis, Massachusetts Institute of Technology (2024)
13. Pataranutaporn, P., et al.: Future you: a conversation with an AI-generated future self reduces anxiety, negative emotions, and increases future self-continuity. In: 2024 IEEE Frontiers in Education Conference (FIE), pp. 1–10. IEEE (2024)
14. Pawliszyn, A.: Archetypal character of the artwork: on art as play with unconsciousness. Agathos **11**(1), 39–40 (2020)

For Intelligent Customer Service Scenarios: Design of a Human-Machine Interface for Customer Service Workspace Integrating Large-Model AI-Assisted Capabilities

Yuan Wu[✉], Tao Shen, and Yan Li

Alibaba Cloud Computing, Hangzhou, China
{wy245053,heitao.st,ruoxi}@alibaba-inc.com

Abstract. This paper proposes a human-machine interface framework called MI-CHMI, designed for enterprise customer service scenarios. By integrating card-based layouts with large-model AI-assisted capabilities, the framework aims to improve the efficiency of multi-threaded task processing and user experience of customer service representatives. The MI-CHMI framework consists of four configurable areas: navigation, conversation queue, chat area, and AI assistance. Each area can be flexibly configured according to users' personalized needs, including card size and position adjustment, customization and sorting of functions to meet the diverse needs of customer service representatives in different industries. Researchers built a high-fidelity interface for simulated testing and compared with the traditional HMI of the Alibaba Cloud Tongyi Xiaomi customer service workspace. Preliminary results demonstrate that the framework significantly improves the efficiency of multi-threaded task processing, enhances customer satisfaction, and facilitates the integration of additional AI-assisted capabilities in the customer service domain. Overall, this framework provides an effective interface design, which helps customer service representatives access relevant information more efficiently when handling multi-threaded tasks, and helps them provide more efficient and accurate services, thereby improving the customer experience. Future work will focus on developing and implementing additional enterprise customer service functionalities within this framework to tackle a broader range of customer service challenges in the commercialization process of enterprises.

Keywords: Human-Machine Interface Framework · Large-Model AI-Assisted · Multi-Threaded Task Processing · Enterprise Customer Service

1 Introduction

Customer service refers to the assistance and advice provided by enterprises to users who purchase or use their products or services through various channels such as phone calls, online chats, in-site messages, or emails. All enterprises require different forms of customer service [1]. High-quality service can help enterprises increase added value, improve customer satisfaction, and build loyalty [2]. For some enterprises, customer

© The Author(s), under exclusive license to Springer Nature Switzerland AG 2026

S. Sundarakannan and O. Knorpp (Eds.): HCII 2025, CCIS 2772, pp. 165–177, 2026.
https://doi.org/10.1007/978-3-032-12767-9_19

service is an intangible asset that distinguishes them from competitors in the industry. A good customer service experience can change customers' perception of the enterprise [3]. With the development of generative AI, more and more enterprises are integrating AI capabilities into their customer service, such as AI chatbots, AI voice bots, and AI assistants. These AI-powered solutions help customers complete simple self-service tasks, thereby reducing labor costs for enterprises [4, 5].

From chatbots to outbound call bots, enterprises will choose different methods to deliver excellent customer service based on their operational needs. Contact centers provide services to customers by integrating the above channels [6]. From a customer's perspective, three core elements of contact centers are particularly important: connectivity, response time, and response quality [7]. As a key player in the customer service, customer service agents can often provide timely services when customers cannot get effective help during the self-service process. The customer service workspace in a contact center is the primary platform for agents to perform their tasks, enabling real-time communication, information retrieval, work order issuance and other operations in various ways. In recent years, enterprises such as Salesforce, Zendesk, IBM, Google, and Alibaba Cloud have incorporated AI capabilities into contact centers, realizing capabilities ranging from automation to predictive analytics and sentiment analysis, equipping agents with intelligent tools to better understand customer needs and improve the customer experience [8]. As direct users of contact center workspace, agents handle hundreds or even thousands of customer requests daily. These tasks are often repetitive and monotonous [9]. Therefore, for contact center workspace, how to improve agent satisfaction and the efficiency of multi-threaded task processing by designing user-friendly interfaces and delivering efficient user experiences are critical challenges for designers. Based on the analysis of current research on contact centers, we found a lack of established methodologies for designing contact center interfaces and this study aims to address this gap.

To address the aforementioned challenges, this study proposes a human-machine interface framework named MI-CHMI (MI-Customer Human Machine Interface). This framework is based on the interface of contact center workspace and is specifically designed for agents. By integrating a card-based layout with large-model AI-assisted capabilities, it aims to enhance the efficiency of multi-threaded task processing and improve the user experience for agents. The MI-CHMI framework consists of four areas: navigation, conversation queue, chat area, and AI assistance. Each area can be flexibly configured according to users' personalized needs. The framework supports not only text-based conversations but also provides automatic speech recognition (ASR) and transcription for voice conversations. Additionally, it offers AI-assisted features such as conversation summarization, intelligent Q&A recommendations, emotion detection, and knowledge base search during and after the customer service process. Researchers developed a high-fidelity interface based on this framework for simulation testing and conducted comparative tests with the traditional human-machine interface of the Alibaba Cloud Tongyi Xiaomi customer service workspace. The study involved 20 participants, experimental results showed an overall satisfaction score of 4.7/5 and a usability score of 4.5/5. Compared to traditional contact center workspace, in text-based conversation scenarios, AI assistance can significantly reduce the time it takes for customer service representatives to handle tasks. However, in voice-based scenarios, the efficiency improvement provided by AI assistance may be influenced by the length of the user's case and dialogue content. Additionally, 90% of participants agreed that MI-CHMI improved work efficiency, while 80% of participants believed it enhanced the user experience during customer service.

Contributions of Our Work:

1. We propose an innovative interactive framework for customer service workspace interface design, offering flexibility and scalability to meet the diverse needs of different users.
2. We integrated AI capabilities based on different business scenarios into the framework, providing effective assistance to agents at different stages of customer service. The framework also supports the extension of AI capabilities.
3. Our preliminary test study (N = 20) validates the value of this framework in improving the work efficiency and user satisfaction of agents in multi-threaded task processing.

2 Related Work

2.1 Interface Design in Customer Service Scenarios

Existing HCI theories applied to customer service scenarios focus on user-centered technology integration, encompassing four dimensions: knowledge management, personalized interaction, ethical design, and human-machine collaboration. Future research needs to further explore dynamic intent recognition, cross-cultural adaptability (e.g., support for Chinese and English data sets [10]), and the controllability of generative AI (e.g., avoiding "hallucinated responses" [11]) to achieve a more natural and trustworthy customer service experience. User acceptance of chatbots is influenced by "perceived usefulness" and "perceived ease of use" [12]. Modern conversational interfaces need to support multimodal interactions, including voice, text, and images. For instance, chatbots that integrate text and images improve accessibility compared to voice-only systems [13]. Through research on the user interface design and emotion recognition of voice-based systems, Ramón et al. [14] emphasized that conversational systems require natural language processing technologies and multimodal interactions, such as speech recognition and emotion detection. Melati et al. [15] demonstrated that conversational interfaces should be intuitive to reduce users' learning costs through the design of a conversational chatbot for online libraries. Similarly, Vannam et al. [16] pointed out that the application of generative AI (GenAI) chatbots in customer service must consider users' technological familiarity and industry-specific characteristics, technologically proficient users prefer advanced features (e.g., personalized recommendations), while less skilled users require simplified processes (e.g., clear operational guidance). However, these studies mainly focus on interface design from the customer's perspective, with limited discussion for customer service workspaces used by agents. Therefore, research centered on interface design for agents has significant potential for further exploration.

2.2 Application of AI Capabilities in Customer Service

Michal et al. [17] proposed the elements and evaluation methods for building an AI Copilot, applying it to the retail sector to enhance personalized shopping experiences for customers. Chris et al. [18] revealed the key engineering pain points in the process of developing AI-assisted products. Maria et al. [12] explored three design principles for AI-powered service robots: human-centric, trust enhancement, and interface, dialogue and robot role design. Amit et al. [19] conducted an in-depth analysis of data from AI-driven sales assistants in retail industry, revealing impact on customer experience in terms of satisfaction, retention and life cycle value. Kirkpatrick [20] investigated case studies of enterprises leveraging AI capabilities in contact centers to improve customer service. Regardless of text consultation, voice calls, or customer email handling, AI has significantly enhanced the user experience. Noyan et al. [21] designed an automatic classification method based on text analysis in the contact center, which has obvious time and labor cost advantages over manual classification. Birjali et al. [22] incorporated conversation summarization and emotion detection into the analysis of agent conversations, which can fully understand the conversation topics and customer emotions, and enhance the company's ability to evaluate customer needs and feedbacks. AI-assisted capabilities should exhibit appropriate proactivity during service processes, such as providing timely assistance without interrupting users [23]. The above studies have discussed methods and principles for leveraging AI to improve customer service satisfaction and work efficiency from both the customer's and agent's perspectives. However, there is still a lack of discussion on integrating AI capabilities with the multi-threaded task processing of agents. Our goal is to integrate AI capabilities with the customer service workspace so that when agents face a large number of customer service requests in their daily work, they can efficiently serve customers through the user interface framework we proposed, which not only improves service efficiency, but also improves user experience satisfaction of customers and agents.

3   MI-CHMI Framework

As shown in Fig. 1, the overall interface layout adopts a modular design. The top header area and the left sidebar consolidate frequently used menus, operations, and status information for customer service agents, enabling quick access and operations. The main interface is dedicated to voice/text chat for real-time interaction, while the assistant area is located on the right side of the chat region. This assistant area supports flexible switching between different functional plugins through a plugin slot on the right. This layout design aims to optimize the workflow of customer service agents and enhance operational efficiency.

Figure 2 compares the new design (with an assistance area) to the original design (without it). The newly added assistance area, positioned on the right side of the interface, is specifically designed to integrate tools commonly used by customer service agents. This area can host various plugins, such as document search, customer analysis, real-time assistance, and other extensible functionalities. By introducing the assistant area, the interface's functionality and flexibility are significantly enhanced, providing comprehensive support for customer service operations.

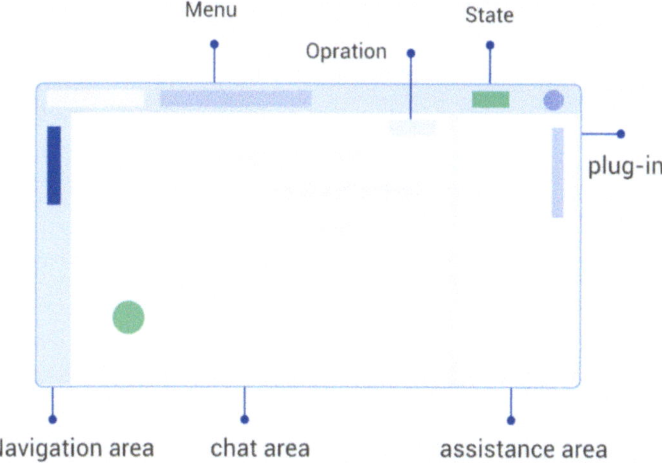

Fig. 1. Main Framework of the Product Interface.

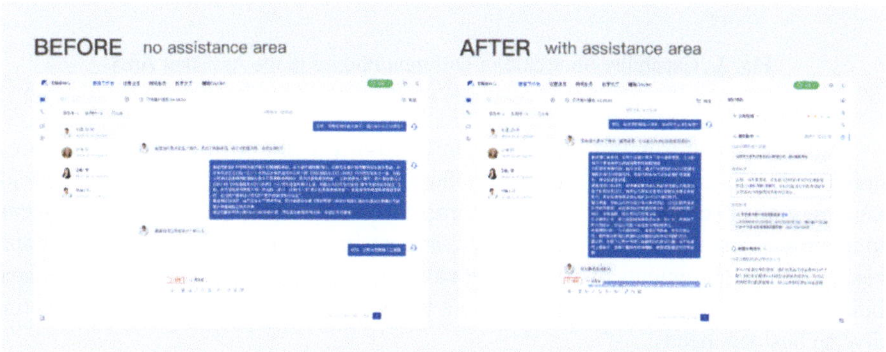

Fig. 2. Comparison of Page Layout Before and After Design.

Figure 3 provides a detailed demonstration of the functional effects of various plugins within the assistant area. The real-time assistance plugin analyzes the context and semantics of real-time conversations between agents and users, automatically detecting service compliance (e.g., whether prohibited words are triggered) to help agents avoid potential risks. The knowledge assistance plugin leverages the enterprise's built-in knowledge base to provide efficient search matching and generate document snippets or summarized answers from large models, enabling agents to quickly retrieve required information. The customer analysis plugin synthesizes historical conversation records, current dialogue content, and system-recorded service data to create precise user profiles, facilitating the resolution of complex issues that span long timeframes.

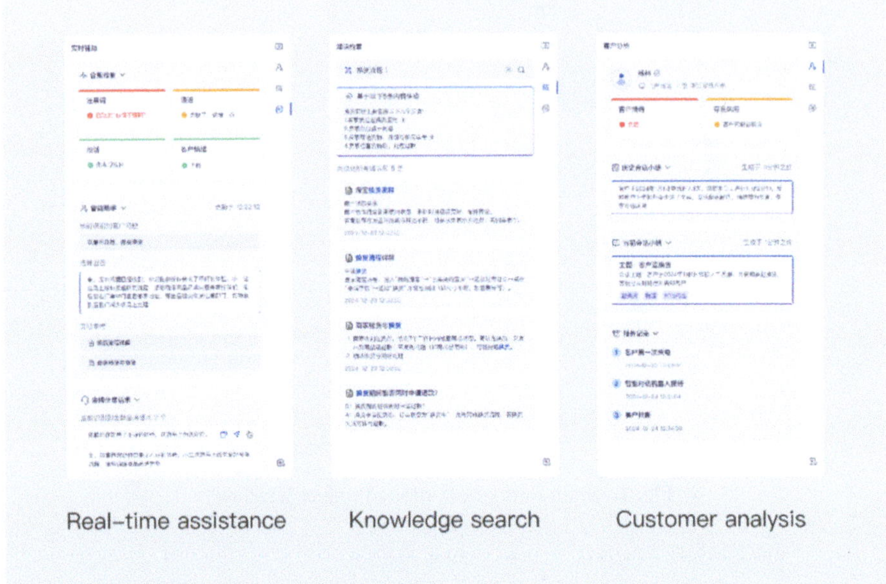

Fig. 3. Capability Showcase of Different Plugins in the Assistant Area.

Figure 4 showcases three extended interaction capabilities of the assistant area: horizontal drag-and-drop adjustment, collapsing and minimizing content, and folding/dragging of content blocks. These interactive features allow customer service agents to flexibly adjust the weight, display area, and position of plugins in the assistant area based on the requirements of different service stages. Through this customization capability, the interface becomes adaptable to a wider range of industry scenarios, meeting diverse business needs.

The overall design focuses on enhancing the efficiency of customer service operations as its core objective. By employing a modular layout, plugin-based extensibility, and flexible interaction capabilities, the interface achieves both high efficiency and adaptability. This design not only optimizes the workflow of customer service agents but also lays a solid foundation for future functional expansions, thereby better serving multi-industry application scenarios.

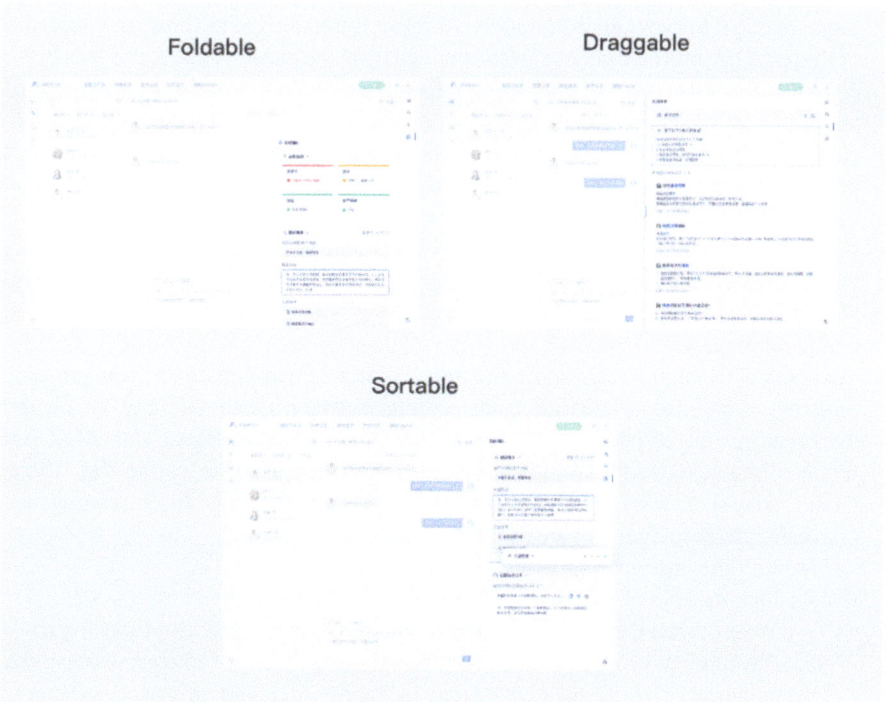

Fig. 4. Extended Interaction Capabilities of the Assistant Area.

4   User Study

4.1   Preliminary User Test

To evaluate the impact of the MI-CHMI on user satisfaction and work efficiency in customer service scenarios, we conducted a preliminary user testing. The test was conducted simultaneously on the enhanced high-fidelity interface and the Alibaba Cloud Tongyi Xiaomi customer service workspace to evaluated the differences in user experience and the improvements in customer service efficiency. A total of 10 participants (5 males and 5 females) were recruited, aged between 25 and 38 years. Ethical approval was obtained before the study, and informed consent was secured from all participants. All participants had basic experience using conversational interfaces, including 11 participants who were active agents in industries such as E-commerce, automobile sales, financial, and 9 participants with interface design and development experience.

To preliminarily explore the efficiency improvements brought by MI-CHMI for agents, we conducted a controlled experiment by randomly dividing participants into two groups: Group A used the high-fidelity interface with MI-CHMI (integrating AI-assisted capabilities). Group B served as the control group, using the Alibaba Cloud Tongyi Xiaomi customer service workspace (without AI-assisted capabilities).

The testing was divided into the following five phases:

1. Setup and Pre-Survey (approximately 10 min). Introduce the purpose and procedure of the test, and informed consent was obtained from the participants. A pre-survey was conducted to collect participants' basic information, including age, gender, experience and usage frequency with conversational products.
2. Knowledge Association Learning (approximately 20 min). To ensure fairness, both groups were provided with the same knowledge document, which served as the source of answers for subsequent tests. To ensure participants were equally unfamiliar with the document content, we pre-assessed their prior knowledge and ultimately selected a knowledge document focused on insurance as the test material. This phase mainly allowed the participants to familiarize themselves with the content so that users could complete the test smoothly.
3. Text-Based Dialogue Test (approximately 10 min). Each participant was presented with two simulated text-based conversations between customers and an chatbot, displayed on the respective interfaces. The high-fidelity interface with MI-CHMI included AI-generated summaries and recommended answers, while the Alibaba Cloud Tongyi Xiaomi customer service workspace did not. After reading each conversation, participants were asked to complete two tasks:
   (a) Identify the customer's request.
   (b) Assume the role of an agent and respond to the request.
      We recorded the time participants took to complete these two tasks to provide data on efficiency improvements. To minimize the impact of conversation content, we prepared two different conversation scenarios and randomly assigned them to the participants.
4. Voice-Based Dialogue Test (approximately 10 min). Each participant acted as an agent, when entered the interface, the experimenter acted as a customer and made twice phone calls to them, simulating real voice interactions to inquire about user requests based on case scenarios, aiming to replicate the real service environment for agents. The high-fidelity interface with MI-CHMI featured real-time AI-detected customer emotions and recommended responses, while the Alibaba Cloud Tongyi Xiaomi interface did not. Between the call, participants were asked to complete two tasks:
   (a) Identify the customer's current emotion.
   (b) Assume the role of an agent and respond to the request based on the customer's emotion.
      We recorded the time participants took to complete these two tasks to provide data on efficiency improvements. To minimize the impact of conversation content, we prepared two different calling scenarios and randomly assigned them to the participants.
5. Post-Test Survey and User Interviews (approximately 20 min). A post-test survey using a five-point Likert scale was conducted to evaluate participants' overall satisfaction, learnability, usability and usefulness of both interfaces. Semi-structured interviews were then conducted to gather qualitative feedback on the efficiency, AI-assisted capabilities, and user experience of the MI-CHMI interface.

4.2 Results

Quantitative Results. All participants completed the test tasks within the specified time. The results (Figure 5) show that participants rated the MI-CHMI human-machine interaction framework with average overall satisfaction score of 4.7 (SD = 0.48), learnability of 4.7 (SD = 0.48), usability of 4.5 (SD = 0.53), and usefulness of 4.9 (SD = 0.32). The Alibaba Cloud Tongyi Xiaomi customer service workspace had an average overall satisfaction score of 2.4 (SD = 0.84), learnability of 3.4 (SD = 1.27), usability of 2.3 (SD = 1.16), and usefulness of 2.5 (SD = 1.08).

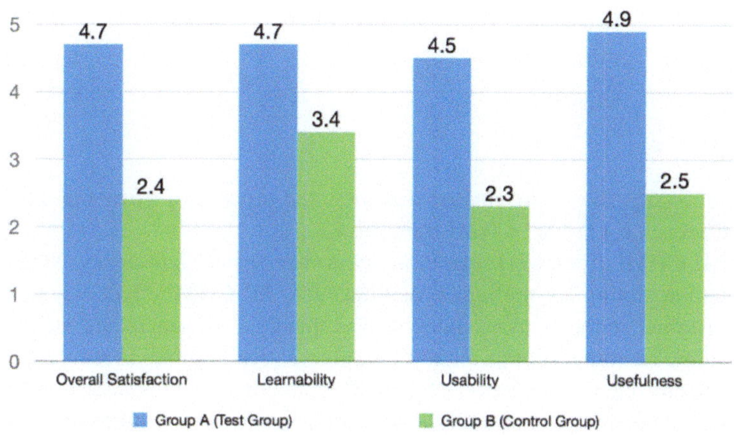

Fig. 5. Five-point Likert scale results of preliminary user test.

Calculate the time taken by users in groups A and B to complete text chat tasks and voice call tasks, respectively. The test results of the users (Table 1) show that: In the two case scenarios of text chat, the task completion time for users in the experimental group with AI assistance (Group A) was significantly lower than that of the control group without AI assistance (Group B).

In the blindness case of the voice conversation, the task completion time for users in the experimental group with AI assistance (Group A) was significantly lower than that of the control group without AI assistance (Group B); however, in the lost luggage case, there was no significant difference between the two groups. We initially speculate that this is because, in the lost luggage case, the customer service representative needs to spend a relatively long time explaining the claims process, thus diminishing the efficiency gains from AI-assisted search.

Based on the above, we can draw the preliminary conclusion that in text-based conversation scenarios, AI assistance can significantly reduce the time it takes for customer service representatives to handle tasks. However, in voice-based scenarios, the efficiency improvement provided by AI assistance may be influenced by the length of the user's case and dialogue content.

Qualitative Results. In the semi-structured interviews, participants were asked to explain their Likert scale ratings to further reveal the reasons behind the quantitative

Table 1. Table of results for independent samples t-test analysis on task completion time.

Test Content	Test Object	Sample Size	Mean(s)	Standard Deviation	Welch's T-Test
Text-Based Injury Scene	Group A	5	52	25.855	T = 3.083 P = 0.024
	Group B	5	91.2	11.819	
Text-Based Rescue Scene	Group A	5	46.4	10.286	T = 4.226 P = 0.010
	Group B	5	119.6	37.34	
Voice-Based Blindness Scene	Group A	5	46.2	10.159	T = 3.104 P = 0.021
	Group B	5	76.6	19.398	
Voice-Based Lost Luggage	Group A	5	74.8	14.721	T = 2.133 P = 0.090
	Group B	5	124.8	50.296	

data. Additionally, they were invited to review the process of using the interface and provide feedback for the MI-CHMI framework.

The MI-CHMI framework enhanced customer service efficiency. 90% of users agreed that integrating AI intelligent assistance into MI-CHMI effectively helped them resolve customer requests more quickly. Specifically, 14 participants mentioned that when handling customer service requests, AI automatically summarized the chat history between the customer and chatbot, which allowed them to quickly understand customer needs. At the same time, it automatically generated solution suggestions for unmet needs, which also saved their time rsearching the knowledge base. 8 participants highlighted that in daily work, they often encounter customers with significant emotional fluctuations. The AI-powered emotion detection feature helped them promptly identify such customers and provide real-time solutions, effectively avoiding further emotional escalation caused by delayed responses or prolonged waiting times. 10 participants noted that the real-time ASR feature during voice calls can converted conversations into text, and AI automatically generated summaries or work orders, which brought convenience for agents to make call records after the conversation. 12 participants stated that if AI assistance could automatically summarize the requests of customers in the waiting queue and generate solutions in advance, the multi-tasking process will be better compressed, which not only saved time for agents but also reduced customer waiting time, enhancing satisfaction for both sides.

Compared to traditional customer service workspaces, the MI-CHMI framework improved user experience. 80% of participants believed that the card-based layout design of the MI-CHMI framework allowed user to flexibly to adjust workspace functions based on different work scenarios, met the personalized needs of different agents. Due to differences among enterprises, the need for AI-assisted capabilities differs among agents. Therefore, enabling flexible adjustments to the plugins in the AI-assisted area can cater to the personalized needs of various agents. Additionally, given the differences between companies, some agents may handle only text-based conversations or voice calls, while others may need to manage both. The ability to adapt the multimodal workspace of the platform based on their work responsibilities provides an optimized user experience. 40%

of participants highlighted that draggable and resizable cards allow the core workspace to be maximized (e.g., minimizing the call section to expand the text dialogue area), which improved space utilization and indirectly enhanced work efficiency. Five participants mentioned that key capabilities should be prominently displayed in the interface design. For instance, AI-generated recommended answers can be visually emphasized using color, and keywords within the answers can also be highlighted to help agents quickly grasp critical information.

5 Discussion

5.1 Discussion and Future Work

Based on the results of the preliminary user tests, we discuss the key insights of the MI-CHMI framework and outline potential future research directions.

AI Credibility Design. AI hallucination is a significant factor affecting user trust. When integrating AI-assisted capabilities into customer service workspaces, if the accuracy of AI-generated content cannot be effectively conveyed through the interface, it will not only fail to improve the efficiency of agents, but will also affect their work due to the obtaining of inaccurate information. Therefore, interface design should prioritize conveying a sense of reliability, such as clearly labeling the credibility of information or citing its sources to help users assess the accuracy of generated content. Additionally, enhancing interactivity within the interface, such as incorporating feedback features that allow agents to mark inaccuracies, which could enable AI to reflect and improve its outputs.

Emotion-Aware Adaptive Interfaces. Currently, the MI-CHMI interface provides a real-time emotion detection module to help agents quickly perceive customer emotions and respond promptly. However, the user interface itself does not adapt to these changes. Drawing inspiration from systems like Nauto's [24] hazard prediction mechanism in driver-assistance systems, when detecting significant emotional fluctuations or when the complexity of a query exceeds a threshold, the interface will automatically switch to "Enhanced Support Mode", such as expanding the agents operation area, highlighting the customer's key information, preloading the emergency plan knowledge base, etc., so as to achieve emotional perception interface adaptation and improve the efficiency of customer service in handling emergency events.

Cross-Language Design. To accommodate the cross-regional business needs of enterprises, the design of customer service workspaces must address multilingual challenges. When hiring agents, enterprises often prioritize candidates from regions with larger user bases, typically without considering multilingual skills. However, when foreign customers make inquiries and the agent cannot understand requests made in another language, AI capabilities could be leveraged to translate the text and display it on the interface. The interface should also allow agents to set their response language, enabling AI to automatically translate their replies into the customer's language, thereby facilitating cross-language communication.

5.2 Limitations

Lack of Real-World Interface Experience. Due to the development timeline, the MI-CHMI framework has not been implemented in actual work. The user test conducted was based on a high-fidelity prototype, which may differ from the final product interface. As a result, the quantitative results obtained in this study might be skewed.

Insufficient Validity of Efficiency Evaluation. It is challenging to fully replicate real-world work scenarios in a laboratory environment. Consequently, the test tasks were designed as simplified comparative tasks to capture the difference in basic task processing efficiency. However, due to the complexity and variability of actual business operations, the efficiency improvement data calculated in this study might not accurately reflect real-world conditions.

Exploration of Efficiency Improvement in Voice Mode. In this experiment, we found that AI assistance significantly improved the efficiency of customer service representatives in text-based test scenarios. However, in voice scenarios, the results were influenced by factors such as the content of the conversation and the complexity of the problem. We speculate that this is because voice-based scenarios place higher demands on the response speed, processing speed, and language organization abilities of customer service representatives. Therefore, in such scenarios, it may be necessary to explore additional designs for voice-based assistance.

6 Conclusion

This paper introduces MI-CHMI, a human-machine interface for customer service workspace integrating large-model AI-assisted capabilities. By combining card-based layouts with large-model AI functionalities, a high-fidelity interface prototype was designed to enhance agents' multi-tasking efficiency and user satisfaction during customer services. The prototype incorporates AI-assisted features such as summary generation, real-time emotion detection, and answer recommendations. Preliminary user testing validated the value of MI-CHMI in improving efficiency and user experience. In future research, we aim to incorporate elements such as AI credibility design, emotion-aware adaptive interfaces, and cross-language functionality into the framework. Additionally, we are committed to developing and implementing more enterprise customer service features within this framework to address practical challenges in customer service during the commercialization process.

References

1. Lucas, R.W.: Customer Service: Skills for Success. McGraw-Hill, New York, NY (2015)
2. Buchanan, L.: A Customer Service Makeover. Inc. Magazine, New York (2011)
3. Swartz, T., Iacobucci, D.: Handbook of Services Marketing and Management. Sage Publications, Thousand Oaks, CA (1999)
4. AI-Enabled Customer Service Is Now the Quickest and Most Effective Route for Institutions to Deliver Personalized, Proactive Experiences that Drive Customer Engagement. McKinsey & Company, New York, NY (2023)

5. Turpin, B.: How Chatbots Can Provide a Better Customer Experience. IBM, New York, NY (2023)
6. Knackstedt, M.: Limitations and Advantages of Voice Bots in Customer Service-Using the Example of a Contact Center. PQDT-Global (2022)
7. Jaakkola, E., Helkkula, A., Aarikka-Stenroos, L.: Service experience co-creation: conceptualization, implications, and future research directions. J. Serv. Manag. **26**(2), 182–205 (2015)
8. Kent, D.: What Is a Contact Center? Definition, Features, and Uses. https://www.nextiva.com/blog/what-is-contact-center.html, last accessed 2024/09/13
9. Abinaya, K., Roy, S.: Are you calling for the vaporizer you ordered? In: Combining Search and Prediction to Identify Orders in Contact Centers. Proceedings of the 4th Workshop on e-Commerce and NLP, pp. 58–69 (2021)
10. Furmakiewicz, M., Liu, C., Taylor, A., Venger, I.: Design and evaluation of AI copilots – case studies of retail copilot templates. arXiv preprint arXiv:2407.09512. (2024)
11. Parnin, C., Soares, G., Pandita, R., Gulwani, S., Rich, J., Henley, A.Z.: Building your own product copilot: challenges, opportunities, and needs. arXiv preprint arXiv:2312.14231. (2023)
12. Hartikainen, M., Väänänen, K.: Towards human-centered design of AI service Chatbots: defining the building blocks. In: International Conference on Human-Computer Interaction. Springer, Cham (2023)
13. Bheemaiah, A.K.: The universality of the conversational UI interface with media in UX design. https://doi.org/10.31224/osf.io/yw6d9 (2019)
14. López-Cózar, R., et al.: Review of spoken dialogue systems. Loquens. **1**(2), 012 (2014)
15. Pratiwi, M.A., Desy Syahbaniar, Azzam Hanif Robbani: WIDYA (Web Information Dialog Your Assistant): AI-Powered Chatbot for Library Online Service Innovation. J. FPPTI, 42–52 (2023)
16. Vannam, L.E., Phung, T.H.: The role of moderators in transitioning from genaı Chatbot customer experience to customer satisfaction in digital marketing. Int. J. Soc. Sci. Econ. Res., v09i07 (2024). https://doi.org/10.46609/ijsser
17. Furmakiewicz, M., et al.: Design and evaluation of AI copilots—case studies of retail copilot templates. arXiv preprint arXiv:2407.09512. (2024)
18. Parnin, C., et al.: Building your own product copilot: challenges, opportunities, and needs. arXiv preprint arXiv:2312.14231. (2023)
19. Sharma, A., Patel, N., Gupta, R.: Enhancing customer experience with AI-powered sales assistants: leveraging natural language processing and reinforcement learning algorithms. Eur. Adv. AI J. **10**(2) (2021)
20. Kirkpatrick, K.: AI in contact centers. Commun. ACM. **60**(8), 18–19 (2017)
21. Ilk, N., Shang, G., Goes, P.: Improving customer routing in contact centers: an automated triage design based on text analytics. J. Oper. Manag. **66**(5), 553–577 (2020)
22. Birjali, M., Kasri, M., Beni-Hssane, A.: A comprehensive survey on sentiment analysis: approaches, challenges and trends. Knowl.-Based Syst. **226**, 107134 (2021)
23. Peng, Z.: Designing and evaluating intelligent agents' interaction mechanisms for assisting human in high-level thinking tasks. In: Extended Abstracts of the 2021 CHI Conference on Human Factors in Computing Systems (2021)
24. Nauto Announces New AI Enhancements for Its Driver and Fleet Safety Platform. https://www.prnewswire.com/news-releases/nauto-announces-new-ai-enhancements-for-its-driver-and-fleet-safety-platform-301307617.html, last accessed 2021/07/08

Psychological Traits Estimation Using Generative Adversarial Networks for Personalized Intervention

Tatsuya Yamamoto[✉] [iD], Shoji Hayakawa, Masahiro Shiraishi [iD], Yuta Masuda, Moe Matsuki, and Takuya Kamimura

Fujitsu Research, Fujitsu Limited, Kanagawa, Japan
{tyamamo,shayakawa,s_masahiro,masuda.yuta,matsuki.moe,
kami}@fujitsu.com

Abstract. Recent developments in behavior change support applications—such as fitness tracking, mental health monitoring, and smoking cessation—highlight the importance of personalized interventions. In particular, users' psychological traits have a strong influence on motivation and adherence. However, self-report questionnaires dominate current assessments. These tools require significant time and cognitive effort, often resulting in high attrition rates. Our study presents a model framework that estimates psychological traits from behavioral logs, eliminating the need for questionnaires. We trained the model using questionnaire-derived labels, designed to infer associations between behavioral patterns and underlying psychological traits. This approach supports future low-burden, adaptive interventions. To address the imbalance and bias in psychological trait data, the framework uses a bidirectional data augmentation strategy with Conditional Generative Adversarial Networks (cGANs). This approach enhances data diversity and model robustness. We conducted field experiments with 176 users of a web-based exercise application designed to promote user wellness. Our method surpassed conventional data augmentation techniques, achieving a maximum classification accuracy of 0.98. We also tested generalization using an independent user group and observed an average accuracy of 0.64. These results demonstrate that generative models can facilitate scalable and low-burden psychological trait estimation in real-world settings .

Keywords: Psychological Traits · Behavior Change · Generative Adversarial Network

1 Introduction

Mobile applications designed to promote behavior change in domains such as health, education, and mental well-being have experienced increasing adoption in recent years [1–3]. These apps promote daily actions, such as step tracking or mindfulness, to support habit formation [4]. However, many users stop using them within days [5], revealing the difficulty of sustaining behavioral change. To enhance engagement, researchers have

© The Author(s), under exclusive license to Springer Nature Switzerland AG 2026
S. Sundarakannan and O. Knorpp (Eds.): HCII 2025, CCIS 2772, pp. 178–189, 2026.
https://doi.org/10.1007/978-3-032-12767-9_20

explored personalized interventions tailored to individual psychological traits [6]. For instance, individuals with high General Self-Efficacy (GSE) [7] tend to maintain positive behaviors, indicating that psychological traits influence habit formation [8]. Traditional assessments rely on questionnaires, yet their length and repetitiveness often cause cognitive fatigue and reduce retention. Moreover, static assessments fail to reflect users' changing psychological states, limiting their adaptability [9].

This study proposes a data-driven approach to infer psychological traits from behavioral logs, aiming to eliminate reliance on traditional questionnaires. Unlike static systems based on pre-assessments, our method utilizes a pre-trained model to analyze usage patterns, with the long-term goal of facilitating adaptive, low-burden interventions in real time.

2   Related Work

Psychological traits have traditionally been assessed through self-report questionnaires such as the Big Five [10] and the GSE scale. While these instruments are well-established, their length imposes cognitive load and reduces engagement in digital contexts [11]. Recent studies have utilized behavioral data, including smartphone logs and sensor outputs, to infer psychological traits with reduced user burden. For example, Kosinski et al. [12] predicted personality traits from Facebook "likes," and Sano et al. [13] estimated stress and sleep patterns using mobile sensing. These findings suggest that behavioral signals serve as proxies for psychological assessments.

Many models rely on large, multimodal datasets that are impractical in constrained settings. Small sample sizes and biased distributions hinder generalizability [14–16]. To address this, researchers have employed data augmentation methods such as upsampling [17], SMOTE [18], and VAEs [19]. While these techniques help balance datasets, they struggle with subjective, high-dimensional labels, such as psychological traits. GANs [20] offer promise in generating realistic data conditioned on specific attributes [21]; nonetheless, their use in psychology remains limited due to concerns about validity and interpretability [22]. Though Manjunath et al. [23] applied GANs to sensor data, the approach did not improve psychological trait prediction.

In summary, while behavioral data and generative models show potential, few studies have integrated them to augment psychological trait labels. This gap limits the adaptability and robustness of current systems.

3   Proposed Method

3.1   Behavioral Feature Extraction

This study estimates psychological traits from behavioral logs to enable personalized interventions without relying on questionnaires. While the current implementation uses questionnaire-based scales as reference labels, the model learns associations between usage patterns and psychological traits. To enhance estimation accuracy under limited data conditions, we incorporate data augmentation techniques.

We collected user interaction logs through a web-based exercise application. These logs include task execution, plan modifications, screen transitions, and input timing. Based on this data, we extracted statistical features across planning, execution, and screen usage dimensions to capture behavioral tendencies relevant to psychological trait estimation. Section 4.1 provides a detailed description of the feature set and processing procedures.

3.2 Target Psychological Traits

In this study, we developed a predictive model that uses behavioral logs as input and outputs psychological traits (Table 1). To classify each trait, we employed Support Vector Machines (SVMs). The modeling process followed three steps: (1) we summed psychological questionnaire scores and treated them as continuous values; (2) we divided the scores into upper, middle, and lower thirds; and (3) we trained separate SVM classifiers for each trait. We defined these three levels to support the selection of appropriate intervention strategies based on individual psychological profiles in future intervention design. For example, we trained three models corresponding to the high, medium, and low levels of GSE.

Table 1. Target Psychological Traits.

Trait Name		Abbreviation
Big Five [10]	Extraversion	EXT
	Neuroticism	NEU
	Conscientiousness	CON
	Agreeableness	AGR
	Openness	OPN
General Self-Efficacy [7]		GSE
Challenge-Seeking Motivation [24]		CSM

3.3 Data Augmentation with Bidirectional-Conditional GAN

Psychological experiments often involve small sample sizes and behavioral data characterized by inherent biases, which limit statistical diversity and may restrict the scope of generalization.

To overcome these issues, this study proposes a data augmentation framework that exploits the relationship between behavioral logs and psychological traits to generate conditionally controlled synthetic data. The framework utilizes Conditional Generative Adversarial Networks (cGANs) [25], comprising a generator and a discriminator. The generator creates data based on specified conditions, while the discriminator assesses the authenticity of the outputs. By incorporating both noise vectors and conditional inputs (e.g., feature vectors or labels), cGANs generate data aligned with specific behavioral or psychological attributes.

Previous work in psychology [23] utilized GAN-based augmentation on sensor data, resulting in synthetic users with shared psychological traits yet distinct behaviors. Although this approach effectively captured one direction of the behavioral–psychological relationship, it did not account for the inverse scenario. In practice, simulating users with similar behaviors yet differing psychological traits is also significant.

To model both directions, this framework integrates two cGAN models (Fig. 1):

- Feature-Conditional GAN: Generates psychological trait labels from behavioral patterns, enabling the synthesis of users with shared behaviors and distinct psychological profiles.
- Psychological Trait-Conditional GAN: Generates behavioral data from psychological traits, enabling the synthesis of users with consistent traits and diverse behaviors.

By incorporating these synthetic profiles into the dataset, the framework improves class balance and enhances diversity. This augmentation strategy strengthens the robustness and performance of downstream machine-learning applications.

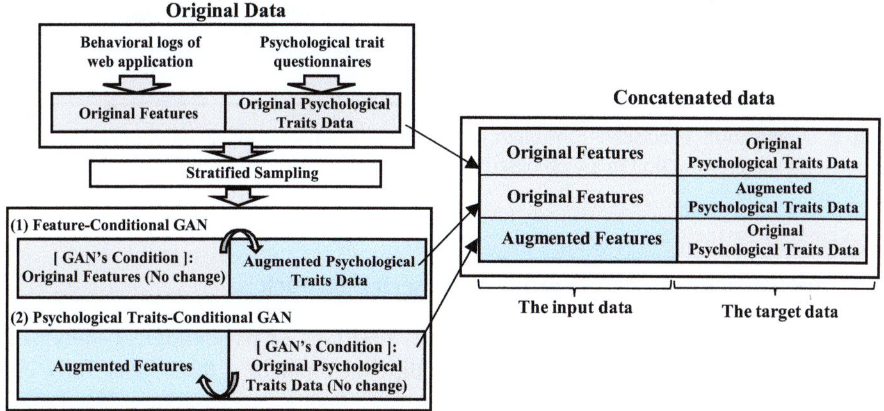

Fig. 1. Methodology of applying the proposed bidirectional cGAN framework.

4 Experiment

4.1 Application and Data Collection

We conducted a field experiment using a web-based exercise application specifically designed for corporate employees (Fig. 2). The application allowed users to create and manage personalized exercise plans, featuring integrated self-monitoring and reminder functions. Throughout the study, the system logged user interactions, including plan creation and modification, task execution frequency and continuity, screen transitions, and input timing. Participants completed standardized psychological questionnaires before using the application. For 4 weeks, the system collected multimodal data, comprising behavioral logs and psychological assessments. We computed weekly statistical features from the behavioral logs (e.g., median, standard deviation) to represent user behavior. These features fell into three categories: planning behavior, execution consistency, and screen usage patterns. In total, we generated 23 features per week, resulting in 92 features across the 4 weeks.

We utilized these behavioral features to train a model for estimating psychological traits. To address data imbalance and improve generalization, we applied a bidirectional conditional GAN-based data augmentation technique and evaluated the model using an independent dataset.

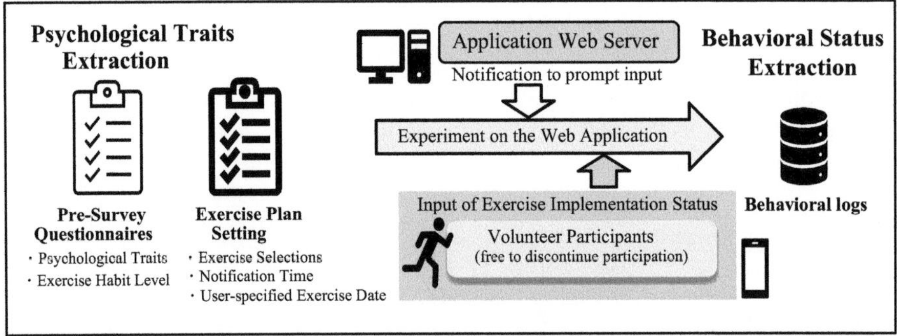

Fig. 2. Application overview: Flowchart illustrating the process of psychological traits and behavioral status extraction in a web-based exercise experiment.

4.2   Implementation of Generative Adversarial Network

The cGAN was configured to generate behavioral logs or psychological traits using a noise vector (dimension $= 500$) and conditional input in a three-layer fully connected network (with up to 512 units). The discriminator processed combined inputs with LeakyReLU, a final Sigmoid layer, and Dropout (0.3) to prevent overfitting. Training used a batch size of 256, a learning rate of 1e-5, and a cosine scheduler over 20,000 epochs. We tested multiple learning rates to ensure stable training and avoid divergence or mode collapse, selecting the most stable configuration.

4.3   Experimental Environment

We conducted two 4-week field experiments (A and B; see Table 2) at a technology company in Asia, utilizing a web-based exercise application, which resulted in 23 features per week and 92 features over the 4 weeks. During the study, we collected behavioral logs and data on psychological traits. We trained and evaluated the predictive model on both the original and cGAN-augmented datasets. At the beginning of each experiment, participants completed standardized psychological questionnaires. Gender was self-reported. While the questionnaire primarily offered binary options (male/female), a small number of participants identified as non-binary. To protect privacy and reduce bias, the model excluded gender and other demographic information, such as age, from its inputs.

Table 2. Details of Experiment A and B.

Experiment	A	B
Number of Participants	75	101
Self-reported Male (%)	62.0	61.0
Average age (years)	38.0	43.0
Standard Deviation (years)	11.8	11.7
Regular Exercise Habits (%)	38.7	29.7

5 Evaluation

5.1 Evaluation Result 1 (Standalone Performance of Experiment A)

We evaluated model performance using accuracy, standard deviation, precision, recall, and F1-score. Proposed-GAN achieved the highest accuracy (max: 0.98, avg.: 0.91) and the lowest variance (SD: 0.052), outperforming all five baselines: No Augmentation, Fixed Scaling [26], Random Scaling [27], Jittering [28], and Base GAN (no conditional input). Wilcoxon signed-rank tests confirmed statistically significant differences between Proposed-GAN and each baseline ($p < 0.001$), with the following W values: No Augmentation (W = 0.0), Fixed Scaling (W = 11.0), Random Scaling (W = 0.0), Jittering (W = 1.0), and Base GAN (W = 9.5). These results demonstrate the consistent superiority of our method over existing augmentation techniques (Fig. 3).

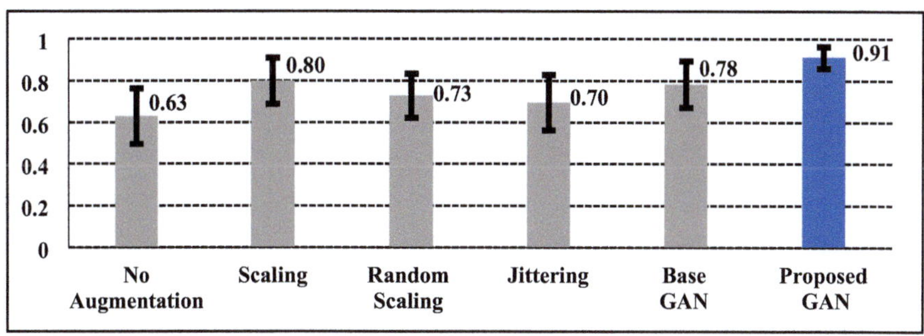

Fig. 3. Comparison of mean performance across baselines and Proposed-GAN models. Error bars indicate standard deviation.

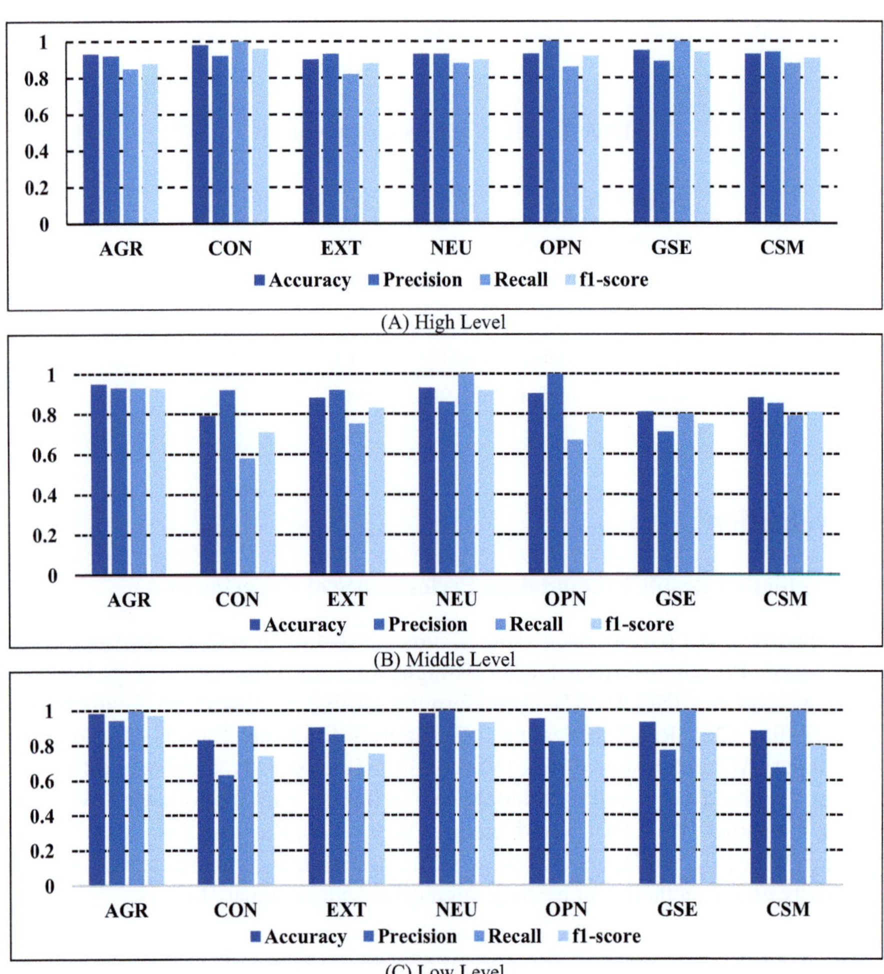

(A) High Level

(B) Middle Level

(C) Low Level

Fig. 4. Model Performance by Target Level.

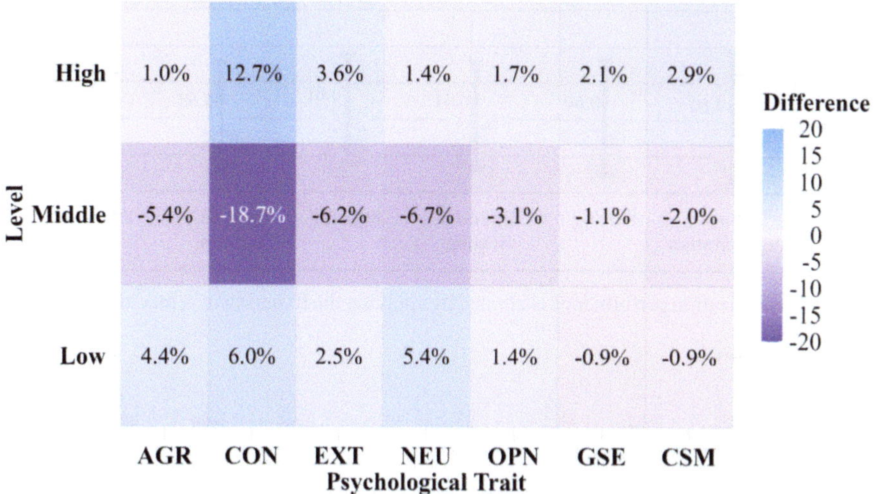

Fig. 5. Changes in class distribution caused by data augmentation and their effect on the classification performance of psychological trait estimation models.

Figure 4 shows that classification accuracy remained high for both High and Low levels across all psychological traits, with a slight drop at the Middle level. CON at the Low level had slightly lower accuracy and precision, while recall declined for EXT (Low) and CON/OPN (Middle). These results reflect the influence of the original distribution's imbalance, which continued to affect performance despite data augmentation.

This interpretation is further supported by the distributional changes shown in Fig. 5, which illustrates how the proportions of psychological traits shifted before and after data augmentation. Negative values indicate a decrease, while positive values indicate an increase. Notably, CON at the Middle level dropped significantly in classification performance (Fig. 4), likely due to distributional shifts introduced by GAN-based augmentation. This result suggests that the synthetic profiles diverged from the original behavioral patterns, reducing the model's ability to generalize in this category.

5.2 Evaluation Result 2 (Cross-Experiment Evaluation Results: Applying the Experiment A Model to Experiment B Data)

To test generalization and rule out overfitting, we applied the Experiment A model to Experiment B data (Fig. 6). Proposed-GAN achieved the highest accuracy (0.84) and average accuracy (0.64), outperforming all baselines. However, it showed higher variance (0.077), mainly due to lower precision for CON and GSE (Middle), and OPN and NEU (High). Wilcoxon signed-rank tests confirmed significant differences ($p < 0.05$) between Proposed-GAN and all baselines: No Augmentation ($W = 0.0$, $p = 1.53 \times 10^{-5}$), Fixed Scaling ($W = 11.0$, $p = 4.20 \times 10^{-4}$), Random Scaling ($W = 0.0$, $p = 2.91 \times 10^{-4}$), Jittering ($W = 2.0$, $p = 2.29 \times 10^{-5}$), and Base GAN ($W = 9.0$, $p = 2.52 \times 10^{-4}$). These results suggest that Proposed-GAN generalizes better by capturing behavioral patterns linked to psychological traits, rather than merely replicating questionnaire data.

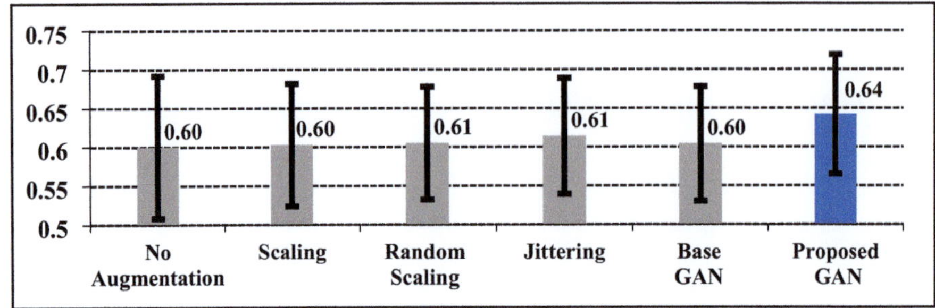

Fig. 6. Generalization performance evaluated by applying the Experiment A model to Experiment B data.

6 Conclusion and Future Work

This study introduces a model that estimates psychological traits—specifically, the Big Five, General Self-Efficacy, and Challenge-Seeking Motivation—by analyzing behavioral logs from app usage, thereby eliminating the need for traditional questionnaires. To improve performance, the approach applies a data augmentation method using Conditional GANs (cGANs). Experiments demonstrate that the proposed method surpasses conventional approaches, particularly in the high-trait class.

However, the model exhibits inconsistent accuracy in the middle and lower classes, underscoring the need to enhance generalization. Given the limited data, the study employs SVMs for classification, leveraging their robustness and interpretability. Building on this approach, subsequent studies could explore deep learning models, including Transformer-based architectures, to more accurately estimate psychological traits.

To enhance data augmentation, the strategy involves refining conditioning methods and modeling the interrelationships of psychological traits. While current conditioning uses complete questionnaire responses, targeting individual traits may yield more precise generation. Further research will investigate regularization, transfer learning, and meta-learning to improve generalization and reduce overfitting.

Ensuring model transparency and ethical integrity—respecting user autonomy and fostering trust—remains crucial for the practical deployment of models. Future efforts will strike a balance between psychological validity and computational efficiency through interdisciplinary collaboration.

7 Ethical Considerations

We conducted this study with corporate employees, taking care to minimize disruption to their routines. Before participation, we provided a comprehensive explanation of the study's objectives and procedures and obtained informed consent via a web form. All participants joined voluntarily and could withdraw at any time without penalty. To maintain high ethical standards, we followed three core principles: (1) protecting participant privacy through anonymized data, (2) ensuring voluntary participation without coercion, and (3) maintaining transparency regarding the study's purpose and data handling. As the study was conducted within a corporate setting, adhering to internal ethical standards, we did not seek formal approval from an external ethics committee; however, we ensured that all procedures adhered to accepted ethical practices for research involving human participants.

Disclosure of Interests. The authors have no competing interests to declare that are relevant to the content of this article.

References

1. Gustafson, D.H., McTavish, F.M., Chih, M.-Y., Atwood, A.K., Johnson, R.A., Boyle, M.G., Levy, M.S., Driscoll, H., Chisholm, S.M., Dillenburg, L., Isham, A., Shah, D.: A smartphone application to support recovery from alcoholism: a randomized clinical trial. JAMA Psychiatry. **71**(5), 566–572 (2014). https://doi.org/10.1001/jamapsychiatry.2013.4642
2. Ben-Zeev, D., Brenner, C.J., Begale, M., Duffecy, J., Mohr, D.C., Mueser, K.T.: Feasibility, acceptability, and preliminary efficacy of a smartphone intervention for schizophrenia. Schizophr. Bull. **40**(6), 1244–1253 (2014). https://doi.org/10.1093/schbul/sbu033
3. Stawarz, K., Cox, A.L., Blandford, A.: Beyond self-tracking and reminders: designing smartphone apps that support habit formation. In: Proceeding of the 33rd Annual ACM Conf. on Human Factors in Computing Systems, pp. 2653–2662 (2015)
4. Kaushal, N., Rhodes, R.E.: Exercise habit formation in new gym members: a longitudinal study. J. Behav. Med. **38**(4), 652–663 (2015). https://doi.org/10.1007/s10865-015-9640-7
5. Eysenbach, G.: The law of attrition revisited—author's reply. J. Med. Internet Res. **8**(3), 73–74 (2006)
6. Hornstein, S., Zantvoort, K., Lueken, U., Funk, B., Hilbert, K.: Personalization strategies in digital mental health interventions: a systematic review and conceptual framework for depressive symptoms. Front. Digit. Health. **5**, 1170002 (2023). https://doi.org/10.3389/fdgth.2023.1170002
7. Miyoshi, A.: Development of the subjective sensation of personality trait self-efficacy scale (SMSGSE). Jpn. J. Dev. Psychol. **14**(2), 172–179 (2003) (In Japanese). https://www.jstage.jst.go.jp/article/jjdp/14/2/14_KJ00001023960/_article/-char/ja/
8. Breso, E., Schaufeli, W.B., Salanova, M.: Can a self-efficacy-based intervention decrease burnout, increase engagement, and enhance performance? A quasi-experimental study. High. Educ. **61**, 339–355 (2011). https://doi.org/10.1007/s10734-010-9334-6
9. Montag, C., Dagum, P., Hall, B.J., Panksepp, J., Elhai, J.D.: Do we still need psychological self-report questionnaires in the age of the internet of things? Disc. Psychol. 2(1), Art 1 (2022). doi: https://doi.org/10.1007/s44202-021-00012-4
10. John, O.P., Srivastava, S.: The big five trait taxonomy: history, measurement, and theoretical perspectives. In: Pervin, L.A., John, O.P. (eds.) Handbook of Personality: Theory and Research, 2nd edn, pp. 102–138. Guilford Press (1999)
11. Bowling, N.A., Gibson, A.M., DeSimone, J.A.: Stop with the questions already! Does data quality suffer for scales positioned near the end of a lengthy questionnaire? J. Bus. Psychol. **37**(6), 1099–1116 (2022). https://doi.org/10.1007/s10869-021-09787-8
12. Kosinski, M., Stillwell, D., Graepel, T.: Manifestations of user personality in website choice and behaviour on online social networks. Mach. Learn. **95**(3), 357–380 (2013)
13. Sano, A., Phillips, A.J., Picard, R.W.: Recognizing academic performance, sleep quality, stress level, and mental health using personality traits, wearable sensors, and mobile phones. Comput. Hum. Behav. **86**, 35–45 (2018)
14. Naz, A., Khan, H.U., Bukhari, A., Alshemaimri, B., Daud, A., Ramzan, M.: Machine and deep learning for personality traits detection: a comprehensive survey and open research challenges. Artif. Intell. Rev. **58**, 239 (2025). https://doi.org/10.1007/s10462-025-11245-3

15. Orru, G., Monaro, M., Conversano, C., Gemignani, A., Sartori, G.: Machine learning in psychometrics and psychological research. Front. Psychol. **10**, 2970 (2019). https://doi.org/10.3389/fpsyg.2019.02970

16. Tay, L., Jebb, A.T., Woo, S.E.: A conceptual framework for investigating and mitigating machine-learning measurement bias (MLMB) in psychological assessment. Front. Psychol. **13**, 867132 (2022). https://doi.org/10.3389/fpsyg.2022.867132

17. Chawla, N.V., Bowyer, K.W., Hall, L.O., Kegelmeyer, W.P.: SMOTE: synthetic minority over-sampling technique. J. Artif. Intell. Res. **16**, 321–357 (2002). https://doi.org/10.1613/jair.953

18. Bunkhumpornpat, C., Sinapiromsaran, K., Lursinsap, C.: Safe-level-SMOTE: safe-level-synthetic minority over-sampling technique for handling the class imbalanced problem. In: Theeramunkong, T., Kijsirikul, B., Cercone, N., Ho, H. (eds.) Advances in Knowledge Discovery and Data Mining: PAKDD 2009, pp. 475–482. Springer (2009). https://doi.org/10.1007/978-3-642-01307-2_43

19. Kingma, D.P., Welling, M.: Auto-encoding variational Bayes. arXiv preprint arXiv:1312.6114 (2014). https://arxiv.org/abs/1312.6114

20. Goodfellow, I., Pouget-Abadie, J., Mirza, M., Xu, B., Warde-Farley, D., Ozair, S., Courville, A., Bengio, Y.: Generative adversarial nets. Adv. Neural Inf. Proces. Syst. **27**, 2672–2680 (2014)

21. Goodfellow, I., Pouget-Abadie, J., Mirza, M., Xu, B., Warde-Farley, D., Ozair, S., Courville, A., Bengio, Y.: Generative adversarial networks. Commun. ACM. **63**(11), 139–144 (2020). https://doi.org/10.1145/3422622

22. Wang, F., Zhong, S., Peng, J., Jiang, J., Liu, Y.: Data augmentation for EEG-based emotion recognition with deep convolutional neural networks. In: Schoeffmann, K., Hussain, T., Culpepper, C., El-Assady, M., Han, J.H., Hu, X. (eds.) MultiMedia Modeling. MMM 2018. Lecture Notes in Computer Science, vol. 10705, pp. 82–93. Springer (2018). https://doi.org/10.1007/978-3-319-73600-6_8

23. Manjunath, N., Li, Z.Y., Choi, E.S., Sen, S., Wang, F., Adler, D.I.: Can data augmentation improve daily mood prediction from wearable data? An empirical study. In: Adjunct Proceedings of the 2023 ACM International Joint Conference on Pervasive and Ubiquitous Computing & 2023 ACM International Symposium on Wearable Computing (UbiComp/ISWC '23 Adjunct), pp. 1–6. ACM (2023). https://doi.org/10.1145/3594739.3612876

24. Horino, M.: Analysis of the components of achievement motivation. Jpn. J. Educ. Psychol. **35**(2), 148–154 (1987) (In Japanese). https://www.jstage.jst.go.jp/article/jjep1953/35/2/35_148/_pdf/-char/ja/

25. Mirza, M., Osindero, S.: Conditional generative adversarial nets. arXiv preprint arXiv:1411.1784 (2014). https://arxiv.org/abs/1411.1784

26. Simard, P.Y., Steinkraus, D., Platt, J.C.: Best practices for convolutional neural networks applied to visual document analysis. In: Proceedings of the Seventh International Conference on Document Analysis and Recognition (ICDAR), pp. 958–963. IEEE (2003). https://doi.org/10.1109/ICDAR.2003.1227801

27. Pialla, G., Devanne, M., Weber, J., Idoumghar, L., Forestier, G.: Data augmentation for time series classification with deep learning models. In: Advanced Analytics and Learning on Temporal Data, pp. 117–132. Springer (2023). https://doi.org/10.1007/978-3-031-24378-3_8
28. Um, T.T., Pfister, F.M.J., Pichler, D., Endo, S., Lang, M., Hirche, S., Fietzek, U., Kulić, D.: Data augmentation of wearable sensor data for Parkinson's disease monitoring using convolutional neural networks. In: Proceedings of the 19th ACM International Conference on Multimodal Interaction, pp. 216–220. ACM (2017). https://doi.org/10.1145/3136755.313 6817

Innovations for Healthcare and Inclusive Design

Integrating Human-Centered Design with ASPE Best Practices to Enhance Standardized Patient Training for Communicating Breaking Bad News in Healthcare Simulation

Swetha Anand[(⊠)] and Cecilia Xi Wang

University of Minnesota, Minneapolis, MN 55414, USA
`Anand172@umn.edu`

Abstract. Standardized Patients (SPs) provide invaluable insights during feedback sessions in simulation training. When faced with the task of delivering difficult news, students often experience feelings of nervousness and unpreparedness in response to the stress, anxiety, and unpredictability associated with a patient's reaction. It is, therefore, crucial for students to be well-equipped for the demanding environment of conveying challenging information, where empathy and compassion play essential roles. In this scenario, SPs also encounter their own stress, as they must communicate effectively while meeting the simulation's objectives. They additionally need to address any knowledge gaps to ensure they confidently convey accurate information to students through constructive feedback, all while managing their own emotions.

SPs must also undergo continuous training to be both physically and psychologically equipped to deliver effective simulation sessions for students. Given the variety of models, frameworks, and scenarios that SPs need to be ready to perform repeatedly, this can be quite demanding. To meet these needs, SPs require comprehensive training that aligns with ASPE best practices. This literature review aims to investigate how human-centred design principles can be seamlessly integrated into the established best practices for SP simulation training systems. By incorporating ASPE guidelines and design thinking into targeted workshops, SPs can engage with a variety of perspectives and scenarios. This approach will empower them to practice effectively, enhancing their readiness to deliver a meaningful and impactful simulation experience for students.

Keywords: Bad News · Standardized Patient · Simulation Training · ASPE Best Practices · Human-Centered Design · Design Thinking Workshop · Communicating Bad News

1 Introduction

Bad news can significantly affect patients' perceptions of their future at the time of the diagnosis or over a period in addition to other factors influencing the illness [19]. Therefore, it is critical for medical physicians to interact with patients and family members

© The Author(s), under exclusive license to Springer Nature Switzerland AG 2026
S. Sundarakannan and O. Knorpp (Eds.): HCII 2025, CCIS 2772, pp. 193–203, 2026.
https://doi.org/10.1007/978-3-032-12767-9_21

thoughtfully when discussing complex and multifaceted topics. Additionally, communicating medical information clearly while being sensitive to the emotional reactions of patients and their families is essential [6]. When communication is handled properly, it can lead to greater patient satisfaction and trust [13].

Simulation provides a safe environment for students to develop both clinical and soft skills [5] before they interact with real patients, which are necessary for effectively communicating bad news. Simulation training has different methodology including Standardized patients (SPs), which help to humanize the simulation process. SPs are trained professionals who portray patients to meet training, assessment, and educational objectives [8, 9, 12]. They also observe students during simulations and provide feedback through debriefing sessions or based on the design of the simulation [5, 8]. SPs positively impact students by helping reduce anxiety during rotations and enhance long-term knowledge retention [5], self-efficacy, communication skills [11], and learning motivation [8]. This experiential learning prepares students for delivering bad news in a safe environment with well-designed scenarios specifically addressing emotionally distressing simulations [5]. Additionally, proper training can also contribute to physicians' well-being and help reduce burnout [4].

During training, SPs are tasked with observing students while they navigate stressful scenarios and providing constructive feedback on communication techniques, including guidance on how to improve their skills [5]. At the same time, SPs may experience emotional distress due to triggers related to their own life experiences. To avoid adverse effects from repeatedly confronting these scenarios, SPs require support and must cultivate self-awareness to cope effectively. It is important for SPs to establish clear emotional boundaries while engaging in complex conversations and to maintain compassion for the students [9].

In this context, SPs also face stress as they must communicate effectively while fulfilling the objectives of the simulation. Additionally, SPs are expected to address their own knowledge gaps to feel confident and consistently convey the right information to students through feedback, all while managing their emotions. In order for SPs to be able to provide good simulation experience for the students in addition to maintaining their well-being, they need appropriate training, which can be achieved by applying best practices from the Association of Standardized Patient Educators (ASPE).

The objective of this research is to explore how human-centered design principles can be integrated into existing Standards of Best Practices (SOBP) for standardized patient (SP) simulation training systems. The following research questions will be examined through a literature review:

RQ1: How are ASPE best practices applied to train SPs in the context of breaking bad news during simulation training?
RQ2: How can design thinking be utilized to create uniformity in existing simulation training?

2 Methodology

To address these questions, a literature review was conducted to understand the best practices in communication for SPs as outlined by the Association of Standardized Patient Educators (ASPE) and to examine how these practices are implemented. Searches were conducted in various databases including SCOPUS, PubMed, Google Scholar, ERIC, MedEdPortal, and MedEdPublish. Additionally, cross-references were included in the review. Only studies focused on SP-based training for communication skills related to breaking bad news were considered, while other types of simulation training were excluded. Papers from the past ten years were prioritized, and the following keywords were used for the search:

"bad news," "standardized patient," "simulation training," "ASPE best practices," "human-centered design," "design thinking workshop," and "communication of bad news."

In total, 5,380 papers were identified during the search. After removing duplicates and excluding those that did not pertain to communication of bad news, 11 papers were selected based on their abstracts. Only papers published in English were included in the final selection.

3 Discussion

Breaking bad news is an essential communication skill that physicians require for strong professional competencies in nearly all medical specialties [4, 7]. This ability is vital, as it significantly impacts both patients and their families, influencing their emotional and psychological well-being [7]. Additionally, medical physicians must interact thought-fully with patients and their family members when discussing complex and multifaceted topics such as diagnosis, prognosis, management options, goals of therapy, and toxicity. It is crucial that they communicate medical information clearly, while being sensitive to the emotional reactions of patients and their families, including discussions about end-of-life information when necessary [6].

Learning to communicate with empathy is vital for students when delivering bad news, as it demonstrates concern for patients and helps reduce the uneasiness they face, especially given that the situation is often beyond their control [2]. Research has shown that physicians frequently lack the skills and confidence needed to communicate bad news effectively [2]. Therefore, physicians need essential skills to be empathetic toward patients while breaking bad news, which requires appropriate training. Without adequate practice, physicians may not be prepared and might develop inappropriate ways of communicating information, leading to emotional repercussions [4] (Fig. 1).

Even though physicians encounter challenging situations on a daily basis in their clinical practice, they may continue to lack effective interpersonal communication skills and empathy, which are crucial in the clinical arena [6]. This can result in negative consequences for patient-physician interactions, where physicians might disengage from patients, prompting them to seek care from different providers [4].

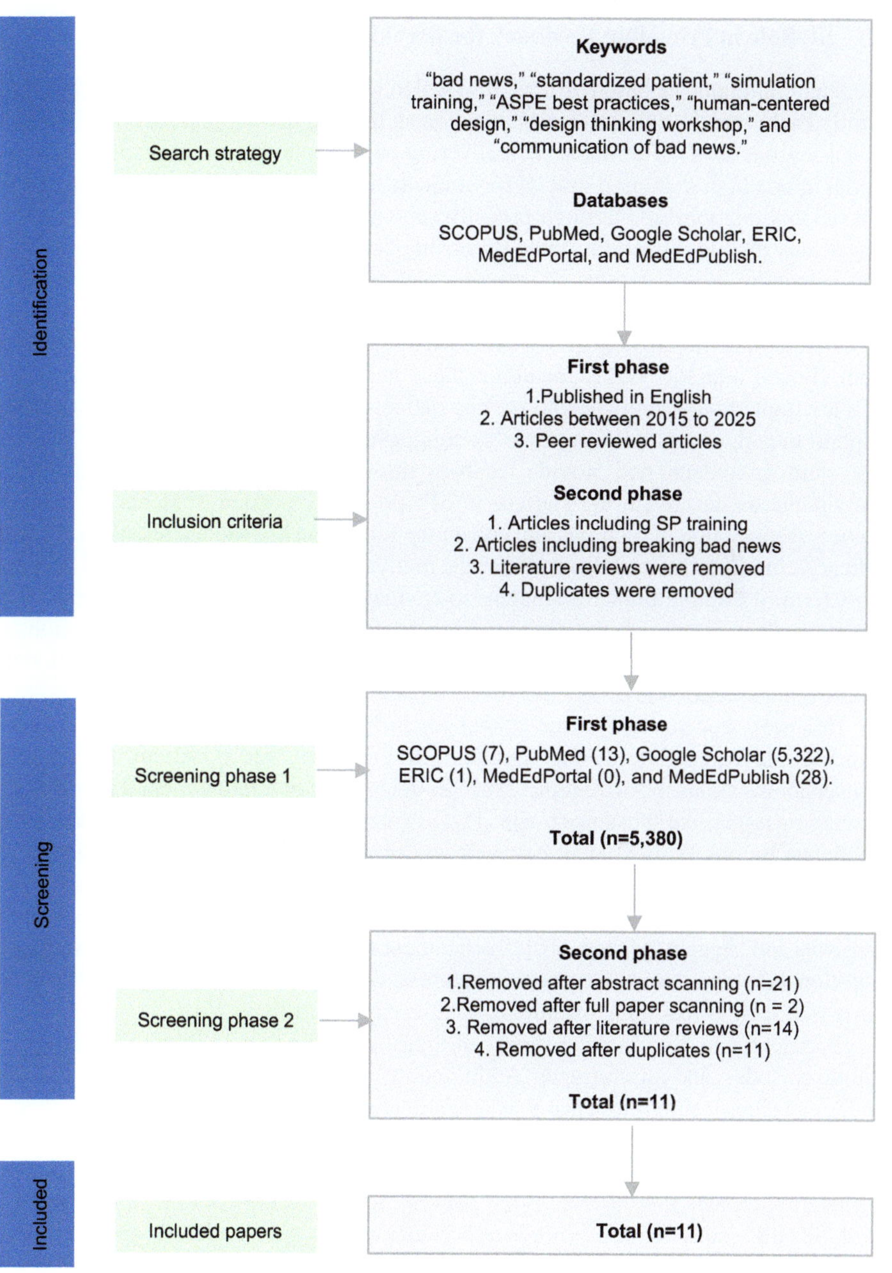

Fig. 1. Flowchart of the selection process.

3.1 SP Role in Providing Feedback for Breaking Bad News

Students communicate based on the individual influences of their lifetime, which include family backgrounds, cultural communication styles, and the training received in educational settings [3, 7]. The impact of delivering bad news to patients lasts long after the initial interaction, making it crucial for students to be trained to foster positive patient-physician's relationships through proactive communication [2, 4]. Additionally, some physicians may feel uncomfortable disclosing full information about bad news [1, 7] and managing illness options due to a lack of knowledge about how to convey such information in an empathetic manner [2].

Simulation with the help of SPs provides a safe environment for students to develop both clinical and soft skills, including those necessary for delivering bad news [5]. SPs are trained professionals who portray patients, family members, and other roles to support the educational objectives of training, assessment, and instruction [8, 9]. They also observe students and provide feedback through debriefing sessions or as part of the simulation design [5, 8]. The use of SPs positively impacts students by reducing anxiety during clinical rotations and enhancing long-term knowledge retention [5], self-efficacy, communication skills, and learning motivation [8] through experiential learning. This form of training prepares students to navigate the complex task of delivering bad news—such as a cancer diagnosis, the death of a loved one, or the implications of mental illness—within a controlled environment using carefully designed, emotionally challenging scenarios [5].

However, students often face challenges in managing the emotional behaviors of patients (played by SPs) during simulation training, and find it difficult to engage in conversations about sensitive topics, such as diagnosing or treating mental illnesses and discussing issues like substance use [9, 11]. SPs are expected to help students address this challenge by observing student behavior and providing timely feedback or debriefing based on the specific case scenario design [5]. Throughout the training process, SPs are expected to prioritize the students, especially since delivering bad news involves many stressors and triggers for them [10]. During these simulations, students often experience emotional distress due to the sensitive nature of the topics and the physical interactions involved, such as touching, examining, and re-clothing patients [5].

Bad news can cover a wide variety of topics, including schizophrenia, autism, psychotic episodes, and miscarriages. Additionally, factors like emotions, beliefs, and attitudes can significantly influence a patient's unique responses to medical staff [2]. This underscores the importance of integrating the patient's voice into medical education, using SPs as a tool to convey tacit knowledge and improve assessments. A patient-centered approach aids in identifying patterns for practicing communication training with SPs that focus on patient needs rather than what may be easier for providers [2].

Moreover, it's essential for providers to demonstrate humanity by being considerate of patient needs and feelings. This involves asking patients about their preferences to develop solutions tailored to their needs, which requires proper training—particularly in verbal communication techniques such as tone of voice [2], as well as non-verbal cues. Recognizing and responding to these cues is critical for delivering empathetic care [2, 5].

Table 1. Table showing medical field and training type used for breaking bad.

Paper	Medical field	Training type
Delivering Difficult News: Simulation-Enhanced Training Improves Psychiatry Residents' Clinical Communication Skills	Workshop	Mental health disorders
Qualitative Assessment of Bad News Delivery Practices during Miscarriage Diagnosis	Objective Structured Clinical Examination (OSCE) using SP training	Miscarriage Diagnosis
Breaking Bad News: A Randomized Trial Assessing Resident Performance After Novel Video Instruction	Objective Structured Clinical Examination (OSCE) using SP training	Obstetrics/Gynecology
Implementation of the REFLECT Communication Curriculum for Clinical Oncology Graduate Medical Education	Workshop (using REFLECT)	Oncology
Resilience Curriculum Improves Skills of Pediatric Fellows in Delivery of Difficult News	Objective Structured Clinical Examination (OSCE) using SP training	Pediatric
The Use of Simulated Participant and Virtual Reality Simulation to Enhance Nursing Students' Communication Skills in "End of Life Care"-A Single-Arm Repeated Measures Study	VR followed by SP simulation	End-Of-Life care
Delivering bad or difficult news. An innovative simulation-based education approach to prepare interdisciplinary fellowships	Objective Structured Clinical Examination (OSCE) using SP training	–
"I Felt The Connection": A Qualitative Exploration of Standardized Patients' Experiences in a Delivering Bad News Scenario.	Online and in-person workshop	Nursing
Experiences of Simulated Patients Involved in Difficult Conversations With Undergraduate and Postgraduate Health Professionals	–	–

(*continued*)

Table 1. (*continued*)

Paper	Medical field	Training type
Development of an integrated milestone assessment tool across multiple early-adopter programs for breaking bad news: a pilot project	–	–
Delivering Difficult News: Simulation-Enhanced Training Improves Psychiatry Residents' Clinical Communication Skills	Problem-Based Learning (PBL) groups	–

Empathetic care can be provided in several ways. For instance, when communicating bad news, healthcare providers should avoid rushing the interaction or focusing on the clock [5]. The empathetic care required by patients can be provided in ways such as, when communicating bad news, physicians should not rush the interaction or focus on the clock [5], Instead, they should allow patients time to process information, using supportive body language, maintaining eye contact and intentional pauses. This approach validates the patients' thoughts and feelings. Another effective communication strategy is rephrasing the patient's words to ensure they feel heard [2]. It's also important to reassure patients and communicate in non-medical jargon, being mindful of language to avoid making patients feel judged [2, 5]. Consequently, many studies indicate that training is primarily focused on developing students' self-efficacy and satisfaction outcomes to tackle the aforementioned communication challenges [1].

Providing care and attention to students has been a motivating factor for SPs, who place emphasis on both verbal and non-verbal behaviors as essential aspects of effective communication [9]. It is important to note that SPs can have both positive impacts, such as encouraging socialization, student interaction, and performance satisfaction, as well as negative impacts, including stress, anxiety, shame, uncertainty, and physical discomfort [5]. These impacts often arise from the roles they play during simulation sessions and the transitions between those roles [9].

3.2 Current Best Practices in SP Training

There is limited research specifically focused on how Standardized Patients (SPs) are prepared for delivering bad news scenarios, primarily due to the complexity of training required to ensure SPs are both emotionally and intellectually equipped [9].

The Association of Standardized Patient Educators (ASPE), a global organization dedicated to human simulation, emphasizes the importance of SP research and support [12]. ASPE has published the Standards of Best Practice (SOBP) for SP training, which serves as a comprehensive guide for various use cases but still has limitations [5]. This document was created with the well-being of SPs in mind [12].

ASPE proposes five key principles for the SP training process: (1) preparation for the training process, (2) role-specific training, (3) feedback training, (4) completion of assessment instruments, and (5) reflection on the training process [12]. These training components are vital to support both the emotional and physical well-being of SPs during simulation sessions for student training.

However, the SOBP is not specifically designed to train SPs in delivering bad news. This creates several challenges. For instance, SPs must maintain emotional balance and develop strategies to portray their roles consistently, ensuring that all students receive equal learning opportunities. Furthermore, it is essential that SPs receive regular training on the various methodologies used in simulation sessions. As outlined in Table 1, these training methodologies can vary significantly across different medical fields and universities. A lack of familiarity with these methodologies may increase SP vulnerability and contribute to elevated stress levels. Therefore, understanding the training methodologies and frameworks discussed below is crucial.

Frameworks Used in Medical Student Training. Communication is an iterative process involving the exchange of verbal and non-verbal messages [14]. Its complexity is heightened by a variety of individual contexts and power dynamics, such as expectations between participants [5].

To navigate the complexities of bad news communication, which often involves significant emotional sensitivity, healthcare education has adopted several frameworks and methodologies, including SPIKES [1, 10], the Kalamazoo Consensus, Motivational Interviewing, the Girgis and Sanson-Fischer Protocol [1], GRIEV_ING, the ABCDE Approach, Patient-Centered Communication Framework [2], and the BREAKS Protocol [7]. The SPIKES model, initially developed in 2000 for communicating bad news to cancer patients, is widely utilized for its structured yet empathetic approach—SPIKES stands for Setting, Perception, Invitation, Knowledge, Empathy, and Summary, encompassing a comprehensive protocol for delivering bad news [7].

Lastly, the REFLECT framework employs a curriculum that incorporates multiple skills through practice and repetition. This framework has been used effectively with radiation oncology residents and medical oncology fellows, utilizing a reflective process to enhance physicians' self-efficacy in delivering bad news [6].

Training Methodologies. Given the challenges of communicating bad news, in addition to frameworks, various methodologies have been implemented to support physician well-being, reduce burnout, and strengthen patient-provider relationships [20]. Learners benefit from information presented in diverse formats. One effective approach is using concise educational videos grounded in best practices, complemented by patient feedback from real-life scenarios [4]. Additionally, training can be conducted through small-group sessions that incorporate peer role-play or SP role-play [2], one-on-one encounters with SPs [2, 13], lectures, discussions [20], clinical observations, and simulations involving standardized patients [3]. Another innovative methodology includes the integration of realistic virtual reality (VR) with SP simulation, which has been shown to enhance students' confidence, provisional skills, and knowledge while increasing engagement in the learning process [11].

3.3 Human-Centered Design Workshop

Given the variety of frameworks and methodologies, it is important to establish a standardized process for training SPs that is tailored to their needs and addresses their challenges. At the core of human-centric design—often referred to as design thinking—is the creation of experiences that prioritize human needs. In this context, SPs become the focal point of the design process.

Design thinking is multidisciplinary, and its definition can vary depending on the designer's methodology and the specific context in which it is applied. Fundamentally, it aims to drive innovation by fostering a deeper understanding of human needs and desires through careful observation [15].

In this scenario, the needs of SPs are paramount for effective simulation training, enabling students to practice empathy and gain knowledge while ensuring their well-being and reducing stress. Recently, design thinking has gained traction in the healthcare sector [16, 18].

Design thinking comprises a six-step nonlinear process: (1) empathize, (2) define, (3) ideate, (4) prototype, (5) test, and (6) implement. This framework can be adapted based on the specific field and context of use. By centering on user needs—specifically those of SPs—collaboration with various stakeholders [15] is essential to develop and execute workshops effectively. This collaborative approach supports SPs' training while establishing a standardized process.

The advantages of integrating a design-driven approach include fostering empathy, collaboration, and innovation, which are invaluable in medical education. Additionally, the qualitative and divergent thinking aspects of design thinking are essential for keeping pace with the evolving medical field 16] [18].. Balancing the essential knowledge and skills with the needs of learners' performance and objectives is achieved through a human-centric design approach [17].

This can be realized by developing workshops in collaboration with diverse stakeholders, allowing the simulation team to bring different insights and perspectives [17]. Such workshops aim to enhance SPs' training, improve educational materials, and develop effective processes for teaching sensitive skills, such as delivering bad news. They contribute to standardizing training processes, continuously building and updating SP training materials, and introducing new insights and scenarios.

Workshops also address the knowledge and skill gaps that SPs may face due to their non-medical backgrounds. This creates a safe learning environment where they can build confidence and ultimately enhance students' simulation training experiences.

Utilizing human-centric design can effectively facilitate collaboration among various stakeholders, including instructors, SPs, SPEs, and students, to gather input for refining training methods for SPs. In the "Empathize" phase, different stakeholders, guided by a facilitator, can plan data collection using various tools such as interviews, site visits, and observations in hospitals and clinics. During the "Define" phase, objectives for SP training should be established using ASPE best practices while addressing challenges related to their implementation. This can involve creating journey maps, mind maps, and utilizing drawings or diagrams to identify patterns and formulate relevant "How might we" questions for the workshop.

The ideation phase can generate a range of scenarios based on experiences shared by different stakeholders, which can be formulated into practice cases. The "Prototype" phase may involve two volunteers acting out each case scenario for refinement. Finally, the "Implementation" phase could see SPs, along with other workshop members, practicing the developed case scenarios. Designers and planners should document the case scenarios and workshop design for future reference by SPs, allowing for broader accessibility.

This workshop will help SPs bridge their knowledge and skill gaps, significantly enhancing the training quality they provide. Moreover, human-centric design promotes continuous improvement of the SP training process, thereby maintaining high standards that benefit not only current students but also future ones, particularly as technology and methodologies evolve.

4 Conclusion

Delivering bad news is a challenging task, and it is essential for students to receive adequate training from standardized patients (SPs). SPs must also undergo continuous training to be both physically and psychologically equipped to deliver effective simulation sessions for students. Given the variety of models, frameworks, and scenarios that SPs need to be ready to perform repeatedly, this can be quite demanding. To enhance this process, incorporating ASPE best practices along with design thinking through workshops can offer SPs diverse perspectives and scenarios while allowing them to practice and ensure they are well-prepared to provide students with a valuable simulation experience.

References

1. Amsalem, D., Martin, A., Mosheva, M., Soul, O., Korotkin, L., Ziv, A., Gothelf, D., Gross, R.: Delivering difficult news: simulation-enhanced training improves psychiatry residents' clinical communication skills. Front. Psych. **12**(649090) (2021)
2. Brann, M., Bute, J.J., Scott, S.F.: Qualitative assessment of bad news delivery practices during miscarriage diagnosis. Qual. Health Res. **30**(2), 258–267 (2020)
3. Beaird, G., Nye, C., Thacker, L.R.: The use of video recording and standardized patient feedback to improve communication performance in undergraduate nursing students. Clin. Simul. Nurs. **13**(4), 176–185 (2017)
4. Shanks, A., Brann, M., Bute, J., Borse, V., Tonismae, T., Scott, N.: Breaking bad news: a randomized trial assessing resident performance after novel video instruction. Cureus. **13**(6), e15461 (2021)
5. Dawson, R.M., Lawrence, K., Gibbs, S., Davis, V., Mele, C., Murillo, C.: "I felt the connection": a qualitative exploration of standardized patients' experiences in a delivering bad news scenario. Clin. Simul. Nurs. **55**, 52–58 (2021)
6. Vern-Gross, T.Z., Laughlin, B.S., Kough, K., Ernst, B., Langley, N., Rule, W.G., Patel, S.H., Ashman, J.B.: Implementation of the REFLECT communication curriculum for clinical oncology graduate medical education. J. Palliat. Med. **27**(2), 231–235 (2024)
7. Turner, A., Gopakumar, S., Minard, C., Guffey, D., Allen, N., Kuo, D., Poszywak, K., Pillow, M.T.: Development of an integrated milestone assessment tool across multiple early-adopter programs for breaking bad news: a pilot project. BMC Med. Educ. **24**(1), 313 (2024)

8. Hillier, M., Williams, T. L., & Chidume, T.: Standardization of Standardized Patient Training in Medical Simulation. (2020)

9. Wiechula, L.A., Chur-Hansen, A., Davies, E.L.: Experiences of simulated patients involved in difficult conversations with undergraduate and postgraduate health professionals. Simul. Healthc.: J. Soc. Simul. Healthc. **19**(6), e127–e134 (2024)

10. Murtha, T.D., Hafler, J., Taylor, E.P., Tala, J., Asnes, A., Massaro, S., Kandil, S.: Resilience curriculum improves skills of pediatric fellows in delivery of difficult news. Rhode Island Med. J. **107**(5), 49–53 (2024)

11. Hall, K., Bhowmik, J., Simonda, I., Edward, K.-l.: The use of simulated participant and virtual reality simulation to enhance nursing students' communication skills in "end of life care" - a single-arm repeated measures study. Clin. Simul. Nurs. **91**, 101543 (2024)

12. Lewis, K.L., Bohnert, C.A., Gammon, W.L., Hölzer, H., Lyman, L., Smith, C., et al.: The association of standardized patient educators (ASPE) standards of best practice (SOBP). Adv. Simul. **2**, 1–8 (2017)

13. Clapper, T.C., Sewell, T.B., Shen, W., Ching, K., Solomon, A.B., Burns, K.P., Martin, P.B., Turetz, M.L., Crawford, C.V., Joyce, C.L., Landres, I.V., Rajwani, K.: Delivering bad or difficult news. An innovative simulation-based education approach to prepare interdisciplinary fellowships. J. Commun. Healthc. **17**(1), 44–50 (2024)

14. Jones, R.G.: Communication in the Real World: an Introduction to Communication Studies. Flat World Knowledge (2003)

15. Brown, T.: Design thinking. Harv. Bus. Rev. **86**(6), 84–92, 141 (2008)

16. Gottlieb, M., Wagner, E., Wagner, A., Chan, T.: Applying design thinking principles to curricular development in medical education. AEM Educ. Train. **1**(1), 21–26 (2017)

17. Schoenherr, J.R., McConnell, M.M.: Human-Centered Design in Health Professions Education. In: Fundamentals and Frontiers of Medical Education and Decision-Making: Educational Theory and Psychological Practice, vol. 3, p. 1 (2024)

18. Moon, S., Chang, S.J.: Comparing the effects of patient safety education using design thinking and case based learning on nursing students' competence and professional socialization: a quasi-experimental design. Heliyon. **10**(9), e29942 (2024)

19. Buckman, R.: Breaking bad news: why is it still so difficult? Br. Med. J. Clin. Res. Ed. **288**, 1597–1599 (1984)

20. Poei, D.M., Tang, M.N., Kwong, K.M., Sakai 4th, D.H., Choi 4th, S.Y., Chen, J.J.: Increasing medical students' confidence in delivering bad news using different teaching modalities. Hawai'i J. Health Soc. Welf. **81**(11), 302–308 (2022)

A Web-Based System for Comprehensive and Accessible Navigation to Exhibits of a Virtual Museum

Despoina Athanasiadou[1], Asterios Leonidis[1,2]($\boxtimes$) , Maria Korozi[1] , Margherita Antona[1] , and Constantine Stephanidis[1,2]

[1] Institute of Computer Science (ICS), Foundation for Research and Technology - Hellas (FORTH), Heraklion, Crete, Greece
`{athandesp,leonidis,korozi,antona,cs}@ics.forth.gr`
[2] Computer Science Department, University of Crete, Heraklion, Crete, Greece

Abstract. The digitization of museum collections has significantly expanded public access to cultural heritage through interactive virtual reality (VR) tours. These web-based experiences provide valuable opportunities for remote engagement with cultural content and are increasingly adopted by institutions worldwide. In this paper, we take a closer look at two such case studies: the Museum of Education and the Museum of Medicine, of the University of Crete. Both museums have implemented VR-based tours that digitally preserve their collections and present them through interactive, web-accessible platforms. However, they often fall short in addressing the needs of users with disabilities, limiting inclusive participation and highlighting the accessibility gap in current immersive systems. To bridge this gap, this project introduces an accessible, web-based version of the university of Crete's virtual museum systems, designed to offer inclusive navigation and interaction for users of all abilities. Built as a single-page Angular application, it incorporates features such as keyboard navigation, screen reader support, high-contrast visual elements, and responsive design, ensuring compliance with the Web Content Accessibility Guidelines (WCAG). Through a user-centered design approach, the system presents multimedia content, including text, images, videos, image galleries, and interactive 3D exhibits, in an intuitive and engaging interface. This work showcases how modern web technologies can enhance immersive digital experiences while ensuring universal accessibility, offering a scalable and adaptable framework for future digital cultural heritage applications.

Keywords: Accessible Web Design · Cultural Heritage · Web Content Accessibility Guidelines (WCAG) · Screen Reader Compatibility · Keyboard Navigation · Inclusive Design · User-Centered Design

© The Author(s), under exclusive license to Springer Nature Switzerland AG 2026
S. Sundarakannan and O. Knorpp (Eds.): HCII 2025, CCIS 2772, pp. 204–214, 2026.
https://doi.org/10.1007/978-3-032-12767-9_22

1   Introduction

1.1   Background and Motivation

Museums are pivotal in preserving and sharing cultural heritage, providing access to history, art, and culture for diverse audiences. Over the years, advancements in technology have transformed the way museums interact with visitors [5,9], introducing immersive experiences such as Virtual Reality (VR) tours [10]. These systems allow users to explore exhibits in a highly engaging manner, breaking physical boundaries and making museum content accessible from anywhere.

However, despite their technological appeal, most existing virtual museum systems remain inaccessible to many users, particularly those with disabilities [3,4] . Key limitations include the lack of support for screen readers and keyboard-only navigation, limited mobile responsiveness, and complex interfaces that may overwhelm users with cognitive or perceptual challenges. As a result, such systems exclude a significant part of the public from fully experiencing cultural heritage content.

The Accessible Invisible Museum Framework. The Museum of Education[1] of the Department of Primary Education and the Museum of Medicine[2] of the School of Medicine, both offer web-based virtual tours that digitally preserve and present important aspects of local cultural heritage. The former was founded with the aim of a) searching, recording, preserving, exhibiting and scientific studying of the educational school past and the history of the teaching profession during the most recent period of Greek history, b) displaying and promoting its archival material conventionally and digitally, c) connecting with the Greek educational and school reality an added European cultural value and an important historical parameter about schooling of the 21st century.

The latter's philosophy is based on a broad exploration of the relationship between humans and medicine. Its collections include hundreds of objects, such as historical medical books, instruments, pharmaceutical utensils, and photographs. The museum organizes its exhibits and activities around five main thematic areas: a) places of healing, focusing on both their physical settings and the people connected to them, b) the human body, the senses, and the brain, c) medical tools and technologies, d) medicinal plants and herbs, and e) the connection between medicine, literature, and the arts. These areas complement one another by offering different perspectives on the role of medicine in human life, ranging from practical applications to cultural and artistic representations. Although immersive and educational, these systems lack accessibility features, making them difficult to use for individuals with disabilities.

The systems are also not optimized for smaller screens or mobile devices, limiting their usability for users without access to larger or VR-enabled setups. Additionally, the dense multimedia content and complex navigation structure

---

[1] https://e-her.org/applications/vr.
[2] https://digital-museum.med.uoc.gr/applications/vr.

can lead to cognitive overload, particularly for users with cognitive disabilities. These issues highlight the need for a more inclusive and universally accessible solution.

1.2 Proposed Solution

This project focuses on adapting existing VR museum tours into accessible web-based formats by developing a solution that ensures universal access to museum content, supports screen readers, keyboard navigation, and high-contrast visuals, and adheres to the Web Content Accessibility Guidelines (WCAG) 2.1 [2]. Key aspects of the work include:

- Analyzing the aforementioned museum VR systems while also identifying the accessibility barriers.
- Designing and developing low and high fidelity prototypes for the accessible version.
- Implementing the accessible version, ensuring compliance with accessibility standards.

2 Design Process

The design process for creating the accessible web-based version of the virtual museum systems followed a user-centered approach, emphasizing iterative development and adherence to accessibility principles [7]. This section outlines the stages involved, including low-fidelity and high-fidelity design, and the rationale behind key design decisions.

2.1 Low Fidelity Design

The low-fidelity mockups were created to establish the structure and functionality of the accessible web-based system while adhering to accessibility principles [1]. A key design decision was to consolidate the entire experience onto a single page, reducing the complexity of navigation and ensuring a seamless flow for all users [8], particularly those with cognitive or motor impairments. Interactions, such as viewing navigation guides or exhibit content, are handled through pop-up windows to maintain context and simplicity.

Main Page Layout. The main page as shown on Fig. 1(a) displays a list of all available exhibits, each represented by its title and type (image,image gallery, video, 3D exhibit). A "Navigation Guide" button is positioned prominently, providing users with detailed instructions on how to interact with the page. This ensures first-time users or those relying on assistive technologies can quickly understand the system.

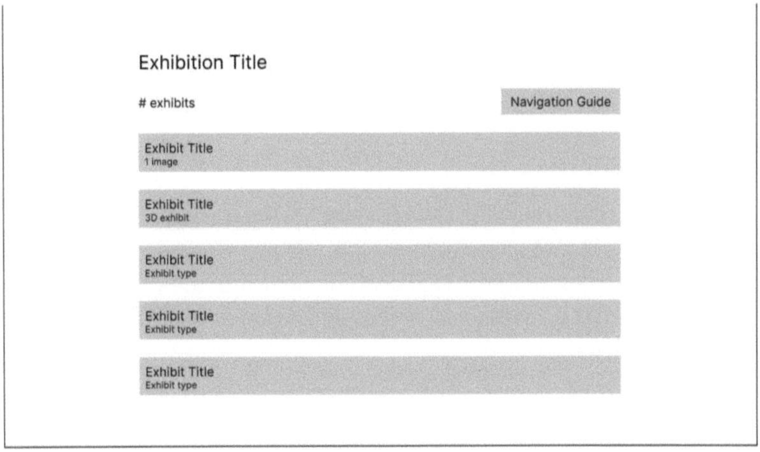

(a) Main Page Layout

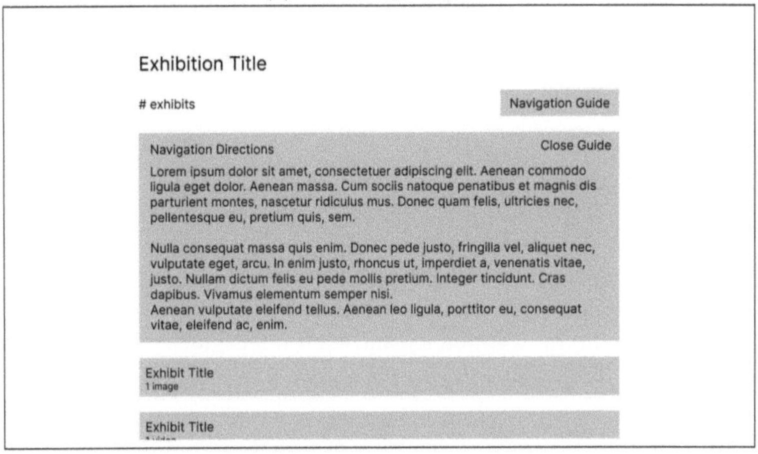

(b) Navigation Guide Pop-Up

Fig. 1. Low Fidelity Mockups

Pop-Up for Navigation Guide. As shown on Fig. 1(b) when the "Navigation Guide" button is clicked, a pop-up window opens, displaying clear and concise directions for navigating the page. This pop-up ensures users can access guidance without leaving the main interface, minimizing cognitive load and improving usability.

Exhibit Details Pop-Up. Each exhibit opens in a dedicated pop-up when selected, tailored to its type, as shown on Fig. 2. When opening a photo exhibit the user can see displayed the exhibit's title, description, and a large, accessible image. Users can close the pop-up to return to the main page seamlessly.

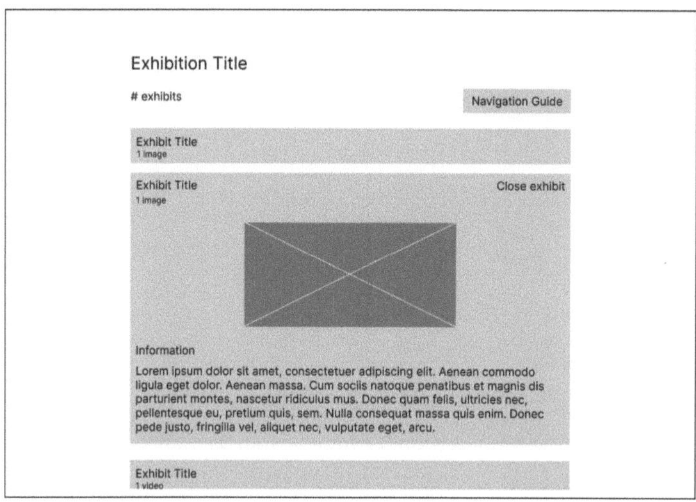

Fig. 2. Photo Exhibit Pop-Up

2.2   Iterative Design Approach

Following the development of the low-fidelity mockups, several areas for improvement were identified, including refining navigation flows, enhancing visual clarity, and ensuring compatibility with assistive technologies. These insights informed the transition to high-fidelity prototypes, where detailed visual elements, interactive features, and accessibility enhancements were incorporated to create a more polished and user-friendly system.

2.3   High Fidelity Design

The high-fidelity designs (Fig. 3) represent a polished version of the accessible web-based VR museum system, incorporating detailed visual and interactive elements to enhance usability and accessibility. These designs build upon the low-fidelity prototypes, implementing improvements to ensure a seamless user experience while maintaining accessibility compliance.

Image-Based Exhibit Pop-Ups. To accommodate exhibits centered around static visual content, the system supports two types of image-based pop-ups: standalone image exhibits and combined image and text exhibits. Both formats are designed with accessibility and readability in mind, maintaining a clean visual hierarchy and compatibility with assistive technologies.

Image Exhibit Pop-Up: Exhibits consisting of a single image are presented in a dedicated pop-up window that displays the visual in a large, centered format (Fig. 4(a)). The image is accompanied by a concise, descriptive title and includes alt text to support screen readers. The layout features high contrast borders,

(a) Main Page Layout

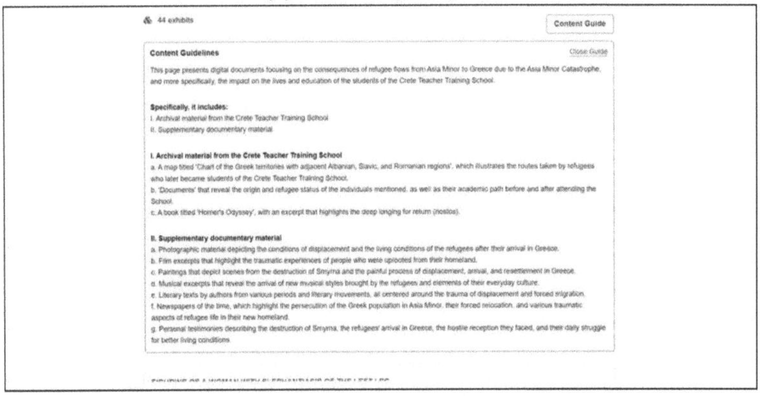

(b) Navigation Guide Pop-Up

Fig. 3. High Fidelity Mockups

generous spacing, and a minimal interface to reduce cognitive load. A clearly labeled, keyboard-accessible close button allows users to seamlessly return to the main interface. This format is optimized for users who benefit from simplified visual presentation and minimal navigation effort.

Image and Text Exhibit Pop-Up: Some exhibits combine an image with a detailed textual narrative (Fig. 4(b)). In these cases, the pop-up window arranges the image and description in a top-bottom layout. This ensures logical reading order and preserves screen reader flow through proper semantic structuring and ARIA roles. The text is presented using high contrast themes to enhance readability, while the image retains alt attributes for accessibility. This format is particularly effective for exhibits where visual elements are enriched by interpretive or historical context.

(a) image exhibit

(b) image and text exhibit

Fig. 4. High Fidelity Mockups

3D Exhibit Pop-Ups. In the high-fidelity version of the system, special attention was given to the presentation of 3D exhibits (Fig. 5). When a user selects a 3D artifact from the main page, a pop-up window appears displaying the exhibit's title, a brief description, and a button labeled "View 3D Model." This interaction preserves the user's position in the interface while offering a clear path to explore more detailed content. Upon clicking the button, the 3D model opens in a full-screen viewer, allowing users to closely examine the object from multiple angles. The interface remains minimal and focused, reducing distractions and ensuring compatibility with assistive technologies such as keyboard navigation and screen readers. This design balances interactivity with accessibility, offering an engaging yet inclusive way to explore complex artifacts.

Video Exhibit Pop-Up. Video exhibits (Fig. 6(a)), are presented within a dedicated pop-up window that includes an embedded video player with accessible controls. Users can play, pause, and adjust volume using the keyboard, ensuring full interaction without relying on a mouse. Captions and descriptive

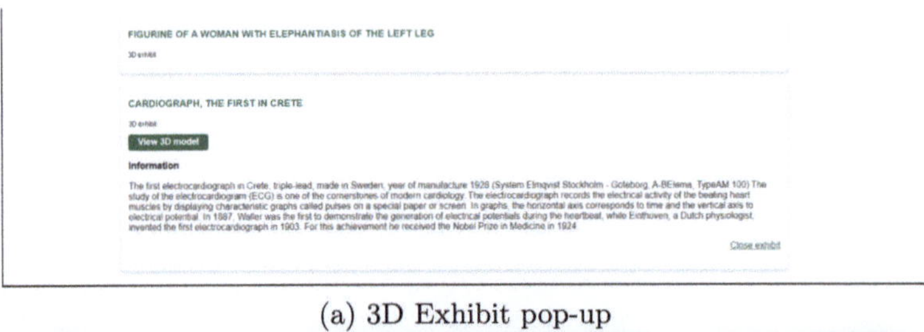

(a) 3D Exhibit pop-up

(b) 3D model viewer

Fig. 5. 3D Exhibit Design

titles are provided to enhance comprehension, particularly for users with hearing impairments. The system integrates the native HTML5 ¡video¿ element as the embedded player, which provides keyboard navigation, tabindex attributes, and alternative text metadata to ensure compatibility with screen readers and compliance with WCAG 2.1 accessibility guidelines.

Image Gallery Exhibit Pop-Up. Gallery exhibits (Fig. 6(b)), contain a scrollable collection of related images, grouped thematically. Each image is accompanied by a caption and is displayed in a clean, high-contrast layout. Navigation buttons and keyboard shortcuts allow users to move through the gallery easily, maintaining both context and accessibility.

3   Design Rationale

The design choices for the accessible web-based VR museum system were guided by the need to create a seamless, intuitive, and visually engaging experience for all users. A single-page layout was selected to simplify navigation, allowing users to access all exhibits and functionality without the need for complex transitions between pages. This approach reduces cognitive load and ensures that all interactions occur in a consistent and familiar environment.

(a) video exhibit

(b) image gallery exhibit

Fig. 6. High Fidelity Mockups

Interactive pop-ups were chosen as the primary method for displaying exhibit details and additional features. This decision was made to preserve the user's context on the main page while providing a focused space for interacting with specific content. The pop-up design also allows for modularity, ensuring each exhibit's content is presented clearly and independently.

Consistency in visual elements was a key consideration. Uniform typography, spacing, and layout styles were employed to maintain a cohesive design and minimize distractions. Each exhibit type was tailored with a specific layout to enhance usability while preserving the unique characteristics of the content [6].

Lastly, the design prioritized clarity and simplicity, ensuring that users could easily navigate the system and understand the content. These choices collectively support the system's goals of accessibility, usability, and inclusivity, creating a foundation for additional accessibility features to be seamlessly integrated.

4   Conclusion and Future Work

The accessible web-based version of the VR museum system successfully addresses the limitations of the original implementation by ensuring inclusivity for users of all abilities. By integrating keyboard navigation, screen reader compatibility, high-contrast visual elements, and a configurable interface, the system adheres to Web Content Accessibility Guidelines (WCAG 2.1) and provides a user-friendly, single-page design with interactive pop-ups. These features make the system intuitive, engaging, and adaptable, preserving the immersive and educational quality of the museum content.

While the current system achieves its objectives, there are opportunities for future enhancements, such as conducting user testing with individuals with disabilities to refine features, expanding personalization options like text spacing and color schemes, and introducing advanced accessibility features like voice navigation. Additional improvements could include content expansion, multilingual support, and integration with VR platforms to provide users with multiple ways to experience the museum. These directions aim to further improve the system's functionality and reach, establishing a benchmark for accessible digital cultural heritage platforms.

Acknowledgements. This work has been supported by the FORTH-ICS internal RTD Programme 'Ambient Intelligence and Smart Environments'.

References

1. Brophy, P., Craven, J.: Web accessibility. Lib. Trends **55**(4), 950–972 (2007)
2. Caldwell, B., et al.: Web content accessibility guidelines (WCAG) 2.0. WWW Consortium (W3C) **290**(1-34), 5–12 (2008)
3. Cemre Kılınç, O.T.: Accessibility of virtual museum spaces in the 21st century in turkey. ICONARP Int. J. Archit. Plann. **11**(2), 879–903 (2023). https://doi.org/10.15320/ICONARP.2023.268
4. Fátima Matos Silva, E.S.: Digital accessibility in art museum webpages and virtual tours. EasyChair Preprint no. 14736 (2024). https://easychair.org/publications/preprint/S4dB, easyChair Preprint
5. Kapnas, G., Leonidis, A., Korozi, M., Ntoa, S., Margetis, G., Stephanidis, C.: A museum guide application for deployment on user-owned mobile devices. In: Stephanidis, C. (ed.) HCI 2013. CCIS, vol. 374, pp. 253–257. Springer, Heidelberg (2013). https://doi.org/10.1007/978-3-642-39476-8_52
6. Kim, S., Leonidis, A., Zidianakis, E.: Interaction styles. In: Interaction Techniques and Technologies in Human-Computer Interaction, pp. 1–44. CRC Press (2024)
7. Korozi, M., Leonidis, S., Margetis, G., Stephanidis, C.: MAID: a multi-platform accessible interface design framework. In: Stephanidis, C. (ed.) UAHCI 2009. LNCS, vol. 5616, pp. 725–734. Springer, Heidelberg (2009). https://doi.org/10.1007/978-3-642-02713-0_77
8. Mourouzis, A., Leonidis, A., Foukarakis, M., Antona, M., Maglaveras, N.: A novel design approach for multi-device adaptable user interfaces: concepts, methods and examples. In: Stephanidis, C. (ed.) UAHCI 2011. LNCS, vol. 6765, pp. 400–409. Springer, Heidelberg (2011). https://doi.org/10.1007/978-3-642-21672-5_44

9. Tosios, A., et al.: CreteAR: enhancing learning experiences through tangible transformable artifacts and extended reality. In: International Conference on Human Factors in Design, Engineering, and Computing, vol. 159, no. 159 (2024)
10. Zidianakis, E., et al.: The invisible museum: a user-centric platform for creating virtual 3D exhibitions with VR support. Electronics **10**(3), 363 (2021)

Accessibility of Small Business Websites: Common Accessibility Compliance Issues and Their Variance Across Business Categories

Bimal Balakrishnan[(✉)] [iD], Hannah Zhou [iD], and Matthew Wong [iD]

Mississippi State University, Mississippi State, MS 39762, USA
bbalakrishnan@caad.msstate.edu

Abstract. This paper reports preliminary findings regarding barriers to accessibility observed in small business websites. The authors conducted a systematic content analysis study of small business websites across multiple business categories to understand compliance with Web Content Accessibility Guidelines (WCAG). Preliminary results indicate that a significant majority of small business websites still lack robust accessibility. These findings underscore the need to increase awareness, advocacy, and training on the importance of web accessibility among small business owners and web developers .

Keywords: Web Accessibility · Small Business Websites · Web Content Accessibility Guidelines (WCAG) · Design for Accessibility

1 Introduction

1.1 Importance of Small Business Websites

Small businesses are a critical component of the economy, particularly in the midwestern United States. In the four midwestern states of Missouri, Kansas, Iowa, and Nebraska, they account for over 99% of all businesses in each state and employ between 44% and 49% of each state's workforce-aged population, according to the Small Business Administration [1]. Given this, small businesses are vital to the economic engine of these states. A closer examination of the overall number of small businesses opening and closing each year in these states reveals significant volatility. For example, between March 2022 and March 2023, 28,519 small businesses opened in the state of Missouri, while 22,834 small businesses closed [1]. According to the U.S. Chamber of Commerce, 42% of small businesses fail due to insufficient market demand [2]. A digital presence is crucial for expanding market reach and driving demand. In 2020, approximately 64% of all small businesses in the United States had a digital presence, typically in the form of a website [3]. The COVID-19 pandemic has accelerated the adoption of digital tools among small businesses. This increased adoption of websites and digital tools heightens the importance of web accessibility and sets a new normal for accessible websites for small businesses and their customers. In 2022, 59% of all small businesses relied on business-owned websites to sell products and services [4]. These facts highlight the critical importance of small business websites.

© The Author(s), under exclusive license to Springer Nature Switzerland AG 2026
S. Sundarakannan and O. Knorpp (Eds.): HCII 2025, CCIS 2772, pp. 215–219, 2026.
https://doi.org/10.1007/978-3-032-12767-9_23

While the importance of small business websites has increased, a substantial barrier to web accessibility remains for individuals with disabilities. The recent WebAIM Million [5] report revealed that their automated analysis showed WCAG 2.2 [6] compliance failures for 94.8% of home pages. The 2019 survey among those with disabilities in the United Kingdom [7] indicated that 69% of respondents click away from the first page of a business website due to a lack of accessibility features, resulting in an estimated business loss of £24.8 billion. Given the importance of small business website accessibility from the perspectives of individuals with disabilities and small business owners, we decided to undertake a systematic study of barriers to accessibility in small business websites. The overall project involves a systematic and detailed content analysis study of small business websites in the midwestern United States to develop a deeper understanding of common web accessibility issues faced by individuals with disabilities. This content analysis study is complemented by planned human subject research.

1.2   Research Questions

In our effort to understand the barriers to accessibility on small business websites, our primary goal was to identify the most common types of Web Content Accessibility Guidance (WCAG) compliance failures observed in business websites. We also wanted to examine whether the type or level of compliance varies based on the type of small business, as the website content and design elements can differ based on the nature of the services provided. A related but future goal is to examine the correlation between adherence to sound design principles and improved accessibility, as previous studies have shown a positive relationship between aesthetics and usability [8] and between visual design and accessibility [9, 10]. In this brief paper, we report the preliminary results from a content analysis study examining barriers to accessibility and compliance with WCAG 2.2.

2   Research Methods

Dataset: We began by creating a list of 22 small and medium-sized towns, as well as large cities, in the four midwestern states of Missouri, Iowa, Kansas, and Nebraska. The towns and cities were classified based on their population as small (under 50,000), medium (between 50,000 and 200,000), and large (over 200,000). We identified small businesses across four common business categories in these towns through multiple sources, including the Small Business Development Center, Chamber of Commerce websites (where available), and online directories such as Yellow Pages. We developed a master list of URLs for over 16,000 small business websites across four categories: accounting and financial services, appliance repair, cafes, and restaurants. We then randomly selected 15 to 17 websites from each category in each state to create a dataset of 259 websites for systematic and detailed content analysis, evaluating their adherence to WCAG 2.2.

Coding for Adherence to WCAG 2.0. Three independent coders successfully completed an online course introducing them to web accessibility and W3C accessibility standards. They were also trained to evaluate websites for conformance with WCAG 2.2 using relevant success criteria. These three independent coders divided the content analysis task and coded for errors or failures to meet each guideline under the four main principles. We have completed coding for the home page of each small business website by one coder. We are in the process of coding by a second coder to establish inter-coder reliability. This detailed coding is an arduous task, and we present only broad and preliminary insights here. Additionally, given that websites are dynamic and subject to changes in content, these findings should be viewed more as a snapshot in time.

3   Preliminary Data Analysis and Results

In our detailed content analysis dataset, we included small business websites from Missouri (N = 64), Kansas (N = 66), Iowa (N = 64), and Nebraska (N = 65) in equal proportions. The 259 websites were distributed relatively evenly across the four small business categories: accounting or financial services (N = 67), restaurants (N = 65), cafes (N = 64), and appliance repair and services (N = 63). Coders identified at least one WCAG 2.2 failure on the homepages of all websites. Key findings are summarized below.

Of the 259 small business websites analyzed, 92.28% failed to provide information and user interface components in a way that users could easily perceive. The most common issues were missing alternative text for non-text content (WCAG guideline 1.1 – text alternative) in 62.22% of home pages, and content presented was not adaptable in 30.89% of websites without losing information or structure (guideline 1.3 - adaptable). Additionally, 76.83% of websites did not have proper contrast to separate the foreground from the background (guideline 1.4 – distinguishable).

When it comes to accessing these websites, 69.88% of them fell short in providing operable user interface components and navigation features that support those with disabilities. Across all websites analyzed, 69.12% of them fell short in providing ways to help users determine their location or navigate to specific content (guideline 2.4). More specifically, 55.6% of websites failed to indicate the purpose of links or had ambiguous links, and users could not understand the resulting action from the link text alone. Additionally, 29.35% of the websites lacked clear headings or labels that accurately described the topic or purpose (guideline 2.4.6).

Another important accessibility principle is that the information and operation of the user interface must be understandable to the user. Of the websites analyzed, 34.36% failed to meet this principle. Specifically, 13.9% of websites were unable to make their text content easily readable and understandable (guideline 3.1). Also, 22.39% of the websites failed to provide labels or instructions for content that required user input (guideline 3.3).

Of the websites evaluated, 4.25% of small business websites failed to provide content that is robust enough to be interpreted by assistive technologies (guideline 4.1).

4   Insights and Future Research

We are completing the data analysis and developing a series of data visualizations to generate insights into common web accessibility issues in small business websites. We believe this content analysis research will help us understand the common barriers to accessibility of small business websites and identify common accessibility failures within the small business category. We are also conducting a detailed content analysis of the same small business websites to assess their adherence to design principles. Future efforts will explore how greater adherence to design principles enhances the accessibility of small business websites.

Our preliminary findings indicate an essential and urgent need to improve the accessibility of small business websites. Initial findings suggest that website accessibility errors vary significantly across small business categories. We are working to complete coding for a fifth category of small business websites related to real estate. This category will complete our dataset. After confirming inter-coder reliability, we will undertake a more nuanced analysis to determine if adherence to WCAG guidelines varies by small business category. Once complete, this will help us gain more nuanced insights into accessibility issues common among small business websites and how they vary across the different business categories. This follow-up analysis will allow us to investigate, identify, and address the root causes of the lack of accessibility compliance on small business websites. These insights can help us determine targeted training strategies across small business categories or locations.

Our broader research project also explores the relationship between adherence to aesthetic design principles and their impact on the accessibility of small business websites. We are scoring the same small business websites for their design quality based on principles of good design. Once this is completed, we will be able to explore the relationship between design principles and accessibility, specifically whether good design also enhances a website's accessibility.

Based on insights from our preliminary results from this content analysis, we are also planning a survey regarding barriers to accessing small business websites. We have developed a detailed online survey instrument and obtained approval for human subjects research from the Institutional Review Board and Office of Research Compliance. The survey population will consist of individuals with disabilities residing in the four-state region of Missouri, Kansas, Nebraska, and Iowa. We are interested in capturing users' experiences with everyday tasks that they typically engage in on small business websites. The survey instrument also aims to capture common accessibility-related challenges faced by those with disabilities.

5   Limitations

Websites, including those of small businesses, often undergo several design modifications or changes within a given timeframe. Constant updates usually pose a challenge for any content analysis efforts. This content analysis should be viewed more as a snapshot in time that provides insight into accessibility compliance issues. Even with this limitation, we believe that insights from our content analysis can inform awareness and training efforts to enhance accessibility.

Acknowledgments. This study was funded by the National Institute on Disability, Independent Living, and Rehabilitation Research (NIDILRR) grant number 90DPAD0007.

Disclosure of Interests.   The authors have no competing interests.

References

1. 2024 Small Business Profiles for the States, Territories, and Nation. https://advocacy.sba.gov/2024/11/19/2024-small-business-profiles-for-the-states-territories-and-nation/, last accessed 2025/05/31
2. Small Business Data Center. https://www.uschamber.com/small-business/small-business-data-center, last accessed 2025/06/06
3. Connected Commerce Council. Digitally Empowered: How digital tools power small businesses amid COVID-19. https://digitallyempowered.connectedcouncil.org/pdf/3C-Digitally Empowered-52720v2.pdf, last accessed March 8, 2020
4. Small Business Sellers Value Online Tools and Marketplaces. https://connectedcouncil.org/wp-content/uploads/2022/05/Small-Businesses-Value-Online-Tools-and-Marketplaces-FINAL-May-2022.pdf, last accessed 2025/06/06
5. Click-Away Pound Survey 2019. https://www.clickawaypound.com/, last accessed 2025/06/06
6. The WebAIM Million. https://webaim.org/projects/million/, last accessed 2025/06/06
7. Web Content Accessibility Guidelines (WCAG) 2.2. https://www.w3.org/TR/WCAG22/, last accessed 2025/06/06
8. Tractinsky, N., Katz, A.S., Ikar, D.: What is beautiful is usable. Interact. Comput. **13**(2), 127–145 (2000). https://doi.org/10.1016/S0953-5438(00)00031-X
9. Abyazani, A.M.: Bridging the Gap: an Exploration of Visual Design Criteria Found in the "Accessibility for Ontarians with Disabilities Act" Unpublished Master's Thesis, York University (2019)
10. Petrie, H., Hamilton, F., King, N.: Tension, what tension? Website accessibility and visual design. In: Proceedings of the International Cross-Disciplinary Workshop on Web Accessibility (W4A), pp. 13–18. Association for Computing Machinery, New York, NY

HealthQb: Design and Evaluation of a Wearable Health Solution to Manage Chronic Stress and Pain

Zohreh Champiri[✉] and Brian Fisher

School of Interactive Arts and Technology, Surrey, BC, Canada
z.champiri@gmail.com, bfisher@sfu.ca

Abstract. Chronic stress is a multidimensional health crisis affecting physical, emotional, and social well-being, often coexisting with conditions like anxiety, depression, and cardiovascular disease. Despite a growing market of over 100 mobile applications targeting chronic pain, few integrate real-time biometric data with the biopsychosocial (BPS) model. To address this gap, HealthQb Technologies Inc. developed a digital platform that pairs psychosocial assessments with biometric data from the Biostrap wearable device. This study evaluates the usability, personalization, and effectiveness of the HealthQb system in managing chronic stress and pain. The platform supports over 1,700 patients and 186 healthcare practitioners. It monitors heart rate variability, respiratory rate, sleep patterns, and oxygen saturation . Combined with Ecological Momentary Assessments (EMA), the system generates personalized recommendations and real-time feedback through a user-facing mobile app and practitioner dashboard. Our UX research engaged 11 patients and practitioners using mixed methods, including interviews, observations, and A/B/C testing. Results showed high usability (67%) but lower equitability (44%) and enjoyability (56%). The "Aha" moment, where users recognize the value, was triggered by viewing personalized ANS/BPS scores and tailored recommendations. However, onboarding challenges, lack of personalization, and UI complexity hindered early engagement. Key improvements include redesigning the UI, refining user personas, and enhancing the recommendation system. These changes led to a 78% improvement in usability and contributed to securing funding. Our findings highlight the critical role of integrated UX research in digital health tools to drive adoption, retention, and real-world clinical impact.

Keywords: Human-Computer Interaction (HCI) · Patient-Centered Design · User Experience (UX) · Chronic Pain · Chronic Stress · Digital Health · Wearables · Biopsychosocial · Personalized Health Recommender Systems · HealthQb

© The Author(s), under exclusive license to Springer Nature Switzerland AG 2026
S. Sundarakannan and O. Knorpp (Eds.): HCII 2025, CCIS 2772, pp. 220–229, 2026.
https://doi.org/10.1007/978-3-032-12767-9_24

1 Introduction

1.1 Research Background

Chronic stress is a silent but pervasive threat to health, gradually contributing to disability, job loss, and social isolation [1]. Up to 88% of sufferers experience comorbid conditions such as depression, anxiety, and cardiovascular diseases, significantly increasing mortality risk [1, 2].

Chronic stress and pain are not merely physical ailments but biopsychosocial phenomena, influenced by biological, psychological, and social factors (BPS) [3]. In 2019, the World Health Organization (WHO) formally recognized this model, emphasizing its role in stress and pain management strategies [4, 5]. Early research also suggests a strong correlation between Automated Nervous System (ANS) activity and the subjective well-being of chronic pain patients [6, 7]. However, effective data capture in after-care settings presents key challenges:

1. Ensuring patient compliance with data collection protocols
2. Enhancing the usability and effectiveness of data interpretation for practitioners

Despite the availability of over 100 pain-related mobile applications targeting conditions like migraines, arthritis, fibromyalgia, and back pain, most focus on [7–10]:

- Tracking symptoms and medication use
- Providing educational content
- Offering relaxation and mindfulness exercises

Only 17% of these apps implement evidence-based interventions, and few incorporate real-time biometric monitoring or the biopsychosocial model critical components in chronic stress and pain management [11–14]. To bridge these gaps, HealthQb Technologies Inc. (Canada) has developed a mobile application that integrates biometric data from the Biostrap wearable device with psychosocial assessments to deliver real-time evaluations and personalized interventions (Fig. 1). Currently, the application supports over 1,700 patients under the supervision of 186 healthcare practitioners.

The Biostrap wristband monitors key physiological parameters, including:

- Heart rate variability (HRV)
- Respiratory rate
- Sleep patterns
- Oxygen saturation levels

These biometric data are synchronized with the HealthQb application, which integrates biopsychosocial assessments to generate real-time insights and personalized interventions for individuals experiencing chronic pain and stress. The HealthQb platform combines biometric data with Ecological Momentary Assessment (EMA) inputs to construct comprehensive biopsychosocial health models (Fig. 2).

The system provides data in two distinct formats:

1. A biopsychosocial baseline report designed for patients, offering insights into their condition and progress.

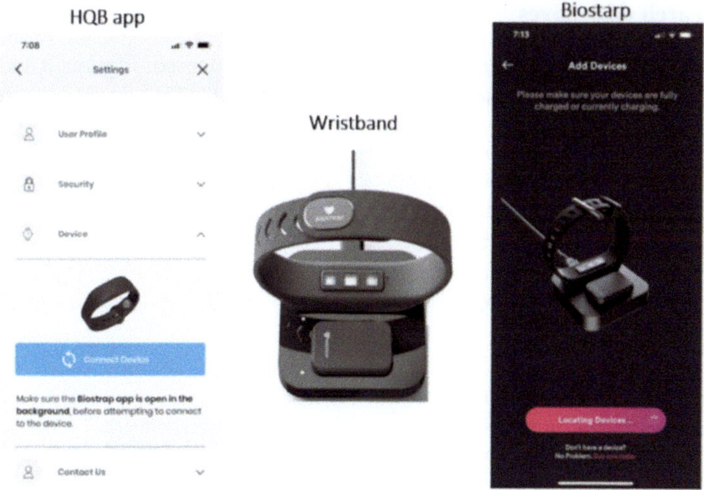

Fig. 1. HealthQb and Biostrap

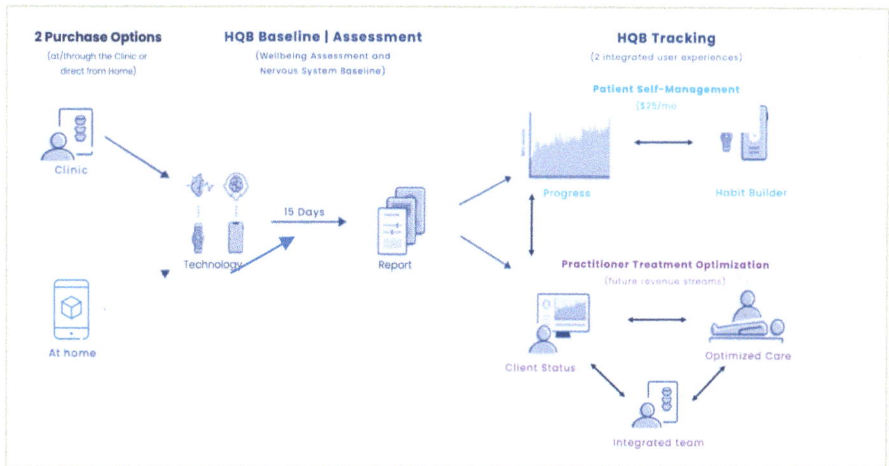

Fig. 2. HealthQb's (HQB) Product Model

2. An executive summary tailored for healthcare practitioners, accessible via a web-hosted dashboard, facilitating clinical decision-making and treatment planning.

This platform is designed to assist allied health professionals in developing personalized treatment plans and tracking patient progress over a six-week period, with a structured reassessment conducted at the conclusion of treatment to evaluate outcomes and adjust interventions as needed.

1.2   Research Objectives

The MVP version of the HealthQb platform has been released. Figures 3 and 4 display selected pages from the app and the practitioner dashboard. This study evaluates the user experience (UX) of HealthQb, with particular emphasis on the following areas:

- Design and usability issues
- The effectiveness of the intervention algorithms in recommending strategies for managing chronic stress and pain
- Platform engagement, retention, and personalization
- Recommendations for UX/UI improvements and the redesign of the HealthQb platform

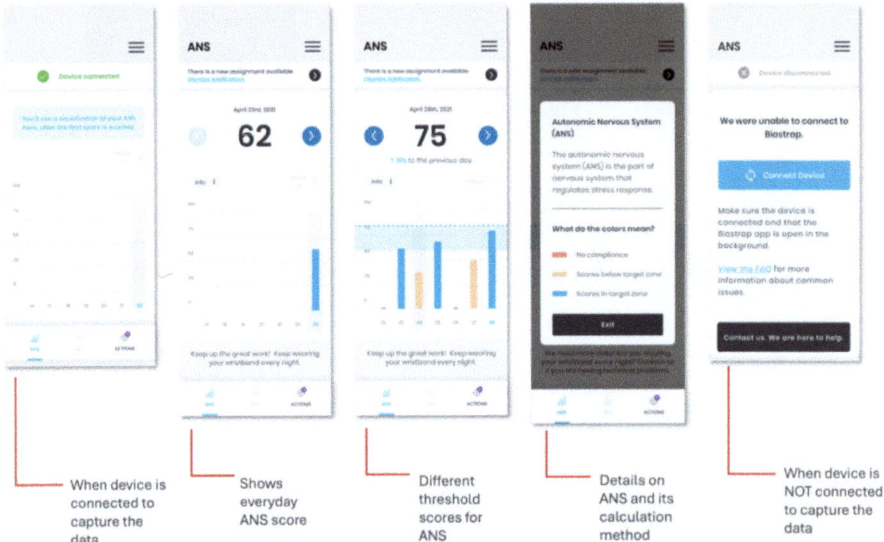

Fig. 3. Selected HealthQb App Pages

Additionally, we will explore the following key questions that are essential for executives to understand:

- When does the 'Aha Moment' typically occur for HealthQb users?
- What are the key challenges in onboarding that blocks the users?
- How much are users willing to pay?

An 'aha moment' refers to the point at which a new user realizes the value of a product. The primary target users for this study include:

1. Patients with chronic stress and pain seeking personalized management strategies
2. Healthcare professionals/practitioners utilizing digital tools to monitor and adjust patient treatments

The UX research explores patient personas, adoption, needs, trust, usage, functionality, satisfaction, privacy, and challenges. For healthcare professionals, it examines usability, data interpretation, value, and obstacles.

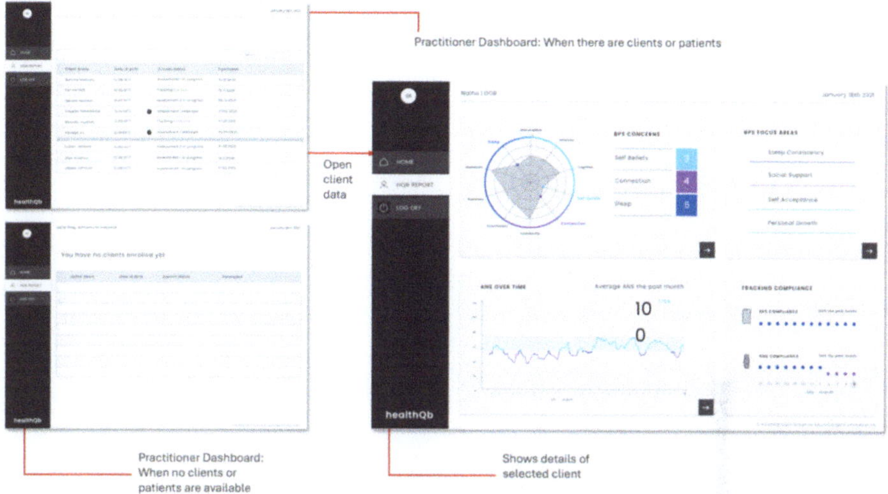

Fig. 4. Practitioner Dashboard

2 Methodology

The study utilizes both qualitative and quantitative UX research methods with 11 patients, incorporating semi-structured interviews, observations, and ABC testing to evaluate usability and identify areas for improvement improvements (see Fig. 3). Key activities include:

- **User Interviews:** Understanding patient and practitioner needs, expectations, and interactions.
- **User Adoption Study:** A 21-day trial for patients, followed by feedback on usability and features.
- **Practitioner Adoption Study:** Evaluating product integration, effectiveness, and challenges.
- **Benefit & Challenge Assessment:** Identifying pain points and user expectations.
- **Design Solutions:** Developing journey maps and UX/UI enhancements (Fig. 5).

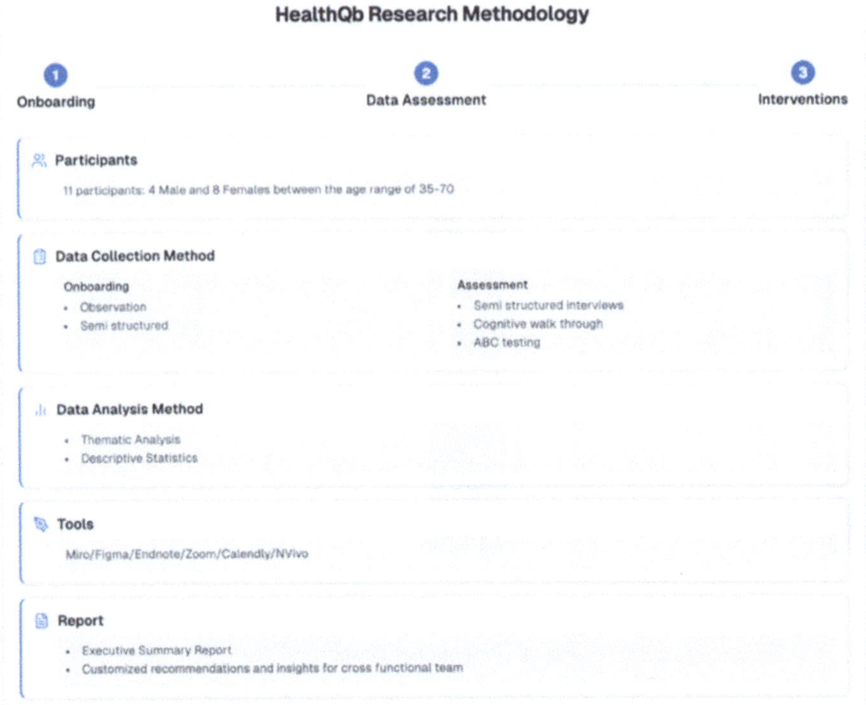

Fig. 5. Research Methodology

3 Results and Conclusion

Selected results are presented below.

3.1 Usability

Four metrics of usability, equity, enjoyability, and usefulness were applied to assess the overall ease of use of the design (Fig. 6). The results indicate that the HealthQb app effectively addresses users' problems. However, participants identified areas for improvement, with equitability rated at 44% and enjoyability at 56%. Usability received the highest rating at 67%, suggesting that the app is generally easy to use.

3.2 Product Value: 'Aha' Moments

The "Aha moment" occurs in two phases (Fig. 7):

- When users view their Automated Nervous System (ANS) and Bio-Psychosocial (BPS) scores and recognize their connection to pain levels.
- When they receive personalized, unexpected recommendations, which often surprise users and build trust [15].

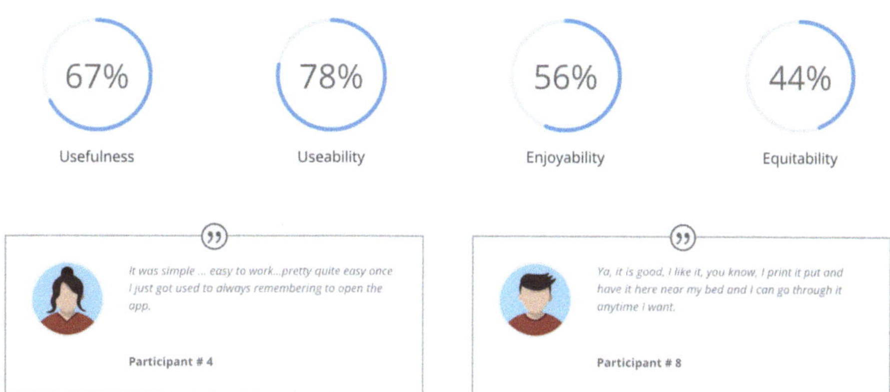

Fig. 6. Usability Metrics and Users' Quotes

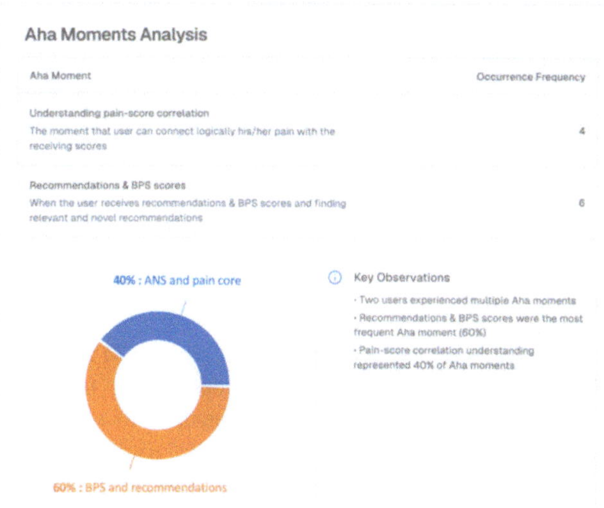

Fig. 7. Aha moments in HealthQb

4   Onboarding Issues (Fig. 8)

- **Unclear instructions:** 55% of users struggled with device charging and syncing due to confusing guidance.
- **Limited support and technical barriers:** 36% found onboarding difficult without human assistance.
- **No "Aha" moment:** Users do not experience an engaging or rewarding moment during onboarding to understand the value of the product.
- **Lack of personalization:** Users prefer a more tailored experience from the beginning and in providing standard recommendations [16, 17].

Fig. 8. Onboarding Issues

4.1 MVP App Price Strategy

67% of respondents indicated that they would not pay for MVP version, while 33% expressed willingness to pay (Fig. 9). Among those willing to pay, none would be willing to pay more than $25 per month, which translates to a maximum of $300 per year. The price strategy should be based on the features users value and are willing to pay for.

Also, the UX evaluation identifies several challenges:

- **UI/UX Design Issues:** Lack of clear visual hierarchy and inconsistent navigation.
- **Content Presentation:** Overloaded text-based content requiring structured information delivery.
- **User Engagement:** Absence of dynamic feedback mechanisms for long-term engagement.
- **User Personas:** Existing personas need refinement to reflect diverse pain management needs.

To enhance usability and clinical effectiveness, we propose:

1. Redesigning the UI for improved accessibility, readability, and interaction flow.
2. Incorporating adaptive interventions based on real-time biometric feedback.
3. Refining user personas to align with diverse pain management experiences.

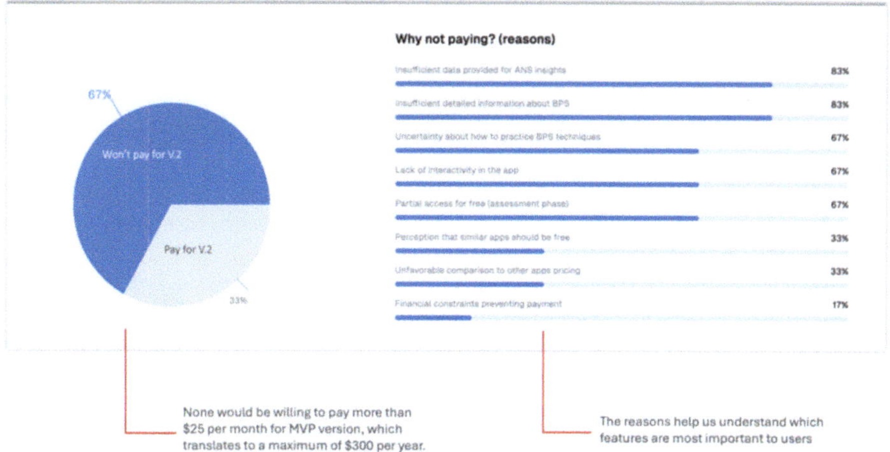

Fig. 9. Reasons for not paying

5 Research Impact

The outcomes and improvements of this research contributed to the following:

- Securing funding by demonstrating the product's value & potential through strategic UX/UI enhancements.
- Improving UX, resulting in a 78% increase in usability metrics (explained in test results in details).
- Refining the recommendation system to deliver more personalized and effective interventions.
- Redesigning the onboarding flow to reduce friction and improve user retention.
- Providing insights and recommendations to optimize the product pricing for better market alignment.
- Designing and implementing a robust habit-tracking system, enhancing user engagement & long-term adherence.

References

1. Meints, S., Edwards, R.J.: Evaluating psychosocial contributions to chronic pain outcomes. Pain Neurosci. Psychiatry. **87**, 168–182 (2022)
2. Raffaeli, W., et al.: Chronic pain: what does it mean? A review on the use of the term chronic pain in clinical practice. J. Pain Res. **14**, 827 (2021)
3. Menagadevi, M., Madian, N., Thiyagarajan, D., Rajendran, R.: Smart medical devices: making healthcare more intelligent. In: Machine Learning Models and Architectures for Biomedical Signal Processing, pp. 487–501. Academic Press, London (2025)
4. Babu, M., Lautman, Z., Lin, X., Sobota, M.H., Snyder, M.P.: Wearable devices: implications for precision medicine and the future of healthcare. Annu. Rev. Med. **75**(1), 401–415 (2024)
5. Del Giorno, R., et al.: Assessment of chronic pain and access to pain therapy: a cross-sectional population-based study. J. Clin. Med. **10**, 2577 (2023)

6. Zis, P., et al.: Depression and chronic pain in the elderly: links and management challenges. Clin. Interv. Aging. **12**, 709–720 (2017)

7. Adams, L.M., Turk, D.C.: Central sensitization and the biopsychosocial approach to understanding pain. Eur. J. Pain. **23**(2), e12125 (2018)

8. Stein, C.: Opioids, sensory systems, and chronic pain. Eur. J. Pharmacol. **716**(1–3), 179–187 (2013)

9. Van Hecke, O., et al.: Chronic pain, depression, and cardiovascular disease linked through a shared genetic predisposition: analysis of a family-based cohort and twin study. PLoS One. **12**(2), e0170653 (2017)

10. Cohen, S.P., Vase, L., Hooten, W.M.: Chronic pain: an update on burden, best practices, and new advances. Lancet. **397**(10289), 2082–2097 (2022)

11. Thurnheer, S.E., et al.: Benefits of mobile apps in pain management: systematic review. JMIR Mhealth Uhealth. **6**(10), e11231 (2022)

12. Bahar, M., et al.: Choroid plexus tumors in adult and pediatric populations: the Cleveland Clinic and university hospitals experience. J. Neurosurg. **132**(3), 427–432 (2017)

13. Berrouiguet, S., et al.: Fundamentals for future mobile-health (mHealth): a systematic review of mobile phone and web-based text messaging in mental health. J. Med. Internet Res. **18**(6), e5066 (2016)

14. Capulli, E., et al.: Ethical and legal implications of health monitoring wearable devices: a scoping review. Soc. Sci. Med. **370**, 117685 (2025)

15. Champiri, Z.D., Shahamiri, S.R., Salim, S.S.B.: A systematic review of scholar context-aware recommender systems. Expert Syst. Appl. **42**, 1743–1758 (2015)

16. Champiri, Z.D., Shahamiri, S.R., Salim, S.S.B., Chong, C.Y.: User experience and recommender systems. In: 2019 2nd International Conference on Computing, Mathematics and Engineering Technologies (iCoMET), pp. 1–5. IEEE, Sukkur (2019). https://doi.org/10.1109/ICOMET.2019.8673410

17. Champiri, Z.D., Fisher, B., Freund, L.: rScholar: an interactive contextual user interface to enhance UX of scholarly recommender systems. In: Kurosu, M. (ed.) HCI International 2020 - Late Breaking Papers. UX Design and Case Studies. HCII 2020. LNCS, vol. 12423, pp. 662–686. Springer, Cham (2020). https://doi.org/10.1007/978-3-030-60114-0_44

Inclusive Design Framework for Suicide Prevention Apps

Lana Cvijic[1] , Bianca Buchgraber-Schnalzer[2] , Beatrice Kaufmann[3] ,
and Kerstin Denecke[1(✉)]

[1] Bern University of Applied Sciences, Quellgasse 21, 2501 Biel, Switzerland
`{lana.cvijic,kerstin.denecke}@bfh.ch`
[2] FH Joanneum University of Applied Sciences, Alte Poststraße 149, 8020 Graz, Austria
`bianca.buchgraber-schnalzer@fh-joanneum.at`
[3] Institute of Design Research, Bern Academy of the Arts HKB, Fellerstrasse 11, 3027 Bern,
Switzerland
`beatrice.kaufmannvatter@hkb.bfh.ch`

Abstract. Suicide remains a major global public health issue, and mobile health apps have emerged as a promising tool for suicide prevention. Evidence suggests that digital solutions can help reduce both suicide attempts and completed suicides. However, the adoption of suicide prevention apps is hindered by usability and accessibility challenges. At present, there is no comprehensive framework to guide the inclusive design of these apps. This study investigates which design elements can enhance the adoption of suicide prevention apps across diverse user groups. The resulting framework with recommended inclusive design elements was developed through a literature review, usability testing of the suicide prevention app SERO and expert evaluation of the initial framework. The resulting framework comprises eight groups of aspects: user interface and visual design, accessibility, educational content, interaction and feedback, customization and user preferences, inclusive language, data security and transparency, as well as emotional support and psychological safety. We conclude the inclusive design of suicide prevention apps goes beyond design elements, but requires a holistic view on the setting these apps are used in and the specific risks of the users .

Keywords: Mental Health · Suicide Prevention · Qualitative Usability Testing · mHealth App · Inclusive Design · Inclusive Design Framework · User-Centered Digital Health

1 Background and Objective

Suicide remains one of the world's foremost public health issues, as evidenced by the statistics published by the World Health Organization (WHO) in 2021 that approximately 727 000 individuals die by suicide each year [1]. This figure underscores the severity and global impact of this problem, which transcends socioeconomic and national boundaries, affecting both developing and developed countries alike. The multifaceted nature of suicide risk factors encompasses a wide array of issues, including mental illnesses

© The Author(s), under exclusive license to Springer Nature Switzerland AG 2026
S. Sundarakannan and O. Knorpp (Eds.): HCII 2025, CCIS 2772, pp. 230–240, 2026.
https://doi.org/10.1007/978-3-032-12767-9_25

such as depression and bipolar disorder and physical health conditions like multiple sclerosis, diabetes and dementia [2, 3]. Sociodemographic factors also play a pivotal role; financial instability, low educational attainment and social isolation are frequently associated with increased suicide risk [3, 4]. Furthermore, the interplay between these factors contributes to the complexity of the problem, making identification and intervention in at-risk individuals a major challenge facing the global healthcare community today.

Mobile health (mHealth) technology, a subdomain of eHealth, is defined by the WHO [5] as "medical and public health practice supported by mobile devices, such as mobile phones, patient monitoring devices, personal digital assistants (PDAs), and other wireless devices". Nowadays, mHealth solutions are widely accepted due to the ease of access to smartphones and can offer an option to use mobile apps within suicide prevention [6, 7]. Studies show that these digital solutions can significantly reduce suicide attempts and completions [8]. Evaluations of mHealth technologies have shown positive effects for individuals at higher suicide or self-harm risk, including decreased depression, distress, self-harm and increased coping efficacy [9]. However, it is critical to note that only a few apps integrate clinical expertise into the design process [6], indicating a need for more clinical integration to improve mHealth effectiveness and safety in suicide prevention. Given the potentially fatal outcomes of suicidal behavior, it is vital that mHealth apps are scientifically evaluated [10] and co-designed with those who have experienced depression or suicidal behavior [11].

Although various mental health apps have been evaluated by research groups [18], no comprehensive framework exists to guide the design of suicide prevention apps. This study explores which design elements can improve the adoption of digital solutions for suicide prevention among a wider range of users. The main objective is to define a framework that includes a set of design recommendations for creating inclusively designed apps aimed at suicide prevention. In the context of digital health interventions, "inclusive design" refers to the deliberate creation of technology-based solutions that meet the diverse needs of all users, considering differences in technological and health literacy, physical and mental abilities, and socio-cultural background [12, 13], ensuring those can effectively use and benefit from these solutions [14]. Digital solutions that prioritize inclusive design can positively impact the user experience (UX) by fostering a sense of belonging [15]. To achieve our objective, we will consider the suicide prevention app SERO.

The SERO app (available in Switzerland for iOS and Android) is an mHealth app developed by Denecke et al. [16] to aid individuals at risk of suicide and their support networks. It assists users in managing their symptoms for enhancing prevention and complements existing mental health treatments. Core functions include an emergency response function, the possibility to call personal contacts, risk assessment functions, a safety plan with the possibility to share it and a treasure chest providing virtual access to personal resources to handle moments of crisis (e.g. videos, or pictures). First insights into user challenges in interacting with the SERO app were collected using a survey shared with all registered users [17]. A structured usability test is still outstanding. Therefore, this study will integrate insights from a systematic literature review, qualitative usability testing of the SERO app and expert evaluations of an initial design framework. Our inclusive design framework is intended to improve the physical, mental and emotional accessibility of the SERO app and similar apps for suicide prevention.

2   Methods

2.1   Literature Search

We searched three scientific databases: IEEE Xplore, JMIR Mental Health, and PubMed for studies on inclusive design in suicide prevention apps. We focused on studies that used participatory or user-centered design methods. Additionally, we conducted a web search. Search terms included were as follows: *mental health intervention user-centered design; design suicide prevention app; framework design mental health app; design recommendations mental health app; inclusive design for mental health.* Studies that described the co-design process of apps for suicide prevention, as well as guidelines and other best practice suggestions for suicide prevention apps were included in the analysis. From the retrieved literature, we collected elements for our inclusive design framework.

2.2   Qualitative Usability Testing

The main objective of the qualitative usability testing was to evaluate the accessibility of the SERO app for users with different socio-cultural backgrounds and to discover potential areas for improvement, with focus on inclusive design.

Participants. According to the literature, in-person qualitative usability tests require three to five participants [19, 20]. Five participants with lived experience of depression and/or suicidal behavior were selected using purposive sampling method [21], with no age exclusions to promote inclusivity. Participants were recruited via a LinkedIn post shared across personal accounts of researchers and through an email to the personal contact network of a researcher who participated in the design and development of the SERO app.

Procedure. We followed user-centered methods [22] to conduct the usability test. An interview guide, prepared in advance, consisted of two parts: four scenario-based tasks in which participants interacted with the SERO app using the think-aloud method [23] and a semi-structured interview with questions on inclusive design aspects. In the scenario-based tasks participants completed the onboarding, created and shared a safety plan, added media to the treasure chest and performed a risk assessment. The semi-structured interview focused on how the SERO app in general and aspects such as inclusive language or visual design in particular can be improved. One co-author (LC) was the facilitator during all usability tests. Testing sessions were recorded, after participants provided an informed consent. Usability tests were conducted in English or German, according to participants' preference. Duration of an hour was allocated for each usability test. Participation was voluntary and the procedure was pretested on a person, who was not included in the study sample. Participants were informed that their anonymized data would be used to enhance the SERO app, with the aim of providing better support to users during difficult times.

Data Analysis. Audio files were transcribed using the noScribe tool [24], then manually reviewed for accuracy. To maintain participants' anonymity, pseudonyms were assigned to participants and identifiable information was removed. Transcripts were organized in MAXQDA, a software for qualitative data analysis [25]. The approach from Rädiker et al. [26] was followed to develop the coding tree and analyze the data. We analyzed transcripts from the test to identify usability challenges and opportunities for inclusive design. Major themes, aligned with scenario-based tasks and interview topics, were documented. One theme focused specifically on inclusive design aspects like accessibility, emotional safety, language, and visual appearance of the UI. To increase the reliability of the coding tree, feedback was collected from two co-authors. Transcripts were coded using the final version of the coding tree. The coding was carried out by one co-author (LC) to ensure consistency across the data. Finally, the thematic analysis was conducted [31].

2.3 Expert Evaluation of the Initial Framework and Final Framework Development

An initial inclusive design framework was created by synthesizing findings from the literature and usability testing of the SERO app. It encompassed the key inclusive design aspects such as UI and visual design, emotional safety and accessibility. This framework, along with three evaluation questions, were sent to six experts in mHealth, inclusive design, psychology and quality assurance in healthcare. Experts were asked the following questions: (1) *What do you find is missing or insufficiently addressed in this inclusive design aspect?* (2) *Which design elements or descriptions within this inclusive design aspect are unclear or could benefit from further clarification?* (3) *Are there any additional considerations or best practices from your field of expertise that you believe would enhance this inclusive design aspect?* Their feedback was analyzed and incorporated into the final framework, which is presented in the results section.

3 Inclusive Design Framework for Suicide Prevention Apps

The following table (see Table 1) presents the inclusive design framework for suicide prevention apps. This framework goes beyond user UI design to encompass accessibility, cultural and linguistic inclusion, emotional support and more.

Table 1. Resulting inclusive design framework for suicide prevention apps.

Inclusive design aspect	Recommended inclusive design elements
User Interface and Visual Design	• Use simple, intuitive workflows. Validate them through usability testing with the target user group • Use an interface that works for desktops, laptops, tablets and smartphones • Provide an overview of the app's functions on the main screen • Add visual elements (e. g., icons) to complement text labels • Display only the essential information per screen to avoid cognitive overload, especially during a crisis • Use both calming and positive colors, and adjust them to the cultural context in which the app is used • Review visual elements for sensitivity to the app's target group (e.g., avoiding visual elements with sharp edges). Validate them with input from both designers and the target user group
Accessibility	• Provide support for visually impaired users via audio formats (e. g., compatibility with screen readers) • Provide support for hearing impaired users via text-based formats (e. g., captions or transcripts) • Offer alternative navigation methods to support users with motor or physical limitations • Allow users to select their preferred font size and enable adaptable color schemes (e. g., to support color blindness and dyslexia) • Provide a clearly visible exit button and immediate help option (e. g., helpful for cognitive decline) • Adhere to existing accessibility standards (e. g., Web Content Accessibility Guidelines - WCAG) • Provide a link to a translation tool to enable the translation • Allow users to skip the onboarding in the app and to access immediate help • Inform healthcare professionals about the app so they can recommend it to patients • Ensure the accessibility to the app in terms of costs • Allow offline and online availability of the app

(continued)

Table 1. (*continued*)

Inclusive design aspect	Recommended inclusive design elements
Educational Content	• Include comprehensive information on coping strategies, self-harm management, emotional regulation and crisis exercises • Provide educational content in text, audio and video format • Ensure all information is expert-verified and sourced from trusted references. Cite all sources for better verifiability and transparency • Tailor educational content to different skill levels (e. g., different health literacy and language proficiency levels) • Use the language appropriate for the target user group, ideally developed in collaboration with users and healthcare experts • Provide phone and text messaging contacts for local support services
Interaction and Feedback	• Enable emotional state check-ins with customizable frequency users can choose (e. g., option for daily, weekly or no check-ins) • Allow the app to detect the negative mood (e.g., negative risk assessments or emotional state check-ins) and explain to user why and how this is done • Provide personalized support when a low mood is detected, such as tailored uplifting content from the user's safety plan or treasure chest (e. g., images) • Base feedback mechanisms on established behavioral or psychological theories to ensure supportive interactions
Customization and User Preferences	• Offer a range of customization options (e. g., choosing avatars or background images) • Support customization of fonts, font sizes and other visual elements to suit individual users' needs and preferences • Allow users to add personal media (e.g., images, videos) and important contacts within the app • Enable users to set the frequency of notifications and messages (e.g., daily check-ins, reminders), with an option to disable them entirely

(*continued*)

Table 1. (continued)

Inclusive design aspect	Recommended inclusive design elements
Inclusive Language	• Use simple and inclusive language throughout the app to support users with varying language proficiencies and health literacy levels • Avoid triggering or stigmatizing terms; use trauma-informed language and avoid assumptions about political orientation, gender or religion • Enable users to customize the way the app refers to them, including their name, preferred form of addressing them (formal or informal) and gender • Offer explanations of underlying clinical models and content in clear terms, avoiding domain-specific words • Provide positive labels for features and content (e.g., "My supportive beliefs", "My positive coping strategies") to avoid misunderstandings • Allow users to choose a male or female voice for audio content • Make content available in multiple languages
Data Security and Transparency	• Clearly communicate how user data is collected, used, stored and who has access, include information about whether data is anonymized and what happens after the app is deleted • Use transparent information, offer both a short summary and a detailed version. Ensure all information is written in clear, inclusive language • Only collect data that is necessary for app's functions • Enhance data security by offering options such as password protection and multi-factor authentication within the app. This should remain optional, as it might be difficult for some users (e.g., older adults) or challenging to use during a crisis

(continued)

Table 1. (*continued*)

Inclusive design aspect	Recommended inclusive design elements
Emotional Support and Psychological Safety	• Provide empathetic, companion-like support (e. g., an icon representing the app's character) to guide users during times of distress • Offer suggestions to promote well-being after detecting a negative emotional state. Provide step-by-step guidance and strategies to help users cope during a crisis or distressing moment • Support users who may not have a personal support network (e.g., friends, family, therapist) • Base emotional support functions on best practices from psychology and psychiatry

4 Discussion

Integrating inclusive design principles into suicide prevention apps is essential to ensure these tools are accessible, usable, and effective for people from diverse backgrounds. Our study has identified several key areas where inclusive design can make a significant impact. These include user interface and visual design, accessibility for users with disabilities, the quality and relevance of educational content, ways the app interacts with users and provides feedback, options for customization, the use of inclusive language, data security and transparency, and emotional support mechanisms.

Some of these aspects, such as intuitive UI design and accessibility, are important for any mHealth app. However, suicide prevention apps have additional, specific requirements. For example, the way the app manages risk and crisis situations is particularly important in this context. Features like personalized emotional check-ins and clear explanations of how the app uses technologies such as mood detection can help users feel understood and informed. This transparency helps users better judge the strengths and limitations of the app, and encourages them to consider alternative sources of help during a crisis [27].

Emotional support and psychological safety are also critical. Suicide prevention apps should be designed to provide empathetic guidance and evidence-based support, especially for users who may lack other support networks. Customization options allow users to tailor the app to their needs and preferences, respecting their individual identities and coping styles. However, there are open questions about how much control users should have—for example, whether they should be able to disable important notifications intended to provide timely support. Future research should explore how such features are best implemented and accepted by users.

UI and visual design should prioritize simplicity, intuitiveness, and cultural sensitivity. Simple workflows and interfaces, developed with input from the target audience, lower barriers for users who may be in distress. Participatory design [28], which involves users in the creation process, helps to avoid unintended triggers and ensures the app is both inclusive and supportive. Visual elements such as icons, calming colors, and culturally appropriate graphics are not only aesthetically pleasing but also support emotional safety and ease of navigation [29].

Accessibility is a foundational aspect of inclusive digital health. The app must support users with visual, hearing, and motor impairments, following standards like the Web Content Accessibility Guidelines (WCAG). Accessibility also extends to ensuring people are aware of the app and can afford to use it. This highlights the need for collaboration with health professionals and the development of sustainable payment models.

Finally, clear and adaptable language is vital. Suicide prevention apps should use trauma-informed and culturally sensitive communication, although it remains unclear if current apps consistently meet this need.

Limitations and Strengths. The study has some limitations. The usability test was conducted only with five participants and by one researcher (LC). Further, a single researcher conducted the literature review, which can introduce selection bias and limit the comprehensiveness of the review. A notable strength of the qualitative user testing of the SERO app in this study is the diversity of the participant group, which included people from different cultural and ethnic backgrounds, as well as people with a migration background. Unlike previous studies, which were limited to German-speaking participants from specific regions of Switzerland [30], this approach included both English- and German-speaking people. The usability test was conducted in a controlled environment. While this approach ensures consistency and minimizes external variables, it may not fully reflect the application's real-world use. Consequently, the results may not capture the full range of usability challenges that users could face in their natural environment. Lastly, the qualitative and thematic analysis of the usability tests was carried out by one researcher, which could lead to subjective interpretations and reduce the credibility of the findings. To address this limitation, the feedback was collected from six experts.

5   Conclusion

Although the identified elements collectively address a wide range of inclusion requirements, the inclusive, participatory design process is inherently iterative and context dependent. It is not possible to anticipate all user needs at the outset, so ongoing participatory design involving diverse populations is necessary to refine and adapt these principles over time. Future studies could examine the impact of considering these design features on safety outcomes and mental health outcomes in the real world. It could be investigated how multiple vulnerability factors, such as age, disability, socioeconomic status and cultural background, interact and impact on shaping digital health experiences. Further, the specific needs regarding design of suicide prevention apps of special populations such as people with neurodevelopmental disorders (e. g., dyslexia, autism spectrum disorder) that are at higher risk of self-harm should be studied carefully.

Acknowledgments We would like to express our gratitude to the experts who participated in the evaluation of the framework developed in this study. Our thanks go to: Elia Gabarron, PhD; Caroline Gurtner-Zürcher, PhD and Carolyn Petersen, MS, MBI.

Transparency Statement. AI tools, specifically ChatGPT and DeepL Write, were used to improve the clarity and comprehensibility of the text when drafting this paper.

Disclosure of Interests. The authors declare no conflicts of interest.

References

1. World Health Organization. https://www.who.int/publications/i/item/9789240110069, last accessed 2025/06/09
2. Ahmedani, B.K., Peterson, E.L., Hu, Y., Rossom, R.C., Lynch, F., et al.: Major physical health conditions and risk of suicide. Am. J. Prev. Med. **53**(3), 308–315 (2017). https://doi.org/10.1016/j.amepre.2017.04.001
3. Turecki, G., Brent, D.A.: Suicide and suicidal behaviour. Lancet (Lond. Engl.). **387**(10024), 1227–1239 (2016). https://doi.org/10.1016/s0140-6736(15)00234-2
4. O'Connor, R.C., Nock, M.K.: The psychology of suicidal behaviour. Lancet Psychiatry. **1**(1), 73–85 (2014). https://doi.org/10.1016/s2215-0366(14)70222-6
5. WHO Global Observatory for eHealth. https://iris.who.int/handle/10665/44607, last accessed on: 2025/06/09
6. Braciszewski, J.M.: Digital Technology for Suicide Prevention. Adv. Psychiatry Behav. Health. **1**(1), 53–65 (2021). https://doi.org/10.1016/j.ypsc.2021.05.008
7. Sellak, H., Grobler, M.: mHealth4U: designing for health and wellbeing self-management. In: Proceedings of the 35th IEEE/ACM International Conference on Automated Software Engineering Workshops. Virtual Event Australia, pp. 41–46. ACM (2020). https://doi.org/10.1145/3417113.3422179
8. Hofstra, E., Van Nieuwenhuizen, C., Bakker, M., Özgül, D., Elfeddali, I., De Jong, S.J., et al.: Effectiveness of suicide prevention interventions: a systematic review and meta-analysis. Gen. Hosp. Psychiatry. **63**, 127–140 (2020). https://doi.org/10.1016/j.genhosppsych.2019.04.011
9. Melia, R., Francis, K., Hickey, E., Bogue, J., Duggan, J., O'Sullivan, M., et al.: Mobile health technology interventions for suicide prevention: systematic review. JMIR Mhealth Uhealth. **8**(1), e12516 (2020). https://doi.org/10.2196/12516
10. Grist, R., Porter, J., Stallard, P.: Mental health Mobile apps for preadolescents and adolescents: a systematic review. J. Med. Internet Res. **19**(5), e176 (2017). https://doi.org/10.2196/jmir.7332
11. Watling, D., Preece, M., Hawgood, J., Bloomfield, S., Kõlves, K.: Developing an intervention for suicide prevention: a rapid review of lived experience involvement. Arch. Suicide Res. **26**(2), 465–480 (2022). https://doi.org/10.1080/13811118.2020.1833799
12. Motta, I., Quaresma, M.: Increasing transparency to design inclusive conversational agents (Cas): perspectives and open issues. In: Proceedings of the 5th International Conference on Conversational User Interfaces, pp. 1–4. Association for Computing Machinery, New York, NY (2023). https://doi.org/10.1145/3571884.3604304
13. Borg, K., Boulet, M., Smith, L., Bragge, P.: Digital Inclusion & Health Communication: a rapid review of literature. Health Commun. **34**(11), 1320–1328 (2019). https://doi.org/10.1080/10410236.2018.1485077
14. Lee, J., Kim, J.: Can menstrual health apps selected based on users' needs change health-related factors? A double-blind randomized controlled trial. J. Am. Med. Inform. Assoc. JAMIA. **26**(7), 655–666 (2019). https://doi.org/10.1093/jamia/ocz019
15. Nielsen Norman Group. https://www.nngroup.com/articles/inclusive-design/, last accessed 2025/06/09

16. Denecke, K., Gurtner, C., Hess, G., Von Kaenel, F., Durrer, M.: Digital solution for supporting suicide prevention: human-centered, participatory development, usage trend analysis and adverse risk assessment. BMC Digit. Health. **3**(1), 12 (2025). https://doi.org/10.1186/s44247-025-00149-5

17. Denecke, K., Von Kaenel, F., Gurtner, C., Durrer, M.: SERO suicide prevention app: a preliminary study of user experiences in real world. Appl. Med. Inform. **46**(Suppl. 2), S29–S32 (2024)

18. Guracho, Y.D., Thomas, S.J., Ammutairi, N., Win, K.T.: Design and development of a mobile mental health application for individuals with depression and anxiety: design science research methods. Behav. Inf. Technol., 1–16. https://doi.org/10.1080/0144929X.2025.2481639

19. Nielsen Norman Group. https://www.nngroup.com/articles/quantitative-studies-how-many-users/, last accessed 2025/06/09

20. Nielsen, S., Carlsen, C., Roke, Y., Schaap, J., Van Daele, T., Bernaerts, S.: Guideline for user participation: adapting digital mental health across borders (2025). https://doi.org/10.13140/RG.2.2.10401.11369

21. Palinkas, L.A., Horwitz, S.M., Green, C.A., Wisdom, J.P., Duan, N., Hoagwood, K.: Purposeful sampling for qualitative data collection and analysis in mixed method implementation research. Admin. Pol. Ment. Health. **42**(5), 533–544 (2015). https://doi.org/10.1007/s10488-013-0528-y

22. Silva, A.G., Caravau, H., Martins, A., Almeida, A.M.P., Silva, T., Ribeiro, Ó., et al.: Procedures of user-centered usability assessment for digital solutions: scoping review of reviews reporting on digital solutions relevant for older adults. JMIR Hum. Factors. **8**(1), e22774 (2021). https://doi.org/10.2196/22774

23. Eccles, D.W., Arsal, G.: The think aloud method: what is it and how do I use it? Qual. Res. Sport Exerc. Health. **9**(4), 514–531 (2017). https://doi.org/10.1080/2159676X.2017.1331501

24. Dröge, K. https://github.com/kaixxx/noScribe, last accessed 2025/06/09

25. MAXQDA. https://www.maxqda.com/, last accessed 2025/06/09

26. Rädiker S., Kuckartz U.: Focused Analysis of Qualitative Interviews with MAXQDA. MAXQDA Press. 125 (2020).

27. Denecke, K., Gabarron, E.: The ethical aspects of integrating sentiment and emotion analysis in Chatbots for depression intervention. Front. Psych. (2024). https://doi.org/10.3389/fpsyt.2024.1462083

28. Denecke, K., Rivera, O., Gabarron, E., Gunti, G., Van HoltenK.: Key components of participatory design workshops for digital health solutions: nominal group technique and feasibility study. J. Healthc. Inform. Res. (2025). https://doi.org/10.1007/s41666-025-00199-4

29. Pakhale, A., Kashyap, V.: User Interface Design Recommendations for Mental Health Mobile Application Design. Springer, Singapore (2023). doi: https://doi.org/10.1007/978-981-99-0293-4_57

30. Werdin, S., Fink, G., Rajkumar, S., Durrer, M., Gurtner, C., Harbauer, G., et al.: Mental health of individuals at increased suicide risk after hospital discharge and initial findings on the usefulness of a suicide prevention project in Central Switzerland. Front. Psych. **15**, 1432336 (2024). https://doi.org/10.3389/fpsyt.2024.1432336

31. Braun, V., Clarke, V.: Using thematic analysis in psychology. Qual. Res. Psychol. **3**(2), 77–101 (2006)

Understanding Developer Misconceptions Between Accessibility and Usability: An Empirical Study on Stack Overflow

Hans Djalali[(✉)], Wajdi Aljedaani, and Stephanie Ludi

University of North Texas, Denton, TX, USA
{hamed.jalali,wajdialjedaani}@my.unt.edu, stephanie.ludi@unt.edu

Abstract. Developers increasingly prioritize accessibility and usability to create inclusive web applications, yet their discussions often reveal misunderstandings between these concepts. We aim to investigate the extent to which developers misclassify or conflate usability and accessibility in Stack Overflow discussions. Our study analyzes 336 posts tagged with both usability and accessibility using a mixed-methods content analysis approach. The result shows that 12.2% of the discussions contain notable confusion between these concepts, particularly at the system level (34.5%), in comparison to feature-level issues (9.9%). The distinction between usability and accessibility becomes particularly challenging when developers discuss broader design decisions. These confusions include the misclassification of issues between the two concepts or the failure to distinguish between them. Our findings show that developers did not make explicit references to usability guidelines in their discussions, while only 20.2% of accessibility-related posts acknowledged standards such as WCAG, highlighting a significant gap between formal standards and their practical application in development contexts.

Keywords: Stack Overflow · Accessibility · Usability · Empirical Studies · Misconception

1 Introduction

In the current web development landscape, both accessibility and usability have become essential non-functional features for evaluating the quality of web applications. Usability refers to how efficiently users can complete tasks and achieve their goals. On the other hand, accessibility is about ensuring that people with disabilities can use, navigate, and complete tasks just as easily. Not all developers clearly differentiate between accessibility and usability in practice. In several Stack Overflow (SO) posts, aspects such as keyboard navigation, color contrast, and focus management are discussed in contexts that may pertain to both usability and accessibility. Having these types of confusions can lead to applications that are neither fully accessible nor optimally usable. It suggests the need for a closer examination of how these topics are addressed from the developers' perspective. To address this need, this study examines how developers discuss usability and accessibility on Stack Overflow (SO). A total of 336 posts

© The Author(s), under exclusive license to Springer Nature Switzerland AG 2026
S. Sundarakannan and O. Knorpp (Eds.): HCII 2025, CCIS 2772, pp. 241–251, 2026.
https://doi.org/10.1007/978-3-032-12767-9_26

tagged with both "usability" and "accessibility" were systematically analyzed. Our empirical, mixed-methods approach involved multiple iterations of manual labeling and content analysis to classify the discussions and identify whether the issues were discussed in relation to established guidelines and standards. For the analysis of usability-related content, we used Nielsen's ten heuristics [13,19].

By manually labeling these SO posts, we aim to explore the details of the challenges developers face in terms of usability and accessibility discussions and answer this research question: **To what extent do developers misclassify or misunderstand usability and accessibility in Stack Overflow posts?**

To the best of our knowledge, there are limited studies that systematically investigate developers' confusion and misunderstandings between accessibility and usability. While previous studies [3,14,21] have acknowledged the overlap and correlation of these concepts, none of the prior studies have explicitly examined developers' perspectives or their challenges in distinguishing and addressing this aspect in practice.

The main contributions of this paper include: (1) empirical evidence showing the extent to which developers confuse usability and accessibility concepts, (2) identification of specific patterns of misclassification, and (3) insights into how confusion varies between system-level and feature-level discussions.

The paper is structured as follows: Sect. 2 discusses related work, Sect. 3 details our study methodology, Sect. 4 presents our findings, and Sect. 5 concludes with implications and future work directions.

2   Related Work

Stack Overflow (SO) is one of the largest and most popular online communities for developers seeking answers to technical questions [9]. As of February 2025, Stack Overflow had 28 million registered users[1] Due to its vast archive of developer discussions, many studies analyze its content to explore various aspects of software development [20]. For example, Alghamdi et al. [4–6] analyzed 8,538 SO posts related to accessibility to identify how developers discuss accessibility guidelines and standards, thereby understanding challenges and trends in web accessibility. Zhang et al. [27] investigated Stack Overflow (SO) posts about Java to understand the common challenges faced by developers. Zou et al. [28] examined 21.7 million SO posts to assess which non-functional requirements developers prioritize. Vendome et al. [26] analyzed 810 accessibility-related SO posts to explore challenges in mobile app development and found that developers often lack familiarity with assistive technologies, leading to difficulties in implementing accessible design practices.

Beyond SO-based research, previous studies have also examined usability and accessibility issues in software development more broadly. Some research has focused on identifying usability concerns by analyzing user reviews [16,22], while others have explored accessibility challenges, such as detecting accessibility barriers and developing automated evaluation techniques [7,8]. Some studies focused

---

[1] Stack Exchange Network - List of Sites. https://stackexchange.com/sites#oldest.

on the relationship between usability and accessibility concepts. For example, Sauer et al. [14] developed a model that connects usability, accessibility, and user experience, suggesting that these elements should be considered together rather than separately. Their work emphasized that accessibility assessments must extend beyond compliance checks to consider broader aspects of user experience. Al-Sakran and Alsudairi [3] evaluated the usability and accessibility of Saudi e-government websites, identifying areas where improvements were needed to meet international standards, such as the Web Content Accessibility Guidelines (WCAG). Their study highlighted key usability and accessibility issues affecting user interaction, particularly for mobile users. Petrie and Bevan [21] provided an overview of accessibility and usability evaluation methods, demonstrating how different assessment techniques, including heuristic evaluations and user testing, influence design decisions.

While our research shares similarities with previous studies analyzing accessibility discussions on SO, particularly Alghamdi et al. [5], our study uniquely focuses on how developers misclassify or misunderstand usability and accessibility in their discussions. Limited studies have focused on developers' perspectives on both accessibility and usability, unlike prior research that primarily examines accessibility challenges or usability heuristics separately. Our work investigates the extent to which developers are getting confused about these concepts.

3   Study Design

In this study, we employed an empirical, mixed-methods approach, as described by Tashakkori et al. [25], to analyze how developers on Stack Overflow discuss usability and accessibility. The goal was to identify patterns in how developers perceive and address these types of issues, as well as to determine whether there is any confusion or overlap in their discussions of usability and accessibility.

3.1   Data Collection

We used Stack Exchange Data Explorer[2] to collect posts related to both *usability* and *accessibility*. Our search targeted posts containing at least one tag from each category (usability and accessibility) to make sure the posts are relevant to both concepts. SO allows only existing tags, and we can not use custom tags. For example, if we have the tag *screen-readers*, we do not have other possible combinations such as *screenreader* or *screen-reader*. To retrieve posts related to each word while accounting for variations in word forms (e.g., usability, usability-testing), we used SQL pattern matching using the LIKE operator with the % wildcard. For example, the query term "'usabil%'" matches any string beginning with "usabil", thereby capturing a range of relevant terms. Additionally, specific tags are automatically grouped, such as *UX* with *user-experience* and *UI* with *user-interface*. Table 1 presents the selected tags and the distribution of collected posts. We also considered the tags *high-contrast, semantic-html, accessible, color-contrast, interface-design, usability-testing, user-testing,* and *information-architecture,* but they did not return any posts in our query. Our SQL query

---

[2] https://data.stackexchange.com/stackoverflow/query/new.

yielded 430 posts, which were subsequently refined through a data cleaning process. Duplicate posts were removed based on post ID to make sure we are analyzing only unique content. The final data set, after the cleaning process, consisted of 336 unique posts. Since SO post bodies contain embedded HTML, all tags were stripped using a regular expression pattern to enhance readability for manual labeling. These 336 posts formed our primary data for the manual labeling process.

Table 1. Distribution of Accessibility and Usability Tags in Stack Overflow Posts

Tag	Accessibility	Screen Readers	WCAG	WAI-ARIA	JAWS	VoiceOver	TalkBack	Section 508	NVDA	Keyboard Nav	Focus	Tabindex	Total
Usability	58	13	3	4	1	0	0	0	0	1	5	2	87
UX	30	2	4	5	0	1	0	1	0	0	3	1	47
UI	62	5	3	3	1	3	1	1	2	1	83	3	168
Responsive	18	3	2	5	0	1	0	0	0	0	3	0	32
Navigation	42	2	2	9	2	0	2	2	2	2	28	3	96
Total													430

3.2   Data Labeling

To analyze how developers discuss usability and accessibility, we conducted a manual labeling process on the collected posts, following a structured three-iteration approach consistent with established content analysis methods [18] (see Fig. 1). Two researchers with expertise in usability and accessibility independently evaluated and classified each post. Afterward, an auxiliary HCI expert resolved the discrepancies between the researchers. The reliability of the labeling is detailed later in this section.

Iteration 1. In the first iteration, we focused on determining the relevance of posts to accessibility and usability. The two researchers independently reviewed each of the 336 collected posts to evaluate whether they contained meaningful discussions on these topics. Posts that were mis-tagged or lacked meaningful content related to usability and accessibility were excluded. During iteration 1, out of the initial 336 posts, we found a total of 35 posts (10.4%) were not relevant to either accessibility or usability and were therefore removed. To elaborate further, a total of 165 posts explicitly focused on accessibility issues, while 141 contained accessibility-related elements. In terms of usability, 11 posts were not related to usability at all. Six posts were misclassified (mis-tagged) as having both usability and accessibility issues when they actually belonged to neither. After the iteration 1 filtering process, our final dataset comprised 301 posts that focused on accessibility and/or usability issues.

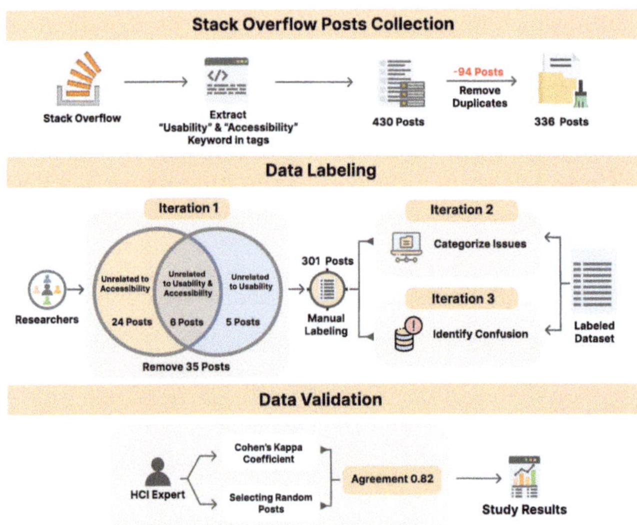

Fig. 1. Study overview.

Iteration 2. In the second iteration, the researchers systematically examined the content of each post to identify the key issues discussed by developers. For accessibility-related discussions, the researchers pinpointed key accessibility concerns by analyzing the terminology used in each post. They labeled posts based on labels used in Vendome et al. [26] and recurring accessibility topics such as screen reader behavior, focus management, WCAG compliance, ARIA attributes, and assistive technology compatibility. Each post could receive multiple accessibility labels if it addressed several distinct accessibility concerns. For usability-related posts, the researchers labeled them based on Jakob Nielsen's 10 usability heuristics [19] to determine whether the issue could be related to one or more of them. The researchers improved the consistency and accuracy of the classifications by independently labeling the posts and subsequently discussing any differences in their classifications.

Iteration 3. In the final iteration, the researchers examined whether developers showed confusion or uncertainty when distinguishing between usability and accessibility concepts. We classified them into three categories: (1) unclear distinction - where discussions could relate to either concept without clear differentiation; (2) accessibility framed as usability - where developers misclassified accessibility issues as usability concerns; and (3) usability framed as accessibility - where usability issues were incorrectly presented as accessibility issues. To further characterize the nature of these misclassifications, we also analyzed how developers expressed their uncertainty. Posts where developers explicitly questioned whether their issue was related to usability or accessibility were categorized as showing "explicit confusion." Posts where developers' framing of issues showed misconceptions without directly questioning the classification were classified as showing "implicit confusion."

3.3 Data Validation

To verify our findings, we recruited an HCI expert (the inspector) to manually re-label a subset of posts that had already been classified. We followed the sampling approach used by Aljedaani et al. [8]. This resulted in a 9% random sample (28 of 301 posts) based on a 95% confidence level and a 6-point interval. The inspector was advised to research any unfamiliar terms during the labeling process. Cohen's Kappa Coefficient [10] revealed an agreement level of 0.82, which Fleiss et al. [12] classify as almost perfect.

4 Study Results

This section presents and discusses the results of our research.

RQ: To what extent do developers misclassify or misunderstand usability and accessibility in Stack Overflow posts?

Results. Among the 301 posts relevant to both accessibility and usability, we observed developers' challenges in distinguishing between them in 37 posts (12.2%). Notably, 19 posts showed an unclear distinction, where the discussion could be related to either concept, but the specific focus remained ambiguous. Additionally, 18 posts presented misclassifications: 6 framed accessibility as usability, and 12 framed usability as accessibility.

To illustrate these categories, we present representative examples from each classification. The **SO question 2883412** asks about the pros of duplicating browser/keyboard functionality and demonstrates an **unclear distinction** between usability and accessibility:

"Is it good for user experience to duplicate browser/keyboard functionality? For example: to provide these links on a web-page. "Back to top" link "Print this page" link "Back" button/link "Text zoom" button alt text Are they really create Site's usability and accessibility?"

The post begins by asking if duplicating browser functions improves "user experience," but later asks whether these elements "create Site's usability and accessibility" without distinguishing between these concepts. The examples in the post (back-to-top links, print functionality, and text zoom) can be evaluated against both usability (efficiency and user control) and accessibility guidelines (keyboard navigation and text resizing). The post, tagged with both usability and accessibility, also indicates that the developer understands an interconnection, but without clear boundaries between the concepts.

The discussion in the **SO question 1520491** presents an example of **accessibility framed as usability**.

"Is there a way to test if a GUI is usable for color blind person? I know that it has many degrees, and I guess that's why simply doing a screenshot in black & white is not the best way to test usability of GUI for a color-blind person. What is the best way or best tool to do it? "

The post inquires whether testing a GUI is suitable for individuals with color blindness. The developer is treating it as a usability concern rather than explicitly recognizing it as an accessibility issue. While usability focuses on ease of use and interaction for all users, accessibility ensures equitable access for individuals with disabilities. The question does not reference accessibility guidelines or specialized tools for accessibility testing; instead, it considers the issue a general UX challenge, which makes it an example of how accessibility concerns can sometimes be misinterpreted as usability issues.

The **SO question 26168231** discusses a proposed toggle mode for accessibility, which is an example of **usability framed as accessibility**:

"We are redesigning our website and there are some concerns internally that accessibility affects the design element. A toggle mode was suggested. Our standard version would still be accessible with the exception of contrast ratio and larger font size, which would be made available when you toggle to accessible mode. Has anyone had any experience with this?"

The problem presented (low contrast and small font sizes) affects readability for all users, not just those with disabilities. However, instead of treating these as fundamental usability improvements, the discussion frames them as separate accessibility features that require activation. It reinforces the false idea that accessibility is an add-on rather than an essential aspect of usability. By isolating these improvements in an "accessible mode" rather than merging them into the default design, the proposed approach creates an unnecessary divide between usability and accessibility.

In addition to categorizing these 37 posts based on their misclassification patterns, we also examined how developers expressed their uncertainty in distinguishing between usability and accessibility. Among these, most cases showed implicit confusion, where developers stated their concerns in a way that revealed uncertainty about classification without directly asking for clarification. In contrast, a smaller subset of posts explicitly questioned whether an issue belonged to usability or accessibility.

For example, the **SO question 2278363** implicitly shows uncertainty about classification when discussing layout choices:

"Instead of giving a 'back to top' button, is it good to make a layout with a fixed header and footer for better usability? Or can this type of layout be a problem for screen readers?"

This post does not explicitly ask whether the issue falls under usability or accessibility, yet it reveals hesitation. The first part of the question suggests that a fixed layout is beneficial for usability (navigation efficiency), while the second part raises concerns about screen readers (compatibility with assistive technologies), which are primarily an accessibility consideration.

In contrast, **SO question 40198097** is an example of explicit confusion. The developer directly asks whether their issue relates to usability or accessibility:

"I am working on a government website that must meet Section 508 ADA standards. A request was made by one of our customers to emphasize a certain piece of content by placing it in two areas of the homepage: Within a slideshow, as well as inside a box underneath this slideshow. Would this be considered a violation of ADA standards or at least, usability practices?"

This post explicitly questions whether content duplication is a usability issue or an ADA (Americans with Disabilities Act) violation. The developer is aware of both usability best practices and accessibility regulations, but is unsure how to categorize the concern. Unlike implicit cases, where uncertainty is embedded in how the issue is framed, this post openly asks for clarification.

In the second iteration, 279 of 301 posts related to both usability and accessibility were classified with at least one usability heuristic. The findings show that the top three heuristics[3] that are directly related to the discussed issues by developers are **H4** (N = 157), **H3** (N = 143), **H7** (N = 62), meaning the issues related to easy navigation, clear choices, and uniform design are more addressed by developers. This focus benefits all users, particularly those who use assistive tools. **H1**, **H2**, and **H9** were less frequently associated with posts. This might mean that developers see these types of problems as already solved, or they might not notice them as much when dealing with immediate practical challenges. It is important to note that researchers manually classified usability heuristics, as developers did not explicitly mention these heuristics in their discussions. Notably, our query for posts tagged with established usability frameworks and guidelines, including Nielsen's Ten Heuristics [19], Shneiderman's Eight Golden Rules [23], ISO 9241-11 [1], and others, returned no results, further confirming the absence of formal usability framework references. Only 20.2% of posts (61 Posts) acknowledged accessibility standards such as WCAG, suggesting that developers may prioritize informal practices over structured guidelines when addressing both usability and accessibility challenges.

We categorized posts into two levels based on the nature of the issues discussed: *system-level* and *feature-level*. System-level issues refer to broader architectural and structural design decisions, such as platform architecture, overall navigation paradigms, and interaction frameworks. Feature-level issues, in contrast, focus on specific UI elements and interactions, such as button contrast, keyboard shortcuts, or the behavior of individual components.

Among the 301 posts analyzed, 29 were system-level, and 272 were *feature-level*. Our analysis shows that confusion between usability and accessibility was more common in *system-level* discussions, where 10 out of 29 posts (34.5%) showed confusion. In comparison, 27 out of 272 feature-level posts (9.9%) demonstrated similar misclassifications. A chi-square test for independence [17] con-

---

[3] Jakob Nielsen's 10 Usability Heuristics: H1. Visibility of system status, H2. Match between the system and the real world, H3. User control and freedom, H4. Consistency and standards, H5. Error prevention, H6. Recognition rather than recall, H7. Flexibility and efficiency of use, H8. Aesthetic and minimalist design, H9. Help users recognize, diagnose, and recover from errors and H10. Help and documentation.

firmed a significant association between discussion level and confusion, $\chi^2(1, N = 301) = 7.82$, $p = 0.0052$, Cramer's V $= 0.16$, indicating a small effect size[4].

Discussion. Developers often get confused about usability and accessibility, with 12.2% of posts showing misclassification or uncertainty. The considerable difference in confusion rates between system-level discussions (34.5%) and feature-level implementations (9.9%) reveals that the extent of misclassification varies substantially based on the abstraction level of the development task. In many cases, developers either treat accessibility problems as usability or vice versa, and some posts discuss both without making a clear distinction. We observed that this confusion is more common in broader, system-level discussions, such as overall layout choices, than in posts focused on feature-level, like keyboard navigation. Only 20.2% of posts explicitly mention established accessibility standards, and no posts explicitly mention any of the usability frameworks and guidelines. Previous studies, such as Lazar et al. [15], suggest that early-stage design decisions, including platform choice and interaction style, can create ambiguity at the system level, making it difficult to distinguish between usability and accessibility. Shneiderman and Plaisant [24] explain that high-level design choices blend usability principles with accessibility guidelines, making it difficult to treat them as separate issues. They emphasize that early integration is critical, as their close relationship makes addressing either separately complicated. Developers' discussions on SO reveal that, despite their efforts to improve their software and create an inclusive design, they sometimes struggle to clearly distinguish usability from accessibility.

5   Conclusion and Future Work

In this study, we analyzed 336 Stack Overflow posts to uncover important insights into the extent to which developers misclassify or misunderstand usability and accessibility issues in their discussions. Our analysis demonstrated a significant level of confusion at the system level, where 34.5% of posts showed an unclear or incorrect framing of usability and accessibility concepts. Feature-level posts followed with a notably lower confusion rate (9.9%). Our findings indicate a significant under utilization of usability frameworks and guidelines, and only 20.2% of accessibility-related posts reference accessibility standards like WCAG. Future research could expand this analysis to other developer communities to determine whether these trends are consistent across different platforms. Additionally, conducting interviews with developers could provide deeper insights into how they interpret and apply usability and accessibility principles in real-world scenarios. Understanding these challenges could inform efforts to improve developer resources and reduce misunderstanding of usability and accessibility concerns.

---

[4] The chi-square test was computed using the standard formula, $\chi^2 = \sum \frac{(O-E)^2}{E}$, comparing observed and expected frequencies.

Ethical Considerations. The study involved only secondary analysis of Stack Overflow posts released in the public Creative-Commons data dump [11]. Because the dataset is publicly available and contains no personally identifiable private information, the work does not constitute human-subjects research and is exempt under 45 CFR 46.101(b)(4) [2]. Consequently, Institutional Review Board (IRB) approval was not required.

References

1. Iso 9241-11: Ergonomic requirements for office work with visual display terminals (vdts) - part 11: Guidance on usability (1998)
2. Protection of human subjects. 45 CFR 46.102 (2018). https://www.hhs.gov/ohrp/regulations-and-policy/regulations/45-cfr-46/index.html
3. Al-Sakran, H.O., Alsudairi, M.A.: Usability and accessibility assessment of Saudi Arabia mobile e-government websites. IEEE Access **9**, 48254–48275 (2021). https://doi.org/10.1109/ACCESS.2021.3068917
4. Alghamdi, A.M., Aljedaani, W., Eler, M.M., Ludi, S.: Accessibility guidelines and standards: Analyzing stack overflow posts. In: Proceedings of the 21st International Web for All Conference, pp. 118–122 (2024)
5. Alghamdi, A.M., Aljedaani, W., Jalali, H., Ludi, S., Eler, M.M.: Understanding developer challenges and trends in web accessibility: a stack overflow analysis. Univ. Access Inf. Soc. (2024). https://doi.org/10.1007/s10209-024-01174-3
6. Alghamdi, A.M., Aljedaani, W., Ludi, S., Javed, Y.: Automating accessibility compliance: Leveraging machine learning to analyze developer challenges with wcag guidelines. In: 2025 8th International Conference on Data Science and Machine Learning Applications (CDMA), pp. 61–66. IEEE (2025)
7. Aljedaani, W., Mkaouer, M.W., Ludi, S., Javed, Y.: Automatic classification of accessibility user reviews in android apps. In: 2022 7th International Conference on Data Science and Machine Learning Applications (CDMA), pp. 133–138. IEEE (2022)
8. Aljedaani, W., Mkaouer, M.W., Ludi, S., Ouni, A., Jenhani, I.: On the identification of accessibility bug reports in open source systems. In: Proceedings of the 19th International Web for All Conference, pp. 1–11 (2022)
9. Antelmi, A., Cordasco, G., De Vinco, D., Spagnuolo, C.: The age of snippet programming: Toward understanding developer communities in stack overflow and reddit. In: Companion Proceedings of the ACM Web Conference 2023, pp. 1218–1224. WWW '23 Companion. Association for Computing Machinery, New York (2023)
10. Cohen, J.: A coefficient of agreement for nominal scales. Educ. Psychol. Measur. **20**(1), 37–46 (1960)
11. Commons, C.: Creative commons attribution-sharealike 4.0 international license. Creative Commons (2023). https://creativecommons.org/licenses/by-sa/4.0/
12. Fleiss, J.L., Levin, B., Paik, M.C., et al.: The measurement of interrater agreement. Stat. Methods Rates Proportions **2**(212–236), 22–23 (1981)
13. Jimenez, C., Lozada, P., Rosas, P.: Usability heuristics: A systematic review. In: 2016 IEEE 11th Colombian Computing Conference (CCC), pp. 1–8. IEEE (2016)
14. Juergen Sauer, A.S., Schmutz, S.: Usability, user experience and accessibility: towards an integrative model. Ergonomics **63**(10), 1207–1220 (2020)

15. Lazar, J., Feng, J., Hochheiser, H.: Research Methods in Human-Computer Interaction, 2nd edn. Morgan Kaufmann, Cambridge, MA (2017)
16. Lu, J., Schmidt, M., Lee, M., Huang, R.: Usability research in educational technology: A state-of-the-art systematic review. Educational technology research and development, pp. 1–42 (2022)
17. McHugh, M.L.: The chi-square test of independence. Biochemia Medica **23**(2), 143–149 (2013). https://doi.org/10.11613/BM.2013.018
18. Nicolai, M., Pascarella, L., Palomba, F., Bacchelli, A.: Healthcare android apps: A tale of the customers' perspective. In: Proceedings of the 3rd ACM SIGSOFT International Workshop on App Market Analytics, pp. 33–39 (2019)
19. Nielsen, J.: Enhancing the explanatory power of usability heuristics. In: Proceedings of the ACM CHI'94 Conference on Human Factors in Computing Systems, pp. 152–158 (1994)
20. Okafor, O., Aljedaani, W., Ludi, S.: Comparative analysis of accessibility testing tools and their limitations in rias. In: International Conference on Human-Computer Interaction, pp. 479–500. Springer (2022)
21. Petrie, H., Bevan, N.: The evaluation of accessibility, usability, and user experience. C Stepanidis (06 2009). https://doi.org/10.1201/9781420064995-c20
22. Reddy, H.B.S., Reddy, R.R.S., Jonnalagadda, R., Singh, P., Gogineni, A.: Usability evaluation of an unpopular restaurant recommender web application zomato. Asian J. Res. Comput. Sci. **13**(4), 12–33 (2022)
23. Shneiderman, B.: Designing the User Interface: Strategies for Effective Human-Computer Interaction. Addison-Wesley (1992)
24. Shneiderman, B., Plaisant, C.: Designing the User Interface: Strategies for Effective Human-Computer Interaction, 4th edn. Addison Wesley, Boston (2004)
25. Tashakkori, A., Teddlie, C., Teddlie, C.B.: Mixed methodology: Combining qualitative and quantitative approaches, vol. 46. Sage (1998)
26. Vendome, C., Solano, D., Linan, S., Linares-Vásquez, M.: Can everyone use my app? an empirical study on accessibility in android apps. In: 2019 IEEE International Conference on Software Maintenance and Evolution (ICSME), pp. 41–52 (2019)
27. Zhang, P.: What topics do developers concern? an analysis of java related posts on stack overflow. In: 2019 2nd International Conference on Artificial Intelligence and Big Data (ICAIBD). pp. 362–368. IEEE (2019)
28. Zou, J., Xu, L., Guo, W., Yan, M., Yang, D., Zhang, X.: Which non-functional requirements do developers focus on? an empirical study on stack overflow using topic analysis. In: 2015 IEEE/ACM 12th Working Conference on Mining Software Repositories, pp. 446–449 (2015)

Usability in Medical Systems: A Case Study on Redesigning Graphical User Interfaces for Intensive Care Units in a Public Hospital in Peru Using User-Centered Design

Miguel La Torre[(✉)], Rony Cueva, and Freddy Paz

Pontificia Universidad Católica del Perú, San Miguel, Lima 15088, Peru
{mlatorreb,cueva.r}@pucp.edu.pe, fpaz@pucp.pe

Abstract. Usability is a key part of software quality, as it affects how easy a system is to understand, learn, and use. In recent years, technology has become more integrated into different areas, including healthcare, where digital tools help with important tasks like patient care. These tools have improved daily work, reduced the time needed for training, and helped medical staff be more productive and satisfied. But even with these benefits, several studies have shown that many medical systems still have usability problems. These issues can make it harder to understand information, slow down patient care, and affect medical decisions. In the worst cases, they could even put patient safety at risk.

This study looks at a public hospital in Peru where the system used in Intensive Care Units (ICUs) shows clear usability problems, especially in its user interfaces. These problems show the need for a redesign that better fits the real needs and work context of healthcare professionals. To understand the situation better, a review of similar cases around the world was carried out. This helped identify common usability challenges, design decisions, and methods used—especially those based on the User-Centered Design (UCD) framework.

Using this information, the study followed the UCD framework to involve real users throughout the redesign process and improve their experience with the system. Techniques such as interviews, User Personas, Journey Maps, and Empathy Maps were used to understand the context of use and define user requirements. High-fidelity prototypes were created and subjected to heuristic usability evaluations in the project's final phase. Iterative cycles within the UCD framework continued until the required usability standards were met .

Keywords: Design/evaluation · Health and DUXU · Heuristics · personas · use scenarios · usability · UCD · user centered-design · hospital · redesign · ICU · intensive care unit · Peru · GUI · graphical user interfaces · user interfaces

1 Introduction

In hospital environments, the use of medical information systems has become a fundamental tool for the efficient management of clinical processes, especially in critical units such as Intensive Care Units (ICUs). However, the effectiveness of these systems

© The Author(s), under exclusive license to Springer Nature Switzerland AG 2026

S. Sundarakannan and O. Knorpp (Eds.): HCII 2025, CCIS 2772, pp. 252–261, 2026.
https://doi.org/10.1007/978-3-032-12767-9_27

depends not only on their functionality but also on the quality of their graphical interfaces and the level of usability they provide to healthcare professionals.

This study focuses on the hospitalization modules of a medical information system used in a public healthcare institution. Through a detailed analysis and the application of the User-Centered Design (UCD) framework, usability deficiencies affecting the medical workflow were identified. With this in mind, a new design for the system's graphical interface was created to make it easier to use, improve navigation, and better support doctors in their daily tasks.

The methodology used in this study helped identify what users actually need and allowed the proposed redesign to be evaluated by experts in Human-Computer Interaction (HCI) through heuristic evaluations. This process led to a redesign focused on improving how medical staff interact with the system, especially in fast-paced hospital environments.

2 Conceptual Framework

This section explains the main concepts that shaped the study. These ideas help to better understand the case being analyzed.

2.1 Medical Systems

Medical systems are digital tools and platforms used to manage health data from different sources, always ensuring ethical access and proper use. They rely on information and communication technologies (ICT) to support public health decisions, improve care delivery, and promote well-being [14].

2.2 Intensive Care Unit (ICU)

An ICU is a hospital area that provides constant monitoring and advanced care to critically ill patients. These units use specialized equipment like heart monitors, ventilators, feeding tubes, and other life-support devices needed to keep vital functions stable [5].

2.3 User-Centered Design (UCD) Framework

User-Centered Design is an iterative framework that focuses on users and their needs from start to finish. It uses different research and design methods to make sure the final product is easy to use and meets user expectations. UCD has four main stages: understanding the context of use, identifying user needs, producing design solutions, and evaluating the design. If the design doesn't meet user needs, earlier steps are revisited until a usable solution is reached [7].

3   Case Study

This section presents the case study carried out to deal with usability problems in the medical system of a hospital in Peru, specifically in the adult Intensive Care Unit (ICU). The process started with a review of international literature to understand how this issue appears in other countries, followed by interviews and a review of local regulations to confirm its presence in the Peruvian context. These findings justified using the User-Centered Design (UCD) framework, whose phases helped involve users and improve their interaction with the system.

3.1   Identification of Issues and Their Relation to the User-Centered Design (UCD) Framework

The literature review pointed out four common issues found in medical systems, each of which connects with a specific phase of the UCD process.

First, many systems fail because they don't take into account the real context in which they're used. There's often a poor understanding of the users' skills, needs, and limitations. This also includes overlooking how medical staff work together (like doctors, nurses, and technicians) and the limitations of the hospital's technology setup [1, 2, 13].

Second, there's usually no clear process to identify what users actually need. This causes a disconnect between those who build or manage the system and those who use it daily. Medical systems are used by professionals with different roles and responsibilities, so their expectations vary. This diversity makes it harder to meet everyone's needs, leading to dissatisfaction and frustration [1, 8].

Third, in the design phase, many interfaces turn out to be confusing or hard to use. Around 60% of usability issues found in studies are related to visual design or navigation problems [15]. Also, these systems often don't allow users to customize the interface or adapt it to future changes [8].

Finally, many systems skip proper usability testing. Without feedback from actual users, it's hard to spot problems or make improvements. This lack of evaluation can slow down healthcare workflows and make daily tasks more difficult for medical staff [10].

These shortcomings reinforce the need to adopt the User-Centered Design (UCD) framework to enhance user experience in medical systems, ensuring their effectiveness, efficiency, and user satisfaction in real clinical settings.

3.2   Problem Analysis in the National Context

According to the regulations and guidelines established by each country, the development and use of medical information systems follow a specific set of principles. In the case of Peru, the *Lineamientos y medidas de reforma del sector salud* (Guidelines and Reform Measures for the Health Sector) were developed in 2013 with the objective of improving and strengthening the national healthcare system. Among its various sections, the document highlights the importance of properly implementing information systems to ensure quality in medical care processes [3].

However, despite the existence of such guidelines, the Peruvian national health system still faces structural fragmentation and limited coordination between central and regional authorities. This situation prevents effective and consistent monitoring of medical information systems across different healthcare institutions. Consequently, several systems in the country continue to exhibit critical problems related to performance, security, scalability, integration, and usability [12].

In this context, a preliminary interview was conducted with a physician working in the Adult Intensive Care Unit to explore the main challenges of the current medical information system. The interview revealed multiple usability problems, including poor visual component organization, ambiguous textual elements, and difficulties in recovering from user errors. These factors negatively affect both the user experience and operational efficiency, causing significant delays in the daily work of the Intensive Care Unit.

The analysis highlights the need for a rigorous User-Centered Design process, which must involve (1) a clear specification of the context of use, (2) the identification and integration of the actual needs of end users, and (3) objective usability evaluation procedures to validate the proposed design solutions. The main problem in this case study is that the interfaces in the hospitalization modules of the medical system used in Adult ICUs are hard to use. This is mostly because the system wasn't designed with the real context of use or the specific needs of the users in mind.

3.3 Preparation for the Study

To collect information for this study, semi-structured interviews were chosen. This method uses a set of guiding questions but gives interviewees the freedom to expand on their answers. It works well when dealing with broad or complex topics that need a deeper understanding of people's views [9].

Because the medical field is complex, it was important to use a method that would give detailed insights into how things work in real clinical settings. That's why semi-structured interviews were a good fit to understand how ICU medical staff go about their work and how the medical system fits into that routine. This method also gave users space to openly share what they expect from the system and what they need.

The interviews were done over video calls, which made it easier to connect with doctors who had little time. To organize everything, a topic guide was prepared along with a consent form that explained the purpose of the interview, how long it would take, the main topics, and other relevant details.

Participants were told that their involvement was completely voluntary and that any personal data collected would be kept confidential. That data was only stored during the study and deleted afterward. Only general information was shared in the results to keep identities anonymous.

All documents followed the official templates and ethical guidelines from the *Pontificia Universidad Católica del Perú* (PUCP), which include recommendations for running interviews in an ethical and respectful way.

3.4 Application of the UCD Framework

The development of the case study followed the four main phases of the User-Centered Design (UCD) framework. Each phase included specific tasks and results focused on improving the usability of the hospitalization modules in the medical information systems.

First phase: Analysis of the context of use. Semi-structured interviews were conducted with five representative users to understand the current interaction environment. Three hierarchical user profiles were identified: resident physician, attending physician (the main user of the module), and chief physician. Based on user feedback, six key system scenarios were defined, and the Hierarchical Task Analysis (HTA) technique was applied to break down complex processes [16]. A detailed list of usability issues was generated based on the difficulties expressed by users. This phase was key in highlighting the lack of user inclusion in the original design, thereby justifying the application of the UCD framework.

Second phase: Identification of user needs. User profiles were characterized using User Personas, reflecting responsibilities, frustrations, and motivations [4]. Based on the identified issues, user requirements and goals were formulated and represented in User Journey Maps to describe their experience in the main scenarios [17]. Additionally, Empathy Maps were created to capture users' thoughts, expectations, and priorities regarding the current system [6]. This phase consolidated the key information required to construct a user-centered design proposal for the hospitalization modules of medical information systems.

Third phase: Analysis of the context of use. Graphical interfaces for the hospitalization modules of medical information systems were designed based on the defined requirements. A style guide inspired by Bootstrap was developed, and both low-fidelity (Balsamiq) and high-fidelity (Figma) prototypes were created. These prototypes were iteratively reviewed and validated by HCI experts and representative users. The feedback received led to adjustments in both the requirements and the solution itself, thereby closing the design loop proposed by the UCD framework.

Fourth phase: Evaluation of the redesign proposal. The initial testing plan for the redesigned interface proposals included the use of heuristic evaluation and the participation of HCI experts in the critical process of identifying usability issues that affected the user experience. As a result of carrying out the plan, clear feedback was gathered that pointed out areas to improve in the design. The necessary changes were made, and the experts approved them, completing the User-Centered Design (UCD) cycle.

4 Results

4.1 High-Fidelity Prototypes and Comparison with the Original Screens

The high-fidelity prototypes created in the study show a detailed and realistic version of the system's interface in the hospitalization modules. They include key visual elements like colors, fonts, layout, and images, closely resembling the final product. The original visual style was kept on purpose to make it easier for current users to adapt.

The redesign mainly focused on improving how elements are arranged on the screen, rather than changing the system's overall look. The adjustments aimed to resolve usability issues that hindered task efficiency during frequent user workflows. Among the most relevant changes were the grouping of related data fields into clearly defined blocks, allowing users to more intuitively identify and differentiate between types of information—such as patient data, clinical information, and care episodes. Additionally, new components were integrated to facilitate navigation, particularly in areas of the system that handle large volumes of records.

Navigation improvements were a key enhancement. Prior to the redesign, users could only browse care records sequentially—moving to the previous or next item—which was inefficient in scenarios involving hundreds of entries. The updated interface introduced advanced navigation options, including direct access to the first and last records and the ability to retrieve a specific entry by entering its identification number. These enhancements were designed to support the most urgent and recurring needs identified during the user analysis phase, directly aligning the redesign with the practical demands of day-to-day clinical operations (Figs. 1 and 2).

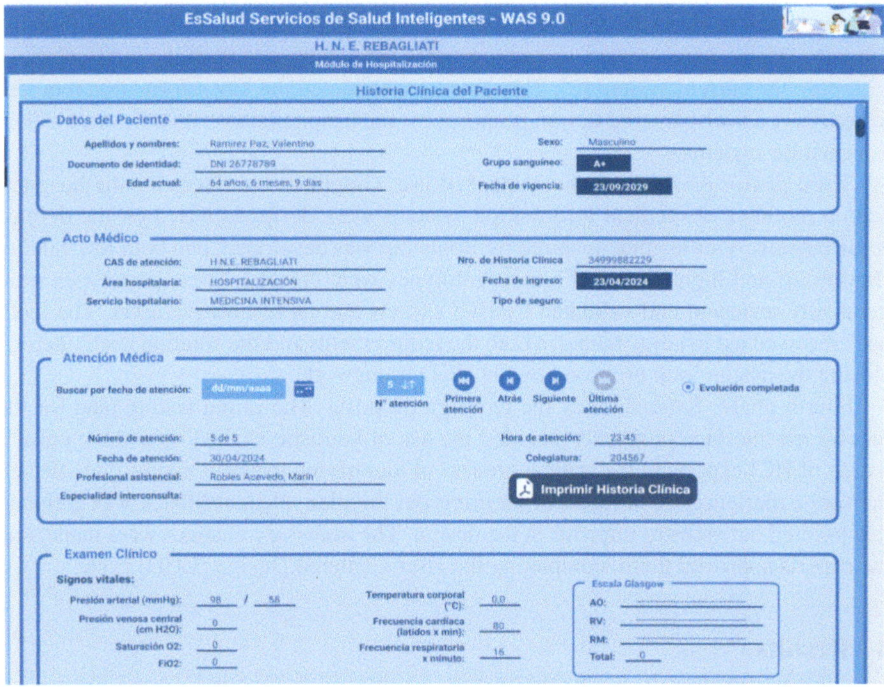

Fig. 1. Redesigned graphical user interfaces of the medical system – Medical Record section.

4.2 Heuristic Evaluation of the Redesigned Interfaces

The heuristic evaluations conducted on the redesigned proposal provided a detailed and critical perspective on the usability of the user interface. Through a rigorous analysis based on Jakob Nielsen's 10 usability heuristics [11], several issues affecting the user experience were identified and prioritized.

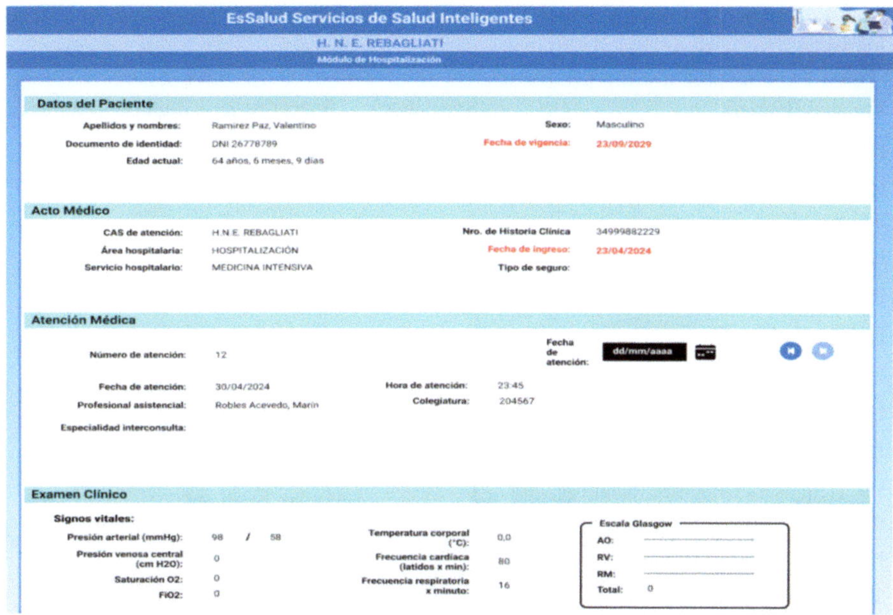

Fig. 2. Current version of the medical system – Medical Record section.

The findings highlighted significant areas of improvement, particularly related to the visibility of system status and the consistency and standards of the interface. Addressing these aspects aims to provide users with clearer system feedback and more predictable interactions during their tasks within the hospitalization modules of medical information systems.

Table 1 summarizes the frequency with which each heuristic was violated, as reported independently by two HCI specialists:

The most frequently identified usability violations were related to H1 (Visibility of system status) and H4 (Consistency and standards). This suggests that certain sections of the high-fidelity prototype for the redesigned hospitalization module interface should be improved to reduce ambiguities that may confuse users, hinder the learning curve, or fail to prevent potential errors—all of which negatively impact the overall user experience.

After addressing all the usability issues identified during the heuristic evaluations, the redesigned interface for the hospitalization modules of medical information systems has evolved into a product that aligns with established usability standards. The applied improvements not only enhance clarity and consistency but also support a more intuitive and efficient user flow. As a result, the system is now better equipped to meet the practical needs of healthcare professionals during their routine tasks, contributing to a more effective and user-centered digital environment.

Table 1. Number of Usability Issues Identified by HCI Experts and Categorized by Violated Heuristics.

Violated Heuristic	Specialist 1	Specialist 2	Total per Heuristic
H1. Visibility of system status	*0*	*0*	4
H2. Match between the system and the real world	*1*	*1*	2
H3. User control and freedom	*0*	*1*	1
H4. Consistency and standards	*3*	*3*	6
H5. Error prevention	*1*	*1*	2
H6. Recognition rather than recall	*1*	*1*	2
H7. Flexibility and efficiency of use	*0*	*0*	0
H8. Aesthetic and minimalist design	*0*	*0*	0
H9. Help users recognize, diagnose, and recover from errors	*0*	*1*	1
H10. Help and documentation	*0*	*0*	0
Total per Specialist	*6*	*8*	**18**

5 Conclusions and Future Works

In summary, a redesign proposal was developed for the graphical user interfaces of the hospitalization modules of medical information systems used in an Intensive Care Unit. The methodological foundation was based on the User-Centered Design (UCD) framework, with the aim of improving the current level of usability and enhancing the experience of the system's representative users, particularly medical professionals.

The UCD framework enabled the creation of an optimized interface proposal that addressed both the actual context of use and the users' needs, integrating the corrections and feedback provided by Human-Computer Interaction (HCI) specialists during the heuristic evaluations. As a result, the redesigned interfaces offer greater clarity, consistency, and efficiency, aligned with fundamental usability principles.

As future work, it is planned to conduct user testing in which participants will be asked to complete a series of tasks using both the current version of the system and the redesigned prototype. This will allow for the collection of objective usability metrics, such as task completion times and scores from the System Usability Scale (SUS) questionnaire, which will be compared to determine whether the redesign has effectively improved the system's usability. Additionally, it is recommended to replicate the user interview process with representatives from Intensive Care Units in other hospitals nationwide, since the redesigned interfaces are based on a system implemented across all healthcare centers of EsSalud (Social Health Insurance of Peru). Once the design phase is completed, the implementation of the proposed redesign can also be approached more effectively and feasibly.

Acknowledgments. This study is highly supported by the Section of Informatics Engineering of the Pontifical Catholic University of Peru (PUCP) - Peru, and the "HCI, Design, User Experience, Accessibility & Innovation Technologies" Research Group (HCI-DUXAIT). HCI-DUXAIT is a research group of PUCP.

Disclosure of Interests The authors declare there are no interest conflicts.

References

1. Ajami, S., Bagheri-Tadi, T.: Barriers for adopting electronic health records (EHRs) by physicians. Acta Inform. Med. **21**(2), 129–134 (2013). https://doi.org/10.5455/aim.2013.21.129-134

2. Chen, W., O'Bryan, C.M., Gorham, G., Howard, K., Balasubramanya, B., Coffey, P., Abeyaratne, A., Cass, A.: Barriers and enablers to implementing and using clinical decision support systems for chronic diseases: a qualitative systematic review and meta-aggregation. Implement. Sci. Commun. **3**(1), 81 (2022). https://doi.org/10.1186/s43058-022-00326-x

3. Consejo Nacional de Salud del Perú: Lineamientos y medidas de reforma del sector salud (2013). http://bvs.minsa.gob.pe/local/MINSA/3044.pdf, last accessed 2023/09/16

4. Dam, R.F., Siang, T.Y.: Personas – A Simple Introduction. The Interaction Design Foundation (2022). https://www.interaction-design.org/literature/article/personas-why-and-how-you-should-use-them, last accessed 2023/11/11

5. Department of Health: Government of Western Australia: Intensive care units (ICUs). https://www.healthywa.wa.gov.au/Articles/F_I/Intensive-care-units-ICUs, last accessed 2025/05/07

6. Gibbons, S.: Empathy Mapping: The First Step in Design Thinking. Nielsen Norman Group (2018). https://www.nngroup.com/articles/empathy-mapping/, last accessed 2023/11/11

7. Interaction Design Foundation: What is User Centered Design? — Updated 2023. *The Interaction Design Foundation.* https://www.interaction-design.org/literature/topics/user-centered-design , last accessed 2023/11/12

8. Jansson, M., Liisanantti, J., Ala-Kokko, T., Reponen, J.: The negative impact of interface design, customizability, inefficiency, malfunctions, and information retrieval on user experience: a national usability survey of ICU clinical information systems in Finland. Int. J. Med. Inform. **159**, 104680 (2022). https://doi.org/10.1016/j.ijmedinf.2021.104680

9. Maguire, M.: Methods to support human-centred design. Int. J. Hum.-Comput. Stud. **55**(4), 587–634 (2001). https://doi.org/10.1006/ijhc.2001.0503

10. Martikainen, S., Viitanen, J., Lääveri, T.: End-user participation in health information systems (HIS) development: physicians' and nurses' experiences. Int. J. Med. Inform. **137**, 104117 (2020). https://doi.org/10.1016/j.ijmedinf.2020.104117

11. Nielsen, J.: 10 Usability Heuristics for User Interface Design. Nielsen Norman Group (2020) https://www.nngroup.com/articles/ten-usability-heuristics/, last accessed 2024/04/10

12. Organisation for Economic Co-operation and Development (OECD): Monitoring Health System Performance in Peru: Data and Statistics (2017). https://doi.org/10.1787/9789264282988-en

13. Paliwal, G., Bunglowala, A., Kanthed, P.: An architectural design study of electronic healthcare record systems with associated context parameters on MIMIC III. Heal. Technol. **12**(2), 313–327 (2022). https://doi.org/10.1007/s12553-022-00638-x

14. Pan American Health Organization (PAHO) & World Health Organization (WHO): Health Information Systems—PAHO/WHO I Pan American Health Organization (2025, junio 12). https://www.paho.org/en/topics/health-information-systems, last accessed 2025/05/09

15. Poncette, A.-S., Mosch, L.K., Stablo, L., Spies, C., Schieler, M., Weber-Carstens, S., Feufel, M.A., Balzer, F.: A remote patient-monitoring system for intensive care medicine: mixed methods human-centered design and usability evaluation. JMIR Hum. Factors. **9**(1), e30655 (2022). https://doi.org/10.2196/30655
16. Roosan, D., Troung, H., Law, A., Karim, M., Chok, J., Roosan, M., Li, Y.: Visualizing medication information using hierarchical task analysis and infographics in a mobile device (preprint). JMIR Mhealth Uhealth. **7** (2019). https://doi.org/10.2196/15940
17. Yale University: User Journey Maps | Usability & Web Accessibility. https://usability.yale.edu/understanding-your-user/user-journey-maps, last accessed 2025/04/02

Periplous: Empowering Visitors Through Accessible, Touch-Based Map Interfaces

Asterios Leonidis[1,2]([✉]) [iD], Alexandra Alexandridi[1], Effie Karuzaki[1] [iD],
Maria Korozi[1] [iD], George Kapnas[1], and Constantine Stephanidis[1,2] [iD]

[1] Institute of Computer Science (ICS), Foundation for Research and Technology - Hellas
(FORTH), 70013 Heraklion, Crete, Greece
{leonidis,alexandrid,korozi,cs}@ics.forth.gr
[2] Department of Computer Science Heraklion, University of Crete, 70013 Heraklion, Crete,
Greece

Abstract. Periplous is an interactive platform for digital mapsthat supports inclusive cultural and geographic exploration in public spaces such as museums, tourist centers, and heritage sites. It allows diverse users—including those with disabilities—to engage with spatial content via a touch-based, multimodal interface. Developed through a user-centered process, Periplous prioritizes accessibility through features like thematic filtering, route planning, and an accessibility mode with tactile input and audio guidance.

Keywords: Interactive Maps · Public Information Systems · Accessibility

1 Introduction

In recent years, public installations have increasingly embraced digital technologies to enhance the accessibility, engagement, and educational value of cultural and geographic content [1]. Interactive systems that support spatial exploration and multimodal information delivery can empower diverse audiences—including tourists, local visitors, and individuals with disabilities—to connect with a region's history, landmarks, and environment in a meaningful and inclusive way [2]. However, despite their growing presence, many existing solutions fall short of meeting the needs of a diverse user base. They often overlook inclusive design principles and provide limited support for users with physical or sensory impairments [3]. This work presents **Periplous**, an interactive platform for digital maps designed to support cultural and geographic exploration in public spaces. Periplous enables users to explore curated Points of Interest (POIs) through a touch-based interface that is both intuitive and accessible. The platform delivers rich, layered content—including text, images, and audio narration—while also offering adaptive interaction techniques for users with different physical and cognitive abilities. Building on principles of human-centered and inclusive design, Periplous aims to balance usability, engagement, and accessibility without compromising the richness of the content presented. The system was developed iteratively through a user-centered design process

© The Author(s), under exclusive license to Springer Nature Switzerland AG 2026
S. Sundarakannan and O. Knorpp (Eds.): HCII 2025, CCIS 2772, pp. 262–272, 2026.
https://doi.org/10.1007/978-3-032-12767-9_28

that involved diverse stakeholder input and real-world deployment scenarios. Particular emphasis was placed on ensuring the platform is both adaptable to different user needs and scalable for various public installation contexts.

2   Related Work

2.1   Interactive Maps as Information Systems

Interactive maps constitute a powerful medium for disseminating information, engaging citizens, and supporting decision-making processes. This domain of research and application intersects various disciplines, including Geographic Information Systems (GIS), human-computer interaction, and cartography, among others. Among the most prevalent applications of interactive maps as information systems are those related to transportation and tourism. In public transportation, interactive maps help passengers navigate by clearly displaying stations, routes, and nearby points of interest. Burch et al. [4], developed an interactive public transport map that visualizes real-time passenger data with statistical views like density plots and line graphs. Similarly, Pun-Cheng [5] describes a web-based map in Hong Kong for real-time route planning based on criteria such as transfers, travel time, or fare. Nagel et al. [6] present a multi-touch tabletop interface for exploring public transit data.

In tourism, interactive maps are used to showcase and promote cultural and historical assets -such as monuments, museums and archaeological sites- while providing relevant contextual information. Research has demonstrated that smart tourism technologies, including smart sightseeing features, significantly enhance tourists' co-creation experiences and contribute positively to their overall perception of a destination [7, 8]. Interactive maps on tourism websites, in particular, play a key role in shaping travel plans, as tourists often explore sightseeing opportunities prior to their visits [9, 10]. The concept of enriching interactive maps with localized data, narratives, and user-specific content has also been embraced by various companies, including Tierraplan[1], Situm[1], Mapme,[1] and others.

2.2   Interactive Maps in Public Displays

Interactive maps deployed on public displays represent a distinct class of information systems characterized by co-located, walk-up-and-use interaction in shared physical spaces such as museums, cultural centers, visitor kiosks, and exhibitions. Unlike personal or mobile interfaces, these systems must address a range of design challenges including multi-user support, situational awareness, discoverability, and accessibility in physically and socially dynamic environments.

Research in public display interaction has emphasized the importance of designing for opportunistic engagement, where users can approach a display spontaneously and begin interacting without the need for prior instruction. This form of casual interaction relies on clear visual affordances, immediate feedback, and intuitive controls to reduce user hesitation and encourage exploration [11, 12]. Studies involving interactive map

---

[1] Tierraplan: https://tierraplan.com/, Situm: https://situm.com/, Mapme: https://mapme.com/

tables in cultural and educational environments have shown that touch-based and tangible interactions can foster both individual learning and collaborative exploration, especially in group settings such as museums or exhibitions [13].

Large-format interactive maps and information kiosks have become increasingly prevalent in public and educational environments, serving as intuitive tools for wayfinding, information access, and visitor support. These systems allow users to search for locations, explore points of interest, and obtain relevant contextual information in a spatial format. Examples include campus-based kiosks that assist students and visitors in locating administrative offices, lecture halls, and university facilities through interactive maps and categorized menus [14, 15]. In tourism settings, kiosks have been developed to guide visitors through local attractions, provide route suggestions, and enable the transfer of navigation information to mobile devices for continued use beyond the display itself [16]. To enhance user experience and engagement, many of these systems incorporate multimedia content, simplified menu structures, and interactive features designed to support diverse user needs. In some cases, they also include feedback mechanisms and content tailored to improve clarity, memory retention, and accessibility for different types of users [14, 17]. Despite these advancements, a recurring design challenge remains: the potential for visual clutter and information overload, particularly when maps present densely packed areas with many overlapping elements.

2.3 Accessibility in Digital Map Interfaces

Accessibility in digital map interfaces is an increasing concern as these systems grow more common on the web and in public displays. Despite advances in map interactivity and visual design, users with visual, cognitive, or motor impairments often encounter significant barriers when interacting with digital maps, which are typically optimized for sighted, touch-based use.

In the domain of web-based maps, research has focused on improving access for blind and visually impaired users through alternative design strategies. Some approaches propose transforming conventional map content into formats compatible with screen readers, often using structured data (e.g., SVG images) and transformation engines to present geographic information through non-visual modalities [18]. Additional strategies include enhancing web pages with screen-reader-friendly structures, providing textual alternatives and descriptive annotations for map pins and points of interest, and designing interfaces that encourage exploration through meaningful, narratively rich content [19–21]. The adoption of multimodal user interfaces that support scalable interaction—such as keyboard navigation, audio feedback, and haptic cues—has also been emphasized as a way to increase usability for diverse users.

In parallel, public display systems face unique accessibility challenges due to their physical format and shared, co-located nature. While these systems are often designed to be visually engaging and intuitive for general audiences, they frequently fall short in accommodating users with disabilities. Studies evaluating interactive kiosks and public map interfaces have highlighted barriers such as unclear navigation flows, lack of tactile or voice input alternatives, and small or densely clustered interface elements that are difficult to interpret [22]. To address these issues, accessibility-centered design efforts have introduced features like linear, scannable content layouts, tactile input devices, voice-controlled navigation, and intelligent interfaces that dynamically adapt to a user's needs [23]. These strategies help transform the typical visually dense and touch-reliant interface into a more inclusive, navigable, and multimodal system.

Overall, while progress has been made in both domains, accessibility in digital map interfaces—particularly in multitouch public displays—remains an underexplored and evolving area. Bridging the gap between personalized web accessibility and the demands of public, walk-up-and-use installations presents a significant design challenge. Periplous addresses this gap by integrating an accessibility mode that restructures visual layouts, incorporates assistive input devices, and delivers multimodal feedback, thereby supporting a broader range of user abilities in collaborative and culturally rich settings.

3 Design Process

Designed for deployment in diverse public contexts, Periplous was developed as part of a broader effort to support meaningful and engaging exploration of geographic and cultural information through an interactive, map-based system. The design methodology followed the AmI-Design Process [24], an iterative framework grounded in Design Thinking principles [25], specifically tailored for the development of Intelligent Environments (IEs) [26]. It supports the design of both intelligent spaces (e.g., smart homes) and the interactive artifacts and applications that operate within them (e.g., smart furniture or wearable devices). The process comprises several stages -Understand, Define, Ideate, Filter & Plan, Design, Implement, and Test- and was systematically applied throughout the development of Periplous.

The design process for Periplous began with the **Understand & Define** phases, which involved an extensive review of literature and existing systems related to interactive maps for public installations, with a particular focus on accessibility and inclusive design principles. This research aimed to establish a comprehensive understanding of the design space, identify user needs, and reveal gaps in existing solutions. In parallel, a series of collaborative meetings with the design team—including UI designers, interaction designers, engineers, and content experts—were conducted, alongside informal interviews with potential end users to define relevant personas and user scenarios. Based on these activities, a list of high-level requirements was established (Table 1).

During the Ideate phase, numerous concepts were generated through brainstorming sessions. The main focus was on how to effectively visualize information and manage the challenges posed by multiple points of interest (POIs) clustered closely together. Key concerns included handling simultaneous interactions for multiple users—such as whether to allow more than one POI's information to be open at a time—and visually differentiating POIs across various categories to enhance clarity. Ensuring the interface was engaging and accessible was also a priority. This involved addressing accessibility challenges, such as how to enable efficient scanning of randomly placed pins and making all interactive elements fully accessible for users with diverse abilities. These ideas were refined through discussions with domain experts, to prioritize solutions that balanced technical feasibility, inclusiveness, and user engagement.

During the Design phase, low- and high-fidelity prototypes were developed through an iterative process. At each stage, UI and User Experience (UX) experts reviewed the prototypes to ensure usability and alignment with user needs before proceeding to implementation. Once the initial implementation was complete, the system underwent a thorough review by an internal Accessibility Team, consisting of experts in accessibility design and assistive technologies. Their hands-on testing led to significant refinements to the scanning behavior, narration structure, and overall interface flow. In addition, every Periplous installation was followed by an on-site pilot phase, during which real users were observed interacting with the system in context. Feedback from these pilot deployments was incorporated into the next iteration of the system, forming an ongoing loop of design, deployment, and refinement.

Table 1. High-Level Requirements.

ID	Requirement
R1	Present Points of Interest (POIs) on an interactive map, accurately positioned.
R2	Allow users to select POIs and view related multimedia content.
R3	Enable zooming and panning of the map for easier navigation.
R4	Display densely clustered POIs in a clear and organized manner.
R5	Organize POIs by category to support thematic exploration.
R6	Present predefined routes with step-by-step directions and visual paths on the map.
R7	Use distinct visual cues (e.g., color-coded icons) to indicate POI categories.
R8	Support navigation for users with diverse physical or visual abilities.
R9	Enable interaction through external accessibility devices (e.g., assistive switches).
R10	Provide a scanning-based mode for sequential input navigation.
R11	Offer text-to-speech (TTS) for all text and alternative text for images.
R12	Place interactive elements within ergonomic reach for all users.
R13	Deliver content through multiple modes, including text, visuals, and audio narration.
R14	Ensure text & icons are readable in varied lighting & enable auto-scroll for long content.
R15	Display idle-time animations or prompts to attract user attention.

4 Periplous Description

The platform can display numerous Points of Interest (POIs), which may represent a wide range of cultural and spatial entities, including archaeological sites, museums, monuments, and natural landmarks (Fig. 1a). Importantly, POIs are not limited to historic or cultural attractions; they may also include contemporary elements such as shops, local businesses, digital service points, parks, and other scenic or functional locations. Each POI is visually distinguished by a unique color and icon corresponding to its thematic category (e.g., historical sites, museums, cultural venues). These thematic categories are presented horizontally along the bottom of the screen as interactive buttons, allowing users to easily toggle categories on or off. This dynamic filtering customizes the map display to align with users' interests or specific inquiries. Users are also able to freely pan, zoom in, and zoom out to explore the map in detail; however, this functionality is thoughtfully constrained to keep users within the designated area of interest and prevent disorientation. When two or more POIs are located very close to each other, the system automatically groups them into a clustered pin, which also reflects the appropriate color and icon of the underlying categories.

Upon selecting a POI on the map, an information panel appears, offering users a detailed exploration experience (Fig. 1b). Users can browse photo galleries that showcase the site or artifact in high detail, watch short videos providing contextual explanations, listen to audio descriptions, and read well-structured textual narratives including both explanatory and practical visitor information such as opening hours or accessibility features. To enhance user convenience and support continued engagement, the system allows users to send selected POI information to their mobile devices. By entering an email address via the on-screen keyboard, users receive the associated text and multimedia content for further exploration at their convenience.

Fig. 1: Snapshot of a map showing (left) Points of Interest, (middle) an active panel displaying details of a selected POI, and (right) a route with **step-by-step navigation instructions**

In order to accommodate both visitors seeking curated cultural narratives and those interested in personalized explorations, the system offers two routing modes. The first mode, Predefined Routes (Fig. 1c), features expertly curated itineraries created by cultural heritage professionals, tourism specialists, local experts, etc. These routes are designed to guide visitors through meaningful sequences of points of interest, whether within interior spaces (e.g., museums, exhibition halls) or exterior environments, including towns, archaeological sites, prefectures, and natural landscapes. The second mode, Custom Routes, empowers users with greater flexibility and control over their exploration. Visitors can select any two POIs on the map according to their personal interests or needs, and the system will calculate the shortest or most convenient path between them using real-world road and pedestrian network data. By supporting autonomous exploration, this mode accommodates visitors who prefer to tailor their experience or who wish to navigate spontaneously based on their preferences.

Both modes are supported by a user-friendly **step-by-step navigation interface**, presented through a floating panel that remains visible throughout the route (Fig. 1c). This panel displays key route information-such as total estimated duration, walking distance, and accessibility indicators-alongside a **predefined set of navigation instructions** that guide the user from one POI to the next. Users have the option to **send the complete**

route directions to their personal email address. This allows them to refer to the instructions at any time making it easier to plan ahead or continue their visit without relying solely on the device interface.

4.1 Accessibility and Inclusivity

Accessibility has been carefully considered throughout the design and development of Periplous to ensure that users with diverse abilities can interact with the system comfortably and effectively. One of the most significant challenges in designing interactive map-based systems -especially those displaying a dense network of POIs- is enabling users to efficiently scan and interpret interface elements without being overwhelmed. This is particularly important for individuals with visual, cognitive, or motor impairments, who may struggle with information overload or small, closely spaced interactive elements. To address these issues, the interface of Periplous includes features that enhance clarity and usability. POIs are thematically grouped and visually differentiated using color-coded icons, helping users distinguish between different categories at a glance. Additionally, most interactive elements are intentionally positioned in the lower portion of the screen, making them easier to reach and interact with—particularly for children, seated users, or individuals with limited mobility—thus reinforcing the system's inclusive design approach.

The system also interoperates with a custom-built accessibility controller to support users with motor or visual impairments. This dedicated device includes four tactile buttons—"Next", "Previous", "OK", and "Enter Accessibility Mode"—enabling users to sequentially navigate through interface elements without relying on touch-based gestures. Once accessibility mode is activated, the interface dynamically restructures itself to facilitate easier interaction. Specifically, thematic categories of POIs are displayed vertically along the left side of the screen, allowing users to scan and select a category using the controller (Fig. 2a). Upon selection, a list of POIs within that category is presented in a structured, linear format, which can then be browsed step by step (Fig. 2b). The scanning mechanism follows an approach similar to the one used in iPhone accessibility scanning: interface elements are grouped into logical, scannable clusters. When a group is entered, a dashed border highlights its boundary, and the user can sequentially scan through the group's contents. Upon reaching the last item, pressing "Next" returns focus to the group border; the user can then press "OK" to exit or "Next" to continue to the next group.

For users with visual impairments, this scanning process is complemented by narrated audio descriptions of each interface element and POI, ensuring that content is accessible without visual input. This approach transforms the otherwise spatial and visually dense interface into a logical, navigable sequence tailored for assistive exploration. Additionally, all visual content is enriched with descriptive alternative text designed for seamless narration by text-to-speech (TTS) systems. In parallel, automatic text scrolling is provided for users with low vision, minimizing the need for continuous manual interaction and helping maintain reading focus. Finally, the physical design of the installation reinforces its accessibility goals (Fig. 2c). The casing structure is designed to support wheelchair access, with a tilted display that accommodates both standing and seated users—including children and individuals using mobility aids.

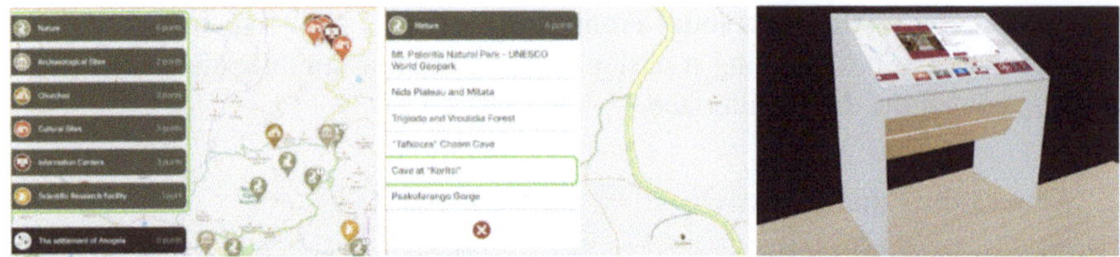

Fig. 2: (left) Categories of POIs presented sequentially in scanning mode; (middle) Selecting a category enables scanning POIs one by one; (right) 3D model of the final system.

4.2 Technologies

The frontend of Periplous is developed using Angular,[2] a robust and widely adopted modern web application framework. Angular provides a modular architecture that ensures scalability, maintainability, and rapid development. It allows for the creation of dynamic, reactive user interfaces that can easily handle asynchronous data and complex user interactions. For map rendering and geospatial interactions, Periplous integrates Leaflet[2], a lightweight yet powerful JavaScript library optimized for interactive maps. Leaflet's extensive plugin ecosystem and ease of customization make it well-suited for delivering a responsive, smooth, and visually appealing mapping experience on large multitouch displays. The base geographic data is primarily sourced from OpenStreetMap[2] (OSM), an open-source, community-maintained map database. OSM provides detailed and frequently updated spatial data including roads, buildings, landmarks, and natural features. Periplous also employs GraphHopper[2], an efficient open-source routing engine that calculates optimal routes based on OSM's road network. GraphHopper allows the system to generate dynamic navigation paths between any two points of interest, as well as support predefined thematic routes curated by domain experts. To support inclusive access, the system uses the browser's native SAPI 5.0 text-to-speech engine by default to provide auditory feedback for interface elements. In addition, it has been tested for compatibility with screen readers such as SuperNova and ChromeVox, ensuring accessibility for individuals with visual impairments.

4.3 Installations

The Periplous system has been successfully deployed in multiple locations, demonstrating its versatility and effectiveness in enhancing visitor engagement with cultural and urban environments through interactive technologies. In the tourist information point of **Kalamata** (Fig. 3a), the system is installed in a coastal pavilion, offering access to information regarding archaeological sites, museums, monuments, and thematic routes extending into the surrounding landscape. Similarly in **Larissa** (Fig. 3b), it guides users through key cultural landmarks such as churches, libraries, and museums, with curated routes that highlight the city's heritage. At the **Archaeological Museum of Messara**

---

[2] Angular: angular.dev, Leaflet: leafletjs.com, OSM: www.openstreetmap.org, GraphHopper: www.graphhopper.com

(Fig. 3c), the platform presents a regional map of archaeological sites and road networks, supporting the museum's educational mission and connecting visitors to local history. In **Anogeia and the Psiloritis Geopark** (Fig. 3d), the system covers natural and cultural landmarks—including caves, trails, and historic churches.

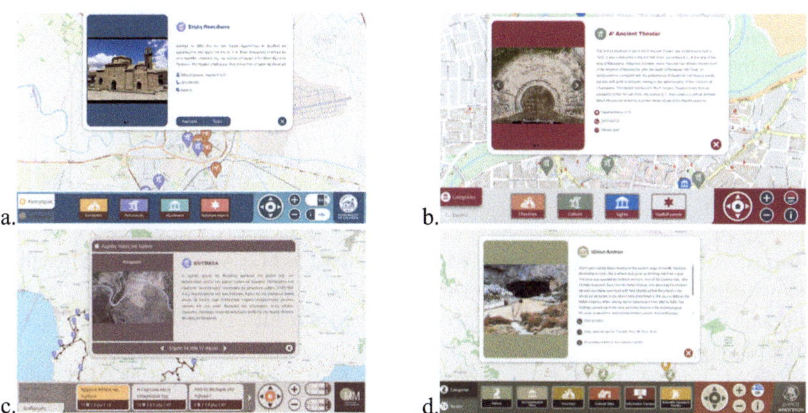

Fig. 3: Snapshots of Periplous UIs in (a) Kalamata, (b) Larissa, (c) Messara, and (d) Anogeia.

Across these diverse deployment sites, informal observations indicate that Periplous effectively attracts and retains visitor attention, encouraging exploratory behavior and prolonged engagement with the digital map interface. Visitors of varying ages and backgrounds demonstrated curiosity and enjoyment when interacting with the platform, often spending more time exploring Points of Interest than anticipated. In several locations, users expressed appreciation for the multimodal content, particularly audio narration and images, which enriched their understanding of local heritage and natural landmarks. Staff and hosts at installation sites reported positive feedback from visitors, noting that Periplous served as a useful orientation tool that sparked conversations and increased interest in lesser-known sites. While some users needed initial guidance, most of them quickly adapted to the intuitive UI. Early feedback suggests the platform fosters meaningful visitor engagement, though formal studies are needed to confirm this.

5   Conclusion and Future Work

This work introduced Periplous, an interactive digital map platform designed to enhance cultural and geographic exploration in public spaces through an accessible, user-centered approach. The platform successfully integrates multimodal content delivery and adaptive interaction techniques to accommodate a diverse range of users, including those with varying physical and cognitive abilities. The deployment of Periplous in real-world public installations demonstrated its potential to engage visitors meaningfully while supporting inclusive exploration of various Points of Interest.

Periplous has consistently attracted interest from multiple venues seeking installations, as well as from investors who recognize its potential impact and scalability. Future work will focus on conducting a large-scale user study to systematically evaluate the platform's usability, accessibility, and overall effectiveness across diverse user groups and contexts. Insights from this study will inform iterative improvements and promote the broader adoption of Periplous as a versatile tool for inclusive cultural and geographic exploration in public spaces.

Acknowledgements. This work has been supported by the FORTH-ICS internal RTD Programme 'Ambient Intelligence and Smart Environments'. The authors would like to thank the Accessibility Team- Stavroula Ntoa & Ilia Adami- and Vanessa Neroutsou for content curation.

References

1. Tosios, A., Leonidis, A., Korozi, M., Stivaktakis, N.M., Apostolakis, E., Roulios, M., Paparoulis, S., Stamatakis, E., Stephanidis, C.: CreteAR: enhancing learning experiences through tangible transformable artifacts and extended reality. Hum. Fact. Des. Eng. Comput. **159** (2024)
2. Fleck, M., Frid, M., Kindberg, T., O'Brien-Strain, E., Rajani, R., Spasojevic, M.: From informing to remembering: ubiquitous systems in interactive museums. IEEE Pervasive Comput. **1**, 13–21 (2002)
3. Bohlmeijer, M.W.: Systematic Literature Review on Interaction Design Used for Museum Learning (2024).
4. Burch, M., Staudt, Y., Frommer, S., Uttenweiler, J., Grupp, P., Hähnle, S., Scheytt, J., Kloos, U.: Pasvis: enhancing public transport maps with interactive passenger data visualizations. In: Proceedings of the 13th International Symposium on Visual Information Communication and Interaction, pp. 1–8 (2020)
5. Pun-Cheng, L.S.: An interactive web-based public transport enquiry system with real-time optimal route computation. IEEE Trans. Intell. Transp. Syst. **13**, 983–988 (2012)
6. Nagel, T., Maitan, M., Duval, E., Vande Moere, A., Klerkx, J., Kloeckl, K., Ratti, C.: Touching transport-a case study on visualizing metropolitan public transit on interactive tabletops. In: Proceedings of the 2014 International Working Conference on Advanced Visual Interfaces, pp. 281–288 (2014)
7. Kapnas, G., Leonidis, A., Korozi, M., Ntoa, S., Margetis, G., Stephanidis, C.: A museum guide application for deployment on user-owned Mobile devices. In: Stephanidis, C. (ed.) HCI International 2013 - Posters' Extended Abstracts, pp. 253–257. Springer, Berlin, Heidelberg (2013). https://doi.org/10.1007/978-3-642-39476-8_52
8. Bashir, M., Asghar, S., Ashfaq, M., Raza, S.S., Zahoor, S.: Digitalizing tourism and interactive navigation: a case study of Pakistan. J. Asian Dev. Stud. **13**, 547–566 (2024)
9. Izumi, T.: Tourism engineering for supporting stroll—what is true travel? In: Systems Design Based on the Benefits of Inconvenience, pp. 69–81. Springer (2022)
10. Young Chung, J., Anuar, F.I., Go, H., Gretzel, U.: Influence of interactive thematic maps on tourist perceptions: a network analysis. J. Hosp. Tour. Technol. **2**, 216–234 (2011)
11. Müller, J., Alt, F., Michelis, D., Schmidt, A.: Requirements and design space for interactive public displays. In: Proceedings of the 18th ACM international conference on Multimedia, pp. 1285–1294 (2010)
12. Alt, F., Shirazi, A.S., Kubitza, T., Schmidt, A.: Interaction techniques for creating and exchanging content with public displays. In: Proceedings of the SIGCHI Conference on Human Factors in Computing Systems, vol. 2013, pp. 1709–1718. Association for Computing Machinery, New York, NY. https://doi.org/10.1145/2470654.2466226

13. Hornecker, E., Stifter, M.: Learning from interactive museum installations about interaction design for public settings. In: Proceedings of the 18th Australia Conference on Computer-Human Interaction: Design: Activities, Artefacts and Environments, pp. 135–142 (2006)

14. Sarmiento, J.R., Capio, A.F., Sison, J.A.L., Nabua, C.J.A., Guadaña, R.R.H.: Ask Billy: An Informative Kiosk in a University. In: 2021 1st International Conference in Information and Computing Research (iCORE), pp. 72–77 (2021)

15. Adam, S.I., Lontaan, R.J., Supit, V.V., Kolibonso, S.C.: Digital information and navigation kiosk application based on progressive web apps and leaflet technology. CogITo Smart J. **10**, 393–402 (2024)

16. Arviola, M., Matienzo, J.C., Peji, J.: Indang Konektayo kiosk: an interactive menu system for tourists. J. Innov. Technol. Converg. **6**, 41–50 (2024)

17. Harper, C., Jefferies, S., Crosser, A., Avera, A., Duke, T., Klisans, D.V.: Exploring hospital wayfinding systems: touchscreen kiosks, apps and environmental cues. In: Proceedings of the International Symposium on Human Factors and Ergonomics in Health Care, pp. 172–175. SAGE Publications Sage CA, Los Angeles, CA (2019)

18. Calle-Jimenez, T., Eguez-Sarzosa, A., Luján-Mora, S.: Design of an architecture for accessible web maps for visually impaired users. In: International Conference on Applied Human Factors and Ergonomics, pp. 221–232. Springer (2018)

19. Buzzi, M.C., Buzzi, M., Leporini, B., Martusciello, L.: Making visual maps accessible to the blind. In: International Conference on Universal Access in Human-Computer Interaction, pp. 271–280. Springer (2011)

20. Klaus, H., Marano, D., Neuschmid, J., Schrenk, M., Wasserburger, W.: AccessibleMap: web-based city maps for blind and visually impaired. In: International Conference on Computers for Handicapped Persons, pp. 536–543. Springer (2012)

21. Manu, S.D., Burghardt, D., Hauthal, E.: Enhancing accessibility of thematic web maps for visually impaired users. KN-J. Cartogr. Geograp. Inform., 1–15 (2025)

22. Lee, Y., Park, S., Park, J., Kim, H.K.: Comparative analysis of usability and accessibility of kiosks for people with disabilities. Appl. Sci. **13**, 3058 (2023)

23. Hagen, S., Sandnes, F.E.: Toward accessible self-service kiosks through intelligent user interfaces. Pers. Ubiquit. Comput. **14**, 715–721 (2010)

24. Stephanidis, C., Leonidis, A., Korozi, M., Kouroumalis, V., Adami, I., Ntoa, S.: Design for intelligent environments. In: Human-Computer Interaction in Intelligent Environments. CRC Press (2024)

25. Brown, T.: Others: design thinking. Harv. Bus. Rev. **86**, 84 (2008)

26. Leonidis, A., Korozi, M., Kouroumalis, V., Poutouris, E., Stefanidi, E., Arampatzis, D., Sykianaki, E., Anyfantis, N., Kalligiannakis, E., Nicodemou, V.C.: Ambient intelligence in the living room. Sensors. **19**, 5011 (2019)

A Human-Centered Approach for Bridging Heritage, Innovation, and Inclusion: The TOFOLA Project's Vision for Accessible Maritime Tourism

Patrik Pluchino[1,2]([✉]) [iD], Valeria Orso[1,2] [iD], Filippo Zordan[1], Anna Spagnolli[1,2] [iD], Claudia Forzan[3], and Luciano Gamberini[1,2] [iD]

[1] Department of General Psychology, University of Padova, Padova 35131, Italy
patrik.pluchino@unipd.it

[2] Human Inspired Technology (HIT) Research Centre, University of Padova, Padova 35121, Italy

[3] Centro Consorzi, Belluno 32036, Italy

Abstract. The Adriatic region encounters ongoing challenges in diversifying its tourism offerings while concurrently ensuring sustainability and inclusivity. The Interreg Italy-Croatia TOFOLA project endeavours to tackle these challenges by developing sustainable and accessible tourism products that are rooted in the maritime heritage of the Serenissima Republic of Venice. This paper articulates a human-centered design approach aimed at creating inclusive tourist boats that serve underrated destinations while guaranteeing equitable access to cultural heritage for individuals with disabilities and elderly users. Through comprehensive participatory design activities that involve target users, caregivers, and nautical experts, we have identified essential accessibility requirements and developed evidence-based design guidelines for the reconstruction of traditional wooden vessels. Besides individuals with motor and sensory disabilities, the informants included nautical professionals specializing in accessible sailing, certified sailing instructors with Paralympic experience. The qualitative analysis has revealed significant insights concerning boarding systems, interior design, assistive technologies, and safety measures that challenge conventional assumptions regarding maritime accessibility. These findings inform the development of boat prototypes that incorporate eco-friendly propulsion systems alongside inclusive design attributes, thereby contributing to both environmental sustainability and social inclusion within maritime tourism. The resulting design guidelines furnish a comprehensive framework that addresses physical access, ergonomic considerations, assistive technologies, stability requirements, and crew training needs, thereby offering a replicable model for accessible heritage tourism throughout the Adriatic region and beyond .

Keywords: Human-Centered Design · Inclusion · Accessible Tourism · Assistive Technology

© The Author(s), under exclusive license to Springer Nature Switzerland AG 2026

S. Sundarakannan and O. Knorpp (Eds.): HCII 2025, CCIS 2772, pp. 273–281, 2026.
https://doi.org/10.1007/978-3-032-12767-9_29

1 Introduction

Maritime tourism represents a significant economic sector in the Adriatic region, contributing substantially to local economies while providing unique opportunities for cultural and natural heritage engagement. However, accessibility barriers continue to exclude substantial user groups from these experiences, limiting both social inclusion and economic potential [1]. The World Health Organization estimates that over 1.3 billion people worldwide experience significant disabilities, representing approximately 16% of the global population, yet tourism infrastructure often fails to accommodate their needs [2].

The TOFOLA project ("Tourism in the Forest and green Lagoons of the Adriatic through historical wooden boats" - ITHR0200352) addresses this challenge through an innovative approach that combines cultural heritage preservation with inclusive design principles. This Interreg Italy-Croatia initiative recognizes that accessibility is not merely a compliance requirement but a fundamental aspect of sustainable tourism development that benefits entire communities [3].

The project's core objective involves reconstructing traditional wooden vessels from the Serenissima Republic era, integrating modern accessibility features and sustainable technologies. This approach reflects growing recognition that cultural heritage preservation and contemporary accessibility requirements can be successfully integrated through thoughtful design processes [4]. By focusing on maritime heritage, the project addresses a particularly underserved area where accessibility challenges are compounded by safety requirements, environmental conditions, and spatial constraints inherent to maritime environments [5].

This human-centered approach ensures that maritime cultural heritage becomes accessible to all users, including individuals with physical, visual, auditory, or cognitive disabilities, as well as elderly travelers. The significance of this work extends beyond immediate accessibility benefits, contributing to broader social inclusion objectives and economic sustainability of heritage tourism [6].

Recent literature emphasizes the importance of inclusive tourism as both a social imperative and economic opportunity, with accessible tourism representing a market segment with significant growth potential [7, 8]. However, maritime environments present unique challenges due to safety requirements, space constraints, and dynamic conditions that hinder accessibility implementations [9]. Our research contributes to this domain by providing empirically-grounded design guidelines derived from extensive participatory design activities involving target users, caregivers, and industry experts.

The paper presents findings from participatory design activities that engaged diverse stakeholders in identifying accessibility requirements and developing practical solutions for inclusive maritime tourism. Through this human-centered approach, we demonstrate how traditional maritime heritage can be preserved while simultaneously enhancing accessibility and sustainability for contemporary tourism applications.

2   Related Work

2.1   Accessible Maritime Tourism

Research in accessible maritime tourism has emerged as a critical area addressing the intersection of transportation accessibility and inclusive tourism experiences. The field encompasses multiple dimensions including physical infrastructure, service design, and regulatory frameworks that collectively determine the accessibility of maritime tourism offerings.

Gillovic and colleagues [7] analyzed how universal design principles with assistive technologies enhance maritime accessibility. They emphasized the effectiveness of adjustable ramps and hydraulic lifts for barrier-free access. The study showed that implementing accessibility features benefits users with disabilities and improves the overall experience for all passengers, supporting the case for inclusive design.

Lemberg [9] conducted extensive analysis of hydraulic boarding systems in ferry services, showing how automated elevation can adapt to tidal changes while ensuring safety. This research demonstrated the feasibility of adaptive boarding solutions for tourist vessels. The focus on automation fills a gap in traditional maritime accessibility, which often depends on manual support.

Aratani and collaborators [10] validated hydraulic lifting mechanisms for wheelchair users in coastal environments. Their evaluations confirmed improvements in boarding efficiency and user autonomy in challenging docking conditions. The research shows that technology can effectively address environmental barriers limiting maritime accessibility.

Musio-Sale [11] introduced adaptive floating dock systems that respond dynamically to water level changes, reducing risks linked to unstable boarding surfaces. This research addresses a key challenge in maritime accessibility, where static infrastructure often fails under changing conditions. It demonstrates the effectiveness of responsive infrastructure for consistent boarding experiences.

Despite useful, the research works reported above focused on advancing the accessibility of the boat from a merely engineering point of view, largely failing to involve the target population to whom those actions were addressed, namely individuals with disabilities.

2.2   Human-Centered Design in Maritime Contexts

Applying human-centered design (HCD) principles to maritime tourism is an emerging yet underdeveloped research area [12]. Traditional maritime design has focused on engineering and safety, with limited attention to user experience and accessibility across diverse populations.

Capulong [13] conducted pioneering work on ergonomic considerations in boat design, showing that user-centered approaches enhance passenger comfort and safety. The research revealed that ergonomic seating and optimized layouts improve accessibility for users with specific needs and enhance the overall navigation experience for all passengers.

Poko [14] provided insights into riverine tourism accessibility, showing the effectiveness of systematic accessible infrastructure in tourism. This work illustrated how comprehensive accessibility planning, including pathways and adaptive boarding systems, can enhance existing tourism operations and service quality.

Ferrari [15] contributed by proposing accessible and inclusive boat designs, stressing early user involvement in design. This work showcased participatory approaches to discover innovative solutions often overlooked in traditional engineering design.

However, participatory design studies with multiple stakeholders are limited in maritime tourism literature. Most research focuses on single-stakeholder perspectives or technical solutions without user involvement. This gap is significant given the complex safety and regulatory requirements in maritime contexts, necessitating a balance between accessibility and safety.

2.3 Assistive Technologies for Maritime Environments

Integrating assistive technologies in maritime environments is evolving and has significant potential for enhancing accessibility and user experience. However, unique maritime challenges, such as safety requirements, environmental conditions, and space constraints, necessitate specialized approaches to technology implementation.

Qiao [16] researched tactile guides and auditory feedback systems for visually impaired passengers, revealing the effectiveness of multi-sensory aids in maritime environments. The study showed that well-designed systems can enhance spatial awareness and independent navigation for users with visual impairments. This research emphasized the importance of adapting assistive technology to address acoustic challenges from engine noise and wind.

Ali [17] delved into the exciting possibilities that Augmented Reality (AR) applications offer for enriching navigation and orientation in tourism, especially in maritime settings. The research highlights how AR systems can deliver real-time accessibility information, interactive navigation aids, and tailored support for users with various accessibility needs. These findings indicate a wonderful opportunity for AR technologies to help overcome the information barriers that often hinder independent navigation in new and unfamiliar maritime locations.

García-Catalá and colleagues [18] presented innovative research on smart lighting and sensory-adaptive environments applicable to maritime contexts. Their study demonstrated that automated illumination systems and color-coded navigation cues enhance spatial orientation for users with visual or cognitive disabilities. The research supports environmental adaptation approaches that modify physical environments to assist users, rather than relying solely on personal devices.

Benitez [19] offered insights on tactile maps and accessibility pathways, highlighting their role in reducing reliance on external assistance. This research work showed that well-designed tactile navigation systems facilitate independent movement and orientation, especially in constrained maritime areas where traditional mobility aids may be lacking.

3   Methodology

3.1   Research Design

We employed a human-centered participatory design approach to gather user requirements and investigate accessibility and inclusivity challenges in maritime tourism contexts. The study received ethical approval from the University of Padua Ethics Committee (2024_262R2).

3.2   Participatory Design Activities

To achieve a comprehensive understanding of accessibility requirements, we engaged diverse stakeholder groups through participatory design activities, including focus groups and interviews.

Focus Groups with Nautical Experts. We held focus groups with nautical professionals specializing in accessible sailing for individuals with severe motor impairments and cognitive deficits. These sessions included experts from Lega Navale Italiana, Venice Section, all with over 10 years of experience sailing with individuals with physical disabilities.

Expert Interviews. Individual interviews were conducted with certified sailing instructors, including Paralympic athletes and coaches with expertise in inclusive sailing practices, allowing for deeper exploration of technical and safety considerations.

Focus Groups with Target Users. Multiple focus groups involved the primary target user groups, including individuals with deaf blindness, physical disabilities, and older adults. To accommodate diverse needs, sessions were held in accessible venues and online via video conferencing.

4   Preliminary Findings

4.1   Expert Insights

The participatory design activities with nautical experts revealed several critical considerations for accessible boat design:

- **Stability and Safety Requirements:** Experts emphasized that boats must guarantee high stability and safety, with particular attention to minimizing capsizing risks. Small boats typically lack sufficient stability for onboard wheelchair lifts, necessitating quayside installations as safer alternatives.
- **Operational Considerations:** The presence of at least two crew members was identified as essential for safe boarding and navigation operations. Stern mooring emerged as the preferred approach, facilitating safer ramp installation and providing more accessible entry points.
- **Physical Limitations:** Significant accessibility challenges were noted regarding boarding, disembarking, and safe onboard movement. Experts highlighted that wheelchairs are generally incompatible with boats shorter than seven meters, which leads to significant design constraints.

- **Technical Solutions:** To address the limitations identified, experts proposed several solutions including specialized lifts for individuals with severe disabilities, wide gangways for safe access, and preference for side docking over bow or stern access. Additional features such as handrails and ergonomic seating were deemed essential for ensuring adequate support during navigation.

4.2 End-User Requirements

Preliminary findings from end-user focus groups provided crucial insights into accessibility needs:

- **Boarding and Disembarkation Challenges:** Participants emphasized the need for specialized features to enhance boarding and disembarking operations. Specific requirements included specialized access ramps and compact mechanical lift systems designed to assist wheelchair users, with rapid deployment capabilities at maritime docking facilities.
- **Onboard Safety and Comfort:** Secure wheelchair anchoring points were identified as fundamental safety requirements. Users expressed needs for ergonomic seating arrangements, weather protection, and clear emergency procedures tailored to their specific accessibility requirements.
- **Independence and Autonomy:** Participants prioritized solutions that would enhance their independence during maritime experiences, reducing dependence on external assistance while maintaining safety standards.
- **Multi-sensory Considerations:** The involvement of individuals with deafblindness highlighted the importance of multi-sensory design approaches, including tactile guidance systems and enhanced communication methods for emergency situations.

5 Future Work

5.1 Evaluation Activities with End Users

All the indications emerged from the participatory design activities have been shared with the project partners appointed to design and build the inclusive boats. After completing the boat prototypes, a thorough evaluation with the direct involvement of end users, including older adults and individuals with disabilities, will be conducted. Specifically, it is foreseen to devise evaluation sessions embedded into short excursions sailing with the TOFOLA boats to resemble as much as possible real-world situations, to facilitate participants' engagement.

The evaluation will use various data collection methods to understand user experience. Questionnaires on inclusivity, accessibility, and user satisfaction will be used to gather quantitative data. Semi-structured interviews will provide qualitative insights into user experiences, challenges, and improvement suggestions. The materials for collecting their feedbacks (e.g., questionnaires) will be purposefully adapted to meet their sensory and cognitive abilities [20].

Additionally, video analysis will examine user interactions during crucial phases such as boarding, disembarking, and time spent onboard. This data will objectively assess accessibility effectiveness and identify interaction patterns not captured by self-reports.

6 Conclusions

The TOFOLA project shows how human-centered design can effectively combine cultural heritage preservation with modern accessibility needs, developing solutions that enhance cultural and social inclusion. Our participatory design approach, including nautical experts, Paralympic athletes, and end users, uncovered insights that challenge traditional views on maritime accessibility and support inclusive design [19].

The design guidelines significantly contribute to accessible tourism and maritime heritage preservation. By addressing access, ergonomic design, assistive technologies, stability, and crew training, our framework offers actionable guidance for inclusive maritime experiences while maintaining cultural authenticity [21]. This approach highlights that effective accessibility solutions must encompass technical, operational, and human factors.

Notably, our finding emphasizes that accessibility issues in maritime settings require specialized solutions, contrasting with terrestrial approaches. Constraints like boat size, stability, and environmental conditions demand innovative technical solutions, such as quayside lifts and special anchoring systems, often identified only through direct user engagement [20]. These insights enhance understanding of accessibility in constrained environments.

The participatory design methodology underscores engaging multiple stakeholders throughout the design process. Nautical experts provided crucial safety constraints, while user involvement revealed intricate accessibility needs that might otherwise be overlooked [22]. This collaboration ensures solutions tackle real-world challenges rather than theoretical user assumptions.

Our research enriches accessible tourism design knowledge while offering practical guidance for maritime heritage operators. Emphasizing the preservation of vessel aesthetics alongside modern accessibility features addresses a key challenge in heritage tourism: balancing authenticity with contemporary standards [23]. This illustrates that accessibility and heritage preservation can be synergistically integrated through thoughtful design.

The broader implications of this work inform accessible design in various heritage and cultural contexts. The efficacy of participatory methods in identifying innovative accessibility solutions suggests applications in historic buildings and cultural sites, where accessibility and preservation intersect [24].

The TOFOLA project's outcomes will serve as a model for similar initiatives across the Mediterranean and beyond, fostering more inclusive tourism infrastructure while preserving cultural heritage. By highlighting the social and economic benefits of accessible heritage tourism, this research supports policies aimed at creating inclusive, sustainable tourism destinations [25].

Future research should examine the long-term impact of accessible heritage tourism initiatives on local communities, visitor satisfaction across diverse groups, and the scalability of successful models in other cultural contexts. Additionally, exploring emerging assistive technologies in heritage tourism offers a promising direction for innovation.

Acknowledgments. This research is supported by the Interreg Italy-Croatia Programme under project TOFOLA (ITHR0200352). We thank all participants who contributed their time and expertise to this study.

Disclosure of Interests. The authors have no competing interests to declare that are relevant to the content of this article.

References

1. Rossato, C., Baratta, R.: Accessibility and Accessible Tourism: The Conceptual Evolution Through the Analysis of the Literature. Springer Briefs in Applied Sciences and Technology (2023)
2. World Health Organization: Disability and Health Fact Sheet (2021). https://www.who.int/news-room/fact-sheets/detail/disability-and-health
3. Costa, M.S., Ferreira, C.A., Gavinolla, M.R.: Accessible tourism: a review of recent research trends and future agenda. In: Tourist Behaviour and the New Normal, vol. 2. Springer (2024)
4. Sica, L.: Inclusivity and responsible tourism: designing a trademark for a National Park Area. Tour. Manag. (2020)
5. Branowski, B., et al.: Hazard analysis of a yacht designed for people with disabilities. Int. Shipbuild. Prog. (2021)
6. De la Fuente, L.: Understanding stakeholder attitudes, needs and trends in accessible tourism: a systematic review of qualitative studies. J. Tour. Soc. (2020)
7. Gillovic, B.: Accessibility and inclusive tourism development - current state and future agenda. Sustainability. **12**(22), 9722 (2020)
8. Vila, T.D., Rubio-Escuderos, L., Alén González, E.: Accessible tourism: using technology to increase social equality for people with disabilities. Tour. Rev. **79**(2), 112–130 (2024)
9. Lemberg, D.: ALL aboard - universal access for small ferries and tour boats. J. Transp. Health. (2018)
10. Aratani, T., et al.: Actual conditions and issues concerning barrier-free access for tourist boats. Transp. Res. Rec. (2023)
11. Musio-Sale, M.: Human factors in yacht design for older adults. Appl. Hum. Fact. Ergon. Int. (2022)
12. Norman, D.A.: Human-centered design considered harmful. Interactions. **12**(4), 14–19 (2005)
13. Capulong, R.: Designing an ergonomic tourist boat in Taal Lake, Talisay, Philippines. In: J. Marit. Eng. (2018)
14. Poko, T.: Accessibility in river cruise tourism: disabled people's opportunity in river cruise tourism on the Danube. J. Tour. Access. (2020)
15. Ferrari, M.: Design proposals for accessible and inclusive boats. In: J. Boat Des. (2021)
16. Qiao, Z.: Accessible tourism: understanding blind and vision-impaired tourists' behaviour towards inclusion. J. Inclus. Behav. (2022)
17. Ali, A.: The intersection of technology, accessible tourism and tourists with intellectual disabilities. J. Tour. Technol. (2022)
18. García-Catalá, M.T., et al.: Sensory navigation system for indoor localization and orientation of users with cognitive disabilities in daily tasks and emergency situations. Sensors. **24**(22), 7154 (2024)
19. Benitez, M.: The accessibility of beaches for blind people and their guide dogs: accessible tourism and inclusion in Spain. J. Coastal Tour. (2023)
20. Orso, V., Spagnolli, A., Gamberini, L., Ibañez, F., Fabregat, M.E.: Involving older adults in designing interactive technology: the case of senior channel. In: Proceedings of the 11th Biannual Conference of the Italian SIGCHI Chapter, pp. 102–109 (2015)

21. Zablocki, M., et al.: Designing innovative assistive technology devices for tourism. Int. J. Environ. Res. Public Health (2022)
22. Joseph, A., et al.: Participatory design approach to sustainable voyage planning—case maritime autonomous surface ships. In: INTERACT 2023 Proceedings (2024)
23. Benedetto, F.: Enabling a sustainable rural-tourism: the challenge of accessibility. J. Rural Sustain. (2023)
24. Medarić, Z., et al.: Lake Balaton as an accessible tourism destination—the stakeholders' perspectives. Hung. Geogr. Bull. **70**, 233–247 (2021)
25. Senkiv, S.: Prerequisites of development of an accessible tourism for everyone in the European Union. J. Eur. Tour. (2021)

Intense Play: A Hysteria Simulator and Designing with Discomfort

Fateme Rafy[(✉)] [iD]

Department of Game Design, Uppsala University, Campus Gotland, Visby, Sweden
maddyrafy@gmail.com

Abstract. This paper presents an ongoing experimental design project that explores gender bias in healthcare by using discomfort as a mechanic in an interactive experience. Drawing on the historical diagnosis of hysteria, a condition used to dismiss and pathologize women's experiences, the project recreates the logic behind hysteria as a system of control. Players engage with a simulated medical app through a series of questions, like a medical diagnosis session and receive haptic feedback based on their responses in the form of electrical stimulation.

Grounded in feminist epistemology, reflective game design, and abusive game design theory, this simulator is intended to provoke reflection, rather than offer a solution. It intentionally disrupts conventional HCI values of usability and comfort and instead uses discomfort as a method for exposing epistemic injustice and systemic dismissal in clinical contexts.

This paper outlines the project's motivation, theoretical framework, and implementation process, along with early user insights that reveal emotional patterns of confusion, frustration, and resistance. While full in-depth analysis is reserved for future work, preliminary findings suggest that discomfort, when used intentionally and ethically, can be a powerful tool in presenting concepts that are otherwise difficult to address. This Hysteria Simulator is an experiential critique of how systems of power continue to frame care as conditional and credibility as gendered.

Keywords: Critical Design · Feminist HCI · Discomfort in Interaction · Gender Bias · Epistemic Injustice

1 Introduction

This project explores a long-standing pattern in healthcare: the dismissal of women's voices and experiences. Rooted in the historical diagnosis of hysteria, this pattern continues today through ongoing forms of gender bias. Across time, women's reports of pain have been consistently met with disbelief, minimization, or false reinterpretation by medical systems.

Hysteria, now a discarded diagnosis, was once used to explain away a wide variety of women's mental and physical symptoms. Its legacy has not disappeared. Instead, it has transformed into contemporary practices under different names and frameworks, often remaining just as reductive. Modern diagnoses like generalized anxiety disorder

© The Author(s), under exclusive license to Springer Nature Switzerland AG 2026
S. Sundarakannan and O. Knorpp (Eds.): HCII 2025, CCIS 2772, pp. 282–286, 2026.
https://doi.org/10.1007/978-3-032-12767-9_30

are frequently used when a woman's symptoms don't fit conventional expectations or can't be "proven" through measurable tests. Meanwhile, their experiences are often questioned or reinterpreted by clinical professionals, leading to feelings of isolation, confusion, and powerlessness. Scholars such as Devereux (2014) and Cleghorn (2021) have demonstrated how the denial of medical credibility to women is not simply an error; it is a form of control. This project builds on that critique, suggesting that this simulator, like the medical system, can create subtle but powerful forms of discipline.

The Hysteria Simulator is an interactive research project that explores the use of discomfort in design. The device draws on the historical context of hysteria to create a limited, scripted interaction in which players engage with a simulated medical evaluation app. They are asked a series of health-related questions while the app gradually tries to manipulate them into believing they are sick. If the players fail to perform the illness the system expects from them, they receive small electric pulse stimulations to their hands. These pulses are described within the experience as a kind of "treatment".

The discomfort is important. It contradicts the logic of "user-centered design," which is mostly common in games and HCI experiences, where interactions are supposed to be smooth, seamless, and productive. Instead, this project argues that sometimes the most honest design experience is one that produces friction, doubt, or even minor distress. When intentional and ethically framed, discomfort can reveal how systems dismiss the very people they claim to support.

This paper introduces the background of the simulator, its design logic, and the early responses from initial test sessions. While no formal data is presented here, these early insights have helped guide future development. The work is still in progress, and a more detailed analysis will be provided in a full-length publication. However, even in this early form, the simulator demonstrates how HCI and critical design can work together to surface difficult but necessary conversations around gender, credibility, and care.

2 Background

The Hysteria Simulator draws on both historical and theoretical frameworks to explore how digital systems can reproduce the logic of medical dismissal. The project uses the legacy of hysteria to highlight how similar dynamics persist in modern care systems, where credibility is often unequally distributed. It is further informed by critical design theories and feminist epistemology, which shape how the simulator operates and what kind of experience it attempts to create.

Hysteria once functioned not just as a medical diagnosis, but as a broader cultural framework for interpreting women's behavior. As Cleghorn (2021) and Didi-Huberman (2003) discuss, it was a way of interpreting women's emotions and experiences through a lens that assumed emotional instability from the start. Hysteria was more aesthetic than functional, defined by visible signs, gestures, and postures that aligned with the expectations of doctors. At the Salpêtrière hospital, Jean-Martin Charcot's photographic catalogues of hysteria reinforced this performative model. Didi-Huberman (2003) describes how women were encouraged to display symptoms to fit the doctor's framework.

The simulator draws from this historical logic without directly reenacting it. It places players in a constrained interactive system that subtly undermines their input. Players encounter a scenario where their answers to questions are subtly reframed, dismissed, or responded to with clinical detachment. If they answer in unpredictable ways, they receive mild electrical stimulation via two pads attached to their hands. Players are led to "perform the illness" the simulator demands if they want to avoid the discomfort or progress through the experience. This mechanic mimics how institutional systems reward conformity and suppress resistance, even when framed as neutral procedures.

The design is grounded in feminist epistemology, particularly critiques of how knowledge is shaped by power. Scholars like Haraway (1988) and Harding (2016) argue that objectivity is never neutral; it is situated and often aligned with dominant social positions. In medicine, this often means the system is believed more than the patient. The simulator makes that imbalance felt it simulates a system that appears to listen but fails to respond in a meaningful way.

The interaction logic draws from game design theory, particularly reflective and abusive game design. Reflective game design, as described by Khaled (2018), emphasizes creating moments that interrupt flow, causing the player to question the experience and reflect on their role within it. Rather than supporting immersion, the simulator uses ambiguity and haptic feedback to destabilize the user's sense of control. Similarly, the approach aligns with what Wilson and Sicart (2010) refer to as abusive game design, where interaction is intentionally uncomfortable, not to punish, but to play with players' boundaries and expose the underlying assumptions of a system. In this simulator, discomfort pushes players out of their comfort zone and creates moments of pause that lead to reflection. These moments of disruption are invitations to reflect on how systems reward compliance and punish deviation, even under the guise of care.

Together, these influences shape an experience that is not designed to explain hysteria, but to simulate the emotional dynamics of dismissal. The simulator's constraint, ambiguity, and discomfort are all intentional, meant to show what it feels like to be disbelieved. In doing so, the project turns interaction into critique, asking what kinds of systems we trust, and who those systems are designed to believe.

3 Method

The Hysteria Simulator was developed using a Research through Design approach, where the process of making is itself a form of inquiry (Zimmerman et al., 2007). This allowed me to use experimental design to explore how discomfort could be incorporated into interaction, not as a flaw, but as an intentional and affective element.

The physical prototype was built to resemble medical equipment, a cold, impersonal object with a TENS (transcutaneous electrical nerve stimulation) unit and a screen. Two conductive pads are attached to the user's hands while they answer a scripted series of health-related questions displayed on-screen. If the player's answers contradict the expected pattern, they receive a mild electric pulse through the pads. The TENS unit was configured within medically safe parameters and calibrated through iterative testing to ensure that the sensation was noticeable, but not painful. Participants were fully briefed before each session, signed informed consent forms, and retained full agency throughout the experience. They could stop the session at any time.

In line with abusive game design principles (Wilson & Sicart, 2010), the simulator removes clear pathways to success. The player can't "win" or change the outcome.

Every choice eventually leads to friction. This reflects how systems of power usually operate. They're designed to control, undermine, or disqualify rather than understand. The simulator mirrors this through intentionally limited interaction. Players are not given room to explain themselves; they are pushed through a loop of questions, responses, and haptic feedback, reinforcing the sensation of being managed rather than heard.

The focus in this method was on observing how people described their reactions, how they shifted in their seats, and how they reflected afterwards. This approach allowed me to explore how an experimental interaction using discomfort can embody social critique. Rather than explain gender bias in healthcare, the simulator attempts to make users feel it through tone, language, and carefully implemented discomfort.

4 Preliminary Insights

Initial play test sessions have provided early insight into how players respond emotionally and physically to the experience. Several participants commented on feeling confused and unsure of what the system expected from them. Players often attempted to appease the system, highlighting how systems of power can influence self-monitoring and compliance. These reactions mirror the emotional dynamics often reported in real clinical settings, especially when care is delivered through impersonal systems.

Through informal debriefings, many users were able to link the interaction to personal experiences in healthcare, relationships, or other evaluative environments. The neutral cold tone and physical stimulation prompted reflections on being dismissed or disbelieved by systems that claimed to help. These intuitive responses and connections drawn by players suggest that discomfort, when carefully used, can lead to reflection.

While these insights are not presented as generalizable findings, they have helped guide refinement of the simulator's language, pacing, and interaction rhythm. The current results are preliminary and will be expanded upon in a forthcoming full-length study, where analysis of player reflection and system interaction will be discussed in more depth.

5 Discussion and Next Steps

The Hysteria Simulator approaches interaction design not through efficiency or clarity, but through deliberate discomfort. It creates an experience that centres confusion and powerlessness, emotional conditions that many, especially women, already associate with medical systems. This is not a project that tries to educate its users with clear goals or instructions. Instead, it creates a space where people can interact with a system that appears neutral but is extremely biased.

The design intentionally disrupts expectations often associated with user-centred systems. It removes direct feedback. It loops. It implements "treatments" without explanation. In doing so, it mimics how institutional systems, especially in healthcare, can operate under the surface. What might appear neutral or procedural from the outside often feels deeply personal and alienating to those being processed within it. By embedding this logic into its structure, the simulator asks players to question what kind of system they are in, and how that system defines truth, credibility, and care.

The discomfort is used to reveal the emotional labour of navigating systems that expect compliance and punish honesty. Through its limited choices and ambiguous logic, the simulator mirrors the emotional pacing of a clinical encounter where the player is made to feel at fault for not fitting the predefined description.

The use of game design principles is central to this logic. Borrowing from reflective game design (Khaled, 2018), the simulator encourages players to question the system rather than succeed within it. Similarly, the experience echoes the logic of abusive game design (Wilson & Sicart, 2010), where control is withheld or broken to expose deeper power dynamics. In this case, the interaction is designed not to immerse, but to interrupt. These breaks, subtle but pointed, are where reflection begins.

At this stage, the simulator is still under active development. While initial testing has offered valuable insights, future phases will include more structured user sessions. These sessions will explore how discomfort is received across different identities and lived experiences.

6 Conclusion

This project uses discomfort as a deliberate design strategy to show how systems of power, more specifically in healthcare, can alienate, control, or dismiss people through procedural interaction. The simulator is not meant to educate or solve, but to stage a controlled experience of discomfort that mirrors how credibility and agency are quietly stripped away in institutional contexts. By compressing that experience into a short, interactive encounter, the simulator invites reflection on how power is felt in systems we're expected to trust. Future work will expand testing and further explore discomfort as a method in critical interaction design.

References

Cleghorn, E.: Unwell Women: Misdiagnosis and Myth in a Man-Made World. Dutton, Penguin Random House LLC (2021)

Devereux, C.: Hysteria, feminism, and gender revisited: the case of the second wave. ESC Engl. Stud. Can. **40**(1), 19–45 (2014). https://doi.org/10.1353/esc.2014.0004

Didi-Huberman, G.: Invention of Hysteria: Charcot and the Photographic Iconography of the Salpêtrière. MIT Press (2003)

Haraway, D.. Situated knowledges: the science question in feminism and the privilege of partial perspective. Fem. Stud. **14**(3), 575 (1988). https://doi.org/10.2307/3178066

Harding, S.G.: Whose Science? Whose Knowledge? Thinking from Women's Lives. Cornell University Press (2016). https://doi.org/10.7591/9781501712951

Khaled, R.: Questions over answers: reflective game design. In: Cermak-Sassenrath, D. (ed.) Playful Disruption of Digital Media, pp. 3–27. Springer, Singapore (2018). https://doi.org/10.1007/978-981-10-1891-6_1

Wilson, D., Sicart, M.: Now it's personal: on abusive game design. In: Proceedings of the International Academic Conference on the Future of Game Design and Technology, pp. 40–47 (2010). https://doi.org/10.1145/1920778.1920785

Zimmerman, J., Forlizzi, J., Evenson, S.: Research through design as a method for interaction design research in HCI. In: Proceedings of the SIGCHI Conference on Human Factors in Computing Systems, pp. 493–502. ACM (2007). https://doi.org/10.1145/1240624.1240704

Design Research on a Wearable Sensing Device with Dual-Perception Compensation Mechanism for Hearing-Impaired Individuals

Chenxi Wang[1] , Wentao Zang[2]([✉]) , and Zhuojin Wei[1]

[1] Taiyuan University of Technology, No.79, West Yingze Street, Taiyuan, Shanxi province 030024, China
[2] Shenzhen University, 3688 Nanhai Avenue, Shenzhen, Guangdong province 518061, China
angel_1545437640@163.com

Abstract. With increasing attention to the construction of barrier-free environments, the "information inequity" faced by hearing-impaired individuals has become more pronounced, especially in scenarios such as lack of auditory alerts and difficulties in decoding social cues. Traditional hearing aids suffer from functional limitations, discomfort in wearing, and high costs, while single-modal sensory compensation solutions are often insufficient to meet complex information transmission needs. To address these challenges, this study proposes a wearable sensing device based on a dual-perception compensation mechanism. By constructing an interactive chain of "sound acquisition—semantic recognition—multimodal feedback," the system transforms environmental sound signals into visual light effects and tactile vibrations in real time, enabling the identification and feedback of two key types of information: "safety alerts" and "social semantics." The system employs lightweight AI models for acoustic classification and keyword recognition, and uses linear resonant actuators and LED flowing light effects to encode information content and spatial direction. It also supports integration with mobile apps to enhance communication efficiency. This research provides a new technical approach toward achieving "information equity," offering broad social application prospects and valuable design insights.

Keywords: Product design · Intelligent interactive hearing aid products · User experience

1 Introduction

Sound signals are a crucial component of the information humans convey. Compared to the general population, people with hearing impairments lack the ability to transmit and receive sound information, making it difficult for them to quickly connect with their surroundings and respond promptly to environmental changes. This "information inequality" not only undermines the confidence of people with hearing impairments in social participation but also poses some safety risks.

© The Author(s), under exclusive license to Springer Nature Switzerland AG 2026
S. Sundarakannan and O. Knorpp (Eds.): HCII 2025, CCIS 2772, pp. 287–295, 2026.
https://doi.org/10.1007/978-3-032-12767-9_31

Regarding how to reduce the barriers caused by "information inequality" for people with hearing impairments, this study primarily considers two typical scenarios: safety alerts (essential needs) and social enhancement (developmental needs). In the field of safety alerts, sound, as the core carrier of danger signals (such as fire alarms, vehicle sirens, emergency broadcasts), has irreplaceable timeliness. However, current public alarm systems severely lack inclusivity for the hearing impaired. A report in——WHO 2023 year pointed out that the injury rate of people with hearing impairments in sudden disasters is 2.3 times higher than that of hearing individuals, mainly because over 90% of public places still rely on single audio alarms, with only 12% of countries mandating the simultaneous deployment of flashing warning devices. On the social enhancement dimension, the lack of paralinguistic information such as intonation and environmental atmosphere carried by sound makes it difficult for people with hearing impairments to capture emotional tendencies and subtext in conversations, leading to social isolation. A 2022 survey by the National Institutes of Health (NIH) in the United States showed that the depression rate among adult people with hearing impairments reached 31%, with 76% attributing it to "social information decoding difficulties." More seriously, while existing hearing assistance technologies can amplify speech signals, they cannot effectively separate target sounds from background noise (IEEE Transactions on Audio, Speech, and Language Processing experiments confirmed that users of hearing aids increase their sentence repetition requests fourfold in noisy environments), resulting in an ever-widening gap in demand for both scenarios.

Based on the above issues, this paper proposes a wearable product for constructing a cross-modal perceptual compensation system to help people with hearing impairments better respond to environmental information, becoming a key approach to bridging the auditory information gap. In conducting various studies on individuals with hearing impairments, researchers have already demonstrated that deaf individuals react more positively to visual flashes compared to those with normal hearing. Some studies also found that some deaf individuals use brain regions typically used for auditory processing to handle vibrations [1]. One firm conclusion is that part of the information content of sound can be transmitted and perceived in ways other than auditory, leading to the inclusion of visual and vibratory tactile solutions as a primary consideration.

The product achieves a complete interaction chain in three steps: semantic information recognition, perceptual compensation, and multimodal interaction. First, the system captures sound wave signals through intelligent sensing devices and identifies them. Through big data analysis training, the information is categorized into "safety warnings" and "social semantics." Next, multi-channel encoding technology converts the signals into perceptible forms such as visual effects and tactile feedback, using visual and tactile sensory experiences for information compensation. Finally, various types of information under "safety warnings" and "social semantics" are further divided, with different subcategories adjusted in terms of color temperature, flicker mapping, vibration intensity, and rhythm gradient, enabling individuals with hearing impairments to quickly distinguish the urgency and importance of different pieces of information.

Wearable technology is highly beneficial for all users, especially those with hearing impairments. In recent years, an increasing number of studies on wearable devices for people with disabilities have shown that such devices can improve their mobility and quality of life. Wearable devices have been used to assist the daily lives of individuals with hearing impairments. This human-machine collaborative perceptual compensation mechanism not only reconstructs the real-time interaction chain between people with hearing impairments and the physical environment but also reshapes their confidence in social participation.

2   Related Work

2.1   Traditional Hearing Aid Devices

Traditional hearing aids typically refer to assistive devices that use auditory stimulation to represent auditory information, such as cochlear implants and hearing aids. Although they are considered the mainstream solution for hearing impairment intervention, their application efficiency has significant limitations, primarily manifested in the limited effectiveness of existing products for congenital deafness, physical discomfort caused by long-term use, and high costs. For patients with severe sensorineural hearing loss due to congenital causes, the lack of acoustic stimulation during the critical language-sensitive period (0–3 years) leads to underdeveloped language centers in the auditory cortex. As a result, even when using hearing aids to receive physical sound waves, the brain cannot interpret them into comprehensible semantic information—the speech recognition rate for these patients is generally below 30%. Additionally, during surveys of non-congenital deafness patients, 45% reported that prolonged use of hearing aids can lead to ear inflammation and other issues. On the other hand, while cochlear implants bypass the cochlea to directly stimulate the auditory nerve, the cost of unilateral implantation ranges from 250,000 to 400,000 RMB, far exceeding four to six times the per capita disposable income of urban residents in China, forcing low-and middle-income families to abandon intervention. This dual constraint of physiological mechanisms and economic barriers makes it difficult for current mainstream solutions to achieve full coverage of auditory accessibility.

2.2   Cross-Modal Information Interaction Devices for the Hearing Impaired

Using non-auditory stimuli to represent auditory information is commonly referred to as synesthesia in the context of artistic aesthetics, cross-modal correspondence in cognitive psychology, and sensory compensation design in barrier-free experience design. Sensory compensation, also known as sensory compensatory plasticity (compensatory plasticity), refers to the phenomenon where the function of other senses (such as hearing) is enhanced when certain senses are impaired. Applying this characteristic in design can improve the accessibility of products and enhance the sensory compensation ability of users with disabilities. To successfully translate sensory modalities, it is first necessary to identify key information features from the original modality, then process or map the information, and finally present it fully in the alternative modality [2].

Tactile Compensatory Auxiliary Hearing Aid Devices. Tactile is the largest sensory organ on the human body, with the dual nature of sensing input and operating intention output. It is a key channel for humans to understand the external environment and communicate emotions. Studies have shown that vibration tactile information is less affected by limitations in an individual's ability to perceive and process information from other sensory modes (such as vision and hearing) [3], So using vibration touch to present information is a typical cross-modal design. Karam et al. developed a humanoid cochlear model (Model Human Cochlea, MHC) deployed on the user's back [4], And the MHC is applied to the interactive haptic chair Emoti-Chair, hoping to provide a more relaxed way for hearing-impaired users to perceive musical emotions. The main limitation of the haptic chair is that it is difficult to be portable and customized, and users cannot easily change the position of the seat or actuator [5]. The United States has developed a new type of doorbell for the hearing impaired. This doorbell consists of two parts: a radio transmitter and a receiver. The transmitter is mounted on the doorbell, while the receiver resembles a watch worn on the wrist of the person with hearing loss. When the doorbell rings, the radio transmitter sends a signal to the receiver in the wearer's hand, causing a thin plate attached to the receiver to vibrate, indicating that someone has arrived [6]. Although this kind of watch can provide prompt information, it can only provide prompt for a single signal. Moreover, for most hearing impaired people, it is a small probability event that someone visits, which leads to the low frequency of use of this product. Most current wearable devices feature vibration alerts (such as electronic watches and wristbands), but they generally use simple on/off vibration states to notify events, leaving users aware of something happening but unaware of the specifics. To convey various auditory messages through different vibration patterns, multiple vibration motors need to be combined to transmit signals. However, wearable devices are typically small in size, have limited internal space, and low battery capacity. Therefore, vibration designs involving multiple vibration motors are difficult to fit into compact wearable devices. Moreover, vibration designs that use a series of vibration modes (each mode consisting of multiple vibration pulses) for continuous information communication can quickly drain the battery of wearable devices [7].

Tactile Compensatory Auxiliary Hearing Aid Devices. Vision is an important channel for human beings to receive information quickly. Sign language and text are the important ways for hearing-impaired people to obtain information based on visual sense. The earliest wearable sensor sign language recognition scheme comes from the data glove invented by Grimes et al in 1983 [8]. The deaf wore gloves on one hand to display the letter movements of American Sign Language and transmit the data to a receiving device to identify the basic movements. In 2010, Fu et al. proposed the use of digital gloves to control virtual keyboards to help the hearing impaired communicate [9]. In the existing technology, wearable sensor sign language recognition technology can accurately obtain hand movements and has a high recognition rate, but it has some problems such as high cost and poor user experience. Writing is a unique advanced cognitive tool of human beings, which can express infinitely complex thoughts and far exceed the information capacity of other animal communication systems. With the development of technology, the design of hearing glasses has broken through the technical barriers, and micro-projection can be used to directly overlay text information in virtual form on the real vision of human eyes. But smart glasses cannot identify which information is the sound source needed by people with hearing impairments, nor can they determine and capture effective sound sources. This results in visual information being muddled. The approach of presenting all information through a single modality significantly increases the visual burden on people with hearing impairments. It is evident that assistive products based on a single modality (tactile/sight) each have their own limitations.

3   Practice Process and Technological Innovation

3.1   Design of Cross-Modal Interaction Model

Signal Type Selection.   This study aims to provide a new type of language sensing tool that helps the hearing impaired quickly perceive external signals by using bimodal (visual and tactile signals) instead of the original modality (audio signals). The study investigated different environmental sound information required by the hearing impaired. During the survey, we found that 23% of the usage scenarios mentioned the need for comfort and portability in hearing aids, 41% focused on safety and alertness, 35% emphasized the directness of communication with hearing individuals and the convenience of recording conversations, and 69% highlighted the importance of timely access to external information.

Cross-Modal System Design.   This study categorizes external sound information into two core scenarios: "safety warnings" and "social semantics." Among these, "safety warnings" primarily include environmental sounds with potential hazards, such as vehicle horns, falling objects, and alarm sounds. On the other hand, "social semantics" mainly refers to calls from familiar circles of people with hearing impairments, like greetings from friends or colleagues. It is worth noting that sound signals serve a dual function: they convey information content on one hand, and help people determine the direction of the sound source on the other. Therefore, in our design, we distinguish between information content (such as safety warnings or social semantics) through different vibration patterns, and indicate the spatial location of the sound source (left or right) by the flow direction of LED lighting effects, thereby achieving multi-dimensional compensation for auditory information. In addition, to address the pain points of "communication barriers" and "inconvenience in note-taking" faced by people with hearing impairments when interacting with those who can hear, our research found that most individuals with hearing impairments currently rely on typing on their phones for communication. However, this process often requires frequent device unlocking, opening chat apps, manually entering text, and waiting for the other party to edit and respond, leading to low communication efficiency. To solve this issue, our study introduced a feature in product interaction design that links with mobile APPs: When it detects "social semantic" sounds and identifies specific greetings, the system automatically activates the corresponding contact's conversation interface on the phone, quickly redirecting to an editable text chat box, significantly enhancing the convenience and real-time nature of communication.

The Principle Framework of Cross-Modal Models.   After receiving the product, users with hearing impairments need to first enter information. They use a keyword recognition model (TDNN) to identify specific names like "Judy" and provide wake word retrieval, ensuring smooth interaction. The interaction process is divided into three steps: sound collection and preprocessing-sound classification and semantic recognition-bimodal feedback triggering.

Sound acquisition and preprocessing: Hearing aids need to capture ambient sounds using high-sensitivity microphone arrays and directional sound collection technology, optimizing signal capture for different scenarios. In social settings with acquaintances, the microphone can focus on human voices within 1–3 m (such as "Judy" calling out); in safety warning scenarios, omnidirectional microphones must quickly respond to high-frequency burst sounds (like car horns). Subsequently, the audio signal needs to undergo noise reduction and feature extraction: deep learning models (RNNoise) filter background noise and extract key acoustic features such as MFCC mel frequency cepstral coefficients and zero-crossing rate. For safety signals like car horns, the system enhances the detection sensitivity in the 2000–4000 Hz frequency band to improve detection accuracy.

Sound classification and semantic recognition: The system employs a two-tier classification strategy. First, a lightweight CNN model (YAMNet) real-time identifies the type of sound as either—safety alerts (such as honking or alarms) or social semantics (human voices). Safety alerts have the highest priority and directly trigger tactile feedback to avoid delays. For social semantics, further recognition is achieved through a keyword wake word (KWS) model to identify specific names (such as "Judy"), which is then combined with a micro speech recognition model (Wav2Vec 2.0 Tiny) to convert speech into text and confirm semantic validity. For example, when a friend calls out "Judy," the system must verify whether this term is in the user's pre-set social vocabulary and match it against a voiceprint database to identify the caller (supporting up to three contacts, with signals from other callers encoded only through vibration).

Dual-modal feedback trigger: Different sound categories correspond to differentiated vibration and light effect codes. Safety warnings (such as honking from a vehicle behind) trigger long-frequency vibrations (lasting 3 s, with 5 Hz pulses), and indicate the direction of risk through different light effects (for example, honking on the left causes the breathing lights on the right to blink from right to left, and vice versa); social semantics (such as being called by a friend) use short-frequency vibrations (0.2-s intermittent pulses), and combine vibration rhythms to distinguish different contacts. The actuator preferably uses a linear motor (LRA) to ensure high-frequency response and programmable waveform output, while automatically switching to the chat dialog box for the corresponding contact to achieve editable and recordable information. For example, when Judy receives a call from a friend, the device outputs a "short-short" code, and when a vehicle approaches, it outputs continuous vibrations that increase in intensity as the distance decreases.

3.2 Product Interaction Process

The design of the product is clipped to the user's collar, allowing it to touch the skin while also being worn as a decorative accessory, reducing the "labeling" of hearing-impaired individuals and enhancing user experience. By emitting signals at different vibration frequencies, the device intelligently responds through an accompanying mobile APP. Upon receiving the device, users first need to personalize the product by entering their name into the product's voiceprint database, and can adjust the personalized mode via the mobile APP (each contact can set a different vibration rhythm). During use, two scenarios are discussed: safety alerts and social semantics.

Safety Alert Scenario: The user is walking outdoors when a vehicle approaches from the left rear. After the vehicle honks, the sound is captured by the microphone array and the direction of the sound is identified. At this moment, the product initiates long-frequency vibration, and the lights flash from right to left. A pop-up window on the mobile APP displays a danger warning: "Vehicle approaching." Social Semantic Scenario: The user is resting at home when their partner calls out in the room to the right, attempting to communicate. The user's name is recognized by the microphone, followed by short-frequency vibration, and the lights flash from left to right to alert the user. Meanwhile, a dialogue box pops up on the mobile APP for quick communication between both parties. Users can modify the mode of the product during the use of the product. For example, users can receive corresponding information by switching the mode (only safety warning/social semantic dual mode) when they do not want to be disturbed by external calls.

3.3 Hardware Composition

The hardware facilities are composed of seven parts: core processing unit, sound perception module, tactile feedback module, visual prompt module, power supply and charging module, auxiliary sensor and interface, structure and protection. The core processing unit consists of a microcontroller (MCU), an AI assistant TPU, and Flash memory. The MCU supports multi-threaded sound classification, tactile and light control. The AI-assisted processor accelerates the inference of sound classification models and achieves low-latency responses. The Flash memory is used to store user configurations, voiceprint databases, and light encoding rules. The sound perception module comprises a digital MEMS microphone with a source localization accuracy of ±10, arranged in a four-element array, along with low-noise operational amplifiers. The tactile feedback module includes a linear resonance actuator that supports frequencies from 10 Hz to 300 Hz, an DRV2605 driver chip, and a tactile encoding circuit. The tactile encoding circuit can independently control the vibration intensity of each actuator. The visual cue module consists of programmable LED lights and an LED constant current driver chip, dynamically adjusting the direction of LED flow based on the source localization results. The power and charging module comprises a lithium polymer battery, a Type-C charging management interface, and a charging chip, responsible for integrated overcharge and undercharge protection. Auxiliary sensors and interfaces mainly consist of physical buttons and a wireless Bluetooth module. Physical buttons interrupt vibrations and switch modes when deaf individuals receive external signals, while the wireless Bluetooth module supports receiving "social semantics" via a mobile APP and connecting to update configurations. The structure and protection are composed of a casing and graphene heat sinks.

4 Test

Finally, our research team conducted product testing and data analysis by visiting local deaf schools and using social media platforms to interview dozens of individuals who met the criteria for congenital hearing impairment and severe hearing loss. To compare the sensitivity of the product with that of human ears, a team member was assigned to record the moment of information capture during each participant's test for reference. The test is divided into two scenarios and three parts, evaluating the product's sensitivity to social semantic signals, safety warning signal detection, and pop-up window sensitivity on mobile APPs under different distances and noise environments (indoor quiet environment / outdoor generally noisy environment). Finally, the scores for the three modules are calculated and statistically analyzed in the ratio of 30%,40%, and 30%, respectively, to derive the final conclusion.

Through the data in the table, overall, this product can effectively capture sound information around people with hearing impairments, basically establishing an inter-action link between them and their physical environment. In indoor environments, the sensitivity score is generally higher than in outdoor environments, especially when there are many people speaking outdoors, which slightly weakens the ability to capture "social semantic" signals. However, overall, users give the product a high comprehensive rating. Additionally, during interviews after experiencing the product, more than three-quarters of the participants mentioned that it is suitable for most daily life scenarios, offering comfortable wear, easy operation, and frequent use.

5 Discussion and Limitations

This study proposes a wearable hearing aid with a dual-perception compensation mech-anism, using acoustic feature classification, lightweight AI models, and multi-channel tactile coding to distinguish and convey environmental danger alerts and social cues to the hearing-impaired. It offers an effective path toward "information equity," enabling users to access essential daily information more comfortably. Our findings reveal that while sensory substitution is common in wearable design, most products rely on single-modal feedback, which is insufficient for the hearing-impaired. Leveraging their enhanced visual and tactile perception, this study employs dual-modal (visual + tactile) feedback to bridge auditory gaps. Tactile vibration encodes message content, while light flow indicates direction. Usability tests showed promising results. Limitations remain, such as the inability to recognize unfamiliar voices due to technical constraints.

References

1. Florian, H., Mocanu, A., Vlasin, C., Machado, J., Carvalho, V., Soares, F., Astilean, A., Avram, C.: Deaf people feeling music rhythm by using a sensing and actuating device. Sens. Actuators Phys. **267**, 431–442 (2017)
2. Yağanoğlu, M.: Real time wearable speech recognition system for deaf persons. Comput. Electr. Eng. (2021)
3. Urai, A.E., Doiron, B., Leifer, A.M., Churchland, A.K.: Large-scale neural recordings call for new insights to link brain and behavior. Nat. Neurosci. **25**, 11–19 (2022)
4. Audio-Tactile Rendering: A Review on Technology and Methods to Convey Musical Infor-mation through the Sense of Touch. https://www.mdpi.com/1424-8220/21/19/6575. Accessed 2025-03-08
5. Gallace, A., Tan, H.Z., Spence, C.: Multisensory Numerosity Judgments for Visual and Tactile Stimuli. Percept. Psychophys. **69**, 487–501 (2007)

6. Karam, M., Russo, F.A., Branje, C., Price, E., Fels, D.I.: Towards a model human cochlea: sensory substitution for crossmodal audio-tactile displays. In: Graphics Interface (2008)
7. Wang, Y., Millet, B., Smith, J.L.: Designing wearable vibrotactile notifications for information communication. Int. J. Hum. Comput. Stud. (2016)
8. Grimes, G. J.: Digital Data Entry Glove Interface Device. US4414537A (November 8, 1983). https://patents.google.com/patent/US4414537A/en. Accessed 2025-03-08
9. Fu, Y.-F., Ho, C.-S.: Building Intelligent Communication Systems for Handicapped Aphasiacs. Sensors. **10**, 374–387 (2010)

Human-Centered Interaction Design and Experience

Development of a Human-Agent Dialogue Interaction System Using Comic Symbols for Enriching Agent Expression

Ayaka Fujii[(✉)] [iD] and Ken Fukuda [iD]

National Institute of Advanced Industrial Science and Technology (AIST),
Tokyo, Japan
`ayaka.fujii.mail@gmail.com, ken.fukuda@aist.go.jp`

Abstract. Comic symbols that express character states and emotions in comics are intuitively easy to understand, and they can be adapted to not only human-like characters but also animals and objects. Previous studies show the usefulness of comic symbols in human-agent interaction. However, these studies only display predetermined or limited types of comic symbols. In this paper, we describe the development of a system that dynamically utilizes comic symbols according to the content of dialogues. For the first step of the research, we focused on human-like characters and annotated a subset of a comic dataset (Manga109) by identifying the types, display positions, and the number of comic symbols. The annotated data were utilized to fine-tune a large language model. With this fine-tuned model, we developed a system capable of determining the appropriate type, position, and quantity of comic symbols based on the conversational context and spoken dialogue. Leveraging this model, we developed an interactive system in which an on-screen 3D agent engages in dialogues effectively using comic symbols. For future research, we discuss the potential application of the usage of comic symbols in human-robot interaction. We plan to develop a system in which robots can communicate emotions using comic symbols by utilizing mixed reality technology.

Keywords: Comic symbol · Human–agent interaction · Agent expression

1 Introduction

In recent years, agents such as 2D/3D characters and robots have begun to play active roles in various areas of society. To foster a sense of closeness between these agents and humans as companions sharing the same environment, it is important not only to facilitate information transmission but also to engage in interactions that include emotional expressions. This study aims to build a general interaction method for emotional expression that can be applied to a wide range of agents, including robots without dedicated hardware for self-expression. Specifically, we

© The Author(s), under exclusive license to Springer Nature Switzerland AG 2026
S. Sundarakannan and O. Knorpp (Eds.): HCII 2025, CCIS 2772, pp. 299–304, 2026.
https://doi.org/10.1007/978-3-032-12767-9_32

focus on using comic symbols (symbolic visual expressions used in comics to represent characters' states) to achieve rich emotional expressions.

Various approaches, such as facial expressions, body movements, and vocal cues, have been shown to be effective in conveying emotions in agents [4,5,8,13]. However, since agents vary widely in form, ranging from human-like characters to arm robots, developing methods of emotional expression that can be broadly applied to these diverse appearances would be useful. Therefore, we focus on comic symbols, which are used not only to represent human and character emotions but also to endow animals and objects with rich expressions in the comics.

Previous research shows that comic symbols are useful means for agents to communicate emotions [7,9]. However, they have been limited to displaying restricted sets of comic symbols, assigning them to emotions to be expressed according to typical usage. In this paper, we describe the development of a prototype of an agent system for using comic symbols dynamically according to the dialogue contents during interaction. We also discuss the future development of the system for presenting comic symbols with robots by using mixed reality.

2   Related Works

Previous research has explored the interpretations and expressive ability of comic symbols. Even the same type of comic symbols can convey different meanings depending on their position and context [2,3]. For instance, a droplet-shaped comic symbol may represent a tear, a sniffle, or a splash of water according to the situation.

Some studies have investigated the application of comic symbols to digital communication. Gemba et al. proposed using comic symbols to enhance avatars' emotional expressiveness, demonstrating that these visual symbols improve the perception of users' emotions in virtual environments [7]. In the field of robotics, KOBIAN-R II can display comic symbols with facial expressions [9]. The robot has flexible displays to show comic symbols such as cross-popping veins and tear marks, and hardware mechanisms to show vertical lines and wrinkles. Koike et al. explored the potential of graphical tropes, such as smoke, water droplets, and bubbles in human-robot interaction [10]. They developed the fluid-based expression system, which can be attached to robots.

While these studies highlight the expressiveness of comic symbols in agents, they generally associate specific emotions and states with the typical usage of comic symbols. To enable richer emotional expression in human-agent interactions, we think that there is a need for technology that dynamically presents suitable comic symbols based on conversational context.

3   Human-Agent Dialogue Interaction System Using Comic Symbols

3.1   Overview

The overview of the system development is shown in Fig. 1. We annotated part of the comic dataset with information on comic symbol types, their display positions, and the number of symbols, focusing specifically on human-like characters. This annotated data was used to fine-tune a large language model, which enabled us to build a system that automatically selects the type, position, and quantity of comic symbols according to conversational context. Using this model, we developed an interactive application in which an on-screen 3D agent incorporates comic symbols into dialogues.

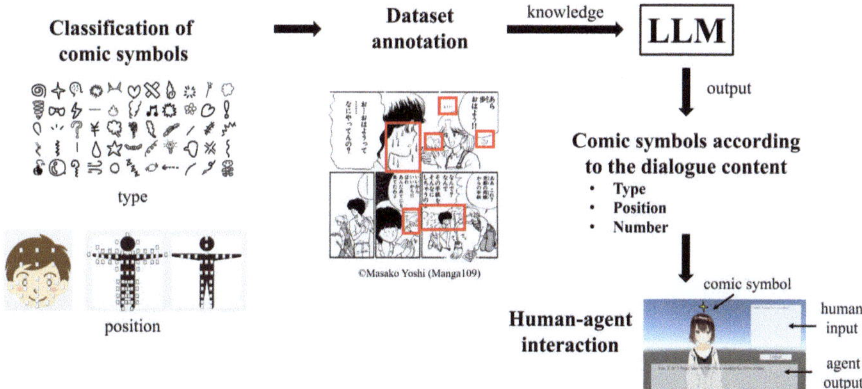

Fig. 1. Overview of the developed human-agent dialogue interaction system using comic symbols.

3.2 Annotation of Comic Symbols Using a Comic Dataset

Manga109 [1,12] was used as the dataset for annotating comic symbols. This is a dataset consisting of 109 Japanese comics, covering a wide range of genres. In the dataset, panels, texts, character faces, and character bodies are annotated. In addition, there is a dataset that maps the dialogues in Manga109 to the characters. However, no annotations are provided for the comic symbols.

We conducted the annotation for the comic symbols, focusing on people and human-like characters. As in our previous work [6], we classified the types and the assigned positions of the comic symbols. Referring to a book [11] and other web sources, 55 types of comic symbols were extracted, excluding onomatopoeia, those related to backgrounds or scenery, and those that could be classified as facial expressions or gestures. With regard to the assigned positions, since we aim to apply the comic symbols to agents, including 3D characters and robots, we used the spatial positions of each body part, such as front, back, outside, and inside. In addition, the number of comic symbols is also important in the expression. The type, assigned position, and number of comic symbols depicted in the comic dataset were mapped to the speech of the character to whom the symbol was assigned, as well as to the speech of the character who appeared just prior to the scene. In the future, we would like to extend the annotation to include comic symbols assigned to animals, objects, etc.

3.3   Generating Context-Sensitive Comic Symbols

To develop a model that can estimate and output appropriate comic symbols according to the conversational context, we fine-tuned a large language model. We employed OpenAI's GPT-4o (gpt-4o-2024-08-06) as the base model. Annotation data, which associates comic symbols with utterances, was converted to JSONL format, which is compatible with GPT-4o, for fine-tuning. In line with the annotation policy, we also enabled the model to acquire information on the type, location, and number of comic symbols related to the conversational content by using the Function Calling function of the OpenAI API.

3.4   Dialogue Agent Capable of Displaying Comic Symbols

We developed a prototype of a dialogue interaction system that aims to enable rich emotional expression by having a 3D CG agent display comic symbols tailored to the conversational context. For the system platform, we used Unity, a game engine well-suited for character control and user interface design. The 3D character model used for the agent was obtained from VRoidHub, a platform for sharing 3D characters.

The user interface has a simple structure. Users input any conversational content as text, and the agent's response is also displayed as text. Simultaneously, comic symbols relevant to the dialogue are shown in alignment with the 3D agent model. The agent's text responses, as well as the type, position, and number of displayed comic symbols, are determined by the fine-tuned large language model.

For the Unity implementation, we prepared the comic symbol image data in the system and set display points linked to the existing bones of the 3D agent model. In response to the output from the large language model, corresponding image data of the comic symbol are interactively added to or removed from the display points as Unity GameObjects, enabling dynamic comic symbol presentation.

4   Discussion of Future Applications of Interactive Comic Symbol Expressions by Robots

In previous studies of robots using expressions like comic symbols, the expressions are realized by integrating dedicated devices such as LED displays and fluid device into the robots [9,10]. However, it is not practical to equip every robot with such display devices. This section discusses a method for presenting comic symbols in accordance with the robot's body by leveraging mixed reality (MR) technology.

In the case in which information about the robot's model, joint angles, and position estimation data from Simultaneous Localization and Mapping (SLAM) is available, the coordinates of the head-mounted display (HMD) wearer can be aligned with the robot's coordinate system, enabling the placement of comic symbols according to the robot's body pose. The use of AR markers can also provide relative positional information between the HMD wearer and the robot.

On the other hand, when the robot's position or joint angle information cannot be obtained, it becomes necessary to estimate the robot's skeleton from different sources, such as images captured by the HMD camera. As an initial investigation, we applied models typically used for human pose estimation, such as MediaPipe and MMPose, to images of robots. The preliminary results showed that for bipedal robots like HRP-4 and NAO, it was possible to estimate the major joints, indicating that existing models could be applied. However, for wheeled robots such as Miroki, it was often difficult to accurately estimate even the upper body. For future work, we plan to develop a skeleton estimator specifically for robots by conducting transfer learning on existing models using data from actual robot hardware or from simulations.

5   Conclusion

In this study, we propose a novel approach to enhance an agent's emotional expression by leveraging comic symbols, symbolic expressions used in comics. We extracted 55 types of comic symbols and organized their placement with a view toward extension into three-dimensional space for humanoid characters. Using annotated data that aligns types, placement, and number of comic symbols with spoken dialogues of characters from a comic dataset, we did fine-tuning of a large language model and developed an agent interaction system capable of presenting suitable comic symbols based on conversational context. We also discussed the future application of comic symbols in the field of human-robot interaction.

In the future, we plan to advance the development of the system that presents comic symbols in MR space aligned with the robot's body and to conduct evaluations through human interaction experiments. In addition, though the current annotation of comic symbols has focused on humans and characters with designs similar to humans, we would like to analyze comic symbols associated with animals and objects and explore ways to present comic symbols for non-human-like agents such as robotic arms and vacuum cleaners. As for the presentation method of the comic symbols, 3D models incorporating dynamic effects and animations could contribute to richer expressions.

We believe that the synergistic use of comic symbols and mixed reality technology is practical and cost-effective and holds the potential to foster a society where humans and agents coexist more harmoniously.

Acknowledgments. This research was supported in part by Tateisi Science and Technology Foundation, Research Grant A (Grant Number 2241023).

Disclosure of Interests. The authors have no competing interests to declare that are relevant to the content of this article.

References

1. Aizawa, K., et al.: Building a manga dataset "manga109" with annotations for multimedia applications. IEEE Multimed. **27**(2), 8–18 (2020). https://doi.org/10.1109/mmul.2020.2987895
2. Akai, Y., Moriyama, Y., Matsushita, M.: Scene Retrieval System based Emotion and Action Scenes in Comics by Using Comic Symbols (In Japanese). IPSJ SIG Technical Report **2017-DCC-15**(42), 1–7 (2017)
3. Akai, Y., Yamashita, R., Matsushita, M.: Giving emotions to characters using comic symbols. In: Proceedings of the 12th International Conference on Advances in Computer Entertainment Technology. ACE '15. Association for Computing Machinery, New York (2015). https://doi.org/10.1145/2832932.2832979
4. Al Moubayed, S., Beskow, J., Skantze, G., Granström, B.: Furhat: A back-projected human-like robot head for multiparty human-machine interaction. In: Esposito, A., Esposito, A.M., Vinciarelli, A., Hoffmann, R., Müller, V.C. (eds.) Cognitive Behavioural Systems, pp. 114–130 (2012)
5. Crumpton, J., Bethel, C.L.: A survey of using vocal prosody to convey emotion in robot speech. Int. J. Soc. Robot. **8**(2), 271–285 (2015). https://doi.org/10.1007/s12369-015-0329-4
6. Fujii, A., Fukuda, K.: Initial study on robot emotional expression using manpu. In: Companion of the 2024 ACM/IEEE International Conference on Human-Robot Interaction, HRI '24, pp. 463–467. Association for Computing Machinery (2024)
7. Gemba, S., Takahashi, T.: Avatar's facial expression with "Manpu (Comic Symbols)" by using multiple biometric information. In: International Workshop on Advanced Imaging Technology (IWAIT) 2020, vol. 11515, pp. 319–324. SPIE (2020)
8. Gomez, R., Szapiro, D., Galindo, K., Nakamura, K.: Haru: hardware design of an experimental tabletop robot assistant. In: Proceedings of the 2018 ACM/IEEE International Conference on Human-Robot Interaction, pp. 233–240 (2018). https://doi.org/10.1145/3171221.3171288
9. Kishi, T., et al.: Development of a comic mark based expressive robotic head adapted to Japanese cultural background. In: 2014 IEEE/RSJ International Conference on Intelligent Robots and Systems, pp. 2608–2613 (2014). https://doi.org/10.1109/IROS.2014.6942918
10. Koike, A., Mutlu, B.: Exploring the design space of extra-linguistic expression for robots. In: Proceedings of the 2023 ACM Designing Interactive Systems Conference, DIS 2023, pp. 2689–2706. Association for Computing Machinery, New York (2023)
11. Kouno, F.: Gigatown Manpuzufu (In Japanese). Asahi Shimbun Publications Inc., Tokyo, Japan (2018). (In Japanese)
12. Matsui, Y., et al.: Sketch-based manga retrieval using manga109 dataset. Multimed. Tools Appl. **76**(20), 21811–21838 (2016). https://doi.org/10.1007/s11042-016-4020-z
13. Saunderson, S., Nejat, G.: How robots influence humans: a survey of nonverbal communication in social human–robot interaction. Int. J. Soc. Robot. **11**(4), 575–608 (2019). https://doi.org/10.1007/s12369-019-00523-0

Application for Locating Dogs in México City Through Pattern Recognition

Rubén Galicia-Mejía[1], Erika Hernández-Rubio[2(✉)],
and Luis Alberto Sosa Sánchez[1]

[1] Instituto Politécnico Nacional, ESCOM, Ciudad de México, Mexico
`rgalicia@ipn.mx`
[2] Instituto Politécnico Nacional, SEPI-ESCOM, Ciudad de México, Mexico
`ehernandezru@ipn.mx`

Abstract. The abandonment and loss of domestic dogs in urban areas remains a critical issue, with an estimated 500,000 cases annually in Mexico - 18 000 of which occur in Mexico City alone. Conventional search methods are often ineffective due to the lack of orientation of the animals and the absence of coordinated community support. This work proposes the development of a mobile application that leverages biometric pattern recognition–specifically nose print identification–to facilitate the recovery of lost dogs. The system enables users to upload digital photographs and share real-time data across a collaborative network of dog owners. By integrating geolocation services and image matching algorithms, the application improves search precision, reduces recovery time, and fosters community participation. The widespread availability of smartphones in Mexico, with mobile penetration exceeding 96% in 2025, provides a solid foundation for deploying this technology on a scale. This work demonstrates the potential of computer vision and mobile platforms to address a growing challenge to social and animal welfare through technological innovation.

Keywords: dogs · geolocation · mobile application · pattern recognition

1 Introduction

According to the November 2024 Subjective Well-being Module conducted by the National Institute of Statistics and Geography (INEGI), Mexico City had a population of 9,209,944 inhabitants. Of this number, 3,284,000 individuals, representing 35. 65% of the population, reported owning at least one pet. Within this group, 2,847,000 individuals identified as dog owners, representing 86. 7% of the pet owners and indicating a strong preference for dogs in the city [1].

It is estimated that hundreds of thousands of dogs and cats are abandoned each year in Mexico, with Mexico City remaining one of the urban centers most affected by this problem. According to recent legislative reports, the capital

© The Author(s), under exclusive license to Springer Nature Switzerland AG 2026
S. Sundarakannan and O. Knorpp (Eds.): HCII 2025, CCIS 2772, pp. 305–315, 2026.
https://doi.org/10.1007/978-3-032-12767-9_33

has become an epicenter of animal abandonment, driven by misinformation, economic hardship, and lack of effective public policies [2]. As a result, many of these animals end up living on the streets, in overcrowded shelters, or in municipal euthanasia centers.

As of early 2025, there were approximately 127 million active mobile connections in Mexico, representing 96.5% of the total population. Additionally, 98.6% of internet users aged 16 and older owned a mobile phone, with 98.3% of them using smartphones [3]. In light of these figures, we propose the development of a mobile application that utilizes digital images of a dog's nose combined with pattern recognition technology as an effective tool to improve the success rate in locating missing pets.

Pattern recognition is a computational method used to categorize input data into objects, classes, or categories based on distinctive characteristics or constant features [4,5]. The decision to implement this technique is grounded in the complexity involved in visually analyzing a dog's nose where subtle traits and shapes may go unnoticed by the human eye, leading to a high margin of error. However, pattern recognition algorithms substantially reduce this margin by improving accuracy and processing efficiency, making the technology valuable for a range of applications, including the identification and recovery of lost dogs.

The proposed mobile application is aimed at individuals who either own a dog or wish to join a digital community dedicated to the recovery of lost pets. This platform will enable users to remain in constant communication and contribute actively to the localization and reintegration of missing dogs.

All information gathered will be shared in real time among users, thereby expanding the reach of alerts and increasing the chances of recovery. The core functionality of the application includes an image-based pattern recognition algorithm capable of analyzing unique characteristics of a dog's nose, captured from one or more digital photographs. Once the relevant data is collected, the system will perform automatic searches based on image-matching criteria, triggering alerts and assisting in pinpointing the location of the lost animal.

2   Related Work

Various mobile applications have been developed to support the recovery and identification of lost pets. Below is a summary of notable platforms currently available:

- **Wizapet:** A collaborative application that allows users to issue alerts and notifications about lost or found pets. It uses geolocation and push notifications to inform nearby users, and includes features such as reward payments and internal chat for coordination [6].
- **Welppy:** Originally designed for emergency alerts (e.g., fires, thefts), Welppy also enables users to report lost pets and receive verified alerts from local authorities. It fosters neighborhood collaboration and includes a historical alert feed and private messaging [7].

– **Akitoy:** A GPS-based tracking application that allows users to monitor the real-time location of pets via a portable device attached to a collar or harness. It includes geofencing and historical route tracking [8].

In addition to these platforms, recent research has explored biometric and AI-based methods for pet identification. Jang *et al.* [9] proposed a muzzle pattern recognition system for dog identification, while Shen *et al.* [10] developed a competitive method for nose-print re-identification. Other studies have applied convolutional neural networks (CNNs) to recognize facial expressions in dogs [11], and ECG-based biometric identification using CNN-LSTM architectures has also been explored [12]. The stability of canine nose patterns over time has been validated by Choi *et al.* [13], and Kumar and Singh [14] have proposed biometric monitoring systems for smart cities.

These developments provide a strong foundation for the proposed mobile application, which integrates biometric nose pattern recognition with real-time alerts and geolocation to improve the recovery of lost dogs.

3   Canine Nose as a Unique Biometric Identifier

The surface of a dog's nose exhibits a complex pattern of ridges and grooves that is unique to each individual, much like a human fingerprint. This anatomical feature has been validated as a reliable biometric marker for canine identification. Recent studies have demonstrated that these nose patterns remain stable over time and are not affected by age, breed, or environmental conditions [13].

Advanced biometric systems have leveraged this uniqueness to develop non-invasive identification methods. For instance, convolutional neural networks (CNNs) and pretrained models such as ResNet50 have been applied to extract and compare nose features with high accuracy [15]. These systems have shown promising results in large-scale datasets, enabling applications in pet recovery, vaccination tracking, and stray animal management.

The integration of nose-print recognition into mobile platforms represents a significant advancement in animal biometrics, combining accessibility, accuracy, and real-time processing to support responsible pet ownership and animal welfare.

4   Neural Networks for Canine Identification

Artificial Neural Networks (ANNs) are computational models inspired by the structure and function of biological neurons. They consist of interconnected layers of nodes (neurons) that process input data through weighted connections and activation functions. Over the past decade, neural networks have become foundational in solving complex pattern recognition tasks, particularly in image classification, speech recognition, and natural language processing [16].

Among the most widely adopted architectures are Convolutional Neural Networks (CNNs), which are especially effective in visual recognition tasks due to their ability to extract spatial hierarchies of features from images. CNNs have been successfully applied in domains such as medical imaging, autonomous vehicles, and animal biometrics [17].

In the context of canine identification, CNNs have demonstrated high accuracy in recognizing breed-specific features and biometric traits such as muzzle patterns and nose prints. For instance, recent studies have employed deep CNNs like Inception and ResNet to classify dog breeds and identify individual dogs based on facial or nasal features [18]. These models are trained on large annotated datasets and leverage transfer learning to improve generalization across diverse image conditions.

Furthermore, hybrid architectures combining CNNs with recurrent layers or attention mechanisms have been explored to enhance robustness in real-world scenarios, such as varying lighting, occlusions, or partial views of the animal [17]. These advances support the development of mobile applications capable of real-time dog identification using only a smartphone camera.

The integration of neural networks into pet recovery systems represents a significant step toward non-invasive, scalable, and accurate biometric identification, reinforcing their role in animal welfare and smart city initiatives.

4.1   Datasets for Model Training

The development and evaluation of neural networks for dog identification rely on the availability of annotated image datasets. The **Stanford Dogs Dataset** contains over 20,000 labeled images across 120 dog breeds and is frequently used for fine-grained image classification tasks [19]. For individual identification, the **Multi-Pose Dog Dataset** offers images of 192 unique dogs captured in a variety of poses [20]. Meanwhile, the **Dog Breeds Object Detection Dataset** by Roboflow includes bounding box annotations optimized for training real-time object detection models on mobile devices [21].

These datasets enable researchers to train and benchmark deep learning models with higher accuracy and robustness, ensuring better generalization across breeds and real-world conditions.

5   Mobile Application

The functionalities and interface of a mobile application called *Salva Lomitos* are described in detail. The application is structured in four main phases: data acquisition, preprocessing, nose pattern identification, and real-time alert dissemination.

5.1   Log in and Post

If an account has already been registered, the user enters their email and password in the corresponding fields and presses *"Log In"*, which grants access to the application's features.

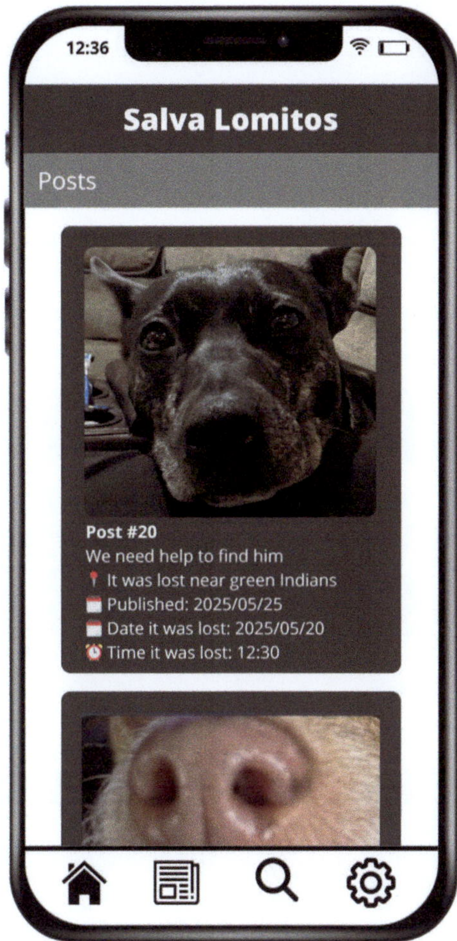

Fig. 1. Screen showing posts created by users.

Upon accessing the system, the first thing the user sees is the list of posts created by other users to report their lost dogs. If the post belongs to the current user, they have the option to edit the information or delete the post (Fig. 1).

When the user selects the *"My Registered Dogs"* option, they are directed to a view displaying each of the dogs they have previously registered (Fig. 2). This interface presents detailed information for each dog and provides options to edit the data, delete the registration, or mark the dog as lost. Additionally, a registration button is available, which redirects the user to a form where they must provide relevant information and upload photographs of the dog, including a full-body image and a close-up of the nose, in order to complete the registration process.

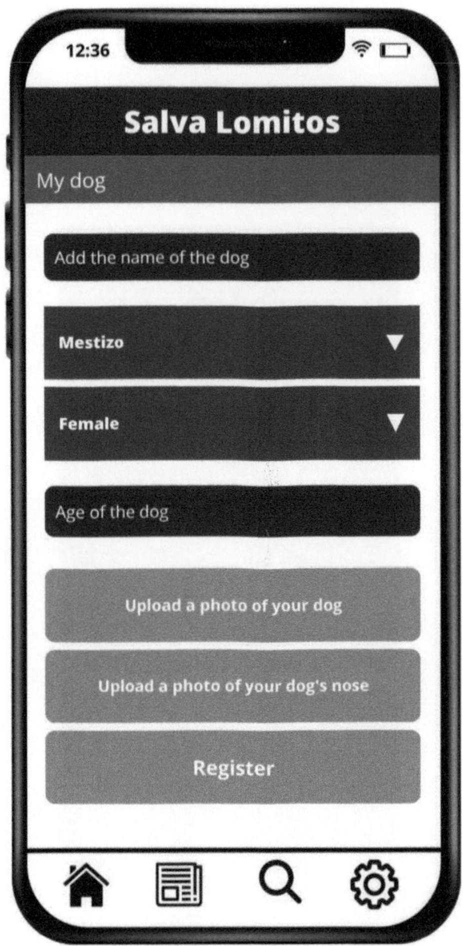

Fig. 2. Screens showing the flow of the "My Registered Dogs" section.

Each registered dog includes a *"Report"* option, which opens a form requesting specific details about the dog's disappearance. The form prompts the user to provide the date and approximate time of the incident, the approximate location, and a description field for any additional relevant information. The dog's image is automatically retrieved from its registration record (Fig. 3).

This reporting flow was intentionally designed to prevent the creation of posts unrelated to the application's intended purpose.

Within the application, under the *"Find the Owner"* tab, users can scroll to the bottom of the view to access a button labeled *"Upload Nose Photo"*. This feature allows users to select an image from their gallery and crop it according to the specified guidelines (Fig. 4). Once the image is uploaded, the user can press

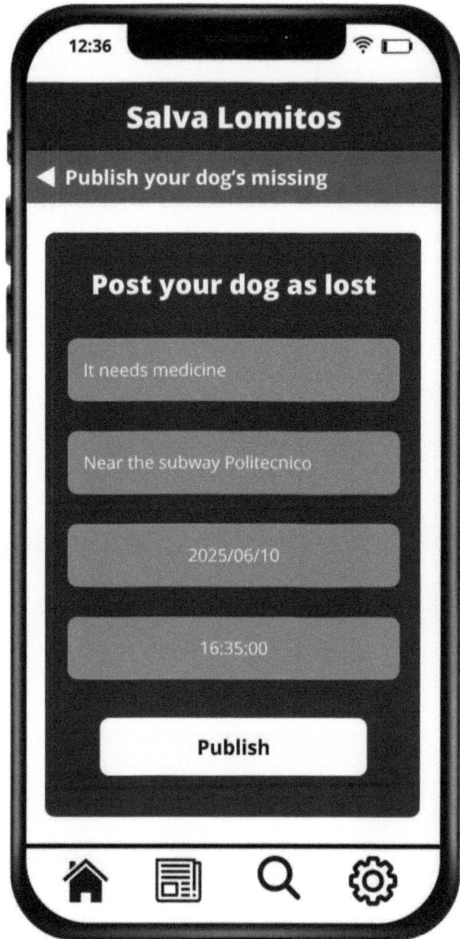

Fig. 3. Screens showing the reporting form for lost dogs.

the *"Start Search"* button, which initiates a comparison between the uploaded photo and all registered nose images stored in the system.

The matching process may take a few seconds, depending on the number of images in the database. This functionality is designed to assist in identifying potential matches between found dogs and those reported as lost, using biometric features extracted from nose patterns.

Once the matching process is complete, the application displays a view showing the best match found based on the uploaded nose image (Fig. 5). This result includes the corresponding dog's profile, allowing the user to review the match and take further action if necessary.

As shown in Fig. 5, the *"View Full Photo of the Dog"* button allows users to display the full-body image of the dog in question, which was provided by the

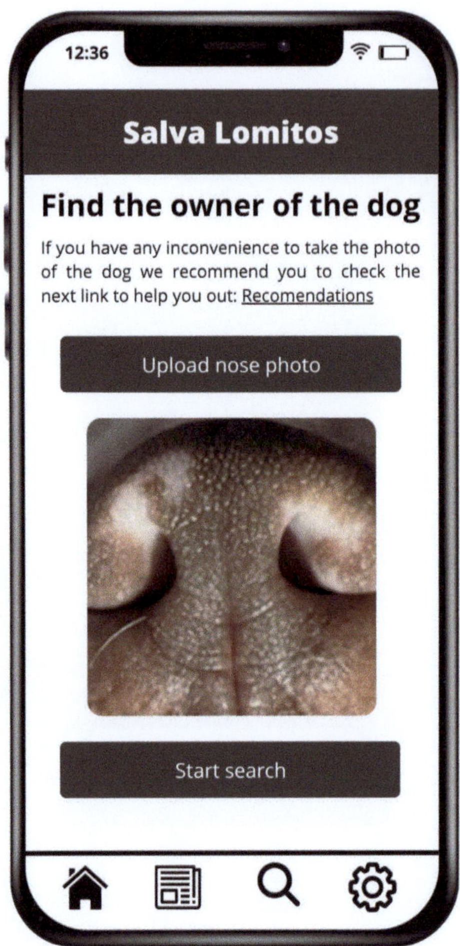

Fig. 4. Interface flow for uploading and searching with a nose photo.

owner during registration. This feature helps confirm whether the dog shown in the match result corresponds to the one that has been found.

If the user determines that the dog is indeed a match, they can select the *"Identify as Correct"* button. If the user reaches the last of the top five best matches without a successful identification, an additional option labeled *"Try Another Method"* becomes available. This triggers a new comparison process using the template matching algorithm described earlier. Once new matches are generated, the verification process is repeated.

Upon confirmation, the current view is closed, and an email notification is sent to the registered owner of the dog, informing them that their pet has been located. Simultaneously, the user who reported the found dog receives an email containing the necessary contact information to reach the owner.

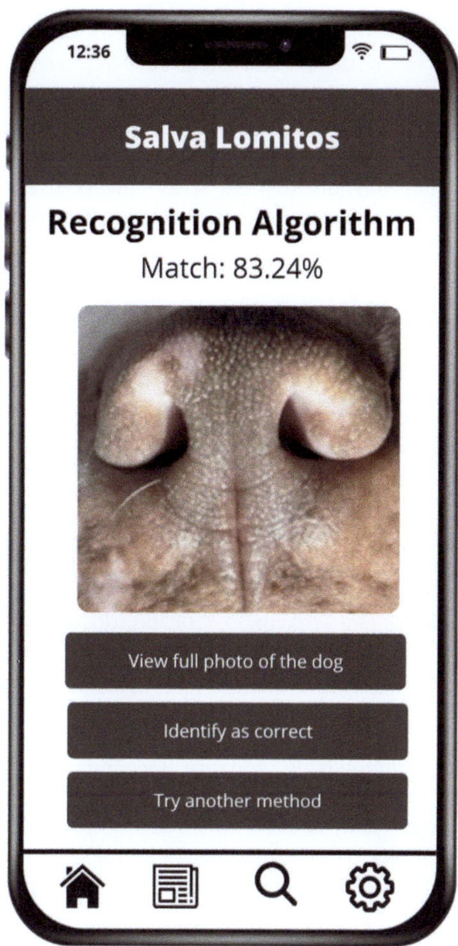

Fig. 5. Screen displaying the best match result after the nose image comparison.

6   Results

One of the most time-intensive tasks in this project was the analysis and evaluation of neural network models and algorithms suitable for the objectives of the application. This complexity stemmed primarily from the high variability in the photographs submitted by users–variations that are inherently uncontrollable in real-world scenarios. Despite these limitations, and in the absence of publicly available implementations addressing this specific problem, we successfully developed an algorithm capable of achieving an acceptable recognition rate under the defined test conditions.

In addition to the technical achievements in image recognition, the project also prioritized user experience. As a result, a user-friendly and intuitive interface was implemented, enabling users to easily access and utilize the system's core functionalities. This combination of robust algorithmic performance and accessible design represents a significant step toward addressing the challenge of locating lost dogs in urban environments such as Mexico City.

Acknowledgments. The authors express their sincere gratitude to the Instituto Politécnico Nacional for the financial support provided through the SIP program under project number 20250537.

Special thanks are also extended to Daira Angelina Aguilar Hernández for her valuable assistance with the editing and preparation of the visual materials included in this work.

References

1. Instituto Nacional de Estadística y Geografía (INEGI), Módulo de bienestar autorreportado, noviembre 2024, Disponible en https://www.inegi.org.mx/contenidos/saladeprensa/boletines/2025/biare/biare2024_Nov.pdf (2025)
2. Macedo, M.A.: Proponen que el abandono animal sea tipificado comodelito con estas penas en prisión". Consultado el 15 de junio de 2025, April 2025. https://www.elimparcial.com/mexico/2025/04/08/proponen-que-el-abandono-animal-sea-tipificado-comodelito-con-estas-penas-en-prision/
3. DataReportal, Digital 2025: Mexico (2025). https://datareportal.com/reports/digital-2025-mexico
4. Theodoridis, S., Koutroumbas, K.: Pattern Recognition, 4th. Elsevier Inc. (2009). isbn: 9780126858754
5. Bishop, C.M.: Neural Networks for Pattern Recognition. Oxford University Press (1996). isbn: 0198538642
6. Wizapet, Wizapet: No lo des por perdido, Disponible en (2025). https://www.wizapet.com/
7. Control Publicidad, Welppy, app para crear y emitir alertas de emergencia (2019). Disponible en https://controlpublicidad.com/empresas-ynegocios-publicidad/welppy-app-para-crear-y-emitir-alertasde-emergencia/
8. Gediros, Akitoy - gps pet tracking app (2024). Disponible en https://play.google.com/store/apps/details?id=com.gediros.akitoy
9. Jang, D., Kwon, K., Kim, J., Yang, K., Kim, J.: Dog identification method based on muzzle pattern image. Appl. Sci. **10**(24), 8994 (2020). https://doi.org/10.3390/app10248994
10. Shen, F., Wang, Z., Fu, X., Chen, J., Du, X., Tang, J.: A competitive method for dog nose-print re-identification (2022). Disponible en https://arxiv.org/abs/2205.15934v2
11. Mao, Y., Liu, Y.: Pet dog facial expression recognition based on convolutional neural network and improved whale optimization algorithm. Sci. Rep. **13**(1) (2023). https://doi.org/10.1038/s41598-023-30442-0
12. Cho, M.K., Kim, T.S.: Canine biometric identification using ecg signals and cnn-lstm neural networks. IEEE Access **11**, 145 732–145 746 (2023). Disponible en https://ieeexplore.ieee.org/abstract/document/10365144. https://doi.org/10.1109/ACCESS.2023.3344452

13. Choi, H.I., Lee, Y., Shin, H., et al.: The formation and invariance of canine nose pattern of beagle dogs from early puppy to young adult periods. Animals **11**(9), 2664 (2021). https://doi.org/10.3390/ani11092664

14. Kumar, S., Singh, S.K.: Monitoring of pet animal in smart cities using animal biometrics. Futur. Gener. Comput. Syst. **83**, 553–563 (2018). https://doi.org/10.1016/j.future.2016.12.006

15. Vaishnavi, P., Aaryan, K.K.M., Bhavanishankar, K.: Ai-driven canine dog nose print recognition, https://ssrn.com/abstract=5124492. Accessed 25 June 2025

16. Mortezapour Shiri, F., Perumal, T., Mustapha, N., Mohamed, R.: A comprehensive overview and comparative analysis on deep learning models: Cnn, rnn, lstm, gru. J. Artif. Intell. **6**(1), 301–360 (2024). arXiv:2305.17473. https://doi.org/10.32604/jai.2024.054314

17. Borwarnginn, P., Kusakunniran, W., Karnjanapreechakorn, S., Thongkanchorn, K.: Knowing your dog breed: identifying a dog breed with deep learning. Int. J. Autom. Comput. **18**(1), 45–54 (2020). https://doi.org/10.1007/s11633-020-1261-0

18. Sonia Devi, V., Satija, A., Kumar, H., Jha, S., Upadhyay, V.: Dog breed identification and classification using convolution neural network. Int. J. Creative Res. Thoughts (IJCRT) **11**(2), 42–349 (2023). https://ijcrt.org/papers/IJCRTAB02042.pdf

19. Khosla, A., Jayadevaprakash, N., Yao, B., Fei-Fei, L.: Stanford dogs dataset (2021). https://www.kaggle.com/datasets/jessicali9530/stanforddogs-dataset. Accessed 25 June 2025

20. Kern, D.: Multi-pose dog dataset: Animal re-identification algorithm for posture diversity (2023). https://github.com/DariaKern/IndividualAnimalReIDDatasets. Accessed 25 June 2025

21. C. Project, Dog breeds object detection dataset (2023). https://universe.roboflow.com/cv-project-ggmi2/dog-breeds-ggciv. Accessed 25 June 2025

From User Needs to Design Solutions: A Hybrid KJ-Kano Approach for Sneaker Customization App

Yitian Guo[1,2], Jiefeng Lv[1,2(✉)], and Jinxuan Lai[3]

[1] Sanya Science and Education Innovation Park of Wuhan University of Technology, Sanya 572000, Hainan, China
664599628@qq.com
[2] Wuhan University of Technology, Wuhan 430070, Hubei, China
[3] Guangzhou City University of Technology, 510800 Guangzhou, China

Abstract. Aim: This initiative aims to conduct a user demand survey for customized sneakers targeting the Chinese market. Building on user research data, we will propose strategies and solutions to enhance the current suboptimal customization process experience, thereby enriching and stimulating the current sneaker consumer market in China.

Methods: Starting from the current market environment and user needs, we employ the KJ method to summarize user demands and pain points in the sneaker customization process, identifying primary and secondary requirements for the app interface design. Subsequently, we employ the Kano model for questionnaire design and analysis, applying the Better-Worse coefficient calculation method to categorize and prioritize functional attributes. This enables us to formulate design strategies for the sneaker customization app interface and conduct design implementation.

Results: The study summarizes authentic user requirements for the sneaker customization app, guiding the development of design strategies across three dimensions: functional service system, visual specifications, and user applicability experience. These strategies informed final design implementation and validation.

Conclusion: The integrated KJ-Kano model effectively prevents designers' subjective assumptions while accurately reflecting authentic user demands in the sneaker customization market. These research outcomes provide valuable references for product development and design studies in customized footwear domains.

Keywords: KJ method · Kano model · sneaker customization · interface design

1 Introduction

China has consistently maintained its position as the global leader in footwear production and exports. However, recent industrial transformations driven by factors such as rising labor costs, technological stagnation in shoemaking, and industrial relocation

© The Author(s), under exclusive license to Springer Nature Switzerland AG 2026
S. Sundarakannan and O. Knorpp (Eds.): HCII 2025, CCIS 2772, pp. 316–326, 2026.
https://doi.org/10.1007/978-3-032-12767-9_34

have significantly altered the global manufacturing landscape. The massive relocation of labor-intensive manufacturing sectors to emerging economies like Vietnam and the Philippines has severely impacted China's traditional footwear industry. Meanwhile, personalized customization has long served as a vital means of individuality expression and personal charisma demonstration. With China's continuous socioeconomic development, consumers increasingly pursue emotionally-driven consumption characterized by personalized and fashionable preferences, creating substantial growth opportunities in the mid-to-high-end footwear consumer market.

Industrial development typically evolves from extensive expansion to refined operations, requiring dynamic strategic adjustments to address market shifts. While China's sneaker market sustained a 12.3% compound annual growth rate (CAGR) from 2000 to 2019 (Euromonitor, 2021), post-pandemic data reveals significant deceleration (6.8% CAGR for 2020–2023). Reduced product refresh cycles for consumer perception stimulation reflect brands' strategic transition from high-frequency product launches to innovation-driven market penetration.

The advent of Industry 4.0 and advancing footwear technologies has catalyzed industry transformation. Batch-capable standardized customization services through digital platforms have become technically feasible, positioning mass-market sneaker customization as the next strategic battleground for brand competitiveness.

Current mobile-based sneaker customization apps in China remain limited, with insufficient empirical demand analysis for this niche market to provide reliable data references. Consequently, this study employs the KJ-Kano hybrid model to excavate and analyze user requirements, distilling core customization demands while eliminating design interference factors, ultimately driving targeted app design implementation.

2 Literature Review and Design Research Analysis

2.1 Related Research Review

The KJ method, also known as the Affinity Diagram or A-type diagrammatic method, is a quality management tool developed by Japanese anthropologist Jiro Kawakita to address ill-structured problems in uncharted domains [1]. It facilitates the identification of intrinsic interrelationships and causal hierarchies among research subjects through systematic pattern organization.

Evolving from Herzberg's Two-Factor Theory (1959) in behavioral psychology, the Kano model was further developed by Professor Noriaki Kano of Tokyo University of Science and colleagues at the 1982 Japanese Quality Control Symposium, formally establishing the Attractive Quality Theory [2]. This model serves as a critical tool for categorizing and prioritizing user requirements, demonstrating the non-linear correlation between product functionalities and user satisfaction, thus proving instrumental in product development and customer experience optimization.

In sneaker customization research, Wallace Brandon et al. posit that customization facilitates cultural resistance against colonialism, empowering marginalized groups to assert individual/collective identities and strengthen regional political solidarity [3]. Trentin Alessio's experimental studies demonstrate customization's efficacy in mitigating consumer aversion toward foreign footwear products [4]. Zeng Dong et al. developed a fuzzy fitness value conversion method for demand ranking in athletic shoe color customization systems, enhancing style preference alignment [5]. Rincon-Guevara Oscar et al. emphasize product modularization and manufacturing configuration complexity as critical enablers for consumer participation in personalized production [6].

Domestic scholars Wang Xiaoxiao and Li Xiaoyan identify supply-side structural reform and internet-plus platforms as crucial drivers for China's footwear customization development through enterprise case studies [7]. Liu Na et al., via PEST analysis of China's customization industry, highlight big data as the key to future service optimization [8]. Jin Guiyang et al. engineered a large-scale flexible customization system for knitted footwear based on ecosystem constituent analysis [9]. Luo Yuhao and Yin Jianguo's consumption behavior research reveals that graffiti-style customization satisfies multi-layered psychological needs, delivering enhanced visual and emotional experiences [10]. Employing mixed methods, Li Chen's market analysis identifies pricing as the predominant factor influencing customized sneaker adoption in China [11].

2.2 Sneaker Customization Interface Design Investigation and Analysis

The research initiated by identifying participants through questionnaires and interviews with prospective sneaker customization app users, including existing consumers and prospective buyers, primarily targeting university students as key youth representatives. Divergent thinking exercises focusing on "App Service Requirements for Sneaker Customization" were conducted to exhaustively capture user needs.

After consolidating these requirements with Donald Norman's Emotional Design Theory [12] and expert consultations, we systematically categorized demands into three tiers: visceral (appearance requirements), behavioral (functional requirements), and reflective (applicability requirements). This analysis distilled three core demand categories and 25 sub-category indicators, as presented in Table 1.

Table 1. Classification Table of User Requirements.

Requirements Collection	
Appearance requirement A	A1 Flat interface design style, A2 Unified color scheme, A3 Sans-serif typography, A4 Trend-driven aesthetic, A5 High-recognition iconography, A6 Waterfall content layout
Functional requirement B	B1 Design sharing, B2 Diversified pricing options, B3 Promotional campaigns;B4 Embroidery customization, B5 Engraving service, B6 Interactive community, B7 Transparent pricing, B8 Material marketplace, B9 Secure transactions, B10 Color editing, B11 After-sales support, B12 Multimode customization
Applicability requirement C	C1 Sneaker culture content, C2 Tutorial repository, C3 Guided design workflow, C4 Intuitive operation, C5 Clear functional labeling, C6 Standardized process, C7 Instant social account login

Building on the hierarchical demand classification derived from the KJ method, the Kano model's questionnaire employs a dual-perspective framework (functional/dysfunctional scenarios) to evaluate features through systematically designed positive/negative inquiry pairs. Effective survey implementation requires three validated phases: (1) operationalizing features through standardized definitions to ensure cognitive consistency, (2) constructing bipolar measurement scales to quantify satisfaction/dissatisfaction thresholds, and (3) conducting pilot testing with diagnostic metrics to verify data integrity and actionable insights generation.

The survey distributed 45 questionnaires through offline and online channels, with 39 valid responses retained after excluding insincere online submissions. SPSS analysis demonstrated acceptable psychometric properties: Cronbach's $\alpha = 0.716$ (good reliability) and KMO $= 0.738$ (adequate validity). Established content validity through preliminary studies enables subsequent analysis.

Using the Kano questionnaire framework, we systematically classified user demands into five quality attributes:

- **Attractive** (Delight-enhancing features)
- **One-dimensional** (Performance-sensitive features)
- **Must-be** (Basic expectations)
- **Indifferent** (Neutral perceptions)
- **Reverse** (Counterproductive elements)

Each demand exhibits 25 possible classification combinations through cross-tabulation of functional/dysfunctional responses.

2.3 Requirement Attribute Classification Based on Better-Worse Coefficient Metrics

In order to improve the accuracy of the experimental analysis, this study introduces the Better-Worse coefficient analysis method, which aids in classifying demand attributes by calculating the satisfaction coefficient (SI) and dissatisfaction coefficient (DSI). This method first calculates the SI and DSI values for each quality attribute, and then determines the demand characteristics by averaging the SI and DSI. Finally, a demand sensitivity matrix is created based on the SI and DSI values to visually delineate each demand attribute. The following are the formulas for calculating Satisfaction Influence (SI) and Dissatisfaction Influence (DSI):

1. Increased satisfaction factor:

$$\text{Better/SI} = (A + O)/(A + O + M + I) \tag{1}$$

2. Dissatisfaction factor after elimination:

$$\text{Worse/DSI} = (-1) \times (O + M)/(A + O + M + I) \tag{2}$$

The Better coefficient indicates the satisfaction coefficient, usually a positive number, after adding a feature attribute. The higher the value of this coefficient, or the closer it is to 1, the greater the impact of the feature on user satisfaction, i.e., the more effective the increase in satisfaction. Conversely, the Worse coefficient represents the level of dissatisfaction after eliminating the feature attribute and is usually a negative number. The lower the value of this coefficient, or the closer it is to -1, the stronger the feature's impact on user dissatisfaction and the more significant the decrease in satisfaction.

The Better-Worse coefficient analysis results were imported into the SPSS AU online data analysis platform for processing. The analytical outcomes were visualized as a four-quadrant diagram (Fig. 1), with the Better index plotted on the vertical axis (Y-axis) and the absolute Worse index on the horizontal axis (X-axis).

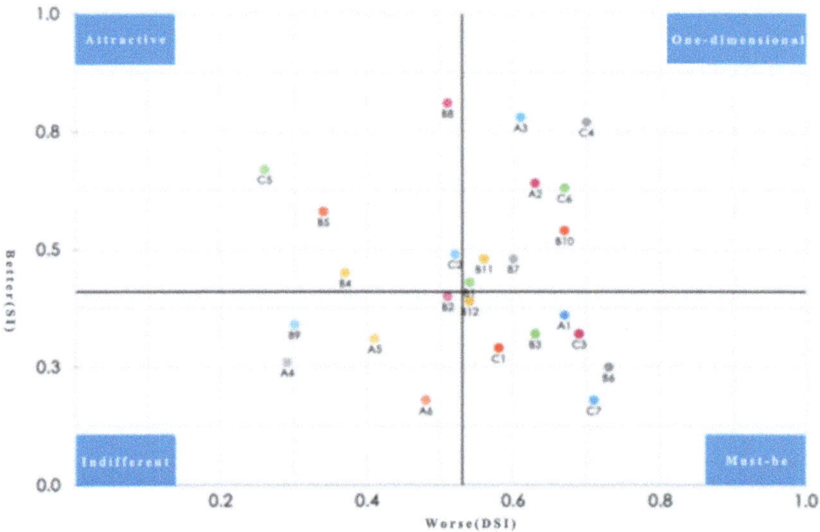

Fig. 1. Quartile Quadrant Diagram: Analysis of Better Worse Coefficient.

The demand items were classified through satisfaction analysis into 7 Must-be attributes, 8 One-dimensional attributes, 5 Attractive attributes, and 5 Indifferent attributes based on quadrant analysis. For functionally equivalent attributes, product development should prioritize those with higher Better coefficients or larger absolute Worse coefficients (Better-Worse priority rule), as these reflect stronger user sensitivity and require prioritized design consideration.

The satisfaction sensitivity (S) metric, calculated as the Euclidean distance from the origin to the (SI, |DSI|) coordinate point [13], determines demand importance. Higher S values indicate greater user satisfaction impact. Figure 2 visualizes this comparison within the sensitivity matrix using SI (X-axis) and DSI (Y-axis).

Following the prioritization hierarchy of Must-be > One-dimensional > Attractive > Indifferent, and integrating sensitivity metrics, we derived comprehensive rankings for primary demand categories:

- Functional   Requirements:
  B6 > B3 > B12 > B10 > B7 > B11 > B1 > B8 > B5 > B4 > B2 > B9

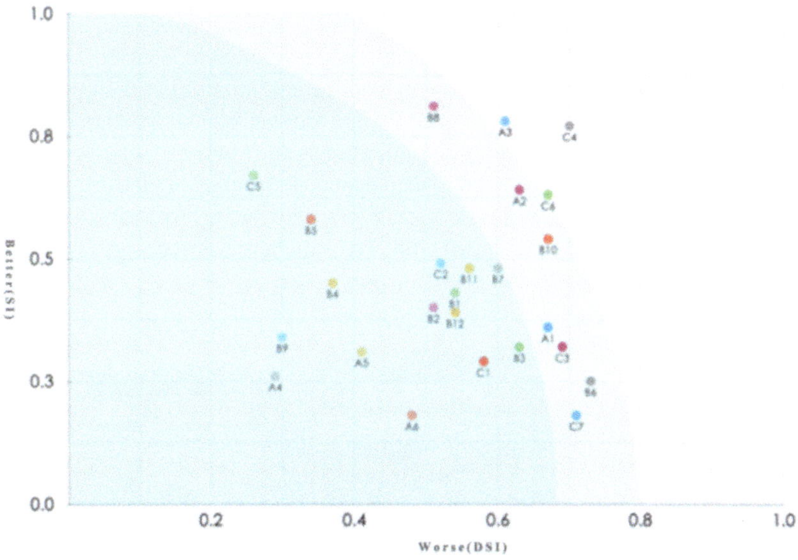

Fig. 2. Requirement sensitivity matrix.

- Appearance Requirements: A1 > A3 > A2 > A6 > A5 > A4
- Applicability Requirements: C3 > C7 > C1 > C4 > C6 > C2 > C5

3 Sneaker Customization App Interface Design Strategy and Practice

3.1 Establishing a Customization-Centric Functional Service System

Empirical analysis and prioritization results identify community interaction and sharing (B6) as a top-priority functional requirement. Given the inherent limitations of single-purpose utility apps in user acquisition and engagement frequency within mainstream markets, establishing a dedicated sneaker enthusiast community platform effectively increases daily active users (DAU) through enhanced immersive experiences and emotional resonance, thereby boosting app stickiness. This social infrastructure addresses users' intrinsic need for identity validation through digital interactions, providing instant content-sharing mechanisms that enable the dissemination of positive emotional experiences during product usage. Such viral sharing not only amplifies user delight but also organically expands brand influence by creating multiplatform touchpoints, ultimately facilitating large-scale content dissemination.

The community interaction and service platform is universally accessible, where sneaker customization enthusiasts can thoroughly discuss and share content, while commercial designers utilize it to promote their products/services (Fig. 3: Recommendation Interface and Follow Interface in the community module).Under the current internet trend of "social commerce ecosystems," establishing mutually beneficial relationships between content creators and platforms constitutes a critical operational element. Seasoned sneaker customization professionals, already proficient in internet-based marketing and sales models, predominantly leverage online communities as their primary sales channels. Integrating this community platform into the sneaker customization app—with optimized designs for product inquiries, purchases, and reviews—effectively attracts both enthusiast communities and experienced designers from other platforms. This strategy fosters direct engagement with core target users, cultivates a professionalized sneaker culture community, expands user bases, and drives the app's virtuous growth cycle.

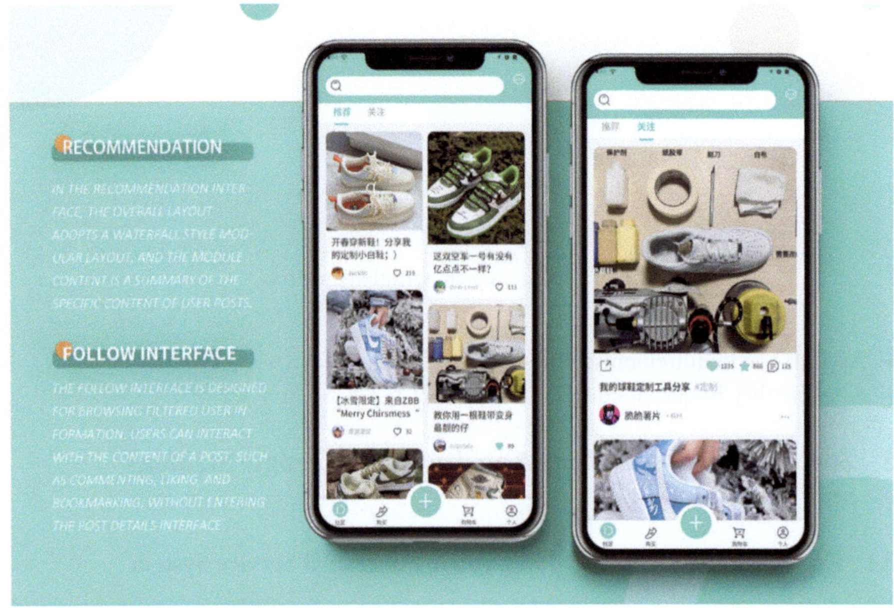

Fig. 3. Recommendation and Follow Interface

Establishing standardized official customization functionalities can significantly facilitate product customization (see Fig. 4: Sneaker Customization Interface). Users simply access the service through the app's designated customization portal, follow step-by-step instructions provided in the service program, and obtain their desired customized results. Due to the constrained functionality of this standardized workflow, users can accurately predict customization outcomes before initiating the process, evaluate results, and decide whether to proceed, thereby substantially improving customization efficiency.

Additionally, analytical results indicate that implementing diverse promotional campaigns, establishing a robust after-sales support system, and creating instant sharing functionality remain critical user concerns.

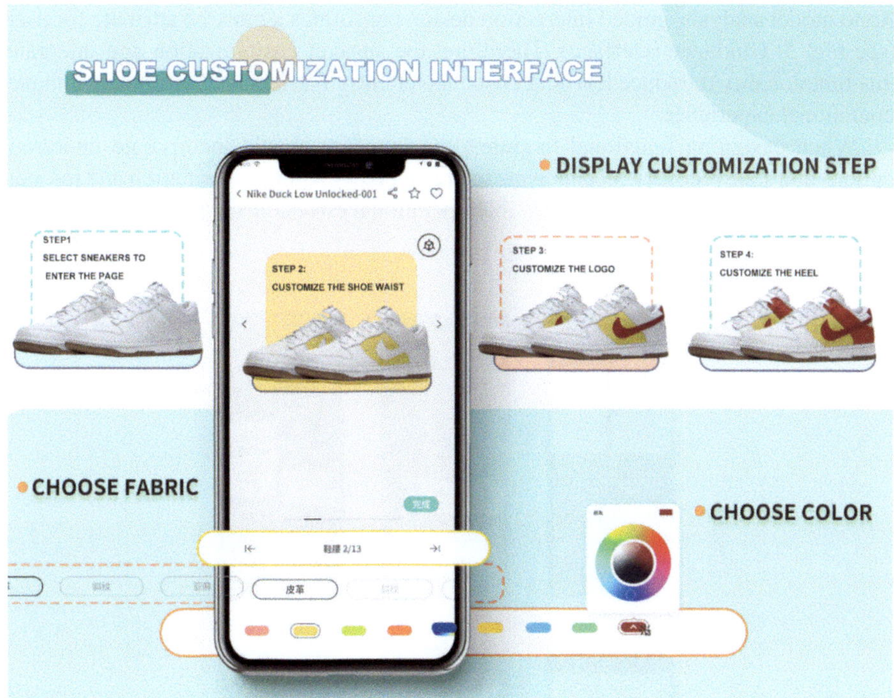

Fig. 4 Shoe customization interface

3.2 Establishing Minimalist Fashion-Oriented Visual Specifications

The primary user base of sneaker customization apps consists of young adults aged 20–30 who prioritize efficiency and convenience. Compared to skeuomorphic design, flat design demonstrates superior advantages through its lightweight implementation, operational clarity, and visual neatness, aligning with the "less is more" design philosophy. By employing clean-cut visual elements and eliminating redundant interactive effects, this approach emphasizes core functionalities while reducing the app's perceptual presence, thereby highlighting products and cultural content to enhance user immersion and experience.

Furthermore, flat design ensures cross-device adaptability – interface components can be proportionally resized for diverse mobile platforms. This universal visual framework effectively reduces cognitive load during interactions, making it ideal for information-intensive apps with rich content diversity.

3.3 Optimizing User Applicability Experience

Functional user interfaces prioritizing product features and user requirements often exhibit a significant discrepancy between their design logic and users' behavioral logic during operation. While designers perceive interface information acquisition and module switching as straightforward, users still face steep learning curves. According to

Kano model analysis, guided interaction design constitutes a must-be attribute for users (see Fig. 5: Guidance interface). Therefore, the sneaker customization app integrates this functionality to reduce learning costs, lower entry barriers, and ultimately enhance operational experience.

When designing functional modules, the interface should incorporate undo/redo options and state recovery mechanisms to prevent navigation disorientation and mitigate negative emotions caused by irreversible operational errors during page transitions.

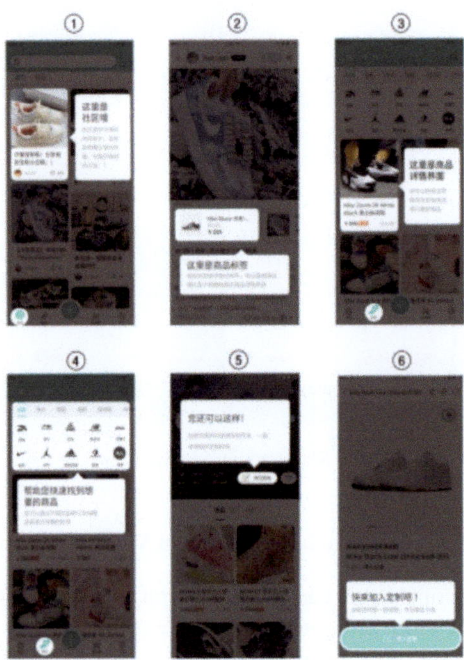

Fig. 5 Guidance interface (layered).

3.4 User Testing

Following the completion of the core design for the sneaker customization app, user interviews and evaluations were conducted to validate the design's effectiveness based on subjective scoring. In accordance with Nielsen's usability testing principles [14], 10 participants aged 21–29 with sneaker customization experience were recruited. The evaluation covered six dimensions: usability, stability, controllability, satisfaction, visual design, and information architecture.

The design was assessed using a 5-point Likert scale (5: Very Satisfied; 1: Very Dissatisfied). Results indicated favorable outcomes, with all average scores exceeding 4 points. For lower-scoring aspects, iterative refinements—such as improving the accessibility of customization features on specific pages—were implemented based on user feedback, which further enhanced the experiential evaluation. Overall, the design achieved the predefined objectives.

4 Conclusions

This study developed a systematic methodology for sneaker customization app design by applying the KJ-Kano hybrid model. Through computational analysis of survey data and interview insights, we established prioritized user demand rankings and formulated interface design strategies based on Better-Worse coefficients, culminating in the "ICREATE" design implementation.

Amid increasing market openness in the global sneaker industry and intensifying challenges faced by traditional manufacturers, customized sneaker services may inject new dynamism into existing markets. Focused on China's customization market, this research explores dedicated app development objectives, providing actionable insights for global software design initiatives in similar contexts. Furthermore, the methodology and findings will undergo iterative refinement and optimization to better support industry advancement.

Acknowledgments. This research was jointly funded and supported by the School of Art and Design of Wuhan University of Technology and Yazhou Bay Science and Technology Park in Sanya City, Hainan Province.

References

1. Gensler, S., Völckner, F., Egger, M., et al.: Listen to your customers: insights into brand image using online consumer-generated product reviews. Int. J. Electron. Commer. **20**(1), 112–141 (2015)
2. Kano, N., et al.: Attractive quality and must-be quality. J. Japan Soc. Qual. Control. **14**(2), 39–48 (1984)
3. Wallace B, Andrews D L. Decolonizing the sneaker: sneaker customization and the racial politics of expressive popular culture. J. Sport Soc. Issues, 2022, 46(6): 524–545.
4. Trentin, A., Aichner, T., Sandrin, E., et al.: Competing through manufacturing: countering a product's liability of foreignness through mass customization. Int. J. Oper. Prod. Manag. **40**(11), 1661–1683 (2020)
5. Zeng, D., He, M., Zhou, Z., et al.: An interactive genetic algorithm with an alternation ranking method and its application to product customization. Hum. Centr. Comput. Inform. Sci. **11** (2021)
6. Rincón-Guevara, O., Samayoa, J.A., Panchal, J.H., et al.: The role of the product design and manufacturing system dyad in efficient personalized production. J. Mech. Des. **144**(10), 102001 (2022)
7. Wang, X.X., Li, X.Y.: Today, have you customized? Customized footwear under "supply-side reform" and "internet plus". China Foreign Footwear [中外鞋苑]. **314**(5), 36–42+35+94-100 (2016)
8. Liu, N., Gao, H.Y., Zhang, L.B.: Business model innovation and implementation of customized footwear based on big data technology. China Leather [中国皮革]. **51**(6), 118–123 (2022)

9. Jin, G.Y., Chen, G., Li, L.J., et al.: Design and development of a large-scale flexible customization ecosystem for knitted footwear and apparel. Knitting Industry [针织工业]. **402**(7), 16–20 (2022)
10. Luo, Y. H., & Yin, J. G. (2019). Graffiti design in modern personalized customized sneakers. Western Leather [西部皮革], 41(13), 93–94, 98.
11. Li, C.: Consumer intention and current status survey of customized athletic footwear in China. Econ. Res. Guid. [经济研究导刊]. **16**, 68–86 (2018)
12. Norman, D.: Emotional Design: why we Love (or Hate) Everyday Things. Basic Books (2007)
13. Chuli, Q., Jing, G., Jing, M., et al.: Research on demand for bus stop facilities based on Kano model and waiting experience. Pack. Eng. **43**(16), 401–409 (2022). https://doi.org/10.19554/j.cnki.1001-3563.2022.16.049
14. Nielsen, J., Molich, R.: Teaching user interface design based on usability engineering. ACM SIGCHI Bull. **21**(1), 45–48 (1989)

Emotional Recognition Using Eye Movements

Rishabh Varsha Vallabh Haria[1(✉)] [iD], Mohamed Abdoulaye Bailo Diallo[1] [iD], Sahura Ertugrul[2] [iD], Louisa Kulke[2] [iD], and Sebastian Maneth[1] [iD]

[1] Department of Informatics, University of Bremen, Bremen, Germany
{haria,mdiallo,maneth}@uni-bremen.de
[2] Department of Developmental and Educational Psychology, University of Bremen, Bremen, Germany
{sahura,kulke}@uni-bremen.de

Abstract. There are two well known dimension of emotions, arousal and valence. In this research we focus on arousal. The PicDisengage dataset consists of 43 users who are shown 30 images for 32 trials per image (1.5 to 2.5 s per image) while their eye movements are recorded using a state-of-the-art eye tracker. For each image the users give a manual arousal rating between 1 and 9. We apply to this data a well known machine learning pipeline for eye tracking data that has been successfull for user prediction and other tasks. By applying this pipeline methods we achieve successful prediction of arousal ratings, as described below. When we do binary prediction of arousal ratings 1–4 versus 5–9 then we obtain an accuracy of 78%. When we do binary predictions of one arousal rating versus the rest of the ratings then we obtain accuracies always above 80% and in some cases as high as 96%. More precisely, for predicting the arousal ratings 5, 6, and 7 against the respective rests we obtain accuracies of around 82%, while for all other arousal ratings our accuracies are above 90%. The three major achievements of our research are: (i) it enables prediction from static images alone (whereas all prior studies on the top use video clips plus possibly other modalities), (ii) it requires very little data (instead of the full 32 trials our predictions achieve similar accuracies when using only 6 trials), and (iii) our predictions are made using *unseen images* (this corresponds to "cross stimulus prediction" which is an extremely challenging and largely unsolved issue within machine learning based eye tracking research).

Keywords: Emotional Recognition · Eye Movement Data · Machine Learning

1 Introduction

Emotions defined by dimensions such as arousal and valence are central to human experience, and their perception is increasingly studied using eye tracking to infer short-term emotional states [16,17,24,29,30,33,37]. This study focuses on

© The Author(s), under exclusive license to Springer Nature Switzerland AG 2026
S. Sundarakannan and O. Knorpp (Eds.): HCII 2025, CCIS 2772, pp. 327–340, 2026.
https://doi.org/10.1007/978-3-032-12767-9_35

arousal, which represents the intensity of emotional experience. Traditionally, researchers have measured emotional arousal using the Self-Assessment Manikin (SAM) [4], which is an icon-based tool, and the Positive and Negative Affect Schedule (PANAS) [34], which uses a list of 20 emotions for people to rate. Although widely used, these methods depend on people reflecting on and reporting their feelings which can take time and may be influenced by personal bias or how well someone can describe their emotions. In contrast, eye tracking provides a faster and more objective way to estimate emotional arousal by analyzing how people's eyes move when they look at different things without needing them to stop and explain how they feel. In the PicDisengage dataset [14] arousal labels are obtained directly from user ratings using a 9 point Likert scale after viewing the image. users were allowed to look at each image for as long as they needed before rating it. This provides a subjective ground truth for emotional intensity. Our study explores a transformative alternative: Recognizing arousal from eye movements. Instead of relying on time consuming self report tests we investigate whether just a one to one and a half minute of picture viewing eye tracking data can yield comparable estimates of emotional arousal. This would mark a major shift in how emotional states are assessed by reducing cognitive load, response bias, and time investment. Such an approach could minimize cognitive load and response bias while enabling real-time, passive emotional assessment, particularly beneficial in scenarios where self-report is impractical [16, 19] This has broad applications: In affective computing, user interfaces could adapt dynamically to arousal states to improve user experience [7]. In clinical psychology, passive arousal monitoring could help identify emotional dysregulation in patients during therapy trial [22]. In education, real time arousal detection could identify disengaged students enabling adaptive content delivery [9].

Recent studies show that eye tracking alone without multimodal inputs like EEG or facial cues can be effective for emotion recognition. Lim et al. [16] provides a comprehensive review, highlighting key limitations in prior work: small datasets, reliance on discrete emotion labels, and lack of focus on continuous emotional dimensions. They advocate for methods that use unimodal signals, predict continuous emotions, and generalize across stimuli. Tarnowski et al. [30] uses eye tracking features such as fixation duration, saccade amplitude, and pupil diameter from 25 users viewing emotion eliciting videos, achieving up to 80% accuracy in classifying valence into three categories (pleasant, neutral, unpleasant) using an SVM classifier. Similarly, Skaramagkas et al. [29] collects data from 48 users watching ten emotional video clips and extracted features from fixations, saccades, blinks, and pupil size. Their deep learning model reached 92% accuracy for binary valence prediction and 81% for binary arousal, demonstrating that eye tracking alone can support robust emotion recognition in dynamic video settings. However, continuous arousal prediction using only eye tracking and static images remains under-explored. Static images lack the dynamic temporal cues of videos making arousal prediction more challenging. To address this gap, we employ the PicDisengage [14] dataset, which includes eye tracking data from 43 users exposed to 30 static images.

Our key contributions and findings include:

1. We demonstrate, for the first time, that arousal levels can be predicted using unimodal eye tracking data with static images, without the need for dynamic or multimodal inputs.
2. Our binary arousal classification achieves up to 78% accuracy, and one-vs-all classification for individual ratings reaches up to 96% accuracy.
3. We show that using only 6 trials (9 to 15 s) per image suffices for accurate predictions, making the approach lightweight and practical.
4. Our models generalize well across unseen stimuli, achieving strong performance in cross stimulus prediction, an open challenge in the field of eye tracking research.

These results align directly with the recommendations of Lim et al. [16], validating that continuous, generalizable emotion prediction using unimodal eye tracking is both feasible and effective.

2 Proposed System

This section describes our emotion recognition architecture including the employed dataset, data processing and segmentation methods, feature extraction, machine learning classifiers, and the accuracy metric used in this study.

2.1 Visual Stimuli

This study utilizes the *PicDisengage* [14] dataset comprising eye tracking data from 43 users (mean age = 22.43 years, SD = 3.73, age range: 18–35 years). The dataset was collected by the Department of Developmental and Educational Psychology at the University of Bremen, Germany, in collaboration with the Department of Neurocognitive Developmental Psychology at Friedrich-Alexander University Erlangen-Nuremberg, Germany. All users are native German speakers with normal or corrected to normal vision and provided written informed consent in accordance with institutional ethical guidelines prior to participation. Users were presented with emotion eliciting images defined as visual stimuli capable of evoking varying degrees of emotional valence (positive, neutral, negative) and arousal. A total of 30 images were selected from two validated and widely used image databases: the *International Affective Picture System (IAPS)* [15] and the *Nencki Affective Picture System (NAPS)* [18,20,25,32,35]. The images are selected ensuring that all images had comparably high arousal values to control for arousal based variability in attentional engagement. Images were categorized by sociality (social vs non-social) and valence (positive, neutral, negative) making six experimental conditions with five images each (total of 30 images). To control for visual differences like brightness and contrast all images are luminance corrected using histogram matching optimized by structural similarity index via the SHINE_color Toolbox [36]. Each image is presented 32 times in a randomized order resulting in 960 trials per user. These 32 repetitions come from the combination of the following variables:

- 2 Competition Conditions: *Competition* (image remains on screen) vs *Non competition* (image disappears before peripheral bar appears)
- 2 Peripheral Bar Positions: Left or Right
- 2 Peripheral Bar Color Schemes: Black White or White Black
- 4 Repetitions for each combination

2.2   Apparatus and Procedure

Each trial begins with a central fixation cross followed by the presentation of a centrally located emotion eliciting image that remains on the screen for approximately 1.5–2.5 s. After this interval a peripheral bar composed of adjacent black and white segments is displayed on either the left or right side of the screen. This peripheral bar functioned as a gaze shift target to measure user's ability to disengage visual attention from the central emotional stimulus based on [12,13]. Figure 1 illustrates the experimental procedure starting with fixation, image presentation, peripheral bar onset, and post task rating.

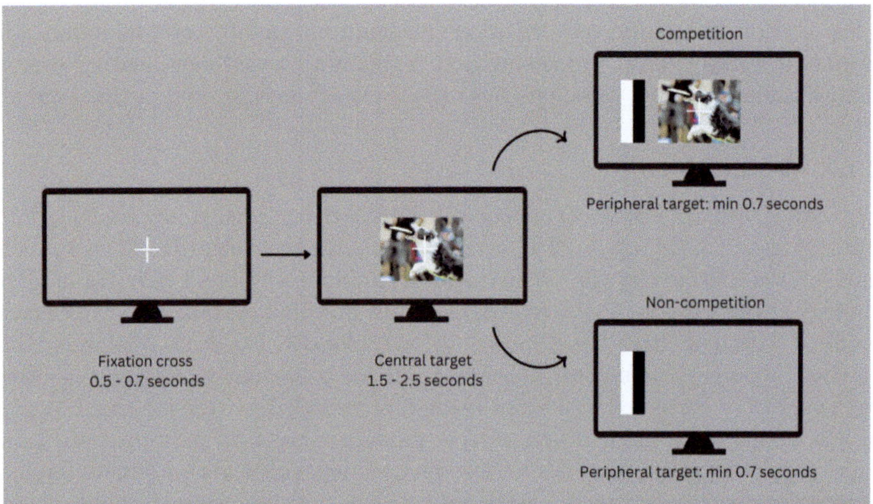

Fig. 1. Schematic of the experimental procedure: each trial begins with a fixation cross, followed by a central image, then a peripheral bar on either side.

Users were instructed to fixate on the central cross and upon appearance of the peripheral bar to shift their gaze to it as quickly as possible. Eye movements were recorded using the EyeLink 1000 Plus eye tracker (SR Research, Ontario, Canada) at a sampling rate 500 Hz for eye movement analysis. Following the eye tracking session users rated each image on two 9 point Likert scales for:
Valence (1 = very negative, 9 = very positive), and
Arousal (1 = very calming, 9 = very arousing).
Three example images are shown in Fig. 2.

Fig. 2. Example images from two experimental conditions: non-social positive and non-social negative.

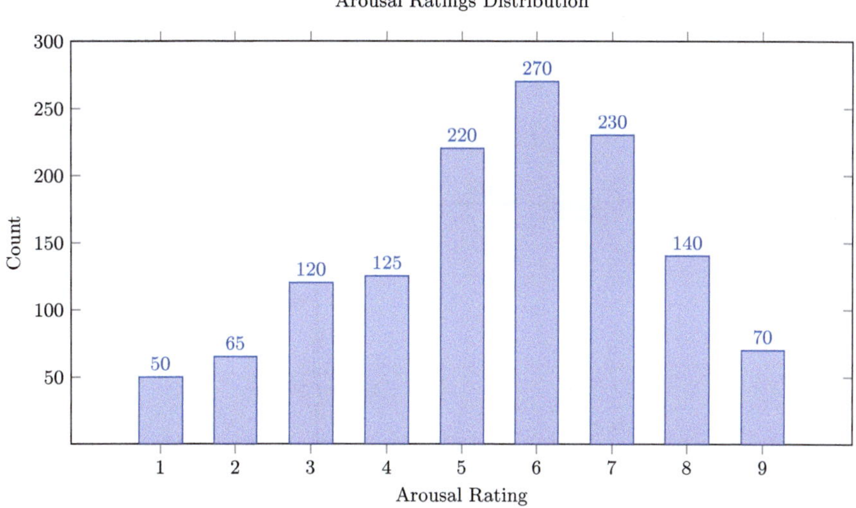

Fig. 3. Arousal Ratings Distribution: The histogram shows the distribution of arousal ratings (1–9) given by 43 users, each viewing 30 static images. Ratings cluster around the midpoint with the most frequent rating being 6. The distribution resembles a slightly left skewed bell shape, with a mean of 5.7 approximately.

2.3   Data Processing and Segmentation

To prepare the PicDisengage dataset for analysis, we apply preprocessing and segmentation techniques to ensure data quality and extract meaningful eye movement features. The raw data is stored in .mat files for each user. Each user views 30 images with each image having 32 trials throughout the experiment. Each trial takes 1.5 s to 2.5 s. For each image eye tracking data from all 32 trial is extracted and concatenated to form a trajectory. This raw data contains noise. We smooth the raw data using a Savitzky Golay filter (polynomial order = 6, frame size = 15). We apply the same Savitzky Golay filter settings used by George and Routray in their study [10]. This filter smooths the raw gaze data and reduces high frequency noise which is common during rapid eye movements like saccades. Since we compute velocity and acceleration from position data the small noise can distort these features. The Savitzky Golay filter helps by fitting a polynomial to each frame of data and minimizing the squared error. Prior work shows this method works well for noisy signals and provides accurate estimates of derivatives [11, 23, 27, 28].

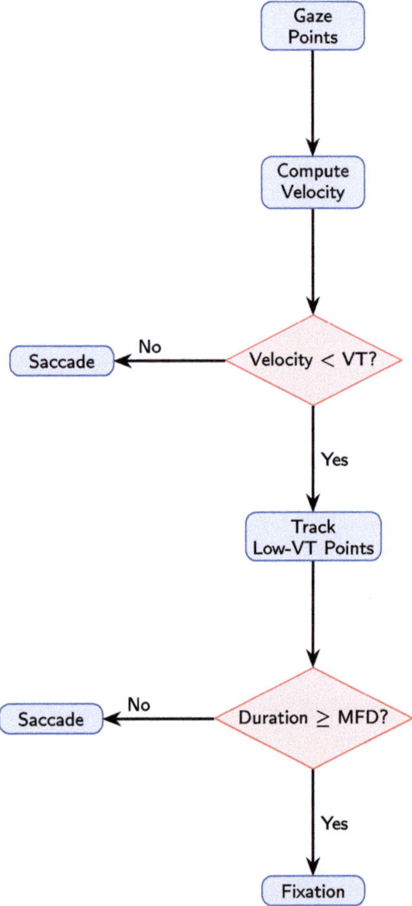

Fig. 4. IVT algorithm logic for classifying gaze points into fixations or saccades based on velocity and duration thresholds.

To analyze visual attention patterns in eye tracking data we segment trajectories into fixations and saccades using the Identification by Velocity Threshold (IVT) algorithm, as described in prior studies [1, 10, 26, 31]. Fixations represent periods of stable gaze where visual information is processed and saccades indicate rapid eye movements between fixations. The IVT algorithm employs two key parameters: the velocity threshold (VT) and the minimum fixation duration (MFD), following the implementation in [10]. The steps of the IVT algorithm are summarized in Fig. 4. It classifies consecutive gaze points with eye rotation velocities below the VT as fixations, provided their duration exceeds the MFD to ensure meaningful visual processing as very short fixations may not allow sufficient time for the brain to register visual input [26]. All other segments are identified as saccades. We evaluate VT values ranging from 1 to 100 deg/s, calculating the mean number of fixations across all users for each VT. At a VT of 60 deg/s we achieve a mean of 1065.42 fixations per user maximizing the fixation count in the PicDisengage dataset. Consequently, we select a VT of 60 deg/s to optimize fixation detection as this value enhances accuracy for specific predictive tasks.

2.4   Feature Extraction

We extract features separately from fixations and saccades using a framework first introduced by George and Routray [10]. Their award winning score level fusion system uses core eye movement metrics for effective recognition including duration, path length, amplitude, dispersion, angular deviation between shifts, and the fixation/saccade ratio (peak velocity divided by duration). This feature set was later extended by Al Zaidawi et al. [1] for user identification. They include higher order derivative features up to the fifth order computed using the forward difference method. These derivatives capture rapid gaze transitions more precisely. We adopt this extended framework for our study. For both fixations and saccades, we compute:

- Core eye movement features: duration, path length, amplitude, dispersion, angular change, and fixation/saccade ratio.
- Higher-order derivatives of velocity up to the fifth order.
- Statistical features for each signal and its derivatives: mean, median, max, standard deviation, skewness, and kurtosis.

This complete feature set, commonly referred to as "M3S2K" [1,31], captures both spatial and temporal dynamics in eye movement behavior. We normalize all features using Z-score standardization [21] to ensure comparability across users. Table 1 provides an overview of the full feature set used in our experiments.

2.5   Machine Learning Classifers and Performance Metrics

The dataset includes 30 images per user from 43 users, categorized by valence (negative, neutral, positive) and sociality (social, non-social) into six groups of five images each. For each user, the data is split into 80% training (24 images) and 20% testing (6 images), ensuring test images are unseen during training.

We perform 9-fold random cross validation using the structure of the stimulus set. The 30 images are divided into six groups based on valence (negative, neutral, positive) and sociality (social, non-social) with five images per group.

Table 1. Fixation and saccade features computed from the eye-movement trajectories, to be used for our SVM classifier in order to predict arousal ratings.

Position based (15 features)					
1	Duration	6	Kurtosis Y	11	Amplitude
2	Path length	7	Standard deviation of X	12	Dispersion
3	Skew X	8	Standard deviation of Y	13	Dist. to previous Fix/Sac
4	Skew Y	9	Fix/Sac ratio	14	Angle with previous Fix/Sac
5	Kurtosis X	10	Fix/Sac angle	15	Average speed
Higher order derivative features (18 features per derivative)					
16–21	Angular velocity*	22–27	Velocity X*	28–33	Velocity Y*
34–39	Angular acceleration*	40–45	Acceleration X*	46–51	Acceleration Y*
52–57	Angular jerk*	58–63	Jerk X*	64–69	Jerk Y*
70–75	Angular jounce*	76–81	Jounce X*	82–87	Jounce Y*
88–93	Angular crackle*	94–99	Crackle X*	100–105	Crackle Y*

*M3S2K-Statistical features: Mean, Median, Max, Standard deviation, Skewness, Kurtosis

In each fold, we select six image randomly for testing and use the remaining 24 images for training. This ensures that the model is always evaluated on unseen images, promoting generalization and providing a robust estimate of real world performance.

To assess classification performance in our emotion recognition task, we report *accuracy* as the percentage of correctly predicted instances out of all predictions, with each prediction corresponding to a single test image. We compute accuracy individually for each user based on their test images, and the final performance is reported as the mean accuracy across all users, expressed in percentage points. We measure how much accuracy varies between users by reporting the standard deviation of their individual accuracies. Performance for each configuration is evaluated using per user accuracy based on their six test images, with results reported as the mean and standard deviation across all users. We train two classifers one for fixation and one for saccades. The final prediction probability for each arousal class i, $P_{\text{final}}(i)$, is computed as the average of the probabilities from both classifiers (fixation and saccade classifer):

$$P_{\text{final}}(i) = 0.5 \cdot P_{\text{fix}}(i) + 0.5 \cdot P_{\text{sac}}(i). \tag{1}$$

The predicted label is the class with the highest $P_{\text{final}}(i)$. We compared the following classifiers: Support Vector Machines (SVM) [8], Random Forests [5], Radial Basis Function Network (RBFN) [6], Naive Bayes [2], and Logistic Regression [3] for comparison. SVM consistently yielded the highest accuracy and stability across the dataset. We use default hyperparameters for each classifier.

3   Emotional Recognition Experiments

In our study, we assess the performance of our model using a Support Vector Machine (SVM) classifier, as discussed in Sect. 2.5, for predicting arousal states using our feature set and building on the preprocessing discussed in Sect. 2.3. We approach arousal prediction in four different ways.

First, we formulate it as a ternary classification task, grouping self-reported arousal ratings (on a 1–9 scale) into three balanced categories: Low Arousal (1–3), Medium Arousal (4–6), and High Arousal (7–9). This setup provides a clear framework for capturing general affective states. Second, we simplify the task into a binary classification problem. We divide ratings into Low Arousal (1–4) and High Arousal (5–9) to explore coarse-grained emotional discrimination. Third, we address fine-grained prediction using a One-vs-Rest (OvR) approach. We train a single SVM to distinguish one specific rating (e.g., Rating 1 vs. Rest) from all others, focusing on isolating individual arousal levels for precise classification. And fourth, we use SVM (in two different ways) to perform the full nine-class prediction of arousal ratings in the range of 1–9 (note that this fourth experiment is only carried out over the "reduced dataset"; see next paragraph). The following presents the results of these approaches (Table 2).

Table 2. Ternary classification performance using arousal ratings grouped into low (1–3), medium (4–6), and high (7–9). Results are shown for all 32 trials and for a subset of 6 trials.

Model	Accuracy (%)	Std Dev
SVM (Ternary)	**52.02**	±2.8

(a) All 32 trials

Model	Accuracy (%)	Std Dev
SVM (Ternary)	**47.84**	±4.3

(b) Subset of 6 trials

To further refine our arousal prediction model and assess its robustness with limited data, we select only 6 trials from the original 32 trials of eye tracking data per image approximately one-fifth of the full dataset. This number is chosen to represent a significant reduction in data volume while still retaining sufficient variability to support meaningful classification. This reduction allows us to investigate whether the model can still distinguish arousal states effectively and testing its sensitivity to smaller datasets. We apply the same three classification approaches ternary, binary, and One-vs-Rest (OvR) as described previously, using the same preprocessing pipeline and the SVM classifier. The results presented in the tables below show the model's performance with this reduced dataset (Table 3).

Table 3. Binary classification performance for distinguishing low arousal (1–4) from high arousal (5–9). Results are shown for all 32 trials and for a subset of 6 trials.

Model	Accuracy (%)	Std Dev
SVM (Binary)	**72.73**	±6.9

(a) All 32 trials

Model	Accuracy (%)	Std Dev
SVM (Binary)	**72.43**	±7.8

(b) Subset of 6 trials

Our experiments demonstrate that eye tracking data processed through an SVM classifier enables arousal prediction across ternary, binary, and OvR paradigms with notable performance in rapid assessment using only 6 trials (9–15 s) per image. The binary classification's robust accuracy of 72.43% ($\pm$7.8) with the reduced dataset highlights the feasibility of distinguishing low (1–4) from high (5–9) arousal in under 15 s, supporting our goal of rapid passive emotional assessment [16]. While the OvR approach achieves high accuracy for extreme ratings 96.21% ($\pm$2.6) for Rating 1 and 79.45% ($\pm$3.6) for Rating 6 its advantage becomes less compelling when compared against a simple baseline.

To contextualize these results and establish a performance floor we compute a majority class predictor baseline. This naive classifier always predicts the majority class i.e., it assumes each sample does not belong to the target class in a One-vs-Rest (OvR) setup. Based on the dataset's class distribution (43 participants $\times$ 30 images = 1290 ratings) we calculate per class frequencies (e.g., class 6 occurs 270 times) and derive the majority predictor accuracy as the proportion of correctly classified "not-class" instances. For example, predicting "not class 6" yields 1290$-$270=1020 correct predictions, or 79.07% accuracy. Repeating this process across all nine classes, we find the average majority predictor accuracy to be 88.90% (Table 4).

Table 4. One-vs-Rest (OvR) classification performance of an SVM classifier for distinguishing each arousal rating (1–9) from all others. Results are shown for all 32 trials, a subset of 6 trials, and a majority-class baseline.

Class	32 Trials		6 Trials		Majority Predictor
	Accuracy (%)	Std Dev	Accuracy (%)	Std Dev	Accuracy (%)
1 vs Rest	**95.21**	$\pm$2.6	**96.21**	$\pm$2.6	96.12
2 vs Rest	93.75	$\pm$2.1	94.96	$\pm$2.8	94.96
3 vs Rest	93.32	$\pm$2.0	92.37	$\pm$2.2	90.70
4 vs Rest	89.87	$\pm$2.4	91.12	$\pm$1.7	90.31
5 vs Rest	82.34	$\pm$3.0	82.21	$\pm$3.0	82.95
6 vs Rest	79.71	$\pm$2.4	79.45	$\pm$3.6	79.07
7 vs Rest	83.97	$\pm$3.8	82.34	$\pm$3.3	82.21
8 vs Rest	89.23	$\pm$2.2	90.48	$\pm$2.5	89.15
9 vs Rest	94.35	$\pm$1.2	94.14	$\pm$2.3	94.57
Average	**89.08**	$\pm$2.41	**89.25**	$\pm$2.67	**88.90**

3.1 Nine-Class Arousal Prediction

We further evaluate a nine-class arousal prediction approach using two different ways. The first involves training a single multiclass SVM that performs direct

9-class classification. The second way involves training nine separate binary classifiers (One-vs-Rest), each tasked with distinguishing one specific arousal rating (1–9) from the rest. At test time, the predicted class is selected as the one whose classifier outputs the highest probability. Using the reduced dataset (6 trials per image) and 9-fold cross-validation, the single multiclass SVM achieves an accuracy of 13.55%, while the One-vs-Rest ensemble approach yields 18.81% (Table 5).

Table 5. Comparison of multiclass arousal prediction methods using reduced trials (6 per image) and 9-fold cross-validation. (a) Single multiclass SVM trained for nine-class classification. (b) Ensemble of nine binary classifiers (One-vs-Rest), with prediction based on the highest probability score.

Method	Accuracy (%)	Std Dev
SVM	**13.55**	±2.8

(a) One 9-class SVM

Method	Accuracy (%)	Std Dev
SVM	**18.81**	±2.6

(b) Nine OvR binary SVMs

4 Discussion and Conclusion

The ability to predict arousal within 9–15 s purely from users' eye movements positions our approach as a low cost alternative to self-reports, enabling real-time applications in affective computing such as clinical diagnostics and human computer interaction [19].

Among all tested paradigms, the 9-class prediction using the maximum probability from nine one-vs-rest classifiers demonstrates the most statistically meaningful improvement over chance. It achieves an accuracy of 18.81%. This means an improvement of 11.11% over the uniform baseline (i.e., random guessing across nine classes) by a factor of 1.7. This indicates that even in a fine grained, limited data setting the model is able to extract meaningful signal beyond noise. Ternary classification (low, medium, high arousal) follows as the next most informative scheme, reaching accuracies of 52.02% and 47.84% under reduced trial conditions. These results represent improvements by factors of 1.56 and 1.43, respectively over the 33.33% baseline. The drop in accuracy highlights challenges in reliably differentiating between three arousal bands in short viewing durations. Binary classification (low [1–4] vs. high [5–9]) remains the most stable configuration, with accuracies of 72.73% and 72.43%, outperforming the 50% chance level by a factor of approximately 1.45. This scheme proves effective for coarse and rapid emotional assessment. By contrast, our approach does not help at all for the OvR (one-vs-rest) task when each class is evaluated independently. Figure 3 illustrates the skewed distribution of arousal ratings, which cluster around the middle particularly ratings 5 and 6. This imbalance makes the majority class predictor a very strong baseline. The OvR strategy achieves average accuracies of 89.08% and 89.25%, compared to 88.90% for the majority-class predictor, yielding only marginal improvements by a factor of 1.002 and 1.004, respectively. These gains are negligible, highlighting the limited utility of class-wise OvR classifiers in such imbalanced settings.

These findings underscore a clear trade-off between prediction granularity and reliability. While coarse and extreme arousal predictions are feasible within short viewing durations, achieving reliable performance in fine-grained or mid-range categories appears to require either longer exposure, or advanced temporal modeling. While our current approach uses handcrafted features and a classical machine learning model (SVM), future work could apply deep learning to raw eye movement sequences, allowing the model to automatically learn more complex and subtle patterns associated with emotional arousal.

References

1. Al Zaidawi, S.M.K., Prinzler, M.H., Lührs, J., Maneth, S.: An extensive study of user identification via eye movements across multiple datasets. Signal Process. Image Commun. **108**, 116804 (2022)
2. Bayes, T.: Naive bayes classifier. Article Sources and Contributors, pp. 1–9 (1968)
3. Bishop, C.M., Nasrabadi, N.M.: Pattern recognition and machine learning, vol. 4. Springer (2006)
4. Bradley, M.M., Lang, P.J.: Measuring emotion: the self-assessment manikin and the semantic differential. J. Behav. Ther. Exp. Psychiatry **25**(1), 49–59 (1994)
5. Breiman, L.: Random forests. Mach. Learn. **45**(1), 5–32 (2001)
6. Broomhead, D.S., Lowe, D.: Radial basis functions, multi-variable functional interpolation and adaptive networks. Complex Syst. **2**(3), 321–355 (1988)
7. Calvo, R.A., D'Mello, S.: Affect detection: an interdisciplinary review of models, methods, and their applications. IEEE Trans. Affect. Comput. **1**(1), 18–37 (2010). https://doi.org/10.1109/T-AFFC.2010.1
8. Cortes, C., Vapnik, V.: Support-vector networks. Mach. Learn. **20**(3), 273–297 (1995)
9. Dagar, A., Sharma, G.: Eye-tracking-based attention analysis in online learning environments: A systematic review. Educ. Inf. Technol. **27**, 1401–1425 (2022). https://doi.org/10.1007/s10639-021-10641-6
10. George, A., Routray, A.: A score level fusion method for eye movement biometrics. Pattern Recogn. Lett. **82**, 207–215 (2016)
11. Krishnan, S.R., Seelamantula, C.S.: On the selection of optimum savitzky-golay filters. IEEE Trans. Signal Process. **61**(2), 380–391 (2013). https://doi.org/10.1109/TSP.2012.2225051
12. Kulke, L., Atkinson, J., Braddick, O.: Automatic detection of attention shifts in infancy: eye tracking in the fixation shift paradigm. PLoS ONE **10**(12), e0142505 (2015)
13. Kulke, L., Atkinson, J., Braddick, O.: Neural mechanisms of attention become more specialised during infancy: Insights from combined eye tracking and eeg. Dev. Psychobiol. **59**(2), 250–260 (2017)
14. Kulke, L., Ertuğrul, S.: Disengaging attention from pictures with emotional and social content. https://doi.org/10.17605/OSF.IO/DX9YT (2021), preregistration, April 1

15. Lang, P.J., Bradley, M.M., Cuthbert, B.N.: International Affective Picture System (IAPS): Affective ratings of pictures and instruction manual. University of Florida, Gainesville, FL (2008), technical Report A-8
16. Lim, J.Z., Mountstephens, J., Teo, J.: Emotion recognition using eye-tracking: taxonomy, review and current challenges. Sensors **20**(8), 2384 (2020)
17. Lu, Y., Zheng, W.L., Li, B., Lu, B.L.: Combining eye movements and eeg to enhance emotion recognition. In: IJCAI, vol. 15, pp. 1170–1176. Buenos Aires (2015)
18. Marchewka, A., Żurawski, Ł, Jednoróg, K., Grabowska, A.: The nencki affective picture system (naps): introduction to a novel, standardized, wide-range, high-quality, realistic picture database. Behav. Res. Methods **46**(2), 596–610 (2014). https://doi.org/10.3758/s13428-013-0379-1
19. Meyer, P., Hildebrandt, M., Pipa, G., Schuck, N.W.: Assessing the quality of emotion recognition systems: A comprehensive review. Sensors **20**(16), 4559 (2020). https://doi.org/10.3390/s20164559
20. Michałowski, B.M., Droździel, D., Matuszewski, J., Koziejowski, W., Jednoróg, K., Marchewka, A.: Set of fear inducing pictures (sfip): the development and validation in fearful and non-fearful individuals. Behav. Res. Methods (2016). https://doi.org/10.3758/s13428-016-0797-y
21. Pedregosa, F., et al.: Scikit-learn: machine learning in python. J. Mach. Learn. Res. **12**, 2825–2830 (2011)
22. Picard, R.W.: Toward machines that recognize and respond to user emotion. IBM Syst. J. **39**(3.4), 705–719 (2000). https://doi.org/10.1147/sj.393.0705
23. Press, W.H., Teukolsky, S.A.: Savitzky-golay smoothing filters. Comput. Phys. **4**(6), 669–672 (1990)
24. R.-Tavakoli, H., Atyabi, A., Rantanen, A., Laukka, S.J., Nefti-Meziani, S., Heikkilä, J.: Predicting the valence of a scene from observers' eye movements. PloS one **10**(9), e0138198 (2015)
25. Riegel, M., et al.: Characterization of the nencki affective picture system by discrete emotional categories (naps be). Behav. Res. Methods **48**(2), 600–612 (2016). https://doi.org/10.3758/s13428-015-0620-1
26. Salvucci, D.D., Goldberg, J.H.: Identifying fixations and saccades in eye-tracking protocols. In: Proceedings of the 2000 Symposium on Eye Tracking Research & Applications, pp. 71–78 (2000)
27. Savitzky, A., Golay, M.J.: Smoothing and differentiation of data by simplified least squares procedures. Anal. Chem. **36**(8), 1627–1639 (1964). https://doi.org/10.1021/ac60214a047
28. Schafer, R.W.: What is a savitzky-golay filter?[lecture notes]. IEEE Signal Process. Mag. **28**(4), 111–117 (2011)
29. Skaramagkas, V., et al.: esee-d: emotional state estimation based on eye-tracking dataset. Brain Sci. **13**(4), 589 (2023)
30. Tarnowski, P., Kołodziej, M., Majkowski, A., Rak, R.J.: Eye-tracking analysis for emotion recognition. Comput. Intell. Neurosci. **2020**(1), 2909267 (2020)
31. Vallabh Varsha Haria, R., Abed, A.E., Maneth, S.: User identification via free roaming eye tracking data. In: International Conference on Human-Computer Interaction, pp. 352–364. Springer (2024)
32. Wakeland-Hart, C., Aly, M.: Predicting image memorability from evoked feelings. PsyArXiv (2023). https://doi.org/10.31234/osf.io/grxdz, preprint
33. Wang, Y., Lv, Z., Zheng, Y.: Automatic emotion perception using eye movement information for e-healthcare systems. Sensors **18**(9), 2826 (2018)

34. Watson, D., Clark, L.A.: The panas-x: Manual for the positive and negative affect schedule-expanded form (1994)
35. Wierzba, M., et al.: Erotic subset for the nencki affective picture system (naps ero): cross-sexual comparison study. Front. Psychol. textbf6, 1336 (2015). https://doi.org/10.3389/fpsyg.2015.01336
36. Willenbockel, V., Sadr, J., Fiset, D., Horne, G.O., Gosselin, F., Tanaka, J.W.: Controlling low-level image properties: The shine toolbox. Behav. Res. Methods **42**(3), 671–684 (2010)
37. Zhao, L.M., Li, R., Zheng, W.L., Lu, B.L.: Classification of five emotions from eeg and eye movement signals: complementary representation properties. In: 2019 9th International IEEE/EMBS Conference on Neural Engineering (NER), pp. 611–614. IEEE (2019)

Evaluating Developers' Knowledge of Usability Guidelines: An Empirical Study on Stack Overflow

Hans Djalali[1]([⊠]), Wajdi Aljedaani[1], Asmaa Mansour Alghamdi[2], Stephanie Ludi[1], and Marcelo Medeiros Eler[3]

[1] University of North Texas, Denton, TX, USA
`hamedjalali@my.unt.edu, wajdi.j1@gmail.com, Stephanie.Ludi@unt.edu`
[2] Jazan University, Jizan, Saudi Arabia
`amalghamdi@jazanu.edu.sa`
[3] University of São Paulo, São Paulo, Brazil
`marceloeler@usp.br`

Abstract. Nielsen's 10 usability heuristics, established nearly three decades ago, continue to be taught as foundational principles in software development. However, it remains unclear whether these heuristics effectively address modern usability challenges and to what extent developers actively apply them. We analyzed 894 Stack Overflow posts to evaluate the effectiveness of these heuristics in identifying modern usability issues and examining developers' explicit use of formal guidelines. Our analysis revealed that while Nielsen's heuristics successfully categorized 75.1% of usability discussions, only 2.8% of posts explicitly referenced any usability guidelines, with platform-specific guidelines being more common than theoretical frameworks. In contrast, a comparative analysis with accessibility discussions showed 27.4% explicitly referenced standards like WCAG and ARIA. This stark disparity suggests that while Nielsen's heuristics remain conceptually relevant for understanding usability issues, a significant gap exists between theoretical frameworks and practical developer discourse, with developers tending to gravitate toward technology-specific rather than theoretical guidance.

Keywords: Usability · Usability Heuristics · Evaluation · Stack Overflow · Empirical Analysis

1 Introduction

Human-computer interaction has undergone significant evolution due to the rapid advancement of technology. These changes have made usability and accessibility essential factors in creating inclusive digital experiences. Jakob Nielsen's ten usability heuristics, established in 1994 [25], have served as foundational guidelines in both academic programs and professional practices [20]. These heuristics are: (1) Visibility of system status, (2) Match between system and

© The Author(s), under exclusive license to Springer Nature Switzerland AG 2026
S. Sundarakannan and O. Knorpp (Eds.): HCII 2025, CCIS 2772, pp. 341–351, 2026.
https://doi.org/10.1007/978-3-032-12767-9_36

real world, (3) User control and freedom, (4) Consistency and standards, (5) Error prevention, (6) Recognition rather than recall, (7) Flexibility and efficiency of use, (8) Aesthetic and minimalist design, (9) Help users recognize, diagnose, and recover from errors, and (10) Help and documentation. Accessibility standards, such as the Web Content Accessibility Guidelines (WCAG), help developers make their digital content accessible to users with disabilities. Despite the value of these guidelines and standards, there is a lack of empirical studies examining their practical application by developers in modern software development cycles.

Usability evaluation is a cost-effective method for improving user experience; however, developers face significant challenges when implementing it in real-world scenarios [17]. Most existing research has focused on usability evaluation from the end-users' perspective, primarily through reviews and feedback mechanisms [15,23], resulting in a considerable research gap regarding how software developers perceive, discuss, and address usability concerns in comparison to accessibility issues. This comparison is critical because while both usability and accessibility aim to improve user experience, they differ in key ways: accessibility often has legal mandates and provides concrete, testable criteria, whereas usability guidelines tend to be more subjective and interpretive. Understanding how these differences influence developer discussions can inform better educational approaches and tool development. This study aims to fill the gap by systematically analyzing developers' real-world experiences as reflected in technical discussions.

We conducted a comprehensive analysis of Stack Overflow[1] posts to examine how developers state and resolve usability and accessibility challenges. We extracted 894 Stack Overflow posts tagged with "usability" or "usability-testing" spanning from September 2008 to November 2024. To create a comparative framework, we compared our findings with an analysis of 5,092 accessibility-related posts from Alghamdi et al. [3–5]. This study complements existing research by examining developer discussions about accessibility using a similar Stack Overflow methodology, enabling us to compare how developers engage with these two related yet distinct aspects of software quality: usability and accessibility. We investigate the following research questions through a thorough manual labeling process:

RQ1: To what extent are Nielsen's usability heuristics effective for identifying modern usability issues discussed by developers on Stack Overflow?

To answer this question, we investigate the relationship between Jakob Nielsen's Usability Heuristics and usability issues discussed on Stack Overflow posts. We focus on identifying patterns in how developers address usability challenges and discuss specific usability issues. Answering this question will allow us

---

[1] Stack Overflow represents one of the most prominent online question-and-answer platforms where software developers exchange knowledge regarding programming-related challenges.

to understand to what extent these heuristics are associated with the modern usability issues discussed by developers.

RQ2: How frequently do developers explicitly reference established guidelines in usability discussions?

This research question examines whether developers are aware of and explicitly mention formal usability guidelines and standards in their technical discussions, and to what extent these guidelines are being used by developers. We also compared the usage of accessibility guidelines with usability to understand how developers approach these concepts.

The primary contributions of this study are: (1) to provide empirical evidence regarding the continued relevance of Nielsen's decades-old heuristics in addressing contemporary usability challenges; (2) to quantify the distinct patterns in how developers explicitly engage with established guidelines across usability and accessibility domains; and (3) to identify predominant usability concerns among developers and reveal gaps between theoretical frameworks and practical implementation, offering insights that can inform targeted developer education and tool design.

2   Related Work

Research into software usability and accessibility encompasses a range of methodologies and data sources. Foundational work includes the development and analysis of usability heuristics [25], with numerous studies focusing on their application in evaluation frameworks and the use of user testing procedures [19,29]. Another stream of research identifies usability concerns by analyzing user-generated content, primarily user reviews from app stores or feedback platforms. For instance, studies have mined user reviews to detect usability issues [8,22,30,34]. Hedegaard and Simonsen [18] analyzed a large corpus of reviews to identify aspects such as memorability and efficiency. Similarly, Diniz et al. [15] examined mobile user reviews for complaints related to Nielsen's usability heuristics. Complementary research has investigated accessibility, focusing on automatic detection methods or adherence to standards [10,12]. Additionally, it has explored the specific usability and accessibility experiences of diverse user groups, such as deaf and hard-of-hearing users in educational contexts [6,7,9].

While these studies provide valuable insights from end-user perspectives or through evaluative frameworks, there is a limited amount of research examining how developers themselves discuss and implement usability in practice. Online developer communities, particularly Stack Overflow, serve as rich sources for such investigations. Unlike prior work centered on user reviews [15], issue reports in open-source systems [31], or specific contexts such as mobile usability from a user's standpoint [26], our study focuses on the discourse of software developers within Stack Overflow. We specifically analyze these discussions to assess the continued applicability of Nielsen's usability heuristics to contemporary problems and to compare developer engagement with formal usability frameworks versus established accessibility standards.

Studies analyzing developer discussions on accessibility within platforms like Stack Overflow have indicated that developers do reference guidelines such as WCAG and ARIA [10,11]. However, to our knowledge, there is limited empirical research that directly compares the extent to which developers explicitly reference established usability guidelines in contrast to accessibility standards in their practical discussions. This study addresses this gap by systematically examining developers' posts on Stack Overflow to evaluate whether Nielsen's heuristics remain relevant for modern web usability challenges and to compare how developers reference formal guidelines in usability versus accessibility discussions.

3   Study Design

In our study, we used a systematic content analysis methodology, as described by Tashakkori et al. [33]. We conduct a manual review and labeling of a statistically significant sample of usability posts. Figure 1 provides an overview of

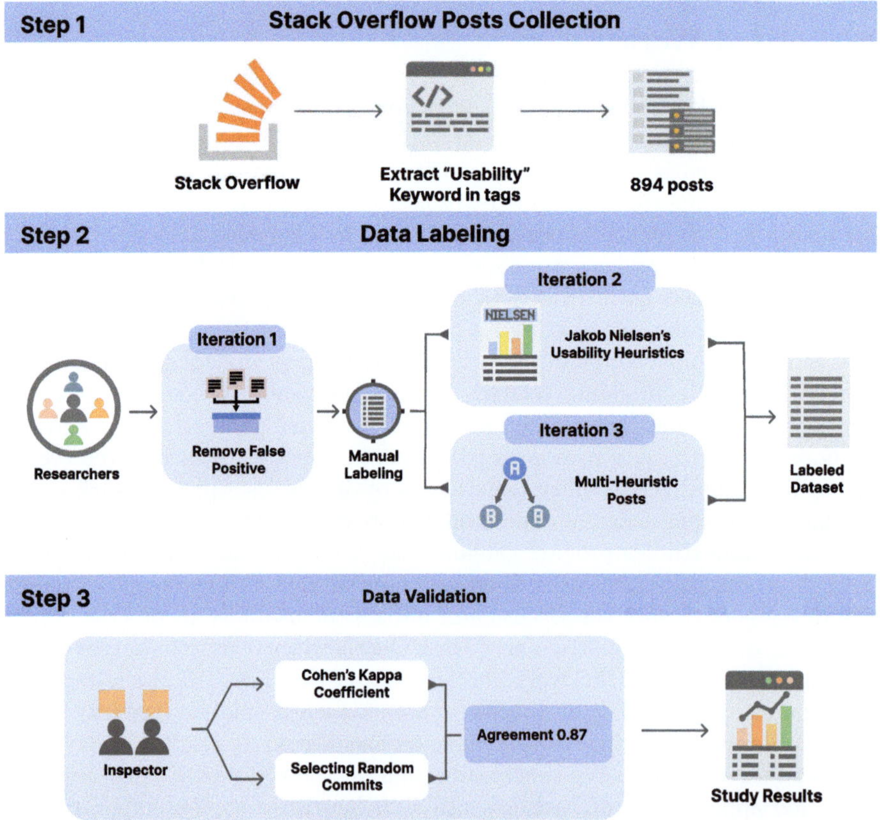

Fig. 1. Study overview.

the methodology used in our study, which comprises three key activities: (1) obtaining a comprehensive and representative Stack Overflow dataset of usability posts, (2) identifying and extracting usability posts, and (3) analyzing the usability posts, including their textual content and metadata. We extract all usability posts that are directly tagged as usability by users. In the following subsections, we provide a detailed description of the methodology and the activities involved.

3.1 Data Collection

Our initial search criteria for tags were any tag that included 'usability', such as 'usability', 'usability-testing', as well as 'Usability-Evaluation', 'Heuristic-Evaluation', and 'Interface-Evaluation'. We utilized the Stack Exchange Data Explorer tool[2] to query posts from Stack Overflow. We observed that many tags, such as 'Usability-Evaluation', 'Heuristic-Evaluation', and 'Interface-Evaluation', had no posts. Also, tags 'reusability' and 'focusability' were returned in the 'usability' query; therefore, we excluded them from our analysis. Our search yielded a set of 894 posts spanning from September 2008, when Stack Overflow was founded, to November 2024, the date we collected the data. Specifically, we found 860 posts related to usability and 34 posts related to usability testing (Table 1).

Table 1. Summary of collected data.

Tags	Number of posts collected	Iteration 1 (classified)	Iteration 2 (classified)	Number of multi-heuristic posts	Data to review
Usability-testing	34	23	3	0	3
Usability	860	763	669	125	669
Total	**894**	**786**	**672**	**125**	**672**

3.2 Data Labeling

Our analysis involved three iterations, which have been previously described in content analysis methods [24,27]. Two researchers with expertise in human-computer interaction (HCI) participated in the analysis. The researchers labeled a total of 894 posts using the following approach:

Iteration 1. In the first iteration of our manual analysis, the researchers separately analyzed 894 posts from Stack Overflow to identify false positives and eliminate non-usability posts. False positives occur when a post is identified as usability-related but is not actually related to usability. This can lead to inaccurate analyses and conclusions. To eliminate false positives, the researchers read through each post and aimed to identify any non-usability posts labeled as usability issues. In this iteration, 108 posts were labeled as false positives.

---

[2] https://data.stackexchange.com/stackoverflow/query/new.

Iteration 2. In this iteration, the aim was to categorize the 786 usability posts that were identified in the first iteration based on Jakob Nielsen's ten usability heuristics. To ensure consistency and accuracy in classification, the researchers employed a set of criteria based on Jakob Nielsen's ten usability heuristics, as defined in [25] and further explained on the Nielsen Norman Group website. After researchers completed the labeling, they discussed the categorizing process to identify any issues that occurred during this iteration. They identified several posts that seemed to be usability posts but were determined to be false positives upon closer examination. The researchers decided to eliminate these false positives, which resulted in a total of 114 reviews being excluded from the final categorization process. The final dataset was a total of 672 usability posts, which were categorized based on Jakob Nielsen's ten usability heuristics.

Iteration 3. In the third iteration, following the classification of 672 usability posts, we focused on posts that related to multiple usability heuristics. We identified 125 posts in this category, with 117 related to two heuristics and 8 related to three. This stage was crucial for preparing for future analyses. By identifying posts that incorporate multiple heuristics, we aimed to acknowledge their presence and establish the basis for analyzing their interrelations in the study results.

Additional Validation: In order to ensure the validity and reliability of the classification process conducted by the researchers, additional validation procedures were used. Following the guidance of Aljedaani et al. [11], a 9% sample (80 out of 894 posts) of the entire dataset was randomly selected for analysis by an auxiliary expert (Inspector). The sample size was determined to meet a confidence level of 95% and a confidence interval of 6. The selected sample was not disclosed to the researchers prior to the analysis. After the labeling process was completed, a comparison was made between the labeled reviews from the original dataset and those from the new dataset to determine the level of agreement between the two datasets. The inter-rater agreement level between the two datasets was calculated using Cohen's Kappa Coefficient [13]. The resulting agreement level was found to be 0.87, which is considered almost *perfect agreement,* as noted by Fleiss et al. [16] for levels between (i.e., 0.811.00).

3.3 Framework Reference Analysis

Following the heuristic classification, we conducted a separate analysis of all 672 usability posts to address our second research question regarding how developers explicitly reference established guidelines. We examined the usability posts for mentions of formal usability guidelines, including Nielsen's heuristics, Shneiderman's eight golden rules, and ISO standards. We specifically looked for direct references to these guidelines by name or clear adoption of their terminology. For comparative analysis with accessibility standards references, we used the quantitative findings from Alghamdi et al. [4], specifically their data on the frequency of explicit accessibility standard references (WCAG, ARIA) in 5,092 Stack Overflow posts. This allowed us to compare reference rates between usability and accessibility domains.

4   Study Results

This section presents and discusses the findings of our study.

RQ1: To what extent are Nielsen's usability heuristics effective for identifying modern usability issues discussed by developers on Stack Overflow?

Results. Our analysis of 894 Stack Overflow posts showed that 672 posts (75.1%) could be categorized using at least one of Nielsen's ten usability heuristics. Figure 2 presents the distribution of posts across each heuristic. Heuristic 7 (Flexibility and efficiency of use) was identified in 140 posts (20.8%), followed by Heuristic 1 (Visibility of system status) with 128 posts (19.0%), Heuristic 5 (Error prevention) with 123 posts (18.3%), and Heuristic 4 (Consistency and standards) with 117 posts (17.4%). We identified 125 posts (18.6%) that were categorized with multiple heuristics, indicating developers often face interconnected usability challenges.

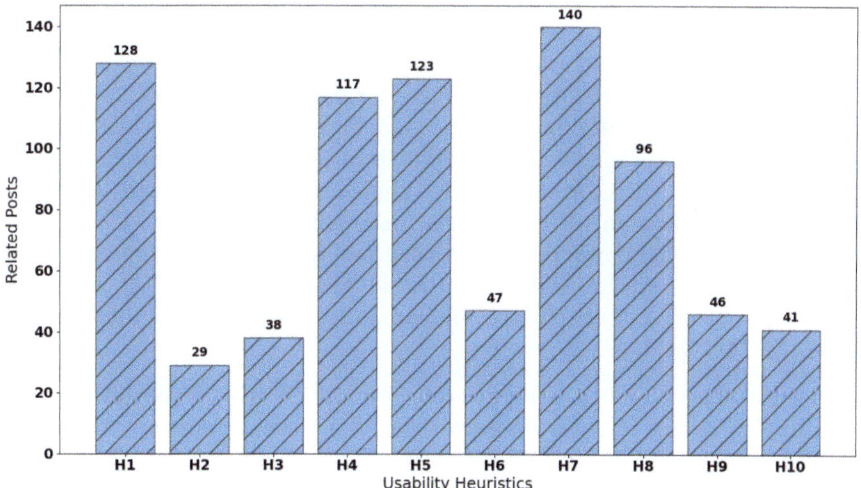

Fig. 2. Distribution of posts by usability heuristic.

Discussion. The high categorization rate (75.1%) demonstrates that Nielsen's heuristics remain effective for identifying modern usability issues despite being established nearly three decades ago. This finding is significant as it provides empirical evidence for the lasting relevance of these principles in contemporary software development. The distribution pattern reveals important insights into the evolution of usability concerns. While all heuristics remain applicable, the strong emphasis on flexibility, visibility, error prevention, and consistency reflects how modern development prioritizes certain aspects of the user experience.

The less frequent identification of Heuristics 2 and 3 contrasts with previous research by Diniz et al. [15], who found Heuristic 2 was more prominent in user reviews. This difference suggests a potential disconnect between user and developer perspectives on usability priorities that merits further investigation. This difference suggests that while users struggle with system-world mapping (H2) and desire more control (H3), developers may be focusing more on technical implementation aspects rather than these conceptual design principles. Additionally, the substantial proportion of posts (18.6%) requiring multiple heuristics to categorize indicates that modern usability challenges increasingly cross traditional categorical boundaries, suggesting that integrated approaches to usability evaluation may be more effective than isolated heuristic application.

RQ2: How frequently do developers explicitly reference established guidelines in usability discussions compared to accessibility discussions?

Results. In our examination of 672 usability posts, we found that only 19 posts (2.8%) explicitly referenced usability guidelines or standards. Among these references, Nielsen's heuristics or related work appeared in 9 posts (including 5 direct mentions of "Nielsen's 10 heuristics"), platform-specific guidelines (Android, BlackBerry, Windows, Kinect) were mentioned in 6 posts, and other resources, including books and ISO standards, appeared in 4 posts. Notably, despite Nielsen's heuristics being effective for categorizing 75.1% of the posts, developers rarely explicitly named these guidelines in their discussions. While we found 9 posts mentioning Nielsen's work within post content, searches for posts specifically tagged with formal usability guideline names such as Nielsen's Ten Heuristics, Shneiderman's Eight Golden Rules [32], or ISO 9241-11 [1] returned no results, indicating developers don't use these frameworks as organizing tags. In contrast, the study by Alghamdi et al. [4] found that 27.4% of accessibility posts (1396 out of 5,092) explicitly referenced established accessibility standards such as WCAG.

Discussion. Nielsen's heuristics are conceptually effective for identifying modern usability issues, but the findings show that developers rarely frame their questions in terms of these guidelines. While not significant, 27.4% of accessibility posts show developers referencing accessibility standards, indicating more awareness and practical application of these standards compared to usability. The predominance of platform-specific guidelines (6 out of 19 references) suggests that developers may be more familiar with practical implementation guidelines tied to specific technologies rather than abstract usability principles. There are several reasons for the lack of usability guidelines compared to accessibility guidelines. Unlike accessibility, which often has legal requirements, such as Section 508, usability does not have similar legal mandates [21]. Additionally, accessibility standards provide concrete, testable criteria, whereas usability heuristics tend to be more subjective [28]. The difference between usability and accessibility guideline references reveals a notable disparity in how developers approach these related topics in their discussions. While our study clearly demonstrates that this gap exists, further study is needed to determine the specific reasons and implications of this difference. The contrast between the high applicability of Nielsen's heuristics (75.1%) and their complete absence in questions suggests potential opportunities for investigating developer awareness of established usability guidelines and how they might be better integrated into development practices. This gap presents an opportunity for the HCI community to better bridge theoretical guidelines with practical development contexts, perhaps through tools that automatically map code issues to relevant heuristics or educational initiatives that connect guidelines to real-world implementation challenges.

5   Conclusion and Future Work

We demonstrated that Jakob Nielsen's ten usability heuristics remain highly effective in identifying modern usability issues, successfully categorizing 75.1% of developer discussions on Stack Overflow. The most frequently identified issues related to flexibility and efficiency (H7), system visibility (H1), and error prevention (H5), with 18.6% of posts addressing multiple heuristics simultaneously. We discovered a significant disparity between how developers engage with usability versus accessibility guidelines: only 2.8% of usability posts explicitly referenced established guidelines, while 27.4% of accessibility posts referenced standards such as WCAG and ARIA. Among the few usability references, platform-specific guidelines were more common than theoretical frameworks, suggesting that developers tend to gravitate toward practical, technology-specific resources.

6   Ethical Considerations

The study involved only secondary analysis of Stack Overflow posts released in the public Creative-Commons data dump [14]. Because the dataset is publicly available and contains no personally identifiable private information, the work does not constitute human-subjects research and is exempt under 45 CFR 46.101(b)(4) [2]. Consequently, Institutional Review Board (IRB) approval was not required.

References

1. Iso 9241-11: Ergonomic requirements for office work with visual display terminals (vdts) - part 11: Guidance on usability (1998)
2. Protection of human subjects. 45 CFR 46.102 (2018). https://www.hhs.gov/ohrp/regulations-and-policy/regulations/45-cfr-46/index.html

3. Alghamdi, A.M., Aljedaani, W., Eler, M.M., Ludi, S.: Accessibility guidelines and standards: Analyzing stack overflow posts. In: Proceedings of the 21st International Web for All Conference, pp. 118–122 (2024)
4. Alghamdi, A.M., Aljedaani, W., Jalali, H., Ludi, S., Eler, M.M.: Understanding developer challenges and trends in web accessibility: a stack overflow analysis. Univ. Access Inf. Soc. (2024)
5. Alghamdi, A.M., Aljedaani, W., Ludi, S., Javed, Y.: Automating accessibility compliance: Leveraging machine learning to analyze developer challenges with wcag guidelines. In: 2025 8th International Conference on Data Science and Machine Learning Applications (CDMA), pp. 61–66. IEEE (2025)
6. Aljedaani, W., Aljedaani, M., AlOmar, E.A., Mkaouer, M.W., Ludi, S., Khalaf, Y.B.: I cannot see you-the perspectives of deaf students to online learning during covid-19 pandemic: Saudi Arabia case study. Educ. Sci. **11**(11), 712 (2021)
7. Aljedaani, W., Aljedaani, M., Mkaouer, M.W., Ludi, S.: Teachers perspectives on transition to online teaching deaf and hard-of-hearing students during the covid-19 pandemic: a case study. In: Proceedings of the 16th Innovations in Software Engineering Conference, pp. 1–10 (2023)
8. Aljedaani, W., Eler, M.M., Keeland, L.E., Jalali, H., Al-Raddah, K., Mkaouer, M.W.: Accessible gaming through better captions: A study on captions preferences and inclusivity of deaf and hard-of-hearing players. In: Proceedings of the 21st International Web for All Conference, pp. 75–86 (2024)
9. Aljedaani, W., Krasniqi, R., Aljedaani, S., Mkaouer, M.W., Ludi, S., Al-Raddah, K.: If online learning works for you, what about deaf students? emerging challenges of online learning for deaf and hearing-impaired students during covid-19: a literature review. Universal access in the information society, pp. 1–20 (2022)
10. Aljedaani, W., Mkaouer, M.W., Ludi, S., Javed, Y.: Automatic classification of accessibility user reviews in android apps. In: 2022 7th International Conference on Data Science and Machine Learning Applications (CDMA), pp. 133–138. IEEE (2022)
11. Aljedaani, W., Mkaouer, M.W., Ludi, S., Ouni, A., Jenhani, I.: On the identification of accessibility bug reports in open source systems. In: Proceedings of the 19th International Web for All Conference. pp. 1–11 (2022)
12. AlOmar, E.A., Aljedaani, W., Tamjeed, M., Mkaouer, M.W., El-Glaly, Y.N.: Finding the needle in a haystack: On the automatic identification of accessibility user reviews. In: Proceedings of the 2021 CHI Conference on Human Factors in Computing Systems, pp. 1–15 (2021)
13. Cohen, J.: A coefficient of agreement for nominal scales. Educ. Psychol. Measur. **20**(1), 37–46 (1960)
14. Commons, C.: Creative commons attribution-sharealike 4.0 international license. Creative Commons (2023). https://creativecommons.org/licenses/by-sa/4.0/
15. Diniz, L.d.N., de Souza Filho, J.C., Carvalho, R.M.: Can user reviews indicate usability heuristic issues? In: CHI Conference on Human Factors in Computing Systems Extended Abstracts, pp. 1–6 (2022)
16. Fleiss, J.L., Levin, B., Paik, M.C., et al.: The measurement of interrater agreement. Stat. Methods Rates Proportions **2**(212–236), 22–23 (1981)
17. Gonzalez-Holland, E., Whitmer, D., Moralez, L., Mouloua, M.: Examination of the use of nielsen's 10 usability heuristics & outlooks for the future. In: Proceedings of the Human Factors and Ergonomics Society Annual Meeting, vol. 61, pp. 1472–1475. SAGE Publications Sage CA, Los Angeles, CA (2017)

18. Hedegaard, S., Simonsen, J.G.: Extracting usability and user experience information from online user reviews. In: Proceedings of the SIGCHI Conference on Human Factors in Computing Systems, CHI '13, pp. 2089–2098. Association for Computing Machinery, New York (2013). https://doi.org/10.1145/2470654.2481286
19. Hermawati, S., Lawson, G.: Establishing usability heuristics for heuristics evaluation in a specific domain: Is there a consensus? Appl. Ergon. **56**, 34–51 (2016)
20. Jimenez, C., Lozada, P., Rosas, P.: Usability heuristics: a systematic review. In: 2016 IEEE 11th Colombian Computing Conference (CCC), pp. 1–8 (2016). https://doi.org/10.1109/ColumbianCC.2016.7750805
21. Lazar, J., Goldstein, D., Taylor, A.: Ensuring Digital Accessibility Through Process and Policy. Morgan Kaufmann, Waltham (2015)
22. Lu, J., Schmidt, M., Lee, M., Huang, R.: Usability research in educational technology: A state-of-the-art systematic review. Educational technology research and development, pp. 1–42 (2022)
23. Morgan, M., Ludi, S., Cook, L., Warren, A.: Impact of usability heuristics on user satisfaction among coding apps for children. In: 2023 IEEE Symposium on Visual Languages and Human-Centric Computing (VL/HCC), pp. 252–254 (2023)
24. Nicolai, M., Pascarella, L., Palomba, F., Bacchelli, A.: Healthcare android apps: a tale of the customers' perspective. In: Proceedings of the 3rd ACM SIGSOFT International Workshop on App Market Analytics, pp. 33–39 (2019)
25. Nielsen, J.: Enhancing the explanatory power of usability heuristics. In: Proceedings of the ACM CHI'94 Conference on Human Factors in Computing Systems, pp. 152–158 (1994)
26. Pachabotla, L.S., Konka, C.: Comparative study of mobile payment apps: Google pay and paypal using nielsen's usability heuristics (2022)
27. Pascarella, L., Spadini, D., Palomba, F., Bruntink, M., Bacchelli, A.: Information needs in contemporary code review. In: Proceedings of the ACM on Human-Computer Interaction 2(CSCW), pp. 1–27 (2018)
28. Petrie, H., Bevan, N.: The evaluation of accessibility, usability, and user experience. In: Stephanidis, C. (ed.) The Universal Access Handbook, pp. 1–16. CRC Press (2009)
29. Quiñones, D., Rusu, C., Rusu, V.: A methodology to develop usability/user experience heuristics. Comput. Stand. Interfaces **59**, 109–129 (2018)
30. Reddy, H.B.S., Reddy, R.R.S., Jonnalagadda, R., Singh, P., Gogineni, A.: Usability evaluation of an unpopular restaurant recommender web application zomato. Asian J. Res. Comput. Sci. **13**(4), 12–33 (2022)
31. Sanei, A., Cheng, J.: Characterizing usability issue discussions in oss projects. arXiv preprint arXiv:2308.09870 (2023)
32. Shneiderman, B.: Designing the User Interface: Strategies for Effective Human-Computer Interaction. Addison-Wesley (1992)
33. Tashakkori, A., Teddlie, C., Teddlie, C.B.: Mixed methodology: Combining qualitative and quantitative approaches, vol. 46. sage (1998)
34. Weichbroth, P.: Usability of mobile applications: a systematic literature study. Ieee Access **8**, 55563–55577 (2020)

Recysack: Text-messaging System for Waste Pickers in Iran

Sahar Kourangbeheshti[(✉)] [iD]

Independent Researcher, Tehran, Iran
saharkb22@gmail.com

Abstract. Informal waste pickers play a crucial role in urban sustainability, yet they lack the needed access to formal systems or digital tools, and they often work in marginalized, unsafe conditions. Empowering waste pickers located in Iran can be achieved through the easing of waste collection, storage, sale, and payment via a low-tech, SMS-based system. We developed and tested RecySack, a low-tech SMS platform for improving waste pickers' working conditions, supported by user-centered research.

RecySack supports direct buyer connections, price transparency, safer working conditions, and economic stability while promoting urban environmental goals and inclusivity.

Keywords: Waste Pickers · Text-messaging System · Inclusive Design

1 Introduction

Globally, informal waste pickers manage 50–80% of urban waste [7, 8], playing a major role in sustainable cities. Still, many are excluded from formal municipal programs [1, 4], facing harsh working conditions and social marginalization [2]. In Tehran, informal waste pickers, especially Afghan migrants, are exploited.

For many in Tehran, collecting recyclables is a survival strategy. Yet unstable prices, poor access to markets, and lack of supporting tech make the work insecure [11]. A low-tech mobile solution could reduce these barriers, stabilize income, and connect waste pickers to a fairer market by addressing these questions:

Social Perspective:

1. What challenges do waste pickers encounter, and how can we honor their autonomy?
2. How can collection systems be organized to improve income and safety?

Technology Perspective:

1. How is price transparency and transactions enabled by way of mobile systems?
2. Which of the services (e.g., tracking, alerts, payments) are most helpful to consider?

Environmental Perspective:

1. Can urban sustainability be increased by technology with regard to waste pickers' contributions?

© The Author(s), under exclusive license to Springer Nature Switzerland AG 2026
S. Sundarakannan and O. Knorpp (Eds.): HCII 2025, CCIS 2772, pp. 352–362, 2026.
https://doi.org/10.1007/978-3-032-12767-9_37

2 Related Work

In this section, we will overview of the research related to mobile phones and marginalized users. We summarize past research that reinforces the importance of digital inclusion among low-income communities and how technologies have been used and evaluated toward this goal.

2.1 Technology Usage and Low-Income Users

Systemic barriers obstruct access by marginalized users to digital technologies. Sambasivan et al. [12] found that shared devices are indeed used, personalization is lacking, as well as intermediaries are often relied on as being key challenges. Katz and Gonzalez [6] found that collective strategies that are shaped by infrastructure gaps and by limited digital literacy are often depended on by low-income families.

2.2 Waste Pickers and Digital Waste Management

Mobile technologies offer some inclusion and a degree of efficiency in some waste systems. However, most of the tools are geared toward municipal tracking or citizen reporting [3, 5, 10]. Mavropoulos et al. [9] and Suruliraj et al. [13] classify waste apps into several informational, functional, and participatory types. However, few of these kinds of apps are tailored well to all of the realities of informal waste pickers.

3 System Design

Waste pickers collect waste daily without recognition and often in an unsafe environment.
    Research indicates that there is little communication between collectors and waste producers(businesses), as intermediaries tend to keep them apart.
    We designed a system with five parts (Appendix):

1. Collecting: Connecting with businesses to receive recyclable materials.
2. Storing: Using designated lockers to keep waste securely and avoid carrying heavy loads.
3. Selling: Providing current prices, buyer offers, and sales reports.
4. Payment: Offering flexible options including cash, store vouchers, or bank transfers.
5. Health and Safety: Providing hygiene reminders, protective gear, and a system for reporting hazardous waste.

3.1 Participants

We recruited 30 waste pickers, 10 businesses, and 5 recycling firms in Isfahan, Iran, between October and November 2024. This study follows a user-centered design approach, combining field research, participatory design, and experimental evaluation. Participants gave informed consent, with support for low-literacy users and strict data privacy protections. Also, those who agreed to be in this study received a gift card at the end of the study.

3.2 Method

We will describe our study method in three phases (Table 1).

Table 1. Research tools used in each phase.

	Pre-study	Study	Follow-up
Waste pickers	Interviews on pricing, tech use, routines	Participatory design (card sorting, feedback on prototypes)	Interviews on system use, privacy, health & safety 1. Material pickup features & clarity 2. Lockers, payments, buyer comparisons, privacy concerns 3. Health tips, hazard alerts, more privacy controls
Businesses	Surveys on waste production, process	Feedback on accessibility and communication	Interviews on system efficiency
Recycling firm	Interviews on buying practices and pricing	Feedback on buyer side design & value	Interviews on system efficiency 1. Safety features 2. Pricing

4 Findings

Participants preferred dignity, travel reduction, and income improvement. Lockers and price transparency were particularly valued. SMS language needed to be short, clear, and repeatable. Human contact, along with repeated experience, did increase trust within the system.

5 Discussion

Recysack, a low-tech mobile system, can support informal labor by providing Economic benefits and reducing exploitation. The system enhanced dignity and autonomy. Future iterations could include savings options and collective bargaining.

6 Ethical Considerations

Since Participants were vulnerable, consent was verbally given, and personal identifiers were not stored. Privacy and autonomy were both given priority. The legal and social risks for undocumented workers were considered throughout the research.

7 Conclusion

RecySack is an SMS-based system that improved the efficiency and earnings of informal waste pickers in Iran. This model can be adapted to other contexts with informal labor in similar contexts.

Appendix

See Figs. 1, 2, 3, 4, 5, and 6

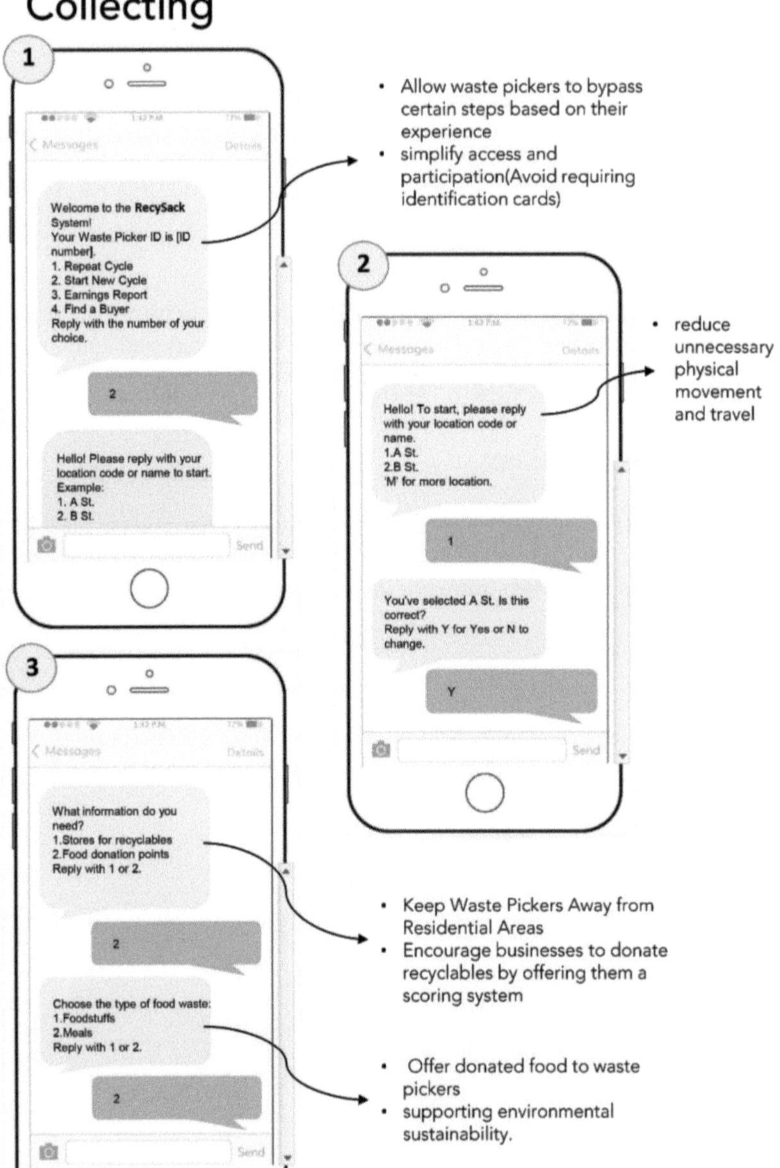

Fig. 1. Recysack overview

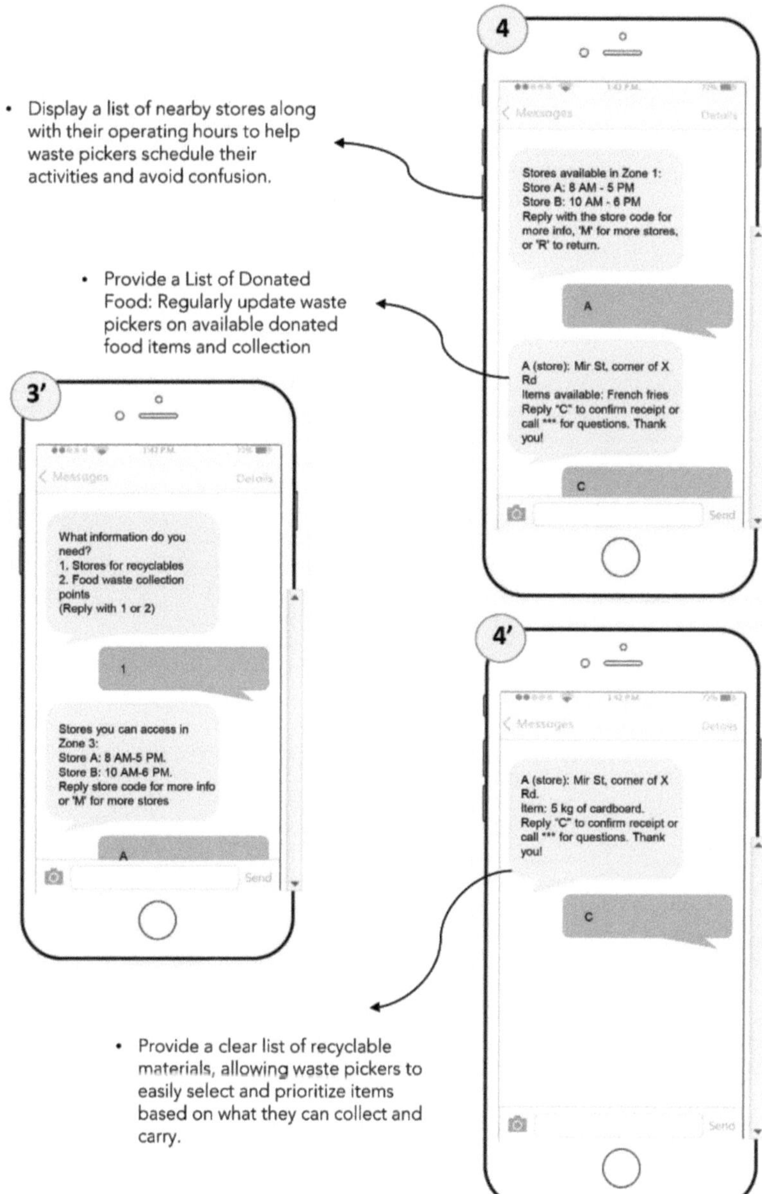

Fig. 2. Recysack overview

Storing

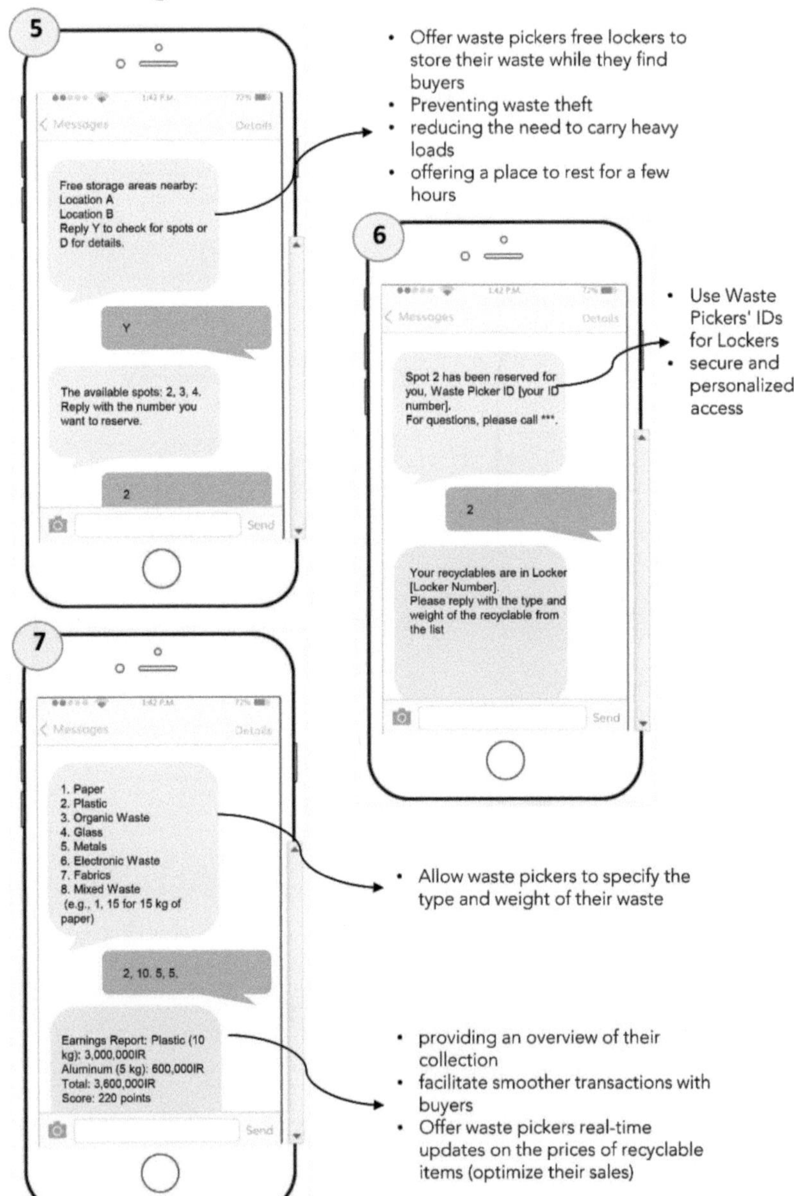

Fig. 3. Recysack overview

Selling

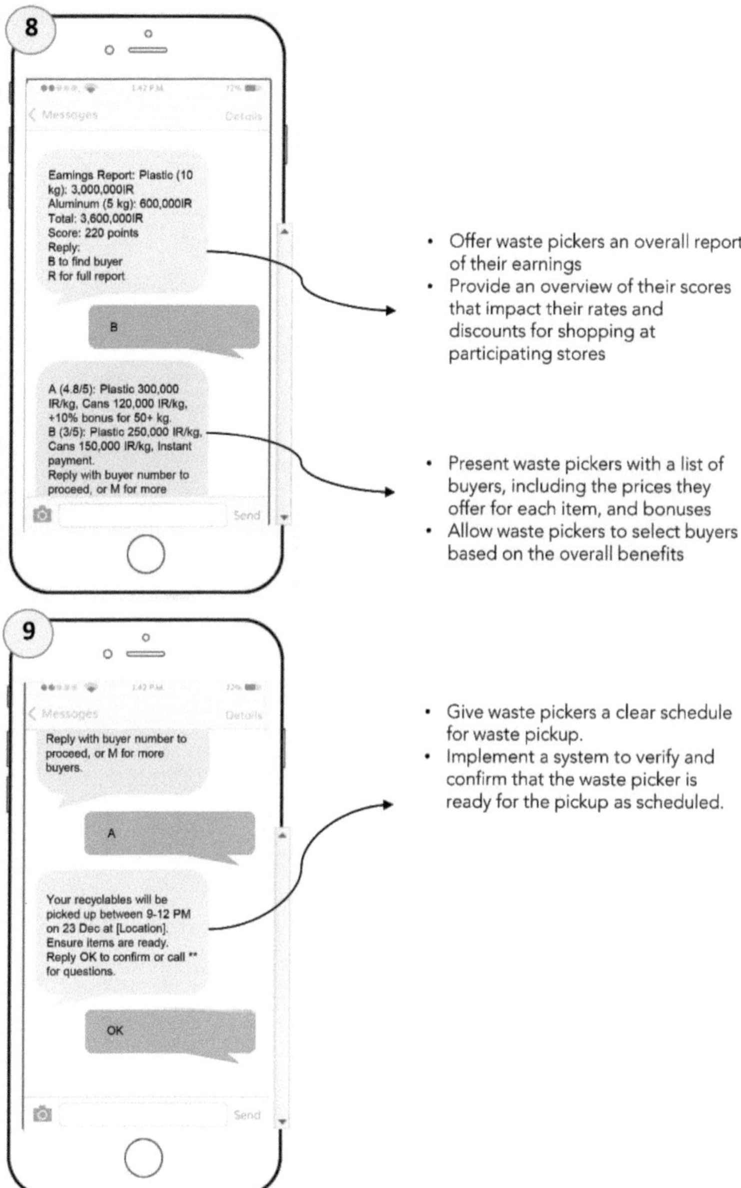

Fig. 4. Recysack overview

Payment

- Provide payment options for those without bank accounts due to identification issues (e.g., Afghan immigrants) and other alternative methods suited to their needs.

- Ensure waste pickers are informed about the final steps of the money transfer
- provide an option to update their account number if needed.

- Final transaction report

- Provide an option for waste pickers to create digital wallets, contingent on establishing the necessary infrastructure.

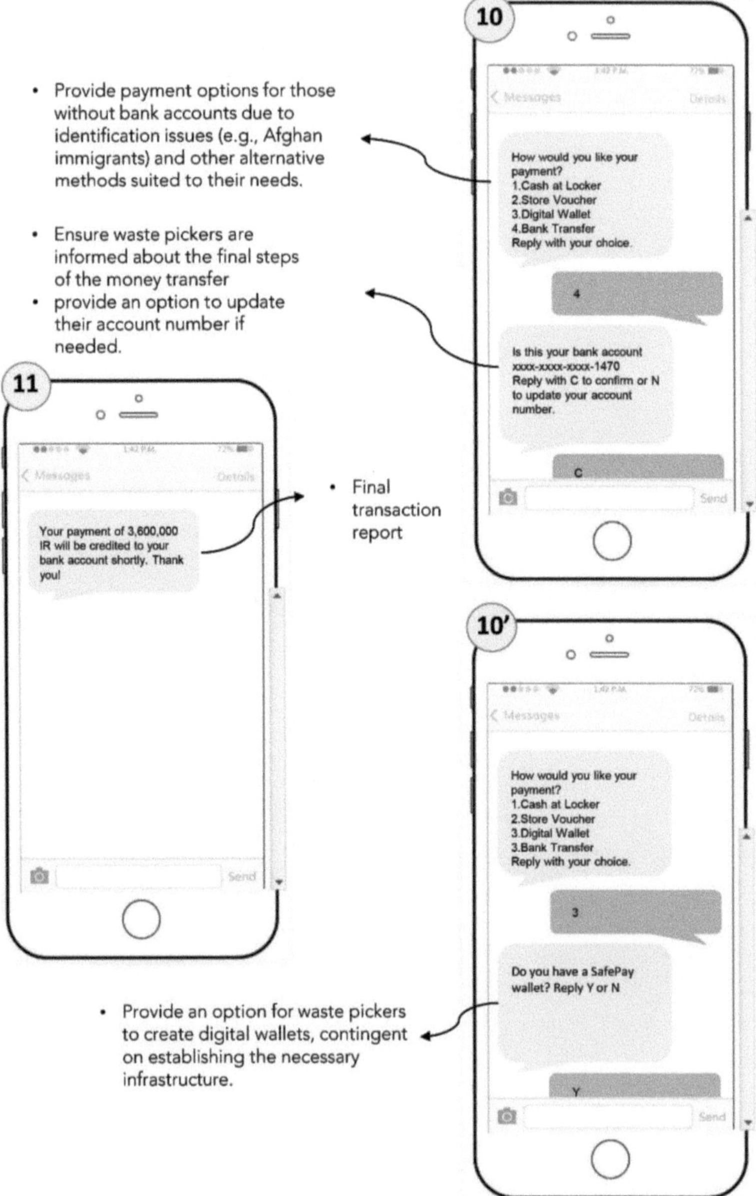

Fig. 5. Recysack overview

Health and Safety

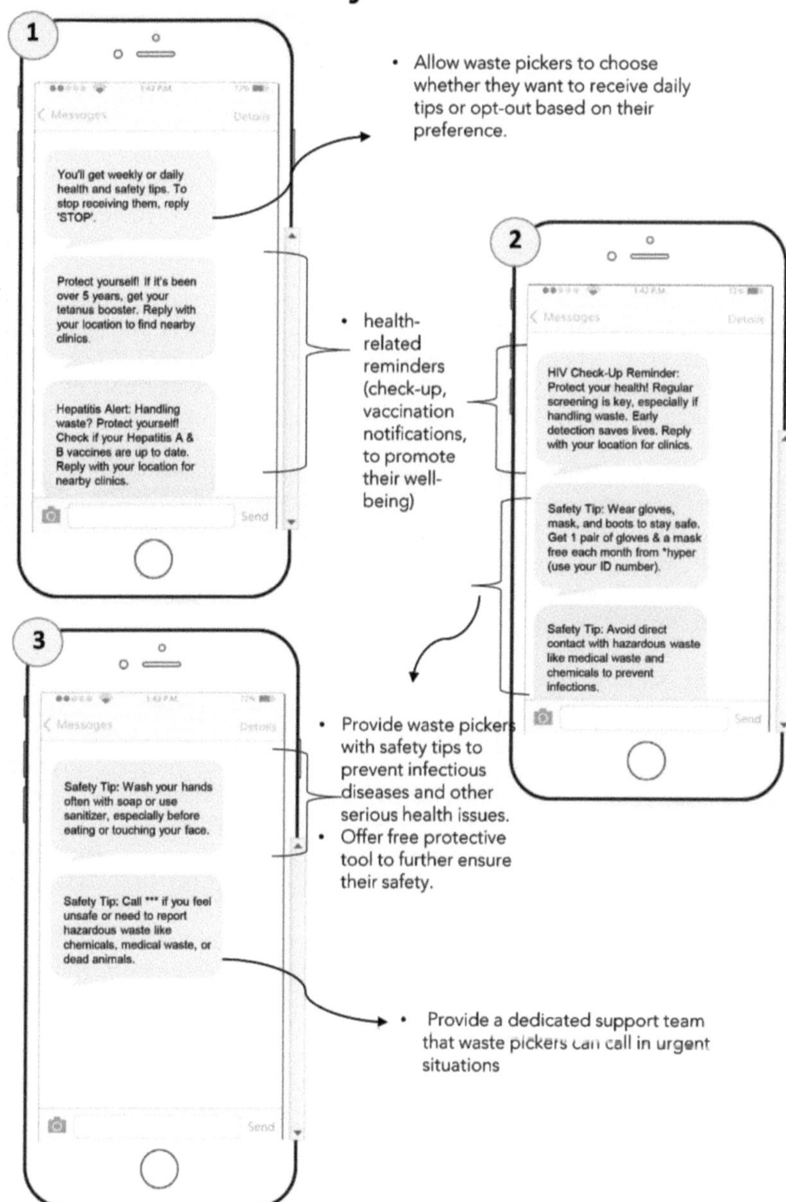

Fig. 6. Recysack overview

References

1. Adama, O.: Marginalisation and integration within the informal urban economy: the case of child waste pickers in Kaduna, Nigeria. Int. Dev. Plan. Rev. **36**(2), 155–180 (2014)
2. Cruvinel, V.R.N., Marques, C.P., Cardoso, V., Novaes, M.R.C.G., Araújo, W.N., Angulo-Tuesta, A., Escalda, P.M.F., Galato, D., Brito, P., Silva, E.N.: Health conditions and occupational risks in a novel group: waste pickers in the largest open garbage dump in Latin America. BMC Public Health. **19**(1), 581 (2019). https://doi.org/10.1186/s12889-019-6879-x
3. Galperin, H., Mariscal, J.: Poverty and mobile telephony in Latin America and the Caribbean. In: Regional Dialogue on the Information Society (DIRSI) & International Development Research Centre (IDRC), Lima (2007)
4. Hartmann, C.: Waste picker livelihoods and inclusive neoliberal municipal solid waste management policies: the case of the La Chureca garbage dump site in Managua, Nicaragua. Waste Manag. **71**, 12–24 (2017). https://doi.org/10.1016/j.wasman.2017.10.008
5. Kumari, R., Vasavada, M.: Digitalized waste management as a way towards sustainable development: a case study of Steel City Jamshedpur. J. Soc. Work Soc. Dev. **12**(2), 160 (2022)
6. Katz, V.S., Gonzalez, C.: Community variations in low-income Latino families' technology adoption and integration. Am. Behav. Sci. **60**(1), 59–80 (2015). https://doi.org/10.1177/0002764215601712
7. Medina, J.P.: Model for Analysis and Simulations (MAS): A New DSGE for the Chilean Economy. Mimeo, Central Bank of Chile, Santiago (2005)
8. Medina, M.: Waste Picker Cooperatives in Developing Countries. WIEGO, Ahmedabad (2005)
9. Mavropoulos, A., Tsakona, M., Anthouli, A.: Urban waste management and the mobile challenge. Waste Manag. Res. **33**(4), 381–387 (2015). https://doi.org/10.1177/0734242X15570316
10. Nagendra, B., Lakshmisha, A., Agarwal, P.: Mobile application in municipal waste tracking: a pilot study of "PAC waste tracker" in Bangalore city, India. J. Mater. Cycles Waste Manag. **21**(3), 705–712 (2019). https://doi.org/10.1007/s10163-018-00819-9
11. Parvin, S., Moradi, A., Donyaie, O., Davoodi, M.: Migration and waste picking: analysis of emerging urban lifestyle. Iran. Popul. Stud. J. **4**(1), 199–228 (2018). https://sid.ir/paper/401000/en
12. Sambasivan, N., Cutrell, E., Toyama, K., Nardi, B.: Intermediated technology use in developing communities. In: Proceedings of the 28th International Conference on Human Factors in Computing Systems (CHI 2010), pp. 2583–2592. ACM, Atlanta (2010). https://doi.org/10.1145/1753326.1753718
13. Suruliraj, B., Nkwo, M., Orji, R.: Persuasive mobile apps for sustainable waste management: a systematic review. In: Gram-Hansen, S., Jonasen, T., Midden, C. (eds.) Persuasive Technology: Designing for Future Change, LNCS, vol. 12064, pp. 182–194. Springer, Heidelberg (2020). https://doi.org/10.1007/978-3-030-45712-9_14

Communication Mentoring System for Connection: A Study on Linking Isolated Users

Jieun Lee[(⊠)]

Kookmin University, Seoul, Republic of Korea
jieunlee@gmail.com

Abstract. This study proposes a non-face-to-face mentoring interaction system between middle-aged and younger adults as a means to provide psychological support for socially isolated individuals. The phenomenon of *hikikomori*, originally coined in Japan, has emerged as a global issue of social isolation, exacerbated by the rapid proliferation of remote work, contactless culture due to the COVID-19 pandemic, and the growing impact of digital addiction. In South Korea, as of 2021, approximately 538,000 young people were reported to be experiencing social isolation, yet systemic support remains insufficient. In response, this study conceptualizes an interaction model that categorizes isolated users by age group and connects them accordingly. It also designs a staged structure for remote communication, aiming to theoretically examine the potential of this approach to enhance psychological stability and foster social connectedness.

Keywords: Emotion-centered design · Psychological profiling · Remote interaction · Digital mental health · Visual character feedback · User experience · Social isolation

1 Introduction

The phenomenon of *hikikomori* was first identified in Japan during the 1990s. Since then, with the advancement of digital technologies and the normalization of remote work, similar patterns of social isolation have increasingly been reported globally [1, 2]. According to a report by the World Health Organization (WHO), approximately one in four (25%) older adults experience social isolation, and 5–15% of adolescents report suffering from loneliness, highlighting the widespread severity of social disconnection across all age groups. A longitudinal study based on the HILDA (Household, Income and Labour Dynamics in Australia) survey (2014–2018) found that 34% of respondents experienced loneliness and 17% reported objective isolation, with particularly high levels of loneliness observed among youth aged 16–24 [3]. In the United States, 34% of adults aged 50 to 80 reported experiencing feelings of isolation in the past year. Notably, although social isolation among the elderly somewhat declined following the COVID-19 pandemic, it remains significantly high [4].

© The Author(s), under exclusive license to Springer Nature Switzerland AG 2026
S. Sundarakannan and O. Knorpp (Eds.): HCII 2025, CCIS 2772, pp. 363–373, 2026.
https://doi.org/10.1007/978-3-032-12767-9_38

In South Korea, socially withdrawn individuals and the broader issue of social isolation have been consistently documented. A 2023 report by the Korea Institute for Health and Social Affairs estimated that, as of 2021, approximately 5% of the 1.776 million individuals aged 19–34 were in a state of social withdrawal [5]. This report identifies key characteristics of socially isolated youth, including social avoidance (avoidance of interpersonal contact), emotional desensitization (reduced emotional expression and empathy), and egocentric thinking. Nevertheless, in contrast to countries such as Japan, the UK, and the US, South Korea has traditionally conceptualized this phenomenon as a subcategory of mental illness. In Japan, the Cabinet Secretariat has established a dedicated department for loneliness and isolation, with local-level counseling services available. In Korea, however, legal recognition of reclusive youth was only added to the Enforcement Decree of the Youth Welfare Support Act in April 2023. This delay reveals the limitations of framing social withdrawal as an individual issue rather than a matter requiring systemic social support [6]. According to Maslow's hierarchy of needs and Weiss's theory of social isolation, failure to fulfill the need for social belonging can result in psychological isolation, depression, and anxiety. Despite the recognized importance of these psychological needs, South Korea still lacks systematic investigations and tailored support programs for socially isolated youth. Based on this context, the central research question of this study is as follows:

RQ1. Can a remote mentoring system be designed in a way that provides emotional support and a sense of connectedness for socially isolated users?
RQ2. Does an intergenerational mentoring approach hold design potential for enhancing emotional stability and psychological support in the future?

2 Background and Related Work

Social isolation is characterized by both subjective loneliness and an objective lack of social interaction, which has been shown to lead to mental health issues such as depression and anxiety, particularly in the absence of emotional support [Weiss, 1973; Hawkley & Cacioppo, 2010]. A study by Mann et al. [10] on digital interventions indicated that digital approaches were both acceptable and potentially effective for individuals with mental health concerns, suggesting a foundation for future rigorous research. Yuen et al. [7] suggested that intergenerational mentoring may contribute to the assignment of new social roles and emotional stability. According to Erikson's theory of psychosocial development [Erikson, 1963], interaction and a sense of belonging are essential to the formation of identity and psychological well-being. Fiske et al. [8] and Moon [9] proposed that digital tools such as chatbots and online mentoring systems may facilitate emotional intimacy among users. Furthermore, a review by Phang et al. [11] emphasized that digital intergenerational exchange programs can reduce feelings of isolation and enhance participants' self-efficacy and emotional connectedness. Notably, automated video calls and educational support mechanisms were found to play a positive role in fostering emotional benefits.

However, several gaps remain in the existing literature. First, from a UX perspective, there has been limited research that closely examines the actual acceptance and lived experiences of digitally isolated users. Second, as highlighted by Mann et al. [10], there is a lack of studies that integrate both quantitative and qualitative data to holistically assess user experiences, thereby making it difficult to fully understand the contextual realities of use. Third, as noted in the comprehensive review by Phang et al. [11], many studies on digital intergenerational interaction have been limited to specific regions or older populations, restricting their generalizability to broader cultural and social contexts. In light of these limitations, the present study proposes a user-centered UX design and a staged communication process, aiming to explore the potential for providing emotional and psychological support to socially isolated individuals in digital environments.

3 Methodology

This study aims to explore the potential for emotional support through intergenerational interaction, grounded in the observation that social and psychological isolation is increasingly prevalent not only among older adults but also among younger populations. According to a WHO report, approximately 25% of older adults experience social isolation, while 5–15% of adolescents report feelings of loneliness. Similarly, findings from the HILDA survey in Australia indicate that 34% of respondents reported loneliness and 17% experienced objective isolation, with comparable trends observed among younger individuals aged 16–24 [3]. Considering these generationally distinct patterns of social isolation, this study proposes the design of a digital communication mentoring system that enables non-face-to-face interaction between different age groups. From a propositional perspective, it further examines whether such an age-tailored structure can theoretically contribute to the provision of emotional support.

3.1 Design of a Remote Mentoring Structure: Four-Stage Interaction Flow

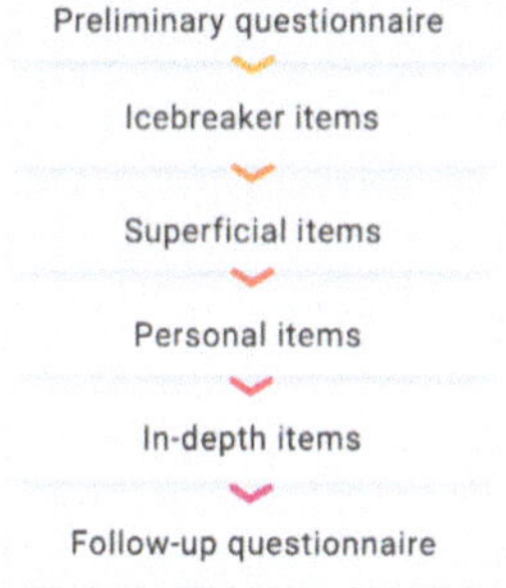

Fig. 1. Stage-Based Conversational Depth Model.

This study theoretically designs a four-stage remote communication process as a means to facilitate emotional exchange among socially isolated users. Each stage (chat session) is structured to last approximately 10 min, with the goal of guiding natural and emotionally attuned conversation flows through an automated chat system in future applications (Fig. 1). The structure is designed to gradually progress from initial rapport building to deeper emotional engagement, allowing for a progressive development of relational intimacy (Table 1).

Table 1. Communication Stage Structure.

Screen Name	Main Function / User State Representation
Loading Screen	User entry, emotional stabilization support
Emotional & Personality Indicator1,2	Brief psychological assessment items based on TCI/MMPI
Character Completion	Character visualization generated based on assessment results; visualizes user's emotional traits and profile
Mood Input	Self-report of current emotional state (e.g., emoji selection)
Action Screen 1 (Based on Input)	Feedback animation reflecting user's emotional state
Action Screen 2 (Based on Input)	Deepened or shifted emotional response
Loading Screen 1,2,3	Visual transition before moving into the next conversation flow
Chat Screen	Chat Screen Beginning of non-face-to-face emotional interaction

3.2 Target Participants

The target groups for the communication structure proposed in this study were determined based on theoretical and policy-oriented criteria. According to international demographic standards and the World Health Organization (WHO), middle adulthood is generally defined as ranging from 45 to 59 years of age. In South Korea, the *Framework Act on Youth* classifies youth as individuals between the ages of 19 and 34. Drawing on these classifications, this study identifies two primary hypothetical participant groups: Middle-aged adults (45–64 years): Individuals who may experience psychological and social isolation due to the burdens of familial and occupational responsibilities, Younger adults (24–37 years): Individuals likely to experience emotional isolation stemming from unstable career transitions and limited social networks. These target groups reflect generational differences in the causes of isolation and serve as a key theoretical foundation for designing structures of intergenerational emotional interaction.

3.3 Data Collection

To theoretically examine the changes experienced by users undergoing emotional and social isolation, this study designed a data collection framework based on pre- and post-intervention surveys. The primary measurement instruments include the UCLA Loneliness Scale (Version 3) for assessing perceived isolation [16], and the Multidimensional Scale of Perceived Social Support (MSPSS) for evaluating perceived emotional and social support [17]. Selected and adapted items from both scales were combined into a 20-item questionnaire, structured using a 5-point Likert scale, and designed to be administered identically before and after the intervention. In addition, self-report items assessing participants' overall psychological state were included to facilitate brief mental health screening. This survey framework is intended to serve as a foundation for future empirical studies, with the potential to be expanded into a comprehensive data collection method for both quantitative and qualitative evaluations of emotional change and user interaction effects (Table 2). (While the post-interaction survey is detailed in this study, the pre-interaction survey—though equally integral to the data collection framework—was not included due to space limitations.)

Table 2. Post-Interaction Survey.

No.	Items (Post-Interaction Survey)	Responses (1–5 Likert scale).
1	After the conversation, I felt less lonely.	1 = Not at all, 5 = Very much so
2	I feel more socially connected than before.	1 = Not at all, 5 = Very much so
3	I feel emotionally closer to others.	1 = Not at all, 5 = Very much so
4	I felt that I was not alone.	1 = Not at all, 5 = Very much so
5	I enjoyed the time spent talking.	1 = Not at all, 5 = Very much so
6	I felt that my emotions were understood.	1 = Not at all, 5 = Very much so
7	Knowing that someone listened to me was encouraging.	1 = Not at all, 5 = Very much so
8	I gained hope for forming social relationships.	1 = Not at all, 5 = Very much so
9	I felt emotionally comforted.	1 = Not at all, 5 = Very much so
10	The conversation helped reduce my sense of isolation.	1 = Not at all, 5 = Very much so
11	I felt that I received emotional support.	1 = Not at all, 5 = Very much so
12	The interaction with the other person was comforting.	1 = Not at all, 5 = Very much so
13	I felt a sense of connection with someone.	1 = Not at all, 5 = Very much so
14	The interaction improved my mood.	1 = Not at all, 5 = Very much so
15	I came to feel that there is someone who can help me.	1 = Not at all, 5 = Very much so
16	I gained trust in relationships where emotions can be shared.	1 = Not at all, 5 = Very much so

(*continued*)

Table 2. (continued)

No.	Items (Post-Interaction Survey)	Responses (1–5 Likert scale).
17	I felt emotionally stabilized.	1 = Not at all, 5 = Very much so
18	I think my psychological state has improved positively.	1 = Not at all, 5 = Very much so
19	I would like to continue having these kinds of conversations in the future.	1 = Not at all, 5 = Very much so
20	I feel that my social support network has expanded.	1 = Not at all, 5 = Very much so

3.4 Preliminary Psychological Assessment Items (Based on TCI and MMPI)

To briefly assess users' emotional characteristics and cognitive response tendencies during the initial interaction phase, this study developed a short-form self-report instrument grounded in validated personality and clinical psychology assessments. The items were designed based on core constructs from the Temperament and Character Inventory (TCI) and the Minnesota Multiphasic Personality Inventory-2 (MMPI-2), and are formatted using a 5-point Likert scale. These items serve as baseline data to explore users' temperament and emotional state upon entry, and are intended to be presented during the loading or initial onboarding screen.

1. TCI-Based Personality Trait Items Based on Cloninger's psychobiological model of personality, the following three items are presented [23]: (1) Novelty Seeking: "Do you feel intensely anxious when unexpected changes occur?", (2) Harm Avoidance: "Do you tend to deliberately avoid risky situations?", (3) Reward Dependence: "Are you strongly motivated by others' praise?"
2. MMPI-Based Emotional and Behavioral Tendency Items

Referencing the clinical scales of the MMPI-2, the following items were designed to assess psychological tendencies [24]: (1) Depression: "Have you frequently felt a sense of helplessness over the past two weeks?", (2) Social Sensitivity: "Do you often feel overly conscious of how others perceive you?", (3) Impulsivity: "Have you ever acted impulsively in response to emotional situations?" These brief assessment items serve as the foundation for a personalized emotional feedback system and are utilized as baseline data for designing emotionally responsive companion characters in subsequent interaction scenarios (Fig. 2).

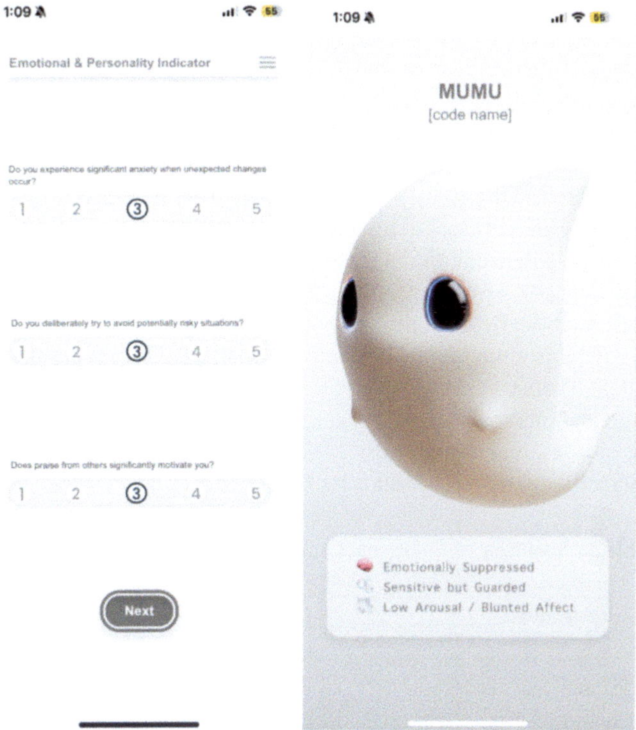

Fig. 2. Psychological Input–Driven Character Feedback Interface.

3.5 Emotion-Based UI Interface Design and User Response Modeling

1. Design of Emotion-Based Visual Elements and Narrative Responses
2. Color Mapping: Based on clinical scales from the MMPI, users' emotional states are visually represented through the primary color tones of the character. The mapping is as follows: a. High Depression Scores (Hs, D): Cold blue hues are applied to reflect introverted and withdrawn affect. b. High Schizophrenia Tendencies (Sc): Grayscale or achromatic tones are used to represent social detachment. c. High Impulsivity/Hyperactivity (Mania: Ma): Intense red tones are used to express emotional volatility and elevated energy. d. High Anxiety (Psychasthenia: Pt): Pale violet and light blue tones are used to reflect sensitivity and emotional fragility. e. High Hysteria Tendencies (Hysteria: Hy): Bright pastel colors are applied to project an outwardly cheerful image.
3. Linguistic and Narrative Response Design: Drawing from TCI personality dimensions [23], the character's linguistic style, dialogical reactions, modes of emotional expression, and narrative context are tailored accordingly. This design enables users to externalize and intuitively interpret their internal emotional states through the character. The character functions as an emotional projection of the user's identity, serving as a mediator for affect recognition and self-understanding.

3.6 Emotion-Centered Visual and Interaction Design

Users engage with a character generated to reflect their psychological disposition within a structured four-stage remote communication process. Each stage is designed to progressively reduce emotional distance and encourage psychological openness between users. The stages' objectives, user states, and corresponding emotional responses are summarized in the following table (not shown here). Color plays a central role as a visual element that directly affects users' emotional immersion and openness. Prior studies suggest that color can regulate emotional states and foster affective connection [18, 19]. For users with experiences of social isolation, the use of non-overstimulating, emotionally stabilizing, and relationally engaging color and language choices is especially important. Accordingly, this study applies principles from UI/UX psychological theory and Color-in-Context Theory to design a visual language appropriate for each stage of the remote communication process. Each stage combines emotionally guided prompts, concise initiating phrases, and emotion-driven color schemes to reduce emotional barriers and gradually facilitate user self-disclosure (Table 3).

Table 3. Summary of Emotional Language and Color Mapping by Stage.

Stage	Objective	User status	color
Ice-breaking	Easing tension and reducing emotional distance	Slightly guarded → Requires a gentle and warm approach	#FFE0C3, #D6F0F5
Surface-level conversation	Sharing everyday interests → Building a sense of empathy	Somewhat open, yet still cautious	#FFF4C1,#CDE8D7
Personal storytelling	Sharing emotions and experiences → Encouraging psychological openness	Begins to share inner thoughts with a sense of emerging trust	#D8CCE8, #E7B8B1
In-depth conversation	Sharing difficulties and providing emotional support	May involve pain, anxiety, or heavy emotions	#A3B1C6, #7E868C

Additionally, a 20-min break is provided after each conversation stage, allowing users to recover cognitive resources through an experience of *soft fascination*—a concept from attention restoration theory rooted in naturalistic engagement—and to maintain emotional connectedness through brief, informal interactions. This structured pause is intended to facilitate a smooth transition toward deeper levels of communication. According to chronemics theory, such temporal pauses and the flow of time influence turn-taking, emotional regulation, and conversational structure [14]. Furthermore, rapport-building theory suggests that this type of nonverbal coordination offers an emotional buffer and establishes a foundation for deeper information exchange [15].

4   Preliminary Results and Discussion

This study is currently in the exploratory phase, focusing on design and theoretical propositions; empirical experimentation and data collection are planned for future research stages. The proposed system is grounded in affective user experience theories [25, 26] and is designed to facilitate emotional expression and empathy for users experiencing social isolation through a tailored UI/UX structure. Additionally, the study adopts a *Positive Computing* perspective [27] to theoretically examine the potential of digital environments to enhance emotional well-being. In particular, visual elements such as color mapping were designed to reflect individual user dispositions, aiming to evoke emotional stability and engagement. Prior research has indicated that warm color schemes promote vitality and intimacy, while cool tones offer calming effects. Aesthetic coherence in design has also been identified as a key factor in fostering user acceptance and eliciting positive emotional responses [12, 13]. Through this design framework, the study theoretically examined the potential for emotion-centered, user-driven UI/UX models to promote emotional exchange and empathy even in non-face-to-face settings. Future research will require empirical validation to assess real-world applicability and user responses.

5   Ethical Considerations

This study is currently in the design and proposal phase, and no user experiments have yet been conducted. All future experimental procedures and data collection activities will be carried out following approval from an Institutional Review Board (IRB). Participants will receive clear explanations regarding the study's purpose, procedures, data usage, and privacy protocols, and informed consent will be obtained through formal documentation to ensure voluntary participation. Given the potential inclusion of emotionally vulnerable individuals, the study also plans to establish supportive measures, including referrals or guidance systems to alleviate psychological discomfort when necessary. All collected data will be anonymized and processed in strict compliance with data protection regulations and research ethics standards.

6   Conclusion and Future Work

This study proposed a non-face-to-face, intergenerational mentoring framework integrated with emotion-centered UX design to support socially isolated individuals, aiming to enhance emotional stability and social connectedness. Although empirical testing has not yet been conducted, the visual and linguistic feedback system—grounded in color psychology and UI/UX theory—was conceptually designed to facilitate emotional disclosure in remote settings. Future directions include pilot-based validation, development of culturally adaptive emotional feedback systems, and NLP integration for real-time emotion inference. Scalable extensions involve function-word-based sentiment analysis (e.g., LIWC, BERT), GPT-driven tone modeling, and long-term emotional regulation tracking to improve the precision of digital emotional support systems.

References

1. Kato, T.A., Kanba, S., Teo, A.R.: Defining pathological social withdrawal: proposed diagnostic criteria for hikikomori. World Psychiatry. **18**(1), 116–117 (2019)
2. Stickley, A., Koyanagi, A.: Loneliness, common mental disorders and suicidal behavior: findings from a general population survey. J. Affect. Disord. **197**, 81–87 (2016)
3. The prevalence of chronic and episodic loneliness and social isolation from a longitudinal survey. https://www.nature.com/articles/s41598-023-39289-x
4. Trends in Loneliness Among Older Adults 2018–2023. https://www.healthyagingpoll.org/reports-more/report/trends-loneliness-among-older-adults-2018-2023
5. Tateno, M., Park, S.C., Kato, T.A., Umene-Nakano, W., Saito, T.: Hikikomori as a possible clinical term in psychiatry: a questionnaire survey. BMC Psychiatry. **12**, 169 (2012)
6. Teo, A.R., Gaw, A.C.: Hikikomori Group: clinical case series of hikikomori in the United States. J. Nerv. Ment. Dis. **198**(6), 444–449 (2010)
7. Yuen, J.W.Y., Yan, W.S., Wong, V.C.W.: Hikikomori phenomenon in East Asia: regional perspectives, challenges, and opportunities for social health agencies. Front. Psych. **9**, 492 (2018)
8. Fiske, S.T., Cuddy, A.J.C., Glick, P., Xu, J.: A model of (often mixed) stereotype content: Competence and warmth respectively follow from perceived status and competition. Psychol. Rev. **126**(6), 1080–1091 (2019)
9. Moon, Y.: Intimate exchanges: Using computers to elicit self-disclosure from consumers. J. Consum. Res. **26**(3), 323–337 (2000)
10. Mann, F., Bone, J.K., Lloyd-Evans, B., Frerichs, J., Pinfold, V., Ma, R., Wang, J., Johnson, S.: A life less lonely: the state of the art in interventions to reduce loneliness in people with mental health problems. BMC Psychiatry. **22**(1), 1–13 (2022)
11. Phang, Y., Lee, Y., Lim, Y.J., Cheong, L.J.: Digital interventions for older adults to reduce social isolation: A systematic review and meta-analysis. JMIR Aging. **6**(1), e41916 (2023)
12. Shakoor, A.: The Impact of Emotional Design in UX. ResearchGate (2024)
13. Color and psychological functioning: a review of theoretical and empirical work. Color Psychology, Wikipedia (2025)
14. Bruneau, T.J.: Chronemics: time and human interaction. Commun.: J. Commun. Assoc. Pac. **6**(1), 1–30 (1977)
15. Duncan, D.R., Joos, K.B., Hickson, G.B.: The meaning of rapport for patients, families, and healthcare professionals. Patient Educ. Couns. **105**(1), 2–14 (2000)
16. Russell, D.: UCLA loneliness scale (version 3): reliability, validity, and factor structure. J. Pers. Assess. **66**(1), 20–40 (1996). https://doi.org/10.1207/s15327752jpa6601_2
17. Zimet, G.D., Dahlem, N.W., Zimet, S.G., Farley, G.K.: The multidimensional scale of perceived social support. J. Pers. Assess. **52**(1), 30–41 (1988). https://doi.org/10.1207/s15327752jpa5201_2
18. Valdez, P., Mehrabian, A.: Effects of color on emotions. J. Exp. Psychol. Gen. **123**(4), 394–409 (1994). https://doi.org/10.1037/0096-3445.123.4.394
19. Elliot, A.J., Maier, M.A.: Color-in-context theory. Adv. Exp. Soc. Psychol. **45**, 61–125 (2012). https://doi.org/10.1016/B978-0-12-394286-9.00002-0
20. Gaines, R., Curry, C.: Color and psychological functioning: a review of theoretical and empirical work. Color Res. Appl. **36**(6), 394–403 (2011). https://doi.org/10.1002/col.20679
21. Kaya, N., Epps, H.H.: Relationship between color and emotion: a study of college students. Coll. Stud. J. **38**(3), 396–405 (2004)
22. Mahlke, S., Thüring, M.: Studying antecedents of emotional experiences in interactive contexts. In: Proceedings of the SIGCHI Conference on Human Factors in Computing Systems, pp. 915–918 (2007). https://doi.org/10.1145/1240624.1240762

23. Cloninger, C.R., Svrakic, D.M., Przybeck, T.R.: A psychobiological model of temperament and character. Arch. Gen. Psychiatry. **50**(12), 975–990 (1993). https://doi.org/10.1001/arc hpsyc.1993.01820240059008
24. Butcher, J.N., Dahlstrom, W.G., Graham, J.R., Tellegen, A., Kaemmer, B.: Minnesota Multiphasic Personality Inventory-2 (MMPI-2): Manual for Administration and Scoring. University of Minnesota Press (1989)
25. Norman, D.A.: Emotional Design: Why We Love (or Hate) Everyday Things. Basic Books (2004)
26. Hassenzahl, M.: The interplay of beauty, goodness, and usability in interactive products. Hum. Comput. Interact. **19**(4), 319–349 (2004)
27. Calvo, R.A., Peters, D.: Positive Computing: Technology for Wellbeing and Human Potential. MIT Press (2014)

HeritageLens: An Interactive Exploration System for Museums and Cultural Exhibits

Asterios Leonidis[1,2]([envelope]) [iD], Maria Korozi[1] [iD], Marianthi Argyropoulou[1],
Effie Karuzaki[1] [iD], Maria Bouhli[1], and Constantine Stephanidis[1,2] [iD]

[1] Institute of Computer Science (ICS), Foundation for Research and Technology - Hellas
(FORTH), 70013 Heraklion, Crete, Greece
`{leonidis,korozi,cs}@ics.forth.gr`
[2] Department of Computer Science Heraklion, University of Crete, 70013 Heraklion, Crete,
Greece

Abstract. HeritageLens is an interactive system designed to support inclusive, curiosity-driven engagement with cultural content in public installations such as museum kiosks. It features a visually rich, non-linear interface that enables users to navigate museum rooms, object collections, and outdoor cultural routes by interacting with thematic image tiles and detailed visuals—like room photos or route maps—augmented with points of interest presented as markers or animated cutouts that signal interactivity. Accessibility is central to the system's design; a custom-built tactile controller allows for sequential navigation, while the interface dynamically restructures into scannable clusters enhanced with text-to-speech and audio descriptions to support diverse user needs. Developed through an inclusive, iterative design process, HeritageLens uses a modular Angular frontend that supports a range of deployment configurations to accommodate different use cases.

Keywords: Exploratory Interfaces · Public Information Systems · Accessibility · Museum Technologies

1 Introduction

Museums and cultural institutions increasingly rely on digital technologies to enhance visitor engagement, support personalized learning, and broaden access to heritage content [1]. However, many existing digital installations remain static or overly prescriptive, offering limited opportunities for exploration and often failing to accommodate the diverse needs and preferences of visitors [2]. There is a growing demand for interactive systems that enable users to engage with cultural material on their own terms -navigating non-linearly, exploring topics in depth, and uncovering connections through intuitive interfaces [3]. As museums work toward greater inclusivity, there is a heightened focus on designing systems that are not only engaging but also accessible to individuals with a wide range of abilities. This includes addressing barriers commonly encountered by users with visual, motor, or cognitive impairments -such as difficulties interacting with dense visual content, small or closely spaced interface elements, and non-standard interaction patterns.

© The Author(s), under exclusive license to Springer Nature Switzerland AG 2026
S. Sundarakannan and O. Knorpp (Eds.): HCII 2025, CCIS 2772, pp. 374–382, 2026.
https://doi.org/10.1007/978-3-032-12767-9_39

We introduce HeritageLens, an interactive exploration system designed to support in-depth engagement with museum exhibits and cultural content. HeritageLens enables visitors to delve into specific objects or topics through a multimodal, visually rich interface that encourages curiosity-driven exploration. The system is built to be generalizable across exhibition types -from historical artifacts to natural heritage- and is intended for deployment in public spaces such as museum kiosks or cultural centers; currently deployed at the "Cultural Interconnection Point" in the city of Larissa,[1] as well as at one of the two new tourist information points in the city of Kalamata.[2]

Additionally, accessibility has been carefully considered across all aspects of the system's design. A custom-built accessibility controller enables sequential navigation using tactile buttons, transforming the interface into a structured, scannable format with text-to-speech support. This approach ensures that users with diverse abilities can interact with the system confidently and effectively, without being overwhelmed or excluded.

2 Related Work

In recent years, interactive technologies have become central to enriching cultural experiences in museums and heritage sites [3]. A wide range of systems -ranging from touchscreen installations to mixed-reality platforms- have been employed to promote storytelling, personalization, and visitor engagement [1]. These technologies aim to move beyond passive consumption by encouraging active exploration and deeper interpretation of cultural content [2].

Touch-based systems are among the most adopted interfaces in museum settings due to their simplicity and familiarity [4]. Multi-touch tables and wall-mounted displays have been used to provide contextual information, interactive timelines, games, and multilingual narratives. For example, various museums have employed large-scale touchscreens to allow visitors to navigate digital archives, explore thematic clusters, or interact with high-resolution images of artifacts [5]. These systems typically support intuitive point-and-click interaction, although accessibility remains a challenge when touch is the sole modality.

Augmented and virtual reality systems are increasingly used to enhance spatial understanding and visual engagement in museums [6, 7]. CreteAR [8] is a notable example, combining a scale model of the island of Crete with XR overlays. Users can interact with a transformable physical model—equipped with mechatronics that reveal showcases -while viewing supplementary content through handheld devices and a companion screen. This hybrid setup bridges physical and digital interactions, offering rich, embodied engagement with regional history and geography.

More recently immersive environments offer novel ways to situate users within reconstructed historical or artistic scenes. FRAMES is an example of such a platform, designed for CAVE-like environments to enable multi-user interaction and cultural immersion [9]. It incorporates personalized interaction, accessibility features, and AR

---

[1] https://ami.ics.forth.gr/en/installation/a-cultural-interconnection-point-for-the-municipality-of-larissa/

[2] https://ami.ics.forth.gr/en/installation/info-points-municipality-of-kalamata/

enhancements. A notable instantiation of this framework is VanoArt, which was tailored for art galleries and demonstrated how immersive technologies can support both narrative depth and social interaction in public heritage contexts.

Mobile apps remain a flexible and cost-effective solution for cultural engagement, often used for indoor navigation, exhibit enrichment, or educational games. Some apps provide museum-wide guidance using Bluetooth or QR beacons, while others offer exhibit-specific content such as high-resolution imagery, curatorial notes, or audio commentary [10]. For younger audiences, mobile treasure hunts and gamified tours have been shown to improve learning outcomes and participation, especially in school-group settings [11]. These systems typically adapt to personal devices, supporting accessibility tools like screen readers and zoom features [12].

A newer area of research explores the fusion of physical objects and digital interactivity to create "smart artifacts" [13]. *AugmenTable* [14] is one such system, designed to augment paper-based content with digital overlays. It supports touch-based interaction and adaptive lighting, enabling users to explore heritage information in a collaborative and embodied way. Another example is the *Smart Interactive Showcase*, developed for the "REVOLUTION '21 REFRAMED" exhibition at the National Historical Museum in Greece [15]. This installation combined a traditional display case with a touch-sensitive surface and projected media content, allowing users to access contextual multimedia presentations by simply touching the glass near an exhibit.

Despite growing awareness of inclusive design, many touchscreen or digital museum interfaces still exclude users with motor or visual impairments. Recent innovations like Touchally [16] offer mechanical and mobile-based solutions for making existing touchscreens usable by blind individuals -enabling tactile interaction and smartphone-based screen-reader access. Other measures, such as tactile keypad interfaces or Universal Key Pads implemented at institutions like the Canadian Museum for Human Rights, support screen-based content with audio navigation and tactile controls [17]. Additionally, initiatives like Museum of Touch demonstrate the value of co-design with visually impaired users, using tactile models, tactile paving, and braille signage to create inclusive physical and digital experiences [18].

3 Design Methodology

The design methodology followed the AmI-Design Process [19], an iterative framework grounded in Design Thinking principles [20], specifically tailored for the development of Intelligent Environments (IEs) [21]. The process began with an exploration of existing literature and technologies related to interactive displays, particularly those used in cultural contexts. Special attention was given to accessibility practices and inclusive design strategies for public installations. In parallel, exploratory sessions were held with stakeholders, including UI/UX designers, software developers, museum professionals, and accessibility consultants. This process helped shape a set of four representative user personas of potential visitors and guided the definition of motivational scenarios. These personas were informed by stakeholder input, and they reflected variations in **age, familiarity with digital technologies, cultural interests, and accessibility needs**. For instance, one persona depicted a visually impaired adult relying on assistive technologies, while another represented a tourist with limited time but a strong interest in discovering cultural highlights. A third persona captured the perspective of a school-age learner motivated by curiosity and play, whereas a fourth highlighted an older visitor with limited motor dexterity but deep cultural knowledge. These personas helped the team to anticipate diverse use cases and avoid overly prescriptive interaction models.

During an ideation phase, a wide range of concepts were explored through brainstorming sessions. Key questions included how to best represent points of interest on an image -should they appear as visual cutouts, overlaid pins, or highlighted areas? How can users intuitively recognize that certain parts of the image are interactive? Accessibility was also a major focus at this stage, particularly how to support efficient scanning of POIs and ensure that all interactive elements were usable by individuals with diverse abilities. These ideas were iteratively refined through consultations with domain experts, helping to prioritize solutions that balanced technical feasibility, inclusivity, and engaging user experience. This process ultimately led to the formulation of high-level requirements.

The design process progressed through several rounds of low- and high-fidelity prototyping. These prototypes were evaluated internally by experts in interface design and assistive technologies to ensure usability and compliance with accessibility standards. Particular emphasis was placed on refining the interaction flow, narration structure, and visual clarity of the interface. Accessibility considerations played a key role throughout, leading to early prototyping of scanning mechanisms and tactile navigation strategies suitable for users with motor or visual impairments.

In addition, every system installation was followed by an on-site pilot phase; these trials offered valuable insight into how users of varying ages and abilities engaged with HeritageLens in context. Observations and feedback from these pilots informed further refinements, contributing to a continuous loop of design, testing, and improvement.

Fig. 1. Snapshots of the HeritageLens landing page as installed at tourist information points. Users can browse museum rooms in Larissa (Left) and hiking routes around Kalamata (Right).

4 HeritageLens Description

HeritageLens offers an intuitive, visually engaging platform designed to facilitate in-depth exploration of cultural content. It allows visitors to explore curated content -like museum exhibits, thematic collections, or even outdoor cultural routes- through a layered, visual interface that supports curiosity-driven engagement.

The experience begins at a visually engaging landing page (Fig. 1), which presents content as a series of clearly labeled image tiles. Each tile corresponds to a distinct category or theme -such as a museum room, a hiking trail, or a curated object collection- and is accompanied by a concise title. This design allows users to browse the available content at a glance and quickly identify topics of interest, fostering an intuitive and inviting entry point into the system.

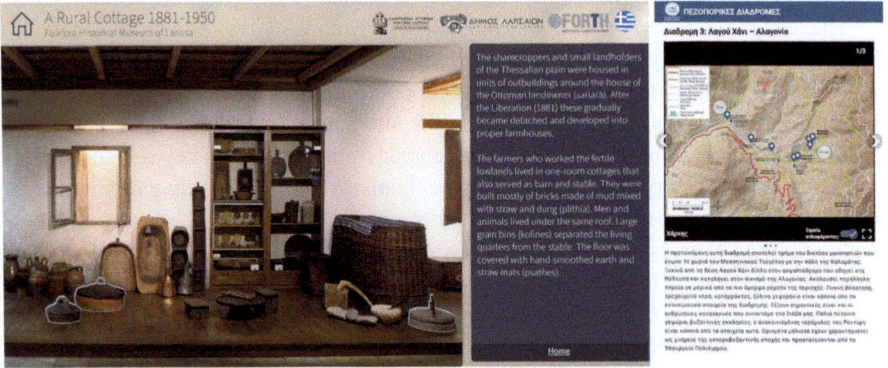

Fig. 2. After selecting a category, users view detailed content: (Left) an image of the museum room with a brief description; (Right) a map of the hiking route and relevant details.

Upon selecting a category, users are presented with a detailed view that combines a general textual description with an interactive visual representation -such as an image of a museum room, a route map, or a close-up of an artifact (Fig. 2). This visual acts as the primary interface for exploration and is augmented with selectable points of interest (POIs), which highlight specific features or sub-elements relevant to the selected category (e.g., objects within a museum room, stops along a hiking route, or motifs depicted on a vase).

POIs may appear as traditional clickable markers (like pins), or they may be integrated directly into the image as cutouts of specific objects (Fig. 3 Left). In these cases, POIs are visually distinguished by a vivid-colored border that subtly fades in and out, signaling interactivity and inviting user engagement without disrupting the natural aesthetics of the visual scene. When a POI is selected, the system reveals additional content, including descriptive text and related photographs, enabling users to explore the topic in greater depth without losing context within the overall experience.

For example, selecting a museum room as a category presents an image map of the room, where items of the room are highlighted as interactive elements. Users can click on these items to access specific information and accompanying photos (Fig. 4).

Fig. 3. (Left) Close-up of selectable POIs; (Middle) details of a selected museum room item; (Right) details of a selected hiking route stop.

In another scenario, choosing a hiking route displays a trail map overlaid with POIs, each offering information such as location-specific descriptions, elevation, distances, and nearby landmarks.

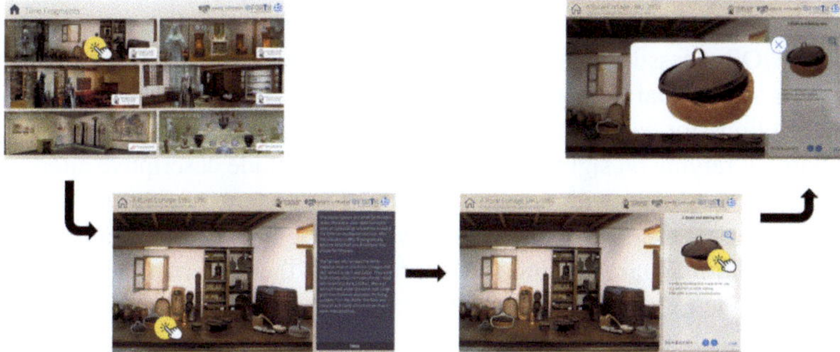

Fig. 4: Interaction workflow showing the step-by-step process: selecting a category, identifying hotspots on the room, retrieving item details, and viewing item photos in full-screen.

4.1 Accessibility and Inclusivity

Accessibility has been an important focus in the design of *HeritageLens* in order to create an inclusive system that accommodates users with diverse physical, sensory, and cognitive abilities. The interface layout follows universal design principles [22, 23], with most interactive elements intentionally placed in the lower portion of the screen to enhance reachability. This positioning benefits a wide range of users, including children, individuals using wheelchairs, and those with limited upper-body mobility .

To further support accessible interaction, HeritageLens interoperates with a custom-built accessibility controller (Fig. 5 Left) designed for users with motor or visual impairments. The controller features four tactile buttons -Next, Previous, OK, and Start Accessibility Mode- that enable users to navigate the interface sequentially, without relying on touch-based gestures or precise pointing. To activate accessibility features, the user

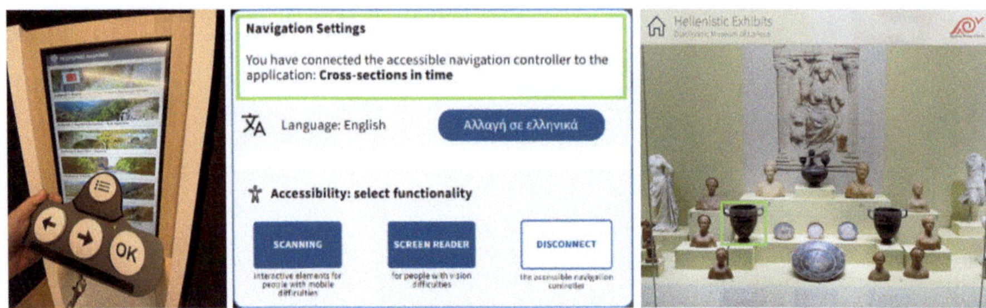

Fig. 5. (Left) Custom-built accessibility controller with tactile buttons for sequential navigation; (Middle) accessibility mode selection popup; (Right) Scannable POIs.

clicks the corresponding button on the controller. A popup appears (Fig. 5 Middle), allowing them to choose between Scanning mode (for users with motor impairments) and Screen Reader mode (for users with visual impairments). Once accessibility mode is activated, the system restructures its interface into scannable clusters of related elements. Each group is visually indicated with a dashed border, and users can cycle through the elements within a group before returning to the group level and continuing to the next cluster (Fig. 5. Right). This scanning approach draws on established paradigms, such as those used in iOS accessibility features, to provide predictable and low-effort interaction.

For users with visual impairments, this scanning process is enhanced with narrated audio descriptions for each interface element and point of interest, ensuring access to content without relying on sight. All visual elements include descriptive alternative text that integrates seamlessly with text-to-speech (TTS) systems. Additionally, automatic text scrolling assists users with low vision by reducing the need for manual navigation and helping them maintain reading focus throughout their interaction. Together, these features contribute to a system that can be comfortably and effectively used by a wide audience, regardless of ability.

4.2 Technologies

The frontend of HeritageLens is built using Angular, a widely supported web development framework known for its modular structure and ability to support complex, interactive applications. Angular enables the creation of responsive and maintainable user interfaces, capable of handling dynamic content and real-time user interactions with ease.

Depending on the installation context, the system can be deployed in both vertical and horizontal screen orientations. These and other configuration options—such as content themes, interface behavior, and underlying data—are defined through external configuration files, allowing the system to be easily adapted to diverse physical layouts and thematic exhibition scenarios.

To support inclusive access, HeritageLens uses the browser's native SAPI 5.0 text-to-speech engine by default to provide auditory feedback for interface elements. In addition, the system has been tested for compatibility with screen readers such as SuperNova and ChromeVox, ensuring accessibility for individuals with visual impairments, particularly in scenarios where the application is deployed in public settings, thus aligning with the system's broader accessibility goals.

5 Conclusion and Future Work

This paper introduced HeritageLens, an interactive system designed to support inclusive, curiosity-driven exploration of cultural content in public-facing settings such as museums and tourist information points. Unlike conventional touch-based systems that often constrain user pathways or exclude visitors with accessibility needs, HeritageLens offers a flexible, visually engaging interface that encourages users to delve into cultural material on their own terms. Its layered interaction model -centered around rich visuals and contextual points of interest- accommodates both in-depth exploration and quick, casual browsing.

A key contribution of HeritageLens lies in its comprehensive accessibility features. Through a custom-built controller and integrated accessibility modes (Scanning and Screen Reader), the system provides tactile and audio-based navigation support, enabling users with motor and visual impairments to confidently interact with the content. The modular, Angular-based frontend also ensures the system can be adapted to different screen orientations, physical settings, and content themes.

Looking ahead, broader deployments in real-world cultural institutions -combined with structured user evaluations- will provide critical feedback on long-term usability, inclusivity, and educational value.

Acknowledgements. This work has been supported by the FORTH-ICS internal RTD Programme 'Ambient Intelligence and Smart Environments'. The authors would like to thank the Accessibility Team -Stavroula Ntoa & Ilia Adami- and Vanessa Neroutsou for content curation.

References

1. Mohd Noor Shah, N.F., Ghazali, M.: A systematic review on digital technology for enhancing user experience in museums. In: International Conference on User Science and Engineering, pp. 35–46. Springer (2018)
2. Vaz, R.I.F., Fernandes, P.O., Veiga, A.C.R.: Interactive technologies in museums: how digital installations and media are enhancing the visitors' experience. In: Handbook of Research on Technological Developments for Cultural Heritage and eTourism Applications, pp. 30–53. IGI Global (2018)
3. Poulopoulos, V., Wallace, M.: Digital technologies and the role of data in cultural heritage: the past, the present, and the future. Big Data Cogn. Comput. **6**, 73 (2022)
4. Horn, M.S., Banerjee, A., Bar-El, D., Wallace, I.H.: Engaging families around museum exhibits: comparing tangible and multi-touch interfaces. In: Proceedings of the Interaction Design and Children Conference, pp. 556–566 (2020)
5. Potenziani, M., Callieri, M., Cignoni, P.: Designing and developing interactive kiosks for cultural heritage: best. In: Interactive Media for Cultural Heritage, vol. 473, (2025)
6. Ibiş, A., Çakici Alp, N.: Augmented reality and wearable technology for cultural heritage preservation. Sustainability. **16**, 4007 (2024)

7. Kyriakou, P., Hermon, S.: Can I touch this? Using natural interaction in a museum augmented reality system. Digit. Appl. Archaeol. Cult. Herit. **12**, e00088 (2019). https://doi.org/10.1016/j.daach.2018.e00088

8. Tosios, A., Leonidis, A., Korozi, M., Stivaktakis, N.M., Apostolakis, E., Roulios, M., Paparoulis, S., Stamatakis, E., Stephanidis, C.: CreteAR: enhancing learning experiences through tangible transformable artifacts and extended reality. Hum. Fact. Des. Eng. Comput. **159** (2024)

9. Pitikaki, V.E., Troulis, E., Leonidis, A., Korozi, M., Stephanidis, C.: FRAMES: a platform for constructing immersive and multimodal extended reality exhibitions. In: Presented at the Digital Heritage 2025, Siena, Italy (2025)

10. Kapnas, G., Leonidis, A., Korozi, M., Ntoa, S., Margetis, G., Stephanidis, C.: a museum guide application for deployment on user-owned Mobile devices. In: Stephanidis, C. (ed.) HCI International 2013 - Posters' Extended Abstracts, pp. 253–257. Springer, Berlin, Heidelberg (2013). https://doi.org/10.1007/978-3-642-39476-8_52

11. Michalakis, V.I., Vaitis, M., Klonari, A.: The development of an educational outdoor adventure mobile app. Educ. Sci. **10**, 382 (2020)

12. Nikolarakis, A., Koutsabasis, P.: Mobile AR interaction design patterns for storytelling in cultural heritage: a systematic review. Multimodal Technol. Interact. **8**, 52 (2024)

13. Duranti, D., Spallazzo, D., Petrelli, D.: Smart objects and replicas: a survey of tangible and embodied interactions in museums and cultural heritage sites. J. Comput. Cult. Herit. **17**, 1–32 (2024). https://doi.org/10.1145/3631132

14. Leonidis, A., Korozi, M., Stephanidis, C.: Enhancing user experience with tangible interactive systems through extended reality. ERCIM News. **2024** (2024)

15. Pattakos, A., Zidianakis, E., Sifakis, M., Roulios, M., Partarakis, N., Stephanidis, C.: Digital interaction with physical museum artifacts. Technologies. **11**, 65 (2023)

16. Li, J., Yan, Z., Shah, A., Lazar, J., Peng, H.: Toucha11y: making inaccessible public touchscreens accessible. In: Proceedings of the 2023 CHI Conference on Human Factors in Computing Systems, pp. 1–13 (2023)

17. Seven awesome accessibility features at the Museum | CMHR. https://humanrights.ca/story/seven-awesome-accessibility-features-museum, last accessed 2025/07/28

18. Reinhardt, D., Holloway, L., Thogersen, J., Guerry, E., Diaz, C.A.C., Havellas, W., Poronnik, P.: The museum of touch: tangible models for blind and low vision audiences in museums. In: Lee, J.H., Ostwald, M.J., Kim, M.J. (eds.) Multimodality in Architecture: Collaboration, Technology and Education, pp. 135–155. Springer Nature Switzerland, Cham (2024). https://doi.org/10.1007/978-3-031-49511-3_8

19. Stephanidis, C., Leonidis, A., Korozi, M., Kouroumalis, V., Adami, I., Ntoa, S.: Design for intelligent environments. In: Human-Computer Interaction in Intelligent Environments. CRC Press (2024)

20. Brown, T.: Others: design thinking. Harv. Bus. Rev. **86**, 84 (2008)

21. Leonidis, A., Korozi, M., Kouroumalis, V., Poutouris, E., Stefanidi, E., Arampatzis, D., Sykianaki, E., Anyfantis, N., Kalligiannakis, E., Nicodemou, V.C.: Ambient intelligence in the living room. Sensors. **19**, 5011 (2019)

22. Emiliani, P.L., Stephanidis, C.: Universal access to ambient intelligence environments: opportunities and challenges for people with disabilities. IBM Syst. J. **44**, 605–619 (2005)

23. Korozi, M., Leonidis, S., Margetis, G., Stephanidis, C.: MAID: a multi-platform accessible Interface design framework. In: International Conference on Universal Access in Human-Computer Interaction, pp. 725–734. Springer (2009)

Optimizing Cognitive Load in Complex Infographics: Design Principles for Effective Reading Navigation

Jiayi Liu[✉] and Han Zhang

Central China Normal University, 152 Luo Yu Road, Wuhan, China
{jiayiliu1998,zhanghan120}@ccnu.edu.cn

Abstract. Complex infographics are effective visual formats for presenting large volumes of information in a clear and coherent manner, often integrating multiple charts, visual elements, or informational sections into a unified composition. While their structural openness allows for flexible exploration, it can also impose substantial cognitive load due to the simultaneous presentation of dense content. This study investigates how reading navigation influences cognitive load in the comprehension of complex static infographics, with a focus on deviations from the intended reading path of the designer. It also examines how specific structural features, such as spatial layout, subheadings, and font size, contribute to guiding interpretation and reducing cognitive demand. Participants viewed a series of infographic samples, identified their own reading paths, and rated the cognitive load associated with each. Based on the findings, this research proposes design principles that support effective navigation and alleviate cognitive burden in complex infographic design.

Keywords: Complex Infographics · Cognitive Load Theory · Visual Complexity · Information Visualization · Reading Navigation

1 Introduction

Infographics are widely used as a visual medium for organizing and conveying complex information. Among these, some designs integrate multiple charts, visual elements, or informational sections into a unified composition, allowing viewers to access different dimensions of a subject simultaneously. In this study, these are referred to as *complex infographics*. Unlike data visualizations intended for expert users, complex infographics are commonly found in journalism, education, public communication, and scientific outreach, where the goal is to communicate multivariate content clearly and efficiently to a general audience. These infographics often contain dense data, intricate layout structures, and high visual complexity. Rather than enforcing a fixed narrative sequence, their visual openness encourages viewers to navigate the initial space independently, supporting exploratory understanding.

© The Author(s), under exclusive license to Springer Nature Switzerland AG 2026
S. Sundarakannan and O. Knorpp (Eds.): HCII 2025, CCIS 2772, pp. 383–392, 2026.
https://doi.org/10.1007/978-3-032-12767-9_40

As a cognitive factor, visual complexity can stimulate both engagement and comprehension, depending on how it is structured. Berlyne's theory of collative variables [1] suggests that moderate complexity in visual stimuli can increase arousal and exploratory motivation, potentially encouraging sustained attention and deeper information processing. However, excessive visual density presented without interaction or staged sequencing may overwhelm the viewer and impede comprehension, especially when multiple elements must be processed simultaneously. This aligns with cognitive load theory [2], which demonstrates that unstructured or poorly organized visual information may impose excessive extraneous load, thus exceeding the limited capacity of working memory and impeding comprehension.

Research in visual narrative, particularly comics, has shown that spatial layout significantly influences reading behavior, as Cohn [3] observed. Empirical evidence reinforces this structure-cognition link: Majooni et al. [4] demonstrated that the layout of the infographic significantly affects the comprehension of viewers and the cognitive load, with certain configurations allowing for more efficient information extraction. Layouts aligned with natural reading patterns (for example, left-to-right flow) were particularly effective at reducing mental effort and improving understanding. In formats such as comics, narrative visualizations, or flowcharts, viewers typically follow explicit structural cues that define a fixed reading sequence essential for comprehension. In contrast, complex infographics present multiple information units in a shared space without a fixed order, increasing viewer autonomy but leaving it unclear how path deviation relates to cognitive load. This gap motivates the present investigation into the relationship between spatial navigation and cognitive demand in complex infographics.

This study introduces the term *reading navigation* to describe how viewers are guided through these visuals. Reading navigation denotes the ensemble of visual strategies (e.g., layout organization, subheadings, spatial grouping, visual proximity) that shape how information is accessed and related. Within this framework, the *intended path* is the sequence implicitly suggested by the designer's layout and content arrangement; the *actual path* is the order in which viewers report processing of the visual regions; and the divergence between them is termed *path deviation*.

In the design of complex infographics, many designers have adopted a 2.5D layout (a visual representation commonly used in games and illustrations, which often simulates a sense of spatial depth on a two-dimensional plane through isometric projection and is understood here as a way of arranging the information) in order to structure the information content. By introducing layer depth and non-parallel compositional arrangements, these designs enhance visual appeal and stimulate exploratory behavior. These spatial configurations may differ significantly from traditional 2D layouts in terms of navigational behavior and cognitive load. Specifically, 2.5D layouts typically provide higher openness and viewer dominance, which may increase the path deviation and affect the overall cognitive load. Therefore, this study distinguishes a category distinction between 2D and 2.5D layouts in experimental design.

Specifically, this study addresses the following research questions:

RQ1: Does path deviation significantly affect viewer cognitive load and information comprehension?

RQ2: What structural features, including spatial configuration (2D vs. 2.5D), subheadings, text size, and the number of visual sections, affect the cognitive load of viewers?

2 Method

2.1 Participants

22 students (8 postgraduate, 14 undergraduate) from Central China Normal University, Wuhan, China participated in the study. All of the participants majored in design (19 in Visual Communication Design and 3 in Digital Media Art) and demonstrated familiarity with layout and infographic structures. The age range of the participants was between 19 and 25 years.

2.2 Stimuli

The stimuli consisted of six complex, static infographics selected from student projects developed under a unified course brief, and were primarily chosen based on award recognition or high performance according to course assessment standards. These works were designed for general audiences rather than expert users, aiming to communicate topics in cultural knowledge or popular science through visually engaging formats. We classified them into two groups: three 2D and three 2.5D compositions. The topics and overall visual complexity were balanced across the two layout types to control for confounding variables related to content, ensuring that the layout structure remained the primary independent variable (Fig. 1).

Each infographic contained between four and seven distinct information areas, based on the designer's specifications. These typically included a title section, core data visualizations, explanatory text, and supporting symbolic elements. The original viewing sequence, as intended by the designer, was used to define the reference reading path. To prevent participants from defaulting to a numerical reading order, the annotated versions shown to participants used alphabetical labels (A-G) instead of numbers. For consistency, all labeled areas were reordered linearly from left to right and from top to bottom, independently of their original visual layout. All infographics were horizontally oriented and presented in high resolution to ensure visual clarity.

Among the six infographics, three featured clearly defined subheadings, while the remaining either lacked subheadings or contained them in visually ambiguous forms. The minimum body text size across the samples ranged from 3 pt to 13 pt on an A2 frame (as defined in the original design files; on-screen display was rescaled, but participants were allowed to zoom freely). These structural variations were documented and used as variables in subsequent analysis.

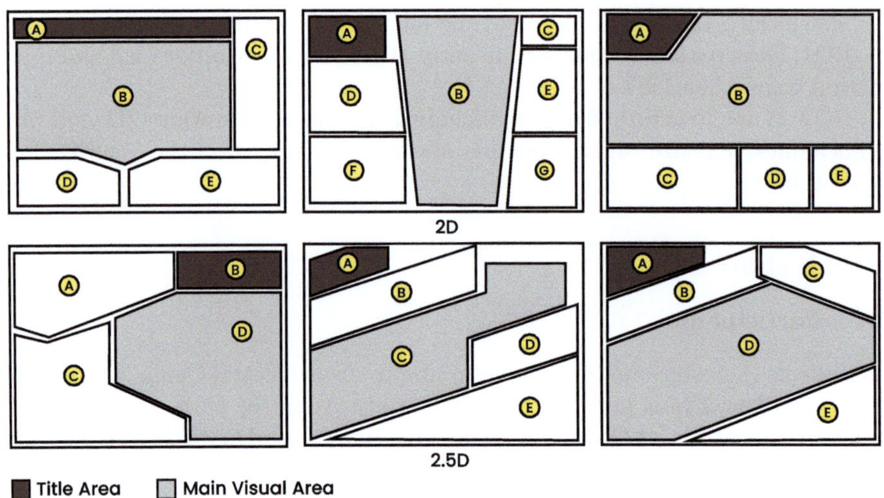

Fig. 1. Annotation Structure Across All Stimulus Images

2.3   Procedure

This study used a centrally administered offline procedure. The experimental process for each round was as follows.

First, the electronic questionnaire randomly indicated which infographic would be shown, and the researcher retrieved the corresponding image. The participants viewed the infographic on a standardized display. Each image was first presented in an unannotated version (30 s) to allow free observation and initial understanding.

Subsequently, the image with the labeled zones was shown and the participants were asked to complete a "reading path sequencing" task. In this task, they identified their subjective viewing order based on their interpretation of the graphic. To avoid prepredicted effects from any pre-set order in the questionnaire, responses were collected through handwritten input. These individual sequences were later compared with the designer's intended order to generate a 'path deviation' index reflecting the discrepancy between actual and intended navigation.

After completion of the sequencing task, participants responded to three follow-up questions (Q1-Q3) in the electronic questionnaire, each addressing a different aspect of visual comprehension.

Q1: Theme Identification (recognizing the main topic of the infographic, typically found in the title)

Q2: Information Understanding (identifying secondary-level information presented in the infographic)

Q3: Inferential Reasoning (integrating multiple elements to infer underlying meaning)

These questions were designed based on the three-level text comprehension model proposed by Kintsch (1998) [5], corresponding respectively to information extraction, structural integration, and meaning construction. This model emphasizes the hierarchical nature of comprehension, where the cognitive load increases with the depth of processing. The three tasks aimed to assess participants' information processing at these levels, reflecting the effectiveness of infographic structure in supporting cognition.

After completing the ordering task, participants rated their subjective cognitive load using a simplified NASA Task Load Index (NASA-TLX) [6] (details in Sect. 2.4). The questionnaire enforced mandatory completion without skipping or reviewing responses. Given the open structure and high information density of complex infographics, participants were allowed to revisit the image while completing the questionnaire. This design choice aimed to simulate a more natural viewing condition. All tasks were performed on a unified digital platform, with the six sections presented in randomized order to minimize order effects. The sessions were facilitated and monitored by the researcher to ensure consistent timing and data reliability.

2.4   Cognitive Load Measurement

To evaluate the perceived cognitive load of participants during the infographic comprehension task, a simplified version of NASA-TLX was used. This self-report instrument originally includes six dimensions of perceived workload; however, considering the visual nature of the task and the controlled experimental conditions, the two NASA-TLX dimensions, Mental Demand and Physical Demand, were excluded due to the characteristics of the task. The ability to revisit the infographic reduced Mental Demand. The absence of physical effort rendered Physical Demand inapplicable. Four key dimensions were selected to reflect the core aspects of cognitive load: Temporal Demand, Effort, Frustration, and Performance.

Each dimension was rated on a continuous sliding scale of 0–21 (0 = very low, 21 = very high). The questionnaire used a forced response mechanism and participants were not allowed to skip or review responses. All ratings were completed immediately after the task was completed to reflect subjective impressions at the time.

2.5   Data Analysis

To address RQ1, we first tested whether the path deviation predicted the cognitive load. Letter-labeled zones were converted to numeric sequences and compared against the designer's intended order. The path deviation for each participant-infographic pair was calculated using a normalized Spearman's Footrule distance:

$$D_{\mathrm{norm}}(P, Q) = \frac{\sum_{i=1}^{n} |P(i) - Q(i)|}{\max F_r(n)} \tag{1}$$

The denominator $\max F_r(n)$ denotes the theoretical maximum possible footrule distance for length n permutations, ensuring that the result is normalized to the interval $[0, 1]$. It can be compactly expressed using the floor operator:

$$\max F_r(n) = \left\lfloor \frac{n^2}{2} \right\rfloor \tag{2}$$

The normalized score D_{norm} thus ranges from 0 (perfect alignment with the intended path) to 1 (maximum deviation), where higher values indicate greater divergence from the designer's intended reading sequence [7].

To evaluate the potential impact of path deviation on cognitive load, a multivariate analysis of covariance (MANCOVA) was conducted using the normalized Spearman's Footrule distance (path deviation) as covariate, with the four NASA-TLX dimensions: Temporal Demand, Effort, Frustration, and Performance, as dependent variables.

To address RQ2, we conducted two sets of multivariate analyses to examine how structural features influenced cognitive load across the four NASA-TLX dimensions.

First, a multivariate analysis of variance (MANOVA) was performed with two categorical predictors: Layout Type (0 = 2D, 1 = 2.5D) and Subheading Presence (0 = absent, 1 = present). This analysis assessed whether these discrete structural features significantly affected participants' cognitive load profiles. Second, a MANCOVA was conducted using two continuous covariates: Minimum Body Text Size (ranging from 3 to 13 pt) and Zone Count (ranging from 4 to 7 zones).

3   Result

3.1   Path Deviation

To examine whether the path deviation had a significant impact on cognitive load, a multivariate analysis was conducted across the four selected NASA-TLX dimensions. The result was not statistically significant (Pillai's trace $= .056$, $F(4, 127) = 1.892$, $p = .116$, partial $\eta^2 = .056$), suggesting that path deviation did not produce a general effect on cognitive load. Follow-up univariate analyses also revealed no significant effects.

3.2   Layout Type

A multivariate test revealed a significant effect of layout type on the four NASA-TLX dimensions (Pillai's trace $= .177$, $F(4, 127) = 6.810$, $p < .001$, partial $\eta^2 = .177$), indicating that 17.7% of the multivariate variance in cognitive load is attributable to layout configuration.

Subsequent univariate tests showed significant effects on Temporal Demand ($p = .001$), Frustration ($p < .001$), and Effort ($p < .001$), but not on Performance ($p = .056$). These results suggest that participants experienced lower cognitive load when interacting with 2D layouts compared to 2.5D layouts, in terms of temporal demand, effort, and frustration.

3.3 Other Structural Features

Subheading Presence. The results showed a significant multivariate effect on the combined NASA-TLX dimensions (Pillai's trace $= .280$, $F(12, 381) = 3.273$, $p < .001$, partial $\eta^2 = .093$). Follow-up univariate tests revealed significant effects across all four dimensions: Temporal Demand ($p = .008$), Frustration ($p = .001$), Effort ($p < .001$), and Performance ($p = .012$). These results suggest that the presence of subheadings can meaningfully reduce perceived task difficulty and enhance user clarity.

Minimum Body Text Size. The results indicated a significant multivariate effect (Pillai's trace $= .119$, $F(4, 127) = 4.302$, $p = .003$, partial $\eta^2 = .119$).

Univariate analysis showed that text size significantly influenced Temporal Demand ($p = .003$), Frustration ($p = .001$), and Effort ($p < .001$), but not Performance ($p = .518$). This suggests that while small text increases perceived difficulty, it may not reduce confidence in task performance–possibly due to participants being able to reference the visuals during the tasks.

Zone Count. In contrast, the number of visual zones did not produce a significant multivariate effect (Pillai's trace $= .035$, $F(4, 127) = 1.149$, $p = .336$, partial $\eta^2 = .035$). Increasing or decreasing the number of segmented sections between four and seven had no substantial impact on the perceived cognitive load of the participants.

Summary of Structural Effects. Among all factors tested, the presence of subheadings showed the strongest and most consistent association with reduced cognitive load. The minimum size of the body text and the layout type were also significantly related to perceived effort, though they had no observable effect on self-reported performance. In contrast, zone count and path deviation showed no significant correlation with any of the cognitive dimensions measured.

4 Discussion

4.1 Key Findings

The number of visual areas (zone count) did not significantly affect the cognitive load. In other words, as long as the layout is clear, even a relatively high number of segmented zones that present various types of information can still effectively support audience comprehension. Post-task interviews revealed that the majority of the participants preferred the two visuals with the lowest cognitive load (13 and 11 votes), while the remaining four visuals received similar preference levels (5, 5, 5, and 4 votes). The participant's preference for the two visuals with the highest cognitive load appeared to be primarily influenced by their visual appeal. These results suggest that clarity and ease of understanding are central to user preference in infographic design, yet visual attractiveness should not be overlooked.

4.2   Design Implications

There is no single correct answer in visual design. The balance between effective information delivery and aesthetic appeal is shaped by a variety of subtle factors, including reading habits, cognitive tendencies, and aesthetic preferences. The suggestions offered below do not aim to prescribe universal rules, but rather reflect insights drawn from the specific conditions of this study. They are intended to serve as references for designers who are navigating the challenges of complex infographic creation.

Prioritize Typographic Clarity. Typography plays a fundamental role in visual communication. Clear, well-sized, and contrast-rich body text reduces viewer fatigue and facilitates efficient reading. Our results indicate that distorted or overly decorative fonts, especially those affected by spatial transformations, can significantly increase perceived effort and frustration. Designers are encouraged to use clean and legible typefaces, especially in dense or information-heavy layouts.

Use Subheadings to Segment Information. Subheadings help structure visual content and provide anchors for navigation. They not only reduce perceived complexity but also improve performance in information retrieval tasks. According to our findings, subheadings significantly lowered cognitive load across several dimensions, suggesting their value as low-effort yet high-impact structural cues in static infographics.

Be Cautious with 2.5D Embellishments. Although the 2.5D effect can enhance visual interest, they may also obscure critical content or impair overall legibility. In our study, such embellishments, especially 2.5D transformations applied to text, significantly increased perceived effort and frustration. These distortions disrupted the fluency of reading and made it harder for participants to extract information efficiently.

It is also important to note that because of the constraints of our experimental design, all selected materials were in a horizontal layout. Moreover, to calculate the path deviation, we excluded flowcharts that might have relatively clear and linear reading paths. In actual design practice, vertical 2.5D visuals and flow charts or a combination of both, which is very common, may function clearly and effectively within well-structured guidance systems. More studies are needed to assess their cognitive impact in such a context.

Allow for Multiple Zones Without Overburdening the Viewer. Based on the experimental materials, which included visualizations segmented into four to seven zones, the results indicate that an increased number of visual zones does not inherently impose a higher cognitive load. When the layout is well structured and visually coherent, viewers are able to process segmented information efficiently.

In particular, the visualization containing the highest number of zones (seven in total) was rated as having the second lowest cognitive load among the six designs. This indicates that segmentation, when accompanied by clear spatial organization, may enhance rather than impair comprehension. However, this effect likely applies only within a limited range. Excessive fragmentation, especially in the absence of strong visual guidance, may still increase cognitive effort and compromise clarity. Further research is needed to better define the upper bounds of effective segmentation.

5   Conclusion

Within the scope of this study, no clear correlation was found between path deviation and subjective cognitive load. However, other structural factors showed stronger associations with the perceived effort of the participants. These included whether the infographic used a 2D or 2.5D design, the minimum size of the body text, and the presence or absence of clear subheadings. In contrast, the number of visual zones (which ranged from four to seven in our test materials) did not significantly affect cognitive load. These findings suggest that neither the path deviation nor the number of segmented sections (within the tested range of four to seven) plays a substantial role in shaping the perceived cognitive load, while other visual features may exert a more pronounced influence.

One promising direction is to further explore how specific structural features influence Path Deviation. Although this study focused on the link between layout design and cognitive load, a deeper understanding of how elements such as the relative size of key components, the balance between titles and visual zones, or the presence of spatial obstructions shape reader navigation remains to be established. Early observations suggest that differences in visual prominence may play a role, and insights from comic layout studies, such as 'blockage' as discussed in Cohn's research [3], could offer valuable analogies. Both comics and complex infographics rely on spatial arrangements to organize juxtaposed segments within a shared visual space, making such comparisons especially relevant.

Another valuable direction involves the use of eye tracking to triangulate the designer's intended reading path, participants' self-reported navigation, and their actual gaze behavior. This method can reveal where visual cues succeed in guiding attention and where they fall short, providing deeper insight into how viewers interpret complex structures in real time. The resulting evidence would enhance our understanding of visual guidance mechanisms and support the design of layouts that reduce cognitive burden while preserving exploratory freedom.

Lastly, future work might expand the scope of visualization types included in the analysis. Although this study focused on horizontally arranged static images with a moderate number of zones, infographics in broader design contexts such as digital formats often incorporate motion or light interactivity. Features such as zooming or panning represent a nuanced middle ground between static and dynamic presentations. Projects like Calculating Empires [8] illustrate how, when carefully designed, these interactive formats can support exploratory navigation while preserving the coherence of highly complex visual structures. Such hybrid approaches may benefit from being examined within a unified classification framework that integrates spatial organization and interaction design.

Ultimately, effective reading navigation is not about simplifying information, but about shaping visual structures that encourage curiosity and support intuitive exploration. The richness of complex infographics lies in their ability to open up interpretive spaces where meaning is not only delivered, but also actively constructed.

Acknowledgments. The authors thank all designers who authorized the use of their infographic works as experimental stimuli. Formal permissions were obtained from all copyright holders prior to the study. We also sincerely thank all student participants for their time and cooperation during the experimental sessions. All participants provided informed consent in accordance with institutional ethical guidelines.

References

1. Berlyne, D.E.: Aesthetics and Psychobiology. Appleton-Century-Crofts, New York (1971)
2. Sweller, J.: Cognitive load during problem solving: effects on learning. Cogn. Sci. **12**, 257–285 (1988)
3. Cohn, N.: Navigating comics: an empirical and theoretical approach to strategies of reading comic page layouts. Front. Psychol. **4**(186) (2013)
4. Majooni, A., Masood, M., Masoumi, A.A.: An eye-tracking study on the effect of infographic structures on viewer's comprehension and cognitive load. Inf. Vis. **17**(2), 1–10 (2017). https://doi.org/10.1177/1473871617701971
5. Kintsch, W.: Comprehension: A Paradigm for Cognition. Cambridge University Press, London (1998)
6. Hart, S.G., Staveland, L.E.: Development of NASA-TLX (Task Load Index): Results of Empirical and Theoretical Research. Human Mental Workload, 139–183 (1988)
7. Fagin, R., Kumar, R., Sivakumar, D.: Comparing Top k lists. SIAM J. Discret. Math. **17**(1), 134–160 (2003)
8. Calculating Empires: A Genealogy of Technology and Power Since 1500. https://calculatingempires.net. Accessed 15 June 2025

A Comparative Analysis of Open-Source Conversational Chatbots in Resource-Constrained Environments

Giuseppe Sansonetti[(✉)] [iD] and Alessandro Micarelli [iD]

Department of Engineering, Roma Tre University, Via della Vasca Navale, 79, 00146 Rome, Italy
`{gsansone,ailab}@dia.uniroma3.it`

Abstract. In this paper, we explore and compare the performance of three conversational chatbots based on large language models, focusing on solutions that are entirely open-source and accessible. The models were tested under realistic computational constraints using Google Colab's free environment. The evaluation covered two tasks: closed-domain question answering (based solely on internal model knowledge) and standard question answering (with external context provided). Both technical performance and user feedback were considered. The technical assessment included over 250 questions, measuring accuracy, speed, informativeness, and language quality. A user survey involving some participants supplemented these findings.

Keywords: Large Language Models · Question Answering · Comparative Analysis

1 Introduction

Nowadays, the Internet has become a ubiquitous companion in our lives [16], enabling continuous access to information and facilitating interaction across temporal, spatial, and social boundaries [33]. Within this digitally mediated ecosystem, intelligent systems such as recommender systems [11,22], play a critical role in shaping user experiences. These systems guide individuals in making decisions about what to read [4], study [18,19], listen to [27], watch [34], play [5], purchase [2,21], or engage with [17]. Increasingly, they also act as proactive agents, offering personalized suggestions for cultural activities [9,20,31], tourist destinations (e.g., restaurants [29,32] and museums [12,24]), multimedia content [25,30], and optimized travel itineraries [8,13]. From a Human-Computer Interaction (HCI) perspective, these developments emphasize a shift in how users engage with digital environments, moving from reactive search-based paradigms to more anticipatory, context-aware interactions. Intelligent systems have evolved beyond being mere tools [10]; they now work as interactive agents embedded in everyday practices, shaping behavior and expectations in subtle yet profound ways [3,14].

© The Author(s), under exclusive license to Springer Nature Switzerland AG 2026
S. Sundarakannan and O. Knorpp (Eds.): HCII 2025, CCIS 2772, pp. 393–401, 2026.
https://doi.org/10.1007/978-3-032-12767-9_41

A particularly transformative advancement in this space is the emergence and rapid integration of Large Language Models (LLMs), which are now widely accessible through Internet-connected devices [35]. These models enable new forms of interaction characterized by natural language dialogue, contextual reasoning, and adaptive feedback, thereby redefining traditional notions of interface design and user support [28]. Contemporary platforms such as OpenAI's ChatGPT[1], Google's Gemini[2], and Microsoft's Copilot[3] exemplify this evolution, providing conversational agents that support a wide spectrum of information-seeking and problem-solving activities. Their widespread adoption has significant implications for HCI, raising new questions about usability, transparency, trust, cognitive load, and the co-adaptive dynamics between humans and AI systems. Reflecting these shifts, the HCI research community has already begun to publish a substantial body of work that explores these technologies from theoretical and applied perspectives [36]. This emerging literature offers valuable insights into how LLM-based systems are transforming user experiences, reshaping interaction paradigms, and prompting reconsideration of long-standing design principles in human-computer interaction [26]. Among the works available in the research literature, there are also contributions presenting the results of comprehensive comparative analyses of currently available large language models, including both proprietary and open-source solutions (e.g., see [6,7,23]). In particular, with open-source alternatives becoming increasingly sophisticated, there is also a growing need to assess which models perform best under accessible conditions. This research investigates this issue by evaluating three popular open-source chatbots in a constrained environment that mirrors typical resource availability for developers and researchers.

2 Research Motivation and Setup

The primary objective of this study is to understand which open-source LLMs offer the best balance in terms of performance and usability, especially when deployed in environments with limited computational resources. Specifically, we used the free version of Google Colab[4], which offers the following computing resources:

- 12.7 GB of RAM;
- 16 GB T4 GPU;
- 70.8 GB of disk space.

These limitations constrain the size of models that can be loaded and used effectively. Models exceeding seven billion parameters typically require optimization techniques, such as 4-bit quantization, to run smoothly. We selected the following three models based on distinct attributes:

---

[1] https://chatgpt.com/.
[2] https://gemini.google.com/.
[3] https://copilot.microsoft.com/.
[4] https://colab.research.google.com/.

- **Llama-2-7b-chat-hf** (from here on simply **Llama 2**), developed by Meta, is among the most popular for its revolutionary architecture within the open-source ecosystem;
- **Falcon-7b-instruct** (from here on simply **Falcon**), created by the Technology Innovation Institute, is known for being the most downloaded 7-billion-parameter model for its reliability;
- **Neural-chat-7b-v3-1** (from here on simply **Neural-Chat**), Intel's contribution built on Mistral-7B-v0.1, was included for its technical excellence.

3   Methodology

We evaluated the models based on their ability to perform two types of Question Answering (QA) tasks [1]. In the closed-domain setting, models were asked to respond to questions using only their pre-trained knowledge. In contrast, the standard QA task provided a context passage along with the question, requiring models to extract and generate appropriate answers based on that context. To evaluate these models comprehensively, we adopted a dual approach [15].

3.1   Technical Evaluation

First, we conducted a technical evaluation by manually assessing model responses to 128 closed-domain and 127 standard QA questions. Each response was rated on a five-point scale for correctness, syntactic quality, informativeness, and response time.

3.2   User Survey

Second, we organized a user survey with 13 participants, whose demographics are reported in Table 1.

Each participant formulated and submitted ten questions to each of the three models using Colab notebooks. Participants rated each model based on overall satisfaction, interface usability, and the perceived quality of responses.

Participants were also asked to evaluate the chatbot interfaces (see Table 2). Over half of them rated the interface as adequate, while a notable portion found it intuitive. Only a few participants rated the interface negatively, suggesting that the user interface did not significantly hinder their experience.

Each participant submitted ten questions to each of the three models, for a total of 130 questions. Table 3 shows that the most common domains related to questions asked by participants were general knowledge, sport, and computer science, indicating a diverse but focused range of interests.

The user survey was performed in accordance with ethical standards involving human subjects. All participants provided informed consent prior to their involvement, and strict measures were taken to ensure the confidentiality and privacy of their data, so that our research protocol complied with national and international guidelines for human subject research.

Table 1. Demographic characteristics of the 13 participants in the user survey (in %).

Characteristic	Category	Percentage (%)
Gender	Male	53.8
	Female	46.2
	Non-Binary	0.0
	I prefer not to answer	0.0
Age	18–29	38.5
	30–49	15.4
	50–64	38.5
	65+	7.6
	I prefer not to answer	0.0
Country of origin	Italy	84.6
	Europe (Not Italy)	0.0
	Extra Europe	15.4
	I prefer not to answer	0.0
Educational level	High School	61.5
	Bachelor's Degree	15.4
	Master's Degree	15.4
	PhD or higher	7.7
	I prefer not to answer	0.0
Average time on the Internet (hr/d)	Less than 1 h	7.7
	1–3 hours	38.5
	3–5 hours	53.8
	More than 5 h	53.8
	I prefer not to answer	0.0
Most used information medium	Television	53.8
	Social media	38.5
	Newspapers	0.0
	Other	0.0
	I prefer not to answer	7.7

Table 2. User ratings regarding interface preferences (in %).

Rating	Percentage (%)
Strongly Dislike	0.0
Dislike	7.7
Neutral	53.8
Like	38.5
Strongly Like	0.0

Table 3. Domains of questions submitted by users (in %).

Domain	Percentage (%)
Automotive	7.0
Cinema	5.0
Computer science	12.0
Economy and finance	4.0
General knowledge	25.0
Geography	9.0
History	5.0
Math	8.0
Medicine	7.0
Sport	14.0
Technology	4.0

4 Results and Analysis

In order to test the three models, we considered the following evaluation metrics:

- Correctness of responses (CRT) (technical evaluation);
- Average response time (TMR) (technical evaluation);
- Syntactic quality (QST) (technical evaluation);
- Quantity of information (QIT) ((technical evaluation);
- Correctness of responses (CRS) (survey);
- Average response time (TMS) (survey);
- Syntactic quality (QSS) (survey).

According to the evaluation metrics, Neural-Chat consistently outperformed the other models across most criteria (see Tables 4 and 5). It generated more accurate and informative answers, maintained higher syntactic quality, and, in the standard QA task, even outperforming Falcon in response time, which had demonstrated superior speed in earlier assessments. LLaMA 2 performed consistently but did not match the levels achieved by Neural-Chat or Falcon in any specific metric.

Table 4. Results of the closed-domain QA evaluation.

Model	CRT	CRS	TMR	TMS	QST	QSS	QIT	Total Value
Neural-Chat	4.55	4.69	3.89	4.00	3.07	3.40	3.33	26.93
Llama-2	4.55	4.07	3.32	3.30	3.21	2.91	3.29	24.65
Falcon	4.00	3.38	4.16	4.61	2.62	2.31	2.61	23.69

Table 5. Results of the standard QA evaluation.

Model	CRT	TMR	QST	QIT	Total Value
Neural-Chat	4.53	3.16	3.16	3.16	14.01
Llama-2	3.75	2.37	2.92	2.54	11.58
Falcon	3.23	3.05	2.47	2.37	11.12

User feedback further supported these findings. As shown in Table 4, the metric values from the user survey (i.e., CRS, TMS, and QSS) indicate that most participants rated their interaction with Neural-Chat positively, particularly appreciating the clarity and reliability of its responses. While Falcon was recognized for its responsiveness, it did not consistently meet expectations regarding answer quality. Finally, LLaMA 2 received moderate ratings and was frequently perceived as less engaging and accurate compared to Neural-Chat (Table 6).

5   Discussion

The results from both evaluation analyses suggest that Neural-Chat is currently the most balanced and capable open-source chatbot among those tested.

Table 6. Overall results of the two evaluations and their mean value.

Model	Closed-Domain QA	Standard QA	Mean Value
Neural-Chat	26.93	14.01	20.47
Llama-2	24.65	11.58	18.12
Falcon	23.69	11.12	17.41

It excels not only in technical performance but also in providing a user-friendly experience, even under resource-constrained conditions typical of Google Colab. The success of Falcon in response speed is notable, but it does not compensate for its slightly lower quality in other areas. LLaMA 2, while popular, may benefit from further tuning or enhancements to compete at the same level. Using a standardized five-point rating scale allowed us to normalize and compare results objectively. This approach was particularly helpful in maintaining consistency across both technical and survey-based evaluations.

5.1   Limitations

While the findings of this study provide valuable insights into the comparative performance of open-source chatbots in constrained environments, several limitations should be acknowledged. First, the evaluation was conducted using a relatively small and homogeneous user sample, which may limit the generalizability of the user feedback. Second, the assessment relied on a fixed set of questions and a subjective scoring scale, which could potentially introduce evaluator bias despite efforts to ensure consistency. Additionally, only three models with similar parameter sizes were tested, excluding larger or differently optimized models that may perform differently under the same conditions. Lastly, using the free version of Google Colab imposes limitations not only on computational resources but also on reproducibility and long-term deployment feasibility.

6   Conclusions and Future Work

Our comparative study confirms that Neural-Chat is the most effective open-source chatbot within the tested environment. Its superior performance in both technical and user-based evaluations makes it a promising foundation for future conversational AI systems. We aim to contribute to the development of more capable, accessible, and intelligent chatbots that align with the principles of openness and user empowerment.

In future work, we plan to extend this work by comparing the capabilities of various chatbots that incorporate conversational memory, which allows the chatbot to retain and leverage previous interactions to deliver increasingly satisfactory responses to users. To this end, we plan to develop a dedicated user interface using modern frontend frameworks to enhance accessibility. We also plan to implement voice interaction capabilities, making the chatbot usable in voice-activated, hands-free scenarios. Finally, we intend to integrate tools and agents, enabling the chatbot to handle complex tasks, such as executing Python code or interfacing with APIs, thereby making it a more general-purpose AI assistant.

References

1. Biancini, G., Ferrato, A., Limongelli, C.: Multiple-choice question generation using large language models: methodology and educator insights. In: Adjunct Proceedings of the 32nd ACM Conference on User Modeling, Adaptation and Personalization, pp. 584–590. UMAP Adjunct '24, ACM, New York, NY, USA (2024)
2. Bologna, C., De Rosa, A.C., De Vivo, A., Gaeta, M., Sansonetti, G., Viserta, V.: Personality-based recommendation in e-commerce. In: CEUR Workshop Proceedings, vol. 997. CEUR-WS.org, Aachen, Germany (2013)
3. Bordoni, L., et al.: The contribution of AI to enhance understanding of cultural heritage. Intell. Artif. **7**(2), 101–112 (2013)
4. Caldarelli, S., Gurini, D.F., Micarelli, A., Sansonetti, G.: A signal-based approach to news recommendation. In: CEUR Workshop Proceedings, vol. 1618, pp. 1–4. CEUR-WS.org, Aachen, Germany (2016)
5. Carloni, L., De Angelis, A., Sansonetti, G., Micarelli, A.: A machine learning approach to football match result prediction. In: Stephanidis, C., Antona, M., Ntoa, S. (eds.) HCI International 2021 - Posters, pp. 473–480. Springer, Cham (2021)

6. Castagnacci, G., Sansonetti, G., Micarelli, A.: User experience with ChatGPT: insights from a comprehensive evaluation. In: Stephanidis, C., Antona, M., Ntoa, S., Salvendy, G. (eds.) HCI International 2024 Posters, pp. 177–185. Springer, Cham (2024)

7. Chang, Y., et al.: A survey on evaluation of large language models. ACM TIST **15**(3) (2024)

8. D'Agostino, D., Gasparetti, F., Micarelli, A., Sansonetti, G.: A social context-aware recommender of itineraries between relevant points of interest. In: Stephanidis, C. (ed.) HCI International 2016, vol. 618, pp. 354–359. Springer, Cham (2016). https://doi.org/10.1007/978-3-319-40542-1_58

9. De Angelis, A., Gasparetti, F., Micarelli, A., Sansonetti, G.: A social cultural recommender based on linked open data. In: Adjunct Publication of the 25th Conference on User Modeling, Adaptation and Personalization, pp. 329–332. UMAP '17, ACM, New York, NY, USA (2017)

10. Deng, Y., Liao, L., Zheng, Z., Yang, G.H., Chua, T.S.: Towards human-centered proactive conversational agents. In: Proceedings of the 47th International ACM SIGIR Conference on Research and Development in Information Retrieval, pp. 807–818. SIGIR '24, ACM, New York, NY, USA (2024)

11. Ferrato, A.: Challenges for anonymous session-based recommender systems in indoor environments. In: Proceedings of the 17th ACM Conference on Recommender Systems, pp. 1339–1341. RecSys '23, ACM, New York, NY, USA (2023)

12. Ferrato, A., Limongelli, C., Mezzini, M., Sansonetti, G.: The meta4rs proposal: museum emotion and tracking analysis for recommender systems. In: Adjunct Proceedings of the 30th ACM Conference on User Modeling, Adaptation and Personalization, pp. 406–409. UMAP '22 Adjunct, ACM, New York, NY, USA (2022)

13. Fogli, A., Sansonetti, G.: Exploiting semantics for context-aware itinerary recommendation. Pers. Ubiquit. Comput. **23**(2), 215–231 (2019)

14. Garcia, K., Mayer, S., Ricci, A., Ciortea, A.: Proactive digital companions in pervasive hypermedia environments. In: 2020 IEEE 6th International Conference on Collaboration and Internet Computing (CIC), pp. 54–59. IEEE (2020)

15. Gena, C., Cena, F., Vernero, F., Grillo, P.: The evaluation of a social adaptive website for cultural events. User Model. User-Adap. Inter. **23**, 89–137 (2013)

16. Graham, M., Dutton, W.H.: Society and The Internet: How Networks of Information and Communication are Changing Our Lives. Oxford University Press (2019)

17. Gurini, D.F., Gasparetti, F., Micarelli, A., Sansonetti, G.: iSCUR: interest and sentiment-based community detection for user recommendation on twitter. In: Dimitrova, V., Kuflik, T., Chin, D., Ricci, F., Dolog, P., Houben, G.-J. (eds.) UMAP 2014. LNCS, vol. 8538, pp. 314–319. Springer, Cham (2014). https://doi.org/10.1007/978-3-319-08786-3_27

18. Hassan, H.A.M., Sansonetti, G., Gasparetti, F., Micarelli, A.: Semantic-based tag recommendation in scientific bookmarking systems. In: Proceedings of the 12th ACM Conference on Recommender Systems, pp. 465–469. ACM, New York, NY, USA (2018)

19. Hassan, H.A.M., Sansonetti, G., Gasparetti, F., Micarelli, A., Beel, J.: Bert, elmo, use and infersent sentence encoders: the panacea for research-paper recommendation? In: RecSys (Late-Breaking Results), pp. 6–10 (2019)

20. Huang, J.: Personalized recommendation method for cultural creative products in tourism cities based on user profiles. Procedia Comput. Sci. **243**, 1133–1142 (2024)

21. Jameson, A., et al.: How can we support users' preferential choice? In: Conference on Human Factors in Computing Systems - Proceedings, pp. 409–418 (2011)

22. Ko, H., Lee, S., Park, Y., Choi, A.: A survey of recommendation systems: recommendation models, techniques, and application fields. Electronics **11**(1), 141 (2022)
23. Li, Z., Wu, X., Du, H., Nghiem, H., Shi, G.: Benchmark evaluations, applications, and challenges of large vision language models: a survey. arXiv preprint arXiv:2501.02189 (2025)
24. Mezzini, M., Limongelli, C., Sansonetti, G., De Medio, C.: Tracking museum visitors through convolutional object detectors. In: Adjunct Publication of the 28th ACM Conference on User Modeling, Adaptation and Personalization, pp. 352–355. UMAP '20 Adjunct, ACM, New York, NY, USA (2020)
25. Micarelli, A., Neri, A., Sansonetti, G.: A case-based approach to image recognition. In: Blanzieri, E., Portinale, L. (eds.) EWCBR 2000. LNCS, vol. 1898, pp. 443–454. Springer, Heidelberg (2000). https://doi.org/10.1007/3-540-44527-7_38
26. Oelen, A., Auer, S.: Leveraging large language models for realizing truly intelligent user interfaces. In: Extended Abstracts of the CHI Conference on Human Factors in Computing Systems, pp. 1–8 (2024)
27. Onori, M., Micarelli, A., Sansonetti, G.: A comparative analysis of personality-based music recommender systems. In: CEUR Workshop Proceedings, vol. 1680, pp. 55–59. CEUR-WS.org, Aachen, Germany (2016)
28. Pozdniakov, S., et al.: Large language models meet user interfaces: the case of provisioning feedback. Comput. Educ. Artif. Intell. **7**, 100289 (2024)
29. Sansonetti, G.: Point of interest recommendation based on social and linked open data. Pers. Ubiquit. Comput. **23**(2), 199–214 (2019)
30. Sansonetti, G., Gasparetti, F., Micarelli, A.: Using social media for personalizing the cultural heritage experience. In: Adjunct Proceedings of the 29th ACM Conference on User Modeling, Adaptation and Personalization, pp. 189–193. UMAP '21, ACM, New York, NY, USA (2021)
31. Sansonetti, G., Gasparetti, F., Micarelli, A., Cena, F., Gena, C.: Enhancing cultural recommendations through social and linked open data. User Model. User-Adap. Inter. **29**(1), 121–159 (2019)
32. Sardella, N., Biancalana, C., Micarelli, A., Sansonetti, G.: An approach to conversational recommendation of restaurants. In: Stephanidis, C. (ed.) HCII 2019. CCIS, vol. 1034, pp. 123–130. Springer, Cham (2019). https://doi.org/10.1007/978-3-030-23525-3_16
33. Suárez Álvarez, A., Vicente, M.R.: Is too much time on the internet making us less satisfied with life? Appl. Res. Qual. Life **19**(5), 2245–2265 (2024)
34. Valeriani, D., Sansonetti, G., Micarelli, A.: A comparative analysis of state-of-the-art recommendation techniques in the movie domain. In: Corvasi, O., et al. (eds.) ICCSA 2020. LNCS, vol. 12252, pp. 104–118. Springer, Cham (2020). https://doi.org/10.1007/978-3-030-58811-3_8
35. Wasti, S.M., Pu, K.Q., Neshati, A.: Large language user interfaces: voice interactive user interfaces powered by LLMs. In: Intelligent Systems Conference, pp. 639–655. Springer (2024)
36. Zhang, C., et al.: Large language model-brained GUI agents: a survey. arXiv preprint arXiv:2411.18279 (2024)

Designing Wine Tasting Experiences for All: The Role of Human Diversity and Personal Food Memory

Xinyang Shan[1], Yuanyuan Xu[1(✉)], Yuqing Wang[1], Tian Xia[2],
and Yin-Shan Lin[1,3]

[1] Tongji University, Shanghai 200292, China
`xuyuanyuan@alumni.tongji.edu.cn`
[2] Shanghai Jiao Tong University, Shanghai 200240, China
[3] Northeastern University, Boston, MA 02115, USA

Abstract. Wine tourism is a rapidly growing sector, valued at \$29.6 billion globally in 2023, with an anticipated annual growth rate of 5.9%. However, traditional wine tasting practices are rooted in Western cultural norms, limiting their appeal to a diverse global audience. This study explores how human diversity and personal food memory can create more inclusive and engaging wine tasting experiences, particularly for Chinese tourists. Over 11 months, we conducted field studies in Xinjiang, Shandong, and Tuscany with 23 Chinese participants. Data were collected through observations, audio/video recordings, and follow-up interviews. The Abilities, Necessities, and Aspirations (ANA) framework was applied to identify cross-cultural adaptation challenges. Our findings reveal that 76% of participants found Western wine terminology difficult to understand, while 83% preferred describing wine flavors using familiar food-related terms like "pickled radish" and "sun-dried plums". Additionally, 68% reported increased confidence and enjoyment when connecting wine flavors to personal food memories. We propose a three-part framework for designing inclusive wine tasting experiences: adapting tasting guides to reflect cultural differences, balancing sensory exploration with social elements, and integrating personal food memory into flavor descriptions.

This study provides practical guidelines for developing culturally sensitive wine tasting experiences, improving engagement and satisfaction among diverse audiences.

Keywords: Wine Tasting · Inclusive Design · Sensory Memory · Cross-Cultural Experience

1 Introduction

Wine tourism has become a significant part of the global travel industry, with wine tasting at the heart of this growing sector. The global wine tourism market was valued at \$29.6 billion in 2023 and is projected to grow at an annual rate

© The Author(s), under exclusive license to Springer Nature Switzerland AG 2026

S. Sundarakannan and O. Knorpp (Eds.): HCII 2025, CCIS 2772, pp. 402–407, 2026.
https://doi.org/10.1007/978-3-032-12767-9_42

of 5.9% over the next five years [1]. However, traditional wine tasting practices remain deeply rooted in Western cultural norms, which may not resonate with consumers from diverse cultural backgrounds [3].

Current wine tasting practices are typically designed for Western consumers, emphasizing sensory analysis and technical language to describe flavors [9]. This creates barriers for consumers from different cultural backgrounds, especially those from China, where drinking culture is more symbolic and socially driven [8]. Recent works highlight how culturally adapted experience management tools [16], AI-supported cross-cultural frameworks [17], emotion-aware interaction design [18], and language model applications [19] can support more inclusive wine tourism experiences. The role of consumer-perceived value in tailoring such experiences has also been emphasized in business-modeling contexts [20].

2   Background and Literature Review

In Chinese culture, wine is often perceived as a luxury product, valued more for its symbolic meaning than for its sensory qualities [5]. Unlike Western dining traditions, where wine pairing is an important aspect of the meal, Chinese culinary customs involve serving multiple dishes simultaneously without strict pairing guidelines [6]. Cultural differences such as these impact how wine experiences are interpreted and appreciated across global markets [16]. Additionally, emotion recognition and user-centric technological support can play a role in addressing such cultural gaps [18].

Western wine tasting tools, such as the wine flavor wheel and Le Nez du Vin, often fail to resonate with Chinese consumers due to their reliance on Western flavor profiles and sensory terminology [10]. Terms like "oak," "minerality," and "tannins" are difficult to translate into Chinese sensory contexts, leading to confusion and disengagement. Typeface and visual language also play a role in shaping user experience and sensory communication across cultures [21].

3   Methodology

To explore how human diversity and personal food memory influence wine tasting, we conducted a series of field studies over 11 months in three major wine regions: Xinjiang, Shandong, and Tuscany.

Three distinct wine tasting events were organized. The first event, held at a family-owned winery in Xinjiang, combined a vineyard tour, grape picking, and a traditional lunch paired with five wines. The second event, conducted in Shandong, involved a structured tasting of five wines preceded by a 30-minute introduction to wine terminology. The third event, in Tuscany, included a vertical tasting of six vintages from 2007 to 2017.

Data were collected using direct observations, video and audio recordings, and post-event interviews lasting 20 to 30 min. The analysis was guided by the Abilities, Necessities, and Aspirations (ANA) framework [4] (Fig. 1).

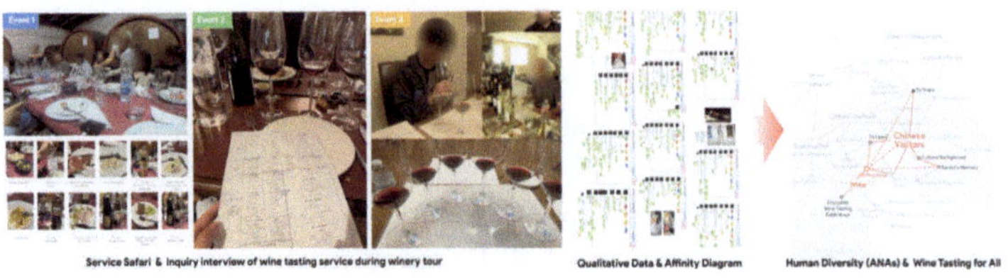

Fig. 1. Overview of the study design and methodology.

Our findings reveal key patterns in how Chinese participants engage with wine tasting experiences.

76% of participants reported difficulty understanding Western wine terminology, such as "oak," "minerality," and "tannins" [10]. These terms lacked cultural relevance, making it difficult for participants to interpret sensory characteristics. Even participants with prior wine knowledge showed limited comprehension.

83% of participants preferred to describe wine using culturally familiar food-related terms [8]. For example, participants described red wine aromas as similar to "pickled radish" or "dried hawthorn" and white wine acidity as "sour plum soup." This suggests that adapting sensory language to local culinary references improves engagement.

68% of participants reported higher confidence and enjoyment when they were encouraged to describe wine flavors using personal food memory [6]. Connecting wine flavors to familiar foods enhanced sensory engagement and facilitated more active social interaction.

Participants engaged more actively in informal tasting events (e.g., vineyard-based tastings) than in structured events held in formal venues. Authenticity and comfort increased when the tasting environment resembled social and family-style settings.

Gender and age differences were observed: female participants showed greater interest in social and symbolic aspects, while younger participants were more open to exploring new flavors. Older participants preferred traditional flavors and described wine using references to Chinese herbal medicine and preserved fruits.

4   Discussion and Implications

The results highlight the need to adapt wine tasting experiences to Chinese consumers' cultural and sensory backgrounds.

Western wine terminology should be adapted to local culinary references. Terms like "oak" and "tannins" have no direct equivalent in Chinese cuisine. Providing bilingual tasting guides with culturally familiar terms (e.g., "hawthorn," "plum," "green tea") can improve comprehension and comfort [10]. Developing a tasting wheel based on Chinese flavor profiles would further support sensory engagement.

Social interaction is central to Chinese drinking culture. Tasting events should incorporate group-based formats and communal sharing to reflect this social dynamic [8]. Including storytelling about the vineyard's history and production process can enhance authenticity and emotional connection.

Personal food memory is a powerful sensory tool. Encouraging participants to describe wine using familiar foods (e.g., "sour plum soup" or "jasmine tea") improves sensory engagement. Training winery staff to integrate culturally relevant terms into tasting descriptions will further enhance this effect [6].

Informal and relaxed tasting settings increase participant comfort and perceived authenticity. Balancing structured analysis with casual, social interaction creates a more engaging experience. For instance, combining sensory analysis with informal food pairings could enhance overall satisfaction.

Gender and age differences should guide the design of tasting experiences. Women showed greater interest in the symbolic and social aspects of wine, while younger participants were more curious about new flavors. Tailoring event formats to these differences can increase overall engagement (Fig. 2).

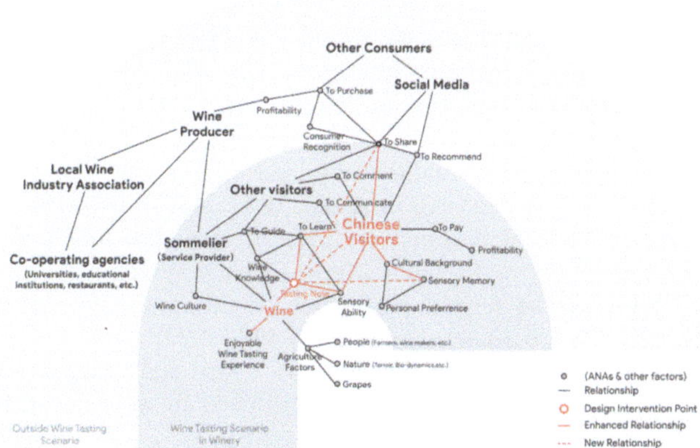

Fig. 2. Proposed framework for designing culturally adaptive wine tasting experiences.

5   Conclusion

This study shows that Western wine terminology creates barriers for Chinese consumers. Adapting tasting language to culturally familiar terms improves comprehension and engagement.

Personal food memory enhances sensory engagement and social interaction. Encouraging participants to describe wine using familiar foods strengthens emotional connection and improves retention.

Social and cultural dynamics influence engagement. Group-based tasting events and storytelling improve authenticity and comfort. Tailoring experiences to gender and age differences increases satisfaction and broadens market reach.

Future research should examine the long-term impact of culturally adaptive tasting experiences on consumer loyalty and winery performance. Cross-cultural tasting frameworks and sensory tools tailored to different markets could further enhance global engagement with wine tourism.

References

1. Santos, V., Ramos, P., Sousa, B., Valeri, M.: Towards a framework for the global wine tourism system. J. Organ. Chang. Manag. **35**(2), 348–360 (2022)
2. Trigo, A., Silva, P.: Sustainable development directions for wine tourism in Douro wine region. Portugal. Sustain. **14**(7), 3949 (2022)
3. Kastenholz, E., Paço, A., Nave, A.: Wine tourism in rural areas-hopes and fears amongst local residents. Worldwide Hosp. Tourism Themes **15**(1), 29–40 (2023)
4. Wu, G., Liang, L.: Examining the effect of potential tourists' wine product involvement on wine tourism destination image and travel intention. In: Current Issues in Tourism, pp. 1–16 (2020)
5. Sun, B.: Chinese National Alcohols: Baijiu and Huangjiu. World Scientific (2021)
6. Yang, Y., et al.: Flavor formation in Chinese rice wine (Huangjiu): impacts of the flavor-active microorganisms, raw materials, and fermentation technology. Front. Microbiol. **11**, 580247 (2020)
7. Schiessl, D.: More expensive wine is really better? The role of positive emotion and consumer power. J. Int. Food Agribusiness Mark. **36**(4), 643–664 (2023)
8. Zhang, J.: Rituals, discourses, and realities: serious wine and tea tasting in contemporary China. J. Consum. Cult. **20**(4), 637–655 (2020)
9. Spence, C.: Multisensory flavour perception: blending, mixing, fusion, and pairing within and between the senses. Foods **9**(4), 407 (2020)
10. Chu, X., Li, Y., Xie, Y., Tian, D., Mu, W.: Regional difference analyzing and prediction model building for Chinese wine consumers' sensory preference. Br. Food J. **122**(8), 2587–2602 (2020)
11. Hanchukova, O., Velikova, N., Koo, B.: Cheers to local! Exploring consumer ethnocentrism in the context of regional wines. Br. Food J. **126**(9), 3584–3603 (2024)
12. Urdapilleta, I., Blanchet-Urdapilleta, H., Demarchi, S.: Cultural sips: exploring sociodemographic and dominance factors in French wine appraisal. Food Res. Int. **187**, 114391 (2024)
13. Wu, D.C., Cao, C., Wu, J., Hu, M.: Wine tourism experiences of Chinese tourists: a tourist-centric perspective. Int. J. Contemp. Hosp. Manag. **36**(8), 2601–2631 (2024)
14. Charters, S., Ali-Knight, J.: Who is the wine tourist? Tour. Manage. **23**(3), 311–319 (2002)
15. Cambourne, B., Macionis, N., Hall, C.M., Sharples, L.: The future of wine tourism. In: Wine Tourism Around the World, pp. 297–320. Routledge (2009)
16. Xu, Y., Shan, X., Guo, M., Gao, W., Lin, Y.-S.: Design and application of experience management tools from the perspective of customer perceived value: a study on the electric vehicle market. World Electr. Veh. J. **15**(8), 378 (2024)

17. Xu, Y., Shan, X., Lin, Y.-S., Wang, J.: AI-enhanced tools for cross-cultural game design: supporting online character conceptualization and collaborative sketching. In: International Conference on Human-Computer Interaction, pp. 429–446. Springer (2025)
18. Xu, Y., Lin, Y.-S., Zhou, X., Shan, X.: Utilizing emotion recognition technology to enhance user experience in real-time. Comput. Artif. Intell. **2**(1), 1388 (2024)
19. Shan, X., Xu, Y., Wang, Y., Lin, Y.-S., Bao, Y.: Cross-cultural implications of large language models: an extended comparative analysis. In: International Conference on Human-Computer Interaction, pp. 106–118. Springer (2024)
20. Xu, Y., Lin, Y.: Exploring the influence of user-perceived value on NEV-enterprises using an empirical computer model. In: Proceedings of the 3rd International Conference on Financial Innovation, FinTech and Information Technology (FFIT 2024), pp. 4–10. Atlantis Press (2024)
21. Tian, G., Xu, Y.: A study on the typeface design method of Han characters imitated Tangut. Adv. Educ. Human. Soc. Sci. Res. **1**(2), 270 (2022)

Designing for Sustainability Through HCI: A Carbon Label System Leveraging TPB and Social Incentives in China

Nahua Shi[✉] [iD], Jie Zhang [iD], Jiaqi Li [iD], Jiaxi Song [iD], and Zhuoran Li [iD]

Beijing Forestry University, No. 35, Qinghua East Road, Haidian District, Beijing 100083, China
Snh20245678@163.com

Abstract. In order to solve the problems of insufficient carbon literacy and low conversion rate of low-carbon consumption behaviour of Chinese consumers, this study proposes a sustainable consumption guidance system that integrates carbon label interaction and mobile application platform. The system takes the graded carbon tag of the traffic light colour ring as the core physical entrance, combines NFC technology to realise the real-time query of the carbon footprint of the commodity, and reduces the cognitive burden of users through the hierarchical visual interface. The five functional modules of the mobile terminal (carbon footprint interaction, game incentives, consumption reminders, low-carbon navigation, and UGC community) form a synergistic effect, organically combining carbon knowledge learning, low-carbon behaviour practice and social communication. Gamified task design stimulates user participation, intelligent recommendation plug-ins directly intervene in consumption decisions, and community interaction uses social norms to strengthen behaviour transformation, and finally builds a complete closed loop from individual cognition to group influence.

Keywords: Carbon Footprint Labeling · Carbon Literacy · Sustainable Consumption · NFC Interaction · Behaviour Guidance · Visual Design · Low-Carbon Transformation · Human-Computer Interaction

1 Introduction

1.1 Background and Significance

The Current State of Carbon Footprint. At present, China's carbon footprint labeling policy has been enacted in the field of electrical and electronic products and services, namely, the "General Rules for Evaluating the Carbon Footprint of Electrical and Electronic Products in China", the standards, methods and procedures for evaluating the carbon footprint of products, and the requirement that electrical appliances produced must contain carbon labels [1]. Work in other areas is also progressing. For example, in 2024, China issued the "Greenhouse Gas Product Carbon Footprint Quantification Requirements and Guidelines" (GB/T 24067–2024), which specifies a common carbon footprint accounting standard. However, carbon labels are not yet popular in China and come in different forms, making them difficult to recognize.

© The Author(s), under exclusive license to Springer Nature Switzerland AG 2026
S. Sundarakannan and O. Knorpp (Eds.): HCII 2025, CCIS 2772, pp. 408–416, 2026.
https://doi.org/10.1007/978-3-032-12767-9_43

The Connotation and Challenges of Carbon Literacy. "Literacy" consists of three components: knowledge, attitude and behavior. The knowledge domain includes low-carbon knowledge and ecological concepts, the attitude domain includes values, sensitivities and control points, and the behavior domain includes behavioral intentions and actions.

Carbon literacy transformation can be reflected through low-carbon consumption behavior, which is also severely lacking among Chinese citizens [2]. For example, in the article Low Carbon Literacy among Exhibitors in China's Exhibition Industry, two authors mention that there is a relative lack of low carbon consumption among exhibitors. For example, factors such as bringing cutlery and reducing bottled water purchases were not prevalent [3].

Correlation between carbon literacy and carbon footprint. The study suggests that individuals with higher carbon engagement, i.e. those who are more willing to engage with information on the topic, do have a smaller carbon footprint. Meanwhile, carbon knowledge was significantly associated with the footprint of dietary choices.

The cueing role of carbon footprint labeling, i.e., carbon participation, and the ecological knowledge of consumers, i.e., carbon literacy, are critical to the emergence of their sustainable consumption behavior, and consumer-led, bottom-up demand is essential to drive sustainable reforms in the production system. Therefore, this study is highly relevant.

1.2 Research Status at Home and Abroad

Current State of Practice of Carbon Footprint System Intervention in Consumers' Sustainable Consumption Behaviour. The main form of intervention in sustainable consumer behavior, sustainable education and sustainable consumption incentives for consumers is currently the creation of carbon footprinting systems through APPs or the Internet [4–6].

For example, Ant Forest is an environmental public welfare app launched by Alipay, where users accumulate virtual energy through low-carbon behaviors, which can be exchanged for real trees planted in desert areas by Alipay's joint public welfare organizations as a way to advocate green living and help ecological protection [7–9].

Four Corners adds carbon labeling to its menu through the Klimato tool, which allows the menu development team and customers to accurately measure the carbon footprint of each ingredient and the entire dish, creating a "climate-friendly" restaurant by influencing consumer decisions and developing and adapting menus.

However, there are still limitations to these practices, for example, there are no carbon footprinting systems that allow for direct interaction between the product and the app, especially for consumers.

Current Research on Carbon Footprinting System Interventions for Consumers' Sustainable Consumption Behavior. Currently, there are three types of carbon footprint labels widely used: those that show absolute carbon emissions, those that use traffic light colors to show the degree of carbon emissions, and those that combine the two.

The study by Meyerding et al. compared the utility of six different carbon footprint labels to assess which label design is most appropriate for consumers. The results showed that qualitative carbon footprint labels using color-coded traffic light labels outperformed labels that claimed to reduce or neutralize climate impacts, as well as those that only showed carbon emissions. However, the impact of carbon emissions on consumers is still limited and significantly lower than information such as price and origin, with a possible reason being the difficulty of understanding the information on carbon labels [10].

Geraldine Holenweger et al. assessed the effectiveness of carbon footprint labeling to increase sustainable food consumption through experimental observation [11]. The results of the study showed that the results indicated that stoplight labeling and the combination of stoplight and absolute emissions labeling increased the odds of choosing low carbon emissions foods. At the same time, there was no interaction between carbon footprint labeling and environmental concerns as well as cognitive reflection for the choice of sustainable food in this experimental scenario, i.e., consumers' choice of food was not determined by environmental concerns as well as cognitive reflection.

A study by AK Edenbrandt et al. investigated how different carbon labels affect the efficiency of consumers in identifying low carbon emitting food products containing labels showing carbon emissions, traffic light color labels, and labels displaying a "Low Carbon Medal" [12]. From a recognition perspective, digital labels outperformed traffic light color labels and logo labels in a task that included different categories of goods.

But now these studies still have limitations, for example, the relevant studies are only limited to the carbon label itself, without considering the synergy with APP, also basically using the questionnaire selection research form, which is different from the real consumption scene.

1.3 Research Objectives and Innovations

This study will be devoted to solving the problem of insufficient consumer carbon literacy and insufficient conversion degree of carbon literacy into low carbon consumption behavior. A carbon labeling and product interaction system that integrates carbon knowledge, carbon participation, and low-carbon consumption behavior reminders is proposed. The system can improve users' carbon participation through low-carbon incentive games and UGC communities, improve users' carbon knowledge by interacting with the carbon footprint labels of products through NFC chips, and directly promote the conversion of users' low-carbon consumption behaviors through the low-carbon consumption reminder plug-in.

2 System Design

2.1 Carbon Label Interaction Design

Label Visual Design. The purpose of the label design is to maximise the user's purchase decision and achieve a certain popular science base, while also serving as a customer acquisition channel for the Mini Programme. The label indicates the absolute carbon emissions to achieve the purpose of science popularisation, and helps users quickly select products with relatively low carbon emissions among similar items through traffic light colour grading.

The colour code design of the traffic light with a strip-like gradient was implemented to avoid visual confusion. The colour matching of "traffic light colour" refers to the Chinese energy efficiency label of electrical appliances, selecting similar colours and grading numbers, which reduces the user's cognitive cost. The logo is brightly coloured, attracting users to interact with the NFC chip of the tag (Fig. 1).

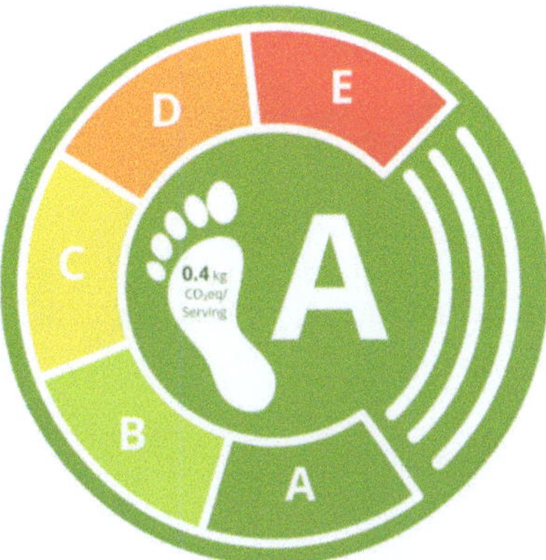

Fig. 1. The carbon footprint label.

The tags are designed to be circular, with the bands of the traffic lights arranged in a circular pattern, indicating where the central NFC chip can interact. The label is composed of semi-rings and "footprints", reminiscent of "carbon" and footprints, making it easy for users to understand the role of labels. The outer contour of the graphic remains intact and closed, which makes the label design conform to human cognitive preferences.

We improve the colour contrast of the interface, visualise the data in the form of data instead of text, combine the design of simple icons and visual elements to improve the aesthetics of the interface, so as to enhance the attraction of users, and combine process charts to reduce the visual burden of users, so that users can understand the distribution of carbon footprints from the perspective of the whole process, and realise the cognitive cost reduction at the user level.

Interactive Processes. Users will put their cell phones close to the carbon label of the product and wake up to the interactive interface automatically through near-field communication technology; the page visualizes the carbon footprint information of the product, with the top displaying the name of the product and the dynamic dashboard of the total carbon emissions, and the environmental protection ratings are reflected through the color of the traffic lights.

The main body of the next page presents the circular decomposition diagram of the supply chain, and the percentage of carbon emissions is displayed according to the links of raw material procurement, production and processing, logistics and transportation, and terminal recycling, etc. Clicking on any block can expand the description of the carbon emissions and the industry benchmark comparison value. Click on any block to expand the description of the carbon emissions of the process and the industry benchmark comparison value. The next page displays a comparison chart, which generates a bar chart comparison view of the product with the industry average with a single click.

2.2 APP Platform Functional Architecture

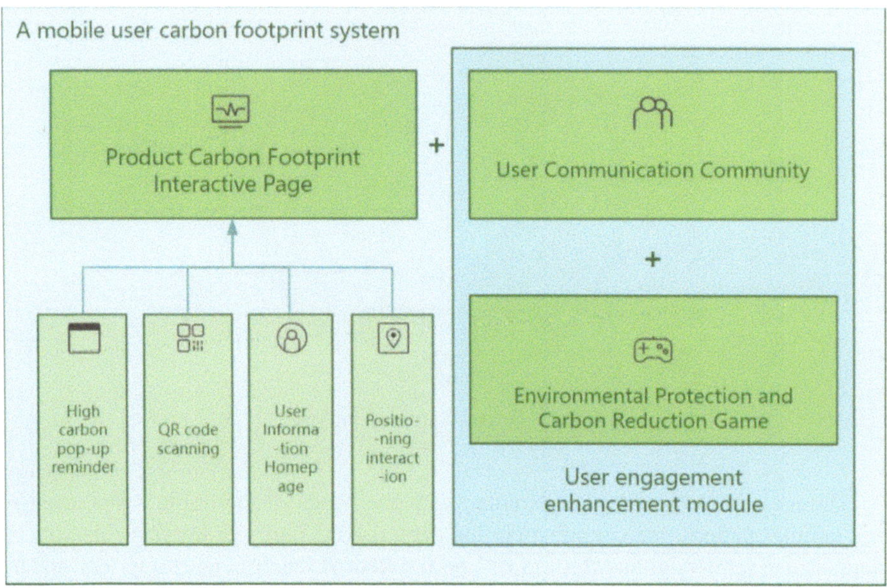

Fig. 2. The user-end carbon footprint system of this project.

From the user's point of view, this product is divided into five major modules, namely, product carbon footprint labeling interaction module, low-carbon game incentive module, low-carbon consumption reminder plug-in, low-carbon navigation module, and UGC community module (Fig. 2).

The Product Carbon Footprint Interactive Module. By touching the NFC chip on the product's carbon footprint tag, the user can enter the interactive interface, which visualizes the carbon footprint of the whole process, helps the user to understand the carbon emissions of the product in each production process, and popularizes carbon knowledge to the user.

The visualization interface adopts a layered display strategy: the first screen displays a dynamic dashboard of total carbon emissions, which intuitively reflects the environmental protection level through the color gradient (green to red); the second level displays a ring diagram of the carbon emissions of each link in the supply chain, which supports clicking on it to view the description of the carbon emissions of the specific process; and the third level provides the function of side-by-side comparison of the same products, which uses the bar chart to present the carbon emissions of the product in the industry. The third level provides the function of side-by-side comparison of similar products, using bar charts to present the percentile ranking of the product's carbon emissions in the industry (Fig. 3).

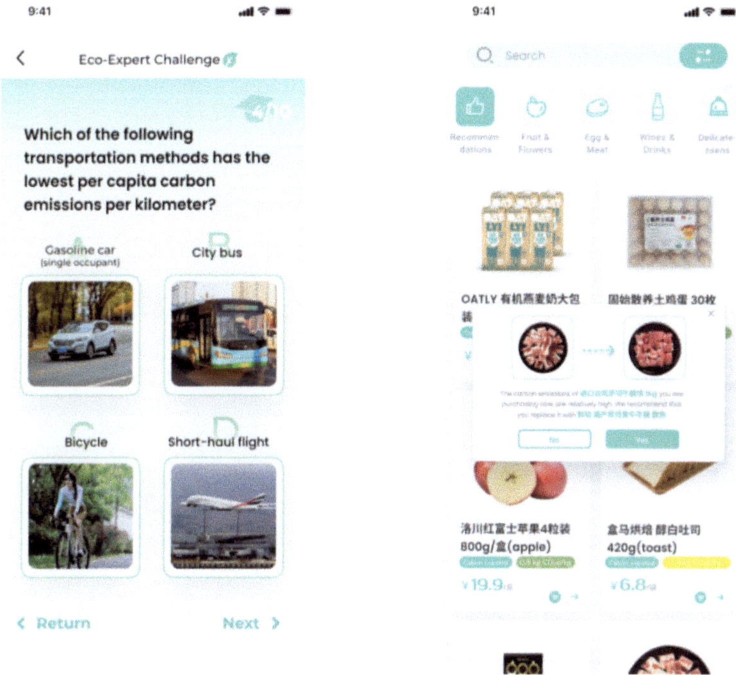

Fig. 3. Game page and pop-up reminder page.

Low-carbon Game Incentive Module. Use serious games to subliminally influence users. Motivate users through casual puzzle games in the form of quizzes and tasks. This module cultivates users' environmental awareness through gamification mechanisms, setting up two types of activity units: knowledge learning and behavior practice. The knowledge learning unit contains daily environmental protection quizzes, covering topics such as garbage classification, energy saving and other life scenarios, with virtual medals awarded for correct answers. The Behavioral Practice unit is designed with contextual simulation tasks, such as the "Weekly Low-Carbon Diet Challenge", which requires users to record their daily meal choices and calculate the amount of carbon emission reduction.

Low-carbon consumption reminder plug-in. Adding expansion on top of a series of shopping sites to label goods with talk label certification status, grade, absolute carbon emissions, etc. The system will recommend low-carbon alternatives to users based on their purchasing habits, reducing the cost of finding sustainable products and decision-making costs for users.

Low-carbon navigation module. Map Navigation. Merchants can upload their own production, low-carbon consumption certification, and after obtaining certification, it will be displayed on the map as a highlighted green location tag, helping users find sustainable products more easily. When recommending routes, the navigation prioritizes green travel routes such as walking and cycling, and predicts the difference in carbon emissions between different modes of transportation.

Navigation within A Specific Supermarket. Highlighted green locator tags are used on supermarket maps to mark products with Carbon Footprint Plaque ratings of lowest carbon and next highest, and navigation to product areas is provided to assist users in making consumption decisions (Fig. 4).

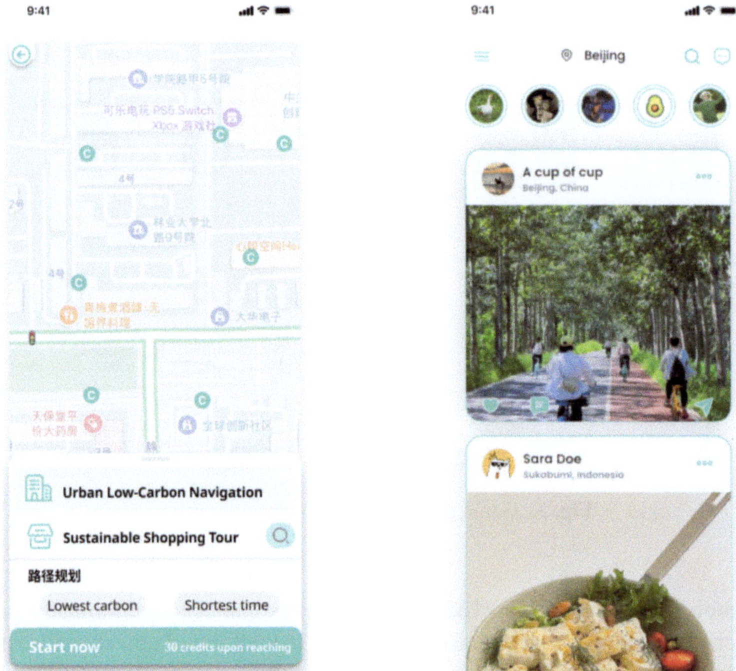

Fig. 4. UGC community page and navigation page.

UGC Community Building. UGC community building is carried out to cultivate users' eco-friendly living habits and low-carbon decision-making habits by utilizing the principle of TPB theory that subjective norms, or social pressures, affect human decision-making. In the community, users can earn carbon points by communicating with each other, and through this reward mechanism, users are encouraged to engage in carbon participation.

3   Conclusion and Future Works

In this study, a sustainable consumption guidance system covering online and offline scenarios is constructed by integrating the physical interaction of carbon labels with a mobile application platform. The system takes the traffic light color ring graded carbon label as the core physical entrance, combines with NFC technology to realize the instant inquiry of carbon footprint of commodities, and reduces the cognitive burden of users through a layered visualization interface. The five functional modules of the mobile terminal (carbon footprint interaction, game motivation, consumption reminder, low carbon navigation, UGC community) form a synergistic effect, which organically combines the learning of carbon knowledge, the practice of low carbon behavior and social communication. The game-based task design stimulates user participation, the intelligent recommendation plug-in directly intervenes in consumption decision-making, and the community interaction makes use of social norms to strengthen behavioral transformation, ultimately constructing a complete closed-loop from individual cognition to group influence.

However, the current study still has certain limitations. The promotion of carbon labels relies on the popularization of hardware and the standardization process, while the domestic carbon labeling policy for commodities is still in the pilot stage, which makes it difficult to be applied on a large scale in the short term [13–15]. The balance between user behavior data collection and privacy protection still needs to be optimized, and the existing anonymization mechanism may not be able to meet the increasingly strict privacy regulations. Experimental validation is mainly based on simulation scenarios, lacking long-term tracking data in real consumption environments, and the low-carbon certification information submitted by merchants on their own faces credibility challenges. These factors may affect the actual implementation of the system, and need to be gradually resolved through technical iteration and system improvement.

To address the above issues, future work will focus on technology optimization and ecological expansion. On the technical level, we will explore the hybrid labeling scheme of QR code and NFC to reduce the hardware deployment cost, and introduce blockchain technology to ensure the tamperability of carbon emission data. In terms of algorithm optimization, we will combine federal learning to improve recommendation accuracy, and improve the low-carbon commodity matching model under the premise of protecting user privacy. In terms of application scenarios, we plan to expand to more categories of commodities such as clothing and daily necessities, promote the standardization of carbon labels in conjunction with industry associations, and develop cross-platform lightweight plug-ins to expand user coverage. In terms of policy docking, we will try to connect user carbon credits with the government's carbon benefits system, and explore the feasible path for individual emission reduction behavior to be included in the regional carbon neutrality target.

Overall, this study bridges the gap between carbon literacy theory and behavioral practice through human-computer interaction design, and provides an actionable technical path for sustainable consumption. In the future, we will deepen the technology development and commercial promotion, and promote the transformation of the system from theoretical model to practical application through pilot verification, policy synergy and social cooperation. The ultimate goal is to form a positive cycle of "User

Emission Reduction - Data Feedback - Industry Upgrade", which will help the overall low-carbon transformation of the society, and provide micro-level support for China to realize the goal of "Double Carbon". This exploration not only expands the boundaries of HCI's application in the field of sustainability, but also provides a new methodological reference for the design of behavior-led systems.

References

1. Zhao, R., Dingye Wu, Junke Zhang: Policy implications on carbon labeling scheme toward carbon neutrality in China. Front. Environ. Sci. **9**, 739943 (2021)
2. Jiang, P., et al.: Building low carbon communities in China: the role of individual's behaviour change and engagement. Energy Policy. **60**, 611–620 (2013)
3. Liu, C.-W., Cheng, J.-S.: Low-carbon literacy of exhibitors in the exhibition industry in China. Sustainability. **14**(4), 2262 (2022)
4. Pourghannad, L.: Reducing Digital Carbon Footprint through Social Media: Educating Users on Sustainable Consumption (2024)
5. Mulcahy, R., Russell-Bennett, R., Iacobucci, D.: Designing gamified apps for sustainable consumption: a field study. J. Bus. Res. **106**, 377–387 (2020)
6. Saari, A.: Changing Behavior Towards Sustainable Consumption Habits With Eco-Feedback Technologies Through User Experience (2021)
7. Shao, Z., Xu, Y.: Moving towards carbon neutral lifestyle through FinTech social media platform: a case study of ant Forest. Front. Environ. Sci. **11**, 1160986 (2023)
8. Wang, J.: The Motivations of Users to Participate in Sustainable Projects on Mobile Applications: The Case of Antforest. MS thesis (2023)
9. Zhang, Y., et al.: The contribution of Fintech to sustainable development in the digital age: ant forest and land restoration in China. Land Use Policy. **103**, 105306 (2021)
10. Meyerding, S.G.H., Schaffmann, A.-L., Lehberger, M.: Consumer preferences for different designs of carbon footprint labelling on tomatoes in Germany—does design matter? Sustainability. **11**(6), 1587 (2019)
11. Holenweger, G., Stöckli, S., Brügger, A.: Carbon footprint labels involving traffic lights foster sustainable food choices. Food Qual. Prefer. **106**, 104813 (2023)
12. Edenbrandt, A.K., Asioli, D., Nordström, J.: Impact of different carbon labels on consumer inference. J. Clean. Prod. **494**, 145020 (2025)
13. Brenton, P., Edwards-Jones, G., Jensen, M.F.: Carbon labelling and low-income country exports: a review of the development issues. Dev. Policy Rev. **27**(3), 243–267 (2009)
14. Liu, T., Wang, Q., Su, B.: A review of carbon labeling: standards, implementation, and impact. Renew. Sust. Energ. Rev. **53**, 68–79 (2016)
15. Taufique, K.M.R., et al.: revisiting the promise of carbon labelling. Nat. Clim. Chang. **12**(2), 132–140 (2022)

Correction to: HCI International 2025 – Late Breaking Posters

Constantine Stephanidis, Margherita Antona, Stavroula Ntoa, George Margetis, and Gavriel Salvendy

Correction to:
S. Sundarakannan and O. Knorpp (Eds.): *HCI International 2025 – Late Breaking Posters*, CCIS 2772, **https://doi.org/10.1007/978-3-032-12767-9**

The book was published with a typo in the book title. The title of the book as "HCI International 2025 – Late Breaking Papers", whereas it should read "HCI International 2025 – Late Breaking Posters" both in the cover and on the Title page of the front-matter correctly. This has been corrected in the book accordingly.

The updated version of this book can be found at
https://doi.org/10.1007/978-3-032-12767-9

© The Author(s), under exclusive license to Springer Nature Switzerland AG 2026
S. Sundarakannan and O. Knorpp (Eds.): HCII 2025, CCIS 2772, p. C1, 2026.
https://doi.org/10.1007/978-3-032-12767-9_44

Author Index

© The Editor(s) (if applicable) and The Author(s), under exclusive license
to Springer Nature Switzerland AG 2026

S. Sundarakannan and O. Knorpp (Eds.): HCII 2025, CCIS 2772, pp. 417–419, 2026.
https://doi.org/10.1007/978-3-032-12767-9

MIX
Papier aus verantwortungsvollen Quellen
Paper from responsible sources
FSC® C105338

If you have any concerns about our products,
you can contact us on
ProductSafety@springernature.com

In case Publisher is established outside the EU,
the EU authorized representative is:
Springer Nature Customer Service Center GmbH
Europaplatz 3, 69115 Heidelberg, Germany

Printed by Libri Plureos GmbH
in Hamburg, Germany